DATE DUE

NOV 01 '05			
OCT 2 7 '06			
NOV 1 8 '06			

D0011422

Part of the Langenscheidt Publishing Group

INSIGHT GUIDE
TURKEY

ABOUT THIS BOOK

Editorial

Project Editor
Melissa Shales
Managing Editor
Emily Hatchwell
Editorial Director
Brian Bell

Distribution

UK & Ireland
GeoCenter International Ltd
The Viables Centre, Harrow Way
Basingstoke, Hants RG22 4BJ
Fax: (44) 1256 817988

United States
Langenscheidt Publishers, Inc.
46–35 54th Road, Maspeth, NY 11378
Fax: 1 (718) 784 0640

Canada
Thomas Allen & Son Ltd
390 Steelcase Road East
Markham, Ontario L3R 1G2
Fax: (1) 905 475 6747

Australia
Universal Publishers
1 Waterloo Road
Macquarie Park, NSW 2113
Fax: (61) 2 9888 9074

New Zealand
Hema Maps New Zealand Ltd (HNZ)
Unit D, 24 Ra ORA Drive
East Tamaki, Auckland
Fax: (64) 9 273 6479

Worldwide
**Apa Publications GmbH & Co.
Verlag KG (Singapore branch)**
38 Joo Koon Road, Singapore 628990
Tel: (65) 6865 1600. Fax: (65) 6861 6438

Printing

Insight Print Services (Pte) Ltd
38 Joo Koon Road, Singapore 628990
Tel: (65) 6865 1600. Fax: (65) 6861 6438

©2005 Apa Publications GmbH & Co.
Verlag KG (Singapore branch)
All Rights Reserved
First Edition 1988
Fifth Edition 1999
Updated 2003; Reprinted 2005

CONTACTING THE EDITORS
We would appreciate it if readers
would alert us to errors or out-
dated information by writing to:
**Insight Guides, P.O. Box 7910,
London SE1 1WE, England.
Fax: (44) 20 7403 0290.
insight@apaguide.co.uk**

This guidebook combines the interests and enthusiasms of two of
the world's best known information
providers: Insight Guides, whose titles
have set the standard for visual travel
guides since 1970, and Discovery
Channel, the world's premier source
of nonfiction television programming.

Insight Guides provide practical
advice as well as a general understanding about a destination's history, culture, institutions and people,
while Discovery Channel and its website, www.discovery.com, help millions of viewers explore their world
from the comfort of their own home
and also encourage them to explore
it firsthand.

How to use this book

The book has been carefully struc-
tured both to convey an understanding of the country and its
culture and to guide readers through
its sights and activities.

◆ The first section, with a yellow bar,
concentrates on providing an
understanding of Turkey and its people, and explains the country's
lengthy and complex **History**. The
Features section looks at the people,
life and culture of Turkey, from the status of women in contemporary society
to the music scene in downtown
Istanbul.

◆ The main **Places** section, with a
blue bar, is a tour of Turkey, region

by region, providing a full run-down of all the attractions worth seeing. The principal places of interest are coordinated by number with full-colour maps.

◆ The **Travel Tips** listings provide a convenient reference section filled with information on travel, hotels, restaurants, sports and festivals. Information may be located quickly by using the index printed on the back cover flap – while the flaps themselves provide handy bookmarks.

◆ **Photographs** are chosen not only to illustrate the geography and attractions of the country but as a vivid portrayal of the lives and moods of the Turkish people.

The Contributors

A dedicated team in Istanbul and London worked hard to update this expanded edition of *Insight Guide: Turkey*. The original project editor, **Melissa Shales**, an English freelance travel writer and editor, and Turkey specialist, updated the information for this version, which was edited by **Cathy Muscat** in the London office. The Travel Tips were edited by **Erica Brown** also in the London office. The book builds upon an original edition project edited by **Thomas Goltz**.

New material for the previous edition was contributed by **Molly McAnailly-Burke** (the Black Sea; Istanbul; Features), **Metin Demirsar** (Central Anatolia; the East), and **Elizabeth Meath Baker** (Travel Tips), all based in Istanbul; and **Bernard McDonagh** (Thrace and Marmara), **Melissa Shales** (the Mediterranean Coast; History) and **Sean Sheehan** (the Aegean Coast).

Contributors to the original guide included **Lale Apa, Selçuk Bakkalbası, David Barchard, Paul Bolding, Nur Bilge Criss, Metin Demirsar, Marian Ellingworth, Tony Gillote, Rasit Gürdilek, Talat Halman, Lyle Lawson, Sevan Nısanyan, Gabrielle Ohl, Virginia Penn-Taylor, Anne Reeves, Canan Silay** and **Barbara Samantha Stenzel**.

The principal photographers were **Semsi Güner, Marcus Wilson-Smith** and **Phil Wood**.

Picture research was undertaken by **Hilary Genin** and **Monica Allende**. The original book was indexed by **Isobel McLean**. The updated edition was proofread by **Emma Sangster**.

Map Legend

—··—	International Boundary
—·—·—	National Park/Reserve
——————	Ferry Route
✈ ✈	Airport: International/Regional
🚌	Bus Station
P	Parking
ⓘ	Tourist Information
⊠	Post Office
✝ ✝	Church/Ruins
✝	Monastery
☾	Mosque
✡	Synagogue
⌂	Castle/Ruins
∴	Archaeological Site
∩	Cave
⚱	Statue/Monument
★	Place of Interest

The main places of interest in the Places section are coordinated by number with a full-colour map (e.g. ❶), and a symbol at the top of every right-hand page tells you where to find the map.

Insight Guide
Turkey

CONTENTS

Temple of
Trajan at
Pergamon

Insight on ...

Information panels

Places

THE LAND OF THE TURKS

*There's something for everyone in Turkey. The trouble is that,
for centuries, almost everyone has tried to grab a slice*

The classical Romans called it *Asia Minor* – that landmass protruding from Asia into the eastern Mediterranean, defined by the Black Sea to the north, the Aegean to the west and the deserts of Arabia to the south, and bordered by Greece, Bulgaria, Georgia, Armenia, Iran, Iraq and Syria. To the ancient peoples who came before them, it was simply *Anatolia* – the Motherland; in 1923, under Atatürk, the country became *Türkiye*, the Land of the Turks.

Since the dawn of time, this sprawling land of mountain ranges, high plateaux and fertile river valleys has been the dividing line between the Orient and Occident. The Persian king of kings Xerxes crossed westwards with his Asian hordes on their way to victory at Thermopylae and defeat at Salamis; Alexander the Great reversed that movement when he led his Macedonians eastwards to India in pursuit of his great empire, leaving Anatolia an indelible Hellenic stamp. The Romans saw in Anatolia a granary and bulwark against their traditional enemies to the east; it was at Zela, east of Ankara, that Caesar uttered his famous words: *"Veni. Vidi. Vici."* – "I came. I saw. I conquered."

Over the next 1,000 years, Anatolia became the nucleus of the Byzantine Empire, with its capital, Constantinople, undoubtedly the greatest, most powerful and magnificent city in the world. It was here that early Christianity first took root, only to be replaced by Islam, first introduced by the 7th-century Arabs, and then imposed by the Seljuk and Ottoman Turks, who pushed the frontiers of the Ottoman empire from the Persian Gulf to the Atlantic and from the Indian Ocean to Vienna. Within, and perhaps because of, all the tragedy, bloodshed and empire-building, Anatolia remained one of the most politically and culturally influential places on the planet for at least 2,000 years.

Defeat during World War I, the ruthless carve-up of the empire, and the decision of the Turks under the leadership of Mustafa Kemal to regain Anatolia and remould themselves, gave modern Turkey a very different role in the 20th century.

Today, as the country struggles to embrace Western-style economics and liberalism within an Islamic, Eastern framework, the nation looks boldly forward to a new future, not as a dividing line or buffer zone between East and West, but as a bridge between them. Meanwhile, the new invasion has begun. This time, it is more friendly and short-lived, with some 7 million people arriving for two weeks each year in search of warm seas, magnificent scenery, echoes of ancient history, fine food and a friendly greeting.

"Hoş geldiniz!" – Welcome to Turkey.   ❏

PRECEDING PAGES: bazaar temptations, Istanbul; village boys paddling at Kale on the Mediterranean coast; feeding time; café culture, near Kayseri, Cappadocia.
LEFT: enjoying a quiet read in a mosque in Diyarbakır.

Decisive Dates

c.6500–5400 BC Çatalhöyük, the world's second-oldest known city (after Jericho), is a thriving community of around 5,000, keeping domesticated animals, irrigating crops, weaving, and trading in obsidian.

c.5400–3000 BC First fortified towns, at Hacılar, Can Hasan and Yümuktepe.

c.3000 BC Interconnected city states trade with Greece and Syria. Sophisticated metalworking is proven by the hoards of treasure found at Troy II in 1873 and at Alacahöyük in the 1930s.

c.1900–1150 BC The Hittite invasion of Central

Anatolia, crushing the indigenous Hattite culture, and creating the area's first advanced civilisation, contemporary with Babylon and ancient Egypt. This is the first era recorded by written histories.

c.1250–650 BC The legendary Trojan Wars, later described by Homer, are followed by successive waves of invaders, known collectively as the Sea People and thought to come from the Troad region of northwestern Anatolia (around Troy). The most powerful are the Phrygians.

850–590 BC The kingdom of Urartu flourishes around Lake Van. Early Greek tribes settle along the coasts. The Phrygian empire is destroyed by arriving Lydians, whose most famous king was Croesus.

546 BC The Persian conquest of Anatolia is begun

by Cyrus and completed by Darius the Great and his son, Xerxes. The area remains under Persian rule for nearly 200 years.

c.490–425 BC Greek historian, Herodotus, lives and works in Halikarnassos (Bodrum).

334–323 BC Alexander the Great marches east, driving the Persians from Anatolia at the Battle of Issos in 333 BC, After his death, Anatolia is divided up between four of his generals – Seleukos Nicator, Ptolemy, Antigonus and Lysimachus.

4th–2nd centuries BC The great age of Hellenistic city states, some of which band together to form democratic federations such as the Lycian League.

282 BC Pergamon breaks away as an independent kingdom, later creating an alliance with Rome.

278 BC Celts arrive in Anatolia, settle near Ankara and attempt unsuccessfully to build an empire.

133 BC King Attalus III of Pergamon leaves his kingdom to Rome. Anatolia eventually becomes the Roman province of Asia Minor.

20 BC Rome signs a peace treaty with the Parthian Persians. The *Pax Romana* lasts 200 years.

AD 45–58 Christianity spreads as several apostles, including St Paul the Evangelist, travel and preach widely throughout Asia Minor.

AD 313 Persecution ends as Emperor Constantine converts to Christianity.

AD 325 The Council of Nicaea proclaims Christianity the official religion of the Roman Empire.

BYZANTIUM

AD 330 Constantine moves his capital to Byzantium, building the world's most glamorous city and naming it Constantinople. This is the official beginning of the Byzantine Empire.

AD 395 Emperor Theodosius divides the Roman Empire between his sons; Asia Minor becomes the centre of the Eastern, Byzantine Empire. The Western empire eventually becomes the Holy Roman Empire in AD 800.

647 The first Arab invasions mark the start of several centuries of constant fighting and the introduction of Islam to Anatolia. Southeastern Anatolia becomes Arab territory. The Bulgars, Armenians and Persians all attack the fringes of the empire.

726–787 Iconoclasts borrow from Islam and ban religious images of the human form. Many Byzantine churches are literally defaced.

1071–1461 Persian Seljuk Turks rout the Byzantine army at the Battle of Malazgirt. By 1078, the Seljuks have built a new empire covering most of Anatolia, imposing their language, culture and name on the people. The Byzantine Empire shrinks to the area immediately round Istanbul, the Aegean and parts of the Black Sea.

1080–1375 Armenia breaks away to form an independent Christian state in the east.

1096–1204 Crusaders heading east to halt the spread of Islam use Anatolian ports for supplies. Edessa and Antioch briefly become Norman, Christian principalities.

1204 The Fourth Crusade sacks Christian Constantinople, ruling it as a Latin kingdom until 1261.

1243 The Seljuks are defeated by the Mongols.

1288 Minor Muslim warlord, Osman Ghazi, with lands around Eskişehir in central Anatolia, begins to build a powerbase which grows steadily into an empire over the next 150 years.

THE OTTOMANS

1453 The Ottomans, under Mehmet II, conquer Constantinople; the last Byzantine emperor, Constantine IX, dies in battle defending the city, which is renamed Istanbul (Islamboul – City of Islam).

1512–20 Selim I consolidates Ottoman rule over all Anatolia, conquers Persia and Egypt, and assumes the title of caliph, head of all Islam.

1520–66 Süleyman the Magnificent reigns over the golden age of the Ottomans.

1683–99 The failure of the Siege of Vienna, defeat at the Battle of Zenta and the Treaty of Karlowitz mark the end of Ottoman expansion in Europe.

1774 The Ottomans lose Crimea to the Russians.

1853–6 The Crimean War. Britain and France side with the Ottomans against Russia.

1908 Young Turks Revolution in support of Western-style liberalism leaves sultan as figurehead to a more democratic government.

1914–18 Turkey enters World War I as a German ally; Mustafa Kemal leads victorious resistance at Gallipoli in the Dardanelles.

THE REPUBLIC

1919 The Ottoman Empire is ruthlessly carved up by the Allies in the Treaty of Sèvres. Mustafa Kemal leads the Turkish War of Independence and, over the next four years, throws out all foreigners.

1923 Mustafa Kemal, now called Atatürk (Father of the Turks), abolishes the monarchy and becomes president of the new republic of Turkey. Almost 1½ million people are moved as Greece and Turkey exchange minority populations.

PRECEDING PAGES: Medusa at Didyma.
LEFT: the siege of Troy, on a 5th-century BC plate.
RIGHT: Mehmet II conquers Constantinople in 1453.

1923–38 Atatürk reforms the constitution, giving votes to women, establishing equal rights, disestablishing religion and adopting the Latin alphabet. He rules as a benevolent dictator and dies in 1938.

1939–45 Turkey remains neutral during World War II, declaring war on Germany in the last few weeks, in time to qualify for UN membership.

1946 Turkey becomes a charter member of the UN.

1952 Turkey joins NATO.

1960, 1971 and 1980 Kemalist military factions lead military coups after political and economic crises. Each time, they restore democracy after stabilising the situation.

1974 Turkey invades northern Cyprus.

1988 Kurdish separatists (the PKK) begin an armed insurrection in the southeast.

1996 The Islamist Refah (Welfare) Party, dedicated to *Shari'a* (Islamic) law, forms a coalition government, but in 1998 is banned and reforms as the Virtue Party.

1999 Earthquake rocks the Istanbul area. Turkey becomes a candidate member of the EU.

2000 The PKK abandons its rebellion.

2002 The AK (Justice and Development Party), a religious party born out of the Virtue Party, wins the election, but promises secular government.

2003 Turkey's refusal to cooperate with the USA in Iraq War rocks NATO. Al Qaeda carries out bombings on British and Jewish targets in Istanbul. ❑

THE CRADLE OF CIVILISATION

Straddling Europe and Asia, Turkey was the junction between

civilisations, crucial in the development of history itself

Since biblical times, Anatolia has played a major part in the history of civilisation. The Old Testament contains a wealth of references to the land and its peoples, from Abraham, father of the Jewish nation, who came from Edessa (now Sanlıurfa), to Noah, whose ark is said to have landed on Mount Ararat. The Euphrates and Tigris rivers, both rising in the mountains of eastern Anatolia, nurtured between them the great civilisations of the Fertile Crescent, while ancient Mesopotamia now lies in southeastern Turkey.

The real story of mankind in Anatolia begins far earlier still. In a cave at Yarımburgaz, about 32 km (20 miles) from Istanbul, a team of archaeologists, working in 1986–7, discovered human remains dating back a million years, the oldest yet found outside Africa. The first people to have left any remains other than bones lived in caves at Belbaşı and Beldibi near Antalya some 10,000 years ago, creating powerful paintings and carvings on their walls.

Within 4,000 years, the evolution from a life of hunting and gathering to settled communities seems to have been complete and some of the earliest towns ever established existed on Anatolian soil. Çatalhöyük, south of Konya, was beaten by Jericho to the honour of being the world's first town, but by 6250 BC, it had a population of around 5,000 and was the first place known to use irrigation for crops such as barley, or to domesticate pigs and sheep. By 5000 BC, people in Hacılar (220 km/135 miles to the west of Çatalhöyük) had streets, houses with doors, and produced pottery so fine it is still acclaimed by archaeologists.

The Bronze Age

Now came the discovery of copper, and the pace of change began to speed up, each new advance catalogued in the successive levels of settlement mounds (known as a *tell* in Arabic

LEFT: monumental Hittite sculpture at Alacahöyük.
RIGHT: the Anatolian Mother Goddess, one of the world's oldest and most potent fertility symbols.

countries, *höyük* in Turkey), formed by many generations of mudbrick houses crumbling on a single spot. We know the Bronze Age Anatolians largely from their pottery – dark, red, or burnished to a metallic sheen.

The most famous of all the mounds is at Troy, where the original city was founded in

about 3000 BC. Few details have survived under the later levels, but this seems to have been a highly sophisticated community, with large houses (one almost 20 metres/65 ft by 7 metres/ 25 ft), while the sturdy city walls indicate that both politics and warfare were flourishing.

By now, prehistory had ended in Egypt and Mesopotamia, but Anatolia, a patchwork of minor kingdoms and city states, had to wait another thousand years for written records. Nevertheless, archaeological sites show continuous occupation, increasing sophistication in house-building and pottery, and growing trade connections. To this period belong Mersin and Troy II, where Heinrich Schliemann was to discover the remains of an impressive city, and 16 hoards of gold and jewellery. He believed they belonged to Homer's Trojans and King Priam, although they are, in fact, much earlier, as was the Treasure of Dorak, sadly only glimpsed briefly by British archaeologist, James Mellart.

Towards the end of the third millennium BC, a devastating invasion of Anatolia from the northwest destroyed the cities, bringing the hitherto prosperous civilisation to an abrupt and bloody end.

WRITTEN IN GOLD

In the Treasure of Dorak, which went missing in the 1950s, was a gold fragment inscribed with the name of Sahure, Pharaoh of Egypt in 2450 BC. This is the first known writing in Anatolia.

an early version of Aramaic, the Semitic sister language of Hebrew and Arabic, which to this day continues to be spoken by a few thousand people around Midyat.

A true history of the second millennium, including people, places, names and dates, is partly made possible by several discoveries of documents written on clay tablets, seals and stone monuments. The first, the records of some Mesopotamian traders who were in the area to buy copper and other metal goods for sale elsewhere in the

The second millennium

When the darkness lifts again several hundred years later, we can finally name some of the people living in Anatolia, although their origins remain a mystery.

Among them were the Hattites (speakers of native Anatolian languages – and not to be confused with the Indo-European Hittites who later conquered them) and newer arrivals, speaking Indo-European Luwian in the north and west, and Hurrian in the south and east.

Beyond the Euphrates River, stretching over southeastern Turkey and Syria, the kingdom of Mitanni was ruled by an Indo-European military caste, although most of its people spoke

Near East, were discovered early this century, near Kanesh (modern Kültepe) near Kayseri.

Shortly afterwards, the Indo-Europeans conquered Hattusas (modern Boğazköy), ending the dynasty of Hattite rulers who had lived there and in nearby Alacahöyük. As he left, the last Hattite king cursed the city, decreeing that it should be abandoned forever. Within two centuries, however, Hittite Labarnas I had made it his capital, at the centre of a powerful empire, stretching to the Aegean coast and Cyprus.

The Hittites

When the immense ruins of Boğazköy were first discovered by Western travellers in the

19th century, they seemed to be a complete puzzle. Memories of the Hittites were limited to the famous Old Testament reference to "Uriel the Hittite" – and even he came from the much later southern Hittite principalities.

Knowledge of the much larger and older Hittite kingdom in the north revived with the discovery of cuneiform and hieroglyphic tablets at Boğazköy. The Sumerian forms could be read at once. Soon after came the realisation that the Hittite language was Indo-European. Some of its words are even close to modern English – such as "watar" for water.

From about 1800–1170 BC, Hittite emperors ruled a feudal patchwork of client kings and princes, using a sophisticated administrative system, based on scribes and writing. They erected great monuments across Anatolia; in Kemalpaşa and Manisa outside Izmir, at Eflatunpınar south of Konya, and near Adana.

Although their records are lost, their hostile, rival neighbours – the Arzawa, Lukka and Ahhiyawa – seem to have been similar but less powerful states, ruled by a warrior class who spoke Luwian, from which, it is thought, the common place name ending *assos*, may derive.

Of the three, the Ahhiyawa are most tantalising. In the *Iliad*, Homer calls the Greeks "Achaeans" (Achaioi). Could it be that the Ahhiyawa are the same people?

The Phrygians

From about 1250 BC onwards, another wave of invasions began and the civilisations of both the Hittites and the Mycenaean Greeks were destroyed so thoroughly that memory of them was all but lost until modern times. Among the casualties was Troy VII, whose story, eventually told by Homer in the *Iliad*, 300–400 years later, still stirs the imagination.

Of the new peoples who moved into Anatolia around 800 BC, perhaps the most attractive are the Phrygians who arrived from Thrace and set up a kingdom covering most of central and western Turkey. They spoke an Indo-European language, with a written script derived from the Phoenician alphabet, still seen on monuments at Midas City (Yazılıkaya) south of Eskişehir. They probably also had written archives, but

excavations at the two Phrygian capitals – Midas City and Gordium, about 100 km (62 miles) west of Ankara – have failed to uncover any written materials, perhaps because they no longer used clay tablets. However, the Phrygians do not count as wholly prehistoric, for we catch glimpses of them through the eyes of their neighbours, the Greeks, who, by this time, had been settled for several hundred years upon the Aegean coast of Asia Minor and were gradually moving east along the Mediterranean.

The mound covering the city at Gordium is built up of many different levels very much like that at Troy. Nearby, a mosaic of many coloured

pebbles, the earliest known anywhere in the world, heralds the emergence of the classical civilisations. Meanwhile, two Phrygian kings live on in legend – Gordius (who gave his name to the city, and the riddle of the Gordion knot, broken by Alexander) and his son, Midas of the golden touch. The massive tomb of Gordius, excavated in 1957, proved incredible wealth but, astonishingly, uncovered no gold.

The Phrygians rapidly succumbed to hostile neighbours, most notably the Lydians, who established a powerful kingdom based in Sardis (near İzmir), yet they survive well into Roman times, with much of central Anatolia speaking Phrygian until about AD 300. ❏

LEFT: a procession of Hittite soldiers march along the rocks at Yazılıkaya.
RIGHT: Urartian tablet inscription, Van region.

THE CLASSICAL YEARS

With the arrival of the Greeks, coastal Turkey entered a millennium

that produced immense wealth and sophistication

For about a hundred years (650–546 BC), the Lydians dominated western Turkey, while remaining on close terms with their Greek neighbours, whose awe at their wealth has survived until today in the expression "as rich as Croesus." Croesus (560–546 BC) was the last of the Lydian kings.

Persians versus Greeks

In 546 BC, Lydia was invaded and conquered by the Persian King Cyrus who captured and imprisoned Croesus. From their capital at Persepolis, in present-day Iran, Cyrus and his successors, Darius and Xerxes, expanded their empire westwards to the Aegean. The Lydian capital, Sardis, became the centre of one of four Persian *satraps* (governors). The cities of Ionia, which had been centres of early learning – and where Homer was probably born in about 700 BC – hated Persian rule, regarding it as stifling and repressive. Yet the situation remained unchanged for over 200 years, until Alexander the Great arrived in 334 BC.

The Persians were notorious for their destructiveness. After a revolt in 494 BC, they wiped out Miletus, said to have been one of the most splendid of the early Ionian cities, while in Xanthos on the Lycian coast, the inhabitants preferred mass suicide to the Persian yoke.

Inland, the situation may have been better. In Cappadocia, where the Persian nobles settled, their culture remained alive for centuries after Alexander's victory. Nevertheless, monuments of the period are few and far between. The best-known survivals are three stelae from Ergili, near Lake Manyas, dating from about 400 BC, which are now on display in the Istanbul Archaeological Museum.

Persian rule inhibited the growth of city-states but did not stop it entirely. Throughout the coastal areas of Anatolia, local populations organised themselves into thriving towns with municipal institutions and sophisticated public utilities, such as theatres and baths.

Alexander and Hellenism

The real cultural history of Anatolia between 700 BC and AD 400 is of the steady advance of Classical Graeco-Roman civilisation.

The most significant catalyst for change was Alexander the Great, the boy king of Macedonia, and one of history's meteors. Only 11 years separate his first setting foot in Anatolia in 334 BC from his death in 323 BC, yet in that time he managed to amass one of the greatest (if most short-lived) empires the world has known. His influence on Anatolia lasted for centuries.

Fuelled by a passionate desire to liberate Anatolia from Persian rule, Alexander spread Hellenistic culture and language everywhere his armies marched, first through the coastal city-states, set up centuries before by Greek traders, then spreading inland and eastwards. Even after his death, the empire remained under

LEFT: the many-breasted Artemis, Ephesus.
RIGHT: Alexander the Great meets his hostage, the empress of Persia, after the Battle of Issos.

Greek control, with his vast territories carved up amongst four of his generals *(see page 263)*.

Although these powerful players stir the soul, the true political unit of these centuries was a strong, complex network of municipal communities which ran their own affairs while paying lip-service and tribute to their political masters.

Walls and water, as much as the *Iliad* and Sophocles, were the basis of Hellenistic and Roman culture in Anatolia. The thriving cities planned streets and

market squares, lined with columns, built high defensive walls with grandiose gates, temples for the gods, baths and gymnasia for hygiene and health, stadiums, theatres and odeons for entertainment. It was a classical age of splendid architecture, erected by slaves. Even the most insignificant communities of the period have left their traces in fine columns and carved capitals. In Anatolia, the most magnificent of all was the altar of Zeus at Pergamon, whose superb friezes are now, controversially, in Berlin. The spread of Hellenistic civilisation into central Anatolia can literally be traced in stonemasonry techniques brought to local chieftains by builders hired from the coast.

> ### WATER FOR ALL
>
> Pergamon's water supply began in the mountains 45 km (28 miles) north of the town, running through a triple-pipe system with no fewer than 240,000 sections.

But as much as the beauty of the buildings, respect should be given to the extraordinary engineering capabilities of these great builders. The end of the classical world coincides almost exactly with the destruction of the aqueducts by Arab invaders.

The era is also marked by the gradual disappearance of local languages such as Carian, Pamphylian, Lycian and Phrygian.

In modern southeastern Turkey, Syria and Palestine, the spreading Hellenistic culture faced a rival written language, Syriac, which it was never fully able to absorb or subdue. Cultural and linguistic tension between the Semitic Syriac-speaking Middle East and Hellenism bedevilled the Roman Empire, prepared the way for the rise of Islam and Arabic, and still has repercussions today.

Elsewhere in the Middle East, Hebrew and Egyptian survived as written languages. Phrygian, the language of King Midas, survives only in a few monuments. Along the coast we have inscriptions in other languages such as Lycian and Pamphylian, but these come from the earlier periods. There seems to have been no major literature in these languages to rival that of ancient Greece and the Anatolian languages faded gradually as first the prosperous classes, and later the peasantry, began to use Greek as a means of communication and for most of their daily purposes.

The overall picture is one of a slow, voluntary and peaceful assimilation of indigenous peoples – until the region came to consider itself the heartland of the Roman world.

The Celts in Turkey

For a generation after the death of Alexander the Great and the establishment of rival kingdoms by his successors, the history of Anatolia was one of constant civil wars between would-be kings.

In 279 BC, the somewhat misguided King Nicomedes of Bithynia invited Celtic mercenaries, who were expanding throughout central Europe, to enter Anatolia, allowing them to settle in what had been eastern Phrygia on the west bank of the Kızıl Irmak River. They called their new land Galatia.

These Celts ("Gauls") were kinsmen of the Gauls who settled in what are now France,

Britain and Ireland. A robust, warrior people, they preyed upon the wealthy Hellenistic city-states in much the same way that the Germanic tribes would feed on the decaying Roman Empire 500 years later. The Hellenistic kingdoms immortalised their barbaric but valiant invaders in the famous sculpture of the "Dying Gaul".

On the whole, however, the Celts left little mark, either positive or negative, on Anatolia, although a kind of Celtic language was spoken for the next 600 years or so. According to the records of St Jerome, the Celtic language of Ankara could still be understood in northern Gaul at the end of the 4th century AD.

was not only a rich area, filled with raw materials, but the power vacuum was in danger of destabilising existing wealthy trade routes. It was ripe for the picking.

Pergamon, by now one of the wealthiest states in Anatolia, sided with the Romans but the growth of Latin power was unpopular with the local people, and it came as a severe shock when, in 133 BC, Attalus III, the last king of Pergamon, bequeathed his kingdom to Rome.

Over the next century, local rulers such as Mithridates, king of Pontus on the Black Sea, tried to stem the Roman advance. There was an anti-Roman uprising in Pergamon itself in

Advent of the Romans

The persistent Gauls were finally turned back by Attalus I, king of Pergamon, in 230 BC, but Attalus also had to contend with the growing political and trading power of the Romans, on the far side of the Aegean Sea.

The confusion surrounding the rivalry for the Anatolian kingdoms had drawn the Romans to the area. Hard-headed pragmatists, they rarely tried to acquire territory unless they had strong economic reasons for it. Anatolia

LEFT: detail of a Greek soldier in full armour, in the Istanbul Archaeological Museum.
ABOVE: Hercules and the lion; detail of a sarcophagus.

88 BC during which a total of 80,000 Romans were massacred in various Anatolian cities. This was quickly countered by a Roman military expedition to quell Mithridates and consolidate Rome's powerful grip on the province.

A series of Roman generals made their reputations putting down the Anatolian revolts. Mithridates was defeated first by Sulla, and then again 12 years later by Pompey the Great who ran the cagey old man to the ground in the Crimea in 63 BC. Rather than be dragged in chains to Rome, Mithridates tried to poison himself but failed – during his long life he had imbibed far too much toxin as a prophylactic against assassination, and was obliged to have a trusted servant run him through with a sword. A 10-day public holiday was declared in Rome upon the news of his death. Pompey, meanwhile, proceeded to clean up the pirate dens in the Mediterranean coastal towns of Alanya and Side, bringing the cult of Mithras with him back to Rome.

A generation later, in 47 BC, at the Battle of Zela (modern Zile, near Tokat), Julius Caesar completed Pompey's work when he defeated Pharnaces, the nephew of Mithridates and uttered the famous boast: *"Veni. Vidi. Vici."* ("I came. I saw. I conquered"). The remaining semi-independent kingdoms in the centre and

themselves into the Greek-speaking, imperial and Christian Byzantines. Yet they continued to call themselves "Romans", which is why the Greeks of Anatolia and Cyprus are known, even today, in Turkish, as *Rum*.

The first few centuries of Roman rule were a mixed affair. The *Pax Romana* (Roman peace) brought security and prosperity to the cities, which grew in size and splendour. But it also meant the arrival of the tax farmer, eager to squeeze all the money he could from the province he had been awarded by auction. These administrators had no interest in the welfare of their province and, inevitably, created

east of Anatolia were gradually absorbed by the Romans over the next 100 years or so, and the eastern frontier was pushed back to the kingdom of Armenia and the Euphrates, though the border often fluctuated during the following centuries, under continued pressure from the Persians, who controlled the area around Lake Van for most of this period.

The Roman centuries

The story of the Romans in Anatolia stretches from the Battle of Magnesia in 190 BC to the fall of Constantinople to the Turks in AD 1453. During these long centuries, the Latin Romans, originally pagans and republicans, transformed

fierce resentment of distant Rome. However, Roman rule also brought many advantages to the less-developed interior. Living standards in Roman Anatolia were well ahead of those at the beginning of the 20th century.

We know of the people of this period from their gravestones. Some are haughty senatorial families with estates all over the Roman world; others are simple farming folk who carved ovens, ploughs, looms and other reflections of daily life on their headstones. Echoes of imperial politics are also to be found in the surviving monuments. Emperors were venerated then worshipped as gods, like many earlier Hellenistic kings. Temple inscriptions honour both the emperors and family members such as Livia, the infamous wife of Augustus, commemorated at Ephesus, and Britannicus, the son and heir of Claudius I, mentioned on an inscription in Samsun.

The tremors of change

Under the Romans, the population of Anatolia reached about 12 million, and they must have thought that history was coming to a triumphant climax with the civilised world united in a single state. But by the 3rd century AD, tremors began to shake the foundations of the empire. Internally, it was challenged by a religion consciously opposed to classical civilisation and its values – Christianity. Externally, its borders were menaced by barbarian invaders.

In AD 258, bands of Gothic tribesmen poured deep into the heart of Anatolia, ransacking many of its towns and cities, as far inland as Ankara and Cappadocia, and kidnapping local people for slaves. During the same century, the Persians renewed their military threat to the eastern borders and a Roman emperor, Valerian, was actually taken prisoner in battle and later executed. Next came the Goths, who were repulsed by Claudius II, a capable soldier who took the name of Gothicus. A column erected in his honour still stands on Seraglio Point in Istanbul.

Reform

Later emperors were to become energetic, often harsh reformers. Diocletian (AD 284–305) reorganised both the army and system of government and tried to combat a more modern problem – inflation. Copies of his famous edict ordering a price-freeze can be seen throughout Anatolia, most notably at Aphrodisias. However, Diocletian's two most radical initiatives failed: he tried to create a new capital for the Roman Empire in Anatolia at Nicomedia (İzmit) and in AD 303, in an attempt to wipe out the religion, he unleashed a ferocious persecution of Christians.

A generation later, Constantine the Great (reigned AD 306–37) tackled the same problems from a different angle and in doing so, catapulted the empire into a new phase which was to last for the next 1,000 years. In AD 313,

the emperor converted to Christianity and declared it the official religion of the empire. In AD 325, he hosted the Council of Nicaea (İznik) which began to formalise the system of belief still stated in the Nicene Creed and appointed the emperor head of the church.

In AD 330, the capital moved to Byzantium (Istanbul), renamed Constantinople. The emperor had been working on the project for nearly six years. Astonished courtiers watched as Constantine marked the bounds of the new city way beyond the edge of old Byzantium. Asked why he did so, he replied that he was following an angelic guide. ❑

FAR LEFT: the imposing Roman theatre, Termessos.
LEFT: Corinthian column at Miletus.
RIGHT: Emperor Constantine I (AD 280–337).

CHRISTIANITY IN ANATOLIA

It was in Anatolia that Christianity really took root, mainly thanks to the tireless evangelising of Paul, a native of Tarsus, between AD 45–58. By AD 100, Christian groups had formed in most major cities of the Roman world. The powerhouse of early Christian thought was at Antioch (Antakya), Peter's base before he transferred to Rome. It remained one of the four chief bishoprics of the early church until the Arab conquest in AD 642. In AD 110, the governor of Bithynia, Pliny the Younger, wrote to Emperor Trajan requesting advice on how to handle the Christians in his province. This signalled the start of persecutions that lasted for the next 200 years.

BYZANTIUM

The Byzantine Empire was a ferment of religious fervour, artistic splendour, palace intrigue and barbarian invasions

The most pressing issue facing the Roman Empire was the struggle for supremacy between paganism and Christianity. Even the converted Constantine was not immune to lingering lapses into paganism and was only baptised shortly before he took his last breath.

The major breakthrough was made during the civil wars of the early 4th century, when Constantine adopted the cross as his symbol before the decisive battle of Milvisan Bridge in AD 312. A decade later, he decided to leave the traditional seat of power (and pagan worship) at Rome and establish a new, Christian city in Asia. He originally chose the site of Troy on the Dardanelles, replete with Homeric associations, for his new capital; the walls were nearly complete when he changed his mind (thanks, he said, to angelic intervention) and selected provincial Byzantium instead. Divine inspiration was to remain a leitmotif of the Christian world thereafter.

No sooner was the city established in 324 than courtiers and senators moved in. Dedicated in 330 and extravagantly decorated with stolen treasures from all over the classical world, the city became the seat of Christianity and the venue of the numerous acrimonious fights over the nature of the True Faith.

The horror of heresy

Christians had been at loggerheads with each other from the very beginning. In 1st century Ephesus, the Apostle John was seen retreating hastily from the baths to avoid Cerinthus, a heretic who believed that Christ was a spirit, not a man. A generation later, Marcion from Sinop was promoting a brand of Christianity which rejected the Old Testament and its God. Between AD 160 and 170 in Phrygia, Montanus, a former priest of the goddess Cybele, converted to Christianity, and two women friends developed a theory of ecstatic prophecy which

LEFT: 6th-century Italian mosaic of the Byzantine Emperor Justinian I (527–65).
RIGHT: detail with cross, Basilica of St John, Selçuk.

held that the Holy Spirit was speaking through them. The movement was banned, but it spread rapidly right across the Roman Empire.

For most of its history, the Roman and later Byzantine Empire was beset by problems of theology which sapped the energy of emperors and scholars, causing sometimes unbridgeable

political and social divisions. Yet these disputes are often virtually impossible to understand.

What was the fuss about? Basically, the new church was being forced to thrash out agreed explanations of its central truths – against the rationalisations of philosophers and diverse cultural and linguistic communities with their own vested interests to defend. The core issue was whether Jesus Christ was God or man, or (as orthodox Christians held) both at once.

At the two extremes were Monophysitism and Arianism. Arius was an Egyptian priest who believed that Christ was not God but more a heroic superman. The Monophysites arose as a reaction, stressing the divinity of Christ.

Between the two positions lay others of every conceivable variation. The semi-Arians said Christ was of similar, but not the same substance as God. He had one mind (Apolloninarianism) or one will (Monothelitism). He was born man and became God (Nestorianism). There were many, many more subvariants and by the middle of the 4th century, the controversy became so acrimonious that no Anatolian bishop was quite sure of anyone's orthodoxy. To solve the mess, Constantine held a Council of the

> ### MONASTIC RULES
> In AD 360, Basil of Kayseri (Cappadocia) wrote a set of monastic rules still used by the Greek Orthodox Church. The Rule of St Benedict is based on them.

attack on paganism. Temples were closed, trashed or converted, statues were thrown out, and oracles shut down. Emperor Julian (361–363), the great-nephew of Constantine, made an attempt to turn the clock back, but was too late: in 363, he was killed at Nusaybin, while fighting the Persians. All the subsequent emperors were Christians.

Perhaps even more influential than the monks were the ascetics, who sought extraordinary ways to demonstrate their faith. St Simeon Stylites lived on top of a pillar near Antioch for 30 years. Daniel the Stylite (409–493) passed the last 33 years of his life on a pillar at Rumelihisarı (Anaplous), attracting visitors like Emperor Leo I and his family. Other holy men, called "dendrites", preferred to live in trees. The church became the physical, social and political focus of every city.

Church at Nicaea (İznik) in 325, which resulted in the Nicene Creed, the declaration of faith still used today. The emperor prepared the way carefully, holding propaganda sessions and banishing as criminals any who refused to sign his version of the creed.

Arianism faded within a few generations. Monophysitism has survived to the present day amongst Syriac and Armenian Christians.

The advance of the holy men

From the 3rd century, the state faced an oblique threat to its authority with the formation of the first monasteries. Throughout the 4th and 5th centuries, the monks spearheaded a fierce

The Byzantine era

While the west was wracked by invading Goths, Vandals, Franks and other sundry barbarians, the eastern empire thrived, largely unaffected by the chaos. In Anatolia, the 5th and 6th centuries were periods of tremendous splendour under emperors such as Theodosius I (378–95), Theodosius II (408–50) and Justinian I (527–65). Greek began to replace Latin as the language of the court and the administration. The educational system became explicitly Christian. Imperial power grew and municipal traditions waned as senators cast off their pagan culture and sought careers as monks or bishops.

Emperor Justinian I has gone down in history as the builder of St Sophia and the codifier of Roman law, but these were only parts of a vast imperial programme which also aimed to reconquer the western territories lost 60 years earlier to the Germanic chieftains. Justinian's armies conquered north Africa and part of Spain relatively easily, but the reconquest of Italy required a long and enervating war.

To finance it and his vision of a strong, centralised empire, Justinian's rapacious minister, John of Cappadocia, squeezed the cities of Anatolia and Greece, weakening what remained of the classical, urban institutions. The contradiction was felt acutely by contemporaries, such as the historian Procopius, who publicly eulogised

Justinian for the buildings he was erecting, while privately lambasting him in his *Secret History* as a devil in human form, married to a prostitute, who delighted in humiliating his foremost subjects.

Justinian's legacy did not endure. Within his lifetime, the empire was struck by a great plague and soon after he rescued Italy from the Goths, it was overrun by the Lombards.

The Slav menace

The empire's northern provinces came under renewed threat at the end of the 6th century. The Danube frontier was attacked by the Avars, a Central Asian people similar to the Huns. The empire battled bravely, but as the frontier collapsed, the Slavs flooded the south. Emperor Maurice (582–602) struggled to contain the challenge but in 602, his armies revolted and he was killed by a usurper, Phocas.

For a period, order collapsed. The northern invasions were matched by others from the east as the Sassanid Persians, hereditary foes of the empire, staged their most successful invasion ever, crossing the entire length of Anatolia to reach the Sea of Marmara at Kadıköy and seizing Byzantine provinces as far away as Egypt. It was Persia's greatest triumph since Alexander the Great's defeat of Darius.

Settled life was impossible for the next 100 years. Most cities were destroyed, although Constantinople and Thessalonika survived, and there was an economic and cultural collapse unprecedented since the long forgotten invasions which had destroyed the Hittite empire 2,000 years before. In 622, Ankara was destroyed and its population was massacred or enslaved. Remarkably, Emperor Heraclius (610–41) was able to muster his army and expel the Persians by 628, but the effort so exhausted both the Persian and the Roman empires that they were unable to resist the sudden appearance of a new enemy on their frontiers – the Arab armies sweeping out of the desert under the banner of Islam.

Islam

The Arab invasions of the 7th century brought Islam to Anatolia – today it is the religion of

LEFT: Byzantine icon of the Apostles.
RIGHT: Emperor Theophilus with his bodyguard, from the Scylitzes Chronicle.

around 99 percent of the population. The Arab armies fought in the name of Allah and his Prophet Mohammed. To the Byzantines, the Arabs appeared to be wild, primitive tribesmen, a notion quickly overturned when the Byzantine host was routed by the Muslim horsemen under Khalid Ibn Walid, the "Sword of Islam", at the Battle of Yormuk (in present-day Jordan).

In 654, Arab armies swept through Anatolia, taking Ankara and other cities. Twenty years later began the first great siege of Istanbul, lasting four years. It was repulsed, as was the second one in 717–18, but the Byzantines lost most of their eastern provinces including

eastern Anatolia. Their new frontier stretched from east of Silifke on the south coast, past Kayseri (the great Byzantine frontier defense station) to a point east of Trabzon on the Black Sea. Tarsus, Malatya and Erzurum became Arab garrison towns from which annual raids were made on Byzantine territory.

Islam brought a new civilisation, religion, language and script. It was a radical departure for an area which had been basically Greek-speaking since the days of Alexander, even if the new religion had some points in common with Christianity. On the whole, however, Islam tolerated people of other Bible-based religions, provided they accepted inferior status and paid special taxes. As a result, those parts of Anatolia under Muslim rule remained multi-ethnic and multi-religious until the 20th century.

Byzantium and the Arabs each influenced the other: in 726, Emperor Leo III copied the Arab caliph in banning pictures and representations of human beings. The result was a new religious crisis as the iconoclasts battled with the supporters of images. The Orthodox leader was Mansur, a Christian Arab and civil servant at the court of the caliph in Damascus, known to the Greek world as St John of Damascus.

Against the Arab threat, the Byzantines emphasised the cross on their coins and city

walls. The unadorned cross can be found in the rock chapels of Cappadocia and in St Sophia (Aya Sofya) as a relic of the emergency period. By 843, the supporters of icons triumphed and images were gradually restored in churches.

Byzantine revival

The turning point came between 856–66, when Byzantium was ruled by Caesar Bardas on behalf of the weak Michael III.

On 3 September, 863, Bardas' brother, Petronas, defeated the Arab armies of Omer Ibn Abdullah, the emir of Malatya, at the Battle of Poson. Just at this point, however, Bardas was murdered by Emperor Michael's homosexual

lover and former groom, a peasant from Thrace called Basil. Basil was a penniless youth of Armenian descent who had drifted from Thrace (Macedonia as the Byzantines called it, hence the name of his dynasty) to the big city as a teenager, sleeping out in churches before he got a job as a groom, first in a wealthy household, and later, in the palace itself where he doubled as a champion wrestler.

Basil quickly became the favourite of the emperor, but neither he nor his master were taken seriously by the men running the empire. After the assassination, Basil was crowned joint emperor with Michael on 26 May, 866.

The sequel was predictable: on 23 September, 867, Basil murdered Michael III to become the empire's sole ruler. From this sordid beginning emerged Byzantium's most glorious dynasty. Over the next 200 years, the frontiers were expanded in all directions, with wars fought and won over the Fatamids in Egypt, the Abbasids in Baghdad, and the Bulgars and Russians to the north.

Under the ferocious Basil II ("The Bulgar Slayer"), the late Byzantine state reached the apogee of its glory. With the aid of Varangian soldiers sent by Vladimir of Kiev (in return for which a royal princess was given to Vladmir on his adoption of Christianity), Basil first crushed the revolt of two generals who meant to usurp and divide the empire between them before turning to the Balkans to deal with the Bulgarian czar, Samuel.

The end came in 1014, when the Byzantine host captured some 14,000 Bulgarian soldiers. They were all blinded and sent back to Samuel, in his last redoubt, in groups of 100, each of which was led by one man who only had one eye put out. When Samuel beheld the gruesome spectacle, he fell into delirium tremens and died within two days. His kingdom was then annexed to the Byzantine state.

Basil II also extended the eastern frontier of the empire to the Armenian kingdom of the Bagratids in the north, and in the south to Amida (Diyarbakır), Edessa (Sanlıurfa) and Aleppo. In the west, he restored much of Italy to the Byzantine sphere, and was preparing for a decisive campaign against the Muslims in Egypt and Syria when he died in 1025, an unmarried warrior with no heir.

In many ways, Basil's death signalled the end of Byzantium, as the ruling house fell into a vortex of complex, sinister intrigues. Basil's ageing, younger brother, Constantine VIII, next took the purple and was succeeded in turn by an elderly, spinster daughter Zoe who was married at his deathbed to Romanus Aryges. The new emperor died in his bath a few years later at the hand of Zoe's young peasant lover, who was crowned Michael IV before attempting to banish his ageing wife to a convent. That backfired and Michael IV was blinded and deposed.

Zoe and Theodora

Zoe then raised her sister, Theodora, to rule as a joint empress. Although aged 63, Zoe was

This could not have occurred at a worse time: to the north, Turkish tribesmen ransacked the Danube provinces; far more ominous were the Seljuk Turks who had replaced the Arab threat. After overrunning Arab lands from Baghdad to Egypt, the new power on the eastern horizon of the empire was now raiding north into the Byzantine empire as far as Cappadocia.

The desperate situation led to the arranged marriage of Romanus IV Diogenes to the widowed Empress Eudocia. Diogenes led a host of some 150,000 mercenaries east to meet 14,000 Seljuk horsemen, under Alp Arslan. On 19 August, 1071, they clashed on the field of

determined to marry again. Her new husband, Constantine IX Monomachus (along with his young lover, who quickly obtained the official title of Sebaste) joined a bizarre triumvirate, which, if nothing else, drained the treasury.

The final break with the Catholic church in Rome isolated Byzantium from its natural allies in the West, while civil bureaucracy castrated the Byzantine war machine, leaving the frontier defenses in the hands of local aristocrats and their personal armies of mercenaries.

LEFT: figures in many frescoes in Cappadocia had their eyes gouged out by iconoclasts.
ABOVE: Christ with Constantine IX and Zoe, St Sophia.

Manzikert, north of Lake Van. It was an utter rout, with large numbers of Armenian mercenaries deserting to the Turks, while Romanus himself fell captive. He managed to ransom himself and signed a treaty with the Turks, but his defeat turned into a total disaster upon his return to Constantinople, when he learned that he had been deposed during his captivity. He was subsequently blinded by the new emperor and died of his injuries in 1072.

The freshly signed treaty between Romanus and the Seljuk prince, Alp Arslan, was no longer valid. Thus Anatolia lay open to the Turks, who quickly began their ineluctable conquest of the country. ❑

AN EMPIRE UNDER THREAT

Faced by the onslaught of colonial imperialism from every direction, the Byzantine
Empire shrank into a tiny enclave around the walls of Constantinople

Byzantium was to struggle on for another four centuries under the new Comneni dynasty, at times seeming to regain some spark of former glory, but ultimately doomed to failure. The population decreased steadily, invaders prowled the edges of the empire, subject peoples saw their opportunity and sought to gain their independence, and foreign armies – such as the Crusaders – came to play an ever greater role in state affairs. The first dire prophesy of doom came at the Battle of Manzikert in 1071, when the Byzantine army faced a new enemy for the first time. The nomadic Turks were sweeping west across the great plains of Central Asia, but who were they?

The Turks

The names of Attila the Hun, Genghis Khan and Timur, riding at the front of their hordes (*ordu* in Turkish, simply meaning army), strike images of bloodthirsty horror into the minds of modern man. However, these figures must be evaluated within the drama of the day – nomads versus settlers, the stirrup versus the plough.

Somewhere in the vastness of Central Asia, a nomadic people ventured from one dried-up waterhole to the next, fighting drought, the torrid heat and the bitter cold of night. It was almost by a primitive law of nature that when these poor herdsmen came upon cultivated lands they ransacked the riches. It is from this stock of people that the Turks emerged.

Language alone sets them apart from the Europeans, Slavs or Semitic peoples. Aside from the modern, Western Turkish spoken in Turkey today, millions of Turkic peoples in parts of Iran, the Caucasus and Chinese Turkestan speak a form of Turkish or other related languages such as Mongolian or Uzbek, which belong to the Ural-Altaic family of languages, along with Finnish, Hungarian, Japanese, Korean and – some say – Navaho.

LEFT: Seljuk Ulucamii (Grand Mosque) at Sivas.
RIGHT: early Seljuk *kümbet* (domed tomb) at Ahlat, on the shores of Lake Van.

The word "Turk" was first recorded in Chinese annals as early as 1,300 BC, when it appears as *T'u-chueh* or *Durko*. The 8th-century BC Orkhon inscriptions found in Mongolia describe the ordeal of bringing tribes under a single authority to stand against a common enemy, the Chinese. The inscriptions, written

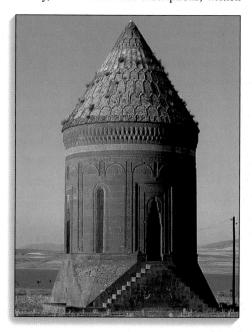

EXPERIMENTING WITH RELIGION

People today think of the Turks as an Islamic people, but this is certainly not the whole story. The ancient religion of the Turkic nomads was shamanism, a polytheistic faith using totems and magic. Gradually, some tribes, such as the Uighurs, adopted Buddhism; while others became Zoroastrians, Nestorians or Manicheans. The Khazar Turks, whose story is depicted in Arthur Koestler's The *Thirteenth Tribe*, adopted Judaism. Today a few Christian Turks, the Gagauz, survive in Poland, and a colony of Jewish Karaim Turks lives in the Baltic States. It was not until the 10th century that Islam penetrated Central Asia and the conversion of the Turks to Islam began.

in runic characters, also reveal the capital cities of the tent-dwellers. An interesting inscription on the east side reads: "If the sky above did not collapse and if the earth below did not give way, Oh, Turkish people, who would be able to destroy your state and institutions?"

One learns more about the lifestyle of these people in the ancient Turkish epic *Dede Korkut*. Ancient Turks were patriarchal, but monogamous. When the wife was unable to bear children it was accepted as fate; taking a second wife was not considered as an option.

Traditionally, the Turks married outside their tribe, establishing blood ties and alliances with

their neighbours, which partially explains the confusion surrounding the Mongols and Turks among the various Central Asian dynasties; Timucin, better known as Genghis Khan – was actually half-Mongol and half-Turkish.

The Turks, like the Mongols, were renowned horsemen and soldiers. The Abbasid caliphs in Baghdad were well aware of their martial qualities and recruited them in large numbers as paid warriors or as superior slave soldiers. The Arabs, it would seem, had not read enough Roman history as regards the hiring and firing of foreigners in the homeguards. By the end of the 9th century, most military command posts of the empire were held by Muslim Turks.

The Seljuks

In the mid-11th century, an obscure Turcoman people called the Seljuks set up a state in Iran, with Isfahan as their capital. The Abbasid caliph in Baghdad was so taken in by their military prowess, that he gave their leader, Toğrul Bey, the impressive title "King of the East and West", designating the Seljuk warlord as his temporal deputy.

However, the Seljuks under Toğrul and his successor, Alp Arslan, were not content with controlling only their piece of the disintegrating Arab empire. Recent and enthusiastic converts to Islam, they persuaded themselves that they were the rightful heirs to all the lands conquered during and immediately after the time of the Prophet Mohammed, in particular, the heretical lands of the Levant and Egypt. In order to secure their own flanks, as they concentrated on their southern conquests, Toğrul entered into numerous negotiations with the Byzantine emperors of Constantinople.

Meanwhile, the day-to-day situation on the borderlands between the Seljuks and the Byzantines was anything but peaceful. Various Armenian and Byzantine landowners enrolled private troops from amongst the ranks of the Turcoman *ghazis* (warriors for the faith; generally a very motley crew) and the Byzantine *akritoi* (mercenaries), all of whom promptly engaged in private looting, leaving the Seljuks and Byzantines to accuse each other of bad faith and breaching the general peace. By the third quarter of the 11th century, the situation was critical. The Byzantines, under Emperor (or *Basileus*) Romanus IV Diogenes, decided to pre-empt the nascent Seljuk power on their eastern frontier and reconquer Armenia.

Using ancient Harput (modern Elazığ) as his base, Diogenes crossed the Euphrates – the classic demarcation of east and west – in order to confront the Seljuk army on the field of Manzikert, north of Lake Van in 1071. Although they vastly outnumbered the irregular Turkish horsemen, the Byzantine Christian troops could scarcely have selected a worse venue: the light-riding Turks feigned a retreat, lured the main Byzantine force into a loop, and showered the heat-exhausted Christian host with arrows before closing on three sides with the scimitar. The booty for the victors on "that dreadful day" included the vanquished Diogenes himself.

Remarkably, the Seljuks did not drag the beaten Diogenes back home in victory, but released him for a ransom and huge tracts of Byzantine land, giving the Turks control over most of eastern Anatolia.

Seljuk settlers

There now followed another long period of often uneasy peace between the Seljuks and Constantinople.

The reigns of Alp Arslan and his son, Malik Shah, were the most glorious years of the great Seljuks of Isfahan; the death of the latter marked the decline of the great Seljuks and by 1192 the dynasty ended in the same obscurity with which it had begun, unable to cope with the pressures from the Crusaders, the caliph and new Turcoman clans arriving from the east.

With no overall power, a number of lesser Seljuk clans began establishing their own small Muslim principalities throughout central Anatolia, making the small Christian states in the area their vassals. Through intermarriage, they facilitated the cultural syncretism of the region.

Continuing to nibble away at the corners of the Byzantine state, the nomads were settling down. What's more, they were doing it in style, which explains the abundance of superb Seljuk architecture in modern Turkey. Some of the best examples of this so-called "poetry in stone" can be seen in Erzurum, Divriği, Sivas and Konya, of which Konya is perhaps the most impressive of all. This was where the Sufi mystic, Jelaleddin Rumi (*Mevlana* or "Our Master") graced the court of master builder, Alâeddin Keykubat, sultan of Rum, and initiated the peculiar whirling dervish ceremony in an effort to seek spiritual union with the Creator himself. The cultural effervescence at Konya, however, met with the same abrupt and unhappy end as the others at the hands of the powerful and indiscriminate Mongol hordes of Genghis Khan (whom the modern Turks oddly and inconsistently claim as one of their own).

The latter were soon to erupt from the deepest recesses of Central Asia to sack much of the known world before returning just as quickly to the frontiers of China. Just as they had overwhelmed the Byzantines two centuries before,

the now settled Seljuks could not resist the most recent wave of nomad arrivals. On June 26, 1243, despite Byzantine auxiliaries sent by the Seljuk sultan's "ally" in Constantinople, the once mighty Turkish army was utterly routed at Köse Dağ, outside the quintessentially Seljuk city of Sivas. Neither Christian nor Muslim was spared the sword.

The remaining Turkish clans scattered westwards, and in the end had to accept their role as mere vassals in the greater scheme of things. Yet no sooner had the Mongol tide surged over the region than it withdrew once more, leaving behind several unimportant mini-states led by

petty chieftains who might have remained utterly obscure but for one of their number, a man with a patch of land tucked between the Seljuk and Byzantine states. Osman, son of Ertuğrul, was destined to found one of the mightiest empires the world has known, stretching from Morocco in the west to Iran in the east; from the Yemen in the south to the Crimea in the north.

The Armenians

If the Turks were unknown nomadic invaders, the Armenians were anything but – they had been living in north and eastern Anatolia for literally thousands of years, retaining their independence for much of that time.

LEFT: the Byzantine monastery at Alahan, one of many Christian institutions to thrive under Seljuk rule.
RIGHT: the great Mongol chief, Timur (c.1336–1405).

The emergence of Armenians dates to the period after the fall of the Urartus in the 7th century BC. Linguistic evidence suggests a wave of Indo-European immigration from the west, apparently related to the Phrygians. A network of powerful and often warring local lords colonised the area bounded by modern Erzincan, the Çoruh valley, Lake Sevan in the Armenian Republic, Lake Urmia in Iran and Lake Van. The first recorded unification of Armenian princes under a proper monarchy occurred in about 190 BC. The following century, King Tigran the Great (95–55 BC) assisted his father-in-law, Mithridates of Pontus, in his struggle against the Romans, then went on to forge an empire extending to Syria and the Mediterranean that survived until the 5th century AD as a buffer between the Roman-Byzantine and the Persian worlds. Christianity was adopted in AD 301 during the reign of King Trdad (Tiridates) through the efforts of St Gregory the Illuminator.

> ### ALPHABET
>
> The Armenian alphabet – which is still in use – was devised in AD 407 by the scribe Mesrob, and heralded a period of literary, scholastic and theological ferment in the 5th century.

This so-called "golden age" ended with the Persian occupation, schism with the Byzantine Orthodox Church and a gradual reversion to the dominance of petty regional dynasties.

One such dynasty, the Bagratids of the Çoruh valley and Kars region, succeeded in establishing its dominance over most Armenian princes during the 9th century. The Bagratid kingdom, centred first in Kars, then Ani, lasted for almost 200 years. It was a period of intense architectural activity whose monuments still dot the landscape of northeast Turkey and Caucasia.

But for all its finery, the Bagratid kingdom was still a pawn between two very warlike kings and in the early 11th century, the dynasty was toppled by Byzantium, which transported many Armenians to Cilicia and left their kingdom vulnerable to conquest. With the rout of the Byzantine army in 1071, the Seljuks simply walked in. Some Armenian princes not only welcomed the Turks, but actually converted to Islam and participated in the subsequent wars of conquest.

Not long after 1071, a network of semi-independent Armeno-Georgian dynasties took control of the Ani region and ruled until the Mongolian devastation. Meanwhile, in the south, the Armenians, resettled in Cilicia by the Byzantines, took advantage of the mayhem to break away and form an independent state, based around Antioch, Malatya, Maraş and Edessa, which sided with the Norman Crusaders and even the Mongols against Byzantium. Further north, Armenian towns and chieftains coexisted with marauding Turkish, Kurdish and Arab beys, tribal coalitions, bandit chiefs and adventurers of unknown origin – in a state of perpetual anarchy – until as late as the Ottoman conquest of 1514.

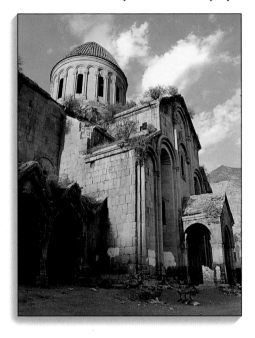

> ### WHERE ARE THEY NOW?
>
> Until the late 1800s, one-third of the population of northeast Turkey remained Christian and Armenian. The disintegration of the Ottoman Empire led to calls for Armenian autonomy; Russia and England entered the fray with a view to their conflicting interests in the region. During World War I, fearing the imminent collapse of its eastern front under a Russian offensive, the Ottoman government tried to deport most of its Armenian population to camps in Mesopotamia; many thousands died. Officially, since the 1920s, there have been no Armenians in eastern Turkey. The country is extremely sensitive to perceived attempts to revive a history it prefers to forget.

The Crusades

The third great threat to Byzantine power came from the most unlikely quarter of all. The Byzantine defeat at Manzikert was a final alarm call to Christian Europe, already facing a steady tide of Muslim expansion from Iberia. Pope Urban II, determined to save the Holy Land, called a Crusade against the infidel Turk.

Byzantium, less troubled by Islam than by the loss of its lands, joined the First Crusade of 1097–8, realising only afterwards that there was a heavy price to pay. The Crusaders' progress across Byzantine land was marked by wholesale pillaging and looting. Reluctantly,

When, in 1175, Byzantium complained of the Westerners' cavalier treatment, Holy Roman Emperor Frederick Barbarossa actually persuaded the Seljuks to attack Constantinople. Byzantium suffered another horrific defeat. The Balkan States took advantage of the moment and broke away. In 1185, matters became even worse when the Normans sacked Thessalonika. Two years later, the Third Crusade took Edirne, while in 1203, the notorious Fourth Crusade gave up all pretence of fighting the Turks and laid siege to Constantinople itself, crowning Count Baldwin of Flanders as head of a new Latin Empire of Byzantium.

the empire was persuaded to allow the Western armies free passage during the Second Crusade of 1146. Again, their lands suffered widespread destruction.

Meanwhile, the Western Crusaders regarded the "heretical" Eastern Orthodox state as little better than the Seljuks. They conquered Antioch, Edessa and eventually Jerusalem, but they set them up as Norman principalities, paying only the most tenuous lip service to Byzantium and eventually breaking away completely.

LEFT: Armenian Öşk-Vank monastery, near Ani.
ABOVE: a cavalry charge by the Knights of St John, during the First Crusade (1097–8).

The Byzantines retreated hastily to Nicaea. Their eventual recovery of the city in 1261 by Michael VIII Palaeologus was little more than an interesting historical footnote. The once powerful empire had been reduced to a rump state, ever more dependent on the Ottoman Turks whose realms were slowly but surely surrounding those of Byzantium.

Still the city struggled to survive for another 200 years until the sultans, their harems filled with Byzantine princesses taken in exchange for peace, finally grew tired of the presence of the ancient city of Constantine in their midst and the Ottomans surged forward to sweep Anatolia clean. ❑

THE OTTOMANS

Out of nowhere, the warlike Osman clan rose to challenge the Seljuk

and Byzantine empires, forming a dynasty that lasted 800 years

As the Mongol forces swept over Anatolia, an exhausted band of retreating Seljuks, led by Alâeddin of Konya, were cornered by a detachment of the Mongol barbarians from the east. Just as all hope seemed lost for the Turks, a wall of horsemen appeared on the crest of a nearby hill, pausing, it would seem, just long enough to determine the victor and claim his side for a division of the spoils. The chieftain of the horsemen signalled his men forward, drawing his scimitar as he charged.

But instead of joining the apparent victors, the horsemen spurred their steeds towards the Mongol flank, and carved their way through to the surprised relief of Alâeddin. Grateful for his life, the Seljuk commander asked the leader of the gallant horsemen his name: Ertuğrul, came the answer, father of Osman.

So legend tells of the emergence of Ertuğrul Ghazi and his 444 horsemen, and the birth of the Ottoman Empire. Even if the historical accuracy of the episode is somewhat doubtful, the fact remains that after his intervention helped stem the tide of the Mongol invasion, Ertuğrul emerged as the possessor of a small fiefdom near the town of Eskişehir in western Anatolia. This was to serve as the base from which the Ottoman Empire spread first across Anatolia into Europe, later expanding to encompass most of the Middle East and parts of Asia.

The beginning

At the time they settled in Eskişehir, the Ottomans had not yet converted to Islam. It is also doubtful that they numbered more than 4,000 souls, including women and children – hardly a force to breach the walls of the Byzantine capital. But in the chaos resulting from the Mongolian sack of Anatolia, coupled with the internal confusion of the late Byzantine state itself, no dreams were, perhaps, too wild for credence. As the power vacuum grew, so did

the need for order, and the Ottoman Turks were waiting for their opportunity.

There were several factors in their favour. Their fief lay on the march between the Seljuk-Muslim lands of Anatolia and the rump Byzantine state around the Sea of Marmara. It was a convenient frontier along which to invite the

LEFT: contemporary European oil painting of Emperor Süleyman the Magnificent.

RIGHT: European image of the Janissary Corps.

DREAMS OF WORLD DOMINATION

Upon his succession as clan chieftain, Osman Ghazi spent the night in the house of a pious Muslim who introduced the young warlord to the Qur'an (Koran). Osman read deep into the night, finally falling asleep on his feet to dream of a giant tree springing from his loins. Its branches grew to such heights as to cover the great mountain ranges of the known world while its roots were watered by the great rivers – the Tigris, Euphrates, Danube and Nile. A wind blew through the vision, turning the leaves of the branches into swords, all pointed in the direction of Constantinople, which appeared as a fabulous, bejewelled ring ripe for the plucking.

Ghazi (Holy Soldier) to war with the infidel. Perhaps more importantly, local confidence in Christianity was at an all time low: wrecked by schisms in the faith which made the road to piety confusing and filled with pitfalls. More to the point, on Ottoman lands, the *Dhimmi* tax cost non-Muslims 50 percent of earnings, while believers paid only a tithe (10 percent). On Christian land, the serfs were still bound to give feudal labour to their overlords. Wedged firmly between a rock and a hard place, untold numbers of Byzantine peasants converted to Islam.

For 12 years, Osman Ghazi's forces grew from his father's reputed 444 horsemen to over

gained effective control of the entire Anatolian hinterland and the remaining Byzantine cities in Asia Minor, chief among which was Bursa.

After a seven-year siege, Bursa's garrison commander finally surrendered in 1326, and he, his forces and most of the city's inhabitants embraced Islam. Osman Ghazi was only able to enter his empire's first capital in a shroud. The founder of the dynasty had died in 1324, before he could see the realisation of his dream, leaving his son and successor, Orhan Ghazi, a firm foundation on which to build. The great tree of Osman's vision was well-rooted, its branches reaching towards the jewel of Byzantium.

4,000 men at arms. In 1301, the Ottoman state came into direct conflict with Constantinople for the first time, near Baphaeon. Although inferior in numbers, the Muslims easily bested Christian morale and routed the forces of Andronicus II Palaeologus.

The defeat of an imperial army by a still obscure Muslim clan sent shockwaves through the recently restored empire. The reverberations (and promise of further booty) brought holy warriors and converts from across Anatolia flocking to join Osman, eager for battle. The next confrontation, against the Greeks, was outside Nicomedia seven years later. Byzantium was routed a second time and the Ottomans

The Ottoman state

The reign of Osman's second son, Orhan Ghazi (1324–59) was marked by reorganisation and expansion. He consolidated the proto-Ottoman state with one religion, Islam; he built mosques and religious schools; and promoted Muslim brotherhoods whose members were known as *Akhis*, the Arabic word for "brother". Bursa, in particular, became one large construction site for religious edifices.

Next, he reorganised the military, changing the enthusiastic waves of religiously inspired horsemen into discreet units ranging from shock troops to a regular cavalry and infantry. Finally, Orhan embarked on a multi-pronged expansion programme. He first conquered the Muslim Turkish-Seljuk lands to the south and east, co-opting them as allies, turning them into vassal states or simply annexing them. Next he set his sights on Christian Thrace, crossing the Dardenelles and Sea of Marmara.

His first actual step into Europe came, oddly enough, at the invitation of the Byzantine pretender, John Cantacuzene, who married his daughter, Theodora, into Orhan's harem in exchange for aid during his civil war against the house of Palaeologue. Muslim Turks stood shoulder to shoulder with Christian supporters of the pretender, besieging the walls of Constantinople as brothers-in-arms. When peace was finally agreed, with Cantacuzene marrying another of his daughters to the legitimate Byzantine emperor, Orhan's role as a king-maker in Constantinople was firmly established along with his first tenuous claim to the crown.

By his death in 1359, Orhan had multiplied his territory several times over, mostly due to invitations from his rivals and enemies. Yet with the succession of Orhan's son, Murat (at times called Amurath in medieval chronicles), this policy of expansion-by-invitation was forgotten; the Ottoman power marched on Europe by force-of-arms and the call of destiny.

Murat I

The second half of the 14th century saw the steady expansion of the Ottoman realm, at the expense of both Constantinople and its would-be heirs in the Balkans. Within 18 months of his succession, Murat I (1362–89) controlled all of Thrace, including Adrianople (now renamed Edirne), which was to become the Ottoman's second capital.

Murat I saw the importance of developing new administrative policies to cope with his European conquests. Unlike the Christians of Asia, who had long been exposed to Islam, and were more easily assimilated, the peoples of the Balkans were tenacious of faith. Short of leaving a garrison in every conquered town to ensure their adherence to Islam, they had to be treated differently. Thus, slowly but surely the system of *Millets* came into existence. Under this system, minority populations – based on

religion – were officially recognised, with their leaders held responsible for the communities' taxes, communal and legal affairs.

Yet this recognition came only after surrender. While campaigning, the Ottoman army was almost entirely male, save for camp followers, and any conquered women instantly became the chattel of the forces – eventually resulting in the extremely heterogeneous bloodline of the modern Turk.

The janissaries

Murat I also began the institution of "taxing" subject families for their most able-bodied sons,

who were drafted into corps of "new troops." These candidates, new converts to Islam and completely isolated from their origins, ensured their absolute and personal loyalty to the sultan himself. Bereft of everything but their own esprit de corps, these *Yeniçeri* (janissaries) would eventually become the terror not only of Europe, but of the Ottoman Empire itself.

Writers, from contemporary historians down to Count von Hammer-Purgstall and Edward Gibbon, have decried these "slave soldiers" as an affront to human dignity. But there was a fundamental difference between slavery in Islam and the Christian world. There was a greater difference still between normal Islamic

---

FAR LEFT: 19th-century portrait of Sultan Orhan.
LEFT: young recruit to the Janissary Corps.
RIGHT: portrait of Yavuz Sultan Selim ("the Grim").

slavery and the servant-warrior janissaries of the Ottomans, and the Mamelukes of Egypt and other Arab lands where slave dynasties were formed by the elite praetorian forces. They even ensured their own legacy by enslaving fresh blood from beyond the *Dar Al-Salam* ("abode of peace," as the Muslim world was known) in the *Dar Al-Harb* ("abode of war" – those lands beyond the borders of the Muslim world).

In 1389, Murat met his end on the battlefield at Kosovo, on the verge of victory over a Slavic

SUCCESSION BY DEATH

For the first 150 years of Ottoman rule, the brothers of each new sultan were strangled with a silken cord – in 1595, Sultan Mehmet III had 19 siblings murdered to safeguard his throne.

through the ages, setting the precedent for all future cases of succession to the power of the Ottoman state. Beyazıt next avenged the assassination of his father by massacring all Serbian notables captured during the campaign. Finally, he married Lazar's daughter, Despina, allowing her brother to retain a quasi-independent Serbia, although he was forced to supply troops to the Ottoman sultan and allow Muslim settlement in his fief. The repercussions are still being felt today.

confederation, assassinated by Milosh Obravitch, the son-in-law of the Serbian leader, Stephen Lazar, who had accused his relative of treason. Obravitch, apparently trying to prove his loyalty with his life, surrendered to Murat, only to run the 70-year-old sultan through with a dagger as he knelt before him.

Beyazıt the Thunderbolt

Murat's son, Beyazıt, was raised to sultan immediately upon his father's death. His first act was to have his younger brother, Yakub, strangled in order to ensure his leadership of the state. This grisly practice of fratricide, allowed by Islamic jurisprudence, continued

Beyazıt and the last Crusade

If the Crusades of the first millennium had been inspired by the desire to re-establish the True Faith in distant Jerusalem, the last Crusade was a desperate effort to forestall the infidel Turks from knocking down the door to Europe itself. In the summer of 1396, an "international brigade", drawn from across Christian Europe, assembled in Hungary, pillaging and raping the lands it was allegedly defending from the Turks. The Crusaders found little to test their military mettle save the women and children of Nish, whom they massacred although they were Christian. Finally, the rampant army made camp around the town of Nicopolis in Bulgaria, hoping to starve the Turkish garrison into sub-mission. At last, scouts reported that Beyazıt had arrived to relieve the town. While Eastern Europeans urged caution, the western knights elected for immediate battle. Believing the Ottoman front guard to be the entire battle line, they charged on armoured steeds, wreaking havoc on the Ottoman auxiliaries. They then dismounted and carved their way to the crest of the hill, only to find, like Custer at Little Big Horn, that they had merely dealt with the vanguard of an army of over 200,000 highly trained and battle-fresh janissaries with ven-geance in their eyes. Some 10,000 knights were slaughtered within hours, with a cower-ing knot of survivors fording the Danube to safety. Middle Europe was left undefended.

Surprisingly, Beyazıt did not press through with his victory, returning to Constantinople to seize the jewel that had eluded his forefathers for over a century. But as his forces once again set up their blockade-siege of the city, a new and wholly unexpected challenge was heard from the east, delivered by yet another cousin/rival – the limping but iron-willed Tatar, Timur, more frequently known as Tamerlane.

Timur the Tatar

Some historians of the Muslim lands refer to "the Big Foot" in central Asia, which periodi-cally kicks out the nomadic elements, sending them in all four directions in search of booty, prosperity and power.

So was it between the established "eastern" power, the Ottomans, and the Mongol hordes of Timur. At the very moment when the Ottomans were relishing their victory over Christian Europe, Timur's mounted archers shattered the late Osman's dream and nearly extinguished the Ottoman line itself.

The build-up to the Battle of Ankara was chiefly due to Ottoman stupidity. Inflated by the success of his European victories, Beyazıt seized lands belonging to eastern Anatolian vassals of Timur, then threatened to cuckold the Tatar ruler. With personal honour at stake, Timur had no choice but to march against his fellow Muslim. In 1402, the two armies closed on the plain northeast of the citadel of Ankara.

Beyazıt's foolish pride still knew no bounds. For several days before the battle, he ordered his troops to drive animals for him to hunt. Timur seized the initiative and positioned his army between Beyazıt's now exhausted forces and the citadel, which should have been the Ottoman's last defence. Beyazıt's doom was assured when the majority of his cavalry deserted to Timur. At the end of the day, the once invincible janissaries lay dead on the field or in headlong flight, with Beyazıt himself taken captive.

Bound in chains, Beyazıt was forced to serve as Timur's footstool; the Ottoman was also

obliged to see his favourite wife, Despina, serve the Tatar overlord naked at dinner, and then raped before his eyes. Christopher Marlowe's drama, *Tamburlaine the Great*, relates how the humiliated Beyazıt was dragged through the streets of Anatolia in a cage, insulted and ridiculed by his former subjects, until in utter despair, he took his own life.

There was, in any case, precious little left of the Ottoman domains: Bursa had been sacked and Timur's hordes ranged as far as Smyrna (modern İzmir) to uproot the last colony of Crusaders on the Mediterranean coast, with the skulls of his victims gathered in a pyramid to mark the occasion.

LEFT: a bloody version of the battle between the Turks and Crusaders, by Antonio Calza (1653–1725).
RIGHT: Ottoman miniature of acrobatic warriors.

Rising from the ruins

Beyazıt was survived by four sons who, as Timur's vassals, were unable to practise fratricide until the old Tatar's disappearance in 1405. Then the wars of succession began in earnest. After a decade of chaos, Beyazıt's youngest son Mehmet I emerged as the victor, his siblings dead around him. In 1421, his son, Murat II, shouldered the title and the responsibility of re-establishing state control.

During his reign, the Ottomans re-expanded in Anatolia, overran Greece and turned the cannons on the walls of Constantinople for the first time. But Murat also had a contemplative turn,

and twice renounced the throne in favour of his son Mehmet II, the son of a Christian slave girl, in order to retire to his palace at Manisa outside İzmir. On both occasions, however, he was obliged to return to Edirne to remove his son from power and to deal with the revolts and aggressions in the Balkans, where Hungarian King Ladislas and his heir, Hunyadi, in consort with the Wallachian Prince Vlad Dracul (better known as Dracula or Vlad the Impaler thanks to his bloody tactics of impaling his Muslim enemies) plotted ceaselessly against the Turks. The Albanian renegade Iskender Bey also managed to inspire sufficient resistance to the Ottomans to force a military confrontation

on the field of Kosovo, in a replay of the famous battle fought there 60 years before. This time, Serbia was absorbed into the empire, and disappeared from history for the next 400 years.

The conquest of Byzantium

In 1453, Constantinople had a population of scarcely 40,000, a shadow of Constantine's metropolis. The Byzantine hinterland, which once had stretched from France to Ethiopia, had been reduced to a few farms near the city walls. For centuries the city had been little more than a Turkish dependency, its princesses married into the harems of various sultans in a desperate attempt to maintain its fragile, humiliating independence. That the city would eventually fall to the Turks was a foregone conclusion. The only question remaining was which sultan would claim the honour of fulfilling Osman's dream. The answer was provided within months of Murat II's death and the subsequent ascension of his oft-wayward son, Mehmet, in 1451.

The young sultan announced the final siege of the imperial city by marching his troops within sight of the Byzantine walls. Next he built the castle of Boğaz Kesen ("Throat Cutter"; now known as Rumelihisarı) on the upper Bosphorus, equipping it with heavy ordnance never seen before in eastern warfare. Pairing it with the earlier castle of Anadoluhisarı on the Asian side of the straits, Mehmet reused the Symphlegades or "clashing cliffs" of Jason and the Argonauts, cutting off any aid to the threatened city via the Black Sea.

The Muslims' cannons were cast by Urban, a Hungarian renegade who had first offered his services to the Byzantines (who had no money to pay him.) So impressed was Mehmet with his work, that the young sultan made an order for a new cannon twice the size of that mounted at the Bosphorus castle. This new "toy" was of such weight that the bridges between Edirne and Constantinople had to be reinforced before the monstrosity could be lugged around to within firing range of the ancient city walls.

Such fortifications and new armaments were in direct contradiction to existing treaties; when the last Byzantine Emperor Constantine XI Palaeologus protested, Mehmet beheaded his envoys. Urban's cannons menaced the walls of Byzantine, and a Turkish fleet materialised in the Sea of Marmara. With no one like Timur to distract the Ottomans, it was evident to all that the fall of the city was simply a matter of time. The only reinforcements to run the Turkish naval blockade were 700 Genoese under the command of Giovanni Giustinani; even more able-bodied men fled the city.

The siege opened formally, with Mehmet petitioning Constantine for a complete and unconditional surrender. The soon-to-be last Byzantine emperor's reply, in equally formal manner, was that it was Mehmet alone who had made the decision to break the peace, and that

DEATH OF AN EMPIRE

Alone among the flames and screams, the last emperor of Constantinople was seen discarding his purple robe and engaging the janissaries in hand-to-hand combat.

attackers and patching up gaping holes in the walls as soon as they were formed.

On May 29, 1453, Mehmet ordered the final assault, promising his men a three-day respite from the fighting to boost their flagging morale. Wave after wave of Ottoman soldiers, accompanied by the roar of cannons and the crash of cymbals, stormed the walls on the promise of spreading the faith. First the shock troops fought and fell back, then regulars, then line after line of the sultan's well-rested

God would favour the righteous. There was to be neither surrender nor mercy.

As Mehmet's cannons and siege machinery battered away at the city's walls, teams of oxen dragged boats over the hill at Dolmabahçe, and down into the Golden Horn, where the Turkish fleet opened up another front against the low harbour walls, stretching the limited number of defenders even further. Still the Christians held out. Giustinani and his men performed military miracles by throwing back wave after wave of

LEFT: a magnificent, gilded Ottoman battle-axe, inscribed with the word "Ali".
ABOVE: medieval painting of Istanbul.

janissaries waded through the human debris in their path to test the ultimate resolve of the city's exhausted defenders. A breach here, closed again; a breach there, once again staunched. Finally, the Genoese commander, Giustinani, fell mortally wounded, and with him, the whole resistance collapsed. The magnificent Byzantine Empire was no more.

The Turks had conquered Constantinople. Mehmet the Conqueror entered the city in true imperial style, wearing his majestic turban and riding on a white stallion. The sultan held prayers at Hagia Sophia which the Turks turned into a mosque. Constantine's Christian city had become "Islamboul" – the City of Islam. ❏

SÜLEYMAN THE MAGNIFICENT

This influential sultan excelled in many roles: as conqueror, statesman, legislator and patron of the arts. This was the golden age of the Ottomans

Süleyman inherited the throne at the age of 26, and reigned for 46 years (1520–66).

Painted portraits offer varying pictures of him, but memoirs and historical records are more consistent about his appearance. He was "tall, broad-shouldered", had a "long graceful neck… aquiline nose…dark hazel eyes…fair skin, auburn hair, beetling eyebrows…long arms and hands."

The young sultan immediately proved himself to be a man of many parts – and many titles. The Europeans dubbed him "the Magnificent" even during his reign; he preferred the title "Kanuni" (lawgiver). His ground-breaking Codex Süleymanicus synthesised Islamic and secular law to establish a fully fledged, comprehensive judicial system with the concept of "justice" as the cornerstone, a guarantee of equal justice for all and a measure of leniency in the penal code.

As caliph and ruler of Islam's holiest places, Süleyman consolidated the Sunni Supremacy over Shia *(see page 82)*, while his skill as a military strategist more than doubled the size of his empire.

At home, he was a great patron of the arts: architecture, painting, calligraphy, illumination, weaponry, tiles and textiles, woodwork, metalwork and literature all flourished during his reign. He himself was an accomplished goldsmith and a fine classical poet whose collected works furnished many proverbs.

▷ **AGE OF KINGS**
Henry VIII and Elizabeth I of England; Ivan the Terrible of Russia; Francis I of France; and Holy Roman Emperor Charles V: these were all contemporaries of Süleyman the Magnificent.

◁ ARTISTS' PATRON
Twenty-nine painters (half of them Europeans) worked in the Palace Studio, producing many albums of miniature paintings depicting Ottoman military campaigns and court life.

▽ CLOTH OF GOLD
Even the clothes worn by the royal family were works of art, lavishly embroidered with silk, and gold and silver thread.

A DEVOTED FAMILY MAN

Until Süleyman, Ottoman sultans traditionally did not marry, enjoying instead large and fruitful harems. But this father of eight sons and one daughter fell in love with and married one of his concubines, Roxelana, later known as Hürrem. During their 25-year marriage, it is thought that Süleyman remained monogamous.

Hürrem was clever and ambitious, the first of many generations of harem women to involve themselves in palace politics. Some of Süleyman's sons died in infancy or adolescence, but she was determined to keep the path absolutely clear for her own disastrous son, Selim.

She persuaded the sultan to order and then witness the execution first of his heir apparent, Mustafa, a favourite of the armed forces, his son Beyazıt and Beyazıt's four sons. All of them were strangled with a silken bow as it was illegal to shed royal blood.

◁ EMPIRE BUILDER
Süleyman's naval forces totally dominated the Mediterranean as his armies swept east, west and south across three continents.

▽ MONUMENTAL GLORY
Süleyman's architect, Sinan, designed some of Turkey's greatest buildings, including the Süleymaniye Mosque.

THE DECLINE AND FALL OF THE OTTOMANS

After the golden age, when Süleyman the Magnificent and his successors ruled the East, the next 300 years were downhill all the way

The Ottoman Empire reached its zenith, not only territorially, but also in statesmanship, management, culture and arts during the reign of Sultan Süleyman the Magnificent *(see pages 50–51)*. But as early as the end of

the 16th century, the Ottoman Empire began a slow and steady decline. Systems which had once contributed to the glory of the empire could not adapt to internal or external changes.

Deterioration of the empire's internal structure began with the breakdown of the janissary military tradition and the system of land-tenure. Both the military and the administration were largely in the hands of Christian "slaves" selected from the most promising recruits rounded up each year as "blood tax," since non-Muslims were exempt from military service. They were sent to Istanbul, converted to Islam, and put through a rigorous Palace School, which ensured their absolute dependency and

loyalty to the sultan. The rest of the boys were settled with a Turkish family in the provinces, and learned a trade and the Muslim way of life before joining the ranks of the janissary corps.

However revolutionary the initial idea was, the janissary system became corrupted when the soldiers were allowed to marry and become involved in commerce, while their sons and other outsiders were admitted to the ranks. Numbers swelled, and there were frequent mutinies to exact more money from the sultan. The "slave soldiers" had in fact become power brokers in the capital, and had the distinction of committing the first regicide to taint Ottoman history. Osman II (1618–22), unhappy with the less than enthusiastic performance of his troops during his unsuccessful Polish campaign, decided to counter janissary domination by forming an Asiatic army of conscripts. Upon learning of the scheme, the janissaries revolted, beheaded the Grand Vizier and forced the young sultan to ride on a broken-down nag amid insults, before raping and then strangling him in the dreaded prison of Seven Towers.

The "gilded cage"

The sultans themselves had also become weak. The macabre bloodbath surrounding the struggle for power and the legal fratricide which accompanied each new succession generally ensured that the best and most popular prince won and there were no further challenges to rock the boat. But Mehmet III (1595–1603) went too far and had all 19 of his brothers killed, even though some were still babies. The attitude towards fratricide changed, and in a welter of popular moral and religious outrage, Ahmet I (1603–17) initiated a new custom. Once the oldest male of the dynasty ascended the throne, brothers and sons were to be kept in luxurious captivity in what was called "the gilded cage", accompanied only by eunuchs, women and an occasional tutor who reported their every move. Many potential rulers of the empire became incompetent and even deranged by this treatment, such as Ibrahim I (1640–48), who personifies the negative image of an eccentric, womanising oriental despot.

The New World disaster

For centuries, the Turks had grown wealthy by controlling the vital trade routes to the east – the Silk Road overland from China, and the sea lanes from India through the Red Sea to the Mediterranean, which in many ways had become a Turkish lake. Indeed, one of the motivations of the Italian sailor Christopher Columbus in sailing west was to find a way to China and India which avoided the fleets of such Turkish admirals as Piri Reis. His success in discovering the New World and Vasco da Gama's later voyage around the Cape of Good Hope to India were unmitigated disasters for the Turks. Not only had they lost their control of the trade routes to "distant Cathay," but the groaning shiploads of silver and gold flooding into Europe from the New World effectively debased the Ottoman currency.

Additionally, the Europeans' daring voyages gave new importance to naval, geographical and military science – and better ships, captains and guns meant better battles. Inexorably, the Europeans took control first of the Atlantic, then the Indian Ocean and finally even the Mediterranean. The Ottoman victory in Cyprus in 1571 (colourfully treated by Shakespeare in *Othello*, who was employed by the duke of Venice "against the general enemy Ottoman") only serves to underline the point. Within months of the Turkish victory at Famagusta, a grand coalition of Spain, the Vatican and Venice surprised the Turkish fleet at Lepanto in the Gulf of Corinth, effectively destroying Ottoman sea power forever.

On an intellectual level, too, the profound astronomical discoveries with their algebraic and geometrical spin-offs were a thing of the past, with a strict and rigorous interpretation of Islam preventing further intellectual growth. This attitude was in sharp contrast to Europe, which was rapidly emerging from the Middle Ages into the full flowering of the Renaissance. Intellectuals, freed from religious dogma, were making huge advances in scientific discovery, rational thought, technology and industry. Even the printing press, which had been used for 250 years in Europe, was only sanctioned by the Islamic clergy in 1727.

The Islamic lands fell further behind, and as the once glorious empire crumbled from within, formerly cowed rivals were eager to nibble away at the edges. The Treaty of Zsitva-Torok gave Hungary to the Hapsburgs, who also stopped paying tribute to the Ottomans in 1606. The second Ottoman siege of Vienna (1683) resulted in failure. Russia gained the Crimea and parts of the north shore of the Black Sea

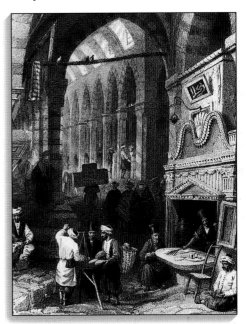

LEFT: a European idea of a janissary execution; most Western images of the Turks involved violence or sex.
RIGHT: Istanbul's Grand Bazaar in Ottoman times.

A TURKISH FANTASY

By the 18th century, Europe had lost its fear of the "Turk", while increased trade and colonial expansion created a market among eager collectors. Images of Turkey began to appear in European music, art and literature: in works such as Mozart's opera, *Abduction from the Seraglio*; in paintings such as Jean Baptiste Vanmour's *A Turkish Hunting Party* (1711), *The Death of Sardanapulus* (1827–8) by Delacroix, Ingres' *The Great Odalisque* (1814) and *The Turkish Bath* (1862); and in romantic literature was typified by Byron's exotic harems and cruel pashas (governors), Coleridge's *Kubla Khan* (1816), and Edward Fitzgerald's *The Rubaiyat of Omar Khayyam* (1859).

in the Treaty of Küçük Kaynarca (1774); while Napoleon invaded Ottoman Egypt in 1789, although nominal Ottoman control of the region was re-established by 1801.

Crimea and capitulations

Throughout the 19th century, the empire's balance of trade went haywire as the European Industrial Revolution turned the fading Ottoman Empire into a source of cheap raw materials and a vast market for manufactured products. Economic concessions given to the Western countries worsened the situation with favours ending as "capitulations". Not only were the

emphasis on cleanliness and hygiene. For her services, she became the first woman in the world to receive a medal of honour from a sultan. Literature of the period was enriched by English Lord Tennyson's stirring epic, *The Charge of the Light Brigade*, while Russian novelist, Tolstoy, wrote the *Sevastopol Tales*.

Large-scale borrowing with high interest rates led to state bankruptcy in 1875. In 1881, the Ottoman Empire came under total Western financial control with the establishment of the Ottoman Public Debt Administration. Despite various attempts at reform throughout the 19th century, territorial losses continued. Russia

postal service, street cars, tobacco, electricity and railway now managed by foreigners, but they also had legal privileges. Any legal matter involving a foreigner or a non-Muslim Ottoman who asked for the protection of a foreign consulate could not be tried in an Ottoman court.

Trade with the empire became so valuable to England and France that the Muslim Ottomans were saved by Christian England, France and Italy when attacked by Russia during the Crimean War (1854). This small but bloody war stirred the public imagination, inspiring an English woman, Florence Nightingale, to establish war hospitals in Istanbul. At these, she invented modern nursing practice, with its life-saving

annexed Bessarabia (1812); Greece became an independent principality (1827); Moldavia and Wallachia became autonomous principalities (1829); and the British occupied Egypt (1882).

Reform attempts

Reform of the Ottoman Empire began in earnest with Sultan Mahmut II (1808–29). In 1826, he abolished the decadent janissary corps. It was a bloody affair. After obtaining the support of the clerics and the people, the sultan asked each janissary battalion to spare 150 men for the new corps he was forming. The janissaries refused and overturned their camp kettles in the traditional signal of revolt. But

Mahmut unfurled the sacred banner of the prophet and opened fire on his own elite corps from the Seraglio. Four thousand janissaries were killed in their barracks, with thousands of others slaughtered in the streets of Istanbul and in the provinces as a general purge began.

Next the sultan produced a generation of French-speaking bureaucrats who were trained in the newly formed translation bureaux. Certain elements within the new bureaucracy desired reform from within, and edicts of 1839 and 1856 attempted orderly tax collection, fair and regular conscription, and the establishment of banks, public works and commerce.

Strangely enough, "equality" held little attraction for many Ottomans, and was resisted fiercely by non-Muslims, who, until then, had been exempted from military service. As prosperous tradesmen and farmers – often under the protection of foreign governments – they had no intention of interrupting business for the sake of a five- to seven-year-period of national service. Although paved with good intentions, the road to reform proved very rocky.

First constitution

In 1876, the Ottoman Empire adopted its first written constitution, and one of its most controversial sultans, Abdülhamid II (1876–1909), came to the throne. Meanwhile, the growing Pan-Slavic movement in the Balkans culminated in a war with Russia, which resulted in independence for Serbia, Montenegro and Bulgaria. Masses of refugees flooded across the frontiers, cutting some of the Ottomans' richest provinces off from the state forever. The crisis prompted Abdülhamid to suspend the new constitution and dissolve parliament. For the next 30 years, the empire lived under oppression and censure, but the sultan's autocracy inevitably fomented opposition, and a secret society, the Committee of Union and Progress, began its work to restore the constitution and, eventually, to depose the sultan.

In 1908, in an uprising which became known as the Young Turks Revolution, army officers in Macedonia revolted, forcing the sultan to call for elections and reopen the parliament. The following year, Abdülhamid II was forced to

LEFT: the Sultanahmet (Blue) mosque.
RIGHT: Sultan Abdülhamid II – the first Ottoman ruler to be photographed.

abdicate in favour of Sultan Mehmet Reshat V (1909–18), who ascended the throne as a mere figurehead. The Ottoman sultanate was a thing of the past, in all but name.

Dissent from within was matched by intrigue from without, as the European powers vied with each other to establish influence on the "sick man of Europe," cajoling and threatening by turns. The most successful of the suitors was the Kaiser's Germany, which, itself a newly formed nation-state, attempted to play catch-up pool with its rivals in the Grand Game of Asia. Military delegations, trade and projects such as the Berlin-to-Baghdad railway were

among the means used to woo the Ottomans to the imperial German side.

World War I

When war broke out in August 1914, the Ottomans hesitated, while the English promptly seized two warships being built in dry dock for the Ottoman fleet. Collections had been made all over the Muslim world to pay for them, and Ottoman fury finally turned the tide. Two German warships being pursued by the English and French navies in the Mediterranean were "donated" to the Ottomans as they steamed towards the Dardanelles. And with a change of uniform but not of crew, the new Turkish warships sailed through the Bosphorus and into the Black Sea to lob shells at Russian ports in the Crimea. To the chagrin of many in Istanbul, Ottoman Turkey discovered that it was a Central Power.

Turkey was scarcely prepared for the war, having still not recovered from its loss of Libya to the Italians in 1911, nor its humiliating defeat by the Bulgarians, Greeks and Serbs during the Balkan War, when Istanbul itself was only saved by bickering and internecine war between the Balkan allies.

A HERO'S DEFENCE

"I am not ordering you to attack; I am ordering you to die", Mustafa Kemal instructed his troops at Gallipoli. Struck near the heart by shrapnel during the fighting, his life was saved by a pocket watch.

Egypt's nominal loyalty was severed when the British ousted the last Ottoman khedive in 1914, and the former province became a major base for English activities in the Middle East, including the Arab uprising against Ottoman rule, led in part by the romantic Lawrence of Arabia. Meanwhile, to the northeast, the forces of tsarist Russia, with the aid of local Armenians, pressed inexorably west as far as Erzurum, successfully annexing large areas within the motherland – Anatolia.

Gallipoli

Within this sea of disaster, the only successful Ottoman military action during the war was the defence of the Dardanelles in 1915, when the combined French, British and Australian–New Zealand (ANZAC) forces landed at Gallipoli. One of the leaders of the "Young Turks" rebellion, a certain Colonel Mustafa Kemal (later to become known as Atatürk, *see page 65*), commanded a brilliant but brutal defence for the Ottomans, winning a reputation for invincibility and heroism that stood him well several years later when he started building the Republic of Turkey.

The Gallipoli campaign was instrumental in the fate of other individuals and nations too: Sea Lord Winston Churchill, the architect of the ill-fated invasion, was obliged to resign and join the doughboys in the trenches in France; Australia and New Zealand acquired a new sense of nationhood as a result of their horrendous casualties, and tsarist Russia, unable to export wheat or import weapons – in interesting contrast to the flow of trade today – collapsed in 1917, to resurface as the Soviet Union.

Armenian deportations

While the Ottoman forces held at Gallipoli, on all other fronts disaster followed disaster. The situation in the remote eastern provinces, where Armenian nationalists were siding with the forces of tsarist Russia on the promise of future independence, was especially critical.

According to the Armenians, what followed was nothing short of genocide; to the Turks, it was nothing of the sort. The bare historical facts point to a double tragedy. The Ottoman government decided to deport the Armenians from their traditional areas of settlement in the eastern provinces of the empire, marching them away to "safer" areas in Mesopotamia. Disease, bandit raids and security excesses resulted in the deaths of tens of thousands of Armenians in a tragedy of the highest magnitude, bitterly remembered by Armenians the world over to this day. However, during the same period, hundreds of thousands of Muslim Turkish civilians and soldiers also perished as a result of combat, disease, malnutrition and attacks by Armenian rebel armies against Turkish villages.

Fighting between the Turks and Armenians did not finally end until the signing of the Treaty of Alexandropol in 1920, two years after the end of World War I. One historian estimates that 40 percent of the total population in Eastern Europe died during the war, making it one of the areas of highest mortality for both soldiers and civilians in World War I.

The end of the empire

When the Ottomans finally capitulated to the Allies with the signing of the Mudros Armistice in November 1918, the once proud empire was but a pale reflection of its former self. The peace treaty eventually signed in Sèvres in 1920 stripped the rump state of many of her former provinces: Iraq and Palestine were

dentist plan to re-establish the Roman Empire, while the tsarist Russians had been promised Istanbul itself, the "key to the Crimea."

Thirty-one "children"

The 500-year reign of the Ottomans was over, but everywhere her "children" sprang up in her wake. Today, 31 nations owe a significant part of their heritage to the Turks, be it as banal as military terminology, as basic as food or sublime as architecture: Albania, Bulgaria, the two nations on Cyprus, Greece, Hungary, Bosnia, Croatia, Slovenia, and the former Yugoslavia in Europe; the Ukraine, Armenia, Georgia and

ceded to the British, while Syria (including Lebanon) was given to France under the new League of Nations' mandate system. Separate Armenian, Assyrian and Kurdish states were also envisioned, all of them to be established in the same eastern provinces – an insubstantial promise that has caused bloodshed ever since. Not even the Turkish homeland of central Anatolia was sacred, thanks to agreements made secretly by the Allies. Italy was to be given several of the southern provinces as part of an irre-

Azerbaijan in the former Soviet Union; the Middle Eastern states of Bahrain, Egypt, Iraq, Israel, Jordan, Kuwait, Lebanon, Oman, Saudi Arabia, Sudan, Syria, the United Arab Emirates and North and South Yemen; and Algeria, Libya and Tunisia in North Africa.

The Turks were the last to emerge as a nation from the ashes of the empire. It took the ignominy of military defeat, invasion by the Greeks and, finally, one man in the right place and time, to ignite the spark that established a national identity and a modern nation state. The place was a harbour on the Black Sea, the time May 1919, and the man, Mustafa Kemal, the hero of Gallipoli. ❑

LEFT: a Pera bar girl before World War I.
ABOVE: the despondent Turkish army had just one great victory in World War I – at Gallipoli in 1915.

THE REPUBLICAN ERA

With the end of World War I and the collapse of the Ottoman Empire,
the stage was set for the rise of Atatürk's republic

On 30 October, 1918, the Ottoman Empire collapsed. Backing the wrong side in World War I had cost millions of lives, huge chunks of territory and, finally, one of the greatest empires the world has known.

The victors showed little regard for the US-proposed Wilsonian Principles, drawn up as a

blueprint for peace and a new order in Europe. The Treaty of Sèvres that the Ottomans were forced to sign in 1920 was literally the death warrant for the pathetic "sick man of Europe," a mere redrafting of earlier secret protocols for the dismemberment of the empire.

The French and British contented themselves with the patronage of the newly created Arab states in the strategic and oil-rich Middle East. The British also occupied Istanbul, nominally still the Ottoman capital, the Bosphorus and the Dardanelles, sought for centuries by the Russian tzars as the gateway to the warm seas. The French occupied a few provinces in southeast Turkey, while the Mediterranean coast and

some Aegean islands went to the Italians. The Armenians, who had paid a grim price for siding with the Russians during the early stages of the war, were granted their own state in eastern Anatolia; as were the Kurds, and a Greek minority on the eastern Black Sea Coast.

The mainland Greeks were after a much bigger prize – the restoration of ancient Greece with its Ionian colonies. Greece was granted eastern Thrace, west of Istanbul, and, more importantly, the principal Aegean port of Smyrna (now İzmir) with its rich hinterland.

The War of Independence

On 15 May, 1919, when the first Greeks landed at Smyrna, it fanned the latent patriotism of the Turks into flame. Four days later Mustafa Kemal, the brilliant saviour of Gallipoli, arrived at Samsun on the Black Sea to supervise the disbanding of the eastern armies. Once safely away from the court and Istanbul, he renounced his rank and titles and devoted all his energy to building a nationalist army. On 23 April, 1920, he convened the first Grand National Assembly in Ankara.

Local committees in the southeast had already fired the opening salvos of the War of Independence. The battle-weary French soon came to terms with the Ankara government and withdrew from Turkish soil. Kemal sent his troops east, swiftly pushing the Armenians and Georgians back to their modern boundaries. The Italians soon followed the French, leaving only the British to aid the Greeks.

Kemal now turned west and, with the aid of İsmet İnönü, a close friend and accomplished tactician, checked the Greek advance from Smyrna. The 22-day-long Battle of Sakarya, fought almost at the gates of Ankara, turned the tide of the war. The Greeks withdrew and dug in. Kemal himself led the two-week-long counter-attack the following year. At the Battle of Dumlupınar, west of Afyon, the bulk of the Greek army was annihilated; its commander-in-chief was taken prisoner; and the ragged army chased back to İzmir – and into the sea.

The liberation of İzmir on 9 September, 1922, followed by a vicious fire for which each side still blames the other, led to the withdrawal of British troops from the Dardanelles and the ensuing armistice, signed in Mudanya.

Rebuilding the nation

Kemal and his circle now turned their attention to the harder task of rebuilding a leaderless nation ravaged and impoverished by conflict. As the Allies sent invitations to peace talks, the Istanbul government, now totally out of touch with modern reality, called for "a joint stand". Infuriated by their stupidity, Kemal announced the abolition of the monarchy on 1 November, 1922. Two weeks later the last, ailing sultan, Mehmet VI, sought the protection of Britain and, under the cover of darkness, boarded the HMS *Malaya*, bound for Malta and exile.

On 20 November, İsmet İnönü addressed the the peace conference in Lausanne, Switzerland. Proving himself a match for such eminent diplomatic adversaries as the British Foreign Secretary, Lord Curzon, he negotiated a peace treaty, signed on 24 July, 1923, that lessened the harshness of Sèvres, and secured territory, sovereignty, and independence for the Turks.

On 29 October, 1923, the Grand National Assembly unanimously and enthusiastically endorsed the proclamation of the Republic of Turkey. Its first president, inevitably, was Mustafa Kemal, as leader of the newly founded Republican People's Party (RPP). For the next 58 years, this was to be a teacher of statecraft to generations of politicians, a medium for authoritarian government, and an experimental laboratory for social democracy.

Kemal and his reformers wanted to model their new nation on the West, but all existing institutions were unmistakably Eastern. What was more, the Turks were conditioned to see themselves more as an *Umma* (Muslim community) than a nation and had long been discouraged from any involvement in politics, industry, commerce or other potential source of power that could challenge the absolute

WHAT'S IN A NAME?

The obligatory adoption of surnames in 1934 set off a race for colourfully patriotic family names. Kemal's surname was awarded by the Grand National Assembly, which named him Atatürk (Father of Turks).

authority of the Ottomans. The government faced the almost impossible tasks of creating a national consciousness, absorbing Western civilisation and reinterpreting Islam. On 3 March, 1923, the Grand National Assembly abolished the caliphate and immediately banished all male members of the royal family from the country.

Wrenching changes

In 1925, all convents run by a host of religious sects were banned, primary

school education was made compulsory and religious law was abolished. In 1928, Arabic script was discarded and replaced by the Latin alphabet. Even wardrobes were touched by the winds of reform. The fez, the headgear of officialdom, and turbans were banned. Hats and caps, personally modelled by Mustafa Kemal, found a surprising acceptance.

The westernisation of women was not merely cosmetic; new political rights led towards greater emancipation. Women were encouraged to compete with men professionally while the civil code adopted from Switzerland ensured their equality before the law, although the reality has still not caught up with the ideal.

LEFT: site of the 1923 Conference of Lausanne.
RIGHT: Greeks escorting Turkish prisoners following the Greek landing at Smyrna, 15 May, 1919.

Building the economy

The Lausanne Treaty abolished the crippling capitulations levied on Turkey at the end of the war, but the jubilant celebrations which greeted the new government masked deep economic setbacks. Debt relief was refused and Ankara's powers to set tariffs were restricted.

However, leaders of the new state refused to be discouraged and reached eagerly towards what they perceived as the key to Western supremacy – capitalism. Banks were set up with state funds to back private enterprise and a vast array of incentives was offered to businessmen. But then in 1929, the Wall Street

Crash and start of the Great Depression had a disastrous effect on Turkey's crop exports, discrediting capitalism in the eyes of Turkey's military-bureaucratic elite, who saw the apparent immunity of the planned Soviet economy from the global catastrophe.

In an economic U-turn, the state took upon itself the burden of development, and newly created State Economic Enterprises (SEEs) were put at the forefront of the drive towards industrialisation. Self-sufficiency and import-substitution became the order of the day. The first Soviet-influenced Five-Year Development Plan (1934–9) helped a rapid build-up of the country's industries.

Changing of the guard

The leaders of the Republic were also casting increasingly worried glances at the regathering clouds of war in Europe. Against such a background, the death of Atatürk on 10 November, 1938, came as a major blow. The great leader, bedridden for months, died of cirrhosis of the liver at the age of 57. Next day, his lifelong friend and comrade-in-arms, İsmet İnönü, was sworn in as the Republic's second president.

İnönü devoted his energies to keeping Turkey out of the general conflagration which erupted the following year. This required not only a skilled tightrope act between the warring sides – and a certain departure from treaty obligations at times – but an iron hand in the country which the "national chief" employed through the RPP bureaucracy. Turkey remained essentially neutral in World War II, but threw its cards in with the Allies and declared pro-forma war on the moribund Nazi state in the closing weeks of the conflict with Germany, just in time to qualify for UN membership.

In the meantime, the honeymoon of the 1920s and early '30s between Turkey and Russia had long since returned to mutual hostility, thanks to Ankara's repeated crackdowns on domestic communists. Now the situation nearly exploded into fresh violence when Moscow demanded control of the Turkish straits and asserted territorial claims over previously Armenian districts on the Eastern borders. The Soviets eventually withdrew their demands only after the United States and Britain firmly backed Ankara, with America dispatching a battleship, the *USS Missouri*, to Istanbul as a symbol of solidarity.

Democracy

Despite Atatürk's commitment to legality and his overwhelming mandate from the people, his rule was viewed by many as autocratic. In 1924, most of the RPP's leading military men quit to form an opposition party, the Progressive Republicans (PRP). It lasted until the following year when a Kurdish revolt in the east (incited by an Islamic fundamentalist dervish leader declaring a *fatwah* on the state) took months to suppress. It gave Atatürk a perfect excuse to ban the PRP – as well as all dervish orders – in the interests of unity. In 1930, after a plot to assassinate the leader was revealed, many deputies and former members of the PRP were accused of involvement and hanged. Another brief experiment with opposition soon after was no more successful, leaving the RPP effectively to monopolise power for 27 years.

Understandably, Turkey saw the United States and its known antipathy to communism as its most likely supporter against the Soviet threat. This courtship had no little effect on the development of a multi-party democracy in Turkey, a pre-requisite for receiving US assistance under the Truman Doctrine. It also led to Turkey's later involvement in the Korean War (1950), admission to NATO (1952), and controversial recognition of Israel.

emerging urban middle class. By 1950, the DP was in control of the government, with Bayar as president and Menderes as prime minister.

Erratic progress

The DP's policies encouraged a continuous flow of US economic and military aid, giving a new, markedly pro-American tone to Turkey's programme of westernisation. In return the country granted the United States facilities for an air base, electronic surveillance stations and bases for Jupiter missiles, later dismantled as part of the package deal ending the Cuban crisis. Despite the strain this placed on relations

In 1945, a group of former RPP members, headed by Adnan Menderes, an active politician and cotton grower, and Celâl Bayar, a banker and a collaborator of Atatürk, formed the opposition Democrat Party (DP). Its platform included the relaxation of state controls over business and agriculture and more freedom of religion, a potent combination which proved enormously popular with an odd cross-section of voters, including feudal landowners, the traditionally conservative rural masses and the

LEFT: İsmet İnönü, close friend and colleague of Atatürk and second president of the Republic.
ABOVE: Democratic Party election rally in the 1950s.

with the country's Islamic neighbours, Turkey proudly stood by her Western friends during the Cold War years and beyond.

Under the DP, populist policies and new incentives to free enterprise led to chaotic expansion. The supply of tractors to farmers boosted production and exports, but massive imports of foreign goods and overly generous rural loans and public spending left the country with a massive trade deficit and national debt leading to repeated currency devaluations. As his popularity declined, Menderes also became increasingly repressive, censoring the press, jailing political opponents and manipulating elections. He was finally deposed on 27 May,

1960, in a popularly supported military coup. A year later he was sentenced to death by military tribunal, along with two of his ministers.

Perhaps strangely, this and later coups still tend to be regarded as progressive by many Turks, who consider the military guard on Atatürk's ideals a safety valve on extremism.

Under coup leader General Cemal Gürsel the constituent assembly drafted a new, more liberal constitution which was then adopted by a national referendum. Albeit inconclusive and unstable, free elections returned in an open-minded atmosphere – the right to strike was confirmed in 1963 and Turkey's first socialist

party was formed. Meanwhile, followers of the now-banned DP flocked to the newly formed Justice Party where conservative Süleyman Demirel emerged to begin a political career spanning more than 30 years. In 1965 and again in 1969, the Justice Party was swept into power, promising commitment to a free market and foreign investment.

The late 1960s saw an explosion of left-wing activism which continued through the following decade while strikes, political polarisation and street violence brought repeated military intervention and the ultimate alignment of Demirel with the far right. Even the socialist leader Bülent Ecevit had to compromise. In the elections of 1973, his reshaped RPP was forced to form a coalition with Necmettin Erbakan's Islamic fundamentalist National Salvation Party: a so-called "historic compromise" which helped several pro-Islamic factions re-establish themselves on the political stage of the nation.

Descent into chaos

Assuming victory, and perhaps hoping to shake off the Islamist portion of the coalition, Ecevit sought early re-election. Right-wing opposition forces closed ranks, and ultimately gained majority control of the government with the aptly named National Front coalition featuring Demirel's Justice Party and the National Action Party of Alpaslan Türkeş, a far right nationalist.

Throughout the late 1970s Turkey's government was a virtual barn dance of extremes, while the economy was in a dire condition – a morass of foreign debts and uncontrolled public spending. Left-right feuding, sectarian violence and separatist activities erupted, leaving some 5,000 dead by 1980, many more tortured or wounded, and the country on the verge of civil war. On 12 September, the generals once again stepped in.

This time, the generals were determined to make a thorough job of re-establishing order. General Kenan Evren and the commanders of the armed forces formed the notorious National Security Council, and assumed totalitarian powers, caring little for domestic or foreign reaction. All political parties were banned and their leaders detained. Tens of thousands of suspected terrorists were rounded up and tried in military courts, with 25 executed for major crimes and massacres, though the radical right and Islamists suffered far less than Marxists, trade unionists, professors and other left-leaning intellectuals.

CYPRUS

In 1974, Ecevit ordered troops into Northern Cyprus to protect local Turks from the military junta in Greece which had deposed President Makarios and planned to invade and reclaim the island. Appeals for British aid under the Treaty of Guarantee (between Ankara, Athens and London, and designed to ensure Cypriot independence) were ignored. Ecevit felt he had no option but to act, and the Turkish army occupied the northern third of the island. Branded as an "invasion" by most of the world, it has always been regarded by Turks as a legitimate intervention to protect its citizens. The controversial Turkish Republic of Northern Cyprus was set up in 1983.

The Özal era

General elections were restored in 1983, but strict controls were imposed, with all pre-coup parties and their leaders banned. This was to usher in the 10-year "Özal era" as voters demonstrated their overwhelming preference for the populist appeal of Turgut Özal and the ANAP (Motherland Party) in a landslide victory which formed the first outright majority in 30 years. Combining a sweeping liberalisation of the economy with Islamist sympathies and a blind eye to profit by any means, Turgut Özal reached the hearts of the common people. There was a sudden relaxation of trade restric-

for blatant nepotism, which set the stage for the corruption that continues to undermine credibility in Turkish politics, and fostering the national obsession with foreign goods.

Özal died in 1993, succeeded in the presidency by Süleyman Demirel. The election of a female prime minister, economics professor Tansu Çiller, shortly thereafter was also intended to promote the image of progressive free-market values and cooperation with the West as well giving a nod to the status of Turkish women. But her later coalition compromises with Necmettin Erbakan and the pro-Islamic Refah Welfare Party and continued financial

tions, an influx of foreign goods and Turkish business people were encouraged to enter the world arena for the first time. Enormous sums of money were spent on developing the tourism sector and foreign investment was welcomed. Inflation soared, but opportunities existed as never before.

Özal is still seen as a hero of Turkey's commitment to free-market capitalism and hailed for his contribution to the country's impressive national growth figures. He is also remembered

LEFT: Bülent Ecevit and Süleyman Demirel.
ABOVE: political rally for the populist Islamic Refah Welfare Party, now banned under the constitution.

scandals have seriously damaged her image.

The brief Islamist victory is now generally viewed as a protest vote against government corruption in the centre-right, mainstream parties, rather than a desire to overturn 75 years of Republicanism. Erbakan and Refah (the Welfare Party) were given their 15 minutes of fame before being gently nudged out of power through careful military manoeuvering, justified by the commitment to Atatürk's secularism, still enshrined in the constitution.

Since the beginning of 1999, there have been even more political shocks, both positive and negative. The Kurdish separatist leader Abdullah Öcalan was finally captured, bringing 15 years of war between the military and the Kurds to an abrupt close. With economic ills rife in the country, many Turks supported his immediate execution, but under pressure from Europe, still, in theory, considering Turkey as a candidate for future EU inclusion, capital punishment has been banned and Öcalan's sentence commuted.

In August 1999, the Izmit earthquake crippled the country's industrial heartland and economy, and sympathy over the devastation led to a rapprochement between Turkey and Greece (George Papandreou visited Turkey in January, 2000, the first Greek foreign minister to do so in 40 years). In December of that year, Turkey

more than a decade of triple-digit inflation under control, but just as things began to look more hopeful, 11th September knocked the stuffing out of Turkey's crucial tourism industry.

In November 2002, the AKP (Justice and Development Party), born out of the ashes of Refah and the Virtue Party, won a landslide in the parliamentary elections, even though its leader, İstanbul Recep Tayyip Erdoğan did not have a seat. Abdullah Gül was appointed as caretaker prime minister until Erdoğan won a by-election and took over in spring 2003. Although the AKP is an Islamic party, it has promised secular government and so far appears to be holding

finally achieved its coveted status as a potential candidate for integration into the EU.

Perhaps the biggest surprise came in May, 2000, when President Demirel's attempt to change the constitution and retain his presidency failed and he was replaced by Turkey's senior judge, Ahmet Necdet Sezer, known for his respect for the law, commitment to corruption-free government as well as a limitation on presidential powers. Early 2001 also saw some of Demirel's relatives caught red-handed in banking scandals. Sezer did not have an easy time as the economy went into freefall, propped up only by the injection of $4 billion – with many strings attached – from the IMF. This has helped to bring

to its word. Meantime, Turkey, as the only Muslim member of NATO and a neighbour of Iraq with huge US bases on her territory, got caught in the wranglings surrounding the build-up to the war in Iraq. To the dismay of the cabinet, who were chasing some US$26 billion of US finance, parliament refused the US permission to use Turkish bases. The government, desperate to avoid a renewed Kurdish conflict in Turkey, threatened to send Turkish troops into northern Iraq. At the time of writing, new deals with the US have kept things under control, but it is early days in the postwar upheavals. ❑

ABOVE: marching in the Nation Day parade, 19 May.

Atatürk:
Father of the Nation

Gigantic bronze statues of Atatürk – the bigger the better for aspiring governors – occupy the choicest spot of every town. His towering figure and cold, blue eyes bore little physical resemblance to the Central Asian ancestors he identified for his people, but Mustafa Kemal is the idol at the heart of one of the most enduring personality cults in modern history, the literal "Father" of the modern Turkish nation.

With their adopted religion of Islam and many centuries of autocratic rulers demanding filial obedience, the Turks have always been accustomed to following a succession of father figures. What sets Atatürk aside for true reverence is his success in reversing the fate of a doomed nation.

Born the son of a customs official in the now-Greek northern Aegean port of Salonica in 1881, Mustafa had his first violent row with the chief "Mullah" of the district religious school at an early age; an experience which seemingly left him with a lasting hatred for religious fundamentalism. Conversely, he had always been favourably impressed by the tight-fitting uniforms worn by the men of the local military academy, and he secretly enrolled by taking the entrance exams.

At the academy, his mathematical prowess soon won him the name of Kemal, or "the complete one". While there he also developed a keen interest in the works of Rousseau and Voltaire, dreaming of future glory as the Napoleon of the East.

His clandestine activities soon resulted in a transfer to Damascus as staff captain – far away from the locus of power. Even so, he set up a revolutionary society which later merged with the pan-Ottoman Union and Progress Party (UPP) headed by the ill-fated triumvirate of Enver, Cemal and Talat. Unlike them, Mustafa Kemal remained a strict legalist, calling for the separation of the military from politics, and evoking the lasting suspicion of the better-known leaders of the time.

In 1911, Kemal volunteered for service in Libya, which was then under attack by Italian troops. However, the break-out of the catastrophic Balkan Wars the following year brought him home to help Enver recapture Edirne, although the latter was given all the credit. Enver went on to drag Turkey into the

mess of World War I, then died in Central Asia at the head of a cavalry charge. When Talat and Cemal also died, assassinated by Armenian separatists, Mustafa Kemal, the only undefeated general of the savaged Ottoman armies, took up leadership of the struggle to save the heartland of the lost empire. He saw himself as the generator of a new and different nation known as "*Türkiye*," or the Land of the Turks. He led the country to victory in the War of Independence, abolished the monarchy and became its first president, secularising the state, liberating women and westernising the nation. He died from cirrhosis of the liver, on 10 November, 1938, at the age of only 57. His

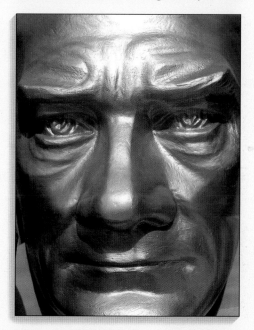

lifelong friend and companion, İsmet İnönü, was sworn in as president to continue his work.

Today, over half a century on, Mustafa Kemal, now Atatürk, is still idolised by his people, a source of often contradictory wisdom for all. Man or woman, rich or poor, right, left or centrist, all look to his quotations, whether those painstakingly translated from the old Ottoman script, or the ones he made up on the spot to suit the occasion.

Above all, the official memory of cadet number 1238 is jealously guarded by the officer corps committed to the preservation of his heritage. And every year, when his number is called out at the roll call of the graduating class of new cadets, there is but one uniform response: "He is among us." ❑

RIGHT: a gold bust of Mustafa Kemal Atatürk.

MODERN TURKS:
A QUEST FOR IDENTITY

With Turkey modernising rapidly, its people have a serious identity crisis as they are torn between agrarian, liberal Islamic values and free-market capitalism

Ne mutlu Türküm diyene! ("Happy is he who calls himself a Turk!"). This famous quotation, taken from Atatürk's speech of 1927 elaborating the future values of an independent Republic, is still inscribed on monuments throughout the country. For all its patriotic sentiment, however, its exact meaning is evermore difficult to define in today's multicultural era of websites and world music. For what is "Turkishness" in a nation which has been populated for 9,000 years by many races and religions, pirates and refugees; a country which regards its heritage as Asian but hankers to belong to Europe and remains so stubbornly attached to its many internal contradictions?

Older people raised on a steady diet of national idealism will, in all likelihood, define themselves by a vague ethnic relationship to the tribes of Islamic Türkic nomads who swept into Anatolia a scant 800 years ago, leaving behind them a rich cultural heritage of which the nation is justifiably proud. However, only a few thousand Turks imposed their civilisation and language (which is Asian in origin, of the Uralic and Altaic family, with grammatical similarities to Finnish and Hungarian) on a much larger indigenous population. Deeper racial links between modern Turks and Central Asia appear more rooted in folklore than fact. Yet the concept is firmly embedded in the Turkish self-image, a heritage from early Republican times when the country's founders rushed to devise a new concept of nationhood which circumvented the centuries of Ottoman rule.

The republican rewrite

After the decay of the Ottoman Empire and the carve-up of its corpse in 1919, the founders of the Republic found it most efficient to deny the

recent past and look further back in history for their national heroes while launching sweeping "Western" style reforms. During Atatürk's stupendous feat of modernisation, when the hat replaced the fez, women were forbidden to wear veils and the Latin alphabet supplanted the Arabic script (leaving generations of Turks removed from 500 years of written cultural heritage), the country was encouraged to view its present in technicolour and its glittering multicultural history in black and white. All things Ottoman were reviled as elitist and backward; any identification with Greek culture was simply incomprehensible. It fell to the short-lived, but glamorous Seljuk Turks to provide a suitable national role model.

Many decades on, the principles that Atatürk laid down are still (officially, at least) the guidelines of the Republic. Turkey's booming cities, new highways, vast dams, spreading tourism

---

PRECEDING PAGES: a gathering of faces, in the old citadel of Ankara; the hopes and smiles of youth.
LEFT: students take a break in Istanbul.
RIGHT: Atatürk demonstrating the Latin alphabet.

infrastructure and commitment to a secular state are all in keeping with the western sense of modernity that he fostered.

Searching for a new outlook

Unfortunately, the cult of personality which developed after the great leader's death and the force-feeding of his ideals through sloganeering has led to an intellectual sloth that finds it easier to repeat clichés than explore changing realities and ask difficult but essential questions.

Some people have begun to ask if the 65 million inhabitants of this developing country have not neglected the "work in progress" because

themselves as a diverse cultural mosaic rather than as a single race. Even 15 years ago, few would admit to having Kurdish, Laz, Circassian, Tatar or Greek roots, while fewer still would admit to belonging to any of the minority Islamic sects which owe as much to pre-Christian mysticism as to the Prophet Mohammed. Today, younger people with a more global outlook are searching for better ways of expressing themselves. The word "Anatolian", meaning "from the motherland", is back in vogue.

Turkey's distinctive character is due to its remarkable location. It is Near-Eastern, but also Balkan and Mediterranean, placed in a web of

they were too satisfied with ideas tailored for 10 million Turks in the traumatic wake of military defeat and economic chaos. Without question, this period of humiliation by the Allies is the source of Turkish sensitivity today. But there are signs of change, not least because of the country's wish to join the EU. Nearly every Turk backs EU membership in theory, but the reforms required for entry, such as an independent or autonomous homeland for the Kurds and limiting of the power of the military, are not always palatable to those of a more nationalist persuasion.

The rate of development and a new sense of worth are helping the Turkish people redefine

relationships spanning the Orient and Occident, to Italy, Spain and the Slavic and Caucasian worlds via the Black Sea. Though young as a modern nation, its long, complex history includes the rise and fall of many great civilisations such as the Hittites, the Phrygians and the Persians. Hellenistic, Roman and Turkish contributions to global civilisation are clear, as is Anatolia's role in the early history of Christianity and the spread of Islam.

Shifting population

Some of the nation's new awareness of its cultural roots may be accidental: Turkey is in the midst of vast demographic change, due to the population explosion and rural migration. Some 3 million Turks now work and live in Europe; more than 2 million of them in Germany. Foreign tourists continue to swarm into Turkey, invading the country's remotest corners. Meanwhile Turks travel and study abroad more, watch foreign films in international festivals, listen to obscure contemporary and jazz labels (including their own) and speak more languages, with an emphasis on English. They also watch representations of themselves from home and abroad

URBAN YOUTH

Sixty-five percent of Turkey's people live in cities. Of a total population of over 65 million, more than half are under 25, a proportion that is still climbing.

Suddenly, providing stiff competition for Western imports, there are Turkish traditional, jazz and rock fusion groups, Turkish fashion designers creating distinctive styles from native cloth, and Turkish film-makers winning awards abroad with images of the country other than political despair. In general, a unique cultural stamp is being forged.

Modern Turkey is an enlightening place in which to watch a "changing of the guard" as young, less inward-looking ideas confront a global future.

on 25 TV channels including state, private, international satellite and cable. Private radio was legalised in 1993 and there are now more than 30 stations. All these changes have had a palpable effect on the nation's global outlook.

Far from the "imposition of foreign culture" which conservatives feared would threaten Turkey's fragile young national identity, there has been an explosion in creativity which has inspired a reassessment and renewed appreciation of Anatolian culture among the young for the first time since the Republic was born.

LEFT: a village wedding in southeastern Turkey.
ABOVE: dreaming of the future.

The pitfalls

This new confidence still masks a country of deep divisions. There have been backlashes against such rapid internationalisation – notably the success of an Islamic party in national elections, an increase in the number of women wearing veils in urban centres, and the surprise refusal of parliament to allow the USA to use Turkish bases during the 2003 Iraq War – a move which lost the country billions of dollars, threatening a barely stable economy.

More importantly, however, fundamental political and economic problems still divide the country. The class gap is frighteningly vast, especially in big cities, where rural migrants are visibly disdained by middle-class, urban Turks. Most employees, including state university professors and civil servants, earn less than $500 a month, yet the shops and nightclubs seem to be packed with high-spending, designer-clad youngsters.

Corruption in the financial and political arena still goes largely unpunished, and attempts to curb a decade of triple-digit inflation in 2000 led to an economic crisis the following year, with a rapid rise in unemployment and ferocious methods of tax collecting that are particularly punitive to blue-collar workers and civil servants. State education is notoriously poor

and though tuition in the universities is largely free, in order to pass competitive entrance exams most young Turks need to study at an expensive private lycée, which necessitates having a rich family.

Unfortunately, even the most well-meant attempts to lodge justifiable political criticism of Turkey are met with defensiveness, a situation grossly inflated when such comments come from a foreigner. Though the culture of nationalism incited by Turkey's sensationalistic media may be on the wane, current reactions against the West are at the base of a new nationalist revival which could have disturbing ramifications. Although the Islamist AKP (Justice and Development Party) currently in power has promised to continue to run a secular state and abide by the constitution, and the vast majority of Turks are pro-Western and welcoming, there are significant anti-American feelings exacerbated by the war in Iraq - something opposed by some 90 percent of Turks.

Images and reflections

Turkey's image abroad – and the country's own sense of how it is perceived by foreigners – remain central to the nation's self-esteem. Propaganda about the 19th-century "sick man of Europe" gave the Turks a palpable national inferiority complex and an appallingly poor, and poorly informed, image elsewhere. There is perpetual exasperation at being prejudicially represented in Western fiction, news and films.

However, as the Turkish people grow in confidence about their unique place in the world, and foreigners become more willing to visit and learn about this complex culture without the baggage of coffee, camels and harems, we can perhaps begin to substitute a more dynamic image of "Turkishness" that will allow the quest for identity to continue without crisis.

Turkish women

How many wives do Turkish men have? One, legally – this is a secular state and the Muslim heritage of four is illegal (though girlfriends or mistresses are not uncommon). Do Turkish women still wear veils? Well, some do, but this is most likely to be a backlash against too rapid and rather vulgar westernisation.

Few topics reveal the psychological distance between "Islamic" and "Western" nations more clearly than that of the status of women. Since the 19th century, European art, literature and popular culture have generally depicted Eastern women as docile, submissive creatures, clad in an all-enveloping black sheet when they are not dancing before their master in exotic, transparent silks. Thus, modern visitors are often surprised when they see Turkish women sitting in a bar enjoying a cocktail after a hard day's work in her chosen profession, such as law or medicine. Equally many modern Turkish women are appalled when they visit their rural sisters, slaving in the kitchen after a day's hard labour in the family field while their husbands return to yet another game of cards or backgammon at the local teahouse. In Turkish divorce law, it is perfectly acceptable to cite "cultural differences" as a reason to separate.

The harem: Following their acceptance of Islam over a thousand years ago, the Turks also began institutionalising its more conservative traditions, including the seclusion of women. The area of the house where the men entertained their guests was called the *selamlık*; the part of the house reserved for women was the *harem* ("forbidden sanctuary"). It was the province of all the women of the household, including daughters and aunts, not a prison for sex slaves.

Today, enough is known about life in the harem to render the more commonly held fantasies associated with this restricted realm either inaccurate or laughable. Anything but a brothel, the harem was essentially the domain of the first wife. In accordance with the dictates of the Prophet Mohammed, who is well known for the difficulties he brought on himself by acquiring too many wives, the Muslim husband required the permission of his first wife before taking another woman. He would also be required to support all his wives in the same style: a gift to one required the same gift to all the others; the same held true for his husbandly duties. Needless to say, most men could simply not afford to practice polygamy, either financially or psychologically.

The harem was, in fact, more like a home and school for women, a place where they were trained in arts and crafts, music, household management and religion. Under Islamic law, slave girls bought for training as servants, nannies, entertainers, or ladies-in-waiting for the wives of an extended family, were to be set free after seven years. Even the famed Topkapı Harem was subject to the same protocol.

A potential paramour was usually chosen not by the sultan himself, but by the Mother Sultan, who carefully trained the concubine before finally presenting her to the ruler. The selected girl had the right to say no.

Winds of change: It took the major social upheavals of World War I and the subsequent War of Independence to change radically the status of women in Turkey. Suddenly, many urban and village women found themselves working in munitions factories. At the same time, the wives and daughters of the elite classes became vocal supporters of Atatürk's fight for independence, and joined his forces in Anatolia. Following the declaration of the Republic in 1923, one of the most significant elements in the social revolution planned and advocated by Kemal Atatürk was the emancipation of Turkish women.

On 17 February, 1926, the country adopted a new code of civil law which significantly altered the traditional family structure. Polygamy and religious marriages were abolished, while divorce and child custody became the prerogative of both women and men. A minimum age

for marriage was fixed and the legal status of women was improved. Women also gained rights of inheritance and equality of testimony before a court of law; previously, under Islamic law, the testimony of two women was equal to that of one man.

Female suffrage was granted at the municipal level in 1930, and nationwide in 1934. In principle, at least, Turkish women were far ahead of many of their Western sisters, and strangely, it was a man – Kemal Atatürk – who was giving them their rights by decree.

Theory and Practice: But theory is one thing, and practice another. Even at the elite level, the traditional Islamic ethic concerning

LEFT: earning one's daily bread.
RIGHT: woman and child in Diyarbakır.

female submission to male authority continues to pervade much of modern Turkish society. Relatively recent changes to Turkish Civil Code have officially allowed married women to keep their maiden name, work without the permission of their husbands, and to be the legal head of the household, but in most cases, the man is still legally regarded as the "head of the family", and his opinions generally hold more sway in the courts. Planned new legislation will finally abolish references to any "head of the family", grant women complete equality in family matters and the right to 50 percent of the family home on divorce.

MARRIAGE

Marriage in Turkey today is completely, and quite unromantically, secular: it is basically a matter of waiting in a queue while state bureaucrats ask a few questions and fill out the proper form. One of the more important legal questions (not always answered honestly) is whether the couple are marrying of their own free will rather than giving in to family pressure for an "arranged" marriage. Religious marriages are not acknowledged by law, yet in areas where female literacy and religious understanding are low and faith high, young women are still sometimes convinced otherwise by their family or the local imam, only to discover later that their "husband" is a bigamist.

Alimony can be very difficult to claim from an unwilling spouse, and inheritance rights are also a big issue for Turkish women, on account of the vast amount of unregistered income in the country. The better-educated and better-off Turkish women make sure their name is included on family property. Needless to say it is the rural, uneducated women who suffer most, with no proper understanding of their legal rights. It's for this reason, according to many women's groups, that so many Turkish women remain in abusive marriages – divorce is still a scandal in religious communities and all too often a woman's own family will not take her back if she leaves her husband. Better education and media coverage are making abuses of the legal system increasingly rare, but the fact remains that there are still three times more illiterate women than men in Turkey.

A matter of class: Travellers in rural areas may notice a fairly relaxed attitude to religion. Many villagers are devout and some even manage the pilgrimage to Mecca, but while most women wear some kind of cotton head covering, it seems more intended to keep the dust out of their hair than cover it up. In the towns, an accute awareness of women's rights tends to be the preserve of the well-off and educated, and sadly many of these women – who may even define themselves as feminists – look with disdain upon their more conservative, traditional sisters. The tragedy is that this mutual distrust is the product of Turkey's vast class divide, especially in the large cities with the highest volume of rural migrants.

It is amongst these, and the urban working class, that many "new fundamentalist" women have emerged, ranging from those wearing the "body bag" black *çarşaf* to the more moderate (frequently middle-aged) "rain-coat brigade" who wear patterned scarves and loose overcoats, often in pastel colours. Younger "new Islamic" women even wear fashionable clothes which cover the wrists and the ankles, but are tight enough to show off their figures, with designer headscarves wrapped alluringly around their throats.

In the main, it is safe to assume a woman's dress style is a matter of free will.

Ethnic minorities

Since the Stone Age, Anatolia has been home to a large number of different races, cultures and faiths, many of which are still found here today.

Over the last decade, the struggle between the Kurds and the Turkish state regularly featured in world headlines, though since the capture of the PKK leader in 1999 the conflict has cooled considerably. There are around 15 million Kurds in Turkey, largely inhabiting the southeast, and most were fighting not so much for independence but for recognition of their cultural rights, such as their distinct language, and representation in parliament.

Kurds, however, are not the only minority who have been suppressed, or had their identity submerged by post-Republic nationalism. The

ganda. Their beliefs are barely acknowledged in the shadow of the Sunni majority.

The Turks: The Central Asian contribution to Turkish blood is comparatively "new" by Anatolian standards. The word "Turk" was first recorded by the Chinese as early as 1300 BC, but most of these Asian-originated tribes (including the Seljuks and Osmanlıs) arrived in Turkey less than 1,000 years ago – in several waves of migration spanning centuries. It is this Turkish ancestry which remains central to the Republic's self-image, and it is certainly from this stock that the Turkish language and Ottoman culture emerged.

Armenian lobby in Europe and the US has drawn world attention to the massacre of up to a million Ottoman Armenians in 1915. In general, Christian minorities in Turkey live at the margins of society, quick to be blamed by nationalists as detrimental to the nation's security. However, it is less well known that the Alevis, a liberal Shi'ite Muslim sect *(see page 81)* which make up about a quarter of Turkey's population, have frequently been the target of attacks as well as the butt of baseless propa-

Ironically, the Ottomans did not consider themselves to be Turks and by the 16th century were so racially intermixed (for one thing, the harem preference tended to be for Caucasian blondes) that finding an Asian identity became irrelevant to them. In general, the Ottoman era was notable for its tolerance of different races and religions.

The Kurds: Ethnically, Kurdish origins are obscure, but it is certainly true that they have inhabited a region stretching from Syria through Iraq, Iran and eastern Turkey since great antiquity. Some claim they are descendants of the Medes, who ruled the area around Lake Van upon the collapse of the Urartian

LEFT: all eyes on the bride on her wedding day.
ABOVE: pious women visiting their patron saint in central Anatolia.

civilisation. Others maintain they are the Car-
duchi encountered in 401 BC by the Greek
general and historian Xenophon, who described them as a "freedom-
loving mountain people".

Whatever their origins, they
are a tribal people who identify
themselves by clan rather than
kingdom, and have numerous
Indo-Iranian language dialects
unrelated to Turkish. They also
include significant religious differences – some are devout Sunni Muslims or
Alevis, others are "Zaza" (thought to be related

HOMELESS

Altogether, there are around
25 million Kurds, across six
countries. The closest they have to
a homeland is in northern Iraq,
now being reintegrated after 12
years of effective independence.

to Zoroastrianism). The two groups traditionally do not mix.

The Caucasians: The Black Sea region
boasts numerous Caucasian cultures such as the
Laz, a unique tribe that traces its ancestry to
the ancient kingdom of Colchis in the Caucasus, where Jason and his Argonauts came to rob
the Golden Fleece. They still speak a language
most closely related to the Mingrelian branch of
pre-Indo-European Caucasian.

Among other things, the Laz are noted for
their independence, energetic style, and dry
sense of humour – but also for their keen business acumen. They are successful in every
Turkish metropolis (especially in the contract-

ing business and the restaurant trade). A particularly distinctive Laz tradition is hawking.

The Hemşınlis of the Kaçkar Mountains are
possibly Heptocomete in origin,
converting to Islam only 150
years ago. They speak a dialect
of Armenian.

The Greeks: Greeks have
lived in Asia Minor since about
the 8th century BC – the south
coast is full of Hellenistic antiquities – and although they
would hate to admit it, most modern Turks have
a healthy dollop of Greek blood.

The Ottomans treated most minorities well,
and the Greek community ("Rum" – as in
Roman – in Turkish) was given a great deal of
freedom to run its own affairs. Until the fall of
the Ottoman Empire, between a quarter and a
third of the population of Istanbul spoke Greek
and professed Orthodox Christianity. The seat
of the Eastern Orthodox Church has been in
Istanbul since the 4th century AD, and the spiritual leader of world Orthodoxy, His All
Holiness Ecumenical Patriarch Bartholomew,
continues to reside at Fener in Istanbul, an
interesting historical neighbourhood at the
entrance to the Golden Horn with a cluster of
Christian and Jewish religious buildings.

But following the War of Independence,
Greece and Turkey agreed to an exchange of
populations. Over a million Greeks were compelled to leave Turkey and about half a million
Turks were sent from Greece. Only Greeks
with Ottoman citizenship were allowed to
remain. Today the Greek population in Turkey
numbers approximately 100,000, with most living in Istanbul. The policy may have seemed
expedient at the time, but it caused a great deal
of suffering and no small loss of property, as
well as the virtual disappearance of a significant cultural group. Many consider it a tragedy
of modern Turkish history.

The Suriyanis: The Tur Abdin plateau,
around Midyat and Mardin in southeast Turkey,
is the home of the 50,000 or so remaining
Suriyanis who continue to speak a sort of proto-
Arabic known to scholars as Syriac. Midyat has
been the centre of the Syrian Orthodox Church
since the 6th century and in medieval times
there were as many as 150 ordained bishops and
80 monasteries in the region. Only three (Mor
Gabriel, Mor Yakub and Deyrulzafaran) still

exist, though most of their community has moved to Istanbul where they have some hope of political representation. A new Syrian Orthodox Church was dedicated in the city in 1963, using stones brought from Tur Abdin. The Suriyanis of Midyat are known throughout Turkey as superb jewellers.

The Armenians: At its peak, Armenian territory stretched from northeastern Turkey to Iranian Azerbaijan. This ancient and once powerful empire was absorbed by the Ottoman Empire in the 16th century.

In the latter half of the 19th century, nationalist sentiment among Armenians was fanned

were murdered or displaced by Turkish nationalist forces in retaliation.

It is particularly tragic to note the Armenian ghost quarters still remaining in some of Turkey's eastern cities; they are living evidence of mass evacuation. Today there are only about 70,000 Armenians in Turkey. The Armenian Orthodox Patriarchate is in Kumkapı in the oldest part of Istanbul.

The Jewish community: Local Jewish history is a happier tale. The remains of Jewish settlements of great antiquity are visible in Sardis and Harran, but most of today's Jewish community trace their ancestry to the summer

by Russia's interest in fragmenting the Ottoman Empire, and during the chaos of World War I some Armenians seized the opportunity to found an independent state by joining the Russian side. The massacres and pogroms that took place between 1915 and 1918 remain a source of immense bitterness and controversy today. An estimated 600,000 Turks and Kurds were slaughtered or dispersed by Russian regiments during an attempt to claim the eastern territory (notably around Van) and even more Armenians

LEFT: Kurdish man, Hakkâri.
ABOVE: Laz fisherman on the Black Sea coast.
RIGHT: nomadic cotton-picker near Harran.

of 1492, when, under the enlightened reign of Sultan Beyazıt II, 150,000 Sephardic Jews were welcomed into Turkey to escape death or conversion under the edict of Queen Isabella and King Ferdinand of Spain, receiving land, tax exemptions, encouragement and assistance from the government. These new citizens established Turkey's first printing press in 1493, and many famous Ottoman court physicians and diplomats were Jewish.

Atatürk also welcomed many Jewish scholars and their families during World War II. But with the founding of Israel in 1948, many Turkish Jews opted to emigrate and today their community, mostly in Istanbul, numbers only

25,000. But many synagogues of historical note remain in the city, mostly near Galata Tower and in Balat.

The Nomads *(Yörük)***:** Sadly, there are few remaining nomadic tribes in Turkey; most live around the Adana region but spend a majority of their time in the Toros Mountains, moving from pasture to mountain pasture – trekkers are sure to encounter them here in the summer months; they are friendly as well as fairly astute concerning politics and the modern world.

Turkish nomads are fairly clear about their tribal structures and consider themselves to belong to some of the original Central Asian gin. Now, hopefully, in this age of pride in multiculturalism, Turkey is beginning to recognise the value of its ethnic and religious differences and their contribution to the kaleidoscopic mosaic that is Anatolian culture.

Muslims

The call to prayer is one of the most evocative sounds heard by visitors to Turkey. Drifting from the minarets of mosques in cities, towns and villages, this is the eerie music of the Muslim world, exhorting the faithful to worship five times a day. Though modern Turkey is a secular republic, most Turks still consider

tribes that entered Anatolia some 800 years ago. Most are nominally Alevi and though the women have a rough time of it, fighting off fleas in the tents (some of which are of the traditional black wool, others US Army surplus) and scraping pots with bark, they have a tax-exempt status and many are quite well off. A notable ethnic feature of Turkish nomads is their startlingly green eyes.

It was only after the foundation of the Turkish Republic in 1923 that a common identity was sought in the pursuit of national unity. However, it is unlikely that Atatürk intended this ideal to efface all cultural differences in favour of a mythological common racial ori- themselves Muslims and at least respect the five duties or pillars of Islam, even though they may not adhere to them themselves. However, the interpretation of Islam in Turkey has always been liberal, bearing little resemblance to its practice in Iran and Saudi Arabia.

Alevis: The majority of Turks are Sunni, but there are also 20 million Shi'ite Alevis, who generally hold more liberal and even left-wing beliefs. The division between these two major sects arose after the death of Mohammed, during a squabble over the ordination of a new caliph. The Sunnis followed Caliph Hasan who believed in consensus rule by a college of *imams*; the breakaway Shi'ites believed in an absolute authority, claiming blood descent from Mohammed through his daughter, Fatima, and her husband, Ali, who is still greatly revered.

Alevism is one of the oldest orders in Anatolia, but it was crystallised mainly in response to the Messianic revolution led by the Shi'ite Shah Ismael of Persia in the 16th century. Through the course of time and due to alienation from mainstream Shi'ite practice, however, distinctive traditions emerged – a system of travelling holy elders (*dede*) replaced the more traditional Muslim structure of authority, for example, and the Qur'anic ban on alcohol was relaxed.

Women have equal status with men and they pray together in what are essentially meeting houses rather than mosques, a custom which has led to foolish allegations of orgies and incest. Their leftist political inclinations may also be at the root of mistrust, primarily among fundamentalists, which has occasionally resulted in violence.

Sufis: Other Muslim minorities include Sufism, based on mystic forms of worship thought to combine elements of pre- and early Christian practice, Buddhism, and neoplatonism. Dancing, music and fire have all been employed to help practitioners achieve a trance or ecstastic state. In Ottoman times, the Sufi brotherhoods formed *tekkes* or lodges, which resembled early Christian orders. Each of these was led by a sheikh, or religious guide, and the novices (*murit*) were attached to a fully fledged dervish. Members were required to embrace piety and poverty, living off alms in their quest for salvation.

The primary Sufi brotherhood still active today is the Mevlevi order, whose "whirling dervishes" follow the mystic poet Mevlana (lord) Celaleddin Rumi who lived in Konya in the 13th century. The Mevlevi Festival, commemorating the death of their founder, is held during the week of 17 December, primarily in Konya and Istanbul, and is a major tourist attraction.

During their religious ceremony, the dervishes wear flowing white robes and conical hats and twirl to the steady beat of drums and strains of mystical music, enacting the death and ultimate union of Mevlana with Allah. Today, the Mevlevis have found new followers among urban intellectuals and young people, especially in Istanbul where the Galata Mevlevihane practises a decidedly "new age" interpretation of Sufism, including the admission of women to the dance ritual.

Bektaşis: The Bektaşi order, followers of a Muslim mystic, Hacı Bektaş Veli (1209–71), is primarily based in the central town of

> **THE PILLARS OF ISLAM**
>
> All Muslims follow five basic rules: the statement of the creed ("There is no God but Allah and Mohammed is his Prophet"), prayer, giving alms to the poor, fasting during Ramazan, and making a pilgrimage to Mecca.

Hacıbektaş, near Kırşehir in central Turkey, where their founder is buried. More worldly than Sufis, they recognise Ali as the rightful successor to Mohammed but regard Hacı Bektaş Veli as their sheikh or *pir*.

The Bektaşis absorbed a great number of non-Muslim rituals, including baptism, and they also celebrate the Zoroastrian festival of light, *Nevroz*, as Ali's birthday. Its dervishes, however, were principally responsible for converting the Christian peasantry of Anatolia and the Balkans to Islam. The brotherhood was long affiliated with the Janissary Corps – the élite Ottoman army unit whose members were Christian converts.

LEFT: Suriyani priest in Mardin.
RIGHT: an elder Muslim devotee reads the Holy Qur'an.

Islam and the Ottomans

Islam played a crucial role in the Ottoman Empire. It helped create solidarity among its diverse Muslim elements and provided a clear ethical and legal structure for its subjects. The Ottoman state was ruled by the sultan, who became the "caliph" or leader of the entire Islamic world following the Turkish conquest of Egypt in the 16th century. Under the Ottomans, Muslim scholars (the *ulema*) laid down the rules on all religious matters, taught religious sciences, operated the mosques and schools, and also controlled the courts.

Early Ottoman theologians were influenced by the views of Al-Ghazali, a Persian scholar living in the 11th century who rejected the idea that scientific knowledge violated Islamic doctrine. As a result, many Muslims achieved fame in the fields of science – notably astronomy, mathematics and medicine. Islamic scholars used mathematics and astronomy to fix the position of the *qibla* (prayer niche in mosques), which had to point towards Mecca. The words "algebra" and "cipher" derive from Arabic, showing the Islamic influence in the field of mathematics.

As the empire declined, however, the Turkish *ulema* became open to widespread corruption,

THE WORDS OF THE PROPHET

Islam is the newest of the three great monotheistic religions, founded in the 7th century AD when the revelations of God to the Prophet Mohammed were conveyed orally and memorised by his followers. These verses, which later comprised the Qur'an, were not written down until after the prophet's death. Little of the "divine word", however, with the possible exception of his recommendations on women and family law, gave much direction as to actual practice of the new religion.

As a result, the *Sunna*, a collection of anecdotes, traditions and sayings *(hadiths)* attributed to Mohammed or based on his deeds and lifestyle, were added as a supplement, forming the basis of much modern Islamic belief and law. It is the wide disparity in interpretation of the Qur'an and the *Sunna* that has resulted in today's diversity of Muslim practice, from the most liberal sects of Alevism to the extremes of enforced *Shari'a* – even the justification for female "circumcision" in Egypt and the Sudan.

In the interests of preserving unity among believers, the *Icma* or "agreement of Islam" allows for practices endemic to local tradition to be assumed and incorporated as authentically Muslim. It is also the *Icma* which allows for tolerance and flexibility in other countries – most notably Turkey.

a development that soon closed the doors on progress. There was even a fatwah on Muslim involvement in the printing press, under pressure from calligraphers. The clergy isolated themselves from intellectual and cultural developments, including in science and technology. In 1580, Sultan Murat III closed an observatory in Istanbul on the grounds that the astronomers were "insolent enough to try to pry open the secrets of the universe" – secrets known only to Allah.

While the European Reformation was making huge strides in the sciences and industry, the Ottoman Empire wallowed in ignorance,

– a measure instituted to help modify their influence on society.

The mid-1990s saw an upsurge in Islamic radicalism within the cities, with "new Islamic" political parties gaining ground in the cities, but the fight back is underway, and Islamist leaders have faced jail sentences or a ban from politics if suspected of contravening the tenets of secularism enshrined in the Turkish constitution.

Curbing extremism

Recent major reforms in the education system have raised the age limit for entry into reli-

guided by a reactionary clergy who were clinging to medieval Islamic ideas.

The secular state

The formation of the modern Turkish republic and the sweeping reforms of Atatürk soon changed all that. He abolished the sultanate and caliphate and replaced *Shari'a* law with civil, trade and criminal codes, which he adapted from those of Switzerland, France and Italy. Today's religious leaders are paid civil servants

---

LEFT: souvenir icons on sale at the tomb of the medieval mystic, Hacı Bektaş.
ABOVE: children in the Ulucami, Manisa.

gious training schools, traditional institutions that proliferated during the mid-1990s. There have also been periodic purges of radical Islamists who have infiltrated the Turkish military – whose commitment to the maintenance of a secular republic is supported by most within its ranks.

There are times when the restraints can seem repressive – there is a continuing debate over the apparently trivial ban of head-coverings in universities and government offices, for example. But with Turkey's unique composition and location, any threat of a return to *Shari'a* remains a source of genuine concern for the vast majority of the population. ❑

KEBABS, SALAD AND SUNSHINE

Take the sun-drenched flavours of the Mediterranean, and season with
just a little olive oil and lemon juice – Turkish food is simple but delicious

For 500 years, the Ottoman Empire ruled much of the medieval world and at the Topkapı Palace in Istanbul, great chefs created a sumptuous cuisine which came to rival the epicurean delights of ancient Rome.

Perhaps due to the infinite variety of fish, fowl, meat, fruit and vegetables produced in

Turkey or to the numerous cultures that took root in ancient Anatolia – archaeologists have recently deciphered a Sumerian tablet that turned out to be a cookbook of sorts, with nearly all the items and spices listed familiar to Turks today.

Today, from the Balkans to North Africa, virtually all the nations share a taste for the savoury kebab *(kebap)*, pilau *(pilav)*, aubergine specialities and the tangy feta cheese whose preparation became an art form in the Topkapı kitchens and the province of Bolu, where young men seeking their fortunes started by peeling vegetables in one of the dozens of exclusive gourmet schools set up by imperial decree.

Even today Bolu remains famous for its chefs.

In early Ottoman times, the riches of the sultan's table owed much to Persian cuisine, notably the Abbassid dynasty banquets which disappeared at the fall of Baghdad after the Mongol invasion. However, the taste for meat charcoal-grilled on a skewer, known today as *şiş* (pronounced "shish") kebab, is more likely to have originated as "fast food" on the steppes of Central Asia or in the shepherds' pastures of Anatolia, while many vegetable- or pulse-based meals can be found in different versions all over the Middle East.

Even today, Turkish tastes are much more notably Mediterranean and meat-based than Persian-influenced, and visitors may notice an odd conservatism in the native palate, which cannot fathom the combination of fruit with savoury dishes, and a reluctance to admit that any world cuisine could match Turkey's.

The result is that "Ottoman" food is difficult to find and not every traveller will be lucky enough to find the best of Turkish cuisine without serious investigation. Though it is all tasty and fresh, and, on the whole, exceptionally healthy, the standard fare in touristic areas can wear on the palate after a few weeks, since restaurant owners play safe and pitch the known quantities of *döner* and *şiş* kebab to the wary and unadventurous, steering you away from strong cheeses and fatty, aromatic meat-balls *(beyti kebabı)* or, God forbid, *koç yumurtası* (ram's testicles) and lamb's brain salad, in favour of pepper steak and hamburgers. If you want to experience the real thing, head for the

FOOD, GLORIOUS FOOD

In the 16th century, court poets devoted love verses to food, and these were written with a delicate sensuality that still survives in Turkish romantic discourse today – "Good night my watermelon, my red wheat waiting in the sack..." Titles of great prestige were given to the finest master chefs, and court recipes were guarded with the greatest of secrecy.

backstreets, working men's cafés or those restaurants which have earned a reputation for authentic Ottoman or eastern Turkish cuisine.

Regional variations

Urban dwellers of Istanbul and Ankara have an aversion to highly spiced food and garlic, associating them with the peasant cultures they disdain. However, as you move south and east, such middle-class prejudices swiftly disappear, and if you recognise the great regional specialities and know what to ask for, there are many surprise delights to please every taste. Foremost, recognise that freshness is essential to the

the 16th century, having originated in China. Further east, towards Alanya, locally grown bananas are smaller and tastier than the imported variety but are being edged out all the same, while the avocado is beginning to put in an appearance. In the south, salad lovers will also find a variety of unusual, spicy herbs appearing along with the standard tomato and cucumber mix, *çoban salatası* (shepherd's salad). *Roka*, the bitter leaf known as rocket in English, is an essential with fish, usually garnished only with lemon and salt; you may also find spiky *Tereotu* (bitter cress), *nane* (fresh mint), or even sorrel *(kuzu kullaşı)*. A spinachy

ingredients used in Turkish food and should be taken into account when ordering meals – a trip to the village market should give you a tip as to what's in season.

The Antalya region is famous for citrus fruits, notably oranges, which are at their best in December, when it is still sunny, and local farmers will frequently invite you to pick all you want off the trees. The Turkish word for orange, *portakal*, is derived from Portugal, from where the fruit first came to Anatolia in

textured vegetable called *semizotu*, often served in garlic-yogurt, is known to us as *purslane*. A strong, white crumbled goat's cheese *(tulum)* is eaten traditionally with walnuts.

The Aegean region is famous for the *çöp şiş*, tiny pieces of lamb threaded onto wooden skewers like satay sticks. People buy four or six at a time and dip them in a spicy mixture of cumin, oregano and hot pepper, then roll them up in a *yufka* – something like a flour tortilla. This is popular truck-stop grub, best eaten by the roar of a highway. The Antalya regional speciality, *hibeş*, is a starter made of sesame paste, lemon, hot pepper and garlic. Heading east of Alanya, the bread changes from the

LEFT: spices tempt the eye and tickle the nose.
ABOVE: the *döner* kebab has become one of Turkey's most famous exports.

European loaf to Middle Eastern unleavened *pide*, similar to pitta or the Indian nan.

Closer to the Syrian borderlands (Şanlıurfa and Antakya), food becomes much spicier. Şanlıurfa is known for its huge spicy *şiş* kebabs (as well as the difficulty of ordering a beer: this is a city of pilgrimage for Muslims) and Antakya for hummus – the chickpea paste with garlic now so familiar in the west. Moving east, you'll find a more heavy-handed use of cumin and red pepper, and odd things like the sweetish *nar ekşisi* (sour pomegranate syrup) – used in tomato and onion salads – which owes more to Persian heritage than most Turkish food.

The Black Sea is famous for *hamsi* (anchovies, usually crisp-fried in cornmeal), cornbread, hazelnuts and dairy products, Edirne and İznik in Marmara for catfish. In central Anatolia, *saç kavurma* is an elegant meat, onion and vegetable stir-fry made in a shallow wok (usually at your table) which tastes rather like a Hungarian goulash. This dish has clear links with the outdoor cooking of Central Asia.

Dining out

When dining out with Turks, you are often asked which you would prefer to eat, fish or meat, so that the best location for one or the other might be chosen. Along with a delicate

palate, sensitivity is extended to include the environment in which food is eaten. Fish should be eaten at a table set alongside the water (preferably with *raki*), while kebabs and other meat dishes are enjoyed in a rural scene. With at least seven months of predictably fine weather in the south, the favoured style of dining here is the outdoor, freshly caught trout restaurant, where one sits beneath spreading plane trees listening to the river sing.

For upmarket dining, however, head for the hotels. Unlike in many parts of Europe, some of the country's finest restaurants are to be found here, many of them specialising in resurrecting old Ottoman menus. They provide exquisite settings for an evening out, but also tend to be more expensive than the local kebab houses and fish restaurants.

Food is served in a variety of establishments from the all-encompassing *restoran* to the *lokanta* (cafeteria serving stews), *salonu* (eating hall), *gazino* (club), *çorbacı* (soup kitchen), *kebapçı* or *köfteci* (kebab stall), or *meyhane* (bar – predominantly male – with simple but usually superb food).

Through the day

Breakfasts are dominated by salty white cheese and olives, with butter, honey, jam, tomatoes, cucumbers and a boiled egg often making an appearance as well. Alternatively, pastry shops serve a variety of flaky pastries with cheese, potato or meat fillings.

The staple of lunchtime cafeterias is *sulu yemek*, which translates literally as "juicy food", meaning vegetable- and meat-based stews. Increasingly, you find the option of *gösleme*, huge eastern Turkish pancakes, served with a tomatoey sauce.

Evening meals usually start with a selection of *mezes* – cold appetisers – which the waiter brings to the table on an enormous platter. This is particularly convenient for foreigners as written descriptions of the dishes often don't do them justice or are eccentrically translated (to wit: "cigarette pie" for *sigara börek*, etc.) Most are cold, cooked vegetable dishes in olive oil, or salads of shrimp and other types of fish, but you can opt for hot *mezes* like *börek* (hot pastries with a variety of fillings, which also make an excellent snack meal), sautéed lamb's liver with onions, or kalamari (deep-fried squid). *Dolma* ("stuffed things") are also a popular addition, which can be made with courgettes, aubergines, peppers, grape leaves, cabbage leaves, tomatoes, mussels or artichokes, filled with a mixture of rice, pine nuts, currants, herbs and spices. They are cooked in olive oil and lemon juice and served hot with meat, or cold with yogurt.

It is also well worthwhile keeping a lookout for regional or less common *meze* delicacies such as *cevizli tavuk* – Circassian chicken, a dish of steamed, boned and shredded breast meat smothered in a sauce of walnuts, bread crumbs, garlic, oil and lemon.

Fish is taken very seriously – there are five separate names for the bluefish alone, from

Some of the most delicious dishes include *kılıq balışı*, swordfish skewered with peppers and tomatoes; *kalkan*, turbot served with lemon wedges; *buşlama*, an exotic fish stew made from any of the larger catch of the day; and *karides güveç*, a casserole of shrimp, hot peppers, tomatoes and cheese (vegetarians should note that a similar dish made with mushrooms is often available). Giant shrimp *(karides)* and clawless Mediterranean lobster are usually available in season, though pricey even then.

Kebab is a word that has figured prominently in Turkish cuisine for over 10 centuries and its meaning has developed to include

yaprak (bay leaf) to *çinakop* or *lüfer*. It is never served more than a day old, and is considered to be at its prime in the autumn. Selections in fish restaurants are likely to include starters such as mussels stuffed with rice, pine nuts and spices; fried kalamari and shrimp; *balık köftesi* (hot fish cakes); or cured fish with fresh dill and vinegar (or even caviar). Main dishes will run to swordfish kebabs and grilled or fried fish of the season – though it is as well to be cautious and ask the price by weight.

LEFT: eating fish is a serious business; the setting and the season are both important to the experience.
ABOVE: trays of appetising stews at a *lokanta*.

meats that have been boiled, baked and stewed. Meat is usually cooked with vegetables; as with the *şiş* kebabs, pieces of green pepper, tomato and onion add flavour to the morsels of meat, or the *güveç* dishes sautéed in a clay casserole with fresh vegetables. Lamb is the meat *par excellence* in Turkey and is used to make various types of *dolma*, stuffed vegetable dishes, or for the classic Konya dish of *tandır* kebab, where a whole lamb is baked in a brick oven, still built in the ground in many villages. Other wonderful kebab dishes, often related to their region of origin, are the *Adana kebab*, ground lamb highly seasoned with red pepper and oregano, wrapped around a skewer and grilled; or *Bursa* and *İskender kebab*, with luscious slices of *döner* meat spread over *pide* bread, smothered in yogurt, tomato sauce and hot butter.

If your main course is a meat dish, it will probably come accompanied by rice, which can be simply cooked with butter and meat broth or, alternatively, richly seasoned with pine nuts, currants, herbs and liver.

Dessert

In restaurants, dessert is usually a selection of seasonal fruits. In spring, this may be green almonds and plums (the latter served with salt),

Winter is the time for citrus fruit and bananas. Melon and white cheese are enjoyed when lingering with drinks after a meal. Even the grandest restaurants will serve fruit, although they may have such luxuries as figs stuffed with almonds, apricots bursting with cheese and pistachio paste, or sugared pumpkin with cream.

Another type of dessert that should definitely be sampled is the *muhallebi*, or milk pudding, served cold and dusted with pistachio nuts or chocolate. Particularly good is *sütlaç*, a rich rice pudding cooked slowly in an earthenware cup. The meal usually ends with tiny cups of ultra-sweet, bitter Turkish coffee.

generally an acquired taste for foreigners. There are strawberries in May, cherries in June, melons in July and August, and apples, pears, pomegranates and grapes in autumn.

VEGETARIAN WOES

Strict vegetarians should take care in most ordinary restaurants. Owners are mystified by the concept and will often tell you a dish is meatless when it has been cooked in stock and has lumps of lamb fat floating in it. In urban centres and fashionable resort areas, however, Western-style "health" food has become trendy and there's more international cuisine catering to vegetarians.

Snacks and munchies

An interesting aspect of Turkish culture is the all-night *işkembe*, or tripe soup parlour. This soup, not unlike Mexican *meñudo*, is considered medicinal after a night out, with crushed garlic from a bowl, red pepper, oregano or vinegar ladled in to taste.

Raisins and dried seeds or nuts are eaten at any time or during any social occasion, and the little shops that sell them are frequently open late at night. Roasted hazelnuts and unshelled black sunflower seeds are the favourites, with powdery dried chickpeas filling in for weight.

Calorie-lovers must seek out the traditional *pastane*, or pudding shop. In earlier days, before rock bars, fast-food restaurants and cafés provided an alternative, young courting couples or families would make the *pastane* a Sunday ritual. Hence you'll notice, particularly in larger cities, that "traditional" pudding shops are frequently romantically decorated in styles from original Art Nouveau to 1950s milk-bar. Even the names of the desserts themselves – Lady's Navel, Lips of the Beloved, and Nightingale's Nests, to name a few, sing of the overblown romance loved by Turkish suitors.

In the *pastane*, you'll find all the traditional Turkish sweets such as the familiar *lokum* (Turkish Delight), syrupy baklava and halva. Profiteroles, supposedly invented in a *pastane* in Istanbul's Istiklal Caddesi, are also popular, as is crème caramel, a pudding made here with shredded pigeon's breast, and *aşure*, a traditional celebratory dish made from all of the 40 different ingredients left in the Ark's kitchen after Noah sighted Ararat.

Sweets such as baklava, rather than alcohol, are the customary gift when one goes visiting.

Drinks

Much of the Aegean region is still bedecked in vines. Wine-making has been popular here since the neolithic era, but despite this long legacy Turks are not great drinkers and many, in keeping with Muslim tradition, do not drink at all. Medium-priced safe bets include fruity whites such as *Villa Doluca*, *Villa Riesling* and *Çankaya*, and hearty reds, *Yakut* and *Dikmen*. But recently, perhaps due to more Turkish contact with the wines of Europe, producers have begun importing and developing vines with tastier grapes, and if you are willing to splash out, try some of the classy newcomers, such as the dark, Bordeaux-style *Karaca* or *Narince,* or the crisp white *Şerefen*. In Cappadocia, small family wineries are producing some excellent, unique vintages.

The more courageous can try the local aniseed-based tipple, rakı, called "lion's milk" by Turks, which goes well with fish. *Efes* and *Tuborg* are the most popular beers.

A taste worth acquiring, as it is both cheap and easy on the stomach, is *ayran*, a yogurt and water frappé. *Ayran* is a much better thirst-quencher than bottled fizz and the salt helps to prevent sweating out all your fluids on a suffocating day's trek around Ephesus. The best *ayran* is served by street vendors, icy cold, slightly salty and as frothy as a milkshake.

Naturally carbonated mineral water *(maden suyu)* is also cheap. Uncarbonated pure water, usually kept very cold, is sold by vendors everywhere in both plastic and glass bottles. Tap water can be risky and is often heavily chlorinated – it does not taste good.

Freshly squeezed juices are also widely available, but best in winter when the citrus season is in full force in the south. Even the

simplest establishments also serve carrot juice, banana milk and apple juice, made to taste.

Strong, sweet, black tea in small curvaceous glasses will usually be served, but there is also a strong tradition of herbal teas, some of which (like sage or even fresh oregano) are unusual to the Western palate but very good. An infusion of *ihlamur* (linden flower) is also popular, especially as a remedy for colds and flu.

Boza and *sahlep* are popular drinks in winter. *Sahlep*, served hot with a sprinkle of cinnamon, often on ferries and by street vendors, is made from the pulverized tubers of the wild orchid. It is considered by some to be an aphrodisiac and is extremely sweet. ❏

LEFT: Turkish pizza, known as *pide* (bread), is topped with cheese, herbs, spinach or even goat meat.
RIGHT: tea seller in Silifke.

ANATOLIA'S ANCIENT ARTS

Anatolia's historic art is infinitely varied – from squat, Hatti fertility figurines to towering Roman temples and delicate Ottoman carvings

When most people think of the art and architecture of Turkey, their first vision is unquestionably of that stupendous Bosphorus skyline which includes Topkapı Palace, Aya Sofya and the glowing minarets of the Blue Mosque lit up at night beneath a golden crescent moon. Here is a fairytale vision

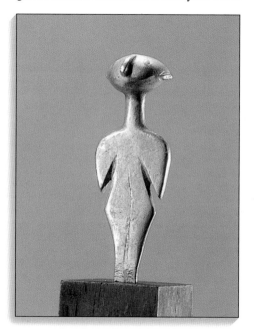

indeed, but these relics of Byzantine and Ottoman splendour mark only one small segment of Anatolia's dazzling visual heritage, for the country has been inhabited by many sophisticated cultures stretching back well before even the earliest Greek settlements.

The first city of art

Ongoing excavations at Çatalhöyük *(see page 285)* have been astonishing even the scholars working there. Nine thousand years ago, these lands were a paradise for some of the world's first farmers, allowing them the luxury of developing sophisticated religion, art and architecture as well as indulging in personal vanity,

evidenced by the quantity of obsidian mirrors, lead and copper jewellery, terracotta stamps, and pots of what may have been body paint found there. Yet most astonishing are the houses, reminiscent of the 2,000-year-old Native American cities in New Mexico and Nevada discovered in recent years. These seem to have been used first as domestic dwellings and later as shrines, and have yielded some of the earliest wall paintings ever found on man-made structures as well as fascinating ritual relief sculptures. Some paintings show exhilarating hunting parties and sexual congress, some a ritual "excarnation" of bodies by vultures or condors, and one a volcanic eruption which may be Hasan Dağ, a twin-peaked mountain known to have been active in the second millennium BC. Many are simply geometric, but may in fact be based on weaving patterns.

The numerous "Venus of Willendorf"-style figurines found in grain bins and graves have suggested a matriarchal culture, while the famed "horned bench" may have been a slab for laying out the dead. In other Çatalhöyük house-shrines, there are bulls' skulls covered with plaster and ranged up the wall, totem-pole fashion, over which a vaguely humanoid form may be riding or giving birth to the animals below. The abstract nature of these works makes interpretation difficult, but nonetheless indicates a high degree of civilisation. There are small but exciting displays at the site itself, while the bulk of the collection is in the Museum of Anatolian Civilisations in Ankara.

The Bronze Age

Third millennium BC Bronze Age finds suggest that the development of sophisticated metallurgy may have been an important influence in the rise of many Central Anatolian kingdoms (such as the Hatti, predecessors of the Hittites). Hordes of gold jewellery and lavish ceremonial objects (such as the commonly seen female double-idols) have been found in graves at heavily fortified and tightly packed settlements such as Alacahöyük *(see page 288)*.

Developments along the coasts during this era also show that Anatolian metalwork was greatly prized in exchange for semi-precious stones and other luxury items from Greece and Syria.

Both the aboriginal Hatti and later Hittites (c.2000–600 BC) knew about astronomy and used the sun disc as a common artistic symbol, together with goddesses, stags, bulls and other animals. Hittite art and architecture is also renowned for its imposing size, epitomised by the fortifications at their capital city of Hattuşa, now Boğazkale *(see page 287)*. Here, gigantic rock-cut reliefs depicting warrior gods and sphinx-like creatures suggest a powerful, militaristic but also highly organised and humane state without the cruelty depicted in Assyrian reliefs. The late Hittite summer palace at Karatepe *(see page 257)* is nearly as impressive, with "real life" depictions of rulers at play in scenes of banqueting, guests surrounded by musicians with lyres and servants with fans.

Remains of the Phrygian (c.1200–600 BC) capital at Gordium *(see page 275)* and elsewhere show superb stone tombs, thrones and fortifications, rock carvings like the wooden gables of buildings with niches for movable cult images and wall surfaces of finely crafted pebble or brick mosaic.

Grave goods were generally vessels of cast bronze while their art displays a taste for strong geometric symmetry, including finds of kilims and gold embroidery as well as crisply designed painted pottery.

The Urartians, who occupied the area around Lake Van in about the 9th century BC, were impressive builders and engineers, leaving behind dense clusters of castles and fortresses, together with superbly crafted rock tombs, cisterns and irrigation channels. Their metalwork was in international demand even in antiquity; especially the large bronze sacrificial cauldrons with human or animal heads which have been noted for their similarity to the exceptional craftsmanship of the Minoans and Etruscans, with high-crowned bearded gods over curling seawave borders under geometric suns.

LEFT: bronze female figure from ancient Anatolia, a style of figurine known as a bird-goddess.
RIGHT: Hittite sculpture in Karatepe.

> **GOD OF THUNDER**
>
> The most powerful god in the Hittites' pantheon (Tashub, Tarhun or Taru) was the god of weather; his wife (Arinnitti or Wurusemu) was goddess of earth and water.

The Hellenic coast

Ancient Caria was a large region on the Aegean coast, and though its culture underwent many periods of transformation, it can still be characterised as Hellenic. Bodrum (ancient Halikarnassos) is a late Carian city, its founder Mausolos committed to Hellenisation of the region. His own pagoda-like *mausoleum* (from whence the word originates) was considered a wonder of the world when built. Sadly, there is little to see today *(see page 209)*; the tomb was pillaged in the

14th century for the construction of Bodrum Castle. However, a tomb discovered accidentally during construction work in 1989 is thought to be that of his sister, Princess Ada, who oversaw the completion of the architectural masterpiece; she came complete with a crown of gold leaves, silk peplos and ornaments intact. Credit for the evidence rests with advanced modern technology; the crowned skull was sent to Manchester University's Medical School for facial reconstruction, and the likeness that it bore to a bust of Princess Ada discovered at Priene (now in the British Museum) is quite remarkable. Her exquisite jewellery and wine goblets are now displayed in glass cabinets in the Carian Princess Hall, Bodrum Museum.

The Lycians who occupied the loop of wild, mountainous territory between Fethiye and Antalya were first documented by the Hittites more than 3,000 years ago as an ungovernable, matriarchal people with a sophisticated culture and intense love of freedom; they succeeded in fending off Roman imperialism until the eleventh hour, preferring to set fire to their cities rather than live in vassaldom.

Given the small population of ancient Lycia, it is unlikely that many "cities" had more than 5,000 people, and, as most of the buildings

were made of wood, archaeologists have only been able to identify the remains of 40. But what has lasted of Lycian life are their distinctive "gothic" sarcophagi. Many of them were highly decorated, graphically detailing the punishment that awaited vandals. In keeping with the times, the Lycians worshipped their ancestors and occasionally sought guidance from the dead through oracles.

There are four basic types of Lycian tombs, the most curious, and no doubt oldest, form being the pillar tomb, where the grave chamber is perched on top of a tapering column; the best examples are at Xanthos (*see page 225*). These may indicate that the earliest Lycians contin-

ued the tradition of their neolithic ancestors by offering mortal remains to the birds – much as the Indian Parsis still do today. Temple tombs, such as those built into the cliffs at Kaunos and Fethiye (*see page 223*) are the more sophisticated version of the intriguing "house tombs" such as those found at Myra (*see page 229*), which were lovingly rock-cut models of the plain wooden Lycian dwellings, often three storeys high.

Xanthos was unfortunately in such a good state of repair when the intrepid Sir Charles Fellows got here in 1838 that a majority of the sculptures and inscriptions were filched and now sit in the British Museum. Excavations carried out since the 1950s, however, reveal enough of the city for the imagination to build on; there is something almost Mayan about Lycian architecture – it is distinctly geometric – no Greek curlicues here. There's the foundation of a temple to the Lycian mother-goddess, and a particularly fine tomb depicting birds with women's heads, either harpies or sirens, carrying away the souls of the dead.

The Classical era

The Graeco-Roman period (1200 BC–AD 300) is considered by many to be the "flowering" of Anatolian art and architecture, especially in the city states along the Aegean and Mediterranean coasts. An indispensable read for those interested in the style and use of Greek and Roman architecture is to be found in the frequently reprinted bestseller, *Ten Books on Architecture,* by Vitruvius, a Roman architect and engineer of the 1st century BC.

The classic "pediment" or triangular roof structure is an early indicator, typical of Hellenistic, Greek and even Lycian and Lydian rock tombs. Of the three famous column designs, the simple fluted Doric column is considered the earliest; the Ionic column, typified by the scroll-shaped top, may have developed in the Carian region, while the ornate, foliated Corinthian column (which later included a composite with the Ionian style) was not much used until the Roman era.

This period saw the birth of modern town planning. The Greeks, who preferred to build

LEFT: the temple Tomb of Amyntas, in Fethiye, is one of the most elaborate of the Lycian rock tombs.
RIGHT: Roman mosaic, Antakya.

their cities on hills, originated the idea of siting the principal temples and treasuries on an "acropolis" (low hill to one side of town) while, below, the "agora" was primarily a market place but was also used for political meetings. The Romans were to rename this area the "forum" and tended to centre their civic buildings and temples nearby.

Greek "theatres" were usually built into natural cavities on hillsides. They usually had temples to Dionysus (patron god of actors) nearby; early theatrical performances were religious in nature and only performed during festivals. Jolly Dionysus himself probably originated as an Anatolian god of fertility and wine, possibly related to the Hittite god of agriculture, Telipinu. Indeed, Hellenistic culture involved a great deal of mingling with beliefs indigenous to Anatolia.

The Roman period began sometime after 190 BC, concluding in the *Pax Romana* (14 BC–AD 191). Ephesus was the original capital of the province of Asia. Roman town planning was similar to Greek design, but the Romans were far more interested in blood sports than high drama; the word "arena" actually comes from the Latin word for sand, which was strewn about to absorb blood and other effluvia from

FIRST-CLASS PLUMBING

The homes of the wealthy occupants of Ephesus are still undergoing restoration, but already offer some of the best-preserved evidence of Roman daily life on the Mediterranean. The houses had central heating and hot-water taps; the walls and floors were adorned with exquisite mosaics and frescoes. However, windows did not look out on the town; the life of the rich was considered private and family oriented. The inward-looking layout of the courtyard houses emphasised a cool dimness and conservation of water; the centre of the roof was open, slanting inwards, and rainwater collected in the *impluvium*, a kind of shallow pool which often had a well beneath.

In one of the houses, a grand, two-seater toilet perhaps tells us something about Roman philosophy, though it is open to personal interpretation. The walls are decorated with frescoes of men, perhaps in the agora, near sundials. "Wait for a Convenient Time or Die" is inscribed in Greek on one wall, on another is "Nine to Five".

Especially astonishing is how tastes have come round full circle since ancient times. Their walls were hand-painted with terracotta floral designs, while the furniture was of marble-topped wrought iron. The roof, which has been rebuilt to its original design, was made of high pine beams with skylights and completely covered with clay tiles.

whatever sport took place there. Semicircular theatres were expanded or built from scratch on flat ground; there are few circular amphitheatres in Anatolia.

The Greek and Roman religious pantheon traditionally begins with some version of Zeus/Jupiter and a host of jealous female consorts, but there is evidence that the influence of Kybele/Kübaba (such as the large female figurines of Çatalhöyük) held sway in Hellenic Anatolia, where a greater attention to goddesses led to worship

Hellenistic either, generally depicted crawling with wildlife and sprouting numerous bulbous protuberances which may represent the testes of sacrificed bulls, eggs, honeybees or breasts. There is little left of the temple, but many examples of Artemis and her predecessors stand in the local museum. The influence of the mother-goddess, in all her many incarnations, cannot be underestimated in pre-Roman Turkey.

Byzantium

In the 4th century AD, the emperor's move to Constantinople and the state conversion to Christianity conspired to help Byzantine architecture veer sharply away from its Roman origins. Buildings of this era are easily recognisable by their square-hewn stonework or double skin of brick and stone filled with rubble that could more readily be curved. Doors and windows are usually constructed as semicircular arches.

Churches have two basic designs. With a nod to the civic architecture of Rome, the early basilica is basically rectangular, twice as long as it is wide, with two rows of columns dividing it into a central nave and side aisles. By the 6th century, the construction of the dome had been perfected. This required transepts (side arms) to maintain its bulk, and thus the cruciform church emerged. In smaller churches, the central plan is of simple circular walls supporting the dome.

Most Byzantine churches were decorated with frescoes or mosaics representing biblical scenes, though most were presented in a folkloric way. Some of the finest extant paintings are found in the cave churches of Cappadocia *(see page 291)*, where they were miraculously saved from the depradations of gravity, Islam and the iconoclasts.

The embarrassing era of the Crusades (11th–16th centuries) wrought vast damage on whatever native architecture it encountered – "pagan", Jewish or Muslim. Temples were pillaged or burned for lime and pedestals stacked horizontally for hastily built warrior's walls. By the Fourth Crusade of 1204, even Byzantine Constantinople was looted – which is one of the primary reasons so little of it remains today. Southern Turkey remains dotted with numerous Crusader fortresses, such as Bodrum

of the increasingly young and slim Artemis of Ephesus, and later had an effect on Christianity in the form of the Virgin Mary.

The Temple of Artemis was built in the 6th century BC, the largest Greek-built structure in the world, not to mention the first monument constructed entirely of marble. There were 127 columns, the 36 standing in front covered with reliefs, giving the impression of a forest. It was a suitable setting for a goddess of nature whose original likeness, according to legend, fell from the sky as a meteor. Archaeologists suspect the temple's design was influenced by Egyptian, Assyrian and Hittite architectural tastes, and the Marble Lady who dwelt inside was not very

Castle, which may be primarily remembered for its restored torture chamber.

Islamic art

Seljuk architecture is noted for its delicacy, influenced by Persia, though the local Muslims did not balk at using animal or human reliefs in their stonework, and they also included Hittite and Hellenistic styles. The most characteristic feature of the Seljuk mosque is a *mihrab* (prayer niche) over the entrance, looking not unlike an elaborate jelly-mould. They are also credited with having perfected the art of geometric tilework, often formed into Arabic char-

culture is primarily noted for its stunning architecture, a unique blend of Asian, Islamic and European styles, best exemplified by the works of Mimar Sinan *(see page 145)*. Another art form perfected by the Ottomans was miniature painting and calligraphy, notably the elaborate monogram *(tuğra)* used by each sultan, which was even engraved on his silverware and is greatly prized by collectors today. Amasya was the centre of calligraphic art in the 15th century; one of its masters, Şeyh Hamdullah, was brought to the capital by Sultan Beyazıt II – his work can be seen in the Beyazıt mosques of both Istanbul and Amasya today.

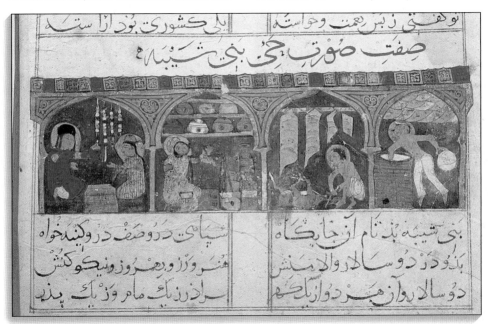

acters or Kufic script; some of the finest examples of which can be seen in Konya *(see page 284)*. The Seljuks were also thought to have introduced knotted pile rugs to Anatolia.

The Ottomans were great lovers of luxury and their early arts are distinctly oriental in style, including Chinese dragons and the classic yin-yang symbol. Turkish shadow puppets (Karagöz) are clearly related to those of Java and came to Turkey via Ottoman occupation of Egypt in the 16th century. However, Ottoman

İznik tilework reached its peak in the 16th century, and there are outstanding examples of İznik tiles in the mosques of Bursa and in Rüstem Paşa Camii in Istanbul. Subsequent attempts to reproduce the tiles' quality and colours (such as the stunning turquoise and tomato red) have failed.

The late 19th and early 20th centuries produced a flowering of Art Nouveau architecture in Istanbul, of which many fine examples still remain, especially around Beyoğlu. In recent years, the contemporary art scene has begun to blossom, too. Yet it is indisputable that the real treasures of art and architecture in Turkey date from more ancient times. ❏

LEFT: the agora of the ruined city, İzmir.
ABOVE: illustrated manuscript of a Seljuk romantic poem, from Konya, c. AD 1250.

JAZZ, JANISSARIES AND ORIENTAL HIP-HOP

*Turkish music has been influencing the world for hundreds of years,
but it is now gaining recognition on its own merits*

Turkey's indigenous music styles vary wildly, from cloyingly sentimental pop and mystical Sufi reed flutes to cutting-edge jazz and the wailing arabesque pouring from your taxi driver's cassette deck. There are

the *aşık* troubadours whose roots go back to the 15th century, but whose laments for justice and equality are at the centre of most Turkish political folk music today, and the frenetic, almost Celtic bagpipe and fiddle dance music of the Black Sea. Sufi ritual music is slow and ponderous, an ideal backdrop for the dance of the whirling dervishes, while arabesque is the Anatolian equivalent of country and western, replete with references to laments for village life left behind in the pursuit of money in the big city. King of the genre, Ibrahim Tatlises occupies a kind of Elvis Presley-like status. His output includes a vast quantity of trashy movies that play regularly on Turkish TV.

Additionally, superb Turkish "alternative" music has developed on the urban scene almost overnight as the vast volume of young people tune in to techno and DJ mixes and begin to blend their own. Jazz has been fashionable among the urban élite since the 1950s – after all, the famous Atlantic Jazz label was founded by two Turkish brothers, Ahmet and Nesuhi Ertegün. Today, their commitment to the contemporary is being upheld by an increasing number of younger, avant-garde musicians and a few newly formed native record companies which are experimenting with a synthesis of New York club sounds and Turkish *meyhane* (gypsy music) or American blues and the 500-year-old Anatolian troubadour tradition.

Drums, flutes and zithers

The best known Sufi *ney* (flute) player today is probably Süleyman Erguner, who gives frequent performances all over Turkey and also collaborates on international experimental projects. However, Sufi music of all types is being widely recorded and it is possible to hear it live at the traditional whirling dervish rituals in Istanbul through the summer and during the Mevlâna Festival in Konya in mid-December. Some of these compositions date back to the early 15th century and include instruments such as the *küdüm* (small drums), *kanun* (zither) and *rebab*, a type of violin accompanying the religious chants. However, the *ney* is the principal instrument, considered by mystic sects to be akin to God's voice. According to the position of the head and the force of breath, it is possible to play an extension of three octaves.

Aşık means "the ones in love", though Turkish troubadour songs are predominantly about spiritual or political yearning rather than romantic pursuit. Generally, the *aşık* is a solo performer accompanying himself on a *saz* (a simple long-necked wooden lute). Most of the bards belong to the Bektaşi and Alevi sects, known for their liberal egalitarianism and the music is often accompanied by the plaintive lyrics of medieval mystic poets such as Yunus Emre and Pir Sultan Abdul.

The Arab influence

Classical Ottoman court music is considered to have reached its peak of development during the 19th century. It shows influence from both the East and West in its modal systems, even borrowing from ancient Greek tradition. Among the Ottoman sovereigns there were many fine composers such as Mahmut I (1730–54) and Selim III (1789–1807). Many women of the harem played the *ud*, a complex type of lute which is Arabic in origin and considered to be the ancestor of western lutes and guitars, brought back to Europe by returning Crusaders. It has a pear-shaped body and fretless keyboard, while its neck protudes at a characteristic angle of 60 degrees. It usually has 11 or 12 strings, tuned two-by-two on C-G-D-A-E-D. More talented women were also taught the *kanun,* a favourite Arabic instrument introduced to Turkey in the 1700s. It is a flat, trapezoidal zither with as many as 100 strings and a complicated system of levers for changing to different keys, in three octaves of minor thirds.

A typical Ottoman classical band will include *tambur* (a larger version of the *saz*), *kanun, ney, ud, küdüm* and *keman* (similar to a western violin), and will often feature female divas. In some ways reminiscent of Sufi ritual music, the difference is in practice. There are regular public performances of Ottoman classical music, which is even played in certain types of restaurants or clubs. Its more contemporary, commercial counterparts, *Sanat* and *Fasıl,* are popular in nightclubs, and concentrate almost solely on the voice. The singers are frequently flamboyantly gay males or transsexuals such as the much beloved Bülent Ersoy.

The long march west

The music of the Ottoman janissary bands, or *mehter*, was developed to intimidate. To the tune of cymbals, clarinets, bagpipes and huge bass drums that produced a fearsome volume, the élite corps marched with blunderbuss and cannon into battle through the Balkans into Central Europe. But defeated at Vienna, they left behind many instruments and a taste for military music, which eventually found their way into works by Mozart, Haydn, Beethoven and even John Philip Sousa. Janissary bands had up to 60 members, and drums so enormous they had to be carted by wagon. Today performances are a tourist attraction in public parks and places such as Istanbul's Military Museum.

Western classical music was introduced into Turkey in 1826, when Sultan Mahmut II invited the Italian conductor Gaetano Donizetti to Istanbul to help form an imperial orchestra, performing French and Italian operas and the occasional

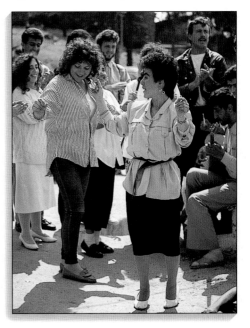

ballet. This taste for Western classical music developed further during Atatürk's reform era; a school for music instructors was opened in 1924 and the State Conservatory in Ankara in 1936. In 1946, Turkey's State Opera and Theatre were founded by refugees from Hitler's Germany such as Hindemith. Composers made a synthesis of Western classical music and Turkish folk rhythms, amongst them Ulvi Cemal Erkin (1906–72), composer of numerous works including five symphonies and the *Köçekçe,* a truly Turkish rhapsody. Another composer, Ahmet Adnan Saygun (born 1907), is famous for adapting Turkish folk music for choirs, the most popular of his compositions being the *Yunus Emre*

LEFT: a Turkish miniature of the *mehter,* or janissary marching band.
RIGHT: an entertaining afternoon in an İzmir park.

Oratorio. Though underfunded, Turkish opera and ballet have reached an international standard; even translating the *Flying Dutchman* into Turkish to make Wagner more accessible.

Rocking round Anatolia

Tastes in music of all types are broadening rapidly as young Turks travel and learn other languages, but it also relates to the growing availability of imported "alternative" music and the proliferation of live-music venues. Jazz groups such as Wax Poetic, headed by New York-based saxophonist Ilhan Ersahin, are the stars of new Istanbul recording companies such

Meanwhile, younger Turkish musicians are reaching into black American blues and jazz to find an international expression of class conflict, linking the arabesque underbelly of Anatolia to the revival of *Rai* in urban Europe. Tarkan has become the first Turkish pop star to make it internationally, thanks, in part, to his singing the 2002 Turkish World Cup anthem, in part to a cover of one of his songs by Australian soap star, Holly Valance. On the club scene, Mustafa Sandal has a growing reputation for good, honest dance music. Most recently, established local star Sertab Erener won the 2003 Eurovision song contest – the first Turkish win in 47 years.

as Doublemoon and its club Babylon, where Romany musicians Laço Tayfa and clarinetist Barbaros Erköse regularly play with visiting US jazz and blues musicians.

Percussionists have also come to the fore, with masters such as "Mısırlı" (Egyptian) Ahmet and Burhan Öçal receiving both international and local acclaim, while "Oriental Hip-Hop" artist Sultana is making waves in Turkey and New York. But we must not forget the old guard: diva Sezen Aksu, formerly a Barbara Streisand-esque performer, has been reclaiming her Anatolian roots as well as collaborating with artists such as Balkan boogie composer Goran Bregovic, and former leftist protest singer Zulfu Livaneli.

Don't be content with tourist-trail belly-dance music; watch for posters directing you to urban jazz clubs or punk dives, and check for the music festivals which take place in almost all Turkish towns today. An opera in the Byzantine church, Aya Irini, in Istanbul is never forgotten, nor is an *aşık* performance in an Anatolian teahouse.

It is worth noting that Turkish-produced CDs are considerably cheaper than imports, and that both can be bought for next to nothing from street sellers specialising in "burned" copies. No one seems to mind.   ❑

ABOVE: *saz* player sings folk songs, surrounded by young girls; Turkey has a strong troubadour tradition.

Festival Fever

I t is a well-known fact among the most progressive minds in Turkey that in terms of promoting a country, the arts move faster than an army of politicians or any expensive tourism campaigns. Turkey has had image problems abroad, some justified and some not, but it is currently in the midst of an arts explosion as international film, theatre, jazz, classical music and visual arts festivities become a speciality of even small villages.

Those events run by the Istanbul Foundation for Culture and the Arts (a non-governmental organisation largely sponsored by private donations) are the best known internationally. Beginning in the spring, the Istanbul International Film Festival brings famous directors from all over the world to meet their Turkish counterparts in panel discussions and competitions, followed by an international theatre festival, and a banquet of classical music and jazz in line with any major European city.

The Istanbul Arts Biennial (held in odd years) is famous for making use of the city's stupendous historical buildings such as the Byzantine church of Aya Irini, and the Yerebatan Sarayı. A vast cultural complex run by the Foundation is currently under construction and is expected to open officially in the next couple of years. Visitors are frequently surprised by the low prices charged for world-class events and are beginning to flock to Istanbul for its festivals; they book out quickly (contact the website: www.istfest.org).

Contemporary music lovers in urban areas should also watch out for Fuji World Music weekends (usually in winter), the International Blues Festival in October, and the marathon rave and techno dance festivals which are taking off with the swell in Turkey's youth population. Even Bursa's traditional month-long festival in June and July has moved to become a world music and dance event (a far cry from its origin as a ploughing competition!). Throughout the summer months stay on the alert for contemporary or classical music concerts taking place in ancient amphitheatres, such as those during the Ephesus and Bergama festivals in May and the Aspendos Opera and Ballet Festival in June. The Eskişehir Arts Festival (mid-October) is highly recommended for the variety of its acts.

RIGHT: Mehter band struts its stuff outside the Military Museum in Istanbul.

The Golden Orange International Film Festival in Antalya each October is bringing in more and more big names to help launch Turkish films on the international circuit.

Flower lovers may appreciate the Istanbul Tulip Festival in Emirgan (last two weeks of April), and the Bursa International Tulip Festival (first week of May). Traditional oil-wrestling competitions take place in Edirne in the second week of June, and again in July *(see page 149)*, and the Kafkasör Bullfights in Artvin (last week of June). Alanya is famous for its sports marathons, from running to rafting (May). Camel wrestling takes place from December to January in Denizli, Aydin and Selçuk.

Islam has several major festivals, all moving with the calendar. Those with a more specific interest in Turkish folk culture should pencil in the Aşık (Troubadour) Festival in Konya in October, followed by the Mevlana Whirling Dervish Celebrations from 10–17 December (Konya and Istanbul).

The month-long fast of Ramazan ends with the three-day Seker Bayram (Sugar Holiday), when everyone is offered sweets. Kurban Bayram (the Feast of the Sacrifice) is a four-day celebration of the sacrifice of Isaac. It involves the ritual throat-slitting of sheep and cows, often in public, so is not appreciated by vegetarians or animal rights enthusiasts. ❑

● *For more information on festivals and public holidays, see Travel Tips at the end of the book.*

HEIRLOOMS OF THE FUTURE

Turkish carpets are among the most beautiful, intricate and
luxurious in the world – but buyers need to be discriminating

An unforgettable part of any Turkish holiday is being pulled off the street by a multilingual carpet dealer and having scores of carpets unrolled before you as you sip Turkish coffee or apple tea from a tulip-shaped glass and listen to the merchant regale you with the origin, meaning and age of each piece.

The Turks claim to have created the knotted pile carpet, which is thought to have been brought here from Central Asia by the Seljuks. But the Turks who settled in Anatolia discovered there was already a thriving indigenous tradition of flat-weave *kilims* whose ancestry stretches back to neolithic times.

Buyer beware

There are basically two types of carpet dealers. Youngsters (often from the east) invest their savings in carpets, rent space in the most popular resort areas then pester the life out of anyone passing, even planting gigolos outside to make passes at glamorous grannies. Although these "commission" boys can sometimes give you the bargain of your life, it is best to steer well clear. Carpet shops run by their owner are usually staffed by older, less pushy men who know a great deal about their stock.

However, all share one common trait: their job is to sell carpets at the highest possible price and most will tell a potential customer anything they want to hear. The goods are generally code-marked to indicate just how far down it is possible to bargain without a loss.

Skirting the minefield

In the past, every village had its own traditions, techniques and patterns that made finished carpets as distinctive as fingerprints. These days, carpet merchants show the villagers pictures of the more popular styles and many of Turkey's carpets use mass-produced designs and colour schemes tailored to foreign tastes. The end product has little bearing on local tradition. This, together with the increased mobility of the population, means that nobody can disentangle the various influences at play and many regional styles are in danger of being lost. Some merchants actually beat or intentionally fade their goods to fake "antiquity". Finding a genuinely unique carpet can be hard work.

Quality control and commitment to heritage is one of the reasons carpet cooperatives such as the DOBAG Project in western Turkey have been set up, to reteach women to use traditional designs and vegetable dyes.

The quest for authenticity also explains the boom in interest in the vivid *kilims* and *sofras* (mats for the family meal, eaten on the floor) produced in the eastern provinces of Hakkâri and Van. These were little valued until about 20 years ago, so escaped the direct influences of the marketplace. Today, they are prized for their vigour and bold but simple abstract design; prices have risen steeply as a result.

Choosing a prize

The quality of a carpet or *kilim* is generally determined by the density of its weave – if you compare the backs of most carpets, it is quite easy to see which are the better made by the clarity of the design. The best-quality pure wool knotted pile carpets are the most expensive – *kilims* are much cheaper. *Cicims* have embroidered designs stitched into them while *sumaks*, *kilims* from Turkistan and the Iraqi borders, have an overlay of figurative stitching. It is also possible to get a wool-and-silk mix which is tough enough to use on the floor. Pure silk carpets cost nearly three times as much and are generally small, delicately coloured, and intricately woven, the very finest containing a staggering 900 knots per square centimetre.

pinks and oranges, which often clash dreadfully to the foreign eye.

It's fairly easy to spot chemical dyes – they don't look natural. If in doubt, dab a little water on a tissue, press it on the carpet and see if any colour comes off. Those pastel shades developed for Western tastes are usually chemically dyed and then chlorine bleached, which will seriously reduce the carpet's longevity.

In the end, though, anyone will tell you that the best way to choose a carpet is personal taste, so resist the pressure and shop around before you buy. Reputable shops will give you a certificate of authenticity.

The quality of the colour is as important as the weave. *Kilims* and carpets using only traditional vegetable dyes are the most prized by collectors today – they have a luminous and subtle quality which the harsh monotony of chemical colours cannot match, and which are much kinder on the wool, making the carpet last longer.

The limited range of very bright colours from natural dyes also serve to curb the Turkish villager's appetite for garish colours such as hot

Getting it home

Many shops offer to post your carpet home for you – but be careful. There have been tales of travellers finding that what they receive is not what they paid for, and it will almost certainly mean paying more import duty as you cannot use your traveller's allowance. It is also surprising how much you can knock off the price by refusing the "free" postage.

You are unlikely to encounter genuine antique carpets in any standard bazaar, but remember that Turkey has very strict laws on the export of antiquities. Any carpet or *kilim* over 100 years old must be cleared by a museum as exportable, in writing. ❑

LEFT: weavers from Hakkâri, southeastern Turkey.
ABOVE: among the myriad shapes and colours, only one is just right.

PATTERNS OF LIFE: CARPETS AND *KILIMS*

Marco Polo, crossing Anatolia in the 13th century, commented on the beauty of Turkey's carpets. Many of today's offerings are equally magnificent

The earliest known Turkish pile carpets (on display in Istanbul and Konya) are the crude but powerful 13th-century Seljuk carpets discovered in Konya and Beyşehir in the early 20th century; flat-weave *kilims* have probably been in production locally since the 6th millennium BC. Until the 1900s, most households had looms to produce carpets, sacks, cushion covers, baby's cradles and other household furnishings. The result is an astonishing range of styles, techniques and designs, which include: the Caucasian-style thick, shaggy piles of the Çanakkale area; the sumptuous carnation motifs of Milas; the hard-edged geometric patterns of Cappadocia; the stylised figurines of Turkoman rugs near the Persian border; and the wild floral and arabesque designs of Ottoman court carpets, woven at workshops in Istanbul and Bursa. The heirs to this tradition today are the finely woven silk-and-wool carpets of Hereke, home to the 19th-century imperial workshops.

Thread for the domestic looms was handspun from wool, goat hair, cotton or linen; silk was manufactured in the imperial factories in Bursa. Each district had its own specialist dyer.

The colours were traditionally obtained from indigenous plants. Madder root produces shades from brick red to orange, pinks and purple. It was a lucrative export crop as one of the only reliable red dyes until the 1860s. Other important dyes were indigo for blue, saffron for yellow and walnut (also exported) for black and brown.

◁ **FIT FOR A SULTAN**
A workshop was established in Hereke in 1844 to weave silk carpets for the Ottoman court, but carpets from here have been famous since the 16th century.

▷ **WOMEN'S WORK**
Weaving is a traditional winter occupation of rural Turkish women; Göreme in Cappadocia has a training and production centre, open to visitors.

◁ **FADING GLORY**
Colours are mellowed in the sun (or to make the carpets look antique); the Milas area is known for its prayer rugs.

▽ **EARTH TONES**
Carpets of the Muğla region are often of muted earth colours, as seen in this 19th-century rug from Fethiye.

◁ **GEOMETRY IN MOTION**
Bold geometric designs have been an intrinsic part of Turkish art since neolithic times; today, they are frequently framed by a border.

LOUDER THAN WORDS

Turkish carpet and *kilim* motifs *(nakıh)* are traditionally handed down from mother to daughter. In accordance with Islamic tradition, animal and human motifs are highly stylised.

Among Turkish nomads, the *elibelinde* or arms-akimbo motif represents good luck, while flocks of birds may stand for home-sickness. The tree of life is a classical spiritual symbol, though the beech tree is thought to relate specifically to Central Asian shamanist beliefs. An eight-pointed star can represent fate, or the Wheel of Life.

Prayer rugs *(namazlık)* frequently show a *mihrab* (prayer niche), to be pointed towards Mecca; a mosque lamp hanging from the arch denotes divine light. Funereal carpets, for graveside worship, may contain images of cypress trees, headstones, and blue skies above the *mihrab*, representing paradise.

The pattern of two triangles, tips touching, often represents a girl, and may be used in a "dowry" *kilim* for luck and light work after marriage. Single triangles may be talismans worn by nomads.

PLACES

*A detailed guide to the entire country, with principal sites
cross-referenced by number to the maps*

This book is nothing but ambitious. Having squeezed Turkey's entire, extraordinary 8,000-year history and modern culture into some 100 pages, the next task is to take the reader on a whistlestop tour of Anatolia, with its mountains and deserts, great plains, fabulous cities and hidden villages.

The country is simply too huge and too complex to treat every sight with the lavish attention it deserves, so the decision was taken reluctantly to concentrate on the more popular and accessible areas. Some parts of Turkey are so remote that it is difficult to reach them without mounting an expedition; others, still recovering from over a decade of political and military upheaval, had not yet had sufficient time to develop a tourism-based infrastructure before being thrown back into potential disarray by the war in neighbouring Iraq.

The Places section has been divided into seven regions, each with a short introduction and detailed map. These are then subdivided into manageable geographic bites. Firstly comes magnificent, stately **Istanbul**, where the old and new cities face each other across the Golden Horn. A separate short chapter describes the banks of the Bosphorus. Wrapped around the city and the Sea of Marmara are the small but fascinating provinces of **Thrace** (European Turkey) and **Marmara**, each in its time the capital of the Ottoman Empire.

Turkey has more than its fair share of warm, turquoise-blue coast, with limpid sands and shady pines. The ancient Greeks knew they were on to a good thing, and so do the millions of tourists who flock here each summer. The **Aegean Coast** (Turkey's west coast) is divided into four areas – the north; the city of İzmir and its surroundings; the south coast, around Ephesus; and the tourist havens of Bodrum and Marmaris. From here, the **Mediterranean Coast** runs east for over 1500 km (1000 miles), through the ancient kingdoms of Lycia (west), Pamphylia (centre, around the major tourist towns of Antalya and Alanya), and Cilicia, before turning south into the Hatay, which has spent much of its history as part of Syria.

Great swathes of **Central Anatolia** focus on Atatürk's modern city of Ankara, around which chapters lead northwest, southwest, east and to the legendary underground cities of Cappadocia. To the north is the **Black Sea Coast**. Geographically, **Eastern Turkey** covers nearly half the land of the country, but much of it is a harsh, sparsely populated and desperately poor land, whose spectacular beauty remains hidden to all but the most adventurous traveller. ❏

PRECEDING PAGES: the unmistakable remains of Nemrut Dağı in eastern Anatolia; the eerie landscape of Cappadocia; the seductive rooftops of waterside Istanbul. **LEFT:** skimming over the barren landscape of Turkey's Far Eastern region.

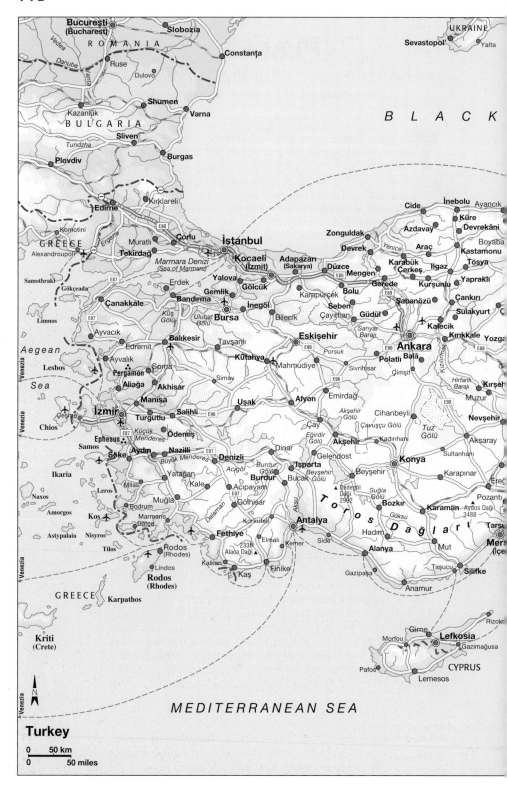

Turkey

0   50 km

0   50 miles

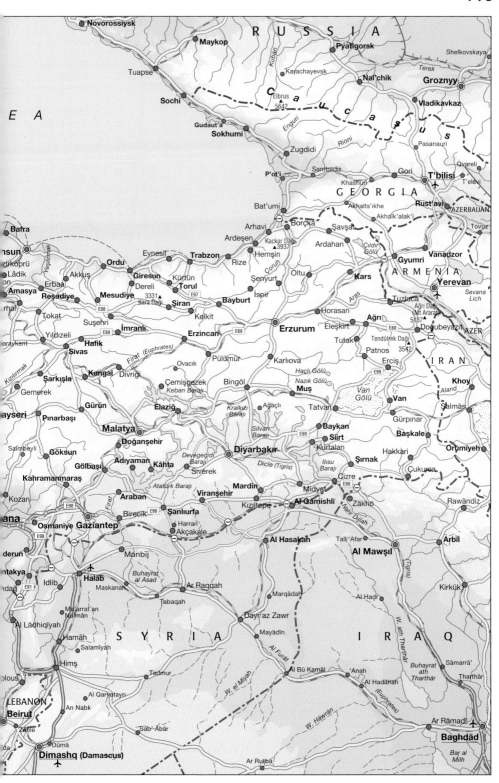

ISTANBUL

Capital of one of the world's greatest empires for over 1,500 years, Istanbul today is a buzzing, cosmopolitan modern city

Over the marble paths, pillars and pomp of the Byzantine and Ottoman empires, a vast jazz metropolis of youth, choking traffic, political contradictions and thriving ideas has emerged. There are times – when standing on a street corner in the inner city, overcome by traffic fumes, with shouting peddlars and the odd riot squad competing with rock bars and swinging young things with pockets full of gold – that the visitor to Istanbul wonders just where the mysterious East has gone.

Your average guidebook is still full of the stupendous ancient sites that can be stumbled upon even in the midst of an urban centre (though chances are they have gone black with pollution and are overshadowed by tower blocks), but those seeking ancient monuments alone may be missing something significant in a city with a massive youth population (65 percent of Istanbul's official population of 12 million is under 25), and where spanking new cultural treasures constantly join the ranks of the venerable past.

Modern Istanbul takes some adjustment, especially if you expect slow-moving waterpipe smokers and odalisques languishing on lush carpets in misty bazaars and bathhouses. For the needs of the present are in stiff competition with history, and you may be surprised at how little regard the average citizen shows for a 300-year-old marble fountain or gravestone plonked along a highway or in the middle of a residential neighbourhood.

The call to prayer still exhorts the true believers to mend their ways and arise at dawn for Allah, and new mosques are constantly being built. But with the exception of firmly religious neighbour-hoods such as Fatih or Üsküdar, these powerful symbols of Islam are all but empty, except on Friday evenings and holidays – everyone's too busy with the money markets. Byzantine and other Christian monuments may also appear largely hidden from view, eclipsed by Ottoman history and rarely well signposted. You must go searching for the oldest churches and architectural remains, and will often find them in the most unlikely of neighbourhoods, where scant regard is paid to their maintenance.

But this dismissal of the past is not due to Islamic or republican sentiment – no one wants to snap off a continuity of civilisation that has existed for 2,000 years. Neither is it the desire to appear more "modern" in the Western sense, replacing the icons of empires with fashion houses and modern apartments. It is simply that Istanbul is running out of room, and its inhabitants are understandably exhausted by the weight of history created by all those empires, emperors and sultans, simply taking them for granted. Those in mega-cities cannot afford to be romantic all the time – they must also be practical. ❏

LEFT: view over the Golden Horn from the Süleimaniye Mosque.

ISTANBUL: OLD CITY

*Istanbul's diminutive but magnificent heart still beats
to the glories of ancient Byzantium, Constantinople
and the Ottoman Empire*

Map
on page
118

According to legend, Istanbul was first established by the Megaran leader, Byzas, in the 7th century BC. After consulting the oracle of Delphi, he was instructed to settle across from the "land of the blind ones". Encountering a community living at Chalcedon on the Asian shore, Byzas concluded that the earlier colonists had, indeed, been deprived of their sight when they overlooked the superb location across the mouth of the Bosphorus in Europe, and the colony of Byzantium was born on top of what is now Seraglio Point.

Remarkably, Byzas was the only one for centuries to see the strategic value of the Bosphorus and, with the exception of the occasional raid by marauding tribes and Persians on the move against ancient Greece, the settlement was left in peace until captured by Septimus Severus in AD 196, when Byzantium was absorbed into the Roman Empire.

Even for Constantine the Great, in search of the ideal position for New Rome, Byzantium was second choice. Constantine initially chose the alleged tomb of Ajax on the field of ancient Troy on the Dardanelles for his new city, and had even started reconstruction of the city walls before he reconsidered and marched on Byzantium to oust its residents, turning their rustic community into the biggest construction site the world had seen.

Officially founded on 26 November, 326, and dedicated to the gods in 330, Constantine filled his new city with the treasures of the ancient world, creating a startling mixture of classical paganism and the more recent Christianity. Never in the West had a city of such magnitude existed, and contemporaries wrote of the city in one hushed and amazed voice upon their admittance through the walls.

Constantinople – the name itself conjured up images of wealth beyond the dreams of the petty kings and princes of medieval Europe, whose capital cities ranked as villages in comparison. The city recorded a startling population of nearly 1 million in the 9th century. Its main streets were not only paved, but covered, and decorated with columns and fountains. The products of state monopolies and the exotic goods traded here made it, in the words of one writer, the "biggest luxury shopping centre in the world."

Precious little remains of the original city today, save the broken remnants of the great walls and the occasional sacred structure, such as Aya Sofya. One theory has it that the closest replica of old Constantinople might be found in the period architecture of Venice, which, emerging as a city of refugees from the Italian mainland, first became Byzantium's lesser partner in trade, then its emulator in sacred and secular architecture, and finally its enemy, allied with the Crusaders to sack the city in

LEFT: a specialist art: making tops for minarets.
BELOW: tea-seller at the Grand Bazaar.

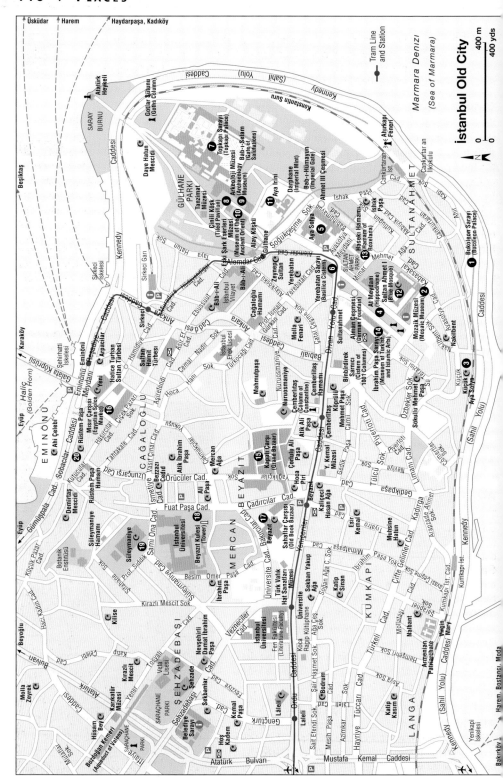

↑ Üsküdar   ↑ Harem   ↑ Haydarpaşa, Kadıköy

Tram Line and Station

Marmara Denizi
(Sea of Marmara)

İstanbul Old City

0   400 m
0   400 yds

N

Kennedy (Sahil Yolu) Caddesi

Atatürk Heykeli
SARAY BURNU
Gotlar Şütunu (Goths Column)
Daye Hatun Mescidi
GÜLHANE PARKI
Topkapı Sarayı (Topkapı Palace)
Bab-ı Selâm (Gate of Salutations)
Arkeoloji Müzesi (Archaeology Museum)
Tanzimat Müzesi
Çinili Köşk (Tiled Pavilion)
Şark Eserleri Müzesi (Museum of the Ancient Orient)
Alay Köşkü
Aya İrini
Darphane (Imperial Mint)
Bab-ı Hümayun (Imperial Gate)
Ahmet III Çeşmesi
Gülhane
İshak Paşa
İshak Paşa
Ahırkapı Feneri
Çankurtaran İst.
İlkokulu
SULTANAHMET
Aya Sofia
Soğukçeşme Sok.
Haseki Hamamı
Hamam-ı Rosetana
Bukoleon Sarayı (Bucoleon Palace)
Nakilbent
Cankurtaran Cad.
Kabasakal Caddesi
Aya Sofia
Mozaik Müzesi (Mosaic Museum)
Sultan Ahmet (Blue Mosque)
At Meydanı (Hippodrome)
Alman Çeşmesi (German Fountain)
SULTAN AHMET PARKI
Atmeydanı
Ibrahim Paşa Sarayı (Museum of Turkish and Islamic Arts)
Binbirdirek Sarnıcı (Cistern of 1001 Columns)
Yerebatan Sarayı (Basilica Cistern)
Zeynep-i Sultan
Bab-ı Ali
İstanbul Vilayet
Çağaloğlu Hamamı
Cağaloğlu
Divan Yolu Cad.
Sultanahmet
Molla Fenari
Nuruosmaniye
Çemberlitaş Column of Constantine
Çemberlitaş Hamamı
Mehmet Paşa
Köprülü Cad.
Piyerloti Cad.
Gedikpaşa
Mosaik
Sirkeci Garı
Sirkeci
Ankara Caddesi
Babıali
Prof. İsmail Gürkan Cad.
Bab-ı Ali
Ankara Cad.
Emniyet Cad.
Hamidiye Cad.
Arpacılar
Yeni
Hatice Turhan Sultan Türbesi
Sultan Hamit Türbesi
Mahmutpaşa
Hoca Han Sok.
Cemal Nadir Sok.
İstanbul Erkek Lisesi
Asir Efendi
Türkocağı Cad.
Atik Ali Paşa
Corlulu Ali Paşa
Y. Kemal Müzesi
Gedik Cad.
Rüstem Paşa
Eminönü Meydanı
Eminönü
Mısır Çarşısı (Egyptian Spice Market)
Çiçek Pazarı Sok.
Hasırcılar Cad.
Uzunçarşı Cad.
Vasıf Çınar Cad.
Hoca
Hani
Yoksu
Yağlıkçılar
Kapalı Çarşı (Grand Bazaar)
Mercan Aga
Hoca Piri
Sokullu Mehmet Paşa
Küçük Aya Sofia
Özbekler Sok.
Tülcü Sok.
Limanı Cad.
Küçük Aya Sofia Cad.
Karaköy
Galata Köprüsü (Galata Bridge)
Ahi Çelebi
Şehirhattı İskelesi
Sirkeci İskelesi
Sehirhattı İskelesi
Sebaclar Caddesi
Kutuoglu Cad.
Demirtaş Mescidi
Rüstem Paşa Hamam
İsmetiye Cad.
Bezzaı Cedid
Atik İbrahim Paşa
Orucüler Cad.
Kaliceci Hasan Ağa
Esir Kemal
Muhsine Hatun
Tiyatro Sok.
Kadırga Liman Cad.
İbrahim Paşa Çeşme Cad.
Çifte Gelinler Cad.
KUMKAPI
Arapade Ahmet Sok.
Mihalpaşa
Mollataşı
Nabant
Kumkapı İst.
Kumkapı Cad.
LANGA
EMİNÖNÜ
Eyüp - Haliç (Golden Horn)
Beyoğlu
Eyüp
Botanik Enstitüsü
Küçük Pazar Cad.
Süleymaniye Hamamı
Süleymaniye
Sami Ona Cad.
İstanbul Üniversitesi
CAĞALOĞLU
Beyazıt Kulesi (Tower)
Fuat Paşa Cad.
BEYAZIT
Çadırcılar Cad.
Sahaflar Çarşısı (Old Book Bazaar)
Beyazıt
Yemberler Cad.
Üniversite
Sıcak Yakup Ağa
Soğan Ağa C. Sok.
Katip Sinan
İbrahim Paşa Çeşme Cad.
Türkeli Cad.
Hemşeri Sok.
Asya Sok.
Molla Zeyrek
Karkatlür Müzesi
Kiliise
Kırazlı Mescit Sok.
Süleymaniye Cad.
Botanik Prof. Sıddık
Sühhane Sok.
Besim Ömer Paşa Cad.
Türk Vakfı Hat Sanatları Müzesi
MERCAN
Prof. Siddık Cad.
İbrahim Paşa
Üniversite Cad.
Vezneciler Cad.
İstanbul Üniversitesi
Fen Fakültesi (Literature Faculty)
Koca Ragıp Kütüphane Sok.
Şair Hasmet Sok.
Mesih Paşa Cad.
Azimkar Sok.
Hayriye Tüccari Cad.
Katip Kasım
Katip Kasım Cad.
Armenian Patriarchate
Ermeni Mary Cad.
Yenikapı İskelesi
Bakırköy
Harem, Bostancı, Moda
MERCAN
Hisam Bey
Atatürk Bulvarı
Molla Çelebi
Kırazlı Mescit
Kırazlı Mescit
Toygar Yatağan Sok.
Vefa Lisesi
Nevşehirli Damat İbrahim Paşa
Şehzade Cad.
ŞEHZADEBAŞI
Şehzadebaşı Cad.
SARAÇHANE PARKI
Bozdoğan Kemeri (Aqueduct of Valens)
Hüsam Bey
Hacı Kadın Cad.
İtfaiye Sok.
Şehbaşı
Şebnem
Kemal Paşa
Hoş Kadem
Laleli Cad.
Laleli
Gençtürk Cad.
Ordu Caddesi
Laleli
Bodrum Sok.
Mustafa Kemal Caddesi
Belediye Sarayı
Tevziye Cad.
Atatürk Bulvarı
Şair Efendi Sok.
Konstantin Suru

Locator markers: 1 Gotlar Şütunu (Goths Column), 7 Topkapı Sarayı, 8 Çinili Köşk, 9 Şark Eserleri Müzesi, 10 Arkeoloji Müzesi, 11 Aya İrini, 5 Aya Sofia, 6 Yerebatan Sarayı, 4 At Meydanı, 14 Alman Çeşmesi, 12 Sultan Ahmet, 2 Mozaik Müzesi, 3 Küçük Aya Sofia, 1 Bukoleon Sarayı, 13 Haseki Hamamı, 15 Çemberlitaş, 16 Kapalı Çarşı, 17 Beyazıt, 1 Yeni, 16 Mısır Çarşısı, 20 Rüstem Paşa, 1 Süleymaniye, 1 Şehzade, 1 Laleli, 1 Belediye Sarayı

1203. The four golden horses atop the portal of St Mark's in Venice, removed from the great Hippodrome in today's Sultan Ahmet Square, were but a part of that city's war booty from Constantinople. Recent improvements in signposting around the Sultanahmet area have made Byzantine Istanbul easier to locate.

Map on page 118

Constantine's city

With the exception of the stunning Aya Sofya, which dominates the Sultanahmet skyline, Constantine's city has largely to be sought out with a magnifying glass, so it is well to do some research before you arrive. Most of what remains is around the area of the Hippodrome – notably the last wall of the **Bukoleon Sarayı** ❶, the Imperial Palace of Bucoleon which towered over the private harbour of the Byzantine emperors on the Sea of Marmara.

It was here that the fabled golden tree with mechanical singing birds once stood. When sacked by Crusaders in 1204 the palace was described as containing 500 interconnected halls and 30 chapels decorated with gold mosaic. First built by Constantine, and the very essence of lost Byzantium, little is left today but a single façade connected to the old sea walls, with three enormous marble-framed windows and the corbels of a vast balcony that must have commanded a view of all strategic naval concerns. Gazing over the ruins 200 years later, Mehmet the Conqueror is alleged to have quoted the Persian poet Saadi:

The spider holds the curtain in the Palace of the Caesars
The owl hoots its night call in the towers of Aphrasiab.

Constantine's original palace is thought to have stretched north to encompass the area around Aya Sofya and the Sultan Ahmet (Blue) Mosque, and to have extended right up to the Yerebatan Sarayı, where early Byzantine tiles were discovered in a stairwell near the museum. The only part of the ongoing excavations currently open is the **Mozaik Müzesi (Mosaic Museum)** ❷ (open 9.30am–5pm; closed Tues; entrance fee), in an alley of the Arasta Bazaar behind the Sultan Ahmet Mosque, which displays one patch of the magnificent mosaic floor contributed by Justinian in the 6th century.

Byzantine churches

There are numerous small, dank and atmospheric early Christian churches which are worth seeking out in the rather dilapidated neighbourhoods off the standard tourist trail. These include the **Küçük Aya Sofya Camii** ❸ (previously SS Sergius and Bacchus), dating from 827, and the **Molla Zeyrek Camii** (formerly St Saviour Pantocrator), built in around 1120.

However, **Aya Irini** (the Church of St Eirene), located inside the first gate of the Topkapı Palace complex, is the oldest Byzantine church in the city. The original structure, dedicated in 360, was the cathedral of Constantinople until Aya Sofya was built. Never converted to a mosque, the breathtaking church was used as an armoury and is now only open when used as a venue for concerts and visual-arts events. Also under-promoted is the magnificent **Kariye Müzsei (Chora Monastery)** on the Golden Horn *(see page 129)*, home to some of the finest Byzantine mosaics in the world.

TIP

All Istanbul museums charge an entrance fee. However, the cost of visiting Aya Sofya and Topkapı Palace is significantly higher, with additional fees for the highlights, as both are in need of funds for restoration.

BELOW: the ruins of the Byzantine Tekfur Sarayı, overlooking the Golden Horn.

The Obelisk of Pharaoh Thutmose.

The Hippodrome

The **At Meydanı ❹** (Hippodrome) itself was initially built by the Roman Emperor Septimus Severus, but it was Constantine who established the arena – with a crowd capacity of over 100,000 people – as the public centre of his city. It was here that Justinian's partner, Theodora, first appeared on the stage of history (so the historian Edward Gibbon informs us) as a dancing girl in a circus troop. The Hippodrome was also the site of the notorious Nika or "victory" riots between the rival Green (lower-class monotheists) and Blue (Orthodox bourgeoisie) religious factions. Some 30,000 died in five days of urban warfare; St Sophia was destroyed for the second time; and Justinian was nearly driven from his throne.

There are three monuments left in the Hippodrome worth noting. The **Dikilitaş (Obelisk of Pharaoh Thutmose)** was brought by Constantine from Karnak in Egypt, during his general plunder of the portable monuments of the ancient world. The **Yılanlı Sütun (Serpentine Column)**, which is formed by three intertwined snakes, stood originally in the Temple of Apollo at Delphi. Perhaps the most curious of the three monuments, it represents Constantine's eclectic (and not necessarily Christian) decorative tastes. The **Ormetaş** or **Column of Constantine VII Porphyrogenitus**, was restored in the early 10th century but is thought to be many centuries older. The original bronze plates covering the column were carried off to Venice after the Crusaders sacked the city in 1204.

Aya Sofya (St Sophia)

BELOW: Byzantine mosaic of Christ in Aya Sofya.

Aya Sofya ❺ (open Tues–Sun 9.30am–4.30pm; June–Oct 9am–7pm; separate entrance fees for the main building and the gallery) – or Haghia Sophia, the Church of Holy Wisdom – is not only the main Byzantine building still standing in Istanbul, unquestionably the most spectacular sight in the city and one of the finest architectural creations in the world, but it is probably also one of the most important. Almost since it was built, this imposing edifice has been a source of political controversy and remains so today. Now and again it comes under dispute between those who would prefer to see it become a mosque, as it was in Ottoman times, and those who are happy that it remains a museum and relic of Byzantium. Meanwhile, government bureaucracy, its pre-Islamic origin, and lack of funding have led to shocking neglect and it is in urgent need of repair.

Dedicated in 536 during the reign of Justinian, the church, actually the third on the site, was the architectural wonder of its time. The first church, built by Constantine's son, Constantinus, burned to the ground in 404, while the second, built by Theodosius in 415, was torched during the Nika riots of 532.

The present structure, whose dome has inspired architectural design for 1,500 years, was basically the creation of Anthenius of Tralles and Isidorus of Miletus, who laboured for nearly six years before the church could be consecrated on 26 December, 537. It was reconsecrated in 563 after repairs following an earthquake that ruined the symmetry of the dome. It now stands 56 metres (183 ft) high and measures

32 metres (105 ft) from east to west and 32 metres (105 ft) from north to south. Thin marble panels absorbed and reflected the light of thousands of candles and lamps, which illuminated the entire building so well that it was used as a lighthouse – though it is dim and mysterious today. The myriad candles possibly accounted for the first great fire that destroyed the original edifice, as well as much of the city.

Tradition maintains that the area around the emperor's throne was the official centre of the world. Also on the main floor is the "sweating column", where Justinian was said to have cured a migraine by resting his head against the stone, leading to the belief that when rubbed, each of the pillars in the church could cure a specific disease. Centuries of visitors touching the spot has resulted in a deep dent, now framed in brass and called the "holy hole".

When Justinian built Aya Sofya, he filled it with decorative mosaics. Later emperors added figurative ones, destroyed by the iconoclasts between 729 and 843. The mosaics in the church today all postdate that period, and were preserved after the Muslim conquest of the city (when it became a mosque), thanks to a simple coat of whitewash. The mosaics were rediscovered during renovations in the 1930s when Atatürk converted Aya Sofya into a national museum.

Most of the mosaics on the main floor are dingy and ill-lit, and you need a pair of strong binoculars to see them clearly. More accessible are those on the eastern wall of the south gallery, showing Christ, John the Baptist and the Virgin Mary. In the last bay of the same gallery is an unmissable mosaic of the Empress Zoë and her husband, Constantine IX Monomachus. The latter's head was superimposed over that of Zoë's first husband, Romanus, the stable boy who seduced the 50-year-old spinster before trying to shuttle her off to a nunnery. He

Map on page 118

BELOW: elegantly piled domes make Aya Sofya one of the world's greatest landmarks.

Detail of one of the Medusa's heads in the Yerebatan Sarayı.

BELOW: the Yerebatan Sarayı was little more than a ridiculously extravagant water tank.

failed and his face – and his life – were removed from all association with the throne forever. The mosaic depicting Constantine and Justinian giving the city of Istanbul and Aya Sofya to the Virgin and Child is situated over the exit door.

The Yerebatan Sarayı

Diagonally across from Aya Sophia, near the top of the Divan Yolu (the Imperial Way), is the **Yerebatan Sarayı** ❻ (open daily 9am–5pm; entrance fee) popularly known as the Sunken Palace or **Basilica Cistern**. This was restored in 1987 after the removal of several hundred years' worth of mud and rubbish. Begun by Constantine but expanded by Justinian in 532 for storing the imperial water supply, it may originally have been accessible from the Imperial Palace complex, but fell into disuse during Ottoman times.

Today, it provides a bizarre attraction, in the form of an eerily lit underground chamber, its cathedral-like ceiling supported by 336 columns. It still contains a few feet of water, over which bridges have been built to give visitors the full effect. So inspiring is the site that it has been used as a film set and for audiovisual installations during the Istanbul Arts Biennial. The early Medusa heads, one on its side, were probably poached from pre-Christian ruins.

A few blocks away, on Klodfarer Cad., the **Binbirdirek Sarnıcı (Cistern of 1001 Columns)** (open 8am–midnight; entrance fee refundable if you eat here) is a second, even older Byzantine cistern, dating back to Constantine's original 4th-century city. Recently restored and opened to the public, this is another extraordinary building, with 264 columns. It was said to hold enough water to support 360,000 for 10 days. Today, it is home to an excellent restaurant, café, hubble-bubble bar, various craft stalls and concerts.

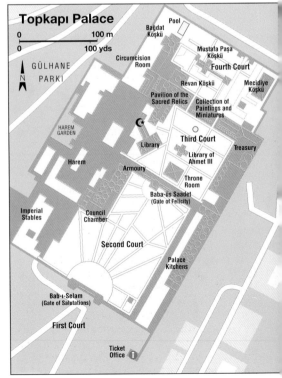

Topkapı Palace

| 0 | 100 m |
| 0 | 100 yds |

N

GÜLHANE PARKI

Pool
Bağdat Köşkü
Circumcision Room
Mustafa Paşa Köşkü
Fourth Court
Revan Köşkü
Mecidiye Köşkü
Pavilion of the Sacred Relics
Collection of Paintings and Miniatures
HAREM GARDEN
Library
Third Court
Harem
Library of Ahmet III
Treasury
Armoury
Throne Room
Baba-üs Saadet (Gate of Felicity)
Imperial Stables
Council Chamber
Second Court
Palace Kitchens
Bab-ı-Selam (Gate of Salutations)
First Court
Ticket Office ℹ

Topkapı Palace

Located behind Aya Sofya is the **Topkapı Sarayı** (**Topkapı Palace**) (open 9.30am–5pm; June–Oct, 9am–7pm; closed Tues; separate entrance fees for the main palace, treasury and harem). The complex is considerably smaller than the original (it used to extend down to the Sea of Marmara, including today's Sirkeci railway station and Gülhane Park), but the grounds are still enormous. You need a full day to appreciate it properly – and to give yourself time to visit the excellent gift shop.

The Topkapı was the nerve centre of the far-flung Ottoman Empire after Mehmet the Conqueror's great-grandson, Süleyman the Magnificent, made the decision to consolidate the seat of the Ottoman Empire and his royal residence. This vast palace became the setting for many events, both sublime and sordid, throughout 400 years of history until the construction of Dolmabahçe Palace *(see page 136)* further along the Bosphorus in the mid-19th century.

Though structurally reflecting Mehmet I's original plans, the sprawling, eclectic compound overlooking the confluence of the Bosphorus, the Golden Horn and the Sea of Marmara reflects no single particular architectural stamp. Every new sultan elaborated on the building according to need, and four major fires did little to preserve whatever architectural unity might have existed. The only original buildings left from the time of Mehmet I are the Raht Hazinesi (or Treasury building), which was Süleyman's original palace, the inner and outer walls, and the **Çinili Köşk** (**Tiled Pavilion**) , just below the palace in Gülhane Park. The latter is now home to the **Museum of Turkish Porcelains**, which displays early Seljuk and Ottoman ceramics as well as some exquisite Iznik tiles from the 17th and 18th centuries.

Next to this is the city's excellent **Arkeoloji Müzesi** (**Archaeology Museum**) ⊙, which contains a number of Greek and Roman antiquities and a magnificent sarcophagus erroneously claimed to belong to Alexander the Great. The newly refurbished and expanded wing of the **Eski Şark Eserleri Müzesi** (**Museum of the Ancient Orient**) ❿ contains Sumerian, Babylonian and Hittite treasures. All three museums are open Tues–Sun 9am–5pm; single entrance fee for all three.

The main Topkapı Palace complex consists of three distinct areas, the **Birun** (Outer Palace), **Enderun** (Inner Palace) and **Harem**, each of them broken down into various courtyards connected by a maze of gates.

At one time over 50,000 people lived and worked on the palace grounds, a veritable city within a city, complete with dormitories for various guards, craftsmen and gardeners, all wearing their own distinctive garb for easy identification. In addition to discreet neighbouring mosques and baths, the palace even had its own zoo, where lions, elephants, bears and other gifts from foreign rulers were kept.

The **Bab-ı-Hümayun** (Imperial Gate) is the main entrance, erected by Mehmet I in 1478. It leads to the First Courtyard where the janissaries, the Praetorian Guards of the Ottomans, were once headquartered. To the left is **Aya Irini** (**St Eirene**) ⓫, the oldest Byzantine church in Istanbul *(see page 119)*.

Map on page 118

TIP

It is best to visit the Topkapı Palace early, since it can get very crowded in the peak tourist season. Book your tour of the harem as soon as you arrive on a timed ticket.

BELOW: the Imperial Hall in the Topkapı.

TIP

Take time when in the Old City to have a bath. The Cagaloglu Hamami, Prof. Kazim Ismail Gürkan Cad. 3, the Çemberlitas Hamami, Vezhirhan Cad., and the Süleymaniye Hamami, Mimar Sinan Cad. 20, are three of the loveliest historic hamams in Turkey. A sybaritic bath, scrub and massage costs less than US$20.

BELOW: the Fruit Room, in the Harem of the Topkapı.

Near the ticket office and the shop, the second gate, built by Süleyman the Magnificent in 1524, is known as the **Bab-ı-Selam (Gate of Salutations)**. This is the entrance proper to the palace. It was renowned for its cypress trees, fountains, peacocks and gazelles designed to create an impression of calm and tranquillity. On the right are the domes and chimneys of the palace's huge kitchens, which now house a vast collection of glass, silver and rare Chinese porcelain,

The **Baba-üs Saadet (Gate of Felicity)** leads to the **Throne Room** and the **Treasury**, home to the Ottomans' almost obscene accumulation of jewels and precious metals. Security is tight for the staggering display of opulence, which includes bejewelled daggers, ivory book covers, huge slabs of emerald and the 84-carat Spoonmaker's Diamond, fifth largest in the world. Also in this courtyard are a collection of early Turkish and Persian miniatures, some holy relics of the Prophet Mohammed and a sumptuous display of Imperial robes.

The Harem

Of all parts of the palace, the Harem, also reached from the Second Courtyard, probably most inflames the visitor's imagination, fuelled by images of odalisques and slaves reclining on divans waiting for the sultan's pleasure. There were over 300 rooms (of which 40 are open today), but half were cramped cubicles for the lesser eunuchs, servants and concubines. Rooms increase in size and opulence as you approach the chambers of favourite concubines and four legal wives. Thanks to the legacy of Roxelana, chief wife of Süleyman the Magnificent, the *Valide Sultan* ("mother of the sultan") was to become effective queen of the domain and could exert great influence – her apartment was second only to the sultan's own voluptuously ornate private rooms.

Even in its most decadent days, the Harem was hardly the den of unfettered sex and iniquity conjured up by many – there was too much competition. Sex with the sultan could hardly be a spontaneous affair – according to records left by one legal wife, he simply requested the Chief Black Eunuch to inform the girl he had chosen, after which she was bathed, perfumed, dressed and sent a gift. Unless she was especially favoured, he then presented himself at her chamber, (only a very few ever entered the sultan's rooms), where the date and time were recorded. If she became with child, that, too, went on record; if the birth resulted in a boy, she acquired the elevated status of *Haseki Sultan*. Some sultans were known to be disinterested in and even hostile towards women, and a preference for boys was not unknown. Osman II even wore spiked shoes in the Harem so that the grating sound would warn the women to get out of his way,

For the first 150 years of Ottoman rule, the brothers of each new sultan were strangled with a silken cord – in 1595 Sultan Mehmet III had 19 siblings murdered to avoid any later power struggles. This could lead to difficulties later if no heir was forthcoming in time and later Ottomans rethought the strategy. The Fourth Courtyard contains a rather disturbing legacy of their solution – the **Veliaht Dairesi** (Gilded Cage), where, in an effort to cut down on such rampant fratricide, the siblings of the heir apparent were kept safely out of the way in indulged isolation, awaiting the possibility of power. The conditions were not ideally suited to producing great leadership, however, and are often considered to have contributed to the fall of the empire. Deli Ibrahim (Ibrahim the Mad) suffered from extreme paranoia after 22 years in debauched isolation – his reign is primarily remembered for the 280 concubines he ordered drowned in the Bosphorus upon hearing rumours of a Harem plot.

Map on page 118

The Kaşıkçı ("Spoonmaker's") Diamond, star of the film "Topkapı".

BELOW: miniature showing a birth in the Harem.

LIFE IN THE HAREM

Daily life in the Harem must have been a squalling racket of babies, competitive mothers and harassed servants. The only men allowed in were the various princes, black eunuchs (colour-coded by job for easy identification) and, in emergencies, the so-called Zülfülü Baltacılar ("Firemen of the Lovelocks"), who wore exaggeratedly high collars to screen their prying eyes. As the empire decayed, the complex became more and more overcrowded; by the mid-1800s, there were over 800 odalisques in the Harem – virtual slaves living in often squalid conditions.

Yet despite its oppressive reputation, real romance could also flourish in the Harem. The 17th-century Sultan Abdülhamid I wrote a love letter to one of his paramours proving that political status can be no match for the arrows of passion: "My Rühhah, your Hamid is yours to dispose of. The Lord Creator of the Universe is the Creator of all beings, and would never torment a man for a single fault. I am your bound slave, beat me or kill me if you wish. I surrender myself utterly to you. Please come tonight I beg of you. I swear you will be the cause of my illness, perhaps even of my death. I beg you, wiping the soles of your feet with my face and eyes. I swear to God Almighty, I can no longer control myself."

BELOW: decoration covers every wall of the Sultan Ahmet (or Blue) Mosque.

Islamic Istanbul

If Ottoman state bureaucracy was stamped into the walls of the Topkapı Palace, the state religion, Islam, found its expression in the dozens of grand mosques whose needle-like minarets spike the city's skyline. The prolific number of mosques in Istanbul makes an exhaustive account of them all quite impossible, and new ones are being built all the time, whether of architectural merit or not. The following brief listing should help locate the most distinctive.

The most famous, if not necessarily the most beautiful, mosque in the old city is the **Sultan Ahmet I Camii (Blue Mosque)** ⑫ (open daily, but closed at prayer times – best to visit early in the morning; entrance is free, but donations are expected on exit), facing Aya Sofya from across Sultanahmet Square. It is a purposefully imposing structure, its interior walls clad in exquisite İznik tiles, built between 1609 and 1616 by the architect Mehmet Ağa. A student of the great architect Sinan, Ağa built the mosque both as a means of showing the world that he had outstripped his master – and the architects of Aya Sofya – and as a tribute to the superiority of Islam. It still maintains that symbolism for many Muslims. The mosque, with 260 windows, associated religious school, hospital, caravansaray and soup kitchen (the *külliye* or "complete social centre" in the Islamic sense) is impressive for size alone. Its six minarets nearly caused a major rift, as this was as many as the great mosque in Mecca; the sultan had to donate an extra minaret to Mecca to quell the row.

In the vaulted cellars, the **Hünkar Kasri (Carpet and Kilim Museum)** is a good place to familiarise yourself with Turkish style and quality without pressure (open Tues–Sun 8.30am–5pm; entrance fee). If you are inspired to buy, the **Hasekı Hamamı** ⑬, built by Sinan in 1556 for Roxelana, the wife of Süleyman

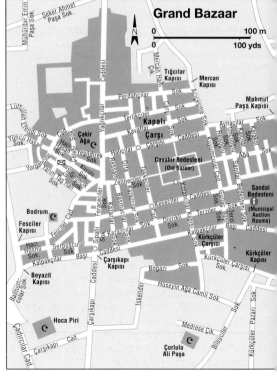

the Magnificent, is now home to the state-run **Turkish Handwoven Carpets Exhibition**, with expert staff and reasonable prices.

Most of the other greatest Ottoman mosques are clustered together a little further west, near the great Sulimaniye Camii, but before leaving Sultanahmet, visit the **İbrahim Paşa Sarayı**, on the Hippodrome opposite the Blue Mosque. This palace houses the **Museum of Turkish and Islamic Arts** ⓮ (open Tues– Sun 9am–5pm; entrance fee), which is considered one of the best museums in Turkey and one of the finest extant Ottoman residential buildings in Istanbul. Originally built in 1524 for another of Süleyman the Magnificent's grand viziers, the quality and location of the structure points to a man of great power, who ruled as second in command for 13 years before Roxelana persuaded Süleyman that the man had become too big for his turban and had him strangled – a not uncommon fate for grand viziers.

The museum specialises in religious artefacts and antique carpets, with some fragments dating back to the 13th century. Don't miss the "Evolution of the Turkish House" exhibition in the basement, which traces the history of Turkish dwellings from the nomadic tent to the more modern Turkish home.

The Grand Bazaar

Heading west towards the city walls, the **Divan Yolu**, once the avenue of state trodden by viziers and paşas (high officials of the Ottoman Empire), is now lined with tourist shops, travel agencies and uninspired restaurants. A perpetually crammed tramway runs out to the city's central bus station and airport. Several blocks west, the Divan Yolu changes its name to **Yeniçeriler Çaddesı** (Avenue of the Janissaries), ending at Beyazıt Square and the entrance to the **Kapalı Çarşı** (**Grand Bazaar**) ⓯ – a favourite tourist haunt, the size of a city street block, where everything from carpets to leather jackets, antiques, silver, icons and gold is haggled over. The selection is superb. Competition also keeps the prices reasonable, but shop around before you commit to heavy bargaining. Don't expect to pick up some rare and dusty item for peanuts; the bazaar is a high-rent area and traders have to be sharp. Some have even written books on their areas of specialisation and all know the international value of real treasures.

Another popular bazaar, closer to the ferry docks at Eminönü, is the **Mısır Çarşısı** (Egyptian Spice Market) ⓰. There are few things on sale that you can't get cheaper elsewhere, but it provides a good range of herbal products, Turkish Delight and basketry, as well as spices. More interesting is the medieval warren of old craftsmen, coppersmiths and woodworkers behind and to the right of the bazaar, home also to the delightful Rüstem Paşa Mosque.

Just west of the Grand Bazaar is the **Beyazıdiye** (Beyazıt Complex) which, among other things, serves as the primary campus of Istanbul University. The **Beyazıt Camii** ⓱, clearly inspired by the domes of Byzantine Aya Sofya, was the earliest of the classical Ottoman sacral buildings which soon covered the Islamic world, replacing the traditional open courtyard structures favoured by the Arabs.

Map on page 118

BELOW: the golden glow of the busy Grand Bazaar.

Map on page 118

Pilgrims at the Eyüp Camii, Golden Horn.

BELOW: mosaic of Christ with Adam and Eve, Chora Monastery.

The spire at the centre of Istanbul University is known as **Beyazıt Kulesi** ⓲. Originally constructed of wood and used as a fire tower, it burned in one of the periodic infernos that have plagued the city since earliest times, and was replaced by the present structure in 1828. Before the relatively recent advent of helicopter rides, the tower was perhaps the best observatory from which to get a bird's eye view of the city, although its 150 wooden stairs are a bit rickety.

Beyond this is the towering bulk of the **Süleymaniye Camii** ⓳, or Sülemaniye Mosque, built by Sinan for the great man himself. It is the second-largest mosque in the city, as well as one of the finest you can find in the world. Construction began in 1550. Inside, the mosque is almost square, measuring 58 by 57 metres (190 by 186 ft); the diameter of the dome is 57 metres (186 ft) and its height 47 metres (154 ft). Much less ornate than most of the other imperial mosques, the structure invites you to find a corner to recline and meditate.

In the peaceful back garden, through a forest of ornate tombstones including two other sultans, are the tombs of Süleyman the Magnificent and Roxelana. Süleyman's tomb is octagonal and covered with İznik tiles, while his wife's is smaller, with a cylindrical base recessed from the corners of the building.

Other mosques that are worth searching out are the **Atık Ali Paşa Camii** (Boğazkesen Cad., Karaköy), one of the oldest in the city, and **Azapkapı** (next to the Atatürk Bridge, Galatasaray), a swan song built by Mimar Sinan in 1577. Especially beautiful, however, is the small **Rüstem Paşa Camii** ⓴, on Kutucular Caddesi, Eminönü, not far from Galata Bridge. Commissioned from Sinan by the grand vizier Rüstem Paşa, husband of Süleyman the Magnificent's favourite daughter, Mihrimah in 1561, it is notable for its superb İznik tile work. ❑

The Golden Horn

The Golden Horn is an inland body of water, once the private playground of sultans and a favourite place to picnic. But the city's population explosion during the 1950s, coupled with ineffective zoning laws, have turned the once pristine waters into Turkey's Lake Erie, in which no living thing could survive. In the 1980s, efforts were made to clean it, but these have proved ineffective. It still smells dreadful in the heat of summer, detracting rather from the view.

However, there are some wonderful sights along the shore which make the 20-minute taxi ride in heavy traffic well worth the effort. For anyone serious about Byzantine culture, the **Kariye Camii Sok** (Kariye Museum), just inside the Edirne Gate, is an essential stop (open 9am–5pm; closed Wed; entrance fee). Originally known as the Monastery of St Saviour in Chora ("in the country"), because it stood outside Constantine's city walls, it was rebuilt several times, and the existing church was the project of the mother-in-law of Emperor Alexius I Comnenus. Its walls are rich with over 100 of the finest Byzantine mosaics in the world, the work of artist Grand Logethete Theodore Metochites in 1315–21. They depict biblical scenes from the annunciation to the Last Judgment.

You can also visit the much touted **Pierre Loti Café** (made famous by a Turkophile French author in the 1800s), for the view over a beautiful graveyard. It's best to go by taxi and bear in mind that due to the religious nature of the area, no alcohol is served. Nor is there any food.

From here, walk down to the **Eyüp Camii** through the cemetery, whose old Ottoman tombs are topped with stone turbans.

Eyüp

"The Süleymaniye is glorious, Sultan Ahmet is beautiful, but it is the Eyüp Mosque which is holy." So the saying goes, and, indeed, the conservative religious nature of Eyüp, on the upper reaches of the Golden Horn, will be instantly noticeable in the number of women in black veils. Visitors are advised to dress accordingly – shorts and halter tops are out. Avoid Eyüp on Fridays, the main day of prayer, since the mosque will be packed with worshippers.

After Mecca, Medina and Jerusalem, the Eyüp Mosque vies with Damascus and Karbala as the fourth most important place of pilgrimage in the Islamic world, so behave respectfully and refrain from taking photographs, especially of veiled women.

The mosque was originally built in the 15th century under Mehmet the Conqueror on the spot where Eyüb Al-Ansari, an elderly companion of the Prophet Mohammed, fell during the first Arab seige of Constantinople in 688. His tomb is enshrined here, and is taken very seriously by the devout. Weekends are an interesting time to visit, when newlyweds arrive after their legal, secular wedding to be blessed by the imam – the bride often wearing a stylish white wedding dress, but with a white satin scarf covering her hair, another of the wonderful ways in which Turkey mixes Eastern and Western culture. ❑

RIGHT: the Pierre Loti Café has a magnificent view across the Golden Horn.

Map on page 131

ISTANBUL: NEW CITY

*Bounded by the Golden Horn and the Bosphorus,
"New Istanbul" is a jazzy mix of Ottoman alleys,
Art Nouveau mansions and steel-and-glass skyscrapers*

I t is perhaps misleading to describe the area loosely termed **Beyoğlu** – which stretches roughly from the 14th-century Galata Tower, overlooking the Golden Horn, to the swinging nightclub district of Taksim – as the "new" city (as any Turk would think of it). Most of the shabby genteel architecture is over a century old, and its history, predominantly one of foreign settlement, dates from the time of Justinian onwards. Most intriguingly, it was the designated European Quarter during early Ottoman times, earning a reputation for both culture and debauchery which attracted many curious Muslims and off-duty janissary soldiers. Later, the area was settled by other minorities welcomed by the Ottomans, and its cultural differences have survived to the present day through the impact of Greek, Jewish, Armenian, Italian, Russian and other settlers, whether merchants, natives or refugees.

Pera was the original Greek name for the area, meaning "beyond" or "across" (from the old city). By the 17th century, it had become synonymous with taverns and bawdy licentiousness. According to Turkish traveller, Evliya Çelebi there were "200 taverns and wine houses where the Infidels divert themselves with music and drinking". Prostitution, both male and female, was (and still more or less is) overlooked by the government and Islamic authorities.

BELOW: the view across the Golden Horn to Galata.

In the 19th and early 20th centuries, the Western powers built their embassies here, imprinting a European stamp on the neighbourhood. Most of these mansions are now used as consulates (ridiculous in the case of Sweden or Holland, who must staff their 30 rooms with no more than two or three functionaries).

At the bottom of the hill, housed in the former Hasköy Dockyard on the edge of the Golden Horn, the **Rahmi M. Koç Industrial Museum** (Hasköy Cad. 27; open Tues–Fri 10am–5pm, Sat–Sun 10am–7pm; entrance fee) is Turkey's only industrial and transport museum with a splendid collection of real and model vehicles including a vintage plane and submarine. Further up, one of the more famous landmarks of old Beyoğlu is the wonderful, century-old hotel made famous by Agatha Christie, the **Pera Palas Oteli ❶**. Built to accommodate passengers from the Orient Express, its lobbies are still cluttered with 19th-century furniture and its plush corridors redolent with intrigue.

Despite the fact that the city was dethroned in 1923, when Ankara was declared the capital of Turkey, Istanbul has remained the commercial and cultural hub of the nation. This is where most major businesses maintain their head offices, where all new trends in art, literature, music and film begin, and where most of the money is made and kept.

This has caused something of a conflict within the social fabric of the city as poor rural migrants, frequently

from the troubled east, pour in looking for employment, only to find themselves treated as second-class citizens. All too often, they become easy prey for the utopian promises of radical Islam. Today, the Galata area is rather conservatively Islamic, settled primarily by rural migrants and lamp manufacturers although fashionable restaurants and teahouses have successfully invaded.

In the face of this conservatism, the area's once famous nightlife has simply moved across to the street opposite **Tünel**. It begins with the "artist's quarter" of **Asmalımescit** (at the last count there were at least 40 artists' studios and a cluster of galleries and bohemian cafés within a four-block radius) and runs through the lively *meyhanes* (boozy, cheap restaurants) of **Çiçek Pasajı** ❷ and **Nevizade Sokak** to Taksim, where many of the "alternative" (gay, transsexual, rave, techno and new jazz) nightclubs are found. Throughout these often decrepit-looking streets are some of the best (and cheapest) small restaurants in town: Russian and Armenian specialities add to classic Turkish fare and the general sense of the internationalism that defines the cultural heart of Istanbul. Nevizade Sokak, which runs off the same fish and vegetable market as the more famous Çiçek Pasajı, and where gypsy musicians and hawkers still stroll the tables, gives more of the original flavour of the district – though it is somewhat rowdier. Get there early in summer or seats may be hard to find.

The bright red restored "historic tram" runs from Taksim to Tünel.

Ecumenical sightseeing

The **Galata Kulesi** ❸ (off Yüksekkaldırım Cad.; open daily 8am–8pm; evening show at 8pm; entrance fee) was built by Genoese settlers in 1348 in defence of their colony, which had been granted free trade and a semi-independent status following the Latin occupation. Take an elevator to the top for a sweeping view of the city.

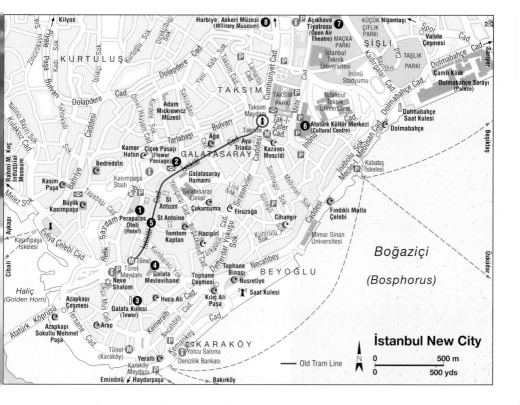

Beyoğlu and Galata are also where those Christian churches still open for business are to be found, from liberal Anglican to Dutch Reform and Roman Catholic establishments. There are also several synagogues in Galata, including the Neve Shalom, which in November 2003 was the target of a massive al Qaeda bomb that killed 25 people. Most of Istanbul's Jewish community is Sephardic, having been welcomed into Turkey when they fled the Inquisition.

Nor are Muslim minorities left out: the public are able to visit the **Galata Mevlevihane** ❹ (open Sun–Mon 9.30am–4.30pm; entrance fee), a particularly open-minded dervish centre that is officially a museum. Although based on the same beliefs as the Konya dervishes *(see pages 81 and 285)*, those in Galata follow a separate *Dede* (master) and are decidedly new age, the first to allow women to participate in the dance ceremony. Performances of their whirling trance-dance form of worship take place approximately every fortnight in summer (Sun 3pm) with information posted outside the building. They also perform regularly during the season around the Mevlevi Festival on December 17. CDs of their music are available for sale.

Moving uptown

İstiklâl Caddesi ❺, which runs from Tünel to Taksim, is several miles long, dedicated to business, shopping and culture, and serviced by an atmospheric old tramway which trundles slowly along the pedestrianised cobbles. There are more cinemas here than in any other part of the city (films show in their original languages), along with numerous fashion houses, Vakko prime among them. İstiklâl is also home to many major art galleries, and at one end is the **Atatürk Kültür Merkezi** ❻, where operas and concerts are staged.

TIP

Contemporary music fans should check the fly posters advertising the new young bands or venues; for more serious concerts, galleries, etc., check the *Turkish Daily News'* Sunday Cultural Supplement, *Time Out Istanbul, Istanbul The Guide* or brochures in hotels, tourist offices and banks.

BELOW: early evening traffic in the New City.

HOW SAFE IS THE CITY?

Considering its size and overpopulation, Istanbul is not a dangerous city. Sexual harassment and bag-snatching are common but, with the exception of tragic street children addicted to sniffing solvents, the city has few of the drug problems that plague European and American cities and serious crime is rare. There are unsavoury neighbourhoods to be avoided – Karaköy becomes a cruising ground at night, and there is a large government-regulated brothel complex off the road running parallel to Yüksek Kaldırım (The High Steps) that is definitely not a tourist attraction. Women on their own are rarely in danger but will be hassled and should follow normal safety precautions.

Foreign men are frequently targeted by touts for the "pavyon" or belly-dancing clubs, which are nothing more than clip joints stocked with whisky dollies whose job it is to get you to buy them drinks at ridiculous prices on the vague but unfulfilled promise of action later. It's safer to ignore any suggestion by a taxi driver or stranger. If you want to see belly-dancing, your hotel should be able to recommend a reputable club. The restaurant on top of Galata Tower offers a dinner and belly-dance package. While something of a tourist trap, the clubs clustered near the Hilton Hotel are at least not seedy.

This is the area to come for nightlife, with Parisian-style bistros and rock bars along the main drag, and trendy nightclubs – straight and gay – down the narrow dark alleys to either side. The area is also well stocked with *pavyons* where red lights glow and the women do business from the doorways.

Map on page 131

Taksim and beyond

At the far end of İstiklâl Caddesi, Taksim is the highrise heartland of business Istanbul, a busy modern district of plate glass, Mercedes Benz and designer restaurants. Taksim Square boasts the **Cumhuriyet Anıcı (Republic Monument)**, created by Italian sculptor, Canonica, in 1928, depicting Atatürk among the founders of modern Turkey. Nearby, on Cumhuriyet Caddesi, the **Taksim Art Gallery** (open Mon–Sat 11am–7pm) has a small display of Istanbul landscapes and a variety of temporary exhibitions, mainly by Turkish artists.

    Conference Valley area, around the Hilton Hotel and Harbiye, just beyond Taksim, is an essential centre for business and entertainment, with many of the city's cultural events, held in venues such as the **Cemal Reşit Rey Concert Hall**, the **Lütfi Kırdar Convention and Exhibition Centre** and **Açıkhava Tiyatrosu (Open-Air Theatre)** ❼. Arts lovers should find out about the **Istanbul Festivals** *(see page 99)* run by the non-governmental Istanbul Foundation for Culture and the Arts, an organisation aiming to bring the city's arts to an international level. Beginning in spring and running until the end of July, an international film festival is followed by a theatre festival, classical music festival and a jazz/contemporary music festival. Ticket prices are reasonable and spectacular performances from all over the world are attracting increasing foreign interest and participation at sell-out levels. The Istanbul Art Biennial, much of it held in Byzantine, "old city" venues, takes place in the autumn of odd-numbered years.

    One place worth visiting in this area is the **Askeri Müzesi (Military Museum)** ❽ (open Wed–Sun 9am–5pm; entrance fee), which has an interesting collection of weaponry, elaborate costumes and some impressive embroidered tents from Ottoman military campaigns. In summer, the Ottoman Mehter Military Band dresses up in janissary finery for concerts at 3pm and 4pm daily, with a short introductory film.

    Harbiye leads to Valikonağı Caddesi, a glitzy shopping area, and on to **Nişantaşı** district. Those interested in Turkish contemporary art should seek out the TEM Gallery (Professor Dr. Orhan Ersek Sok. 44/2) and Galeri Nev (Maçka Cad. 33/8), while distinctive gold and silver jewellery, paintings and sculptures can be found at Urart (Abdi İpekçi Cad. 18/1). **Teşvikiye** and **Maçka** are also home to some of the city's best galleries and boutiques.

    From here to the upmarket residential neighbourhoods of **Etiler** and **Levent**, Istanbul's trendy restaurants and malls leave street people, rural migrants and disgruntled Islamists far behind. But monied Istanbul also runs down to the older, more village-like neighbourhoods such as Bebek, Tarabya, Arnavutköy and Rumelihisar, with their beautifully restored wooden houses, fashionable bars and lines of delightful waterfront fish restaurants overlooking the Bosphorus. ❑

BELOW: modern architecture around Taksim Square.

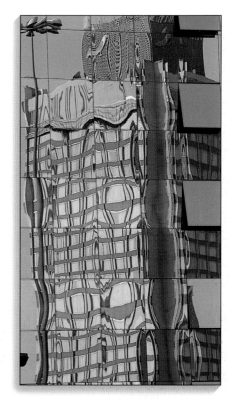

BOSPHORUS

*This romantic, strategically vital stretch of water divides
Europe from Asia and connects the Black Sea
to the Mediterranean*

Map on page 137

According to legend, the Bosphorus (the "Ford of the Cow") gained its name when Zeus, playing away from home as usual, had an affair with the beautiful goddess Io. Jealous Hera sent a swarm of gnats to irritate Io who, for some inexplicable reason, turned herself into a heifer to swim the channel and escape. Since Greek times, the deep, 32-km (20-mile) strait linking East and West has been one of the most strategically significant waterways in the world, witnessing the passage of Jason's Argonauts and the arrival of the first Greek settlers of Byzantium. Because of its unique strategic value, the 1936 Montreux Convention declared the Bosphorus an international waterway and Turkey can only police vessels flying a Turkish flag. In 1936, around 150 ships passed through the straits; today that number is more like 45,000 and growing, due to the exportation of Russian, Central Asian and Caucasian oil. Understandably, there are real safety fears, and control of the Bosphorus has become a political hot potato. When you see tiny fishing boats and laden commuter ferries zipping beneath the bows of the giant tankers, it seems astonishing that no major disasters have occurred so far.

Summer retreat

Over a century ago, the shore north of Üsküdar and Beşiktaş was much less developed than it is today, occupied by villages and summer residences for aristocrats and wealthy citizens attracted by the cool breezes, forests and opportunities to row their brightly painted *caïques* (boats). The paşas built airy stone palaces and other privileged members of Istanbul society erected beautifully carved wooden mansions *(yalı)*. Some of these are still standing, though many fell victim to fire, storms or ships running aground through their lower storeys. The Asian side still boasts plane trees with Byzantine roots (or so the coastal teahouse owners tell you). Both coasts are now lined with superb seafood restaurants and modern dwellings as expensive as any in Paris. By far the best way to see them is on a Bosphorus cruise – which enables you to avoid the traffic along the coast roads and gives you a welcome chance to relax after sightseeing in the city.

Cheap city-run circular cruises leave from a **ferry dock** on the Eminönü side (near a restored Ottoman summer palace) as well as from Beşiktaş. There are three sailings daily in summer and one in winter (check times), taking two hours each way with a stop for lunch at one of the many fish restaurants in Anadolu Kavağı. For information, call 522 0045. A number of private companies also run Bosphorus cruises, such as Plan Tours (tel: 230 8118; www.plantours.com), which offers dinner cruises. *(See also page 373)*

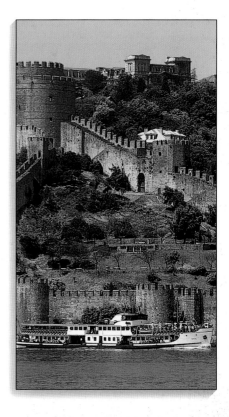

LEFT: crossing from Europe to Asia on the Bosphorus Bridge.
BELOW: the fortress of Rumelihisar.

Golden tea urn in the Domabahçe Palace.

BELOW: the overly ornate Domabahçe Palace took over from the Topkapı in the 19th century.

Landmarks of the Bosphorus

The circular tour first passes out of the mouth of the Golden Horn, with the Topkapı and Seraglio Point to your right. Mid-stream is **Leander's Tower**, a Greek watchtower rebuilt as a lighthouse in the 12th century, while the **Dolmabahçe Sarayı ❶**, in all its outlandish glory, is on your left, at the bottom of İnönü Caddesi leading down from Taksim to the Bosphorus (open Oct–Feb 9am–3pm, Mar–Sept 9am–4pm; closed Mon and Thur; guided tours only; entrance fee).

This 19th-century palace was built by Sultan Abdülmecid to compete with his European rivals. It represents everything incongruous about Istanbul aesthetics, with tons of gold being wasted on over-elaborate decoration, bankrupting the state, although there are also some stunning carpets and *objets d'art* to be found here. Atatürk died here, his simple room a stark contrast to the general impression the palace conveys of complete irresponsibility and overwhelming kitsch. Many of the treasures and the building itself are now in a sad state of neglect. A janissary band performs here on Tuesday afternoons in summer.

Abdülmecid died shortly after the palace's completion; his successor and brother, Abdülaziz, was apparently so disgusted with the building that he built his own palace, the **Beylerbeyı ❷**, across the Bosphorus, ignoring the fact that there was no money left in the till. This lavishly furnished 19th-century summer palace is considered to be one of the loveliest in Istanbul (open 9.30am–4pm, except Mon and Thur; entrance fee).

Next along the European waterfront is the **Çirağan Sarayı ❸**, also built by Abdülaziz. Burnt to a shell in the 1920s, it has been restored as the luxury Çirağan Hotel Kempinski complex. Behind it, on the slopes leading uphill, is the attractive **Yıldız Park**, once part of the sultan's private grounds but now

favoured by courting couples and wedding parties. In **Beşiktaş** ❹, the **Yıldız Palace Museum** (Barbaros Bulvari; open 9am–5pm; closed Mon; entrance fee) houses an exquisite porcelain collection commissioned by Sultan Abdülhamit. Near the ferry dock stands the **Deniz Müzesi** or Maritime Museum (open Fri–Tues 9.30am– 5pm; entrance fee) which displays the elaborate *caiques* used by the sultans to move between their waterfront palaces.

Beneath the first **Bosphorus Bridge**, built in 1973 and, at 1074 metres (3,525 ft) one of the world's longest single-span suspension bridges, the once modest village of **Ortaköy** ❺ has given over its waterfront to trendy lanes of galleries, gift shops and ambitious bars and restaurants as well as a pricey flea market on Sundays.

Arnavutköy ❻ (Albanian Village) is filled with surviving wooden mansions in the classical Ottoman style, all now refurbished and selling at astonishing prices. In **Bebek** ❼, the former home of distinguished 19th-century Turkish poet Tevfik Fikret, now houses the **Aşiyan Museum** (Aşiyan Yokuşu; open 9am–5pm; closed Mon and Thur; entrance fee).

Asian **Anadoluhisar** ❽ (Anatolian Castle), reached by local boat, and European **Rumelihisar** ❾ (Thracian Castle) mark the gates to the Black Sea. The two castles look quaint and harmless enough, but Rumelihisar (open 9am–5pm; closed Wed; entrance fee) was built in 1452 when Sultan Mehmet used the two castles in tandem to choke off all aid to beleaguered Constantinople during the final siege of the city.

The ferry jags across the Bosphorus to the Asian side and quiet suburbs such as as **Beylerbeyı** and **Kanlıca** ❿ (famous for its delicious yogurt), while in **Sarıyer** ⓫, back on the European shore, two fine old mansions house the **Sadberk Hanım Museum** (Büyükdere Caddesi 27–29; open 9am–5pm; closed Wed; entrance fee), with its evocative displays of archaeology, ethnography and 19th-century life. ❑

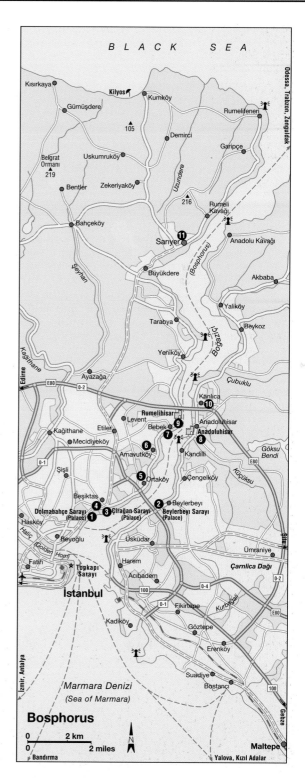

Bosphorus

0   2 km
0   2 miles

THRACE AND MARMARA

East officially meets West here, with European Thrace and Asian Marmara wrapped around the Sea of Marmara

Thrace and Marmara are important areas of Turkey, attracting a large number of visitors each year. Those in search of history find a land of ghosts – from the warriors of ancient Troy who divided nations for the sake of a pretty face to the many thousands who died in the horrific battles at Gallipoli. Though the area is physically close to Istanbul, it differs substantially in character from that great city. Its people are intensely proud of their history and rich local traditions.

Thrace (Trakya) is that small area of northwest Turkey which remains part of Europe. With an area of 23,764 sq km (9,368 sq miles), it occupies about a quarter of the ancient province of the same name. It is a land of bare, rolling, windswept hills, tracts of fertile farmland, areas of melancholy bogland and vine-covered hills that tumble down to the sea, bisected by the E80, successor to the Roman Via Egnatia and Turkey's main road link with Europe.

This is the land of the Dardanelles, that strategic stretch of water between the Sea of Marmara and the Aegean where so many bloody battles took place during World War I. Its principal city, Edirne, which replaced Bursa as the Ottoman capital, stands within a few miles of the border with Greece and Bulgaria, and, unsurprisingly, has a busy, cosmopolitan air. A string of small resorts, popular with Istanbulers but largely unknown to foreigners, decks the coastline.

To the south, **Marmara** is an area of great physical variety. The hills around İznik are soft and rounded. On the fertile plain to the west of Bursa are two great lakes – Ulubat Gölü, where visitors can see the remains of ancient Apollonia, and Kuşcenneti (Bird Paradise), where a national park is home to many species of birds and animals. From the summit of Mount Ida on the southern edge of the region, the gods watched the progress of the Trojan War. There are small coastal resorts like Gemlik, Erdek and Çanakkale to explore, islands such as Marmara Adası and Gökçeada to visit, and spas like Yalova and Gönen where visitors may rest and recover from their exertions. The region's produce is rich and varied – wine from around İznik, the best onions in Turkey from Karacabey and prize cattle and horses from the former Ottoman stud farm at Hara. Of the ancient sites in the region, the most famous, if not most photogenic, is Troy, where Schliemann's spirit still broods over the plundered hill. ❏

PRECEDING PAGES: Büyükada Island, in the Sea of Marmara, near Istanbul.
LEFT: the quiet, timeless streets of Bursa.

THRACE

The last remnant of European Turkey, Thrace was also once the capital of the Ottoman Empire – a dual heritage that leaves the region rich in architectural splendour and military tragedy

Maps:
Area 148
City 144

According to the philosopher Xenophanes (*c.* 570–478 BC), the ancient Thracians were a blue-eyed, red-haired people very much like the images of their gods. Known as being quarrelsome in the extreme, Herodotus said they would have been invincible, if only they could have agreed with one another. Modern Thracians still maintain the reputation of their ancestors for being good fighters. The standard of living in Thrace is higher than in much of Anatolia; neat, well-kept houses of the towns and villages, and lucrative products including tobacco, wine and root crops are evidence of this. The region is known for its independent, liberal spirit, and neither radical politics nor religion thrive here. However, border areas adjacent to Greece and Bulgaria have become something of a lawless no-man's land due to disputes, corruption, smuggling and illegal immigration, and are best avoided.

Edirne

There have been settlements at the junction of the Meriç and Tunca rivers since the 7th century. The modern city of **Edirne** ❶ (estimated pop. 210,000) now occupies this strategic position on one of the main routes linking Asia Minor with southeastern Europe. Emperor Hadrian visited the town in AD 125. It became a garrison town, and was renamed Hadrianopolis in his honour. The Romans then established an armaments industry here, producing shields and weapons. Under Diocletian (245–305), it became capital of one of the four provinces of Thrace. It was attacked by the Avars in the late 6th century, by the Bulgars in the 10th century, and sacked twice by Crusaders before falling to the Ottomans in 1362.

Now renamed Edirne, the growing city became the forward base for Ottoman forays into Europe, serving as the empire's capital from 1413 to 1458, when it was said to have had nearly 300 mosques. Emperor Süleyman the Magnificent (1520–66) liked to hunt in the local countryside, returning to Constantinople only when the croaking of the unconquerable marsh frogs made sleep impossible.

By the early 19th century, Edirne had become a quiet provincial backwater. However, its tranquillity was not to last. It was occupied by the Russians in 1829 and 1878 and, briefly, by the Bulgarians in 1913. Recaptured by Enver Paşa in the same year, it was taken by the Greeks in 1920 and held by them until 1922. Not only was Edirne the scene of occupation, hardship and privation, it became a safe haven for thousands of refugees from the former European provinces of the Ottoman Empire, its population fluctuating tremendously during those troubled times.

LEFT: a turkey in Turkey outside the Selimiye Camii.
BELOW: gypsy boy with a painted wagon.

Today, the magnificent Selimiye Camii and the city's other fine Ottoman buildings are among Turkey's top attractions and visitors will find Edirne pleasantly upbeat. It is a university town with a youthful population and busy cafés. Despite an abundance of religious buildings the atmosphere is decidedly secular. Being located near the E80, Turkey's main road link to Europe, Edirne has also developed into a major business centre, so finding accommodation is not always easy. Rooms are best booked in advance through the **Tourism Office**, Hürriyet Meydanı 17, near the Semiz Ali Paşa Arasta; tel: 0284-213 9208 (open Mon–Fri 9am–5pm; open Sat and until 6pm in summer).

The devşirme *system, which existed from the end of the 14th century to the mid-17th century, was a levy of Christian boys, aged 8 to 20. It was imposed at between three-year and seven-year intervals on farming communities in the Ottoman Empire. Converted to Islam, they became janissaries, government officials or royal pages.*

The master's masterpiece

The magnificent **Selimiye Camii** 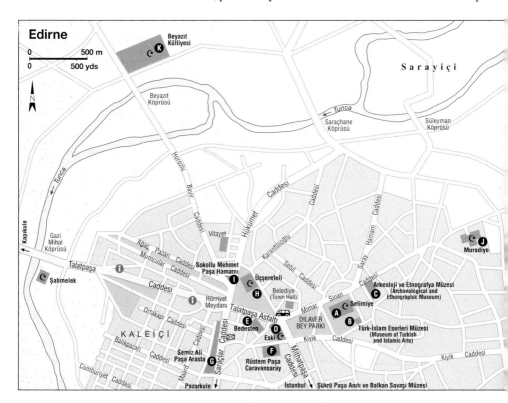 **Ⓐ** towers over Edirne. Considered by many to be the highest attainment of Ottoman architecture, it was built between 1569 and 1574 by master architect Sinan for Sultan Selim II (1566–74).

Sinan was 79 years old when the Selimiye was completed in 1575. The enormous *külliye* (mosque complex), comprising the mosque itself, the *avlus* (courtyard) and *medrese*, occupies the Kavak Medanyı (Square of the Poplars), which stands high above the city centre. It is approached through a pleasant garden where children play, their elders take the evening air, and couples meet beneath the small bowers. The *arasta* (shopping arcade), where souvenirs and religious objects are sold, is the work of Sinan's pupil, Davut Ağa.

The Selimiye epitomises Sinan's great mosque design plan: a succession of 18 small domes lead the eye to a great central dome framed by four slender minarets. Soft red Edirne sandstone has been used extensively and effectively in decorative details, particularly over the arches of the arcades in the courtyard.

Inside, one is awed by the extraordinary sense of space and light conveyed by the great floating dome (31.28 metres/103 ft in diameter and 43.5 metres/143 ft above the floor), supported by eight giant, stately pillars in an orderly circle. The mosque's rectangular plan is cunningly masked by the arrangement of the side galleries – those on the lower floor open to the outside while the upper floor opens inwards. The lower part of the *mihrab* and the sultan's *loge* (balcony) are clad in fine İznik tiles and there is a beautifully carved marble *mimber* (pulpit).

The medrese behind the mosque is now the **Türk-İslam Eserleri Müzesi** (Museum of Turkish and Islamic Arts) **B**. Its collection, set around a garden courtyard, includes an embroidered satin tent used by Ottoman viziers, copies of the Qur'an, embroidery, weapons, glass, photographs and records of oil-wrestling matches (open Tues–Sun 8.30am–5pm; entrance fee). The nearby **Arkeoloji ve Etnografya Müzesi (Archaeological and Ethnographic Museum)** **C** (open Tues–Sun 8.30am–5pm in summer, until 4.30pm in winter; entrance fee) has Thracian ceramics; bronze fibulae; marble busts; jewellery; Greek, Roman and Byzantine coins; and a Roman copy of a Greek statue of Apollo found in Lüleburgaz among its treasures. Its ethnographic section has embroidered costumes, kilims, scimitars, bows, axes, maces and guns.

The city centre

The restored **Eski Cami** **D** in the city centre was constructed between 1403 and 1415. Modelled on Bursa's Ulu Camii, it is a square building divided into nine domed sections. Its upkeep was paid for by revenues from the **Bedesten** **E**, built in 1418 to store and sell valuable goods; according to the 17th-century Turkish traveller, Evliya Çelebi, 60 night watchmen guarded its treasures.

Maps:
Area 148
City 144

Architectural detail on the portal of the Eski Cami.

BELOW: Sinan's masterpiece, the Selimiye Camii.

SINAN, ARCHITECTURAL GENIUS

Mimar Sinan (1489–1588), the greatest of all Ottoman architects, influenced religious and civic architecture during his lifetime and for centuries after his death. Born into the Greek Orthodox faith, this youth from the Karaman was selected under the devsirme system for janissary training in the imperial schools. He rose rapidly through the ranks, ending up as commander of the Infantry Cadet Corps. His ability as a designer and builder of military constructions eventually brought him to the attention of Sultan Süleyman the Magnificent, who appointed him Darüs-saadet, "Architect of the Abode of Felicity", i.e. Constantinople.

For the next 40 years Sinan devoted himself to a prodigious output of architecture. In addition to minor works from aqueducts to fountains, he was involved in the design and construction of 34 palaces, 79 mosques, 33 hamams, 19 tombs, 55 schools, 12 caravansaries, 16 külliyeler (charitable institutions) and 7 medreses. He regarded the Sehzade Camii in Istanbul as the work of his apprentice days; the Süleymaniye, also in Istanbul, as the work of his maturity; and the Selimiye in Edirne as his chef d'oeuvre. He was buried in a simple tomb in the garden to the northwest of the Süleymaniye mosque.

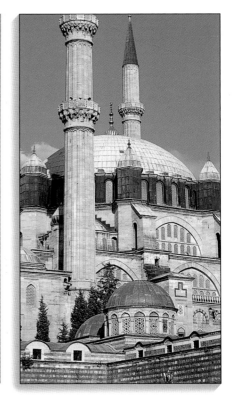

BELOW: the Rüstem Paşa Caravansaray, now a hotel.

Nearby are two of Sinan's buildings, the great **Caravansaray** built for the grand vizier Rüstem Paşa (now a hotel; *see page 383*) and the **Semiz Ali Paşa Arasta** (market). Shop here for books and Edirne's speciality soap, shaped like fruit and vegetables. Other local specialities, catering for the sweet of tooth, are lokum (Turkish delight), Badamezmesi (marzipan) and deva-i-misk (a hard, high-energy sweet).

Across the road, the **Üçşerefeli Camii** (the Mosque of the Three Balconied Minarets; 1438–47) represents a stylistic innovation in early Ottoman architecture. For the first time a massive central dome was placed over a rectangular floor plan. It was a dramatic concept that the architect evidently found difficult to realise; the dome is supported by massive pillars with awkwardly wedge-shaped areas filled by small, turret-like domes at the sides. Yet although patently experimental, the interior breathes strength and reassurance, while the exterior has beautiful decorative details in the mellow local red sandstone. The courtyard, festooned with arcades of pillars, was the first built by the Ottomans, while the three minarets, each decorated in a different stone pattern, were the tallest in Edirne until the construction of the Selimiye Mosque. Each of the balconies is approached by separate staircases within the same minaret, an engineering miracle.

Near the Üçşerefeli Camii is **Sokollu Mehmet Paşa Hamamı** (open daily, women's section 10am–6pm, men's section 10am–8pm; entrance fee), also built by Sinan and still a functioning traditional bath, with a fine dome and plasterwork. Sadly, its İznik tiles have disappeared. Behind the hamam stands the last remaining tower of the **Castle of Edirne** which was built on the foundations of the Roman fort. The castle was allowed to collapse when Edirne was a prosperous Ottoman town. The sole surviving tower is used as a fire station.

Beyond the centre

On a hillock a short distance west of the Archaeological Museum is the **Muradiye Camii** , built by Murat II in 1435 as a lodging for the Mevlevi dervishes. Later the dervishes moved into a *tekke* (convent) in the garden and the main building was converted into a mosque. Its once glorious interior was wrecked when the tiles were stolen in 2002 and it is now closed to the public.

A *dolmuş* (bus) from near the Hamam will take you northeast over bridges and dykes out into the countryside, to the **Beyazıt Külliyesi** . This gleaming white complex, built from 1484–5 by Beyazıt II, comprised a mosque, hospital, medical school, soup kitchen, pharmacy, hamam, *medrese* and kitchens. It was one of the great charitable foundations of the Islamic world. Here, Lady Mary Wortley Montagu took the revolutionary step of having her children inoculated against smallpox, a practice still virtually unknown in most of Europe. The hospital is to the right when facing the complex. The asylum's hexagonal cool white stone treatment room had domed alcoves where the patients were soothed by the sound of water, by music and by flowers. According to Evliya Çelebi, visits to the tranquil asylum were one of the favourite pastimes of the gilded youth of Edirne. The hospital section is now run as a slightly eccentric museum of health (tel: 284-212 0922; open Tues–Sun 9am–5pm; entrance fee) with wax figures of patients being soothed musically, cases of medical instruments and copies of some lurid 15th-century pictures of operations in progress.

Walk back to the city and you will not only have a chance to look more closely at the many elegant Ottoman bridges over the deep Meriç and Tunca rivers, but can inspect the complicated system of dykes that protect Edirne from floods.

At the highest point of the town, the **Şükrü Paşa Anıtı ve Balkan Savaşı**

Maps:
Area 148
City 144

BELOW: Beyazıt II's extensive hospital.

Müzesi (off Talatpaşa Asealtı; open Tues–Sun 9am–5pm; free) is a memorial and museum dedicated to the seige of Edirne during the 1912–13 Balkan War, built around the tomb of the leader of the defense forces, Sükrü Paşa.

The Balkan War that foreshadowed World War I was caused by Serbia, Bulgaria, Greece and Montenegro challenging the ailing Ottoman Empire. Edirne was beseiged for 5.5 months in 1912 before surrendering. It was recaptured by Turkey in July, 1913.

Outside Edirne

Uzunköprü ❷, east of Edirne on the road to Istanbul, gets its name from a kilometre-long bridge, with 174 arches, at the north of the town, built during the reign of Murat II. Uzunköprü is an official rail entry/exit point to Turkey. In **Lüleburgaz ❸**, the **Sokollu Mehmet Paşa Külliye**, built by Sinan in 1569–71, comprises a mosque, *hamam* (baths), *medrese* (religious school), *türbe* (tomb) and market. Born in Bosnia, Sokollu Mehmet was a product of the *devşirme* system *(see page 144)*, and came to power in the 16th century.

Just outside **Çorlu ❹** (ancient Cenuporio) are the ruins of a **Roman bridge** built as part of the Via Egnatia. Two tragic events occurred here. Emperor Aurelian (reigned AD 270–75) was murdered here by his generals while campaigning against the Persians, and Sultan Beyazıt II died here, probably from poison administered on the orders of his son and successor, Selim I (reigned 1512–20).

Along the Sea of Marmara

From Istanbul, a coast road follows the curve of the shore round the Sea of Marmara to Eceabat, on the Dardanelles. As you approach **Silivri ❺** (ancient Selymbria), look for a fine Ottoman bridge, one of many built by Sinan in this area. Süleyman the Magnificent liked to hunt here and once had a narrow escape from a flash flood, climbing on to the roof of a pavilion to escape the torrent. There are some late Roman and Byzantine architectural fragments from Selym-

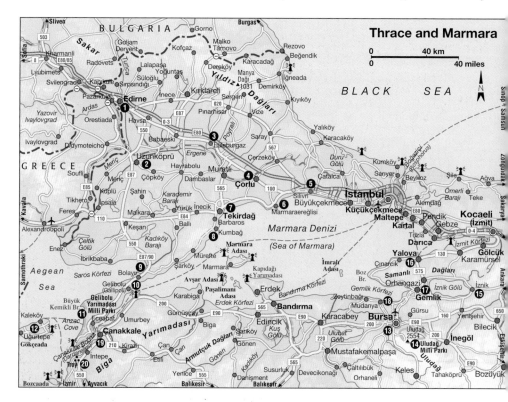

bria in the Kale Park. At **Marmaraereğlisi** ❻ are the fortifications, harbour, theatre, acropolis and stadium of the Samian colony of Perinthus Heracleia.

Tekirdağ ❼ is a seaside town popular with Turkish holidaymakers while its fish restaurants draw patrons from as far away as Istanbul. There are regular ferry services from Tekirdağ to Marmara Adası, Avşa Adası and Erdek.

The **Rüstem Paşa Camii** and the **Bedesten** were both designed by Sinan. The **Arkeoloji ve Etnografya Müzesi** (Archaeological and Ethnographic Museum; open Tues–Sun 9.30am–noon, 1.30–5pm; entrance fee), housed in the elegant Naval Club, has collections from the Greek, Roman and Byzantine periods, as well as Ottoman jewellery, embroidery, utensils and costumes.

Hungarian Prince Ferenc II Rakoczi (1676–1735), invited to Istanbul in 1717 to help fight the Austrians, spent the last years of his life in Tekirdağ. The project was abandoned but the prince never returned to his native land. His house, converted into a **museum** (open Tues–Sun 8.30am–4.30pm; entrance fee) by the Hungarian government in 1932, has a collection of Hungarian weapons, documents, memorabilia, paintings and Prince Rakoczi's flag.

Stop for a swim at **Kumbağ** ❽, 8 km (5 miles) west of Tekirdağ, whose sandy beach is surrounded by pine trees. The surrounding hills are coated with vineyards – this is the start of Turkey's best wine region.

Gelibolu (Gallipoli)

Bolayır ❾ marks the narrowest point of the Gallipoli Peninsula. Here one can see both the Saros Gulf and the Dardanelles. Süleyman Paşa, favourite son of Orhan Gazi, had an accident and died here while engaged in falconry. His tomb, surrounded by cypress trees, is just outside the village. This is one of the most

Map on page 148

Onions and root vegetables are a Thracian speciality.

BELOW: oil wrestlers struggle for a slippery hold.

OIL WRESTLING

Turkish Yaglı Güres (oil wrestling) is a summer sport. According to legend, it began as a means to train soldiers to fitness. The competitions began in 1360, when Süleyman Pasa invited 40 champions to wrestle for Allah and the sultan. By dawn the next day, the last two were dead, but where each hero fell a spring gushed from the ground. To this day the festival is held at Kırkpınar ("40 springs"), just outside Edirne. The basics of the sport remain the same. The majority of modern wrestlers are farm boys dreaming of instant riches.

Each year, about 1,000 wrestlers, covered with diluted olive oil parade to the sound of gypsy music. They compete in classes as young boys, mid-height, full-height and complete-height (the championship Pehlivan class). Betting is brisk, a listless performance booed, and no quarter is given by the Pehlivan class. Referees only monitor illegal holds and announce the winner after a wrestler's shoulder is forced to the ground or a contestant collapses. Matches last on average half an hour, some go on for up to three hours. After a victory, they pair off again until only one remains standing.

To find out more about this unusual pastime, visit: www.kirkpinarwrestling.com.

beautiful regions of Turkey – and one of the most tragic. Once treeless, the peninsula is now covered in lush pine forests, part of the Gallipoli National Park, where any shallow scrape of earth can still dislodge the remnants of an unlucky soldier. The monuments to the dead on all sides are enough to bring a tear to the most jaded eye. Yet it is an unspoilt natural paradise, cool and breezy in the height of Turkish summer temperatures, with a wealth of bird and animal life, and, due to lack of heavy traffic, uniquely suitable for bicycles.

Gelibolu ⑩ is the starting point for visits to the battlefields of World War I. It is an attractive little fishing town, with a small tower museum dedicated to the Dardanelles campaign and the great 17th-century Turkish admiral, Piri Reis. However most visitors stay in Çannakale, from where there is a regular car ferry across to Eceabat, on the peninsula.

There are two official museums and information points, at the **Çamburnu Park Headquarters**, 1 km south of Eceabat, and at the moving **Kabatepe Military Museum**, also the official Turkish memorial, at the centre of the peninsula. Both are open daily 8am–noon, 1pm–5pm; entrance fee.

"Damn the Dardanelles! They will be our grave!" wrote Admiral Fisher to Winston Churchill in a letter dated April 5, 1915. Those words were to haunt the Allied Naval Forces. Under the control of Churchill, in his first major role as First Lord of the Admiralty, a combined Allied force of nearly half a million men tried to force a passage through the Dardanelles to Istanbul, to defeat Turkey.

General von Sanders, the German commander of the Ottoman armies, could not have guessed what forces he had set in motion when he ceded command to Mustafa Kemal, his junior officer. Kemal climbed to the top of the Çonkbayır mountain range from where he could observe the activities of the entire Allied

fleet. During one of the many desperate struggles that followed, he gave his exhausted soldiers the historic command: "I am not ordering you to attack, I am ordering you to die." They did so and won the campaign.

It takes a good day to visit all the battlefields, cemeteries and memorials. The most famous are the Lone Pine Cemetery and **Anzac Cove** ⓫, where Australian and New Zealand troops lie. The British landings were in the far south. The **Turkish Memorial** at Anzac Cove, unveiled on Anzac Day, April 25, 1985, bears an eloquent message of reconciliation written by Atatürk.

> *There is no difference between the Johnnies and the Mehmets to us,*
> *Where they lie side by side here in this country of ours,*
> *You, the mothers who sent their sons from faraway countries, wipe*
> *   away your tears;*
> *Your sons are now lying in our bosom and are in peace after*
> *   having lost their lives on this land,*
> *They have become our sons as well.*

Every year on 25 April, surviving Anzac and Turkish veterans return to this historic place to remember their dead and renew their friendship.

Gökçeada

The island of **Gökçeada** ⓬ (formerly Imbros), northwest of the entrance to the Dardanelles, is best reached by ferry from Çanakkale. It served as the Allied HQ during the Gallipoli campaign and was ceded to Turkey by the Treaty of Lausanne in 1923, with neighbouring Bozcaada. There is a ruined **castle** built by Süleyman the Magnificent at Kale on the north coast. Deep-sea anglers can fish for sea bass and tuna in the clear, blue waters of the Aegean. ❑

Map on page 148

TIP

A set of multi-lingual plaques, with an accompanying guidebook, available from the information points, guides the dedicated visitor around all the Anzac battlefields, cemeteries and memorials.

BELOW: Kilitbahir Castle on the Dardanelles.

Maps:
Area 148
City 153

MARMARA

This green and fertile province south of the Sea of Marmara has wrapped itself in legends, from Karagöz shadow plays to the Wooden Horse of Troy

In classical times the area south of the Sea of Marmara (ancient Propontis) was divided between Bithynia and Mysia. According to Herodotus, the Bithynians were a fierce, warlike people who came originally from Thrace. After the expulsion of the Persians from Asia Minor by Alexander the Great they formed an independent kingdom with its capital at Nicomedia (modern İzmit). According to Homer, the Mysians were allies of the Trojans, but there is no record of a Mysian kingdom. It was, rather, a geographical term for the Troad, Aeolis and Pergamon. Before the Romans made it part of the Province of Asia in 129 BC Mysia had been ruled by the Lydian, Persian and Pergamene kings.

Bursa

The historic city of **Bursa** ⓭ is dominated by the great bulk of the 2,554-metre (8,377-ft) **Uludağ**. Until a few years ago the Turks talked of *"Yeşil"* Bursa ("Green" Bursa) because of the city's sylvan setting. Unfortunately, due to a spate of building, concrete underpasses, overpasses and new high-rise structures now disturb its symmetry and skyline. Some lament that Yeşil Bursa has become "Çimento Bursa". Fortunately, the *hamams* (bathhouses) and spas remain, and are justifiably famous.

According to the Greek geographer Strabo *(Geography* 12.4.3), Bursa was founded by the Bithynian King Prusias I Cholus "the Lame" (reigned 228–185 BC), and he also gave his name – altered to the Hellenistic "Prusa" – to the city. Legend has it that the great Carthaginian General Hannibal helped him to choose the site.

In 74 BC, Bithynia was willed to Rome by its last ruler, the vicious and ineffectual Nicomedes IV. Prusa prospered under Roman and early Byzantine rule, but suffered greatly from the 7th- to 8th-century Arab raids and fell to the Seljuks in 1075. Subsequently, it was fought over by the Crusaders, Byzantines and Turks until, in 1326, it was conquered by Orhan Gazi, whom the 13th-century Arab traveller, Ibn Battuta, described as "the greatest of the Turkmen kings, and the richest in wealth, lands and military forces."

Bursa was the first Ottoman capital in the true sense of the word, and its rulers lavished money and care on it. Orhan issued his first coins here in 1327 and set up a trading centre with a *bedesten* (inn/market/warehouse) in 1340. Apart from recent urban development, the present form of the city still follows Ottoman lines, with the main area surrounding the mosques and religious foundations built by the first six Ottoman sultans. Today, Bursa is the fifth-largest city in Turkey and it still glows with the same civic pride felt by its first Turkish citizens in the 14th century.

BELOW: studying the Qur'an in a Bursa mosque.

True, its industrial prosperity has produced a certain unsightly proliferation of warehouses, factories and offices and there is too much traffic, nevertheless, the old quarter presents an unrivalled display of early Ottoman architecture including some of the loveliest buildings in Turkey.

Çekirge

The elegant suburb of **Çekirge**, west of the city centre, is probably the best place to stay. Mineral water, rich in iron, sodium, sulphur, calcium, bicarbonate and magnesium, gushes from the mountainside at temperatures ranging from 47–78°C (116–172°F), and is used in the treatment of rheumatism, gynaecological and dermatological problems. The **Eski Kaplıca**, erected on the site of Roman and Byzantine baths and the **Yeni Kaplıca A**, built in 1552 by grand vizier Rüstem Paşa, are two of Bursa's many historic mineral baths. Many of the local hotels also sport their own deluxe mineral baths. Of them all, Bursa's oldest luxury hotel, the **Çelik Palas Oteli B**, traditional haunt of kings and statesmen, has a beautiful marble pool, Turkish bath and sauna in its grand Art Nouveau building *(see Where to Stay, Travel Tips)*.

You may be able to catch a shadow puppet play at the **Bursa Karagöz Sanat Evi** – the Karagöz Theatre and Museum – at Çekirge Caddesi 3, where there are performances at 2pm and 8.15pm; the museum is open Tues–Sat noon–5pm. Further information is available from the Karagöz Antique Shop.

Shadow puppet plays probably came with the Turks from Central Asia. A popular form of entertainment in Ottoman society, they were often performed in coffee houses. The stories feature Karagöz (Black Eye) and his stooge Hacival in a series of comic, often rather bawdy, routines. The two characters were

Bursa's traditional shadow puppets are made from camel hide, oiled to make it translucent, then painted. The Karagöz Antique Shop in the bazaar at Eski Aynalı Çarsısı 1-17 (tel: 0224-222 6151) has an interesting range of puppets for sale and organises performances.

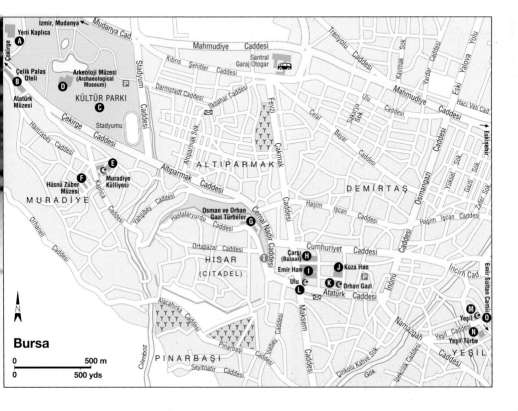

originally based on workmen who laboured on the construction of the Ulucamii. Their antics were found so amusing by the other workers that they held up work on the building of the mosque and, as a result, were executed on the orders of the angry Sultan Beyazıt!

Mosque and Türbe of Murat I

There are over 125 mosques in Bursa. Of these the most important, most interesting and most beautiful were those created by the first Ottoman rulers, many of whom are buried here.

Also in Çekirge are the **Mosque** and **Türbe of Murat I**, built from 1366 to 1385. Murat, known as Hudâvendigâr ("Creator of the World"), spent most of his reign at war. The mosque is based on the usual inverted T-plan, but has unusual features which are sometimes attributed to its possible design by a captured Italian architect. On the ground floor was a *zaviye* (dervish lodging), upstairs a *medrese* (religious school). Some suggest that this was for teaching "orthodox" Islam and that its position above the dervish quarters represents some kind of victory over heterodox mysticism. Today only the lower floor is open to visitors.

The tomb of the warrior sultan lies across the road in a lovingly tended garden, his sarcophagus resting between eight columns which support the dome. The complex's *imaret* (soup kitchen) has disappeared, but the elaborate toilet, with two washrooms, five cubicles and a central fountain, is still in use.

Heading towards the old city, you reach the **Kültür Parkı** ◉ (Çekirge Cad.; always open; entrance fee), one of the social centres of the city, with pleasant gardens, a small boating lake, and a variety of restaurants and nightclubs. At its centre, the **Arkeoloji Müzesi (Archaeological Museum)** ◉ (open Tues–Sun 8:30am–noon, 1–5.30pm; entrance fee) has an interesting collection of artefacts and ethnographic objects, including statues of Cybele, a bronze youth, Roman jewellery and coins from Prusa, Nicomedia and Nicaea.

BELOW: each cocoon must be unravelled into whisper-thin fibres to make silk.

THE STORY OF SILK

It was the Chinese who first realised that the small white worms that infested the leaves of the mulberry trees spin themselves a cocoon, whose gossamer threads can be used to produce a fabric of filmy lightness and incredible strength. For about 4,000 years they jealously guarded the secret and monopolised the market.

It was Byzantine Emperor Justinian I (AD 527–565) who persuaded two Persian monks to smuggle silkworms hidden in bamboo canes from China to Constantinople. Silk production became a state monopoly, based in Bursa. The Ottomans encouraged local production and imports from the Far East, producing magnificent fabrics and carpets. Among the 2,500 items on display in the wardrobe section of the Topkapı are many superb silk brocade and velvet garments, made in Bursa.

The silk industry had collapsed by the 1800s, but today, state intervention has revitalised it. Some 300 Bursa companies now make silk, about 70 percent of it used for weaving silk carpets, especially the Hereke type. However, villagers seem increasingly reluctant to farm the troublesome silkworms, and merchants are now complaining that they cannot buy enough silk. Whether the trade will last is questionable.

The Muradiye complex

Just to the south of the Çekirge Caddesi, the **Muradiye Külliyesi**  was built between 1425 and 1426. It comprises a mosque, an *imaret* (soup kitchen), *medrese*, the tomb of Murat II (1421–51) and the tombs of a number of other Ottoman royalty. The site is open daily 8.30am–5.30pm in summer, 8am–5pm in winter; there is an entrance fee, and you may have to tip the *bekçi* (porter) to see some areas (which are open in rotation). Above the portico of the mosque, brick patterns highlighted in azure tiling depict the heavenly spheres, while thunderbolts in blue glazed tiles are set into the marble to the right of the entrance. The so-called *eyvan* design of this mosque, based on a central covered hall surrounded by rooms, was developed by the Ottomans from the plan of Selçuk Medrese in Central Anatolia and the mosques of Central Asia and Iran. Around the *mihrab* are bold plain blue and white tiles.

In the lovely gardens are 12 tombs of various styles. Murat's tomb lies under a dome raised on antique columns. Like all the early Ottoman sultans, Murat was a renowned fighter on the battlefield, the scourge of Europe, but, as recorded by Edward Gibbon, "he seldom engaged in war till he was justified by a previous and adequate provocation. In the observance of treaties his word was inviolate and sacred." Attracted to the life of the mystic and contemplative, and eschewing pomp and circumstance, he chose to be buried here under the rain and the stars; his tomb's simplicity is in contrast to that of his father in the Yeşil Türbe.

Deeper in the garden, past beds of roses and lilies edged with box, is the tomb of Cem Sultan, one of the tragic figures of Ottoman history. After the sultan's death, court intrigue and janissary meddling prevented Cem, the favourite son of Mehmet II, from reaching Istanbul before his brother Beyazıt,

Maps:
Area 148
City 153

Bursa, the official end of the Silk Route, is still an excellent place to shop for silk, from scarves to shirts, at bargain-basement prices.

BELOW: the Muradiye complex.

who proclaimed himself sultan. The two fought briefly, then Cem fled abroad where he was used as a pawn in the intrigues of international politics. He died in Naples on February 25, 1495, probably from poison administered at Beyazıt's instigation. A man of action, culture and poetry, had Cem ascended the throne Ottoman history might have been very different. His verses evoke the bitter pain of separation from his homeland. Now he rests in a tomb built for his nephew, a structure of great beauty lined with gilded octagonal blue tiles.

Nearby, Süleyman the Magnificent's son, Şehzade Mustafa, lies in a tomb lined with İznik tiles depicting hyacinths, tulips and blossoming shrubs.

The Muradiye is in one of Bursa's old quarters. Across from the mosque is the 17th-century **Ottoman House Museum** (open Tues–Sun 9am–5pm; entrance fee), arranged as it would have been in Ottoman times. And a couple of streets away, the **Hüsnü Züber Müzesi** ❻ (Uzunyol Sok 3, Kaplıca Cad.; open Tues–Sun 10am–5pm; entrance fee) is a restored Ottoman guesthouse, built in 1836 with lavishly carved woodwork. Some of the current owner's own carvings are also on display.

From here, climb up the steep hill, along Kaplıca Caddesi, to the **Hisar** (**Citadel**) and the **Osman ve Orhan Gazi Türbeler** ❼, tombs of the first Ottoman leaders, who are buried in the ruins of a Byzantine church overlooking the walls. There are a few pieces of mosaic from the church near Orhan's tomb. The terrace behind them offers a good view of the lower part of Bursa.

The market quarter

The **Çarsı** (**Bazaar**) ❽, founded by Orhan Gazi in the 14th century, was the heart of the old city and is still the commercial centre of Bursa. Work began here

BELOW: the tomb of the Ottoman ruler, Orhan Gazi.

during the rule of Orhan, but it was substantially extended by subsequent sultans. The busy shopping area is still crowded with locals inspecting wares laid out in the narrow alleys and passages lined with small shops. At the heart of the bazaar, the **Bedesten**, built by Sultan Beyazıt I on the site of Orhan Gazi's earlier building, is an impregnable structure still used for storing and selling gold and silver jewellery and other valuable goods. Its massive doors are locked every night. Some of the revenue of the Bedesten went to aid Orhan Gazi's nearby mosque; most supported Beyazıt's Ulucamii, an example of the link between commerce and good works and piety under the Ottomans.

Maps:
Area 148
City 153

Amid the narrow, bustling streets is a group of *hans* (markets) built around quiet courtyards shaded by trees and cooled by fountains. Orhan built the **Emir Han ❶**, the earliest example of an Ottoman *han* constructed in accordance with the requirements of inner-city commerce. Much restored, it had a courtyard, pool and trees surrounded by rooms which could be used as shops, storage areas or dwellings. The rather grand two-storied **Koza Han ❷** is also built around a courtyard, in the centre of which there is a tiny octagonal *mescit* (small mosque) built over a fountain. Dazzling rolls of coloured silks cascade over the counters of the tiny shops surrounding the courtyard.

Window detail of the Yeşil Camii (Green Mosque) in Bursa.

Not far from here is the much restored **Orhan Gazi Camii ❸**, built in 1339. Despite its massive five-bay porch adorned with Byzantine columns, it appears simple and unassuming in the bustle of the surrounding commercial district. Perhaps this is appropriate. Orhan Gazi was an unpretentious fighting man, though he was the brother-in-law of a Byzantine emperor, the friend and ally of the Genoese and near master of Thrace. The mosque is an early example of the *eyvan* plan, with a central domed hall. Originally there was probably a basin beneath to catch the rain. The *mihrab* faces the entrance of the central hall, which is surrounded on the other three sides by domed chambers. It is believed that dervishes lived in some of them.

BELOW: view over Bursa from the Ulucamii.

Bursa's great mosques

Along Atatürk Caddesi rises the massive bulk of the **Ulucamii ❹ (Grand Mosque)**, built by Beyazıt I (reigned 1389–1403). It is said that before going into battle at Nicopolis in Macedonia in 1396 he promised that, if victorious, he would build 20 mosques. He cheated and built one mosque with 20 domes! The Ulucamii dominates the surrounding area like a great fortress. The walls of rough-hewn blocks of warm yellow limestone are pierced at intervals by windows, while doors on three sides are surrounded by carved marble portals. It is believed that the door on the north side was added by Timur when he occupied Bursa in 1402. Five rows of four domes, supported by huge pillars, ornamented with inscriptions from the Qur'an in stylised calligraphy, divide the interior space. Beneath the central dome, somewhat higher than the others, is the *şadırvan* (ablutions fountain).

From here, walk in an easterly direction to the **Atatürk monument**, known colloquially as the "*heykel*", from the Turkish for statue. Then follow the yellow signs to the **Yeşil Camii (Green Mosque) ❺**, built in 1419 by Mehmet I (reigned 1413–21). The

outside is almost entirely marble. Its name comes from the turquoise-green tiles which once covered the roof and the tops of the minarets. Note the delicate carving and a band of turquoise tiles around the windows.

Inside, the eye is overwhelmed by the richness of the decoration. Circles, stars and geometric motifs on turquoise, green, white and blue tiles succeed and supplant each other in an endlessly changing composition which is both harmonious and complex. By the beautifully decorated *mihrab*, an inscription in Persian states that they are the work of the master craftsmen of Tabriz.

The Yeşil Camii, like others in Bursa, is an *eyvan*-type mosque with a şadırvan in the middle of the central hall and raised prayer halls on all four sides. To the right and left of the central hall, doors open to rooms with elaborate stucco shelving and fireplaces. The function of these rooms is not known with any certainty, but they may have been dervish quarters or used by government officials. Immediately to the right and left of the entrance, narrow stairs lead to the richly decorated sultan's *loge* (theatre box) which overlooked the prayer hall. You may need permission to see this.

Across the road, Mehmet I's **Yeşil Türbe** (**Green Tomb**)  (open daily 8.30am–noon, 1–5pm) is perhaps the loveliest building in Bursa. Walk slowly around the tomb to enjoy the extraordinary turquoise of the plain tiles and the richness of the patterned tiled lunettes over the seven windows. The inside walls, apart from the elaborately decorated *mihrab*, are ornamented with plain turquoise tiles on which are set lozenges of patterned tiles. The elaborate, almost frivolous but empty sarcophagus of the sultan is flanked by those of his close family. Muslim law does not permit burial above ground. From the terrace, there is a fine view over the city and the plain beyond.

BELOW: the interior of the Yeşil Türbe (Green Tomb).

Slightly to the right, set among the cypresses of a large cemetery, is the **Emir Sultan Camii** . Rebuilt at the start of the 19th century in an over-elaborate style popular at that time, it was constructed originally in the 15th century in honour of Emir Sultan, the dervish, counsellor and son-in-law of Beyazıt I.

To reach the twice-restored **complex of Beyazıt I**, walk down through a quiet neighbourhood of small houses, then climb a steep slope to the outcrop on which the complex stands. Built between 1390 and 1395, it consisted originally of a mosque, *imaret*, two *medreses*, a hospital, palace and Beyazıt's *türbe* (tomb). Today only the mosque, *türbe* and one *medrese* remain. Beyazıt's body was brought back to Bursa by his son Süleyman Çelebi after his unhappy captivity and death at Aksaray, as a prisoner of Timur. Reviled by subsequent sultans for his defeat (Murat IV visited Bursa with the express purpose of kicking the tomb), Beyazıt rests under a plain sarcophagus.

Out of Bursa

Just south of Bursa, at an altitude of 1,900–2,500 metres (6,235–8,200 ft), the richly forested, mountainous **Uludağ Milli Parkı** ⑭ ("Big Mountain" National Park) claims to be Turkey's premier ski resort, although it is noticeably quiet even in mid-winter. It has hotels, chalets, ski-lifts, chairlifts, slalom and giant slalom courses as well as nursery slopes.

Climb Uludağ the easy way – on the 5km-long cable car.

In spring and summer, the national park attracts people who are more interested in natural history, offering long walks by tumbling brooks and across slopes carpeted with wild flowers to the tarns near the summit. Some of the hotels are open throughout the year. *Kendin Pişir* (grill your own) meat restaurants abound, particularly in the Sarıalan picnic area. A cable car leaves several times daily from the city centre, but the service may be cancelled during bad weather. The ascent by road takes about an hour.

BELOW: autumn in the Uludağ National Park.

About 10 km (6 miles) from the city centre, on the eastern slopes of Uludağ, the village of **Cumalıkızık** is a picture-perfect Ottoman village with a small museum, mosque, hamam and some delightful houses, most in urgent need of restoration.

Nicaea – İznik

İznik ⑮ (formerly Nicaea) lies 80 km (50 miles) northeast of Bursa. Now just a small lakeside town, it contains some of Turkey's best Byzantine sights. It was founded in 316 BC by Antigonus I (the One-Eyed) and named Antigonia in his honour. Around the year 301 BC, it was renamed Nicaea by Lysimachus, after his deceased wife. The city prospered under Roman rule. Pliny the Younger, governor of Bithynia (AD 111–113), lived here and rebuilt the theatre and gymnasium.

The town has played an instrumental role in the history of Christianity. In AD 325, Nicaea was the venue for the First Ecumenical Council, which condemned the Arian heresy and formulated the Nicene Creed still used by most Christian denominations. The iconoclastic controversy was settled by the Seventh Ecumenical Council, held in the Basilica of St Sophia in 787. Occupied by Byzantines, Persians, Mongols

Maps:
Area 148
City 153

On August 17, 1999, an earthquake measuring 7.8 on the Richter Scale, centred on the industrial heartland of Izmit, but rippled across 640 km (400 miles) of the Bosphorus coast including Yalova, Çınarcık, and Gölcuk, and reaching as far as Istanbul. Government statistics put the death toll at 23,000, though the number of fatalities is reckoned to be closer to 40,000.

BELOW: minaret of the Yeşil Camii (Green Mosque) in İznik.

and Turks at various times, Nicaea was both refuge and capital for the Byzantine Lascarid dynasty during the Crusader occupation of Constantinople in the 13th century. It was taken by Orhan Gazi in 1331 and renamed İznik. The basilica was turned into a mosque. Skilled craftsmen brought here from Tabriz in Iran by Selim the Grim (reigned 1512–20) set up the ceramic industry which made İznik tiles famous. Those used to adorn the great classical Ottoman mosques were all produced here; production moved to Kütahya in the 17th century.

İznik sights

İznik merits a visit just for its beautiful lakeside situation. There are many pleasant walks along the banks, and anglers will enjoy the fishing. Some of the town's best hotels and restaurants are situated here, too.

The city's ancient walls and four great gates are largely intact, while in the ruined Byzantine **Basilica of Aya Sofya** (open daily 9am–noon, 1–5pm; entrance fee), sections of the mosaic pavement of Justinian's 6th-century church and part of a 7th-century fresco of the Deisis are still visible. During its 57 years as Lascarid capital, Nicaea hosted the coronation of four Byzantine emperors and substantial additions were made to its fortifications and church buildings.

The **Hacı Özbek Camii**, built in 1333, is the earliest Ottoman mosque in Turkey which can be dated accurately. Nearby the **Yeşil Camii** (**Green Mosque**), built from 1378 to 1392 by Candarlı Kara Halil Paşa has particularly harmonious proportions. Sadly, the original İznik tiles on the minaret disappeared a long time ago and have been replaced by inferior substitutes from Kütahya.

İznik's **Arkeoloji Müzesi** (**Archaeological Museum**) is housed in the Nilufer Hatun İmareti. Nilufer Hatun, wife of Orhan Gazi, was a beautiful and distinguished Greek princess, daughter of Emperor John VI Catacuzenos, who remained a Christian after her marriage. Orhan Gazi trusted his wife completely, leaving her in charge of affairs of state during his many military campaigns. In the museum (open daily 8.30am–5pm; entrance fee) there are some fine İznik tiles, Roman glass, plates and bowls. Note the inscription on the tombstone of an Ottoman lady who expressed a pious wish that there would be plenty of dancing boys in heaven.

Yalova

Yalova ⑯, a historic spa town on the southern shore of the Gulf of İzmit, is popular with middle-class Turkish holidaymakers. Accessible from Bursa by road, it is also connected to Istanbul by a regular car-ferry service. There are numerous good hotels with bathing facilities in the forested spa area, 12 km (7 miles) inland from Yalova. The original bathhouse has one particularly hot steam room. The springs were popular with the Romans and Byzantines; interest in them revived at the beginning of the 20th century. A few ruins attest to Yalova's historic past, while Atatürk's house is now a **museum** (open Tues–Sun 8.30am–noon, 1–5pm; entrance fee).

Gemlik ⑰ (**ancient Ciucius**) is one of the most beautiful small resorts on the Sea of Marmara. Nearby, according to Strabo (*Geography* 12.4.3.), Hercules lost

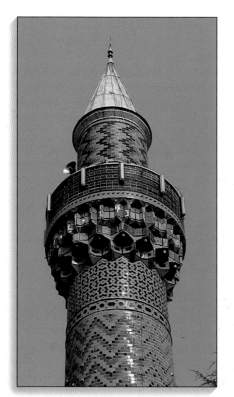

his lover, Hylas, after sending the boy to fetch water from the spring of Pegae. The resident nymphs were so overcome by his beauty that they pulled him under the surface, so they could keep him forever. Gemlik's small hotels are usually full of Istanbulers but the sea is so polluted that swimming is discouraged.

Map on page 148

Mudanya

The small town of **Mudanya** ⑱, on the coast to the north of Bursa, is also popular with Turkish tourists. In 1922, Turkish nationalists negotiated an armistice here with Britain, Italy and France, thus avoiding a fresh war with the Allies who occupied substantial parts of the country including Istanbul and Thrace. Catamaran and ferry services operate daily between Mudanya and Istanbul. On the beautiful coastline to the west of the town there are some interesting small fishing ports. None of them have hotels, but there are places you may camp, with permission.

Çanakkale

Because of its position it is likely that there were settlements here from the very earliest times – control of the Dardanelles brought wealth and power. The straits get their name from the maiden Helle (*see panel*). It was here that the Persian King Xerxes built his bridge of boats across the narrowest part of the straits to land 100,000 troops in Thrace. His planned conquest of Greece ended in defeat at Salamis and Plataea. Ever since, the Dardanelles have remained a crucial control point between the European and Asian continents as well as between the Aegean and the Sea of Marmara and the Black Sea beyond.

Çanakkale ⑲ is only a few hours by car or bus from Istanbul, with long-distance buses using the ferry link with Eceabat. The town became an active

With Phrixus, her brother, Helle fled on the back of a winged ram from their evil stepmother, Ino, who wished to kill them. Tragically, she fell from the ram's back and drowned in the strait that for ever after bore her name – the Hellespont.

BELOW: the Yalova landscape offers an idyllic rural dream.

Relaxing by the harbour.

trading and transit point between Asia and Europe after Sultan Mehmet II built a fortress here in 1452. Although it may not have reclaimed entirely the status it enjoyed in the 19th century, when it was home to scores of consulates and customs houses, Çanakkale has improved considerably in recent years. The harbour area has been refurbished and there is an attractive seaside promenade. Visitors to Troy, the Troad and Gallipoli frequently base themselves here.

The local restaurants maintain their reputation for serving freshly caught seafood. Enjoy a glass of tea or a beer in one of the cafés while you savour the bustling activity of the port and its never ending parade of large freighters, fishing boats and *caïques* (boats). To get a bird's-eye view of the area, walk to the small promontory near the entrance to the military installation at the north end of town. From there you have a spectacular view of old Çanakkale extending into the straits, its old Ottoman fortress (now a military museum), the harbour and, beyond, the broad panorama of the Dardanelles.

The **Çanakkale Archaeology Museum** (1.5 km/1 mile south of the town centre on the road to Troy; open daily 8.30am–noon, 1–5.30pm; entrance fee) exhibits artefacts, sculpture and ceramics from Troy, including a crystal amulet and lion-head (Troy II), a pot cover in the form of a female head (Troy III), goblets (Troy VI) and beautiful terracottas (Troy VIII). There are also collections of costumes; Roman, Byzantine and Ottoman coins; and a display of Atatürk's military clothing. In the garden are sarcophagi, stelae and funerary urns.

Troy

BELOW: pumpkins and squashes sold at a roadside stall.

The name **Troy** conjures up visions of the star-crossed lovers Helen and Paris, of Greek and Trojan heroes, of betrayal and revenge, of cunning and deceit, of a huge wooden horse, of the destruction of a great city and of blind Homer who immortalised them all in two epic poems, the *Iliad* and *Odyssey*. Did Helen and Paris, Agamemnon and Clytemnestra, Achilles and Odysseus ever exist? Did these events actually take place? Was there really a siege of Troy?

Whether you regard Homer as just an early minstrel and wandering entertainer, or as the source of history's most profound legends, the adventures of these heroic figures have become an integral part of the world's literary heritage, and their fates have enthralled and moved countless generations.

A little history

In 333 BC, Alexander the Great came to Troy, where he made a propitiatory sacrifice to the spirit of Priam, received a gold crown from a citizen of Sigeum (where, it was believed, the Greeks had beached their ships), and exchanged his weapons and armour for some kept in the Temple of Athena – thought to date from the time of the Trojan War. He then anointed his body with oil and ran naked to the mound where Achilles was buried. His lover, Hephaestion, did the same at the tomb of Achilles' companion, Patroclus.

Troy was destroyed during the Mithridatic War of about 82 BC and rebuilt by Julius Caesar. It received special honours from several emperors because it was the birthplace of Aeneas, the legendary founder of

Rome. When Emperor Julian the Apostate (AD 361–63) visited Ilium Novum, as Troy was then known, he was greeted by the bishop, Pegasios, who offered to show him the sights of the ancient city. Julian was astonished to find a fire smouldering on an altar at the tomb of Hector and the statue of the hero covered in oil.

The bishop explained: "Is it strange that they [the people of Troy] should show [their] respect … as we show ours for our martyrs?" Because of the growing importance of nearby Alexandria Troas, the city soon began to decline. This was accelerated by the silting of its harbour.

Christoboulos of Imbros relates how Sultan Mehmet II "… inspected the ruins… [was] shown the tombs of Achilles, Hector and Ajax [and said] "It is to me that Allah has given to avenge this city and its people… Indeed it was the Greeks who before devastated this city, and it is their descendants who after so many years have paid me the debt which their boundless pride had contracted… towards us, the peoples of Asia."

The early 17th-century Scottish traveller William Lithgow was not particularly impressed by Troy. "I wot I saw infinite old sepulchres, but for their particular names and nimonation of them I suspend: neither could I believe my interpreter, sith it is more than three thousand odd years ago that Troy was destroyed!"

In May 1810, Lord Byron seemed to be preoccupied with rather more earthy matters. "The only vestige of Troy, or of her destroyers, are the barrows supposed to contain the carcases of Achilles, Antilochus, Ajax but Mt Ida is still in high feather, though the Shepherds are nowadays not much like Ganymede".

Map on page 148

BELOW: view of the South Wall of Troy.

Map
on page
148

In recent years the wooden horse that once symbolised military cunning has been turned by Turkish school children into a symbol of peace. Each August they release a white dove from it shouting in unison, "Peace, Peace, Peace."

BELOW: a modern wooden horse captures the imagination of children at Troy.

Schliemann's great discovery

Towards the end of the 19th century Heinrich Schliemann, a wealthy German businessman and amateur archaeologist, began to excavate at Troy using the *Iliad* as his guide. Accompanied by his second wife, a beautiful Greek woman named Sophia, who had been selected for him by the Archbishop of Athens, he dug a great trench into the mound of Hisarlık. For over four months he led his team of more than 150 workers, while the academics laughed at the mad German who was squandering his wealth so foolishly. But Schliemann found gold. First a necklace, then gold cups, daggers, lance heads, silver vases and two extraordinary golden headbands worn, he judged, by royalty. In fact he had not found Homer's Troy, his treasure came from the remains of an earlier Bronze Age civilisation – about 1,200 years earlier.

Ongoing controversy

Subsequent investigations by other archaeologists have revealed more than nine separate levels of occupation at Hisarlık. Professor Blegen, leader of the University of Cincinnati expedition in 1932–8, maintained that Troy VII was the city of Priam and that it was destroyed in about 1260 BC, at roughly the same time as the fall of Mycenae. But Professor Finley countered that the archaeologists were basing their claims on a single bronze arrowhead and that there was no evidence of a hostile coalition, let alone a Mycenaean coalition at Troy. A recent colloquium on the Trojan War reached a similar conclusion, stating that "on present evidence there is neither room nor reason for Mycenaean hostilities against Troy". The late George Bean, a lecturer in Classics at Istanbul University, maintained there is no evidence from Hisarlık to connect the destruction of Troy with a Greek invasion. He also claimed that the paltry remains of Troy VII bear little resemblance to the fine city of Priam as described by Homer. Turkish archaeologists are of the view that sub-level Troy VI is Priam's city. The debate goes on.

Another point of controversy is the Trojan Horse itself, or rather its modern replica. Many visitors find it garish and out of place; for others it is a point of pleasant frivolity at an otherwise visually dull site. Others are reminded of the moment when the stunned defenders realised that they had been duped and that their city was doomed. As in the original, the reconstruction can be entered from underneath, and you can look out over the ruined city and the plain of Troy and see with modern eyes what Homer could only imagine.

The site (open daily 8am–7.30pm in summer, 8am–5pm in winter; entrance fee) has little to show for its illustrious pedigree, and viewing requires a good imagination. Begin your tour at the massive tower in the great wall of Troy VI. Continue through the east gate, passing the carefully constructed houses of Troy VI, to the more careless constructions of Troy VII. From the summit you look over the plain to Homer's "wine-dark sea". Here, you can see Schliemann's great north-south trench. Northwest of the paved ramp, against the wall of Troy II, he found his golden treasure. It may have been through the west gate beyond that the Trojan horse was brought into the city. ❑

Treasure Seekers

In 1829, a seven-year-old German boy, Heinrich Schliemann, received a Christmas gift, Jerrer's *Universal History*. In this there was a striking engraving which showed Aeneas fleeing from burning Troy bearing his father Anchises on his shoulders and leading his son Ascanius by the hand. Deeply impressed, the precocious child pestered his father with questions, deciding then and there that one day he would find Homeric Troy.

The adult Schliemann amassed a fortune, trading in arms, fur, indigo and gold, learned classical Greek, revived his Latin and studied several European languages. In 1868, finally ready to realise his childhood dream, he visited sites in Greece and Turkey, producing a book, *Ithaca, the Peleponnese and Troy*, which named the mound of Hisarlık as the site of Troy. Classical scholars, who regarded the *Iliad* and the *Odyssey* as nothing more than poetic myths, ignored him.

In 1871, with Homer in his pocket, Schliemann began to dig a huge trench through the 32-metre (105-ft) high mound, convinced that Homeric Troy lay at the lowest level. In 1873 he found the ruins of a fortified city and a quantity of jewellery which he called the "Treasure of Priam". In fact, his discoveries were much older, the remains of a prehistoric Bronze Age civilisation. Assisted by experts he made three more excavations at the site before his death in 1890.

He has been criticised for the cavalier way he treated the mound, but there was no canon of established practice for him to follow. His use of trenches is still a fundamental technique and his determined publicity of his finds, both at Troy and Mycenae, helped stir the public imagination. He is now saluted as one of the fathers of modern archaeology.

His illegal removal of the treasure is harder to excuse. His wife wore some of it for a while before presenting it to the German nation. Since then, it has had a chequered history. Stolen from Berlin by the Red Army in 1945, it is now the subject of a dispute involving Greece, Turkey, Germany and Russia.

RIGHT: Heinrich Schliemann, obsessed by a dream, helped create modern archaeology.

Schliemann is the most famous of them, but other Western "treasure hunters" also plundered Turkey. Motivated by a desire "to lay bare the wonders of Lycia" – and enrich collections in the West – Sir Charles Fellows was responsible for rediscovering 13 ancient cities. With the sultan's permission, he shipped 78 cases of Lycian sculpture and architectural fragments to England in 1842, removing a further 27 cases of sculpture from Xanthos two years later. However, every piece was charted, assessed for damage and numbered first. Thomas Newton, who later became Keeper of Antiquities at the British Museum, took a statue of Demeter and a carved lion from Knidos, together with some colossal seated figures from the Sacred Way at Didyma. Fellows' and Newton's spoils now grace the galleries of the British Museum.

All three treasure hunters must be censured for their arrogant rape of Turkey's patrimony, but Schliemann did have permission to dig, if not remove the finds, and the others were given permission by the sultan. Their intentions, at least, were honourable.   q

THE AEGEAN COAST

From classical pagan temples to thumping discos, the Aegean coast has sights to both stir the mind and satisfy the body

The northern Aegean coast is the beginning of Asia Minor. Over the course of time, this long peninsula forming the westernmost part of Turkey (and indeed, of Asia itself) has witnessed the march of ancient history, but where once the great armies of antiquity clashed, now only a gentle wind blowing off the azure-hued Aegean caresses the ancient monuments and ruins of the past to remind newcomers of what came before. Even the most seasoned international traveller will be struck by the unparalleled geographical variety and historically significant locations found in the area.

Between Troy and İzmir, the main tourist destination is the ancient city of Pergamon, served by the agricultural town of Bergama and requiring a whole day to see its wealth of sites. Alternative attractions are provided by the myriad mountain villages and beach resorts, pine forests and lush fields of Turkey's most fertile agricultural region, which conspire magically to make the northern Aegean area one of the most rewarding and relaxing places to visit in Turkey. Conveniently, most of the major sights are located along a coastal highway, and are easily accessible from either Istanbul or İzmir.

İzmir itself is a large urban centre, uncharacteristic of the Turkish Aegean coast but interesting in its own right and a very convenient base for a trip to the limestone cascades at Pamukkale and the ancient Roman city of Hierapolis. However, for anyone seeking a seaside base for their explorations into the surrounding countryside the resort of Kuşadası is a prime contender. Here one can combine nights of hedonistic pleasure while devoting the day to virtuous sightseeing, with Priene, Milet (Miletus) and Didyma only a short trip away. At least a day is required for Efes (Ephesus), probably the single most visited site along the entire Aegean coast. The nearest town to Ephesus is Selçuk, a small town recommended as an attractive place to stay for a night or two, offering affordable, pleasant accommodation as well as several decent restaurants.

South of Kuşadası, the coast becomes more Mediterranean in flavour, with pine forests and ragged grey rocks plunging down to the sand, and winding peninsulas reaching like gnarled fingers out into a turquoise sea. Bouncy Bodrum, its Crusader castle at odds with the pervasive disco beat, is the largest resort here, but the area is better characterised by Marmaris, renowned for its pine-scented honey, as well as a welcoming collection of bars, restaurants and discos. Both resorts offer exciting day trips by boat and longer sailing expeditions along the Gulf of Gökova, the famous Blue Voyage. ❑

PRECEDING PAGES: the magnificent limestone cascades at Pamukkale are Turkey's most dazzling natural wonder.
LEFT: the Library of Celsus is the country's most famous Roman monument.

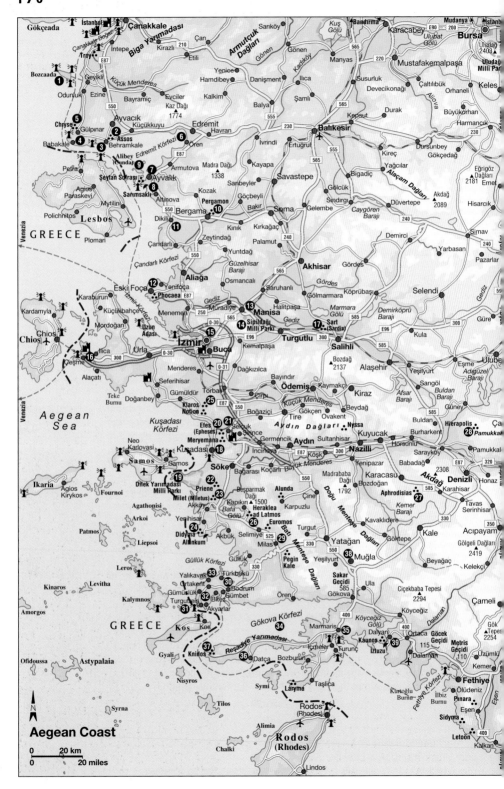

Aegean Coast

0   20 km

0   20 miles

THE NORTH AEGEAN COAST

Troy may be famous, but Assos and Pergamon,
on the northern Aegean coast, are of greater interest,
while the coast itself is sufficient to charm any visitor

Map on page 170

Astonishing as it may seem, there are still areas on the north coast of the Aegean that have not been overrun by tourists. Head only a short distance from the resorts and it is still possible to see many traditional aspects of Turkish village life, with shepherds guiding their wayward flocks, donkeys burdened by heavy loads, busy farmers working their fields and everywhere the ruggedly beautiful and constantly changing landscape.

Bozcaada

The small island of **Bozcaada ❶**, only 5 km (3 miles) across, lies south of Troy and about 60 km (37 miles) southwest of Çanakkale. According to Homer, this is where the Greek fleet moored while the canny Odysseus and his men were tucked inside the Wooden Horse, waiting to surprise the Trojans. It is a surprisingly pleasant place, with a huge Byzantine **citadel** (open daily Apr–Nov 10am–1pm, 2pm–7pm; entrance fee). Otherwise, there are three wineries in town, good unspoiled beaches in the south and southeast of the island and enough small guesthouses and fish restaurants around the harbour to warrant more than a passing visit. To get there, catch a ferry from Çanakkale or **Yükyeri İskelesi**, roughly 60 km (37 miles) south.

Assos

The ancient city of **Assos ❷** (open all year daily 8.30am–sunset; entrance fee) is strategically located on the Bay of Edremit, near the main highway, 100 km (60 miles) south of Çanakkale. To get there, head through Ezine to the picturesque small town of **Ayvacık**, set in rolling farmland a few kilometres from the coast. In late April, visit the annual *panayır*: derived from a primitive Greek festival, this is an unusual and exciting week-long celebration of food, dance and music which brings together all the people of the area. Like several other local towns, Ayvacık is a centre for weaving DOBAG carpets, with guaranteed natural dyes *(see pages 100–104)*.

From here, turn right and follow signs to Assos, along the narrow, winding mountainous road for 20 km (12 miles). Eventually, the road emerges into a low, flat valley, and crosses a splendid 14th-century Ottoman bridge. Rising majestically in the distance is the acropolis of ancient Assos, with the village of Behramkale *(see page 173)* winding its way through the ruins on the steep hillside. Increasingly narrow streets hairpin past typical houses, several small shops and a way of life that hasn't changed significantly in centuries. Near the top, a mosque converted from a church, with a cross and Greek inscription above the door, reflects the time when Assos was part of the Byzantine

BELOW: the colours of the harvest.

Empire. The magnificent citadel is built on an outcrop of solid granite, with hefty stone walls, which stand up to a height of 14 metres (46 ft) high in places. They are nearly 3 km (2 miles) long.

Assos: Temple of Athena

Within the walls of the citadel are the remnants of the **Temple of Athena**, built in about 530 BC at the top of a near vertical drop of 240 metres (750 ft), and dedicated to the daughter of Zeus. Athena was known as a goddess of both war and handicrafts. The temple was excavated by a team of scholars from the American Archaeological Institute in 1881–3. Destroyed as an unwanted reminder of the recent pagan past by the Byzantines, all that remains here are a few Doric columns and the platform of the acropolis itself. Yet no description can effectively convey what can be experienced as you walk among the remaining columns and stand on the temple platform looking out over the Aegean. From here, a breathtaking panorama spreads out before you, nearly to the horizon of the Gulf of Edremit, across the Greek island of **Lesbos** (Midilli), 10 km (6 miles) away, to the deep blue Aegean Sea beyond.

In ancient times, the eunuch Hermeia, called the Tyrant of Atarneus, ruled the Troad (the area around Troy and Lesbos). He had been a student of Plato's in Athens and had sought the master's advice in developing this territory into the ideal city-state described by Plato in his famous political work, *The Republic*.

Aristotle, Plato's most famous student, was invited to Assos and spent more than three years living and working there. He married Hermeia's niece, founded a school of philosophy and conducted his early exploratory work in zoology, biology and botany. A peaceful stroll among the remaining columns still evokes

According to local mythology, it was Athena who taught the women the craft of weaving; the Behramkale area is still famous for fine rugs and carpets.

BELOW: Lesbos looms in the mist.

the atmosphere in which the great rhetorician and thinker lived and worked.

From the main village, a precipitous road crawls down the cliff, past the old walls and ruined sarcophogi, to the harbour area and narrow ribbon of seashore, home to the now fashionable fishing village of **Behramkale ❸**, which consists of some 300 houses and numerous small hotels, restaurants and *pansiyons*. Some of these were converted from abandoned chestnut-storage depots.

Behramkale has become an oasis for many of Istanbul's artists, actors and academics, who find this secluded port irresistible. They inevitably stay longer than they planned, and almost always come back in subsequent years. Tourists – some of whom come here primarily to enjoy the chance to bathe in the nude – have also started to discover the pebbled beach at nearby **Kadırga Bay**.

Map on page 170

Babakale

Turkey offers even the most jaded traveller many unexpected discoveries and rewards, both large and small. One of these is the drowsy traditional village of **Babakale ❹**, at the westernmost point of Asia Minor. It can be reached by a short 45-minute drive back from Behramkale along an unmarked road that hugs the jagged coastline. It seems to run out at Babakale, where the children rush out from under the shade of the giant Ginar (Plane) tree in the village square to greet visitors with happy smiles and a warm welcome.

About 3 km (2 miles) along the rugged coast north of Babakale is the perfect place for those craving secrecy and anonymity. Dominated by an Ottoman fortress (currently under restoration), the working fishing village has a small number of hotels, some holiday villas, and, at nightfall, the most dramatic sunsets in the northern Aegean.

If you are tempted to stay in the vicinity, it is also worth visiting the ancient site of **Chryse ❺** (open daily 9am–sunset; entrance fee), signposted as **Apollo Smintheon** from the village of **Gülpınar**. The actual ruins do not amount to much but Chryse is rich in Homeric significance, as the place from where Agamemnon took the daughter of the priest of Apollo. The priest was able to call on the gods for help and, although his daughter was eventually returned, Agamemnon demanded the mistress of Achilles as compensation. This led to a feud between the two Greek warriors that permeates the whole story of the *Iliad*.

From Behramkale, return to Ayvacık to pick up the highway which continues southeast along the coast. The small town of **Edremit** hardly justifies a stop, unless you are travelling by public transport and must wait here for a connection. Of far more interest is the modest little resort of **Ören ❻**, reached via the village of Burhaniye, from where a *dolmuş* (mini-bus) service runs to the resort. The beach is the best feature of the place and there is no shortage of accommodation along the road heading west to Küçükkuyu and Ayvalık. There is a regular ferry across the gulf to Akçay.

A sleepy Greek town

The highway curves around a broad, flat bay lined by ever-present olive groves, a ribbon of low-budget,

BELOW: the last remaining columns of the Temple of Athena, Assos.

Ayvalık has the largest olive-oil and soap factories in Turkey, exporting oil around the world. They have been at the centre of an environmental storm as the waste "black water" from the presses has a higher nitrogen content than sewage.

uninspiring Turkish holiday hotels and through charmingly green mountains before eventually reaching **Ayvalık** ❼. Ayvalık refers to 'place of the quince', but its pride and joy are its luscious olives grown on huge plantations in the surrounding area. En route, stop at one of the many stalls selling olive oil and soap. Ayvalık is a large resort town with a picture-book perfect fisherman's harbour overlooking a glistening bay across which some two dozen deep-green islands are scattered like thrown dice. The traveller will long remember sitting on the quay while a misty lavender sunset slowly transforms the distant isle of Lesbos into a thing of mystery. To an extent a victim of its own success, Ayvalık is relatively unknown to foreigners, but extremely well known to the local market, boasting some of Turkey's most extensive beaches, some of the best seafood dining in the country, and sadly, as in much of Turkey, too many jerry-built high-rise apartments on the outer fringes of the town.

Old Ayvalık is a sleepy town of handsome wooden houses lining meandering lanes that are more reminiscent of Greece than Turkey; indeed, the town was almost entirely Greek until the population exchange of 1923. Many of Ayvalık's well-off families are said to have come into their riches without much effort as a result of this exchange of neighbourhoods. The departing Greeks, convinced that they would one day return, mortared their gold and jewellery into the walls or squirrelled them under the floorboards, only for them to be discovered by the joyous new residents.

Local lore also has it that the reason for the construction of the maze of narrow back alleys that threads the entire town was to assist smugglers trying to escape from the authorities. Alas, today many of the older houses are falling steadily and surely into dilapidation due to quarrels over inheritance and the

BELOW: the harbour at Ayvalık.

inability of the owners to raise enough cash for repairs or renovations. Two Greek Orthodox churches in the town centre have been converted into mosques, another is closed – allegedly for restoration.

Map: on page 170

Sarımsaklı

For fun-in-the-sun lovers, **Sarımsaklı** ❽, 8 km (5 miles) to the south, has it all, with the finest white-grained sandy beaches in the whole of Turkey, windsurfing and a whole range of other activities, including daily group excursions by yacht. The waterfront promenade comes to life at night, with its scores of hotels, cafés, discos, bars and restaurants. The hotels range from low- to high-priced establishments along the beach to more interesting converted mansions dotted along the southern shore of Ayvalık Bay.

Perched on the highest point of land in the Ayvalık area, Şeytan Sofrasi (the Devil's Table) affords a spectacular view of Ayvalık Bay and the nearby pine-covered islets that meander gently off towards distant Lesbos.

Across the bay, a walking tour of **Alibey Adasi** ❾, an island also known as Cunda, will reveal beautiful bays, places to swim, interestingly ruined ancient walls and an occasional eccentricity. Its natural charms have managed to attract notables including Ptolomey, the Plinys Elder and Younger, and the German geographer Phillipson. Alibey is connected to the mainland by a causeway, but the boat journey from the quayside at Ayvalık is more pleasant.

On the island, the ancient village of **Cunda** has survived the Hellenistic, Roman and Byzantine periods and continues to thrive with an active little harbour lined by good seafood restaurants. The architecture of the town reflects the Greek style and there is a beautiful old Greek Orthodox church that is well worth a visit even though it's now in a deplorable condition. The vandalised religious frescoes show Matthew, Luke, John and Father Nikolai being released from a dolphin's mouth and deposited on the shore after 40 days of hiding.

Bergama

After leaving Ayvalık, the highway leads you south through ancient Aeolia, veering inland past boundless verdant fields, where farmers use modern tractors to prepare the soil for the new planting season, and the occasional huge open-cast gold mine. Along the road, traditional colourful horse-drawn wagons bring the workers (usually women) back from the fields. Periodically, gypsy camps huddle under a cluster of trees, their wagons pulled together for shelter.

On approaching **Bergama** (population 70,000), along the valley of the Bakır Çayı (the ancient Caicus River), you'll notice two odd-looking hills or mounds just outside the city, built overnight (so the story goes) to protect Bergama from invasion. Happily, foreigners are no longer feared, and Bergama is an important and fascinating destination for all, whether your own interests lie in rugs or in ruins. The town centre is busy and alive with character, worth a walk if you have the energy after the ruins. The colourful annual Bergama Festival, which lasts five days in early June, highlights local crafts, dance, music and food.

BELOW: a latter-day Venus arising from the surf.

Ancient capital on display in Bergama Museum.

RIGHT: the colonnaded Sacred Way (Via Tecta) on the Aesclepion.

Pergamon

Towering 300 metres (1,000 ft) above the city, the ruins at **Pergamon** command an extraordinary 360° view. One can understand how the city dominated the entire region, casting its long shadow over the realm. This great Hellenistic city was once a centre of culture, commerce and medicine to rival the other centres of Mediterranean Hellenism such as Ephesus, Alexandria and Antioch.

Pergamon rose to fame only during the carve-up of the empire in the years after the death of Alexander the Great, when his general Lysimachus "inherited" the settlement and its wealth. After his death, general Philetarus, in turn, passed the city on to his son Eumenes, founder of the Attalid dynasty, who ruled Pergamon, erected superb public buildings and defeated the invading Gauls. The city possessed a library as famous as that at Alexandria; it was here that parchment was invented after the jealous Egyptians cut off the supply of papyrus. As F.E. Peters says in his authoritative book *The Harvest of Hellenism*, Pergamon was not merely the hub of a thriving west-Anatolian economic complex, but was also an intellectual centre that possessed famous schools of grammar and medicine.

It came into particular prominence with Galen (AD 129–99), who studied medicine and philosophy in his native Pergamon and became known as the greatest physician and medical authority of ancient times. He began by practising medicine in a gladiator's clinic and greatly influenced medical developments in both East and West. Pergamon was also an important religious centre; worship of Zeus was succeeded by the cult of emperor worship and finally of exotic Egyptians deities.

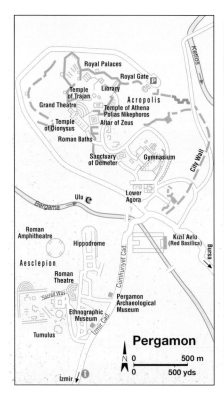

Pergamon

N 0 — 500 m
  0 — 500 yds

Allow a full day to visit the ruins; there are two main areas – the Aesclepion and the Acropolis – as well as many minor ruins and several sites within Bergama itself. Visitors without their own transport should consider a package tour that includes transport to and from both sites because they are some 8 km (5 miles) apart, and the steep road up to the Acropolis makes taxi rides inevitable. The best place to find a taxi is in the centre of town near the museum. Both sites are open daily 8.30am–5.30pm, until 7pm in summer (separate entrance fees).

**Maps:
Area 170
Site 176**

The Aesclepion

The ruins of the **Aesclepion** are about 1 km up the hill from the town centre and just about feasible to walk, if the day is not too hot. Initially dedicated to Aesclepius, the God of Healing, this was not your average medical clinic but the first complete health spa in history.

According to legend, Aesclepios, Apollo's son, was a doctor in Agamemnon's army at Troy, who used the blood of the Gorgon to restore slain men to life.

The process went something like this: a tired, overwrought Greek or Roman businessman, politician or military leader would arrive at the Aesclepion to be greeted by attendants. He was then led down the colonnaded **Via Tecta** (the Sacred Way, a busy bazaar of merchants and advisers) before choosing from a variety of services or sensuous experiences designed to eliminate his stress and relieve him of the burdens of the day. The prospective patient could seek out psychotherapy treatment (where dreams were analysed, 2,000 years before Freud), browse through good books in the library, or go for a dip in the sacred healing springs, and then round it all off with a visit to the 3,500-capacity theatre, for an exciting production of a play by Sophocles and some socialising with friends. The process could take as little as a few hours, but one usually spent a couple of days relaxing and recuperating from the strains of stressful Graeco-Roman life.

BELOW: all that is left of the Temple of Zeus; the rest is in Berlin.

The **Temple of Aesclepios**, easy to recognise due to its circular shape, is worth a closer look, if only to appreciate the fine skill of the stonemasons who created it. It was designed as a miniature of Rome's pantheon, and archaeologists have since found an underground tunnel that brought in water from a nearby spring. In the far southwest corner it is also worth seeking out the ruins of the well-preserved public latrines.

Back in town, stop at the small but satisfying **Pergamon Arkeoloji Müzesi** (Archaeological Museum; open daily 8.30am–5.30pm; entrance fee), on the main street near the tourist office. This is one of the earliest museums to collect artefacts from Pergamon and the surrounding area. Unfortunately, the best exhibits are in Berlin, and the museum has to content itself with a model of the impressive Temple of Zeus. Walking from here towards the Acropolis, you will pass several of the town's better restaurants.

Kızıl Avlu (Red Basilica)

Next, as you approach the Bergama Çayı, you come upon an imposing structure straddling the river, the **Kızıl Avlu** (Red Basilica; open daily 8.30am–5.30pm, until 7pm Apr–Oct; entrance fee). Dating from the 2nd or 3rd century AD, it was originally a vast temple to the Egyptian god, Serapis. Two underground tunnels carried water from the Selinus River, beneath the building's foundations. Later, it was converted into a basilica by the Byzantines, dedicated to either St John or St Paul, and was one of the seven churches of Asia Minor referred to in the Book of Revelation. Originally, the red-brick building was covered in marble but this has long been stripped off and nowadays only the floor paving retains its marble finish.

BELOW: the Red Basilica, Bergama.

There are a couple of interesting antique shops in the vicinity of the Red Basilica, but it helps to know something about what you want because the merchandise is a mixture of genuine antiques, old pots and pans and the odd fake. Just across the river, in the fascinating old Turkish Quarter, is the **Ulucamii** (Grand Mosque) commissioned by Sultan Beyazıt I in 1398–9.

Maps:
Area 170
Site 176

The old Turkish Quarter is a great spot for lunch, with its intriguing narrow streets, restaurants and brightly coloured shopfronts overloaded with perilously heaped goods. Bergama is particularly known for goatskins, fresh white cheeses, fruits, tulips, honey, yogurt, pistachios and the world-famous Bergama carpets. These strikingly exquisite deep red-and-blue patterned carpets hang in front of shops all over town, like the elegant laundry of a sultan.

The Acropolis

From the old Turkish Quarter, cross the Bergama Çayı, turn left and follow the road up a steep hill, past the Lower Agora and the Sanctuary of Demeter until you reach the car park of the fabled **Acropolis**. As you pass through the royal gate, you enter one of the greatest centres of Hellenist civilisation. The natural impulse is to wander around this vast site on your own at random, but it is probably more rewarding to follow the posted signs which provide helpful information to guide you along.

The Turkish Baths in Bergama.

Some background is also necessary to put the evolution, history and full contribution of Pergamon into perspective. Rather than opposing the invading Seleucids of Antioch, Philetarus joined forces with them in a win-win deal that created a powerful network of alliances. Pergamon made a deal to use large gifts from their treasury for presentation to nearby Greek coastal cities. Philetarus' successors, the Attalid dynasty, established the kingdom as a buffer state between the unruly Gauls and the Roman Empire. The kingdom grew to encompass the area from Cappadocia, the Mediterranean at Antalya, and the Aegean coast including Ephesus. At home, they were responsible for erecting the fine palaces, temples and other buildings that made Pergamon a glittering city to rival Athens or Alexandria.

BELOW: Bergama's rich red carpets are among the finest in the country.

In 133 BC, King Attalus II saw that his erratic nephew, Attalus III, had allowed the city to deteriorate to such an extent that he wished to cut him out of the succession. Therefore, upon his death, he willed his entire kingdom to the Romans, who gladly accepted it and transformed it into the capital of the Roman Empire in Asia Minor. From this toehold, they stretched out to conquer all of Anatolia.

To the left of the royal gate is the **Temple of Zeus**, of which nothing but the foundation remains. The altar itself was removed to the Pergamon Museum in East Berlin in the 19th century, where it was rebuilt in all its former glory. Turkey has petitioned the German government for its return. The altar is 12 metres (39 ft) high and its reliefs highlight a mythical battle between giants and the gods. Ironically it was the accidental discovery of a mosaic from the Temple of Zeus, in the 1870s, that led to the full-scale excavation of the site.

Your walk continues past the **Temple of Athena Polias Nikephoros**, the oldest temple in Pergamon, built in the Doric style at the end of the 4th century BC and dedicated to the city's patron goddess Athena "who brings victory".

Especially impressive, at least in one's imagination, are the ruins of the famed **Library of Pergamon**, once filled with over 200,000 volumes written on parchment and collected by King Attalus I, making it one of the most famous libraries of the times. It was later presented to Cleopatra by Antony as a wedding gift in Alexandria and perished with the rest of the huge Alexandrian collection in early Christian times.

Nearby stands the massive **Temple of Trajan**, dedicated to the deified Roman Emperor Trajan I, and completed during the reign of Hadrian II. From here, there is an excellent view of the geographical formation of the valley below that reveals how the sea once came all the way up to the base of the Acropolis.

Finally, you come to the dramatic **Grand Theatre**. The structure itself is impressive, with 80 rows divided into three tiers allowing seating for nearly 10,000. Its setting – right on the edge of the cliff, with the horizon stretching to infinity behind the actors – is incomparable. The steepness of the hill is very apparent, but this did not deter the builders from their task. Standing at the top and gazing down at a precipitous angle on to the stage with its long terrace, orchestra and royal box, it is difficult not to conjure up fleeting images of a solemn Greek chorus and the beginnings of modern drama: unforgettable characters like Medea, who slaughtered her children after being scorned by Jason, and, of course, Oedipus tearing out his eyes after learning he had slept with his mother. If you walk to the back of the orchestra it is still possible to make out the holes which received the temporary posts set up to create a scenic backdrop

In 240 BC, Livius Andronicus produced the first large-scale Greek plays in Rome. But Roman tastes were rather coarse, and the elegant Greek dramas degenerated into bawdy burlesque, pantomime, and spectacles such as wild beast shows and mock naval battles.

BELOW: Pergamon's spectacular theatre.

appropriate to whatever drama was being played out. This screening also hid the beautiful Temple of Dionysos, god of wine and pleasure, on the terrace below, so had to be removed between performances.

After these flights of fantasy, try testing the vaunted acoustics of the theatre. An actor (or tourist) standing centre-stage and talking in a normal voice can be heard even at the top. It is a lesson in design often forgotten in our electronic age.

Of all these important ruins, however, the **Gymnasium** is most interesting for it was here in the ephebeia that the young minds of Pergamon were shaped and guided. The institute of the ephebeia was initially conceived of as a two-year paramilitary course of study in the late Periclean age. Originally aimed at forming "sound bodies and sound minds" through military skills, it eventually evolved into something far broader and ambitious than mere drill and tactics. Indeed, the "curricula" we study in most schools and colleges today are based on this early idea, as expanded on by Aristotle and the ancients. Beyond the ephebeia, essentially a civic institution, lay the world of higher education. For the more serious and professionally inclined, there could be a career at one of the four major philosophical schools at Athens, or perhaps, even the medical school at Pergamon, an early and very busy university town. The substantial remains of the **baths** that can be seen date back to Roman times and it is still possible to make out the washbasins made of marble.

As you leave Pergamon take special notice of the **enclosure walls** of the ancient city, which show clear evidence of former restorations made during the Ottoman period when rocks, stones and bricks held together by mortar were used instead of the mortarless tight fit of granite slabs.

Maps:
Area 170
Site 176

BELOW: the Temple of Trajan, on the Acropolis.

Dikili, Foca and Candarlı

A short distance west of Bergama, **Dikili ⑪** is a small seacoast port where an enjoyable, breezy walk along the Kordon Promenade offers the visitor several fresh seafood restaurants, a number of modest hotels and an occasional view of ocean liners temporarily anchored in the bay. From Dikili it is a short journey south to **Çandarlı**, 40 km (25 miles) southwest of Bergama on the coast. The most direct route is south along the highway, passing rich valleys and beautiful coastline, before turning right at the village of Zeytindağ. A series of ancient Aeolian cities can be visited along the way if time allows, but their ruins consist of little more than a few walls and fragments of columns.

The fishing village of Çandarlı occupies a small peninsula jutting into the bay, dominated by a 14th-century Genoese fortress in excellent condition (closed to the public). Each summer the village comes alive with a modest influx of Turkish families on holiday, but although Çandarlı is the site of ancient Pitane, there is precious little to see. It is a quiet neighbourhood best seen on a Friday when the village square is at its liveliest for the weekly market.

Getting back to the highway, continue on around Çandarlı Bay (Çandarlı Körfezi) to **Aliağa**, another Aeolian city at the southern end of an inlet connected to the bay. Unfortunately, Aliağa's chief claim to fame

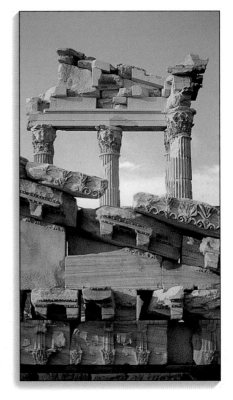

now seems to be the petrochemical complex which has been pouring waste into the beautiful blue waters of the nearby bay.

A few kilometres beyond Aliağa, a turning off to the right winds through the hills to eventually emerge along the coast, revealing a series of dramatic vistas and finally ending at the twin villages of Eski Foça and Yenifoça.

Most guidebooks, if they mention Foça at all, refer to **Eski Foça** ⓬, the site of ancient Phocaea on the southwest end of the peninsula, referred to by Herodotus: "The Phocaeans were the pioneer navigators of the Greeks, and it was they who showed their countrymen the way to the Adriatic, Tyrrhenia and the Spanish peninsula as far as Tartessus." To achieve these naval feats, the Phocaeans solved the problem of sailing heavily laden boats in shallow waters by designing a new flat-bottomed vessel. They were the founders of many colonies in the Sea of Marmara, the Black Sea and the Mediterranean, including the French city of Marseilles.

A Genoese fortress on a promontory divides the bays and once protected the harbour, around which are a number of charming Ottoman-Greek houses, many now restored as *pansiyons* and fish restaurants. It is also a reminder of the important trade in alum, used in cloth dying. The coast at Foça is one of the last haunts of the Mediterranean mark seal – about 400 are believed to survive globally – and local university students participate in a World Wildlife Fund protection project. It is worth driving on to the charming village of **Yenifoça**, which is surrounded by beautiful countryside and also has several restaurants, small hotels and *pansiyons*.

BELOW: a tempting beach between Foça and Aliağa.

Manisa

Returning to the main highway near the village of Buruncuk, turn right until you reach Menemen (also the name of a well-known breakfast dish of eggs,

tomatoes and peppers), then turn left and continue due east towards Manisa. This is a pleasant drive through dry but verdant low valleys rich in a variety of agricultural products – including corn, wheat, sunflowers, grapes and tobacco – until the land slowly flattens out into the sprawling plain of Gediz. Gradually, outlined sharply against the horizon, you will be able to pick out the great mountains of Bozdağ and Mt Sypilus, after which the ancient city of Magnesia ad Sypilum was named.

Map on page 170

Spread out below it, **Manisa** ⓭ is an unexpectedly interesting modern city, whose history boasts an imposing list of conquerors from the earliest Hittite cave-dwelling civilisations through the Greeks, Persians, Seleucids and Egyptians. The original settlement dates back to the time after the fall of Troy, although most of what you see today was rebuilt after the town was destroyed by Greek forces during their retreat in 1922. It was said that only a few hundred buildings, in a town that had contained almost 20,000 people, were still standing after they had left. What couldn't be taken away was Manisa's impressive location, with magnificent mountains looking down on the town. The workaday character of the town can come as a welcome relief after one too many visits to classical sites and, although relatively few tourists come here, there is enough to see to spend half a day or more in the town.

The tourist office in the centre of town dispenses a useful town map which pinpoints three interesting old mosques, some of Manisa's impressive variety of splendid Seljuk and Ottoman religious buildings. The finest is the **Muradiye Camii**, built in the 16th century by the great Turkish architect, Sinan. The *medrese* (religious school) next door now houses the **Archaeological Museum** (open Tues–Sun 9am–noon, 1–5.30pm; entrance fee), which has a fountain and mosaics from the synagogue at ancient Sart (Sardis).

BELOW: the tear-stained rock of Niobe, outside Manisa.

In a small park next to the Muradiye Camii, stands a statue of Tarzanı, celebrated citizen of Manisa. The story goes that every day, dressed only in loincloth, Tarzanı ran to the top of a nearby mountain, planted forests of pine trees all day and then ran back down to pray and meditate on the teachings of Mevlana, the founder of the mystical whirling dervish sect.

Walking downhill to the west, at the base of the Sandıkkale citadel, is the famed **Crying Rock of Niobe**, part of **Sipildağı Milli Parkı** ⓮ (National Park). This is allegedly the petrified remains of proud Niobe, the arrogant daughter of Tantulus (from whom we get the word "tantalise"). Her 14 beautiful children were slain by the goddess Leto to teach Niobe humility, after which the unfortunate Niobe begged Zeus to change her into stone and end her pain. Alas, the bereaved mother continued to weep, day and night, the very stone wet from her tears. Unhappily, the tale is more evocative than the site itself, which appears to be nothing more than weather-worn rock. A good time to visit Manisa is in April, when the weather is cool and the annual Mesir Bayramı (Spiced Candy Festival) is in full swing. Some say that the *mesir*, the candy in question, made of 41 different spices, has special healing properties; others tend to associate the tradition with the ambrosia and nectar of the Olympic gods; some experts say the candy has aphrodisiac qualities. ❏

İZMIR AND SARDIS

Old and new mix in İzmir, in a stunningly beautiful position by a perfect half-moon bay on the Aegean coast, while the modern world has left ancient Sardis untouched

Map on page 170

Turkey's second-largest port and third-largest city, **İzmir** ⑮ (ancient Smyrna) is also one of the country's major industrial and commercial centres, underlined by the important International Trade Fair held here each September. For international travellers, the city has traditionally been used as a base for excursions to the more imposing and well-known archaeological sites and ruins that lie to the the north (Pergamon) and south (Ephesus).

Ancient Smyrna

Things have not always been rosy. History shows that İzmir has experienced centuries of harsh rule by successive waves of occupying armies and jealous conquerors – all lured by her ideal geographic location and mild climate.

During the prehistoric period, the tiny initial settlement of Bayraklı, northeast of the centre, grew in size and importance under the Ionians, who took over the Smyrna region in the 9th century BC and turned it into a prosperous settlement. After a period of decline in the 4th century BC, Alexander the Great moved the settlement to a new citadel built on top of Mount Pagus and named it Smyrna.

In the 1st century BC came the Romans, who ushered in an era of peace and prosperity and, in their customary manner, added many grand civic buildings, of which only a few traces now remain. The city thrived as the harbour of its rival Ephesus silted up. Smyrna was one of the seven churches of Asia Minor and its octagenarian bishop, Polycarp, was martyred for refusing to sacrifice to the emperor.

Smyrna's salad days were brought to an abrupt halt when an Arab armada swept into the bay and sacked the town on its way towards the conquest of Constantinople. At the beginning of the 11th century, Seljuk Turks captured the city, only to be ousted by Crusaders, whose fleet sailed triumphantly into Smyrna's harbour, thereby placing the city in the hands of the Knights of Rhodes. It was next sacked by the Mongol hordes of Timur before falling finally to the Ottomans in 1415. Throughout the Ottoman period, the city remained predominantly Greek Orthodox, a wealthy terminus on the Silk Road with a cosmopolitan lifestyle.

Smyrna burns

After World War I, the city was taken over by Greece, who saw it as the centrepiece of a new Hellenist Empire. Their efforts failed and, in 1922, the Greek army found itself at the harbour in a desperate evacuation of Greek troops from Anatolia. One evening, a mysterious fire suddenly began to burn deep in a Turkish quarter of the city. First from shore, and then from a unique position aboard the British warship, *Iron Duke*, the British correspondent G. Ward Price,

LEFT: classical beauty.
BELOW: a contemporary portrait.

Tile detail on the Konak Camii, İzmir.

wrote a dramatic eyewitness account of the spreading blaze. "Without exaggeration," he wrote, "tonight's holocaust is one of the biggest fires in the world's history." Pandemonium broke loose and thousands of crazed people gathered on the quay waiting to be rescued by the British boats. Untold numbers of others perished in the inferno. Who started the blaze? And why? Price left the big questions unanswered.

One of the consequences of these traumatic events was the great population exchange of Asia Minor in 1923, when the entire remaining Greek population was sent to Greece in exchange for the ethnic Turks who resided in Greece and the Greek islands. Aside from a few Levantine families, İzmir's population today knows almost nothing of its rich Greek past.

İzmir today

Once the equal of the fabled city of Troy, and a rival to Pergamon as a centre of education and medicine, İzmir now attracts throngs of less privileged Turks from all over Anatolia and the East searching for work to support their families. As the city develops, it is forced to confront the familiar problems of the modern era – rapid expansion and sprawling urbanisation. Still, the centre feels cosmopolitan and lively. The main **tourist office**, Gaziosmanpaşa Bulvarı, tel: 0232-445 7390, lies between the Efes and Hilton hotels.

The imposing fortress of **Kadifekale** Ⓐ on Mount Pagus rises up majestically behind the city and offers an unparalleled view of the harbour and city below. The grounds of the "Velvet Castle" contain a wonderful mixture of people: picnicking local folk, well-dressed citizens out for a stroll, and young romantics smiling deeply into each others' eyes over glasses of Turkish tea in one of the

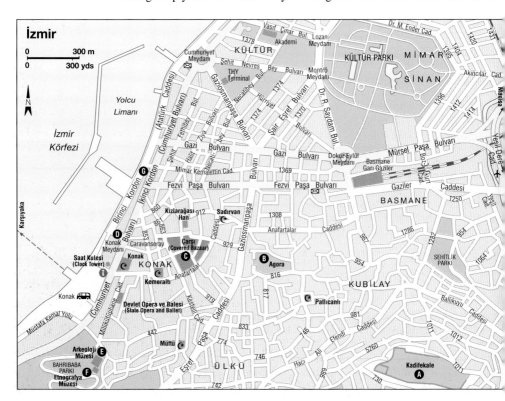

gently shaded outdoor cafés. Just inside the main gate, climb up the steps lead-ing to the top of the wall overlooking the city. Every few steps you take along this parapet reveal another view of the city from a different perspective, from Çeşme on the southern horizon, towards Karşıyaka across the bay, and to Manisa and the mountains in the northeast.

Shopping then and now

Smyrna's ancient marketplace is reached via a network of narrow streets filled with friendly people, playing children and lots of cats. The **Agora** **B** (open daily 8.30am–noon, 1–5pm; entrance fee) dates back to Alexandrian times, but what you see today is a relatively small clearing surrounded by a fence and containing a variety of colonnades around a central esplanade built during the reign of Marcus Aurelius in the 2nd century AD.

On leaving the Agora, turn right towards the main street, Gaziosmanpaşa Bulvarı. Cross this road and after about 100 metres/yards, take one of the small streets on the left into the **Çarşı** (Covered Bazaar) **C**. Although it cannot be compared to the one in Istanbul, it does possess character and atmosphere. Most of the stalls and shops are closed on Sundays.

Pushing through its crowded, narrow and winding streets, you finally emerge on the waterfront at **Konak Meydanı** (Square) **D**, with its distinctive clock tower and statue dedicated to the first Turkish citizen who gave his life to stop the Greek invasion of İzmir in 1920. There is also a charming **mosque**, dating from 1748, ornately decorated with Kütahya tiles. Now a pedestrian area, Konak combines its roles as a park and a ferry dock for commuters to Karşıyaka, which lies directly across the bay. Nearby, off Fevzi Paşa Caddesi,

Maps:
Area 170
City 186

TIP

The easiest way to get to the Kadifekale is by bus No. 33 from the Konak bus station (buy the ticket first from the small booth at the bus stop).

BELOW: one of the many ferries to serve İzmir port.

the **Kızlarağası Han** is a reconstructed Ottoman market, now housing a variety of entertaining craft workshops, shops and a courtyard café.

İzmir's best museums are just south of Konak in Bahribaba Park and can be reached on foot within a few minutes. The **Arkeoloji Müzesi (Archaeological Museum)** (open daily 8.30am–5pm, to 6pm in summer; entrance fee) has a varied and interesting collection of Roman monumental art downstairs, while the other floors are devoted to Greek art from archaic to Hellenistic times. The exhibits in the neighbouring **Etnografya Müzesi (Ethnographic Museum)** (open Tues–Sun 9am–noon, 1–5pm, to 5.30pm in summer; entrance fee) have a wider appeal and include a reconstructed Ottoman pharmacy, a bridal chamber and a circumcision room. There is also a display devoted to the art of manufacturing the blue beads that serve as an antidote to the evil eye, as well as exhibits on camel wrestling and rope-making.

Just after sunset, take a leisurely stroll along the palm tree-lined **Birinci Kordon** and watch hundreds of locals come out each night to promenade along the splendid bay from Cumhuriyet Meydanı to the Atatürk Museum. Take a seat on the quay and feel the *imbat*, the famous gently cooling breeze of İzmir, and enjoy this justly famous city and its softly seductive Mediterranean caress.

Çeşme

One hour's drive (80 km/50 miles) west of İzmir, on the tip of the peninsula, is the strikingly beautiful and very popular resort town of **Çeşme** ⑯, which was originally sought out for its healing thermal baths at nearby **Ilica**. Çeşme is easily reached by car or public transport from İzmir, and there are regular ferry services to the Greek island of **Chios** and the Italian port of Brindisi.

İzmir has a sizeable black population – the descendants of Sudanese slaves used as domestic servants from the 16th–19th centuries. Many remained with their families after the abolition of slavery.

BELOW: lightly roasted tourists on a beach near Çeşme.

There are many small hotels and one may easily settle in to enjoy the special experience that is Çeşme: the slow pace, well-preserved Ottoman domestic architecture, a Turkish bath, and freshly caught seafood at any of the restaurants that line the promenade looking out to sea. There is a small but helpful tourist office near the 14th-century Genoese **castle** where the international Çeşme Pop Song Festival is held every year in late July. It also contains an uninspired small archaeological museum (open Tues–Sun 9am–noon, 1–5.30pm; entrance fee).

Visitors do not come to Çeşme for an exciting nightlife, but for more active entertainment visit neighbouring **Ilica**. It is only a couple of miles to the east and here you will find a good beach, pubs and discos.

Maps:
Area 170
City 186

Sart (Sardis)

Sardis ⑰ (open daily 8am–5pm; entrance fee) is inland, 99 km (59 miles) east of İzmir. It has been occupied for over 3,000 years, developing from a prehistoric lakeside community to a major Roman and Byzantine city. Along the way, it was the capital of the Lydian empire, which had the curious custom of eagerly condoning the prostitution of young girls in order to earn their dowries. An early king, Candaules, allowed one of his bodyguards to glimpse his beautiful wife naked; discovering this, the queen gave Gyges, the bodyguard, the option of death or of murdering her husband. Gyges was the ancestor of Croesus, the last of the Lydian kings, who gave away at least 10 tons of gold and funded the building and decoration of the lavish Temple of Artemis at Ephesus. The expression "rich as Croesus" is still applied to someone who flaunts his riches.

Anyone in search of a cash injection today should stop at the Pactolus stream, which flows next to the unpaved road that leads off the main highway to the

The Agamemnon thermal baths near Çeşme.

BELOW: the Marble Court, Sardis, in its reconstructed glory.

Temple of Artemis. It was said to have been affected by Midas's "golden touch" when he bathed in its headwaters.

The Lydians also claimed to have invented all of the pastimes that were common to them and the Greeks, including dice and knucklebones. A more significant invention attributed to King Alyattes, the father of Croesus, was the invention of coins, first made of "electrum", an alloy of gold and silver. Usually these were without inscriptions and bore only the lion's head – the royal emblem of Sardis. Croesus introduced coins of pure gold and silver.

The most spectacular structure at Sardis is the **Temple of Artemis** (separate entrance fee), whose massive scale – about 45 x 100 metres (150 x 320 ft) – rivals the three great Ionian temples at Ephesus, Samos and Didyma. Construction began around 550 BC, but it was destroyed in the Ionian revolt and Alexander the Great paid for repairs. The temple is in the Ionic order with eight columns at the short end and 20 on the sides. The capitals are some of the most beautiful in existence. The altar sits at the west end of the temple, a peculiar feature perhaps built to avoid making it face towards the slope of the hill.

The Acropolis and other sights

Bozdağ (Mount Tmolus) looms above the broad plain of the Gediz Cayı (ancient Hermus River). Behind the city is the Acropolis, considered impregnable. Legend says that a Persian soldier saw a defender drop his helmet over the walls and climb down to remove it. Using this route, the expert Persian climbers were able to break through and Croesus lost his empire in about 547 BC.

The ascent to the acropolis takes about 45 minutes and requires sturdy walking shoes, but the fantastic panoramic view from the peak makes the

An early method for collecting gold dust was to lay sheepskins in a shallow part of the stream to catch the particles. The legend of the Golden Fleece was supposed to have developed in this way from a gold-bearing branch of the Phasis River.

BELOW: the 1st-century synagogue at Sardis.
RIGHT: detail of a mosaic at Sardis.

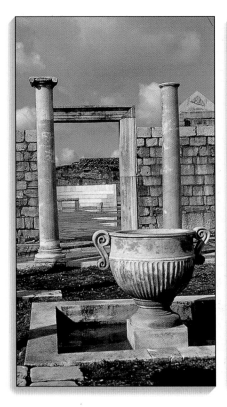

breathless effort worthwhile. On the far side of the plain is the Lydian **royal cemetery**, whose numerous eerie burial mounds give it the name Bin Tepe or "Thousand mounds". Just beyond Bin Tepe lies **Marmara Gölü**, the Gygaean lake, on whose shores there were settlements in the 3rd century BC. These natural landmarks played a part in Latin and Greek literature. In the *Iliad*, Homer sang of the Gygaean lake, "snowy" Mount Tmolus and the "eddying" Hermus. In Ovid's *Metamorphoses*, a personified Tmolus judged the musical competition between Apollo and Pan.

Return to the main highway and cross the road to a fascinating complex of buildings. The **Marble Court** is a grandiose entrance to the Roman gymnasium and bath complex, constructed in the 2nd century AD and carefully reconstructed over a 10-year period. Its columns are decorated with heads of gods and satyrs, including the memorable "Laughing Faun", a masterpiece of carving, whose mischievous smile and features show Greek influences.

The remains of the largest ancient **synagogue** ever found are in a large hall on one side of the **gymnasium**. A marble table with eagles on the legs was set up at the altar end and a wallshrine preserved at the other, apparently in defiance of Judaism's ban on human and animal representation in temples. South of the bath-gymnasium complex is the **House of Bronzes**, which owes its name to the bronze utensils found inside, including an ash shovel decorated with a cross and two dolphins.

The nearest accommodation is 9 km (6 miles) away in the nondescript town of **Salihli** – most people stay in İzmir. There is a basic, though adequate, restaurant on the main road just opposite the Roman remains. Even better, take a picnic and spread out on the grass near the Temple of Artemis. ❑

Map on page 170

BELOW: cultivated fields pattern the landscape.

THE SOUTHERN AEGEAN

*The Southern Aegean not only offers hedonistic nightlife,
shopping and dining but is also home to a host of spectacular
ancient sites that vie for the visitor's attention*

Map
on page
170

The town of **Kuşadası** ⑱, which means "bird island", is set in a superb gulf and is known for its sparkling water, broad sandy beaches and large marina. Less than 20 years ago, sleepy Kuşadası was considered only as a stopover on the way to Efes (Ephesus); now dozens of hotels and holiday villages line its shores, and an ever-increasing number of seafood restaurants and discos cater to tourists, both Turkish and foreign. Traditionally, the carpet and leather shops also do a brisk trade with passengers from the many cruise ships that dock for the day, allowing enough time for a trip to Ephesus and a serious shopping expedition. However here, as in much of Turkey, a stream of bad luck, including the 1998 earthquake and more recent global political events, has hit Turkey's coastal tourism badly. The surviving businesses compete agressively for the remaining custom; expect to be hassled. At night, the tempo is more relaxed.

The tiny **Güvercin Adası (Dove Island)** is connected to the mainland by a causeway. Its romantic setting includes a well-maintained garden, filled with flowers, surrounding the restored 14th- or 15th-century fortress that now houses a thumping disco. Beaches close to town tend to get quite crowded in summer. The best is **Kadınlar Denizi**, 2.5 kms (1.3 miles) from town. Otherwise, the town has a couple of hamams (Turkish baths), but little in the way of sightseeing.

LEFT: shimmering pools at sunset, Pamukkale.
BELOW: Dove Island, Kuşadası.

Day trips from Kuşadası

If you want greater tranquillity, head for the **Dilek Yarımadası Milli Parkı (Dilek Peninsula National Park)** ⑲ (open daily 8am–6.30pm; entrance fee), 28 km (17 miles) south of Kuşadası, though the park can get crowded at weekends. Lush forests include laurels, red and black pines, and several types of lime, chestnuts and oaks found only in northern Anatolia. Seals and turtles are government-protected, living and breeding along the coastline. Numerous species of reptiles, birds and mammals proliferate in the mountainous terrain.

Day trips can also be made from Kuşadası to Ephesus, Priene, Miletus and Didyma. Some tours cram a visit to all four sights into one day but these are not advisable since Ephesus alone is so huge that it requires the best part of one day to take it in. Even the one-day tours to Priene, Miletus and Didyma may induce temple fatigue, which is particularly regrettable when Didyma – the most interesting and enjoyable of the three sites – is left until last. You can visit any of the sights by public transport from Kuşadası, changing bus at Söke.

Another alternative is to ask for a guide at one of the tourist agencies and hire a taxi which will take you to Ephesus, the museum of Selçuk, the Church of the

BELOW: Harbour Street, downtown Ephesus.

Seven Sleepers and the House of the Blessed Virgin (Meryemana). Guides, who congregate outside the entrance at Ephesus, are more interested in getting you into their tourist shop than they are in informing you.

Efes (Ephesus)

Unmatched by any archaeological site anywhere in terms of sheer magnitude, **Efes (Ephesus)** ⑳ appeals to every visitor, from the serious archaeologists delighted by the visual evidence of long pondered facts and figures, to the casual visitor titillated by ribald hints of brothel complexes.

Information on the origin of the founders of Ephesus is inconclusive. Strabo and Pausanias agree that the city was founded by the legendary Amazons, but that the majority of the population were the Carians and Lelegians. According to Herodotus, the Carians considered themselves Anatolia's oldest inhabitants; Halicarnassus (Bodrum) was their capital.

Athenaeus relates the colourful legend of how the original settlement came into being: it seems the founders could not decide on a location for a site, so they consulted an Apollonian oracle which gave them suitably cryptic instructions to establish the city at the spot indicated by a fish and a boar. Androklos, the son of Kodros, the king of Athens, and his friends wanted to fry some fish while contemplating this advice. A fish jumped out of the frying pan, scattering live coals and setting on fire a thicket in which a boar was hiding. The boar rushed out and was killed by Androklos, thus fulfilling the prophesy. The new city was founded at the northern foot of Mount Pion.

By the 6th century BC, Ephesus had prospered, which is perhaps why it was the first city chosen for conquest by King Croesus of Lydia in 560 BC. The

Ephesians naively stretched a rope from the Temple of Artemis to the city and retreated behind it, believing the goddess would protect them. The Lydian army entered the city without a struggle, but contrary to expectations Croesus treated the captives as friends.

The **Archaic Temple of Artemis** (564–546 BC) was still under construction at that time. To please the Ephesians and the goddess, Croesus presented the temple with a set of column capitals carved with reliefs, one of which had his name inscribed on it. These relics are now in the British Museum, London.

In 356 BC – tradition states it was the night of Alexander the Great's birth – the temple was set on fire by a lunatic named Herostatus who wanted to be remembered for posterity, a goal he apparently achieved. The Ephesians at once began work on an even finer structure which, when completed, ranked as one of the Seven Wonders of the World. Work was still in progress when Alexander arrived in 334 BC. He was so impressed by their industriousness that he offered to pay for all expenses if he could be permitted to make the dedication inscription in his name. The offer was politely refused on the grounds that one god should not make a dedication to another. Today, a lone Ionian column rests on a few foundation blocks, often submerged in the marsh – a pitiful reminder of what was once a glorious stone structure. The site of the temple is passed on the road between Selçuk and Ephesus but is hardly worth a detour.

The worship of the mother goddess, called Cybele in prehistoric Anatolia, Isis in Egypt, and Vesta in Rome and Latin–Arab territories continued straight down to Roman Artemis, who is often depicted with three staggered rows of nodes on her chest. These were originally thought to be an overabundance of breasts. Later interpretation has identified them as eggs, also a symbol of fertility.

Maps:
Area 170
Site 195

BELOW: the Celsus Library, Ephesus.

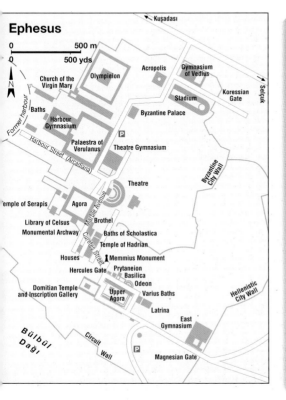

Ephesus

0 ⊢—————⊣ 500 m
0 ⊢—————⊣ 500 yds

Kuşadası

Church of the Virgin Mary
Olympieion
Acropolis
Gymnasium of Vedius
Stadium
Koressian Gate
Selçuk
Baths
Harbour Gymnasium
Byzantine Palace
Former Harbour
Harbour Street (Arcadiana)
Palaestra of Verulanus
Theatre Gymnasium
P
Byzantine City Wall
Theatre
Temple of Serapis
Agora
Marble Avenue
Library of Celsus
Brothel
Monumental Archway
Baths of Scholastica
Curetes Street
Temple of Hadrian
Houses
Memmius Monument
Hercules Gate
Prytaneion
Basilica
Domitian Temple and Inscription Gallery
Upper Agora
Odeon
Varius Baths
Hellenistic City Wall
Latrina
East Gymnasium
Bülbül Dağı
Circuit Wall
P
Magnesian Gate

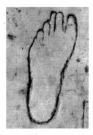

Detail from a supposed brothel advertisement on a wall at Ephesus.

Ephesus entered a golden age during the Roman era, when Augustus declared Ephesus the capital of the province of Asia Minor in place of Pergamon. An inscription from Ephesus at this time calls itself "the first and greatest metropolis of Asia", and indeed it was. As the permanent residence of the governor of Rome, it had a population of 250,000, and was the trade and banking centre of Asia; the only threat to its prosperity being the constant silting up of the harbour by the Cayster River. Despite many inspired or misguided attempts to deepen the channel or divert the river, Ephesus now lies 5 km (3 miles) from the sea.

St Paul arrived in AD 53, and gained enough followers to establish the first Christian church of Ephesus. A backlash against the new religion was spurred by secular rather than sacred interests. The jeweller Demetrius and the others who had a lucrative business selling silver statues of Artemis were incensed by Paul's proselytising, and arranged a rally of thousands in the theatre shouting, "Great is Artemis Ephesia!" St Paul, whose friends Gaios and Aristarhos were dragged into the theatre, wanted to face down the crowd but was restrained from doing so, departing shortly thereafter for Macedonia. Yet the new religion spread quickly in Ephesus and eventually supplanted the worship of Artemis. St John later spent several years here.

The ruins

BELOW: statue of Scholastica at the entrance to her baths.

Most of the surviving ruins of Ephesus belong to the Roman imperial period. An outstanding exception is the **Circuit Wall**, built by Lysimachus and a fine example of a Hellenistic fortification. It has disappeared on the lower ground, but still stands along the crest of **Bülbül Dağı** (Nightingale Mountain), to the south of the city, where anyone energetic enough to climb up will find the wall well-preserved and incorporating gates and towers of high-quality workmanship.

The road leading from the Kuşadası highway to the ruins brings one to the **Gymnasium of Vedius**, a 2nd-century gift to the city from a wealthy citizen. In typical Roman fashion, the building combines both the gymnasium and the baths, which had hot, cold and tepid water, rich mosaics and statuary. The horseshoe-shaped **Stadium** was built during the Hellenistic period but restored to its present condition during Nero's reign (AD 54–68). Across the road to the south is the **Church of the Virgin Mary**, built in the 2nd century as a museum and converted to a basilica in the 4th century. This was the first church in Christian history dedicated to the Virgin.

The city's most impressive road, **Harbour Street** (Arcadiana), is named after Arcadius, who remodelled it in AD 395–408. It stretches between the harbour and the theatre. About 500 metres (1,600 ft) long and 11 metres (36 ft) wide, both sides of the streets were covered with porticos paved with mosaics; behind these were the stores. One of the excavations unearthed an inscription that was a startling revelation. It indicated that the colonnaded street was lit at night by 50 lamps, at a time when only Rome and Antioch shared this distinction.

Beside the road, the imposing 2nd-century **Harbour Bath** is one of the largest structures in Ephesus,

Maps:
Area 170
Site 195

with a 30-metre (100-ft) long elliptical pool and 11-metre (36-ft) marble columns supporting a vaulted brick roof. Next door, the **Harbour Gymnasium** has a colonnaded courtyard, paved with mosaic.

The **Theatre**, constructed during the reign of Lysimachos and carved into the slopes of Mount Pion, is still an impressive structure, large enough to hold 24,000 people and still used for the Ephesus Festival, held each spring. From the top seats, there is a splendid view of the entire city. Its excellent acoustics were further enhanced in ancient times by the judicious placing of clay or bronze sounding vessels. Below the theatre stands the **Library of Celsus**, an edifice so grandiose that it is easy to imagine it as part of a movie set left behind after the shooting of a Roman spectacular. It was actually built in AD 114–17 by Tiberius Julius Aquila for his father Tiberius Julius Celsus, whose sarcophagus is in a tomb under the library. The fabulous façade has been reconstructed from the original fallen masonry. Behind it, a stepped road passing the **Agora** leads to the **Temple of Serapis**, which had eight massive columns with Corinthian capitals that individually weighed 57 tons, although there are indications that the structure was never completed.

At the library, the street turns and becomes the **Curetes Street**, which stretches to the **Hercules Gate**. At the beginning of the street on the left stand the **Baths of Scholastica**, built in the 1st century and reconstructed in the early 5th century by the lady whose headless statue can be seen in the entrance hall. The three-storeyed building was very popular during the Roman Empire, when both the poor and the rich could use the complex of heated rooms and pools free of charge, although only the rich could afford the time to linger for hours, discussing politics and gossip while being massaged by their servants.

In his will, Aquila left 25,000 denari to help maintain the library and buy new works. At its finest, the library contained 12,000 scrolls, which were kept in an inner chamber, surrounded by an outer wall and air cushion to help steady the temperature and humidity. The library was destroyed by invading Goths in AD 262.

BELOW: the Arch of Hadrian.

About 1.5 km (1 mile) from Ephesus is the Cave of the Seven Sleepers, a network of catacombs where seven early Christians hid from persecution in the 2nd century, and were walled in by the Imperial Guard. Legend has it that they fell asleep and awoke 200 years later once Christianity had become the state religion.

BELOW: the İsa Bey Camii, Selçuk.

Next door, a peristyle house known as the **Brothel** because of an inscription found in the lavatory has some delightful mosaics, and traces of frescoes. An overly endowed clay Priapus found in the well is now in the museum.

One of the most memorable sights in Ephesus is the fascinating **Temple of Hadrian** on Curetes Street. Built by AD 138, the four Corinthian columns support an arch with a bust of Tyche, the patron goddess of the city, in the centre. The plaster cast on the site of the original frieze (now in the Ephesus Museum), has three 3rd-century panels depicting gods and goddesses, including Artemis Ephesia, and a 4th-century addition of the Byzantine Emperor Theodosius and his family. This is remarkable when one considers Theodosius's position as a vehement opponent of paganism. A number of private homes and smaller shops are also open to the public, offering a compelling portrait of everyday life.

Selçuk

The small town of **Selçuk** ㉑, some 20 km (12 miles) northeast of Kuşadası, owes its importance to its proximity to Ephesus and the Ephesus Museum. From the tourist office, near the main bus stop, it is a 30-minute walk to Ephesus, though in the heat of summer even this short journey can be exhausting. Taxis, however, are plentiful. There are also a number of decent restaurants in Selçuk, any one of which is preferable to those located immediately outside the entrance to Ephesus itself. Given that the town also has some attractive accommodation possibilities to suit most budgets, plus a couple of lively bars, it is worth considering an overnight stay here.

The **Ephesus Museum** (open Tues–Sun 8.30am–noon, 12.30–5pm; entrance fee) has an exceptional collection, all thoughtfully displayed and labelled.

Mosaics and frescoes from the houses at Ephesus, statues, coins and relics all create a vivid impression of the rich decoration of the ancient city. The most famous exhibits include the bronze statuette of Eros on a dolphin; two marble statues of the "many-breasted" Artemis; a fresco of the philosopher Socrates, with a Greek inscription; a marble statue of Priapus, balancing a tray of fruit on his pride and joy; and a reconstruction of a Roman house. Also take a look at the museum's small ethnographic section.

The **Basilica of St John** is located south of the Seljuk fortress on the hill of Ayasoluk. St John is said to have lived the last years of his life here; after his death, a shrine was located over his grave. Emperor Justinian erected a monumental basilica here in the 6th century, its central dome surrounded by several smaller domes forming the shape of a cross.

The burial chamber of St John is at the end of the central nave, raised by two steps and covered with marble reproductions of the original mosaics. The dome is supported by marble and brick pillars, between which are blue-veined marble columns bearing the monograms of Emperor Justinian and his wife, Theodora. The chapel has frescoes showing St John, Jesus and a saint. The baptistry was constructed in the 5th century, before the main church. At the foot of the hill are the ruins of the elegant late-14th-century **İsa Bey Camii** (usually open, except at prayer times).

According to one tradition, the Virgin Mary came to Ephesus with St John and lived here from AD 37 until her death in AD 48. Her house, the **Meryemana** (8 km/5 miles south of Selçuk; open dawn–dusk; entrance fee), is worth a visit if only for the refreshing wooded paths and mountain streams. It has been converted to a chapel and is a popular place of pilgrimage for both Christians and Muslims, who venerate Mary as a saint. The icons are reputed to have curative powers attested to by the crutches and braces left here by healed pilgrims.

Şirince, an old Greek town only 8 km (5 miles) east of Selçuk, makes a delightful destination after visiting Ephesus. There is nothing of archaeological or historical significance, just fresh air, old Greek houses and an atmosphere of repose and relaxation.

Priene

The ancient Ionian city of **Priene** ㉒ (open daily 8am–5.30pm, to 7.30pm in summer; entrance fee) is reached by a short drive from Kuşadası through some of the most beautiful scenery in Turkey. The road winds through silver-tinged olive groves, fields of cotton bursting with delicate rosebud blooms or fluffy white balls of ripe cotton, and pine-covered hills, past peaceful hamlets surrounded by hot-pink oleanders.

Priene is in a spectacular location, resting on a slab of hillside above the Maeander Valley, with the pine-clad spur of Mount Mycale presiding majestically over the ruins. Once an active port, the town was landlocked by rising silt along the Maeander River. By the 4th century BC, it became necessary to find a new site. New Priene was laid out in a strict geometric gridiron pattern devised by city planner Hippodamos of Miletus in about 450 BC.

Maps:
Area 170
Site 195

Embroidered slippers fit for a sultan.

BELOW: modern gladiators in the ancient stadium.

One of the first structures seen after entering the site through the northwest gate is the small, horseshoe-shaped **Theatre**, built in the classical Hellenistic style with an altar at the centre, used for sacrificial offerings to Dionysus.

Immediately below the theatre are the foundations of a Byzantine church. Nearby is the **Agora**, the central market of the ancient city. The most important monument of Priene is the **Temple of Athena Polias**, designed by the architect Pytheos, who also planned the Mausoleum of Halicarnassus. It was considered so beautiful that its design was used as a template of Ionic architecture for over 200 years.

Milet (Miletus)

The present ruins of **Milet (Miletus)** ❷❸ (open daily 8.30am–5.30pm, to 7.30pm in summer; entrance fee) date from its second foundation after the original city was destroyed by the Persians in 494 BC. Like Priene, the new town was planned according to the principles of Hippodamus. Ephesus may enjoy greater fame today, but early Miletus was the most important city of the Ionian league. Its favourable position, on the Gulf of Latmos, and spirit of enterprise made it not only the wealthiest emporium of its time but also an intellectual centre.

Herodotus relates that the site was inhabited by Cretans and Carians until the arrival of Neleos, son of Kodros of Athens. The intruders had no women of their own, so they slaughtered the men and married their wives. However, this did not lend itself to domestic tranquillity as the women swore an oath never to sit at a table with their new husbands or to call them by their name.

BELOW: the theatre at Miletus.

The best time to visit Miletus is in spring when flowers blanket the site. The finest surviving building here is undoubtedly the 1st-century BC **Theatre**, which

sits on a hillside facing the car park and seats 15,000 people. On several front-row seats are inscriptions – such as "place of the Jews also called the God-fearing" or "place of the goldsmiths of the Blues" – reserving a seat for those individuals or groups whose names they bear.

Map on page 170

Most of the buildings to the east are badly ruined. The city's main sanctuary was the **Shrine of Apollo Delphinius**, whose earliest levels date back to the 6th century BC. The pinkish Hellenistic building was reconstructed in Roman times. Nearly 200 inscriptions found here have proved crucial in recording the early history of the city.

The **Bouleuterion** (Council Chamber), built between 175 and 164 BC, during the reign of Seleucid King Antiochus IV Epiphanes, is one of the oldest buildings surviving in Miletus. Inside are the remains of an altar dedicated to the Roman imperial cult. Opposite, there was a three-storey **Nymphaeum**, built in the 2nd century AD and elaborately decorated with reliefs of nymphs. It was fed by a now ruined aqueduct which distributed water to the entire city.

The best-preserved buildings in this area are the **Baths of Faustina**, built in about AD 150 as a gymnasium and bath complex. They were dedicated to Empress Faustina, the extravagant wife of Marcus Aurelius, and modelled on the Roman *thermae*, the forerunner of the Turkish *hamam*. The exercise field was to the west of the bath's long entrance hall. A number of small rooms, used for lectures and discussions, lead off the main hall. The **Hellenistic Stadium**, which could hold 15,000 spectators, has two monumental gates.

Bursting cotton buds drift like snow across the arid summer landscape.

A short distance from the main site are a small **museum** (open daily 8.30am–12.30pm, 1.30–5.30pm; entrance fee) and the beautiful **Ilyas Bey Camii**, built in 1404 by a member of the Turkish Menteşe dynasty which ruled this part of Anatolia before it was claimed by the Ottomans. Ilyas Bey built the mosque to celebrate his return, after being held hostage in Timur's court. The minaret has collapsed but the handsome design, delicate grillwork on the massive doors and the carving on the sacred niche make it a masterpiece.

BELOW: waiting for wisdom at the Didyma temple.

Didyma

The single most impressive single monument on the west coast is at **Didyma ㉔** (open daily 8am–5.30pm in winter, 9am–7pm in summer; entrance fee). If you visit only one of the local classical sites (other than Ephesus), it should be Didyma's **Temple of Apollo**. The oracle's earliest recorded prophesies date to the 6th century BC. This early phase in Didyma's history ended when it was sacked by the Persians in 494 BC. Didyma remained silent for 150 years until Alexander the Great arrived, when the dry fountain of prophecy gushed to life and the oracle announced that Alexander was the son of Zeus, a result which pleased him so much that he retrieved the cult statue of Apollo from Persia and ordered the building of a new super-temple, which can still be seen today.

Take time to sit in one of the small cafés and contemplate the site, especially just before sunset, when the marble of the immense columns takes on softened shades, and the riveting Head of Medusa, with furrowed brow and tight ringlets, looks most sympathetic.

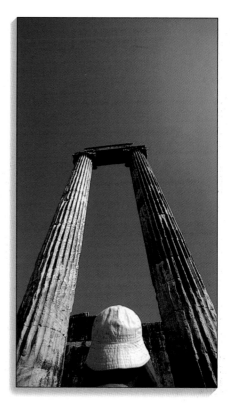

Altınkum is a small resort at the tip of Didyma's peninsula, a few miles south of the Temple of Apollo. Altınkum (Golden Sand) Beach lives up to its name and a growing number of hotels and restaurants is springing up to service summer visitors. The area is best known for Turkish family camping holidays.

Little remains of the ancient Greek town of **Notion**, on the coast some 25 km (15 miles) northwest of Kuşadası, but the site is picturesque. At **Klaros ㉕**, less than a mile away, there is a little more to see. In ancient times Klaros was known for its temple and oracle of Apollo dating from the 4th century BC, built with huge Doric columns; this is now being excavated. The site of the sacred spring that inspired the oracle can still be identified.

Lake Bafa and Heraklea

If you want to take refuge away from the trendier coastal areas, head for **Bafa Gölü (Lake Bafa)**, once part of the sea but cut off by the silting Maeander; its clear, blue water is now fresh. Across the lake is **Heraklea ad Latmos ㉖**, one of the most romantic and compelling ancient sites in Anatolia (entrance fee). It can be approached by land off the main Söke-Milas highway, or by boat from the shore of Lake Bafa (take the road south from Söke). Although situated on the Ionian coast, the city belongs in character to Caria.

The serrated crest of **Mount Latmos**, some 1,500 metres (4,921 ft) high, led to its name of Beşparmak (Five Fingers). A bastion of this wild and formidable mountain curves down to the village of **Kapıkırı**, while the classical walls of ancient Heraklea run up the ridge. They are an outstanding feature of the site, their gates, towers, parapets and roofs lending a fairytale atmosphere to the setting. An excursion to the remote hermitages of Mount Latmos is only

BELOW: Aphrodisias won a reputation as a statue factory.

recommended with a guide, for as writer Freya Stark said, one might be "curiously uncertain as to where the confines of reality end or begin." Around the village of Kapıkırı itself there is plenty to see and signposts indicate the directions to take. One sight not to be missed is the curious **sanctuary of Endymion**, on the inland side when approaching the Zeybek restaurant. Only the bases of the columns remain but the rounded wall built seamlessly between the existing rock is still impressive and it remains possible to conjure up the pagan spirit of this ancient shrine. Also walk across the fields in the direction of the ruined Byzantine castle on the shore to the Carian rock tombs. Some of their stone lids still lie open, as they were left by early grave robbers.

Aphrodisias

Named after the goddess Aphrodite, synonymous with the celebration of sensual love and exquisite femininity, the ancient city of **Aphrodisias** ㉗, which has been occupied since about 2,800 BC, became renowned throughout Asia Minor as a centre of medicine, philosophy, sculpture and the arts.

Buried by a series of earthquakes during late antiquity and abandoned by the survivors after attacks by the Arabs, the once splendid city was largely forgotten by the world until the late Professor Kenan Erim of New York University began a series of excavations, funded by *National Geographic*, in the early 1960s revealed an unparalleled cache of sculpture carved from the nearby white marble quarries; these appear to have been the mother lode of much of the statuary of the Roman age. Signatures on statues found at the extensive site corresponding with others found throughout the Roman world, from Spain to the Danube, point to a distinctive and influential school of sculpture.

Map on page 170

A spicy harvest of red hot chilli peppers.

LEFT: the Temple of Aphrodite at Aphrodisias.
BELOW: Lake Bafa.

TIP

Aphrodisias (open daily
9am–8pm, to 5pm in
winter; museum open
9am–6.30pm in
summer, to 5pm in
winter; separate
entrance fees for site
and museum) is 40 km
(24 miles) southeast of
Nazilli, reached by
turning south off the
main Aydin-Denizli
highway. The nearest
restaurants are in
Karacasu, 13 km (8
miles) west, but there
are also tours from
Kusadası and other
resorts.

BELOW: the mineral
pools at Pamukkale.

The well-preserved **Theatre** had its orchestra and stage converted into an arena for fights between gladiators and wild animals in the 2nd century. The **Stadium**, which could hold 30,000 spectators, is one of the finest Graeco-Roman structures in the world and was once the setting for athletics, drama, music and sculpting competitions. In the **Baths of Hadrian** the floor tiles are still visible, the monumental remains of the **Temple of Aphrodite** are well worth seeing, while the **museum** has a substantial collection of sculptures.

The frozen falls

Magical **Pamukkale** ㉘, the "Cotton Castle", lies 19 km (12 miles) north of Denizli, off the main highway from Aydin (officially open daily 24 hrs; entrance fee). It is a shimmering white cascade, formed by limestone-laden hot springs that have created stalactites, potholes and magical fairy-tables. The water is reputed to be beneficial to the eyes and skin and to alleviate rheumatism, asthma and dermatitis. Wading in the little pools on the plateau is now forbidden, but you can swim in the Sacred Pool at the Pamukkale Termal (open dawn–11.30pm; entrance fee). It's exhilarating to paddle through what feels like heated soda water while gazing at the ancient fragments of columns below the surface.

As much fun as the baths are, don't neglect to visit the splendid **Hierapolis** (open daily 8am–6pm, to 7pm in summer; entrance fee). The ruins spread over a mile from the city founded by Eumenes II of Pergamon and bequeathed by Attalus II to Rome. It was levelled by an earthquake in AD 17 but was rapidly rebuilt and enjoyed prosperity in the 2nd and 3rd centuries. The **Theatre** is vast and the intricate friezes of the stage building have undergone restoration. Below the theatre is the small cave of the Plutonium, where you can hear gushing

water. A grill seals the cave now, but it was believed to be an entrance to hell and only the priests could brave poisonous gasses issuing from it. East of here are the very substantial remains of Roman **Froninus Street**. Look out for the impressive remains of Roman public toilets, just before reaching the **Domitian Arch**. The **museum** (open daily 8.30am–noon, 1.30–5pm; entrance fee), next to the Pamukkale Termal in the town centre, houses various finds from the site.

Map on page 170

Milas

Milas ㉙, with its own airport and easy transport from Kuşadası or Bodrum, is a delightful agricultural town. The Milas Market (Tuesdays) is something special. The town is famous for its fine fabrics, coarse goat-hair rugs and shoulderbags, as well as for the distinctively coloured geometric-patterned carpets.

Milas also has some fine examples of Ottoman architecture, often with intriguingly ornate chimneys, and three interesting mosques including the **Ulucamii** built during the Menteşe Empire in 1370. Also worth seeing is the Roman gate known as the **Gate with an Axe**, after the double-headed axe carved into its stone on the north side. Adjacent to the Ulucamii is a **museum** (open daily 8.30am–5.30pm, to 7pm in summer; entrance fee), with many well-displayed finds from ancient **Iassos**, 8 km (5 miles) from Milas. The early-Roman tomb west of the town is a mini-replica of the Halikarnassos Mausoleum *(see page 209)*.

Some 13 km (8 miles) outside Milas on the road to Söke, the magnificent Corinthian Temple of Zeus at ancient **Euromos** (open daily 8.30am–7pm in summer, 8.30am–5.30pm in winter; entrance fee) is one of the six best-preserved in Asia Minor. Its 16 chunky columns, which sit on a base in a grassy field, are easily viewed from the highway. ❏

BELOW: enjoying a dip at the Pamukkale Termal.

BODRUM AND MARMARIS

*Bodrum is a good starting point for a journey along the
Carian coast, with its aura of mythology and history,
and spectacular sandy beaches, rocky coves and fjord-like inlets*

Map
on page
170

Situated on a peninsula facing the Greek island of Kos, **Bodrum** ❸⓿ is one
of the most popular resorts in Turkey. As Halikarnassos, this was the home
town of Herodotus (c. 485–425 BC), known to some as the "Father of History"
but to others as the "Father of Lies" because of his fanciful travel accounts. Another
label for him might be the "Father of Quotations", due to the many pithy observations quoted by travel writers.

Yachts and parties

Until not long ago Bodrum was just a pretty fishing village known for its
sponge-divers. Today, it is the yachting centre of Turkey and continues its ancient
tradition of shipbuilding, specialising in elegant wooden-hulled yachts known
as *gulets*. The town is an excellent base for organising a sailing trip and for the
inexperienced there should be little problem finding a boat complete with a
crew, via one of the many travel agents between the tourist office and the marina.
A one-day boat trip usually begins with a visit to the nearby island of **Karaada**
for a therapeutic mud bath and then on to the beach at **Ortakent** for lunch. On
the return journey, there is often a stop at the Aquarium, a particularly attractive
stretch of water with a wealth of marine life – perfect for snorkelling.

Bodrum's striking, whitewashed, cubist-style houses
are draped with cascades of bougainvillea and give
little indication of the town's contemporary devotion
to the hedonistic pleasures of boating, bronzing and
boozing. The town also has a well-developed shopping scene and some of the better restaurants to be
found along the Aegean coast. Its tourist season gets
longer each year as its reputation as a "party town"
spreads among boaters and landlubbers alike.

Bodrum Castle

Yet history buffs will not be totally disappointed: the
towers and battlements of the Crusader **Sen Piyer
Kalesi** (**Castle of St Peter**) dominate the town as a
major survivor of its past. Standing on a promontory
by the harbour, the castle was built by the Knights of
St John, who plundered the Mausoleum *(see page 209)*
for materials; you can see its column bases in the castle
walls. The Knights of St John arrived in 1402 and
continued to work on their castle throughout the 15th
century. The building was finally completed in 1522,
but the knights were forced to abandon the fortress
shortly afterwards, when Muslim forces under Ottoman
sultan, Süleyman the Magnificent, captured Rhodes.

The inner castle is reached after passing through
seven gates embellished with coats of arms and
inscriptions. Beyond the courtyard, adorned with a
handsome collection of amphorae recovered from

LEFT: anchored in
paradise, on a Blue
Cruise.
BELOW: being taken
for a ride, Bodrum.

BELOW: the Castle of St Peter in Bodrum, beautifully floodlit at night.

excavated wrecks, there are colour-coded walks to guide visitors through the complex of buildings and special exhibitions located inside the castle.

The **Museum of Underwater Archaeology** opened in 1960 with a collection of artefacts from a 7th-century Byzantine wreck, discovered nearby at Yassiada. The displays include treasures from the *Şeytan Deresi* wreck in Gökova Bay as well as the richest haul of Mycenaean objects to be found outside Greece.

The **Glass Wreck** exhibition, perhaps the most interesting of the special exhibits, includes a flat-bottomed Fatimid-Ottoman ship, thought to have sunk in 1075, found in Serçe Harbour, 40 km (24 miles) from Marmaris and meticulously restored by archaeologists. It had been carrying a cargo of glass and the delicate, multicoloured glass fragments have been painstakingly reconstructed into exquisite cups, bottles and plates, many with designs in relief. Another exhibit that whets one's appetite for more is a small-scale replica of an underwater excavation team at work.

The **Uluburun Wreck Hall** contains one of the world's oldest ships, which sank in the 14th century BC off Kaş. Excavations revealed a trading cargo of tin, glass, resin, two swords, a two panel "book" formerly containing wax and the seal of Nefertiti. The French Tower now contains the **Hall of the Carian Princess**. Her tomb, discovered by accident in Bodrum in 1989, was found to contain the remains of a woman who lived in about 360 BC, complete with her jewellery and gold appliquéd clothing. A team of British specialists reconstructed the skull and facial features, recreating the princess from her remains. The richness of her tomb suggests royalty; hence the title of the Carian Princess though she could have been Mausolus's queen – the dates are contemporary. From outside this exhibition room it is possible to climb up to a higher

level from where there are panoramic views of the town and harbour. Children may not be too impressed by the remains of the princess but they will enjoy a visit to the **English Tower**, which is packed with armour and trophies of war. Adult visitors to the tower can enjoy a drink of local wine, served by staff in medieval costumes. Another attraction for children is the Crusaders' dungeons, in the lower levels of the **Gatineau Tower**, where sound effects help conjure up the horrors of those unfortunate prisoners incarcerated here. The motto above the door declares *Inde Deus Abest* ("Where God does not exist") – even more chilling when you realise that it was put there by monks.

Mausoleum of Halikarnassos

To the ancients, the **Mausoleum of Halikarnassos** (open Tues–Sun 8am–noon, 12.30–5pm; entrance fee) was one of the Seven Wonders of the World. Consecrated to the memory of the ambitious Mausolus, a ruler of Halikarnassos in the 4th century BC (who was awarded the Persian title of *satrap* or provincial governor), the mausoleum was commissioned by his sister/widow, Artemesia, who then drank a macabre cocktail of wine mixed with his ashes daily until her death two years later. She employed the world's best sculptors to create a monument topped with a pyramidical roof and a chariot with effigies of Mausolus and herself in triumph. Much of this was raided by the knights, as a convenient local quarry, and the best remains are in the British Museum.

The women here were powerful. Another earlier queen, Artemesia I, joined forces with Xerxes against Athens in about 480 BC; she took command of her ships and proceeded to destroy the Rhodian fleet. This victory caused the great King Xerxes to say he wished all of his admirals were women.

Map on page 170

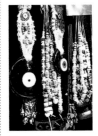

Many Turks wear blue beads to ward off the evil eye.

BELOW: the Mediterranean charms of backstreet Bodrum.

The magical city

Traditionally, Bodrum has tolerated – indeed, encouraged – eccentricity. Its fame as a bohemian artistic centre began during the infancy of the Turkish Republic when Cevat Şakir Kabaağaçli, the "Halikarnassos Fisherman", was exiled here in 1923, writing a number of fascinating books and stories about Bodrum that attracted other writers and artists to the restful locale. "When the moon comes up, the universe turns into a fairytale," he wrote.

Bodrum's nocturnal setting is magical; its nightlife is invigorating and often continues until dawn. Cocktails at one of the bars along the promenade can be followed by dinner at a harbourside restaurant. After an evening meal the night is still young in Bodrum and midnight approaches before the disco scene comes alive. At the eastern end of Cumhuriyet Caddesi is the famous **Halikarnas Disco**. Located on a prominent slope at the end of the beach, this immense Bodrum phenomenon has become internationally famous. Its monumental temple pillars topped with torches are bordered by gushing fountains lit by garish strobe lights and dramatically sliced by laser beams.

Bodrum beaches

Bodrum has a few sandy pockets on Cumhuriyet Caddesi and some rocks next to the castle, but the water is not always very clean. To find the best beaches it is necessary to leave town. In fact, many visitors opt to stay out of town in one of the villages on the peninsula. They are all easily accessible, with regular buses from Bodrum. **Gümbet**, 5 km (3 miles) from Bodrum, has a long sandy beach dotted with motels and *pansiyons*. Gümbet means "water cistern", referring to the many domed raincatchers in the vicinity. The resort has a large windsurfing school and offers diving courses. A small *caïque* (boat) service runs from the popular beach to Bodrum.

BELOW: picnic under the windmills on the Bodrum peninsula.

Bitez, on a bay a few kilometres west, also has a windsurfing school and wooden piers from which to swim. It is backed by thick tangerine orchards. While Gümbet is very popular with young people, Bitez is more upmarket and attracts an older crowd.

Ortakent, off the main highway west of Bodrum, is popular with Turkish families. Its beach is considered by many to be the best on the peninsula, and there are several restaurants and motels, and some unique tower-houses. The oldest, the Mustafa Paşa house (1601), is given a stately appearance by its rampart-size walls and a peaked roof formed by cannon embrasures.

The waterfront of **Turgutreis** ❸ is lined with restaurants, hotels and boutiques, and there is no shortage of bars or discos. Its beach, though not especially sandy, is very popular because it remains shallow for quite some way out, making it safer for young children. Be warned, however, that Turgutreis is entirely dedicated to tourism, so if you prefer more isolation you should head for one of the quieter areas off the road to Akyarlar; a long sandy beach near the lighthouse usually attracts a few swimmers.

Akyarlar itself is an ideal place to sample typical Turkish village life. Its small sandy beach sits in a sheltered harbour lined by restaurants offering temptingly fresh fish.

Gümüslük ㉜ is more popular for its secluded setting than for its beach. Since it has been designated an archaeological site, no drastic alterations are allowed to the landscape. Gümüslük is the site of ancient **Myndos**, and its harbour and western beaches are adorned by a fortification wall, ancient tower and submerged sea walls. If you walk towards the south end of the sand and gravel beach, you will be able to swim very close to some of the ruins of ancient Myndos. Alternatively, dine at one of the beach restaurants; you will not believe just how close to the sea they are until, seated at your table, you stretch out a foot and dip it into the water.

The beach at **Yalıkavak** ㉝ is not spectacular but the place is relaxing. This was one of the last sponge-fishing villages but tourism has taken over and now villas abound. The hills around the village are ideal for picnics and walks, especially in the spring when they are covered with a brilliant profusion of wild flowers. One of the still functional seaside windmills is over 300 years old. In a large bay northwest of Bodrum, the lovely little villages of **Türkbükü** and **Gölköy** cater to families and independent travellers who want to spend quiet contemplative days absorbing the fantastic natural beauty, and evenings in quaint seaside eateries.

Blue cruising

Apart from its other charms, Bodrum also serves as one of the major centres for the growing trade in *Mavi Yolculuk* (Blue Cruises) into neighbouring **Gökova Körfezi** ㉞ and other inlets around the Datça peninsula. Several agencies cater to the yachting crowd, and boats are available at various rates. The cruises into Gökova Bay usually include an overnight dock at **English Bay**, where several

Map on page 170

LEFT: toasting in the midday sun.
BELOW: ready for frying and serving.

German cruisers were sunk during World War II, at the village of **Türkevler** and then at **Cleopatra Island**, allegedly a favourite resort of Mark Antony and his Egyptian bride.

Legend has it that the fine grained sand on Cleopatra Island – found nowhere else along the Turkish coast – was imported from Egypt to make the Queen of the Nile feel more at home.

Avoid the common mistake of underestimating the amount of liquid needed to sustain yourselves throughout a long day and night; bring twice the amount you think you will need. While non-alcoholic drinks cater for common thirst under burning summer skies, alcohol may also be desired. Don't expect to dine on fresh fish every night as Gökova has been largely fished-out. Buy extra food and pack it away in the ship's hold.

Don't feel shy about telling your captain to linger a little longer at a place you like, or to pull up anchor and sail on if he docks with his other captain friends in an overcrowded cove. You are paying for the journey, and you should be able to call the shots.

The Marmaris peninsula

The resort of **Marmaris** ❸ is reached along a 32-km (20-mile) road off the highway between Muğla and Fethiye, which starts with a splendid avenue of eucalyptus trees. Unfortunately, however, the trees are too close together for modern traffic needs. A new and larger road now serves cars while the old road is left to donkeys and horse-drawn carriages. The name Marmaris is traced back to the days when Süleyman the Magnificent, mounting an attack on Rhodes, expressed his anger at the state of the fortress in Marmaris, exclaiming *mimarı as* ("hang the architect"). Lord Nelson was more impressed by the area's potential when he used the large bay to prepare his fleet before attacking (and defeating) Napoleon's navy at Abukir in 1798.

The near-perfect natural harbour and splendid setting ringed by pine-clad mountains are indeed worthy of admiration and Marmaris deserves to vie with Bodrum as the starting point for cruises along the Turkish coast. Offering plenty of entertainment, shopping and eating, Marmaris is more downmarket. Both resort towns have their beer-swilling bar streets but Marmaris also caters to families and package-tour holidaymakers with better beaches and English food in abundance.

The Marmaris peninsula as a whole is much less developed than the Bodrum area but still offers plenty of accommodation. A useful water taxi plies its way regularly between Marmaris and the Munumar Hotel at **İçmeler**, the resort closest to Marmaris itself. Although only 8 km (5 miles) from the main resort town, İçmeler is noticeably more relaxed and subdued. The beach curves around the bay for half a mile and the usual watersports, including windsurfing, are available. The swimming area close to the beach is safely cordoned off from jet skis and the like. Bars and discos are not hard to find, though they tend to close earlier than their counterparts in Marmaris or Bodrum. This, along with the more upmarket accommodation, helps to keep the crowds at bay.

Turunç, 10 km (7 miles) from Marmaris, has awakened slowly to its potential as a package-tour destination away from the relative brashness of the

BELOW:
shopping from the mobile grocer's.

mega-resort. For a long while, this was a quiet backwater visited mostly by sailing folk. Now it is being discovered as a pleasant little town offering peace and relaxation, a coarse sand beach, watersports and a modest choice of restaurants and bars.

The picturesque village of **Bozburun**, with its yachting harbour, makes an interesting detour off the main road to Datça. It has accommodation and several small restaurants, but there is no beach.

Map on page 170

Datça and Knidos

A favourite stopping point for yachtsmen, attractive, sleepy **Datça** ❸ is inexorably waking up to the tourist potential of being virtually surrounded by sea. The ancient city of **Knidos** ❸ (open daily 8am–7pm; entrance fee) may be reached either by sea from Datça, or at the end of a 90-minute bone-shaking drive off the main road just outside town.

The site itself is almost permanently windy, as it was in antiquity when it was infamous among sailors. It occupies a fascinatingly beautiful location at the tip of the peninsula, partly on an island, and with protected harbours. Experts are debating whether this was the sight of the earliest settlement, or whether the town was moved here from present-day Datça. It's under excavation and the initial survey has shown the city to be huge; the island section is off-limits.

The terraced site was laid out on a grid-plan and incorporated a **theatre** – situated to the right of the main road as you approach the village. Other ruined buildings overlooking the twin harbours include the foundation of a small round building known as the **Temple of Aphrodite**, believed to have housed a statue of the goddess which was created by the Greek sculptor Praxiteles (390–330 BC)

Just a perfect day... hot sun, fine sand and an empty mind.

BELOW: boats and houses juxtaposed at Marmaris.

and was famous throughout the ancient world. That discovery was made by the American Professor Iris Love whose other, more controversial, claim is that a battered head she found in a basement in the British Museum is that of the Aphrodite statue.

Of the two harbours that served the ancient city, the southern one benefits tourists with a selection of restaurants and the daily ferry between Bodrum and Datça.

Muğla

About 50 km (30 miles) north of Marmaris, the pretty town of **Muğla** ❸ is revered, for having clung to its architectural heritage. Only in Safranbolu, in the Black Sea region *(see page 305)*, have as many old Turkish houses, caravansarays, fountains and mosques been preserved and kept still in use by the townsfolk. The tourist office in the centre of town dispenses a handy town plan which helps you to find your way up the hill, where the best examples of domestic Ottoman architecture are to be found.

Dalaman and Dalyan

Returning to the main Muğla to Fethiye highway and continuing eastwards, there is a turn-off for **Dalaman**, a small, rather uninspiring town, best known for its airport. Opened in the early 1980s, this was one of the better ideas of Turkey's tourism masters. Daily charter flights from many European locations and scheduled services from Istanbul mean easy access to a wide selection of resorts in the southern Aegean and western Mediterranean.

A short way south is the riverside resort town of **Dalyan** ❸. The name means "fishery", and a complicated system of barriers has been built among the reeds

BELOW: Muğla has cherished its pretty Ottoman houses.

to allow the grey mullet and sea bass that breed in Köyceğiz Lake to be caught as they head for the sea. In **Ilica**, at the northern end of the lake, are a series of open-air thermal mud baths, whose gloriously messy contents (which reach 40°C/104°F) are said to improve male potency, solve gynaecological problems and alleviate rheumatism.

A road of some 25 km (15 miles) winds past blooming hibiscus along the river from Dalyan to the beautiful, remote **İztuzu "Turtle" Beach**, one of the few places in the Mediterranean where giant loggerhead turtles come to lay their eggs. Development of the beach is limited, and access forbidden at night.

Map
on page
170

Kaunos

For seven centuries, under the Persians, the Greeks and the Romans, **Kaunos** (open daily 8.30am–5.30pm; entrance fee) was one of the leading towns of ancient Caria. It was always known as an unhealthy place – the yellow skin of its inhabitants mentioned by Herodotus may have been due to malaria – and whether it was abandoned because of mosquitoes or because of the silting of the harbour is not clear. Today, most visitors arrive by boat from Dalyan.

Alongside the river, south of Dalyan, is a series of Lycian-influenced rock tombs, of which the largest one was never completed. It shows clearly the method of construction – starting at the top. Most people are unlikely to climb to the city walls, but the ruins of a Roman theatre, a huge Byzantine basilica and a Roman fountain house with a long inscription are easily accessible. The acropolis is impressive, standing on a bend in the river, and the traveller who has taken a one-way trip to the landing stage beyond here can easily return by waiting on the Dalyan side of the hill to flag down any passing craft. ❑

LEFT: the lagoon at Dalyan.
BELOW: mud, glorious mud, and it's healthy too.

WATER, WATER EVERYWHERE

Surrounded on three sides by the Black Sea, the Aegean and the Mediterranean, Turkey has always placed great importance on the sea

The sandy beaches and crystal-clear waters that act as a magnet for visitors today also attracted the ancient Phoenicians, then the Greeks and later the Romans. They came across the sea to trade, and to fish, and the Greeks established more colonies along the Aegean coastline of Turkey than anywhere else in the Mediterranean.

As technical advances in underwater archaeology continue, sustained explorations are becoming manageable at deeper levels, and the finds serve to confirm the continuity of the importance of the sea around Turkey. In the past, as now, fresh fish added taste to what otherwise might have been a bland diet; and apart from being a source of food, Turkish waters yield molluscs, which produce a colour-fast purple dye, and sponges up to 1 metre (3 ft) in diameter.

Ancient sea-going vessels hugged the coast for safety and underwater archaeologists are particularly drawn to the stretch of coast between Bodrum and Antalya, where the Greeks and Phoenicians were particularly active, in their search for wrecks. In this area, a journey today is called a Blue Cruise or a Blue Voyage *(mavi yolculuk)* because the water really does appear a glorious turquoise-blue. Provisions and cooking are handled by the crew while voyagers are free to swim, snorkel, fish or frolic. One popular route is from Bodrum across the Gulf of Gökova, before anchoring in a secluded bay on the Datça peninsula. A day is usually spent at uninhabited Sedir Island, where Antony is reputed to have transported the sand to satisfy a whim of Cleopatra's, while evenings unfold serenely after a meal on land close to where the boat anchors for the night.

▽ **SCRUB DOWN**
Turkey is the largest source of natural sea sponges in the world, and around Bodrum many young Turks make a living out of sponge-diving. You will see sponges for sale everywhere.

◁ UNDER SAIL
Everyone is catered for, with everything from day trips that operate on the basis of a shared taxi to a chartered yacht either with or without an experienced crew.

▽ GULETS
Gulets, elegant traditional motor yachts used along the coast, are up to 23 metres (75 ft) long, and built from red pine, and teak, with a pointed bow and flat stern.

◁ THRILLS AND SPILLS
Every conceivable watersport is available at some beach resort, and there are lots of recognised courses for would-be sailors and scuba-divers.

△ LIFE'S A BEACH
There is no shortage of fine beaches; some are over-crowded but there are also secluded coves where you can have the sand to yourselves.

△ ANCIENT WINE BOTTLES
Storage pots, or amphorae, were stacked in layers on a ship with the pointed ends of one layer fitting between the necks of those laid under them.

▷ UNDERWATER RAINBOWS
A snorkel and mask open a window on a kaleido-scopic world around the shipwrecks dotted along the coast.

A STRUGGLE FOR SURVIVAL

Between May and October each year, huge female loggerhead turtles *(caretta caretta)*, weighing up to 180 kg (350 lbs), drag themselves up onto 17 beaches around Turkey.

Once above the water line, they dig a hole in the sand and lay about 100 leathery eggs. Two months later, around three-quarters of the eggs hatch at night. It can take a couple of days for the baby turtle to struggle out of its buried shell, but once it reaches the surface it instinctively scurries towards the water's edge, seemingly attracted by the moonlight on the water. The confusion caused by the dazzling lights of beachside tourist developments are just one of the hazards they face in their struggle for survival. Plastic bags and oil slicks pose other dangers, as do the natural predators such as fish and gulls.

Several favourite nesting beaches such as Dalyan and Patara are now sanctuaries, with safe-guards for the incubating eggs and carefully controlled access to the hatching grounds.

THE MEDITERRANEAN COAST

Wild cliffs, ancient cities, Crusader castles and gentle turquoise seas make this area a holiday paradise

The Turks call their share of the Mediterranean the *Akdeniz*, or "White Sea"; others, familiar with its translucent waters and spectacular vistas prefer to call it the "Turquoise Coast" – and a very special place it is indeed.

Long neglected by all but the most intrepid travellers, the area is now rapidly developing as a major destination for sun and sea seekers, serviced by three international airports (at Dalaman, Antalya and Adana). Massive new construction of giant resort hotels crams ever more people onto the once deserted beaches. Former fishing villages have become boomtowns, and archaeological sites such as Side have discos around the temple walls. Development is running out of control, with seemingly few planning restrictions to halt the inexorable concrete sprawl. For now, you can still find enchantment away from the mass-market resorts; the question is… for how long?

For this book, the coast has been divided into four sections, based roughly on the ancient kingdoms. Lycia, in the west, is undoubtedly the most scenically beautiful with the wild Taurus mountains plunging straight down to a coastline of cliffs and coves, the waves crashing thunderously into mysterious sea caves. Resorts here come in all shapes and sizes: the backpacker heaven at Olympos; Kalkan and Kaş, two of the smaller, more upmarket resorts; and Kemer, which is decidedly mass market.

Pamphylia is bounded by cities, stretching from sophisticated Antalya in the west to Alanya in the east. Much of the land between is a fertile plain, less inspiring scenically, but with long golden beaches and fabulous archaeological sites such as Perge, Aspendos and Side to compensate.

Western Cilicia (roughly Alanya to Adana) has some of the most spectacular cliffs on the Mediterranean; its eastern plains, some of the most hotly contested real estate in history, are now home to a booming industrial complex. Before the Greeks arrived, this was part of the great Hittite Empire. It has relatively few ruined cities – most of its ancient settlements such as Mersin or Tarsus are still thriving. The area's blood-stained past is most visible in the many hundreds of medieval castles that sprinkle the landscape.

Turn south into the Hatay, around biblical Antioch (Antakya) and you enter a region quite different from the rest of Turkey. This was only briefly part of the Ottoman Empire, spending much of its history as part of Armenia and even enjoying a couple of centuries of Norman Christian rule. More recently it was part of Syria, and Arabic is still widely spoken. ❏

PRECEDING PAGES: the waters of the Turquoise Coast live up to their name.
LEFT: the Lycian legacy is a scatter of elaborate rock-carved tombs.

Map
on pages
222-3

LYCIA

*Enchanting Lycia was home to a proud, independent people
who looked to the sea for trade and fish, and who remained
aloof from Anatolia until only a few years ago*

The independent-minded Lycians, believed to be related to the Hittites, settled the wide peninsula between present-day Fethiye and Antalya from around 1,400 BC. They had their own unique language, still to be seen on inscriptions, but are best known today for their spectacular tombs.

From the 6th century BC onwards, at least 20 cities in this sophisticated region banded together in a loose federation. In 540 BC, however, Cyrus II conquered western Anatolia, and Lycia fell under Persian rule. The Hellenistic era began when Alexander the Great arrived in about 333 BC and the cities of Lycia surrendered one by one, some with positive glee. Shortly afterwards, the Lycian League, a political alliance in which each city voted according to its tax contribution, was formed, acquiring economic as well as political prominence. The Lycian language died out gradually, to be replaced by Greek.

In 197 BC Lycia was conquered by Antiochus III of Syria. In turn, he was defeated by Rome in 189 BC and Lycia joined the empire. Awarded to Rhodes, the Lycians rebelled and, within 20 years, the Senate had given the troublesome cities autonomy. After the Battle of Philippi in 42 BC, control passed to Mark Antony, who gave the territory its freedom, leaving it the only part of Asia Minor not under Roman domination. A century later, Emperor Vespasian (AD 69–79) brought the joint province of Lycia and Pamphylia back under Roman control.

Though Lycia became immensely wealthy from coastal trade during the 1st to 3rd centuries, a disastrous earthquake in 241 caused its decline, and from the 6th century it became a remote, backward area. Only in the 1980s were its spectacular coastal bays connected to the rest of the country by proper roads. Now, even the tiny villages have been discovered by the tourists hordes.

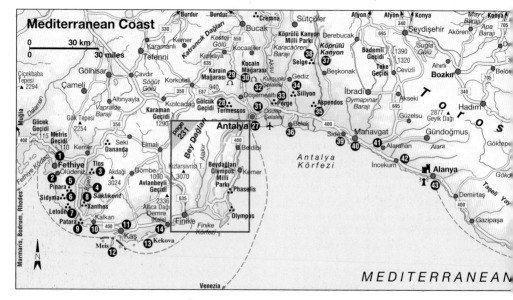

Fethiye

At the western edge of Lycia, **Fethiye ❶** is a small, attractive port town tucked between a broad bay and the sheer cliff face of Mount Cragos, the western end-stop of the Taurus Mountains. There has been a town here since the Lycians built Telmessos, about 2,500 years ago. It was last renamed in 1934 to honour Fethi Bey, a local pilot who died heroically during the War of Independence.

Most of the town is brand-new: it was virtually flattened by earthquakes in 1856 and 1957 which destroyed a temple to Apollo but left several huge Lycian sarcophagi untouched. The damage these relics have suffered has all been inflicted by humans.

Little else remains of the ancient city except for a series of Lycian rock tombs in the cliff behind the town. The largest of these is the grandiose temple **Tomb of Amyntas** (up the steps from Kaya Caddesi, behind the bus station; open daily 8.30am–sunset; entrance fee). Its occupant was identified from a 4th-century BC inscription, but nothing else is known of him. The **Theatre** just behind the **tourist office** (İskele Karşısı 1, opposite the main harbour; tel: 0252-614 1527) is being restored, and on top of the mountain are the last remnants of a 14th-century **Crusader fort** (open access). The town's small **museum** (off Atatürk Caddesi; open Tues–Sun 8.30am–5pm; entrance fee) contains finds from various local archaeological sites, including Xanthos and Kaunos.

Fethiye, now the hub of a thriving tourist destination, has tidied itself up considerably in recent years, with waterfront restaurants and an attractive promenade beside a busy working harbour, where supply ships and fishing boats rub shoulders with elegant yachts and day-tripping *gülets*. Local operators run diving, fishing and adventure excursions. Several old buildings in the bazaar have been converted to attractive stores, restaurants and clubs.

Ölüdeniz

Fethiye itself has no beaches; the nearest beach resort is **Çalış**, 4 km (2½ miles) west of town, with a cluster of giant resort hotels. Otherwise, those wanting to swim must take a *gület* to one of the many bays or islets in the gulf of Fethiye, or cross the peninsula to **Ölüdeniz ❷**, the "Dead Sea", 25 km (15 miles) away.

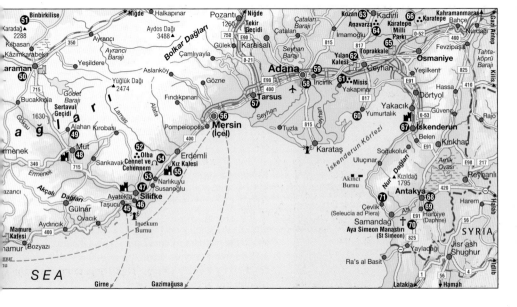

Featured on the cover of many tourist brochures, this was once one of the most beautiful beaches on the Mediterranean, a turquoise and cobalt lagoon encircled by platinum sand, with stone pines leaning crookedly over the water. Virtually unrestricted development turned the narrow spit of sand between the lagoon and the open sea into a car park, while the scattering of *pansiyons* and camp sites found along the approach road a decade or so ago gave way to a whole town of hotels and apartments. A minuscule circle of land surrounding the lagoon itself has been declared a national park, and efforts are now being made, too late, to reclaim the waterfront and ban noisy watersports. If mass-market holidays, with endless cheap accommodation, restaurants, burger bars and beach umbrellas is your cup of tea, then this is definitely for you. Those who remember the lagoon's idyllic past can only weep.

The eerie ghost-town of **Kaya** makes a fascinating excursion, reached most easily off the main road between Fethiye and Ölüdeniz. A more interesting, if difficult, route runs directly up from Fethiye, starting from the street at the foot of the rock tombs. Kaya was home to about 3,500 Greeks until the deportations of the 1920s. The Macedonian Muslims who were due to take over the village believed it to be cursed and refused to move in and so the whole settlement of some 400 homes stands silent. The church and a few houses on the fringes have been restored using EU money.

Heading inland – turn off the N-350 to Korkuteli after 22 km (13 miles) and follow signs to Yakaköy – you reach the ruins of **Tlos ❸** (open access; entrance fee), known to the Hittites in the 14th century BC. The Ottoman castle was inhabited until the 1800s. This little-known sight also has many Lycian "house" tombs. One of the most elaborate, supposedly belonging to the legendary Bellerophon, slayer of the Chimaera, shows the hero astride his winged horse, Pegasus. Below, near the river, are the remains of a wealthy Roman city.

Nearby **Saklıkent ❹**, 44 km (26 miles) southeast of Fethiye (3 km/2 miles from the main road), is a popular hideout from the burning summer sun of the coast. This cool, dark gorge, carved by the turbulent Eşen River, about 300 metres (1,000 ft) high and 18 km (12 miles) long, is used by the more adventurous for canyoning expeditions that involve abseiling down the spectacular waterfalls. For the rest of us, a wooden catwalk leads about 150 metres/yds into the gorge and there are several good restaurants nearby.

The coastal cities

Back on the coast, the serious student of ancient cities will be kept happy for weeks by the long line of well-documented, but often unexcavated, settlements that crowd onto every suitable piece of flattish ground. **Pınara ❺** (open daily 8.30am–6pm; entrance fee), 40 km/24 miles southeast of Fethiye, was a 4th-century BC colony of Xanthos which became a prominent member of the Lycian League in its own right. To drive there, turn off the main road through Minare village and fork left to the car park, 3 km (2 miles) past the turning. The earliest town is built at the top of a sheer cliff honeycombed by Lycian tombs. The Roman city is on the smaller hill nearer the car park.

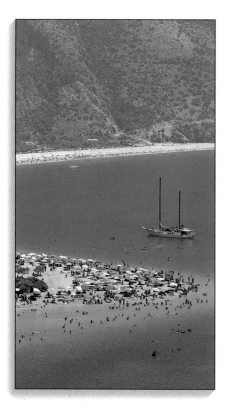

BELOW: the lagoon at Ölüdeniz.

About 10 km (6 miles) southwest, the scattered remains of 2nd-century BC **Sidyma** ⑥ have almost been swamped by the modern village of Dodurga, much of which has been built with ancient stones (open access). The site – 29 km (18 miles) north of Kalkan and 50 km (31 miles) from Fethiye – is 7 km (4 miles) off the N-400, with the last few miles on a steep, rough road.

Three kilometres (2 miles) southeast, another turning, just west of Kınık, leads 4 km (2½ miles) down a side road to the small, but much more rewarding ruins of the **Letoön** ⑦ (open daily May–Sept 7.30am–7pm, Oct–Apr 8.30am–5pm; entrance fee). Partly submerged by the rising water table, and now clad in reeds and inhabited by frogs, terrapins and water birds, this is the site of three adjacent temples dedicated to Leto (said to have been the lover of Zeus) and her children, Apollo and Artemis, the ruling deities of Lycia; they were probably built over a 7th-century BC shrine to the Mother Goddess.

It was here, according to legend, that Lycia received its name. When Leto became pregnant she fled from Mount Olympos, to protect her twins from jealous Hera. The local shepherds drove her off, but the wolves sheltered and fed her and the babies. In gratitude, she named the area to Lycia (*lykos* is the Greek word for wolf), while the unhelpful shepherds were turned into frogs.

A well-preserved theatre has 16 masks above the entrance to the vaulted passage beneath the upper seats on the southwest. French archaeologists have started a restoration programme.

Xanthos

Xanthos ⑧, located 1 km (½ mile) from the turning off the N-400 in the centre of Kınık town (open daily May–Oct 8am–7pm, Nov–Apr 8am–6.30pm; entrance fee), was the leading town of Lycia, known for pride so fierce that twice it preferred to self-destruct than surrender to an overwhelming foe. The first time was in 540 BC. Herodotus reported that when the Persian general, Harpagos, advanced across the plain and besieged the citadel, rather than submit, the men of Xanthos enclosed their women, children and slaves within the walls and burned the place to the ground. "Then, having sworn to do or die, they marched out to meet the enemy and were killed to a man."

In 42 BC, two years after the murder of Julius Caesar, Brutus besieged Xanthos but again the people fought to the death and he gained control of a city that had been razed. The historian Appian relates in great detail how the Xanthians dug a great ditch around their clifftop city, to keep out the invaders. Brutus managed to have it filled in again and a dramatic battle ensued with siege engines, ladders and many of the attackers falling to their deaths. Some 150 of the townsfolk lived, as prisoners, to tell the tale. Following Mark Antony's victory over Brutus, he poured money into rebuilding Xanthos, which became the capital of Roman Lycia.

The site was virtually intact when British explorer Sir Charles Fellows arrived here in 1838. He returned four years later in *HMS Beacon*, whose sailors spent two months carting away the monuments for exhibition in the Lycian Room at the British Museum.

Map on pages 222–3

In 1984, French archaeologists found inscriptions spelling out the dress code for visitors to the Letoön. Anyone entering the sanctuary had to wear a plain dress and simple shoes; jewellery, elaborate hair-dos and broad-brimmed hats were banned, as were all weapons.

BELOW: a few miles inland, Lycia remains a land of peasant farmers.

Today, two tombs that tower above the upper seats of the theatre, and an inscribed "obelisk" (in fact also a tomb) have become the trademarks of the site. The so-called **Harpy Tomb** takes its name from an early interpretation of the reliefs around the top depicting winged women. At first thought to be Harpies, the foul-smelling ugly monsters of Greek mythology, historians now believe them to be Sirens, carrying away the souls of the dead to the Isle of the Blessed. The other is a regular sarcophagus standing atop a short pillar. Pottery found inside dates the **Pillar Tomb** to the 3rd century BC but a relief on the side, since removed, was of the 6th century BC and had apparently been reused.

The **obelisk** is tumbled at the corner of the agora. Mainly inscribed in Lycian, with a few lines of Greek, it recounts the life and exploits of the local hero, 5th-century BC prince, Kerei, whose remains it contained. Elsewhere are the remnants of the 1st-century AD **Arch of Vespasian**, Nereid monument (c. AD 4), whose friezes also decorate the British Museum, a later agora, basilica, monastery and the Byzantine city walls. The view across the Esen Çayı is impressive, and one can picture vividly the tragic scene as the Xanthians fought to the last man, their proud city burning to cinders around them.

Patara

Patara ❾ was another powerful Lycian city. Today, it is known for its 18-km (11-mile) white sand beach, the longest and widest in Turkey and one which, unlike much of the Mediterranean, has a tide that allows body surfing. This giant sand-pit is as popular with breeding turtles as it is with baking tourists, and the land behind the dunes is a vast archaeological site. As a result, the beachfront area is a national park and the long line of hotels is confined to the village of Gelemiş.

To reach the ruins of ancient Patara, turn off the N-400 9 km (5½ miles) west of Kalkan; the site is 8 km (5 miles) from the main road. (The ruins and nearby beach are open daily May–Sept 7.30am–7pm, Oct–Apr 8.30am–5pm; entrance and parking fee). Legend has it that this was the winter home of the sun god, Apollo, and Patara had an oracle as famous as the one in Delphi. The town was also the 4th-century AD birthplace of St Nicholas, better known today as Santa Claus and associated, for no reason whatsoever, with snowy winters in the northern hemisphere *(see page 230)*. Before the sand engulfed the river in the Middle Ages, Patara was a prosperous trading port. Today, the ruins are scattered over a huge area among the fields and dunes, many of them overgrown or hidden under the shifting sands that have drifted across much of the site.

At the official entrance to the old town stands a triple monumental **arch** (1st century BC), which doubled as part of an aqueduct. Further in, the **theatre** (2nd century BC) is intact but has been virtually filled by sand. From the top, there is an excellent view of the other remains and of the coastline. The most important recent discovery is the **Stadiasmus**, a survey of the Roman roads of Lycia, inscribed on a huge monument. The **granary of Hadrian** stands to full height. The temple and oracle of Apollo have not yet been found. A boardwalk leads from the ruins to the beach, which has little natural shade and few drinks stands, so go prepared.

The Greek legacy

In the years immediately before the massive exchange of population in 1923, the area at the base of the Lycian bulge was inhabited mainly by Greek fishermen whose attractive, whitewashed towns of Kalkan and Kaş would still seem more at home in the Dodecanese than in Turkey.

Tiny **Kalkan ⑩** has become one of the most sought after resorts on the Mediterranean coast, with narrow streets of overhanging Ottoman-Greek houses clinging precipitously to narrow alleys that swoop down into a harbour carefully restored to attract the yachting crowd. In spite of its size and total lack of a proper swimming beach, Kalkan in summer has delightful *pansiyons*, boutiques for rich shopaholics, a proud collection of some of the best restaurants outside Istanbul, and spreading suburbs of wealthy villas. The mosque near the harbour appears to have been converted from a Greek church by little more than the addition of a minaret.

The waters around Kalkan are a favourite for spear fishermen, with many natural springs providing the opportunity for a freshwater shower when divers surface at the shore; offshore this strange phenomenon makes the surface much colder than deeper waters. For those in search of sand, regular *dolmus* run the 19 km (12 miles) west to Patara.

The dramatic cliff-hugging route eastwards winds around several small sandy coves, linked to the road above by steps. The best is tiny **Kaputaş Beach**, 6 km (3½ miles) east, which also acts as the official beach for Kaş. From here, you can swim round to beautiful blue-green phosphorescent sea caves.

Superb views mark the entrance to **Kaş ⑪** (107 km/64 miles southeast of Fethiye; 181 km/109 miles

BELOW: the streets of Kalkan are only this quiet during the winter months.

Map on pages 222–3

TIP

Kaş has an efficient
and friendly tourist
office on the main
square (Cumhuriyet
Meydanı 5; tel: 0242-
836 1238), with staff
who speak good English
and are happy to
provide information
on almost anywhere
between Fethiye and
Antalya.

southwest of Antalya, on the N-400), a sophisticated resort that has begun to stabilise after years of rapid growth. Thankfully, the big developers have been put off by the lack of beaches, leaving this as a delightful centre from which to explore the coast. The larger hotels are strung out along a winding peninsula, about 5 km (3 miles) from the town centre.

The town of Antiphellos, on the site of present-day Kaş, began to develop in Hellenistic times and by the Roman period was one of the leading ports of the region. Relatively little has survived as the site remained inhabited, but there is a well-preserved Hellenistic **theatre**, with the Mediterranean as its astounding backdrop, less than 2 km (1 mile) west of the town on Hastane Caddesi (towards the peninsula). Rock-cut **Lycian tombs** can be seen on the cliff-face above, while the sarcophagus-style Lycian Lion Tomb stands on Uzun Garşi.

As a resort, Kaş has style, with some of the best shops and restaurants on the Mediterranean coast. An influx of fashion designers and artisans have made the town a centre for arts and crafts, jewellery and textiles. It also has numerous excellent restaurants, a healthy array of trendy bars and cafés, and a sprinkling of noisy discos. The traveller hoping to get to sleep before 3am may want to find somewhere to stay away from the harbour.

Off-shore

The island of **Meis (Kastellorizo)** ⑫, just out to sea from Kaş, is the easternmost of the Greek islands. Elderly Greek women who have made the day trip to Kaş may be seen shopping or sitting on the benches along the harbour, waiting for the ferry home. It is easy to organise a day trip by boat, with so many of the tour operators in Kaş harbour offering excursions. But be warned

BELOW: the wider
the better.

that an overnight stay will render your day-long Turkish visa invalid and you may have problems getting back in.

The other, even more popular, boat trip is to the island of **Kekova** ⑬. Plenty of organised excursions leave from Kaş or Andriake, the seaport of Demre *(see below)*. Alternatively, you can hire a boat in **Üçağiz**, about 30 km/18 miles east of Kaş; to drive there, turn off the N-400 after 11 km (7 miles) and follow the signs. Üçağiz is a tiny fishing village but it has several decent seafood restaurants. A day out on the water, visiting Kekova Island or Kale (Simena), provides an idyllic combination of sunshine, swimming and historic ruins *(see below)*. The only drawback in high season is that your particular boat will probably be surrounded by about 50 others as the boatmen queue to point out a submerged Lycian tomb, sea cave, the occasional shaggy goat or the smouldering pyramids of wood used locally to make charcoal.

Almost next door to Üçağiz is the Lycian necropolis of **Teimiussa**, its chest-type tombs spread out along the shore. Along the edge of Kekova Island facing the mainland lie the half-submerged remains of a **sunken city**, destroyed in Byzantine times by a vicious earthquake. The authorities have given up the unequal struggle to keep people out and it is now possible to dive or snorkel among the ruins. You can also go ashore for a swim, walk or beach barbecue further west, near the crumbling remains of a Byzantine chapel.

Further round the coast, still on the mainland but accessible only by water, the village of **Kale** (ancient **Simena**) sits below the crenellated ramparts of an Ottoman castle, within which is a small Greek theatre, seating only about 300 people. Down in the harbour a cerulean sea laps at the feet of waterside restaurants offering simple Turkish menus including locally caught fish. A lone Lycian sarcophagus standing in a few inches of water at the western side lures visitors to pose beside it for photographs, an operation made more delicate by the resident spiny sea urchins.

Demre and Myra

Officially – and confusingly – also called Kale, **Demre** ⑭ is an expanding modern town, set in an ugly sea of tomato-growing greenhouses. This blot on the landscape is one of the most unattractive spots in Lycia, but the town does have several sights worth visiting. There are a couple of hotels, but it would be better to stay elsewhere and do a day trip.

Myra (open daily May–Sept 7.30am–7pm, Oct–Apr 8am–5.30pm; entrance fee), 1 km north of the town centre, was founded in the 5th century BC. It grew into one of the most important cities in the Lycian League, and later into a Christian bishopric, visited, among others, by St Paul. It was destroyed by the Arabs in the 7th century, but they left intact some of the finest examples of Lycian funerary architecture in the country.

There are two impressive sets of rock tombs, and many of them have log-cabin features carved into the rock – presumably reflecting the domestic architecture of the period. A few of the more accessible tombs have inscriptions in Lycian script. The carvings above are mostly in poor repair but the overall effect of this jumbled architecture of death is dramatic.

Map on pages 222–3

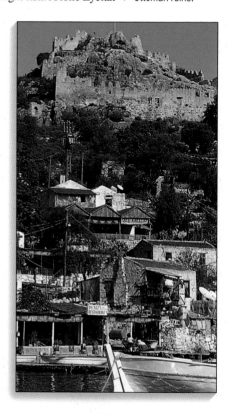

BELOW: Kale (Simena), with its Ottoman ruins.

The Roman city below the cliff is dominated by a large theatre – 150 metres (490 ft) in diameter. Much of the seating is intact, but part of the stage building has collapsed. However, many of its carvings and inscriptions are still visible, and the cavernous tunnels and access ways to the side have been cleared. A macabre set of carved comedy and tragedy masks, presumably from the frieze, lie upside down among the rubble on stage. Further tombs, the agora and an early fort are scattered in the vicinity for the more enthusiastic visitor. Visit as early as possible in the day to catch the morning sunlight.

In the town centre, the **Noel Baba Kilesi** (Church of St Nicholas; open daily 8.30am–4.30pm; entrance fee) is a charmingly painted reconstructed Byzantine church on the site where St Nicholas was bishop in the 4th century AD. The existing church was built in the 6th century over his tomb, repaired by Emperor Justinian, extended by Constantine IX in 1043, and by the Russians in the 19th century. The whole thing is now swamped by a hideous protective canopy and has sadly suffered bad flood damage in the last few years. However, it is still worth a visit. Guides happily point out St Nicholas' tomb even though his remains have not been here since 1087, when a band of merchants carried them off to Bari, Italy, where the Basilica of San Nicola was built to receive them.

A good 3-km (1½-mile) road leads from the N-400 along a marshy riverbed down to **Cayağzı** (ancient **Andriake**), which has been Demre's harbour since prehistoric times. Today, it is trying hard but unsuccessfully to compete with neighbouring resorts, but it does have a few seafood restaurants, a boatyard, a seafront walkway, and a vast 2nd-century AD Roman granary, built by Hadrian as a central supply depot for the entire empire, and reached across a footbridge.

Ask the man himself... checking up on St Nicholas.

BELOW: enjoying a smoke *al fresco*.

SANTA CLAUS

St Nicholas was born in Patara in about 300 AD, later becoming bishop of Myra, where he died. He was a leading member of the church and a delegate to the Council of Nicaea in 325, known both for his immense kindness and the miracles he performed in his lifetime. The link with Father Christmas stems perhaps from two legends: that he cast three bags of gold coins into the home of a merchant who had hit hard times, enabling his daughters to marry, and that he restored to life three boys who had been cut up by a local butcher. The first of these stories is also said to be the origin of the three gold balls that are still used today as the sign of a pawnbroker. Eventually, this busy saint became patron of Greece, Russia, prisoners, sailors, travellers, unmarried girls, merchants, pawnbrokers and children.

The Dutch, who corrupted his name to Sinterklaas (hence the name Santa Claus) began to celebrate his feast day on 6th December by filling the children's clogs with presents. This custom was soon attached to Christmas and the shoe became a stocking. The jolly man in red with a white beard was the 20th-century invention of the Coca Cola company – one of their most enduring advertising campaigns.

Map:
pages
222 & 231

The apple-blossom route

Finike ⓯ (ancient Phoenicus) is famous throughout Turkey for its huge sweet oranges, meltingly juicy honeydew melons and plump scarlet tomatoes. The town has deliberately steered away from the mass tourism development nearby, with relatively few low-key hotels. It is cheerful and clean and has some fine Ottoman houses and sandy beaches but little else to offer save the recollection that this was the site of the "Battle of the Masts" in 655, the first major naval victory of the Muslim Arabs over the Byzantines. The Arabs managed to overcome the enemy's "Greek fire" and turned the fight into one of hand-to-hand conflict by tying each of their ships to one of the Greeks'. The Arab chronicler Al-Tabari describes how the water became thick with blood.

Finike marks the southern end of one of the few roads to cross the mountains to the interior of Lycia, offering what is either a spectacularly beautiful excursion, away from the madding crowd, through the rugged Taurus Mountains and across the Anatolian plains, taking in ancient Limyra and Arykanda, or an alternative route through to Antalya. It gets its poetic name from the many apple orchards of the upland areas.

Head north from Finike on the N-635. After 7 km (4 miles), when you reach Turunçova, turn right for **Limyra** ⓰, which is 3 km (1½ miles) off the main road, along a narrow road through the villages. This was the 4th-century BC capital of Pericles, ruler of a section of Lycia, whose tomb, the **Heroön**, topped the highest point of the most extensive necropolis in Lycia (open access); the elaborate carvings are now in Antalya Museum. It is a steep 40-minute climb up, but the views of the coast are astounding. Less energetic visitors have plenty to occupy themselves with the mausoleum to Gaius Caesar, grandson of Augustus,

BELOW: the alluring Lycian coast – in this case, Olympos.

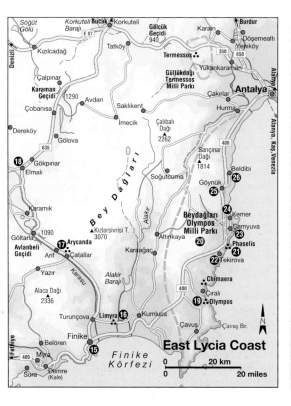

TIP

The yellow sign marking the turning to Arykanda is hidden round a steep, blind bend. The rough, single-track gravel access route to the site (about 1 km/½ mile) is just about passable by car and there is limited parking space. If possible, park near the restaurant and walk.

BELOW: the Roman architects of Arykanda chose their setting well.

who was destined to be emperor but died here of battle wounds before he could wear the purple robe. Near the **theatre** is the freestanding 4th-century BC **Tomb of Catabara**, with reliefs of a funeral banquet and the judgement of the dead. Many of the other tombs were painted. The buildings near the river belonged to a Byzantine convent.

Return to the main road for a further 21 km (13 miles) to the mountain hamlet of Arif and the stunningly beautiful Roman city of **Arykanda** (entrance fee). This is one of the most remote and least known of all Turkey's ancient cities, sited at the end of a plunging valley sprinkled with wild flowers and surrounded by peaks, snow-capped in spring. The lower area is centred on a bathhouse built in the 4th century AD from recycled materials. The sheds above cover the mosaic floors of a large **Byzantine basilica**, while further up the hill are the odeon, theatre, stadium and agora of the 1st–2nd century AD Roman city. From here, the path twists round the mountain to a superb **bathhouse** and gymnasium with 10-metre (33-ft) high arched ceilings, picture windows with views that stretch forever, and mosaic floors. Beyond that are a temple and the cemetery.

Return to the main road which continues north, crossing the huge shallow lake of Göltarla, which dries to a shimmering pan in summer, to the market town of **Elmalı** ⑱, on the slopes of 2,269-metre (7,442-ft) Elmalı Dağ ("Apple Mountain"). The town has a tiled 15th-century mosque and creaking but elegant timber-framed Ottoman mansions. There were several important Bronze Age settlements nearby, at Karataş-Semayük, Kızılbel and Karaburun, but none are open to the public; most of the finds are in the Antalya Archaeological Museum.

From here, the road continues through Korkuteli to Termessos, the Karain Cave and Antalya *(see page 234).*

The Olympic coast

The beautiful ancient city of **Olympos** ⑲ (open access) is tantalisingly close to the main road, but difficult to reach down a steep roller-coaster road of narrow hairpin bends. Once there, the visitor is offered the shattered remains of a monumental gateway, an acropolis, a river port, a small theatre and two sets of baths, all so overgrown that the site doubles as a wildlife sanctuary.

Olympos also has one of the longest large-pebble beaches in Turkey (as beach cafés are now banned here, bring your own drinks). Walk along it and ford the river, or take a second winding turning from the main road to the increasingly popular backpackers' hangout of **Çıralı**. A small hill at the back of the village is the site of an extraordinary natural phenomenon – a natural fire belching flames from tiny fissures in the rock, apparently the result of leaking methane gas. It is thought to be the origin of the Greek myth of the **Chimaera**, the fire-breathing monster with a lion's head, a goat's body and a serpent's tail that was finally destroyed by Bellerophon. The people of Olympos constructed a sanctuary here, dedicated to Hephaestus (Vulcan), the god of fire. It is a 20- to 30-minute walk to the unquenchable flames, which are best seen at dusk. The surrounding mountains all belong to the **Beydağları Olympos Milli Parkı** ⑳, which has a wide selection of hiking trails through the woods.

Phaselis ㉑ (open daily May–Oct 7.30am–7pm, Nov–Apr 8am–5.30pm; entrance fee) is probably the most accessible of the cities along the Lycian coast. It lies 18 km/11 miles south of Kemer, the site itself being about 3 km/1½ miles off the N-400 (1 km beyond the ticket booth). It is also one of the most charming – set on a wooded peninsula between three curved bays, all used as harbours by this busy trading port, which specialised in timber, rose oil and perfumes. Supposedly founded in the 7th century BC by colonists from Rhodes (who paid for the land with dried fish), its citizens were so wily that they were distrusted throughout the ancient world. Demosthenes (c. 383–322 BC) called them "the most scoundrelly and unscrupulous of men". Though the place is crawling with tourists who arrive by the bus- and boatload, it is worth taking some sunblock, a towel and a picnic and settling down for a serious day's sunbathing and swimming, interspersed with bouts of sightseeing.

North of Phaselis, the mountains pull back a little way from the coast, leaving stretches of sandy beach and flat building land that the developers have been quick to exploit. **Tekirova** ㉒ and **Çamyuva** ㉓ are so new that the ink is hardly dry on the maps, but already they have summer populations of thousands as their steadily increasing rows of hotels bulge at the seams with European and Russian tourists on two-week package tours.

The once gentle fishing village of **Kemer** ㉔ is now the hub of this tourist haven. It still has some ordinary folk, citrus farmers and fishermen, but most of its shops now sell carpets and sunglasses. The harbour is full of yachts that gleam in the bright sunshine, and the seafront pulses to a disco beat. Hotels come in all shapes and sizes; the vast all-inclusive resorts are laid out in regimented strips a few kilometres towards Antalya, at **Göynük** ㉕ and **Beldibi** ㉖. ❑

Map on page 231

The Chimaera at Olympos – mythical monster or natural phenomenon?

BELOW: pebble beach at Olympos.

Maps:
Area 222/3
City 235

PAMPHYLIA

Less proud and more pragmatic than Lycia, Pamphylia was happy to cooperate with Alexander and the Romans, assuring itself a good share of the conquerors' largesse

For years, increasing numbers of tourists have poured into ever bigger hotels along this relatively flat stretch of coastline, which provides good beaches and building land. The results are mixed. The influx has been good for conservation, with several of Turkey's finest Graeco-Roman cities on proud display; but while larger cities such as Antalya are flourishing, smaller coastal towns are being swamped, and the post 9/11 downturn in tourism is causing significant hardship for people who have come to rely too heavily on tourism.

Antalya

The hub of Turkey's Mediterranean coast is **Antalya ㉗** (ancient Attaleia), a city of nearly two million whose population swells by another 3–500,000 for most of the 300-day-long summer season. The city could hardly ask for much more in the way of natural assets: its stunning harbour, pretty old town and long, languid climate have made it a favourite port of call for many a European yachtsman. Those who prefer terra firma are pretty well done by too, for town planning has been carried out with taste and intelligence. Acres of parkland skirt the clifftops arching east and west of the harbour, giving a bird's-eye view of the port and some delightful walkways. Behind loom the misty purple Taurus Mountains. If Antalya wears a smug smile of complacence, she can well afford to do so, for this is perhaps Turkey's most beautiful city – small enough to allow everything central to be seen in a few days, and charming enough to make you long to stay.

The city was founded in 158 BC by King Attalus II of Pergamon and bequeathed to Rome in 133 BC. Although badly battered by the Arab invasions of the 7th century, it remained in Byzantine hands until the Seljuks arrived in 1206, and was a regular staging post for Crusaders on their way to the Holy Land. In the 1390s, control was handed to the Ottomans and remained with them until the area was occupied by Italy in 1919. Three years on, it was returned to Turkey.

Kaleiçi

The heart of the city is the beautifully restored old citadel of **Kaleiçi ㊫**, next to a harbour which now shelters vessels both sleek and seedy in a setting that could hold its own on the Riviera. The quayside and the citadel walls above are lined with outdoor seafood restaurants and cafés along with a veritable swarm of souvenir shops. A few old fishermen, their regular marina teahouse having been razed to make way for the tourist trade, continue to mend their nets, and pretend not to notice the change. Others ferociously hawk sea charters to the foreigners. Most of the crews speak rudimentary German or English. The small,

BELOW: cigarette seller.

modern amphitheatre on the waterfront is used for live performances in summer.

Before plunging into the mayhem of the old walled city, pause for a moment beside the magnificent equine **Atatürk Heykeli (Monument)** ❸ in Cumhuriyet Square. The statue itself is worth inspecting, but more importantly, it offers the best vantage point in the city.

Just to the left, the fortified **Saat Kulesi (Clock Tower)** ❻ at Kalekapısı, built in 1244 as an integral part of the city's defences, marks the entrance to the old town. Beside it is the 18th-century **Tekeli Mehmet Paşa Camii**. Just opposite (north of) that is a noisy bazaar selling everything from plastic buckets and *çorap* (hand-woven socks as long, colourful and thick as boots). All the other shops in the old town are given over to the tourist trade, with everything for sale from flimsy fake watches to exquisite jewellery and carpets fit for a sultan. Sadly, window shopping is trying in the extreme due to the aggressive sales techniques of the touts.

Directly ahead of you, the **Yivli Minare (Fluted Minaret)** ❿, the symbol of Antalya and the city's oldest Seljuk monument, dates from the reign of Sultan Alâeddin Keykubat I (1219–38). Exquisite turquoise and blue tiles are set into the 8-metre (26-ft) high minaret itself, while the pool in front is of marble.

The **Eski Camii** next door was built in 1373 by Mehmet Bey. In the grounds, a huge, ancient olive tree has grown up to enclose the grave of a wise muezzin. If you write your request on a piece of paper, wrap it in an olive leaf and leave it in the hollow trunk, your wish will, of course, be granted.

Nearby is a simple and elegant octagonal *türbe* (tomb), made of fine white masonry, built in 1377 in the tradition of central Asian Turks. The big white-washed building to the side, dating from the 14th century, was formerly a dervish

Painted dolls are a speciality of Alanya.

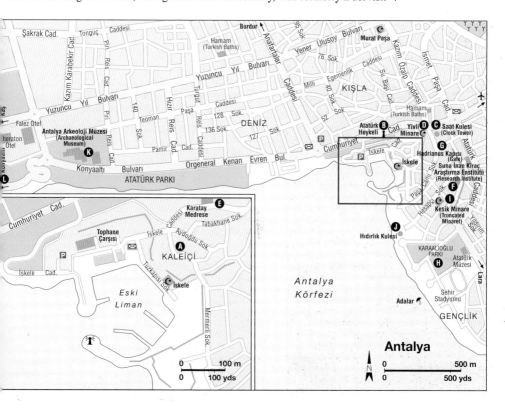

The Kesik Minare, cut off in its prime.

convent. From here, roads meander downhill to the harbour or west along the line of the walls to the other section of the old town, where a number of historic houses have been charmingly restored as hotels and *pansiyons*.

Carry on down the hill and you reach the triumphal entrance of the recently restored **Karatay Medrese** ❺, a religious school built by a Seljuk vizier in 1250. The 13th-century **Ala'addin Camii,** just to the west, is thought to have once been a Byzantine church.

Within the maze of alleys overhung by wooden-frame houses, two Ottoman mansions and the Greek Church of Agios Georgios have been turned into the **Suna-İnan Kiraç Araştirma Enstitütü (Research Institute)** ❻ (Kocatepe Sok 25; tel: 0242-243 4274; open Thur–Tues 9am–noon, 1–6pm in winter; 9am–noon, 2–7.30pm in summer; entrance fee), with exhibition space dedicated to the archaeology, history, ethnography and culture of Mediterranean civilisations. The exhibitions, including displays from the Kiraç family's private collection, are constantly changing.

A few blocks away, **Hadrianus Kapısı (Hadrian's Gate)** ❼ is a stately triple-arched structure of white marble, built in honour of the Emperor's visit in AD 130. Step through it back into the modern world of **Atatürk Caddesi,** a jazzy street, home to Antalya's trendiest cinemas and burger bars, which leads down to **Karaalioğlu Parkı** ❽, atop the cliffs to the east of the harbour, a peaceful shady park ideal for sitting out the heat of the day. At the eastern end of the park, the decapitated minaret of the **Kesik Minare** ❾ is all that remains of a 13th-century mosque that was struck by lightning in 1851 – before the introduction of lightning conductors. Originally a 5th-century church dedicated to the Virgin Mary, it was constructed using 2nd- and 3rd-century spoils.

On the clifftops above the harbour stand the old city walls and ramparts built by the Greeks and restored by the Romans and Seljuks. The skyline is broken by the 13.5 metre (44 ft) tall **Hıdırlık Kulesi** ❶. The sombrely designed lower square section is believed to have been a Hellenic tomb, while the tower itself was built by the Romans in the 2nd century AD as a lighthouse, and adapted by the Seljuks for defence. There is a tiny beach below, reached by steep stone steps from the restaurant on the east side of the harbour.

Konyaaltı

The **Antalya Arkeoloji Müzesi (Archaeological Museum)** ❸ (at Cumhuriyet Cad., 2 km/1 mile west of the town centre; tel: 0242-238 5688; open Tues–Sun 8.30am–5pm; entrance fee) is one of the finest in Turkey, with magnificent exhibits, beautifully displayed, and a children's room with a model village and tables where children can play safely under supervision.

Most of the finds come from the surrounding area, including many millennia of prehistory from the Karain Caves, Bronze Age jewellery and toys from Elmalı, and exquisite classical statuary from Perge and Aspendos, beautifully displayed in the Perge Gallery. The Hall of the Gods displays statues of the Greek gods, Emperors Hadrian and Septimius Severus and their empresses, while the Sarcophagus Gallery even contains the elaborate tomb of a much-loved dog, Stephanos. Other exhibits include part of a stunning mosaic collection from Xanthos depicting the infant Achilles being dangled by his mother into the River Styx. A display of icons includes the familiar portrait of St Nicholas and a box which once contained his "relics". Facing it is a superb collection of 6th-century church silver, part of which was illegally looted and ended up in

Maps:
Area 222/3
City 235

BELOW: Roman sarcophagus at Antalya Museum.

Dumbarton Oaks Museum, Washington. There is also a broad-based ethnographic collection with displays on Turkish lifestyle, dress, musical intruments and carpets. Allow plenty of time, as this museum is a real treat, with an excellent gift shop and garden café.

To the west stretches the pebbly 3 km-long (2-mile) **Konyaaltı Beach** . In recent years, this has been upgraded to provide Antalya with a really attractive and entertaining seafront, with two of Antalya's finest hotels, a number of good restaurants, tennis courts, mini-golf, an aqua-park, funfair and all the other beachfront jollities. The beach itself is almost always overcrowded.

Most of Antalya's mass-market hotels march in serried ranks along the clifftops of **Lara**. This area, stretching for nearly 12 km (7 miles) east of the city, has become an entire suburb of monolithic hotels and holiday apartments which offer a full range of prices and facilities including swimming pools, helicopter landing pads, tennis courts and a host of aquatic sports. Many have steep staircases down the cliff to private swimming platforms. Good beaches are easily reached from the Lara *dolmuş*. The best local beaches are Büyük Çaltıcak and Küçük Çaltıcak, 10–12 km (5–6 miles) west of the city.

North of the city

In addition to its intrinsic charms, Antalya is an immensely useful base, with an international airport, well-placed for easy excursions to such echoes from the ancient world as the cities of Perge, Aspendos, Side, Phaselis and Termessos.

The ancients knew a good beach when they saw one, but they also had a taste for inland vistas, and the plateau behind Antalya, a separate ancient kingdom known as Pisidia, is as studded with ruins as the shores of the Mediterranean.

BELOW: inscription at Termessos, the ferocious "Eagle's Nest" of ancient Pisidia.

Maps:
Area 222/3
City 235

One of the most remarkable of these inland sites is **Termessos** ❷❽ (open daily 8am–7pm; entrance fee), high in the mountains, 37 km (22 miles) northeast of Antalya, off the N-350 to Korkuteli. The car park is about 9 km (5½ miles) along a forest road from the main road; there is then a steep, 2-km (1-mile) walk to the site. There are no refreshments so you'll need to take your own.

The defences of this Pisidian city so daunted Alexander the Great when he came conquering in 333 BC that he raised the siege, burnt down their olive groves and slunk away. It is easy to understand why: the steep, winding road and the remains of the stout defending walls are enough to show the visitor a little of what the Greek adventurer would have faced.

The origin of the city is uncertain but the founders, who called themselves the Solymians, are identified with the Pisidians who occupied the lake district further north (around Burdur and Eğirdir). They called their city the "Eagle's Nest" with good reason. It is perched between summits at about 900 metres (3,000 ft) facing the rugged Güllük Daği, across a narrow canyon. The distant view of the coast alone is magnificent, but the ruins are also fascinating. The vast, cut stones of the walls and the superb theatre lie in a jumble as if tossed around like a giant's playthings – the great earthquake of AD 527 destroyed the majority of the towns on the coastal plain, and left all in a state of ruin. Other remains include an agora, a gymnasium, an odeon, five enormous water cisterns, carved into the rock, and some 1,000 tombs climbing the hillside to the fire-watch tower above.

The site is part of the **Güllükdaği Termessos Milli Parkı** (National Park), an area of dense forest, famed for its birds and butterflies, with several fine hiking trails. Across the main road, the village of **Teniköy** is famous for producing fine Doşemealtı carpets, with strong reds and blues and geometric designs.

The caves of **Karain Mağarası** ❷❾ (open daily 8.30am–5pm; entrance fee) are 27 km (16 miles) northwest of Antalya, off the N-650 to Burdur, about 6 km (3½ miles) from the main road. Finds from these remarkable caves go back to the paleolithic (Old Stone Age), some 30,000 years ago. People lived here for nearly 20,000 years and excavation has yielded tools, axes and other crude implements, the skull of a Neanderthal child, and the bones of an ancient elephant, hippopotamus and bear. Most are on display in Antalya and Ankara, but there is a small site museum. All three caverns have stalactites and stalagmites.

A short distance away as the crow flies, but a long road trip, is **Kocain Mağarası** ❸❶. This is Turkey's largest accessible cave, an awe-inspiring 633 metres (2,000 ft) long and 35 metres (100 ft) high, with giant stalactite pillars. At present, you can only visit on your own, with a torch and good boots, but there are plans to improve access. Take the Burdur road for 27 km (16 miles), then turn off to the villages of **Karataş** and **Karavelıler**. It is a two-hour walk up to the cave.

The limestone country around Antalya is riddled with waterfalls, of which the most famous are the **Düden Şelalesi** ❸❶, two separate cascades on a powerful underground river. The Upper Falls, which have carved out a pretty gorge 14 km (8½ miles) northeast of Antalya, are a popular local picnic spot. The 20-metre (65-ft) high Lower Düden Falls crash

BELOW: Düden Falls.

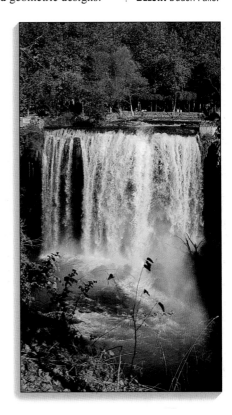

The word Pamphylia means "land of all tribes" in ancient Greek. Historians agree that the fall of Troy in c. 1184 BC brought about the real settlement of the area as refugees flooded in looking for a new start. Their descendants were unable to find peace, however. Pamphylia has been subjugated at least 10 times in the succeeding millennia.

BELOW: the Roman and Hellenistic gates at Perge.

over the cliff into the sea at Lara, 10 km (6 miles) east of Antalya. They are best seen from one of the many boat trips leaving from Antalya harbour.

The **Kurşunlu Şelalesi** 🐘, about 23 km (14 miles) east of Antalya (7 km/4 miles off the main road), are even more popular because of their proximity to Perge and Aspendos. The unusual green-coloured water is surrounded by walkways, picnic tables, a children's playground, souvenirs and even camel rides.

Perge and Aspendos

The most impressive ruins on the Pamphylian coast are at **Perge** 🐘, 15 km (9 miles) east of Antalya along the N-400, 2 km (1 mile) from Aksu, though they are not on the scale of Ephesus or Pergamon. The site is open daily May–Sept 9am–7.30pm, Oct–Apr 9am–6pm; entrance and parking fee.

Known to the Hittites as far back as 1300 BC, the city was a successful trading centre, which kept itself alive and healthy through pragmatism – it had no defensive walls until fortified by the Seleucids in the 2nd century BC. Alexander the Great was welcomed in, and used the city as a base throughout his Anatolian campaigns. The city finally declined during the Byzantine era when the river silted, stranding the port 12 km (7 miles) from the sea.

The red **Hellenistic Gate** towers still stand almost at their original height, but most of "modern" Perge – the 14,000-seat theatre, stadium, hamams and colonnaded street – belongs to the period of Pax Romana. The resplendent **agora** belongs to the 4th century AD. The **stadium** (234 metres/775 ft long and 34 metres/110 ft wide, with seating for 12,000) is one of the best preserved of the ancient world. Of its 30 outward-facing chambers, 20 were used as shops; several wall inscriptions reveal the names of their proprietors as well as their trade.

The truly magnificent finds from this ancient city on display in Antalya Museum *(see page 237)* include a 2nd-century sarcophagus depicting the 12 labours of Hercules and numerous colossal statues of gods and emperors. One name that crops up frequently on statue bases is that of a woman, Plancia Magna. She was the daughter of the governor and a priestess of Artemis, goddess of the moon and patron of the city, in the 2nd century AD. Her legacy contributed approximately 20 statues to the city; her tomb, or what remains of it, lies just outside one of the city gates.

To reach **Sillyon** 🐘 (open access; guide recommended), turn off the N-400 7 km (4 miles) beyond Perge, follow the road for 8 km (5 miles) to Asar Köyü, then climb up the steep unmarked dirt track to the site. The flat-topped acropolis was once the site of a city as old and rich as Perge (but never conquered by Alexander). Sadly, its ruins were badly damaged during massive landslides in 1969 and today it is usually ignored in favour of its more spectacular neighbours.

Some 45 km (25 miles) east of Antalya and 5 km (3 miles) off the main road, imposing **Aspendos** 🐘 (open daily May–Sept 8am–7pm, Oct–Apr 8.30am–5pm; entrance fee) is graced by one of the finest surviving Roman **theatres** in the world. Built during the reign of Emperor Marcus Aurelius (161–180 AD) and seating 15,000, the elaborate structure is nearly intact except for part of the upper cornice. Its architect was

Xeno, a local lad, whose secret formula for creating such perfect acoustics has not yet been discovered – a coin dropped from the orchestra pit can be heard distinctly from the galleries. The Seljuks used the theatre as a caravansaray in the 13th century; Atatürk suggested that it be used for oil wrestling. For 1,800 years neither earthquakes, the ravages of war, nor time have taken their toll. Today, the ancient theatre hosts concerts and an important opera and ballet festival in June and July.

Behind it lie the ruins of the acropolis, agora, nymphaeum, and what may be the best surviving example of a Roman aqueduct. The annals inform us that the river was navigable as far as Aspendos and the city was used as a naval base, although this seems fairly improbable today. It certainly prospered from trading luxury goods, a tradition kept up by local shopkeepers today. The nearby village of **Belkıs** has several very upmarket souvenir superstores, with some of the finest jewellery, carpets and leather on sale outside Istanbul.

The new coastal resort of **Belek** ㊱, only a stone's throw from Antalya airport, is growing so fast that residents are afraid to blink. It has a wonderful white-sand beach, currently shared by a burgeoning line of seriously upmarket resort hotels and some rather beleaguered turtles, while inland is a growing sea of cheap apartment blocks and anonymous mass-market hotels, centred on a very small shopping centre. The most popular attractions here are the four golf courses.

Köprülü Kanyon

A short distance beyond Aspendos, a tarmac road cuts off the main coastal highway leading to the beautiful, cool, green **Köprülü Kanyon** ㊲, a high mountain gorge sliced by the tumbling milky turquoise Köprülü Gayı

The familiar masks of comedy and tragedy grew from Greek theatre.

Map on pages 222–3

LEFT: the great theatre at Aspendos.

HIGH DRAMA

In the 6th century BC, the ancient Greeks began to create a series of religious dance and music dramas in honour of Dionysus (god of revelry and inspiration). In 534 BC, the first public drama competition, the City Dionysia, was held in Athens. It was won by a masked actor/writer called Thespis, who played all the characters, supported by a large chorus. The performance space was originally a dusty circle (the orchestra) in front of the altar. This was transformed by the mid-4th century BC by the addition of seating into a ("place of seeing").

The festival developed until three playwrights each had to produce three linked tragedies (for example The Oresteia by Aeschylus) and a satire, to be performed on the same day, sponsored by a wealthy citizen, a choregon. The first classic play to survive, *The Persians*, also by Aeschylus (who added a second actor), was performed in 472 BC. At much the same time, a winter festival, the Lenea, was dedicated to comedy, much of it broad political satire. Sophocles added a third actor and by the time of Euripides, characters (for example, Medea) were much more psychologically rounded, the chorus more background comment than crucial to the plot. Very few complete plays survive.

(Eurymedon River). The tarred road ends a few kilometres past **Beşkonak** after 43 km (26 miles). Fishing for brown trout is technically illegal, but the authorities seem to turn a blind eye.

The gaggle of waterside restaurants are eager to feed you on pellet-fed rainbow trout, while teenage guides urge you to follow them on walking trails to the dramatic Roman bridge which gave the canyon its name (about 1 km/½ mile downstream on the far side of the river). Beşkonak is also the base for several whitewater-rafting companies offering half- and full-day trips (most will collect from hotels throughout the Antalya area).

Those with good shock-absorbers should continue carefully up the road for a further 14 km (8½ miles), across a high plateau, its soft volcanic rock carved and twisted into columns ("fairy chimneys") by the wind, to the village of **Altınkaya (Zerk)** and the ruins of ancient **Selge** ❸ (open access). Very little remains aside from the magnificent Greek-style theatre with its backdrop of the snow-capped peak of Bozburun. The stadium has been turned into a terraced field for one of the local families. The Roman road, forum, Byzantine basilica and twin temples to Artemis and Zeus are more imagination than fact. Once the swarms of children calm down, they will lead you to the few remains of the ancient town's reliefs and statues, hidden in rock slides and undergrowth.

Side: old crowds and new

Although founded as long ago as the 7th century BC, the peninsula town of **Side** ❸ has undergone its most startling transformation over the past 20 years. Until the beginning of the 21st century, it was a sleepy fishing village; most of today's *pansiyon* and restaurant owners were yesterday's fishermen who have

BELOW: tickle the trout while eating their cousins.

lost interest in the humble hook and line. Tourism has become big business, and the Greek, Roman and Byzantine ruins are totally overshadowed by the mushrooming of hotels, restaurants, carpet shops and snack bars. Still, with the discos and cafés stuffed between ancient columns, Side retains its charm, and is unique in Turkey as a living open-air museum in a spectacular setting.

Perhaps this is because Side (meaning "pomegranate" in Anatolian) is no stranger to crowds. With a population of some 60,000, it was the largest, richest port on the south coast, with an unsavoury reputation. Alexander the Great's biographer Arrian recorded that when his master captured the city in 333 BC, its people spoke a tongue unknown to the invaders – in fact it remains undeciphered to this day. Rampant piracy flourished, with prisoners sold as slaves in the town agora to be sent next to the island of Delos, a notorious depot for human merchandise in antiquity.

The incoming road is a maze of twists and turns littered with Byzantine ruins. Suddenly, past the entrance gate and Vespasian monument, the vast Roman **theatre** (seating 25,000 people) looms into view. Beside it are the **agora**, the remains of a 24-seat public lavatory, a Byzantine basilica, episcopal palace, and remnants of the city wall, beyond which is access to the beach.

Across the road from the theatre, the old **Roman Baths** now house the town **museum** (open Tues–Sun

Map
on pages
222–3

9am–noon, 1.30–6.30pm; entrance fee) displaying finds from local excavations, including many fine, headless statues; St Paul was so convincing as a speaker that the newly converted Christians rushed out and, in a fit of wild overenthusiasm, decapitated their former pagan deities. In fact, Side served as a bishopric in the Byzantine period and most of the monuments lying in such profusion around the village are relics of the early Christian era. Safe parking is a little further along, just before the main shopping street.

Ancient Side declined in the 7th century under relentless Arab attacks, and was finally abandoned in 1150 after earthquakes, too, had taken their toll. Sand drifts now cover most of the southeast section of the old city. Take a walk off the beaten paths, and one has that special sense of being the first to find this ancient wall or shattered cistern, buried in thistles and weeds.

Beaches line either side of the peninsula, so swimming is invited; diving off the rocks and foundation stones of the old harbour is pleasant but frustrating: too many other divers have had the same thought, and few fish remain. Finally, with the setting sun, make for the headland and the twin **Temples of Apollo and Athena**, for a superb show of flaming colour over a wine-dark sea.

If Side is bulging with tourists, neighbouring **Manavgat ⓐ** is a bustling Turkish business and farming community. Monday is market day and a good opportunity to buy the local crafts, old coins or rugs found among the fruit, vegetables and squawking chickens. The only real reason to visit the town is for an excursion by boat up the river to the pleasant but unspectacular **Manavgat Falls**. Boats leave from Side and from the quay beside the main bridge in town. Natural vegetation forms a tropical curtain over the river; be prepared to get out and dig as the river mouth sometimes silts up overnight.

Pamphylia's friendship with Pergamon and Rome assured its citizens had the finest things in life.

BELOW: sunset at the Temple of Apollo, Side.

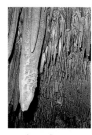

Damlatas Cave, whose weeping rocks cure human ills.

A few kilometres on, a yellow sign points up a scenic road to **Alarahan** ⓪, a well preserved and atmospheric Seljuk **caravansaray** on the banks of the Alara River, constructed in 1231 by Sultan Alâeddin Keykubat I. On a rocky crag above sits **Alara Castle**, its fortress wall running crazily along the summit, a long tunnel leading down through the mountain to the river, where white-water rafters sport in the spring.

İ**ncekum** ⓫, about 20 km (12 miles) west of Alanya, is blessed with one of the finest, longest golden-sand beaches on Turkey's Mediterranean coast. The result has been an explosion of giant resort hotels which line the road as far as the eye can see. Almost all are self-contained; some are all-inclusive – the mainly German guests stay within the grounds, eat at the hotel restaurants, use the hotel's watersports facilities, drink themselves stupid and end up in the local hospital with alcohol poisoning. The village of İncekum has a few newish shops but has benefited little from the annual invasion of tourists.

Alanya

BELOW: the Seljuk Kizil Küle, Alanya.

The rapidly expanding modern city of **Alanya** ⓭, 110 km (70 miles) east of Antalya, sprawls along two broad bays, an elegant, broad-avenued town, which is justifiably one of Turkey's most popular resorts, with a fine harbour and a peaceful, unhurried air. The city centre is sliced emphatically in two by a magnificent 250-metre (800-ft) high promontory of sheer red-gold rock jutting out into the Mediterranean. On the summit, nearly 7 km (4 miles) of ancient curtain walls with 150 bastions wind around three towers, forming the most spectacular and effective fortress on the Turkish coast. There are dizzying views of the sea on three sides, and the orchard-covered foothills of the Taurus Mountains behind. You may notice Turkish visitors throwing pebbles from the summit. Legend says that condemned prisoners were given the same chance. If they threw a pebble into the sea (no mean feat), they were set free; if not, they were hurled immediately to their deaths on the rocks below.

Although the exact foundation date of Alanya is unknown, it traces back to Hellenistic times, when it was named Coracesium, with the Romans, Byzantines, Armenians, Seljuks and Ottomans all taking their turn at power. Pirate chieftain Diototus Tryphon built his fortress on the peak in the 2nd century BC. This was the last bastion to fall to the fury of the Roman General Pompey in his crusade to wipe out the pirates in 65 BC. Later, Mark Antony presented the land to Cleopatra, who made good use of its fine timber, both to rebuild her fleet and for export.

As the Byzantine Empire declined, the south coast was poorly defended, and various Armenian dynasties took advantage of the weakness. In the 10th century Alanya proved no exception to this change of fortune. When the Seljuks tried to wrest control of the fortress in 1222, they found it to be a formidable target. Legend has it that Sultan Alâeddin Keykubat I, at his wit's end, gambled on a last desperate bid. He conscripted into his army hundreds of wild goats. Tying a lighted candle to each of their horns, he shepherded his new recruits ahead of his army up the cliffs. The

enemy, upon seeing the obvious strength of the invaders, surrendered at once and were exiled to Konya – but not before Keykubat had married the daughter of the ousted leader. Keykubat renamed the city *Alaiye* ("city of Ala") in his own honour. It was captured by the Ottomans in 1471.

Today, the markedly different contributions of the Romans, Byzantines and Seljuks to the fortress are clearly discernible. There is a domed Byzantine church (6th-century) dedicated to St George, a flight of red brick stairs said to have been used by Cleopatra when she descended to the sea to bathe, store rooms, numerous cisterns – the largest of which could hold 120,000 tons of water – a hefty advantage during protracted sieges. Just outside the wall, the *bedesten* (inn), now once more restored and operating as a hotel, lies within an attractive tangle of virtually ruinous stone houses, vines and fruit trees.

The road to the castle is a steep 5-km (3-mile) climb and a taxi or *dolmuş* to the top is a wise investment. Save your energy for the walk downhill through carob and fig trees, and scented jasmine, with stunning views of the harbour below. There are regular teahouses and drinks stands en route.

Just west of the fortress at sea level, next to the tourist office, is the **Damlataş Mağarasi** (open daily 6am–10am for patients, 10am–7pm for the public; entrance fee) or "Weeping Cave", an exquisite grotto with curtains of dripping stalactites and stalagmites 15,000–20,000 years old. Its claimed 80 percent success rate in curing respiratory ailments, especially asthma, is apparently due to the atmosphere: 90–100 percent humidity, constant temperature of 22–23°C (71–73°F), high levels of carbon dioxide, natural ionisation and radiation. People come from all over Turkey for this cure, for which a doctor's certificate is required: four hours per day for 21 days. Knots of bescarved women while away the hours as

Map on pages 222–3

BELOW: the fishing fleet in port, Alanya.

Map on pages 222–3

they knit, sew and crochet their way to a clearer respiratory system in this warm, damp enclave. For those interested, doctors in Alanya will examine you and write the necessary report. People with heart ailments may have breathing difficulties here as the dense air pressure makes the heart work overtime.

Just round the corner, the compact **Alanya Museum** (Azaklar Sok, south of Atatürk Cad.; open Tues–Sun 9am–noon, 1.30–6.30pm; entrance fee) has sections on archaeology and ethnography. The exhibits are carefully chosen and well labelled, and the garden contains antique farming implements.

Directly to the east of the citadel is the city harbour, heavily fortified by Sultan Alâeddin Keykubat I. Chief among the defences was the 35-metre (115-ft) octagonal **Kızıl Küle** (Red Tower), designed in 1227 by a Syrian architect, which is now home to a small **ethnographic museum** (open daily 10am–8pm; entrance fee). There are fine views from the battlements. Round the point, at the harbour entrance, is another tower, the **Tophane Küle** (**Arsenal Tower**), used as a cannon foundry by the Ottomans. Between the two is the **Tersane** (open access; best seen from the water), a series of five huge open workshops which were the centrepiece of the Selçuks' naval dockyard, also built in 1227.

Today, the harbour is humming with activity, lined by pavement cafés, with fishing and tourist boats jostling for space along the quays. Alanya's coast has a host of grottoes, and boat trips can be arranged to any or all – Pirate's Cave, Lovers' Grotto, one where phosphorescent pebbles shine up from the sea bed; or to the "wishing gate", an enormous natural hole in the rocks. It is said that barren women who go through this gate will gain the ability to conceive.

Each side of Alanya boasts good, somewhat grey sandy beaches, backed by a host of hotels; the eastern part of the town sports a wider selection. ❑

BELOW: the golden sand of Alanya beach.

Flora

Although it is little known for its flora, Turkey is a paradise for nature lovers, with every region offering a new climate and ecosystem. More than 9,000 species of plants exist in Turkey, of which 3,000 are endemic, only growing in Anatolia. There are some 40 national parks and forests.

Heavy rainfall throughout the year, combined with warm summers and mild winters along the eastern Black Sea coast, cover the mountain slopes with beech, oak and maple. Between them stretch velvet emerald blankets of tea plantations. Gigantic, ageing sycamore, chestnut and pine forests cover much of northwestern Turkey, turning every autumn into a kaleidoscope of colour. Vivid yellow sunflowers brighten Thrace and Marmara in summer, while cluster pine forests cascade down the mountains to the seashores of the southwest, and fragrant pink and white oleanders grow along the Aegean and Mediterranean. On the steppes of central and eastern Turkey, a wide variety of spiky cacti bloom during the long, dry summers.

Istanbul residents seeking respite from the cacophony of the city in a natural preserve drive to the **Belgrad Ormanı** (Belgrade Forest), 40 km (25 miles) north; those in Bursa head for the **Uludağ National Park**.There are also excellent botanical gardens outside both cities where tulips are amongst the many indigenous flowers on brilliant display.

Many bulbous plants and flowers, including *kardelen* (snowdrops or *Galanthus nivalis)*, *karcicegi* (snowflakes or *Leucojum)* and cyclamen are commercially grown and exported. Farmers in Isparta province cultivate roses for their oil (attar of roses), which is exported to France as an essential ingredient in the perfume industry.

Red Anatolian poppies *(Gelincik)* grow wild throughout Turkey, but are commercially produced around Afyon to provide opium for use in codeine medicines.

Oriental tobacco, known for its short stalks, small leaves and aromatic flavour, is grown on sun-drenched slopes in western Turkey, the Marmara region, the Black Sea coast around Samsun and throughout southeastern Turkey by thousands of farmers. Turkey produces 3 percent of the world's tobacco crop and 40 percent of all Oriental tobacco, which requires no irrigation, except normal seasonal rains, and is sun-cured.

Hazelnuts are cultivated all along the Black Sea Coast of Turkey, from Akcakhoca in the west to Rize in the east. Turkey is the world's biggest producer and exporter of hazelnuts, which are consumed alone or used in the chocolate and bakery industries in Europe and the United States.

Turkey is also the world's sixth-largest producer of cotton, which is grown in the fertile valleys of the Aegean Coast, the Çukurova in southern Turkey and now in the arid southeast of Turkey, as a result of major irrigation projects along the Tigris and Euphrates rivers.

Sugar beet is cultivated all along the Kızılirmak, Sakarya and Yesilirmak rivers that run through central and northwestern Anatolia, providing the raw materials for the country's 30-plus sugar manufacturers. ❑

RIGHT: spring flowers add a splash of colour to the Anatolian hills.

Map
on pages
222–3

İstanbul
● Ankara

CILICIA

*The road snakes along soaring cliffs above crashing waves,
while Hellenistic, Byzantine and Seljuk ruins stud the
tiny coves of this most dramatic coast*

The first few kilometres across flat farmland east from Alanya to **Gazipaşa** give no clue as to what comes next – nearly 200 km (124 miles) of fabulous coastal scenery, enough to send vertigo sufferers into total meltdown. Pine forests and mud-plastered houses cling absurdly to the cliffs, terraced banana plantations step resolutely down into the sea, and tiny coves jostle for space. The views are superb, and the journey justifiably famed; even better, there is an almost total absence of Western tourists.

Anamur ❹, 130 km (80 miles) east of Alanya and several kilometres inland, has no particular claim to fame. Its seaside suburb of İskele, 5 km (3 miles) south, is a nice small resort with several good basic hotels and fish restaurants along a white-sand turtle beach, a colony of monk seals and a small **museum** (İskele Cad., tel: 0324-814 1677; open Tues–Sun 8am–5pm; entrance fee).

About 5 km (3 miles) west of town, on the southernmost tip of Asia Minor, slumber the ruins of ancient **Anemurium**, meaning "windy cape" (open daily 8am–8pm; entrance fee). Founded by the Hittites in about 1200 BC, the city became a great trading centre and Byzantine bishopric, thriving until a devastating earthquake in AD 580 was too closely followed by Arab invasions. The well-preserved ruins of the town are overwhelmed by the cemetery, a vast sprawl of some 350 domed tombs. Recruit a guide to show you frescoes and buried mosaics. The setting and the ruins themselves are intensely atmospheric and adjoin a swimming beach and picnic area.

Five km (3 miles) east of Anamur town, on the N-400, **Mamure Kalesi** (Anamur Castle; open daily 9am–5.30pm; entrance fee) stands romantically with one foot in the sea. The first fortress here was built in the 3rd century AD, but it has had many other incarnations: as a 10th-century pirates' lair, and as the property of 11th- to 12th-century kings of Armenia. The surviving magnificent castle was built in 1226 by the great Seljuk Sultan Alâeddin Keykubat I; the mosque and rooms overlooking the sea from the upper battlements were added by Karamanoğlu ruler Mahmut Bey (1300–08). In the late 14th century, it became a mainland toehold for the crusading Lusignan kings of Cyprus, until it was seized by the Ottomans in 1469. It remained in use until the end of World War I.

Ascending and descending in a series of hairpin turns, passing several more aesthetically pleasing but anonymous castles, the coastal road finally hits the Göksu delta near **Taşucu** ❺, one of the two ferry embarkation points (the other is Mersin) for the Turkish Republic of Northern Cyprus. One hydrofoil service and one car ferry leave from here daily. Taşucu itself is a bustling ferry port with several hotels and *pansiyons* on the waterfront to the east of town.

BELOW: taking the oranges to market.

About 5 km (3 miles) further on, at **Ayatekla** ㊻, just left of the highway, a ruined Byzantine basilica towers near the underground hermitage of St Thecla, one of St Paul's first converts. On hearing Paul preach the virtues of chastity in Iconium (Konya), she promptly renounced her betrothal; on a later visit to the apostle in prison, she too was arrested and sentenced to be burned at the stake and tied naked to a pyre in the arena. A divinely inspired deluge doused the flames. Wild beasts were brought in to devour her, but "there was about her a cloud, so that neither the beasts did touch her, nor was she seen to be naked," according to Acts of Paul and Thecla, written in the 2nd century by an unknown Asian presbyter. Once the Romans had given up, she set up a nunnery near ancient Seleucia, where her miraculous cures were said to have taken business away from the town doctors. Eventually, she flew bodily up to heaven.

Anemurium's ghostly city of the dead guards the southern point of Anatolia.

Silifke

Like all coastal cities in Turkey, **Silifke** ㊼ has ancient roots, but precious little remains of ancient Seleucia ad Calycadnum, which was one of nine sister cities founded by Seleucos Nicator in the 3rd century BC after he gained control of Syria on the death of Alexander the Great.

The town is dominated by a vast hilltop **castle** (open daily 8.30am–5pm; entrance fee), which is 4 km (2½ miles) from town and reached from the Konya road. Built originally by the Byzantines but heavily altered by the Armenians and Crusaders, it was captured by the Turks in the late 13th century. From the ramparts there is a superb view, with all the town's other monuments laid out like a map at your feet. Directly below are the Roman necropolis, aqueduct and a vast Byzantine cistern carved from the bedrock. The **stone bridge** over the

BELOW: Anamur, a perfect medieval castle, perfectly positioned.

TIP

Those tackling the coast road east from Alanya to Silifke should set out early in the morning. The road is long and treacherous and the afternoon sun in your eyes is hazardous. If travelling by bus, book a seat on the right to make the best of the superlative views.

Göksu River also has ancient origins (it was first built by Vespasian in AD 78) while the riverside park surrounds an unexcavated *höyük* or tell (archaeologica mound), first fortified by the Assyrians in the 8th century BC. On the right o Inönü Bulvarı stands a single column of the 2nd- or 3rd-century AD **Temple o Zeus**; no sign has yet been found of the city's famous oracle of Apollo Sarpedonios. The **Ulucamii** is of Seljuk origin, and while no trace of decoration remains, the *mihrab* and the entrance are original.

The local tourist office (Gazi Mah. Veli Gürten Bozbey Cad. 6; tel: 0324-714 1151) is enthusiastic and there is a pleasant little **museum** (open Tues–Sun 8am–noon, 1.30–5pm; entrance fee) with a remarkable hoard of Seleucian coins on Taşucu Caddesi, the main Antalya road.

The road north

Silifke marks the real end of the tourist coast. From here on, the landscape flattens into dreary coastal plains and industrial wastelands, although towns such as ancient Tarsus are atmospheric. Many choose to take the road north over the mountains to Konya (*see page 284*) and Cappadocia (*see page 290*), two of the most captivating places in Turkey. Even the road itself, the N-715, is breathtaking, worth doing as a side trip if you are planning to continue east.

The early stages follow the turbulent path of the Göksu River. The Third Crusade came to an abrupt end some 16 km (10 miles) north of Silifke, when Holy Roman Emperor Frederick Barbarossa drowned while bathing on his way to Jerusalem in 1190; a **memorial** marks the spot. He was a long way from home and in order to preserve his body until they could get him to Antioch for burial on Christian land, he was stored in a barrel of vinegar. He was later taken

BELOW: whitewater rafting is a popular pastime at Silifke.

back to Germany. Upstream is the town of **Mut** 🔀, worth visiting, with a 14th-century mosque, the Lal Aği Camii, a fortress and two domed tombs. About 20 km (12 miles) north of town, the beautiful 5th-century **Monastery of Tarasius** **(Alahan)** 🔀 teeters on the edge of the wild Göksu Gorge, with traces of fresco still visible in its baptistry and churches.

The road now rises over the Sertauul pass, where migrating birds of prey congregate in spring and autumn. Another 70 km (45 miles) from Alahan, **Karaman** 🔀 was a powerful autonomous emirate from 1277–1467, so famous that early travellers referred to the entire coast as Karamania. Three fine religious schools, the Hatuniye Medresesi, the İbrahim Bey İmareti and the Ak Tekke; a mosque, the Yunus Emre Camii; and a ruined castle are all that remain of a glorious past; while the small museum also contains finds from Canhasan, about 13 km (8 miles) northeast of town, a settlement dating back to the 6th millennium BC.

About 30 km (19 miles) north, a turning to the left leads to a mountain rising sheer above the plain. On its north flank are the village of **Maden Şehir** and the once majestic Byzantine **Binbirkilise** 🔀 ("A Thousand and One Churches"). For two periods, from the 5th–6th and 9th–14th centuries, the area was almost as packed with monasteries and painted churches as Cappadocia. There are some ruins, but most have sadly been pillaged for building by the local farmers.

There is one other side trip to make before leaving the Silifke area. Tucked high in the Taurus Mountains, at the now remote upland village of **Uzuncaburç**, 30 km (19 miles) north of town, the ancient city of **Olba** (**Diocaesarea**) 🔀 (entrance fee) suns itself in past glories. Founded by the Hittites, this is a stupendous conglomeration of Hellenistic, Roman and Byzantine ruins.

The **Temple of Zeus**, built in 295 BC by Seleucos I Nicator (321–280 BC), is one of the oldest such sanctuaries in Asia Minor. During the 2nd century BC, its priests evolved into a powerful dynasty of priest-kings, the Teukrides, who ruled the surrounding town with a rod of iron right through the Roman era. Thirty columns remain standing today, four still with their capitals, the earliest Corinthian capitals in Asia Minor. It was converted to a church in Byzantine times, when the sanctuary was destroyed and walls and new doors inserted between the columns. Nearby are a five-storey tower (late 3rd century BC), a monumental gate with Corinthian capitals and five columns of the **Temple of Tyche** (Fortune), each made of a single piece of granite nearly 6 metres (20 ft) high, brought from Egypt in the 1st century AD.

The city gate is a massive structure of three richly ornamented arches. At a distance is the ancient cemetery, an eerie valley of rock-cut tombs.

Wonderful wildlife

South of Silifke is the **Göksu Delta**, part of which has been designated a nature reserve. A superb range of water birds inhabit the marshes and reeds. Purple gallinule and black francolin survive the predations of hunters in very limited numbers, and the beaches are home to gulls and turtles. Migrating raptors gather here to feed before resuming their journey across the

Map on pages 222–3

Silifke specialises in unusual drinks – kenger kahvesi, made from prickly acanthus fruit and ada *and* dag *("island" and "mountain") herbal teas. The latter, made from sage, is said to settle upset stomachs.*

BELOW: the Cilician plains are soaked in the blood of successive invading armies.

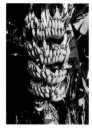

Bananas grow in profusion along this stretch of coast, which is also a land of strawberries, thick-skinned oranges and yogurt as solid as England's Devonshire clotted cream.

BELOW: which way to choose?

Mediterranean to Africa. Information about the birds is available from the ÖCKK (Environment Ministry) agency, near the Ayatekla site, tel: 0324-713 0888.

Some 20 kilometres (12 miles) east of Silifke, **Narlıkuyu** ⓓ, translated as "Well of the Pomegranate", is a pleasant cove lined with seafood restaurants. It is also home to the remains of a famous Roman bathhouse with a dusty 4th-century AD mosaic floor representing the Three Graces. The spring water was claimed by the ancients to enhance grey matter.

Just south of Narlıkuyu is **Susanoğlu** and the **Mausoleum of Priape the Fearless Satrap**. From this massive monument, in all its erect glory, juts the sculptured yard-long phallus of the god of fertility. Legend recounts that Priape was the illegitimate son of Zeus and Aphrodite, and that Hera, jealous wife of Zeus, deformed the child, giving him a phallus equal to his height. He was abandoned out of shame by his mother near the Dardanelles, and was brought by shepherds to Lapsacus (Lapseki).

Heaven and hell

Three kilometres (2 miles) north and inland of Narlıkuyu lies your chance to glimpse paradise and hell without abandoning the comfort of Earth. The **Corycian Caves**, better known as **Cennet ve Cehennem (Heaven and Hell)** ⓔ, were formed by underground chemical erosion. But, like all the best natural phenomena, they are considered sacred by pagans, Christians and Muslims alike. Heaven (Cennet Deresi) is larger than Hell, with 452 stairs leading down to a Byzantine chapel, dedicated to the Virgin Mary. This, in turn, blocks the entrance to a cave-gorge with an underground river, thought by some to be the Styx. The cave at the far end was home to an oracle. Just north is the gloomy pit

of Hell ("Cehennem"), happily inaccessible without climbing equipment as the sides are concave. It was here that Zeus imprisoned Typhon, the many-headed, fire-breathing monster serpent, father of Cerberus, guard dog of Hell. The caves under the souvenir shop have beautiful stalactites and stalagmites, and an atmosphere beneficial to asthma sufferers (open daily 8am–5pm; entrance fee).

A few kilometres east, **Akkaya** has its own Pamukkale in miniature, with smooth white rocks curved like waves, and excellent swimming. On both sides of the highway to Mersin are regimented rows of oranges and lemons, crops of Roman and Byzantine ruins, the last scattered arches of giant Roman aqueducts and an increasingly cluttered forest of corrugated iron and billboards.

Twin castles

Five kilometres (3 miles) east of **Narlıkuyu** stand famous twin medieval castles. On terra firma, 13th-century **Korykos Castle** reuses materials from a city first mentioned by Herodotus in the 5th century BC. On an offshore island, across a 200-metre (650-ft) channel, is its sister, **Kız Kalesi ⑤ (the Maiden's Castle)**, which was a refuge for pirates before it was fortified by Byzantine Admiral Eugenius, in 1104, as a link in the empire's border defences during the Crusades. It was later appropriated by the Armenians, Turks and, in 1482, the Ottomans. Both castles are open daily 8.30am–5pm; entrance fee. You need to negotiate with a local boatman if you want to get across the water.

Kız Kalesi is a pint-sized town, but growing as a tourist resort, best appreciated in early summer, before the *pansiyons* and restaurants fill up with the well-to-do of Adana. From here until Adana, the coast is lined with holiday villas and beach-side restaurants, making it hard to see the waves from the busy road.

Map on pages 222–3

Legend, of course, has its own say with the tired but charming belief that the Maiden's Castle was where King Korykos sequestered his daughter after a dire prediction that she would die from a snake bite. Naturally, a basket of grapes sent to her by a lover contained a viper.

BELOW: Korykos Castle.

This striking statue seems to evoke the confidence of Mersin.

The factory and the Bible

The best thing about the port of **Mersin (İçel)** ③⑥ is that there are two ways to get out in a hurry. Boats leave daily for Cyprus, and inter-city buses are frequent. This is a big, largely modern city with a population of around 1.5 million. The best bit is along the waterfront, where there are broad boulevards, shady parks, a decent supply of restaurants and a small **museum** (Atatürk Cad.; open Tues–Sun 9am–noon, 1–4.30pm; entrance fee). For those inclined to archaeology, **Yumuktepe**, a huge mound 9 km (5 miles) south of the town centre in suburban Soğuksu, has revealed 23 levels of civilisations dating from the 12th century AD back to 6300 BC. The city is also known for its relative gaiety, especially around the permanent market area, perhaps due to the number of sailors who frequent the town.

Sandwiched between the industrial giants, 25 km (16 miles) east of Mersin, **Tarsus** ③⑦ is frequently and foolishly overlooked, despite a resplendent history reaching back to at least 3000 BC (local legend claims it was founded by Seth, son of Adam). Because the site has never been abandoned, the ancient city lies 15–20 metres (50–65 ft) below the modern one, while the ravages of war and time have destroyed most vestiges of the past. However, Tarsus is one of the oldest continuously inhabited cities in the world; it was the birthplace of St Paul; and it was certainly here that Cleopatra met and seduced Mark Antony. The sheer weight of history sends shivers up the spine.

When the engineers of ancient Tarsus cut a pass through the northern mountains to the **Cilician Gates**, they created one of the most significant mountain routes of all time; traders and troops have poured through the narrow gorge ever since. Xerxes and Alexander the Great passed here; the latter almost lost his life after bathing in the icy waters of the River Cydnus (Tarsus Suyu). A fearful and haunted pass, it was named the "Gates of Judas" by the Crusaders.

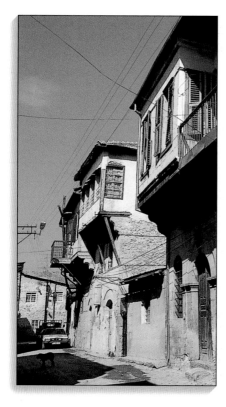

BELOW: backstreet Tarsus, little changed since St Paul played here.

On the back of the trade route grew and flourished one of the richest and most powerful cities of the ancient world. In 41 BC, following his victory at Philippi, Mark Antony sent for the Ptolemite queen of Egypt to punish her for her aid to Cassius.

According to Plutarch, Cleopatra arrived "sailing up the river Cydnus in a barge with gilded stern, outspread sails of purple, and silver oars moving in time to the sound of flutes, pipes and harps. Dressed like Aphrodite, the goddess of love, Cleopatra lay beneath an awning bespangled with gold, while the boys like painted cupids stood at each side fanning her." Mark Antony was so enamoured that he forgot to scold her and, instead, gave her large chunks of the Anatolian coast.

A few decades later, a local Jewish tentmaker named Saul experienced a blinding revelation on the road to Damascus and was transformed into St Paul. **St Paul's Well**, with its curative water (tested every day for purity) supposedly stands on the site of his family home in the old town. It probably has nothing to do with the apostle, and was named by the Byzantines or the Crusaders, both of whom had a vested interest in liberally applying biblical names to relics and places of minor pilgrimage. **Cleopatra's Gate** (also known as the Gate of the Bitch) certainly had nothing to do with the Egyptian Queen. On the other hand, both the well and gate are Roman, while parts of a colonnaded **Roman road** have been uncovered in the bazaar, surrounded by narrow alleys and crumbling Ottoman houses. More modern generations are represented by two mosques, a converted 14th-century Armenian church, the Kilise Camii, and the Makam Camii, opposite. Nearby is the Kulat Paşa Medrese, built in 1570. A collection of attractive cafés surrounds the Şelale (open Mon–Fri 8am–noon, 1–5pm; entrance fee), a wonderfully cooling waterfall on the edge of town, and an excellent small museum.

Map on pages 222–3

Adana

A further 40 km (25 miles) east, **Adana** ❸ has grown rich on heavy industry, cotton and citrus. This is the fourth-largest city in Turkey (after Istanbul, Ankara and İzmir), with a population of over 2 million and the only commercial airport in the region. It is an extraordinary enclave of Mercedes cars and designer boutiques, its hotels and restaurants almost entirely dedicated to business travellers.

Few people outside Turkey know of the city's most awe-inspiring sight – the **Sabancı Merkez Camii** (**Central Mosque**), an enormous, beautiful new mosque whose white marble reflection sparkles in the Şeyhan River, when it hasn't dried up. Opened in 1999, it is second in size only to the Sulemaniye Mosque in Istanbul, with six minarets, a 51-metre (167-ft) high dome and space for 30,000 worshippers, while the elaborate tiles and gold leaf inside are based on the spectacular interior of Istanbul's Blue Mosque. Future plans include a huge open plaza and museum of Islam. The equally beautiful 16th-century **Ulucamii**, with its black-and-white stripes and octagonal minaret, has been dwarfed.

There are few sights besides the new mosque. The drab **Archaeological Museum** (open Tues–Sun 8.30am–noon, 1–5pm, to 5.30pm in summer; entrance fee), next to the Merkez Camii, has some fine exhibits, including classical, Hittite and Urartian statuary, screaming for attention. There is a well-designed but tiny **Ethnography Museum** housed in a Byzantine church (Özler Caddesi, on the roundabout opposite the Çetinkaya shopping mall; open Tues–Sun 8.30am–noon, 1.30–5pm; entrance fee).

One of the city's most eminent sons is novelist Yaşar Kemal, whose pen drips with the ochres and reds of the surrounding Çukurova Plain. His most popular work, *Ince Mehmet* (Mehmet My Hawk), has been translated into a dozen languages and has made the author a perennial candidate for the Nobel Prize for Literature. The film starring Peter Ustinov was disowned by the author as a travesty of his work. The leftist filmmaker Yılmaz Güney also used the city and the surrounding villages as the backdrop for his works on social dislocation and poverty. However, all of Güney's work was banned after his escape from prison and flight to Paris, where he died in 1985.

About 25 km (16 miles) east of Adana, the enormous **İncirlik Air Base** is home to 5,000 US troops. **İncirlik** ❺ village, with its pizza and hamburger joints and dollar economy, is currently closed to non-military personnel for security reasons. ❑

BELOW: Adana is big, brash and modern.

Map
on pages
222–3

THE HATAY

A narrow finger of land pointing south to the Arab lands, the Hatay feels more Arabic than Turkish. This is the true beginning of the Middle East

The drive east from Adana is along the busy N-400, clogged with thundering, belching juggernauts en route to Iran. Some 30 km (19 miles) east of Adana, a road leads south to the Turkish oil refinery of **Yumurtalık ⑥⓪**, which also claims to have a beach resort. Unfortunately, the sand is tarred by the oily discharge of tankers, making the experience less than ideal.

Forty km (25 miles) east of Adana, and 3 km (2 miles) off the N-400, the village of **Yakapınar** is the site of **Misis ⑥①**, said to have been founded by the Hittite King Mopsus. The small Mosaic Museum (open daily 8.30am–noon, 1–4.30pm; entrance fee) is actually only one large, but sadly damaged mosaic, thought to represent Noah's Ark. There are plenty of other ruins, including a Roman stone bridge, city walls, an aqueduct, temple, theatre, unexcavated *harak* (tell or mound), and an Ottoman caravansaray. A walk around the village pays dividends.

Fortifying the land

BELOW: Karatepe's relief sculptures tell a story as vividly as a comic strip.

Today the vast alluvial flats of the well-irrigated Çukurova Plain are devoted to cotton and other cash crops, tended by thousands of migrant farm workers in shabby tent cities, but many castles still dot the plain, most built during the Crusades or under Armenian rule. **Yılan Kalesi ⑥②** ("Snake Castle"; open daily 8.30am–5pm) dominates the plain from its perch above the Ceyhan River. The access road is good; the climb to the castle is difficult.

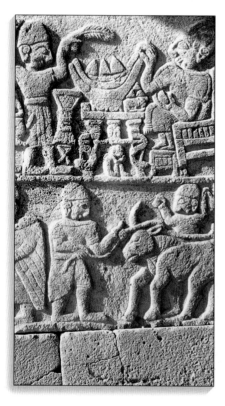

Probably built by Armenian king Leo III (ruled 1270–89), the fortress walls and battlements are still proud, but the buildings inside are wrecked. The origin of its name is obscure; some say the castle had to be abandoned because of snakes, but the best version ascribes it to an apocryphal "king of the Snakes", an evil half-man, half-snake who terrorised the region and was eventually overcome and killed in Tarsus while attempting to kidnap the daughter of the king. A statue of him still stands in the centre of Tarsus. Today, while lizards scurry over turrets and walls, snakes, thankfully, are nowhere to be seen.

Just beyond Yılan Kalesi, a road turns north, forking left after 35 km (22 miles) to the farming village of **Kozan ⑥③**, shrunk from former glories as capital of Cilician Armenia. An unmarked road in the middle of town leads steeply upwards and turns through a series of outer walls to the gate of the castle, built by Leo II (1187–1219). The main walls, ringed by 44 towers, form a saddle linking the twin summits of the long, narrow hill. The capture of the castle and King Leo VI, by Egyptian Mamelukes in 1374, marked the end of the southern Armenian kingdom.

Graeco-Roman **Anavarza (Dilekkaya) ⑥④** is hard to reach and is perfect for those with a sense of adventure: turn off the N-400 at Ceyhan, and after 23 km (14 miles) turn right towards Ayşehoca; from here it is 4 km (2½ miles) to Anavarza. The site has a stadium, theatre, baths, triumphal arch, tombs and mosaics, as well as a heavily fortified Armenian citadel. Anavarza is entirely unexcavated and earthquakes have left rubble strewn across the paths like a giant Lego set.

With the greatest density of oil tankers anywhere in the world (many undergoing repair along the road), **Osmaniye**, 75 km (46 miles) east of Adana, is best avoided. The massive black fortress of **Toprakkale ⑮** (open daily 8.30am–5pm) is surrounded on all sides by a motorway junction, demonstrating graphically its crucial position at the crossroads of international trade and invasion routes. Built by the Byzantine Emperor Nicophorus II Phocas (AD 963–9), the fortress was used as a base for his successful campaign against the Arabs who had held Antioch since the beginning of the 7th century. Later taken over by the Knights of St John, who remodelled it on Krak des Chevaliers (in Syria), it was eventually abandoned in 1337.

Originally built in the 8th century BC, as a combination castle and summer palace by a local king, Asitawanda, and later becoming the neo-Hittite capital, **Karatepe ⑯** was sacked by the Assyrians the following century. Today, the ruins stand on a U-shaped outcrop in a pretty national forest overlooking a reservoir on the upper Ceyhan River. A 1-km (½-mile) circular path loops through the woods between the fort's two main gates, which stand *in situ* protected by tin roofs. Karatepe's chief claim to fame is as the place where Hittite hieroglyphic writing was first deciphered, by comparison with matching inscriptions in Phoenician script. These entertaining Hittite hieroglyphs are actually deeply serious, recording the building of the city, praising the peace and prosperity of the kingdom, and heaping divine retribution on anyone who dares disturb the gate. Other reliefs consist of bizarre carvings, such as spear-toting soldiers with hooved feet, and several lions.

The reservoir abounds in catfish and carp, there are walking trails in the local woods, while villagers produce carpets and flat-weave *kilims*.

Alexander's triumph

From Osmaniye, the route south heads across the plains of **Issos**, past a turning to the Sokullu Mehmet Paşa caravansaray, *medrese* (religious school) and mosque complex. Right opposite a seashore Crusader castle, the buildings are superbly lined with coloured marbles and include a marble bathhouse. Local legend claims that it was here that Jonah was cast from the belly of the whale. More certainly, blood soaks the peaceful soil, for this is where Alexander and his army of 35,000 met and defeated Persian Emperor Darius and an army of over 100,000 in 333 BC, changing the course of world history.

His triumph is marked by the town he founded and named after himself immediately after the battle, **İskenderun ⑰**. Most of the modern city was built during the French Mandate, and has a pleasant, Levantine feel with a fine promenade and good fish restaurants. Any attributes pale, however, against the stinking smog from local steelworks. In summer, the

TIP

To reach Karatepe, fork left at Osmaniye, and follow the signs; the first 20 km (12 miles) are on potholed tar, the final 10 km (6 miles) along a decent dirt road. The site opens daily May–Sept 8.30am–5.30pm, Oct–Apr 8am–3.30pm; with a break for lunch. Guided tours only. Photography is forbidden.

BELOW: İskenderun exists in a chemical haze.

pollution is enough to drive you to the hills. To the south, as the road climbs a mountain pass known as the Gates of Syria, the small town of **Belen** is the area's most desirable suburb.

The scenery softens and flows into green rolling hills watered by the Orontes River until the end of the valley pushes against the first outcroppings of the lesser Lebanon mountains. Here stands **Antakya** , the magnficent biblical Antioch, a city that once rivalled the glories of Rome.

Antakya: the past

Following Alexander's death, one of his lesser generals, Seleucos Nicator, established himself as the *satrap* (governor) of Babylon. During the following internecine wars between the rival Macedonian generals, Seleucos traded most of his territory in India for 500 war elephants, which won the day against the forces of Antigonus ("The One Eyed") at the Battle of Ipsus in western Anatolia in 301 BC. The victory established Seleucos as a Mediterranean power. In 300 BC he built his capital across the trade route at Antioch-on-the-Orontes.

Initially conceived of as a polis, or city, of some 5,300 male citizens – close enough to the ideal number of Hellenic home-owners advocated by Plato – Antioch soon swelled to a population of nearly half a million, becoming the pre-eminent centre of Hellenic civilisation in the region. The Seleucids lavished attention on their city, building theatres, baths, gymnasiums, a stadium that hosted a revived Olympic Games, and other public buildings, all connected by colonnaded streets.

The Seleucids themselves were chased out of Asia Minor by the Romans after several disasters and defeats, starting with the Battle of Magnesia when the

BELOW: Poseidon mosaic in Antakya museum.

Map on pages 222–3

Seleucids' famed war elephants stampeded and destroyed their own troops. They next became embroiled in the unsuccessful revolt of the Maccabees in Palestine and a series of destabilising wars in the east with the Parthians, and in the west with Egypt. The Seleucids were finally conquered in 83 BC by Armenian King Tigranes, son-in-law of the the redoubtable scourge of Rome, Mithridates the Great. Within 20 years, Roman legions had taken possession of Antioch, which became the capital of the newly formed province of Syria.

During the Byzantine period, the city was sacked with cyclical regularity by the Persians. An earthquake in the 5th century killed 250,000 people and it finally fell to the Muslim Arabs in AD 638. Reconquered by Byzantium in 969, it fell again to the Muslims in 1084, and, after a long siege in 1097, it became capital of one of the four Crusader states in the Middle East. When the Mameluke leader, Baybars, captured the city in 1268, he slaughtered 16,000 soldiers, hustling a further 100,000 off to slave markets in Cairo.

Selling vivid scarlet peppers at a market in Antakya.

Antakya: the present

Today, the material remains of Antioch's former glory are precious and few. Yet the city has an intense atmosphere that seeps through the narrow alleys of the bazaar and around the minarets, making it one of the most charming and entertaining cities in southern Turkey. The city is divided neatly in two by the Orontes River; to the left are the wide boulevards and art deco of the French colony (1918–38), to the right the narrow, noisy Arabic old town.

The **Hatay Museum**, on the roundabout beside the main bridge, is home to a world-class collection of some 50 Roman mosaics (Gündüz Cad. 1; open Tues–Sun 8.30am–noon, 1.30–5pm; entrance fee). Most of them, carefully removed from Roman villas in Harbiye, date from the 2nd and 3rd centuries, and seem to leap off the walls. Here is a life-size "Oceanus and Thetis", with the creatures of the deep clustered around them; there the "Happy Hunchback", dancing in glee with erect penis; here again the "Drunken Dionysus" swaying towards the next winery, aided by a small satyr. The Department of Antiquities is often criticised for not removing the phenomenal collection to Istanbul or Ankara, where they would be more accessible; Antakya is hanging on for grim death to its one real draw.

Across the river, the edges of the old town, now one huge bazaar, are marked by minarets. Near the 3rd-century **Rana Köprüsü** ("Old Bridge"), its old stones disguised by modern steel and tarmac, is the **Ulucamii**; up the hill, on Kurtuluş Caddesi, is the **Habib Neccar Camii**, formerly a Byzantine church.

During Roman rule, Antioch had a large Jewish community and became a crucial staging post in the history of early Christianity. St Peter lived here from 47–54 AD, frequently joined by the much-travelled Paul of Tarsus and St Barnabas. As a result, Antioch became the seat of the powerful Patriarchate of Asia, a rival Christian centre to Constantinople – chiefly notorious for its heretical scholars. The tiny cave church of **Sen Piyer Kilisesi** (**St Peter's Cave**), 2 km (1 mile) off Kurtuluş Caddesi, northeast of the city centre, is generally regarded as the first Christian

BELOW: St Peter's Cave, the world's first official Christian church.

church (open Tues–Sun 8am–noon, 1.30–5.30pm; entrance fee). It was here that the saints gave their new religion a name, "Christianity" (Acts 11:26). The fancy façade was built by the Crusaders. Beyond the church, the mountain road winds 15 km (9 miles) to the ruined **Citadel** (3rd century BC–10th century AD).

Daphne (Harbiye)

Some 8 km (5 miles) south of Antakya on the road to Syria are the remains of the **Grove of Daphne**, known locally as **Harbiye** ⓭, a favourite place for picnics and recreation for some 3,000 years. Daphne was a local beauty who was turned into a laurel bush to escape the unwanted attentions of Apollo. Apollo wove himself a wreath from the leaves, the origin of the laurel of victory.

The Seleucids built a massive temple and oracle complex dedicated to Apollo in the valley, serviced by very real "nymphs" whose duties included delighting the self-deified royal family who claimed descent from the Sun God. Antony and Cleopatra were married here by Egyptian ritual in 40 BC, while the surrounding hills became a wealthy summer resort whose treasure trove of villas produced most of the mosaics now in the Hatay Museum. In Christian times, the bones of a bishop were reinterred here to silence the pagan oracle, but when the Byzantine Emperor Julian ("The Apostate") visited the shrine in AD 362, he found only one priest clutching a sacrificial goose instead of the requisite bull. Enraged, Julian removed the bones of the bishop and Christian activists burned the temple down the next day. Even in licentious Antioch, the pagan age was over.

Today, the ancient buildings vanished, Daphne has been spoiled by the free-for-all refreshment concession stands: tables and chairs are set amid babbling streams of water, and plastic bags clutter the bushes; trout is the major dish.

BELOW: the citadel of Antakya.

Simon on a stick

The early church attracted many extremists, including a growing number of ascetic monks and other spiritual acrobats who expressed their devotion to God by a complete and utter abnegation of the world.

The most famous of these anchorites was St Simeon the Elder, who devoted his life to sitting atop an increasingly high pillar, while pilgrims flocked to watch him rail against such human frailties as the desire for a good meal and a clean pair of sheets. Local priests even started marketing the saint's waste to the pious for a fee, with the promise that their contributions helped ensure them a place in heaven. "Simonry" was thus launched as a Christian concept.

Following Simeon the Elder's death in AD 459, a younger Simeon was so inspired that he, too, embraced the holy life. In AD 521, at the age of seven, he climbed his own column on a windy promontory of **Samandağ** (Simeon's Mountain). Over the next 25 years, as he fasted, prayed and preached, and the columns grew in height – culminating in a 13-metre (43-ft) stone pillar – a thriving monastery grew around his feet. Pilgrims and meditative monks liked nothing more than to see the pious miracle of the young boy sitting atop his pillar in all weathers. Finally, and perhaps blissfully, an earthquake brought the entire complex into its present state of ruins. Today, **Aya Simeon Manastırı (St Simeon's Monastery)** ⑳ (open access) is a strange and fearful place, well suited to meditations on the relative freedom of thought in our own time.

Seleucia ad Piera

Back down the mountain, turn left for the coast and **Samandağ**, a supposed resort town which is actually ugly, sprawling and filthy, its beaches covered in

Map on pages 222–3

TIP

The approach to St Simeon's monastery is difficult. Leave Antakya on the Samandağ road. After 22 km (13½ miles), look for a yellow sign and turn left. From here, a rough gravel road loops up the mountain, for about 8 km (5 miles).

BELOW: bringing home the bread.

Map on pages 222–3

Hızır's Holy Tree is massive and very old; local claims that it is 35 metres (115 ft) in circumference seem about right, but it is patently not 100 metres (328 ft) high. Trying to dissuade locals from a belief that it is the largest tree in the world is a futile exercise.

BELOW: slave-carved sluice at Samandağ.
RIGHT:
St Hızır's tomb.

debris and the sea polluted by chemical waste from İskenderun. About 5 km (3 miles) north, the village of **Çevlik** ("The Little Cave") ⑦ is built in and around Antioch's ancient port of **Seleucia ad Piera**. The area is riddled with the tombs and graves of Roman notables as well as remnants of the harbour walls. The most impressive feat of engineering in the area is the **Titus Tüneli**, a huge canal, up to 30 metres (98 ft) deep, gouged from the living rock during the reign of the Roman emperors Titus and Vespasian (1st century AD) in a vain attempt to divert mountain streams from silting up the port.

St Hızır

From Mağaracık village, a good asphalt road cuts uphill to the village of **Musadağ** (**Moses Mountain**) where, according to Muslim tradition, Moses learned to eat crow ("humble pie") prepared by the obscure Prophet Hızır. Moses demanded to know of God whether there was anyone more favoured than himself. God replies that indeed there was, a man named Hızır. Moses met the saint on the beach outside Samandağ, and asked permission to learn from him. Hızır agreed on condition that Moses never questioned his actions. One can guess the rest: Hızır killed a child, built a wall over a pot of gold about to be discovered by an old, poor couple and sank a fishing boat in the harbour. Moses, enraged, demanded an explanation. Hızır calmly explained that if he had not done so, the end result in each case would have been far worse, making his apparently cruel acts "good deeds." Moses walked away perplexed. Hızır planted his staff in the ground near a stream, washed his hands and also went on his way, leaving the staff behind to grow into a massive tree still to be seen (and revered) at **Hızırbeyköy**, about 10 km (6 miles) above Samandağ. ❑

Alexander

Born in 356 BC, Alexander was the son of Philip II of Macedonia and Olympias (daughter of King Neoptolemus of Epirus). Brought up in court, he had the best of tutors, among them the great philosopher, Aristotle, who taught him science, philosophy and medicine and filled the young prince's head with the glories of Greek civilisation and a burning desire to liberate the ancient Anatolia from the Persians.

Winning his first battle at the tender age of 15, Alexander was a firm favourite of the Macedonian army by the time his father was assassinated in 336 BC. His succession to the throne, at the age of only 20, was assured. Philip had already planned the invasion of Asia; Alexander paused only to tighten his grip on the Greek heartland before heading east, landing in Anatolia in 334 BC, at the head of an army of about 30,000 foot soldiers and over 5,000 cavalry.

It took a little under two years for him to drive the Persians from Anatolian soil, culminating in the decisive Battle of Issos. Unsatisfied, he pressed on, to take Egypt, Palestine and Syria, then Persia itself. He had added Afghanistan, modern Pakistan and northern India before his troops mutinied and forced him to turn back in 327 BC.

Alexander was undoubtedly a superb general, with brilliant strategic insight and tremendous luck. He was courageous, always to be found in the thick of the action, and enormously charismatic, inspiring total devotion and even worship from his troops. He was also manipulative and pragmatic, using any means at his disposal to win, from military conquest to marriage. He was adopted by the sister of the *satrap* in Halicarnassus (Bodrum); while in Egypt, he sacrificed to the god, Apis. In 327 BC, he married Roxana, the daughter of the Bactrian chief Oxyartes (he later took Emperor Darius' daughter, Stateira, as his second wife). He founded some 70 new cities and was the catalyst for the great wave of Hellenisation that swept Central Europe and the Near East.

Yet he was also a Boys' Own adventurer who was far more interested in conquering new lands than ruling the ones he had. In Macedonia, he dreamed of being Greek; once in Anatolia, he coveted Persia. Having conquered Persia, he dressed in Eastern robes and demanded to be treated as a deity (one of the few occasions on which his men refused his wishes). He drained Macedonia of money and manpower so thoroughly that it never recovered and simply left local governors in place as he passed. He hated to be crossed, executing those he felt to have betrayed him, including several of his closest friends and advisors. He destroyed Thebes on a whim and torched the Persian royal palace on a drunken spree.

On June 13, 323, after prolonged illness, Alexander died, at the age of only 32. He had reigned for 12 years and 8 months. Without his force of personality, his empire was doomed, but it is unlikely to have survived much longer, even had he remained alive; it was too big and too unwieldy and its emperor was a warrior, not a statesman. ❑

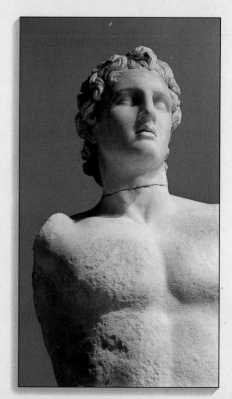

RIGHT: Alexander the Great, a great inspiration to his soldiers.

CENTRAL ANATOLIA

The rolling steppes of inland Anatolia are home to strangely beautiful landscapes and civilisations

Central Anatolia is a vast plateau, circled by rugged mountain chains, its land characterised by flat, fertile steppes and gentle rolling hills, broken by occasional mountains such as the snow-capped Mount Erciyes, an extinct volcano rising 3,917 metres (12,926 ft) above sea level.

Some of mankind's earliest settlements are found in Central Anatolia. It was here that man probably first abandoned hunting and gathering for agriculture, the domestication of animals, and trade, about 10,000 years ago. Dating back to around 6000 BC, Çatalhöyük, south of Konya, is the world's second-oldest town. Some way north, Boğazkale was the capital of the Hittite Empire which flourished from about 1800 BC, at the same time as the Pharaohs of Egypt.

Throughout history, however, few civilisations have survived the relentless tramp of the invading armies. Julius Caesar marched his Roman legions through the territory against Pharnaces II, the son of Mithridates, who had taken possession of the Pontus province in 47 BC. In AD 1402, the Mongol despot Timur (Tamerlane "The Lame") and his hordes thundered across the region, defeating the army of Ottoman Sultan Beyazıt in a battle on the plains of Ankara. Beyazıt was captured and paraded through the streets in a cage to ridicule him for campaigning against other Turkish princes; it nearly put a premature end to the Ottoman dynasty. In 1919, the Greek army invaded the region in its ill-fated campaign to reconquer all of Anatolia. A resurgent Turkish army under Mustafa Kemal (Atatürk) fought back and pushed the Greeks into the sea after bitter fighting.

These broad plains make ideal agricultural land and Central Anatolia served as a granary to both the Roman and Byzantine empires. Its capture by the Turks in the 11th century deprived the Byzantine Empire of its agricultural wealth and helped speed its eventual downfall. Even today, the region produces most of Turkey's wheat, barley and oats. Konya, Turkey's largest province, is one of the world's leading wheat-producing areas. Sugar beet is grown along the sweeping arc of the country's longest river, the Kızılirmak.

Today, travellers to the region pay homage to Atatürk, buried in state in the country's bustling modern capital, Ankara; gasp at the remains of the great Hittite settlements; and visit the superb Museum of Anatolian Civilisations, covering 10,000 years of history. They visit Konya to see the religious monuments of the world-famous whirling dervishes. Above all, they flock to Cappadocia, to see its extraordinary conical fairy chimneys, and the underground cities, huge anthill-like monasteries, early rock churches, stables and homes that have been chiselled into the soft rock. ❏

PRECEDING PAGES: Cappadocia's fairy chimneys, a landscape to outdo any science fiction scene. **LEFT:** a wooden mosque in Kastamonu.

Map on page 270

ANKARA

In only 80 years Ankara has grown from a small and dusty market town of 20,000 people to a vibrant city of more than three million

In 1923, Atatürk chose Ankara to be the new capital of Turkey for several reasons. Not only was it central geographically, but it was not associated in any way with the imperial powerbase of the hated Ottomans. In the last 80 years, Ankara has become a thriving metropolis with a lively cultural and social scene. However, it has also had a distinguished past. It was a flourishing trade and administrative centre in Roman times; it is said to have been the place where King Midas, of the golden touch, was born; more certainly, in around AD 400 Ankara became the summer capital of the Roman emperors who moved their entire administration there in order to escape the sultry summer heat.

Today, it is a residential rather than a touristic city, with its own subtle charms. Ankara is a place where you can eat out in style, go to a club, tour private art galleries or explore the varied antique shops.

Centre of a revolution

Start your historic sightseeing in **Ulus Meydanı Ⓐ**, where the statue of Kemal Atatürk on horseback forms part of Turkey's history. The inscription is written in Ottoman (Arabic) script since the statue dates back to the time before Turkey adopted the Latin alphabet in 1928. Downhill and across the road is the building which housed the first Grand National Assembly, from where Atatürk masterminded his three-year war against the Greeks and the Western powers backing them. This is now home to the **Kürtülüs Savası Müzesi (Museum of the War of Independence) Ⓑ** (TBBM Binası, Cumhuriyet Bulvarı 14, Ulus; www.turkey.org/tourism/ankara; open Tues–Sun 9am–noon, 1–5.15pm; entrance fee).

From the end of the boulevard, proceed straight down until you reach Çankırı Caddesi. About 50 metres (160 ft) further, on the right is the **Vilayet Binası (Governorate of Ankara) Ⓒ**, while close by is the **Jülyanüs Sütunu (Julian's Column) Ⓓ**, erected in about AD 360, probably in honour of Emperor Julian the Apostate, after whom it is named. Whatever the case, it is one of the few surviving Roman columns in Anatolia outside Istanbul and evidently impressed the medieval world, for it figures in one or two Arab travellers' tales.

Further along Çankırı Caddesi, on the left, the **Hamamları (Roman Baths) Ⓔ** (open daily 8.30am–12.30pm, 1.30–5pm; entrance fee) consist mainly of brick foundations, but there are also many pillars, tombstones and other remnants of the Roman city collected here. Many tombstones are designed in the shape of a door – the so-called "Phrygian doorway". The dated Armenian inscriptions on one or two of them show that they were reused in the 19th century.

BELOW: windows on the future in Ankara.

A short detour from Julian's Column will take you to the Hacı Bayram Camii, which was built on part of the Temple of Augustus. The **Hacı Bayram Camii ☻** is one of the oldest mosques in the city, dating originally from the 15th century, and still in use. Inside is the tomb of the "Holy Man", Hacı Bayram Veli himself, who died in 1430. He was the head of a dervish order that continues to help the poor and needy.

The **Augustus Tapınağı (Temple of Augustus) ☻** was built by the Phrygians and co-opted for Augustus. His Byzantine descendants later turned it into a Christian church. Near the entrance a long Roman inscription, written in both Latin and Greek, relates the deeds of the Emperor Augustus, a sort of resumé of his achievements posted here by Augustus himself, towards the end of his reign. It remains one of our most important sources of knowledge about Augustus and the time in which he lived.

Walk up the main road towards the citadel. On the left side are the fragmentary foundations of a small **amphitheatre** discovered in 1984.

Julian's Column, home to generations of artistocratic storks.

The citadel

Between AD 622, when it was taken by the Persians, and AD 838, when it was conquered by the Arabs, Ankara lived under constant threat from invaders. Its defenders numbered only a fraction of the population of the earlier city, and rather than quarry new stone, they reused material from the classical buildings to build up their defences.

Until 1915, the open ground between the outer and inner walls of the city was the Armenian quarter. Several hundred Armenians still live in Ankara with occupations as diverse as tailors, contractors, civil servants and university professors, although most follow traditional crafts such as goldsmithing and jewellery.

BELOW: a haircut, shave and update on the gossip.

The walls of **Ankara Kalesi ☻** (Hisarparkı Caddesi; entrance fee) are more spectacular: to the west, a line of triangular towers, rather like the prow of a ship, jut out from the wall. Step through the main gate, and a winding path through little streets, where houses have hardly changed in the last hundred years, takes you left to the innermost point of the castle. Unfortunately, the **Ottoman tower** is kept locked, but from its base, there is still a fine view.

The **walls**, built in the mid-7th century, did not always prove effective. In AD 838, the Arabs under the Caliph Mutasim sacked the city and killed or took prisoner its entire population. About 10 years later, the Emperor Michael III restored its walls. Walk through the winding streets down to the south gate of the inner walls and, a few yards above the road, you will see the remains of a large **tower** which was probably the residence of the Byzantine governor who ruled a large province called Bucellarion. To the right is the **Alâeddin Camii ☻**, a charming little mosque lined with classical columns; it is one of the earliest Muslim buildings in the city.

An inscription in Byzantine Greek, quoting the Psalms: "Rejoice, Oh Zion", is engraved around the top of the walls near the south gate. Look carefully and you will also see a number of Byzantine crosses

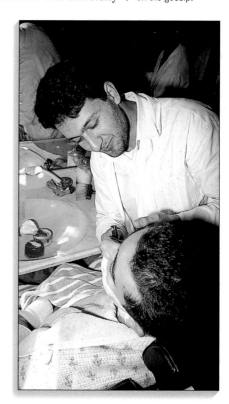

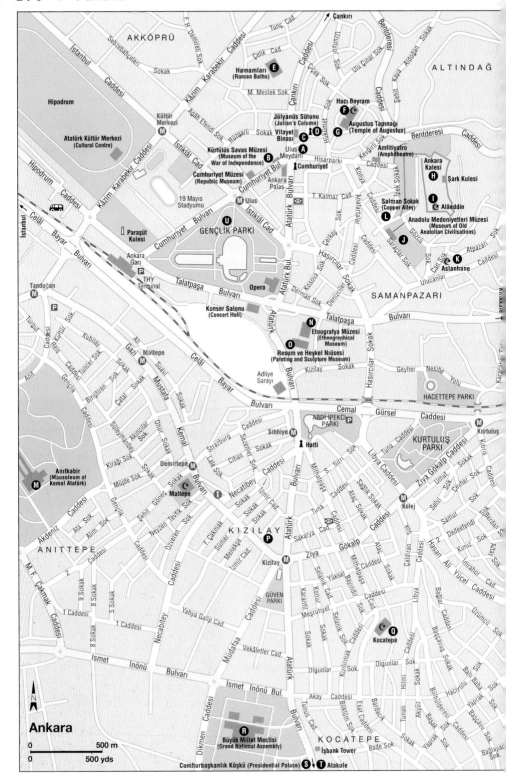

Ankara

0 — 500 m
0 — 500 yds

above the windows. These were intended to work like charms against hostile Islamic invaders from the south and east.

Map on page 270

In Ottoman times, the Muslim population lived inside the walls and the non-Muslims, the bulk of the city's merchants, around the edges. Their houses, with painted plaster walls and elaborate woodwork, one or two of them dating back to the 18th century, are found in the older cities all across Turkey. Nowadays they are usually divided inside and inhabited by several families. Many of those within Ankara citadel have been restored to past splendour and turned into gift shops, coffee houses and restaurants with stunning views of the city below.

Carry on to the south gate in the outer walls and you reach a square in front of the 19th-century **Clock Tower**. To the left is a street which would feel more at home in any small Anatolian town than in the country's capital. Many of the shops here belong to the wool and goatskin industry, a reminder that "Angora" – the old form of the city's name – was a world-famous wool centre.

To the right, down a slope to the west, is the **Anadolu Medeniyetleri Müzesi (Museum of Old Anatolian Civilisations)** ❿ (Kadife Sokak, Ankara Kalesi; tel: 312-324 3160; open Tues–Sun 8.30am–5.15pm; entrance fee). Housed in a former *han*, a market with workshops, built by grand vizier Mahmut Paşa, this is one of the finest museums of its kind in the world. It is designed to emphasise the pre-classical civilisations of Anatolia, and contains relics and artefacts from various digs around Turkey. Its displays start in the Palaeolithic, take in Neolithic Çatalhöyük, the Assyrian traders of Küllepe, and pre-Hittite Alacahöyük, before progressing to the Phrygians and Romans. There are also special collections from the Hittite, Urartian and Late Hittite eras. The contents of the Great Tumulus at Gordium include some very fine Phrygian woodcarvings in astonishingly good condition after 2,700 years. Other things to look out for include Neolithic frescoes from Çatalhöyük, vast Hittite stone sculptures, and the emblems of the Bronze Age reindeer gods found in Alacahöyük. The basement contains an exhibit on Roman Ankara.

Modern icons, the cover girls of glossy magazines.

BELOW: ancient icon, a Hittite fertility god.

Due east from the square by the clock tower is the 12th-century Seljuk **Aslanhane Camii** ⓚ, whose brick minaret still retains a few traces of the blue ceramics that once covered it. Inside, the mosque, built upon the foundations of a Roman temple, has an elaborately carved wooden roof, held up by a forest of wooden pillars. At the top of each column is a whitewashed reused classical capital, some of which came from the temple which once stood on this spot. To the left, facing downhill, a stone doorway with a lion beside it leads into an old dervish *tekke*, a medieval convent whose Roman stonework indicates that it was also built onto a Roman house of some kind.

Copper Alley

The side streets in this part of town are full of little craftsmen's shops, catering to the needs of an agricultural population coming in from the villages. Turn into **Salman Sokak**, to the right of the Aslanhane Mosque, and you are in one of Ankara's most famous shopping attractions. **Copper Alley** ⓛ (as Salman Sokak is known among Ankara's foreign residents, even though *salman* means "straw") is exactly

Gleaming heaps of copper pots turn Ankara's bazaars into Aladdin's Cave.

what its name suggests. You can find brand-new copper here, but old pewter plates and copper jugs (lined with tin if they are to be used), candlesticks, clocks, antiques and curios of all sorts are also on display. A few years ago, ancient coins and other valuable objects would be stealthily displayed to foreign visitors in some of these shops, but these days, most of the "ancient objects" on sale are fakes. If you want something genuine, try a splendid 19th-century plate with a Greek, Ottoman or Armenian inscription.

Atatürk's resting place

All travellers to Ankara should visit the **Anıtkabir** , the **Mausoleum of Kemal Atatürk** (Anıt Cad., Tandoğan; tel: 312-231 7975; open daily 9am–noon, 1.30–4pm, to 5pm in summer, with an evening sound-and-light show in summer). Official visitors never miss this national treasure, as protocol requires that they pay their respects to the founder of modern Turkey. The first thing that any new Turkish government does upon taking office is to pay a visit to the mausoleum and write a message in its album.

The mausoleum, built in a mixture of styles, partially recalls Hittite and ancient Anatolian architecture. Each province of Turkey contributed stone to the mighty hall which contains Atatürk's tomb. His body, however, is not kept in the stone *catafalque* on display to visitors, but is buried in a chamber far below. Within the complex, the **Anıtkabir Museum** (entrance fee) contains such personal items and artefacts as Atatürk's library, uniforms and even some of his visiting cards. Vehicles which were used by the great man are parked outside. On the opposite side of the square is the tomb of Atatürk's deputy and comrade-in-arms, İsmet İnönü, who later become Turkey's second president.

BELOW: Atatürk's mausoleum.

There are several other museums in Ankara. For Turkish handicrafts and costume, go to the **Etnografya Müzesi (Ethnographical Museum)** , on Opera Meydanı (open daily 8.30am–12.30pm, 1.30–5.30pm; entrance fee). Next door is the **Resum ve Heykel Müzesi (Painting and Sculpture Museum)** ◯ (Opera Meydanı; open Tues–Sun 9am–noon, 1–5pm; entrance fee), which exhibits early Republican period art of undistinguished quality. For contemporary Turkish art, visit some of the private art galleries. There is a cluster near Zafer Çarşışı, but others are spread out in various parts of the city.

The **Konser Salonu** (State Concert Hall), close to the railway station, stages Presidential Symphony Orchestra concerts every Friday night and Saturday morning during winter months. Apart from the state opera and two state theatres, there is also a whole host of smaller private theatres, many of them in the vicinity of the Ankara Sanat Tiyatrosu, just off İzmir Caddesi near the Atatürk Bulvarı at **Kızılay** ◯.

The main shopping areas are around Kızılay, along Tunalı Hilmi Caddesi and in the Karum Centre, near the Hilton and Sheraton hotels. Gankaya, the area around Ataküle, and Orhan Mumcu Caddesi have upmarket stores.

Kocatepe Mosque

One of the most impressive sites in the city is the **Kocatepe Camii** ◯, on the hill southeast of Kızılay. Ankara's biggest mosque, the shrine combines the aesthetics of 16th-century Islamic architecture and the technology of the 20th century. The monument is a replica of Istanbul's Blue Mosque, although it has only four minarets instead of six. Taking 20 years to build, the Kocatepe Mosque opened to the public in the early 1980s. To enter the mosque, take the staircases to the white marble courtyard. With a practical modern twist, there is an underground multistorey car park and shopping mall beneath it.

Many of the government ministries are bunched together south of Kızılay, on either side of Atatürk Bulvarı, the main street through Ankara, running north-south. Further south, on the right-hand side of the same street, are the buildings of Turkey's parliament – the **Büyük Millet Meclisi (Grand National Assembly)** ◯. Anyone wishing to visit must obtain special permission from the Public Relations Office (tel: 0312-420 5000).

Most of the foreign embassies are located along Atatürk Bulvarı and Cinnah Caddesi, which continues uphill to Çankaya – crowned by the presidential palace, **Cumhurbaşkanlık Köşkü** ◯. In the well laid-out grounds is a *köşk*, which was Atatürk's residence (open Sunday and holidays 1.30–5.30pm). Also here is **Atakule** ◯ (open 10am–10pm, until 3am if restaurant is open), a 125-metre (413-foot) tower with a shopping centre and a revolving restaurant on the top floor. Since it opened in 1989, this monument has become one of Ankara's best-known landmarks.

Gençlik Parkı ◯, between the railway station and Ulus, is one of the city's most popular recreational areas, with an amusement park, mini-train, and Ferris wheels for children, and many moderately priced pubs and outdoor restaurants beside an artificial lake. ❏

Map on page 270

Rail enthusiasts should head for the small Railway Museum on Platform 1 of the station which has the carriage given to Atatürk by Hitler, and the rusting collection of old steam engines (many German and American) in the Open Air Museum across the tracks.

BELOW: people still live in the huddled alleys of the citadel.

NORTHWEST ANATOLIA

*The population is sparse and much of the landscape
is naked hillsides with hardly a tree to be seen,
but this is the heartland of ancient Phrygia*

Map
on page
274

Three roads head roughly northwest out of Ankara up to the Sea of Marmara and, eventually, on to Istanbul. The first, via Eskişehir, and the second, a remote ramble through the mountains to Beypazarı, Nallıhan and Göynük, connect at Bilecik; the third follows the main highway almost due north into the Black Sea region.

Due west from Ankara

In a famous corruption trial in Ancient Rome, the orator Cicero – who was defending a sticky-fingered Roman governor of Phrygia – managed to ridicule the prosecution witnesses by describing them as "ignorant Phrygians who had never seen a tree in their whole lives." This rather cruel joke of Cicero's comes to mind as you take the E-90 highway out of Ankara through Polatlı and due west to Eskişehir. It is one of the great roads of history: Alexander the Great, the Crusaders, and most of the great armies of the Byzantine and Ottoman empires have travelled on it at some time. It is still the main road connecting Europe to Asia.

Those who plan to drive here should heed a word of warning – although in places it is a good dual-carriageway, this road links **Ankara ❶** with some of Turkey's major cities and on unimproved stretches it may be heavily congested with slow-moving trucks which do not hesitate to overtake on blind corners going uphill – even if they don't have the acceleration to move quickly. Needless to say, accidents are common. Do the journey in daylight when there are fewer trucks on the route.

About an hour out of Ankara, the town of **Polatlı ❷** is chiefly notable for having been the furthest point reached by the Greek invaders of Anatolia in 1921. The hightide mark of the Greek invasion is, quite literally, marked in concrete on the hill to the north of town. Today, Polatlı is the headquarters of an army tank brigade; it is also located at the centre of a cluster of fascinating sights.

Myths and legends

About 10 km (6 miles) northwest of Polatlı, at Yassıhöyük, lie the ruins of **Gordium ❸** (open daily 8.30am–5.30pm; closed Mon in winter; entrance fee), capital of Phrygia under the reign of the fabled King Gordius and his golden son, Midas, in about 800 BC. It remained a moderately important city into classical times, though it was later eclipsed by Ankara. Gordium is chiefly for the archaeology enthusiast. There are no romantic classical remains here. There is also little shade, which can pose a serious problem if you visit in summer.

Its most impressive features today are the huge burial tumuli of the Phrygian kings, found in the 1950s.

BELOW: donkeys are still used in the smaller villages.

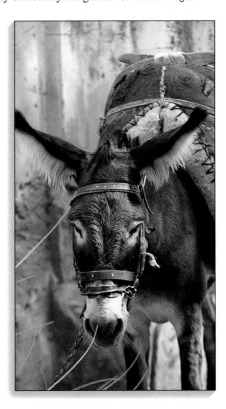

The highly intricate Gordion Knot, which tied together the yoke and pole of Gordius' chariot, was kept in the temple for 500 years. Tradition said it could be undone only by the future conqueror of Asia. The puzzle defeated all contenders until Alexander the Great simply sliced the knot in two.

The tomb of Gordius is an astonishing 50 metres (164 ft) high and 300 metres (985 ft) across. When excavated, the tomb of Midas was filled with a vast variety of objects, although, disappointingly, nothing golden. A special tunnel has been constructed to enable visitors to walk to the centre of the mound where they can inspect his burial chamber, built out of huge cedar trunks which the centuries have turned to stone. The actual remains of the king and the objects buried with him can now be viewed in Ankara's Museum of Anatolian Civilisations *(see page 271)*. Nearby, you can also see the world's earliest mosaic, made out of black and white pebbles, and the walls of the Phrygian capital, still within the mound that eventually swamped the city.

A road south from Polatlı leads to **Haymana** N, famed for its **Therapeutic Baths** which date back to Roman times (open daily 7am–midnight; entrance fee, free to visitors staying in local hotels). For centuries, people suffering from rheumatism, neuralgia, ailments of the joints, paralysis and orthopaedic problems have been coming here in search of relief.

Near Dereköy village, about 40 km (25 miles) northeast of Haymana, on a separate road back to Ankara, is the Hittite castle of **Gâvurkalesi** N (open access) where two gods are carved on a stone cliff on the edge of a small fortress, with a burial chamber. Just before the town of Sivrihisar, the road passes Nasrettinhoca, the birthplace of Nasreddin Hodja, the "wise fool".

Sivrihisar N lies about 30 km (18 miles) further down the road which forks at this point, running due west to Eskişehir, while the E-96 branches south for Afyon, and eventually the south and west coasts. The town has an interesting 13th-century **Ulucamii (Great Mosque)**, one or two Ottoman monuments and also a large 19th-century Armenian church, with an inscription on its front in

BELOW: Gordium is more fascinating to archaeologists than to tourists.

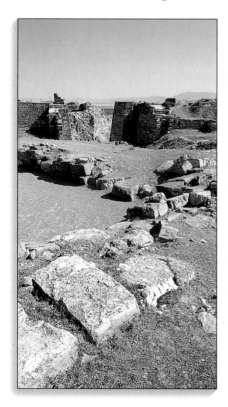

NASREDDIN HODJA

Philosopher and humourist, Nasreddin Hodja (1208–85), lived in northwest Anatolia when the region was under siege by Mongolian invaders. He studied in the religious schools at Sivrihisar and Aksehir, a city 200 km (130 miles) southwest of Ankara. He died in Aksehir, where he is buried.

Turkey's most famous folk hero, Nasreddin Hodja figures in endless jokes throughout the Middle East. His stories, many of which end in a moral twist or clever epigram, are popular among all Turkic peoples. His tales, set in homes, marketplaces, bazaars, streets, courts and mosques, describe everyday life. His jokes and tales ring of the common sense of the Anatolian people and are subtle without intending to disparage anyone.

One story goes: "The Hodja brought home a kilo of delicious lamb one day, asked his wife to prepare it for the evening, and set off to the teahouse to spend the rest of the day. Unable to wait, his wife cooked the meat and shared it with her friends. Returning home, the salivating Hodja was told that the cat had eaten the meat. Puzzled, Hodja grabbed the family's mangy cat and put it on the weighing scales. To his surprise, it weighed exactly one kilo. He barked at his wife, 'If this is the meat, then where is the cat?'"

Armenian script. It now serves as the town's power station – you can make out its shape on the north side of the town, as you drive past on the main road. In the crags behind the town is a Byzantine citadel.

About 19 km (12 miles) south of Sivrihisar, at Ballıhisar, are the Roman ruins of **Pessinos** ❼ (open access), one of the three great centres of Roman Galatia. In recent years, archaeologists have uncovered a temple dedicated to Cybele, the Roman equivalent of the Anatolian mother goddess, Kubaba. Fragments of various Roman buildings are found scattered across an extensive area around the stream running through the present-day village of Ballıhisar.

Pessinos was situated in the middle of the Phrygian plain and historians believe that it was abandoned when the age of invasions began after 600 AD and its people moved to the safety of present-day Sivrihisar.

Map on page 274

Ottoman heartland

Eskişehir ❽, the Roman and Byzantine Dorylaeum, lies about another hour's drive west of Sivrihisar. Its name means "Old City" in Turkish but there are few traces of its past. There is a good provincial **museum** (Hasan Polatkan Bulvarı; open daily 8.30am–noon, 1.30–5pm; entrance fee) with mosaics and statuettes of the Roman period. The **Meerschaum Museum** (open daily 10am–5pm; entrance fee), in the Yunus Emre Culture Building, contains a collection of local meerschaum pipes; modern ones are sold nearby. The meerschaum mines are located at Sepetçi Köyü and Kozlubel.

Today, the city is chiefly a regional industrial powerhouse with factories turning out cement, textiles, clothing and household appliances. Eskişehir also has the state railways factory for diesel engine locomotives and train cars, a

BELOW: spring in Anatolia.

big university and Turkey's largest air-force base with F-16 jet fighters constantly flying over the city and countryside on military manoeuvres.

Visitors will notice many people in the streets with oriental features. These people are the descendants of Crimean Tartars who settled in this part of the country after the Turkish-Russian War of 1878.

A little way west is **Inönü**, the scene of two decisive battles in Turkey's War of Independence against the invading Greeks after World War I.

Directly north of this lies the Sakarya Valley and the rolling landscape from which the Ottoman Empire burst into the world. The small town of **Söğüt** ❾ has the distinction of being the birthplace of the world-famous dynasty which ruled Turkey, the Balkans and much of the Middle East until well into the 20th century. The first of the great war leaders, father of the Sultan Osman I, was a frontier warrior named Ertuğrul Gazi who ruled a minor fiefdom in Söğüt in the late 13th century. His **tomb** can be visited there today (open daily 9am–5pm). Outside, the area is adorned by the busts of the greatest rulers of all 17 Turkish states in world history.

To the east, across the river and due north of Eskişehir, the village of **Mihalgazi** ❿ was home to a Byzantine Greek local warrior chief, Mihal Gazi, who joined forces with Osman, helping his meteoric rise to serious power. His grave, neglected and forlorn, lies in a grassy meadow to the south of the village. It is a reminder of how the first Ottoman ruler made the transition from village raider to self-styled sultan in a single generation – and how easily his allies were forgotten in the heady rush to power.

BELOW: autumn in the Seven Lakes National Forest.

Keep heading northwest from Söğüt and you come to **Bilecik** ⓫, where Osman's wife and his father-in-law, Edibali, lie buried. A few crumbling fragments of wall mark the site of the Byzantine castle which was captured by one of the very first Ottoman war bands. Almost due south of Bilecik, **Bozüyük** has become a regional industrial centre with factories producing tiles, radiators and household appliances. Many of the plants have been relocated from their original sites in Istanbul's Golden Horn.

Northwest from Ankara

This route is definitely the backroad from Ankara, leading through remote hills to visit a succession of small hill and mountain towns – Güdül, Beypazarı, Nallıhan, Murdurnu and Göynük – so little disturbed by time that they have managed to preserve much of their 19th-century appearance and a semblance of Byzantine or Ottoman splendour. **Mudurnu** ⓬ has one of the finest of all early Ottoman mosques, with remarkable carving on the *mihrab* and gallery.

Göynük ⓭ especially deserves to be better known than it is. The approach road is a lonely winding track through the mountains, so go fully prepared. Once there, you can visit the **Tomb of Akşemsettin**, the first *hodja* to give the call to prayer from Aya Sofya in 1453 after the Turkish conquest of Istanbul. It is lavishly maintained with gifts from the Muslim world.

At the far end of the mountain road, just before you reach Bilecik, are **Taraklı, Gölpazarı** ⓮, with a most unusual early Ottoman caravansaray, and **Geyve**.

The Ankara–Istanbul highway

The main route between Ankara and Istanbul is along two parallel highways – the Trans-European Motorway (TEM) and the E-89. The TEM is an express road with very few exits; the E-89 is one of the most scenic routes in the country, running through gloriously wooded mountains which often remind the traveller of Switzerland.

Kızılcahamam ⓯, with its hills and woods, is a favourite picnic and resort spot, famous for its mineral waters, Turkish bath, hot springs, and water bottling plant. This is also a favourite area for wild-boar hunting with animals often growing to the size of small cows.

Fork off the main road and you pass through the town of Çerkeş ⓰, famous only for having Europe's biggest integrated meat plant, Aytaç Gıda. On your way north to the Black Sea region, with its steep, wooded valleys, you pass the seldom visited towns of **Tosya** and **Osmancık**, the majestic **İlgaz Mountains**, with their small ski resort, and **Safranbolu**, filled with delightful Ottoman provincial domestic architecture *(see page 305)*.

Alternatively, keep going along the main road to Dörtdivan and take the side road leading to **Kartalkaya** ⓱, a small winter sports resort with a dozen ski lifts and three hotels. **Bolu** is a nondescript Anatolian town, a centre for Turkey's lumber industry. There is little reason to stop here, but about 32 km (20 miles) west, tucked in the woods is the spa-and-hotel complex of **Abant** ⓲, on the shores of a jade-coloured crater lake. North of the road are the gourmet centre of **Mengen**, still known for the quality of the chefs turned out by its catering colleges, and the **Yedigöller Milli Parkı** (Seven Lakes National Forest), with much-photographed walks around the lakes, best in autumn colours. ❑

Map
on page
274

BELOW: bleak mid-winter on the central plains.

Map
on page
274

BELOW: Afyon's legal
opium harvest
colours the summer
landscape red.

SOUTHWEST ANATOLIA

*Lakes, poppies, pottery, migrating birds, whirling
dervishes and the usual historic cast of thousands:
there is something for everyone here*

In the lush, green area around **Afyon** ⑲, southwest of Ankara, the farmers
grow June-flowering poppies for their opium. The name Afyon even means
"Opium" in Turkish, and this is the centre of the country's opium industry,
with a state-run alcholoid factory which refines opium gums for the pharma-
ceutical industry. A white marble is also excavated, cut and polished here and
is used for flooring, gravestones and work surfaces.

The distinctive black crag at the centre of Afyon has also helped make this one
of the best-known cities of provincial Turkey. Afyon was not a Roman city but
there is thought to have been a Hittite stronghold here and the high rock was also
used as a refuge by the Byzantines in the war against the Arabs. The climb up
some 700 steps to **Afyon Castle** (open access), is not for the faint-hearted. The
town below has a number of interesting 19th-century Ottoman buildings and
several mosques, including the 13th-century Seljuk **Ulucamii** (**Great Mosque**),
the **Kuyulu Mescit** (**Mosque of the Well**), with a tiled minaret, and the 14th-
century **Kubbeli Mescit**. (A *mescit* is a small, simple mosque equivalent to a
Christian chapel.) In the **Archaeological Museum** (Kurtuluş Cad.; open
Tues–Sun 8am–noon, 1–5.30pm; entrance fee) are gathered relics of the Hittite,
Phrygian and Lydian periods, found in and around the city.

North of Afyon

A series of villages that once made up the heart of the
ancient Phrygian kingdom of King Midas lies north of
Afyon. At **Ayazin** ⑳ are rock churches similar to those
of Göreme, while **Kümbet** ㉑ has a Phrygian tomb
from the Roman period, with lions carved upon it. Most
splendid of all the monuments are those at **Yazılıkaya**
(**Midasşehir**) ㉒ (Kunduzlu; open daily 9am–5pm),
where flat landscape gives way to hills and woods, setting the once great Phrygian city of Metropolis in a hilltop landscape worthy of an Italian Renaissance painting.

By far the most striking sight here is the giant **Midas
Monument** (*c.* 6th century BC), to the east of the hill,
with its curious and undeciphered inscription in the
Phrygian alphabet. It probably contained a shrine to
Cybele (also known as Mida and, according to Greek
legend, the mother of King Midas). On the north slope,
there are Roman tombs and one or two Hittite reliefs
which show that the site has a history stretching back
at least a thousand years before Midas. On the summit
is a stone throne, which, local folk will tell you, is
where King Midas sat with his wives.

About 30 km (19 miles) north of Midasşehir, a
superb Bektaşi *tekke* (convent) crowns the hill to the
west of the town of **Seyitgazi** ㉓. In some ways, it is
even more spectacular than the headquarters of the
Bektaşi organisation at Hacıbektaş.

Seyitgazi is named after a legendary Arab warrior who died in the siege of Afyon in AD 740, during the Arab-Byzantine wars. Legend has it that a Byzantine princess fell in love with him, and seeing some soldiers creeping towards him, dropped a stone to warn him of the danger. Alas, it fell on his head and killed him. His tomb, which is about three times the length of a normal man, can be visited. Beside it is a smaller one which is said to be that of the princess. The buildings are a mixture of Ottoman, Seljuk and Byzantine architecture.

Kütahya: ceramic capital

Kütahya ㉔ is one of the most picturesque towns in Turkey with old streets and a **citadel** ringed by a curious Byzantine fortress. It is a highly conservative town, where women may be seen wearing colourful Anatolian costumes. Under the Ottomans, Kütahya became the home of the best faïence and pottery in Turkey, its tiles used on countless mosques, its jugs and bowls found in every upmarket home. The craft has been revived in recent years. There is an interesting small **Tile Museum** (Gediz Cad.; open Tues–Sun 8am–noon, 1.30–5.30pm; entrance fee) in a former soup kitchen behind the 15th-century **Ulucamii** (Great Mosque), one of several fine mosques.

Nearby, the small **archaeological museum** is housed in a theological school (open Tues–Sun 8.30am–noon, 1.30–5.30pm; entrance fee). The **Kossuth Evi** (open Tues–Sun 8.30am–noon, 1–6pm; entrance fee), a fine Ottoman mansion preserved as it was in the mid-19th century, is worth a visit.

A drive 27 km (15 miles) southwest of the town takes you to **Çavdarhisar ㉕**. Because it lies off the beaten track, the site of ancient **Aizanoi** (open 9am–noon, 1–5pm; entrance fee) is seldom visited, but it is worth the drive, with a fine temple and a huge vaulted chamber beneath. In its day, the city claimed to have been the birthplace of the father of the gods, Zeus himself.

The Lake District

South of Afyon is a green and attractive region commonly known as Turkey's "Lake District". There are at least seven significantly large lakes, some saline, along with many smaller ones, attracting a huge variety of birds to keep the twitchers happy.

Isparta ㉖ is chiefly famous for rose oil (attar of roses), an essential ingredient in perfume. The town was founded by Greeks from Sparta and remained an important Greek town until the deportations of the 1920s. A few ruined Greek churches can still be found in the backstreets.

A winding drive of an hour or so east of Isparta brings the traveller to the town of **Eğirdir ㉗** at the southern tip of beautiful **Eğirdir Gölü**, the second-largest freshwater lake in Turkey. The pretty town was founded by the Hittites and became a regular stop on the King's Way, an important trade route between Ephesus and Babylon in the 5th century BC. It has been popular with tourists ever since and has a fine collection of old Greek and Ottoman houses on its narrow streets. Two tiny islands are joined to the town by a causeway and the furthest, **Yeşilada**, has several attractive *pansiyons* and an old Greek church

A giant urn at the town entrance advertises Kütahya's main industry.

BELOW: Kütahya's ceramic factories still flourish.

Towering walls still ring the lakeside city of Eğirdir.

BELOW: Lake Eğirdir's reedy shores attract thousands of migrating birds.

which is under restoration. The ruins of an old **Seljuk fort** stand in the town near the 15th-century **Ulucamii (Great Mosque)** and the Dündar *medrese* (religious school), with a beautifully decorated portal, now used as a small shopping arcade.

The drive up the more attractive eastern side of the lake leads to **Yalvaç** , the ancient Antioch ad Pisidia, much visited by Christian pilgrims because of its associations with St Paul. As written in the New Testament (Acts: Chapter 13), it was here that Paul made his first recorded sermon. This was so successful that the Gentiles pleaded with him to speak again the following Saturday and the synagogue was packed. The Jews, out of envy, drove Paul from the city.

Antioch ad Pisidia (open 9am–5pm; entrance fee), founded between 301 and 280 BC on the site of a Phyrgian settlement by Seleucus Nicator, was later a Roman colony for veteran soldiers. Today, it is under excavation by the Turkish authorities. The triumphal arch leads to a main street with the theatre on the left, to the courtyard, built by Tiberius below the temple to his adopted father Augustus and to Zeus. Huge baths, a nymphaeum, the aqueduct and an early synagogue (later a church) are also visible. The small local **museum** (open Tues–Sun 9am–noon, 1.30–5.30pm; entrance fee) houses relics from the site and the nearby temple to the god men, dating from colonial days. The garden contains many inscriptions in Latin rather than the usual Greek.

You may wish to go on from here on the country road which loops back round the top of the lake and heads southwest, via **Senirkent**, past numerous fruit orchards to **Keçiborlu**. Continue west and the road to Denizli and Pamukkale, with its famous waterfalls, passes **Dinar**, a town levelled by an earthquake in 1995, and a large, sterile salt lake, **Acıgöl** . Alternatively, head

south, down the scrubby shore of the vast saline expanse of **Burdur Gölü**, to the town of Burdur. The lake has shrunk considerably and the flamingo population is difficult to spot.

Burdur **30** itself is dull, but it does have a 14th-century **Ulucamii** (Great Mosque) and is home to a small **regional museum**, in Gazi Caddesi (open Tues–Sun 8.30am–noon, 1.30–5.30pm; entrance fee). Its contents include finds from Kremna and Sagalassos *(see below)* and 6th-millennium BC Hacılar.

About 10 km (6 miles) south of the town, signposted left off the main road, the well-lit **İnsuyu Mağarası 31** is one of the few open caves in Turkey, with 600 metres (190 ft) of tunnels, seven underground lakes and dramatic displays of stalactites (open daily 8.30am–6pm; entrance fee).

Ancient Pisidia

Some 25 km (15½ miles) east of Burdur, off the N-685 to Isparta, follow signs through the village of Ağlasun to find the ruins of **Sagalassos 32** (open daylight hours; entrance fee). This was the second city of Pisidia after Antioch; it is also under excavation and reconstruction, this time by a Belgian team. Set 1,500 metres (4,920 ft) above sea level on the slopes of craggy Mount Akdağ, it is potentially one of the most complete cities in Asia Minor – its superb 9,000-seat theatre remains just as an earthquake left it. The city centre, including a library, two nymphaea, the upper forum, which includes a bouleterion (circular debating chamber) and a monument to the Emperor Claudius, and the lower forum with huge baths, is almost completely excavated. Partly reconstructed finds are assembled in a purpose-built workshop in Ağlasun, due to become a fine museum. Superb computer reconstruction drawings illustrate the major vistas and explain the site; the work is a technical masterpiece, and includes investigation of local land-use, road and water systems and plant and animal life in early historical times.

If you keep heading south towards Antalya, you'll reach **Bucak**, the turning point for the ruins of **Kremna 33** (open access), about 13 miles (8 miles) from Bucak. Getting there requires a little endurance and puff. The approach road winds attractively along a pine-clad valley, to a spectacular clifftop city overlooking the Aksu Çayı.

Kremna has yielded a full picture of how the Romans conducted a siege. After a long campaign, ending in AD 278, the forces of Emperor Probus succeeded in retaking the town from a ruthless brigand named Lydius. An inscription tells how Lydius drove out of the city all those too old or too young to be of use. The Romans, however, drove them back, whereupon Lydius hurled them into the ravines around the city. He even dug a tunnel under the walls to allow residents to steal food, which worked until an informer told the Romans. Lydius' downfall came when one of his commanders defected after a severe dressing-down and pointed out to the Romans the gap in the wall from which he liked to watch the battle. A marksman took aim and mortally wounded him, whereupon the rebellion collapsed.

A massive earthwork used by the Romans to reach

Map on page 274

BELOW: in summer, Tuz Gölü, the great salt lake, dries to a shimmering pan.

The dervish order was founded by Mevlana Jelaleddin Rumi, an Islamic mystic born in Afghanistan, who travelled to Konya at the invitation of the Seljuk sultan to write mystical poetry in Persian (the court language of Seljuk Konya). He died in 1273 and is buried in Konya.

the height of the Kremna walls is still visible today since the soil is a reddish colour compared to the grey-brown of that around it. The remains are late-Hellenistic and Roman but many of the buildings have been badly damaged by earthquakes and general decay. The best preserved is an arched structure which formed part of the baths. Its walls stand to their full height and house some fine inscribed statue bases. Archaeologists have also recently found evidence of the complex hydraulic system of aqueducts and animal-driven wheels which brought water to Kremna from a lower altitude.

Konya

The road south from Ankara to Konya forks off from the Mersin-Adana road (E-90) after about 100 km (62 miles). The journey between Ankara and Konya is swift (it can be done in under three hours) but unexciting. Some of the small settlements along the way date from Roman times, and you will occasionally see a Roman gravestone or column. To the east of the road is the vast salt lake known as **Tuz Gölü** ❸, a favourite spot for goose hunters.

Konya (Konium) ❸ was the capital of the Seljuk Empire between 1071 and 1308, and remains the centre of Sufic teaching and a pilgrimage centre for devout Sunni Muslims. It was visited by St Paul several times around AD 50. The city has become an industrial centre in the last few decades and is now surrounded by bleak concrete suburbs before you get to the Seljuk monuments which lie at its heart. The citizens are renowned for their religious piety. Although the city has one of Turkey's biggest breweries, alcoholic beverage sales are banned in stores and restaurants, and the city has been a stronghold for Islamic parties during the Republican era.

BELOW: Mevlana's tomb, Konya.

In the city centre is a huge *höyük* (tell or mound), the **Alâeddin Tepesi**, built up by successive settlement over the centuries. On the top, with an excellent view over modern Konya, are the last remaining wall of the **Sultani Sarayı** (Palace of the Seljuk Sultans) and the **Alâeddin Camii** (12th and 13th centuries). Some of the oldest carpets in the world were discovered earlier this century lining its floors. The other major Seljuk monument in the town, the **Karatay Medrese**, an Islamic school built in 1251, is now a Ceramics and Tile Museum (Hastane Cad., Alâeddin; open daily 9am–noon, 1–5pm; entrance fee) housing, among other things, tiles showing pictures of Seljuk princesses. After their first 70 years in Anatolia, they still seem distinctly oriental.

Home of the dervishes

Every visitor to Konya wants to see the **Mevlana Tekkesi** (Kışla Cad., open daily 9am–5pm, from 10am Mon; entrance fee), the home of the whirling dervishes *(see page 402)*, founded around 1231. At the heart of the complex is the tomb of Mevlana ("Our Master") Celâddin Rumi, founder of the order. The function of the dervishes was essentially to find a mystic union with God through song and dance. They also appealed to the native Christian population of Anatolia and bridged the gap between them and their Seljuk rulers. Mevlana preached tolerance, forgiveness and enlightenment, and his poetry, even in a translated version, has an uncanny knack of tugging at the heartstrings.

The dervish convent was shut down in 1925 on the orders of Atatürk, but the Mevlana Festival of the Whirling Dervishes is still held every December, although it now takes place in a local gymnasium. In their long white robes, the dervishes spin in a kind of ballet, hoping to achieve a mystical union with the deity. The piety of most of the audience makes it clear that the *sema* (whirling ceremony) has not lost its religious significance. Performances are given daily for tourists in summer (check locally for details).

The local **Archaeological Museum** (Sahip Ata Cad.; open Tues–Sun 9am–noon, 1–5pm; entrance fee) has some fine ancient sarcophagi and some of the finds from nearby Çatalhöyük, although the finest of them have been taken to Ankara.

About 10 km (6 miles) outside Konya is the former Greek village of **Sille ㊱**, in which are the remains of the Church of St Michael and a spring dated 1732.

Çatalhöyük ㊲ (open daily 8am–5pm; entrance fee), just off the road south to Karaman, has been designated a World Heritage Site by UNESCO.

From about 6250–5400 BC, Çatalhöyük was a prosperous town of some 5,000 people. Rich and poor lived crowded together in houses which ran directly onto one another with no streets between them. The only way to gain entry was by climbing through their roofs. It is the first place in the world known to have used irrigation or keep domesticated animals. The community wove textiles, had simple carpets and traded in luxury goods, making their money from black glass-like obsidian, a mineral widely prized for making axes, daggers and mirrors. Most striking of all are the shrines with their paintings and statuettes, showing bulls and what seem to be fertility rites. ❑

Map on page 274

A turret of turquoise tiles is the showy highpoint of the Mevlana Tekkesi.

BELOW: dervishes still whirl, for Allah and the tourists.

EAST OF ANKARA

*The journey east of Ankara takes travellers to spectacular ruins
of ancient civilisations, the old Anatolian countryside
and to the rock churches of Cappadocia*

Map
on page
274

A nyone staying in Ankara should think seriously about a visit to the Hittite capital at Boğazkale, a drive of two to three hours east of the city along the E-88 highway towards Kırıkkale and Çorum. About 26 km (18 miles) east of Ankara, a road known as the "Nato Highway" forks left to the ski resort of **Elmadağ ㊳**, with a small ski lodge and mechanical lifts.

Kalecik ㊴, 80 km (50 miles) northeast of Ankara, has a Roman castle with medieval additions and an Ottoman bridge over the Kızılırmak River. Further north along the same road, en route to Kastamonu, the main sight in **Çankırı ㊵** is the Taş Mescit, a green-domed 13th-century insane asylum built by the Seljuk Turks, where music therapy helped people adapt to the social upheaval caused by marauding bands. The town's **Ulucamii (Grand Mosque)** was built in 1558 by Süleyman the Magnificent, who visited the town on his way east to fight the Iranians, and rebuilt after an earthquake in 1936.

Further along the E-88, due east from Ankara, the nondescript Anatolian town of **Kırıkkale** is home to Turkey's biggest state munitions factory, producing everything from rifles to explosives. It is also possible to approach Boğazkale from the south, climbing a minor road through wild mountains, from Yozgat.

State capital

At the height of its prosperity in about 1400 BC, the ruined city known today as **Boğazkale ㊶** and to the Hittites as **Hattuşaş** (Sungurlu; open daily 8am–noon, 1–5.30pm; entrance fee) was the capital of an empire which stretched south to Cyprus and west to the Aegean. Its massive size (about 2 km/1 mile) across and majestic setting are unrivalled. Though the higher slopes are now largely bare, it is not difficult to people them in the mind's eye with homes, warriors, priests, clerks, saddlers, cobblers and slaves. The sight is made more evocative by the knowledge that, not long after 1200 BC, the imperial city was stormed and burned and never recovered its former greatness.

The city is best explored by car as the distances can take their toll under a burning summer sun. Begin on the ramparts, looking down at the **King's Gate** and **Lion Gate**. A section of the stonework is kept clear of rubble and weeds, so that it is possible to see the great stone ramparts more or less as they looked in Hittite times. Further proof of the formidable nature of Hittite architecture is also provided by the **Yerkapı**, a 70-metre (229-ft) tunnel under the walls.

Lower down, on an outcrop of the hill overlooking the valley, the **Büyükkale** (Citadel) was the site of the Imperial Palace and it is here (in rooms on the south side) that the majority of the 3,350 clay tablets from the emperors' archives were found. Thanks to

LEFT: the fairy chimneys of Cappadocia await.
BELOW: chilly inland Anatolia offers good skiing in winter.

them, this great, vanished civilisation, virtually unknown 100 years ago, now has a detailed written history. Lower down are the clearly preserved foundations of the **Büyük Mabet** (**Great Temple**), which, in its day, may have been the largest building in the world, dedicated to the weather god, Hatti, and the sun goddess, Arinna. It, too, has proven to be a rich source of cuneiform tablets. In 1986, archaeologists unearthed a bronze tablet engraved with the terms of a treaty.

Temple to 1,000 gods

The religious heart of the Hittite kingdom lay slightly over 2 km (1 mile) north-east of Boğazkale, in the rock shrine of **Yazılıkaya ㊷** (open daily 9am–5pm; entrance fee). What survives today dates largely from 1275–1220 BC, when the shrine was enlarged by two Hittite emperors. There are two main galleries carved from the bedrock, their walls covered by reliefs of deities wearing long, conical caps. Many of the gods' names are not Hittite at all, but Hurrian or Hattite, showing how the culture and religion of the Hittite warrior aristocracy blended seamlessly with the beliefs and traditions of the indigenous people they had conquered. The galleries are superbly photogenic, but to catch the light at its best, visit Yazılıkaya well before midday. Sungurlu has a museum with reconstructions of the site *(see below)*.

Alacahöyük

A 20-minute drive further along the road will take you to the third great Hittite centre in the area, **Alacahöyük ㊸** (Sungurlu; open Tues–Sun 8am–noon, 1.30–5.30pm; entrance fee). Many of the most famous ancient Anatolian emblems, including the deer and the sun disk which have become symbols of

The Hittites' curious multi-angular stonework is called "cyclopaedean" because the Ancient Greeks, living about 500 years later, assumed this type of stonework could only have been the work of a vanished race of giants.

BELOW: dwelling on the past?
BELOW RIGHT: hi-tech wheat-farming on the plateau.

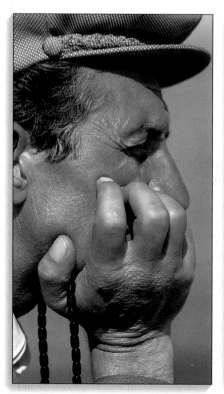

modern Turkey, were discovered here at excavations during the 1930s. However, Alacahöyük is generally far less picturesque than its neighbours, sprawling across the plain. What one can see clearly here is the ground plan of the Hittite and pre-Hittite buildings. The **Sphinx Gate** is the most impressive sight here; the other reliefs have been removed for safety and are now on display in Ankara.

Map on page 274

Other sights in the area

Although the Hittite cities are undoubtedly the stars, there are other places in the area worth a visit. Northeast of Alacahöyük, the city of **Çorum** ❹ dates back to Roman times, fell to the Seljuks in the late 11th century and was conquered by the Ottoman Sultan Beyazıt the Thunderbolt in 1398. The city's fine 13th-century **Ulucamii** was built by Seljuk Sultan Alâeddin Keykubat.

South of Boğazkale, **Yozgat** ❺ was founded by the Çapanoğlu dynasty, a Turkic clan that was influential in the region in the 17th century. The city is dominated by the Çapanoğlu **Mustafa Paşa Camii**, a grand mosque built in 1779.

Kırşehir ❻, southwest of Yozgat at the northwestern corner of Cappadocia, stands on the site of the Byzantine city of Justianopolis Mokyssos. It has a number of prominent Muslim monuments, including the **Mausoleum of Aşik Paşa** (1272–1333), in honour of a mystic Anatolian poet whose works are still quoted today by poets and politicians. The 19th-century Alâeddin Kale Camii is used as a warehouse of the city's **Archaeology Museum** (Kültür Merkezi Içi; open daily 9am–noon, 1–5pm; entrance fee). Other shrines include the 13th-century **Caca Bey Camii** and *medrese*, built in the 13th century as an observatory and later converted to a mosque, and the **Melik Gazi Türbesi**, the mausoleum of a regional Turkish ruler. ❏

BELOW: powerful Hittite statues at Alacahöyük.

Map on page 291

Istanbul
Ankara

CAPPADOCIA

Cappadocia is famed for its eerie lunar landscape, astounding underground cities and spectacular rock churches, their walls decorated with vivid Byzantine frescoes

A French Jesuit scholar, Père Guillaume de Jerphanion, discovered the rock churches of Cappadocia almost by chance during a journey on horseback across Anatolia in the summer of 1907.

"Our eyes were astounded. I remember those valleys in the searingly brilliant light, running through the most fantastic of all landscapes," he wrote.

Even now, when the valleys around the town of Ürgüp are relatively easy to reach (it takes three to four hours by car either from Ankara or Mersin), Cappadocia seems like a lost world to the arriving traveller. It took the 20th century – and perhaps the invention of photography – to make people appreciate this extraordinary region. Several of the most important fathers of the early Church lived in this district; none of them mentions what it looked like.

What we call "Cappadocia" today, if only for simplicity, is only a small part of the Hellenistic kingdom and subsequent Roman province which bore the same name. The original province stretched for hundreds of miles further east and west. The name is older still. The region is first mentioned in a monument bearing the trilingual epitaph of Persian King Darius as *Katpatuka* (the "Land of Beautiful Horses"). Today, it is known more for its donkeys, an essential means of transportation for local farmers, than for its magnificent stallions.

A 10th-century history tells us that its inhabitants were called troglodytes "because they go under the ground in holes, clefts, and labyrinths, like dens and burrows." In the 18th century, a French traveller thought he saw pyramids being used as houses, and weird statues of monks and the Virgin Mary.

Ancient upheavals

The reality is both more straightforward and more bizarre than any of the legends. The whole region is dominated by **Erciyes Dağı ❶** (ancient Mt Argaeus), the third-highest mountain in Anatolia, at 3,916 metres (12,848 ft). The Romans believed that anyone who managed to climb to the top of its eternally snowy summit would be able to see not only the Black Sea but also the blue of the Mediterranean.

Millions of years ago, Erciyes erupted, smothering the surrounding landscape with a torrent of lava stretching hundreds of miles in what must have been one of the greatest upheavals on the planet. Later, floods, rain and wind sawed away at the table of lava, creating deep valleys and fissures, while the slopes were carved into astonishing cones and columns.

Though the white dust from the rocks looks like sand, it is in fact much more fertile than the soil of the surrounding Central Anatolian steppes. Trees, vines and vegetables grow easily in it, attracting a dense population of farmers from the earliest times. And the

first men in these parts quickly discovered that the stone of the rock valleys is as magical as it looks. For it is soft until it comes into contact with the air, making it a perfect medium for carving entire buildings, sculpted out of living rock.

Generations of local people have carved innumerable doorways and rooms in the rocks over an area of several hundred square miles. Some were homes for farmers, others became dovecotes or stables. Some may have been the quarters of the Byzantine Army; many were used as chapels, cells, and refectories for monks and hermits. People still live today in the perfectly insulated rock dwellings, which are cool in summer and protected from the cold in winter.

The result is a fairytale landscape, a child's delight, where dwarves, elves, fairies and other supernatural beings seem to have just stepped round the corner, or perhaps vanished through a little doorway in the rock.

Three thousand rock churches

Many visitors only make a brief excursion to the cones and rock churches of Göreme, and spend an hour or two in **Zelve** or **Ihlara**. That's a pity because Cappadocia is best explored in a leisurely fashion by car or even on horseback. Several local firms are now hiring out horses for trekking expeditions. There are an estimated 3,000 rock churches in the area between Kayseri, Niğde, Gülşehir and the Ihlara Valley; and new caves, "underground cities" and even churches are still being discovered from time to time.

The main roads from Ankara and Konya join up at **Aksaray ❷**, founded by King Archaelais of Cappadocia. The town contains many Islamic shrines, including the 15th-century **Ulucamii** (Great Mosque), and the 13th-century **Eğik Minaret**, Turkey's answer to the Leaning Tower of Pisa.

The sight and sound of chickens and other farm animals are never far away in rural Turkey.

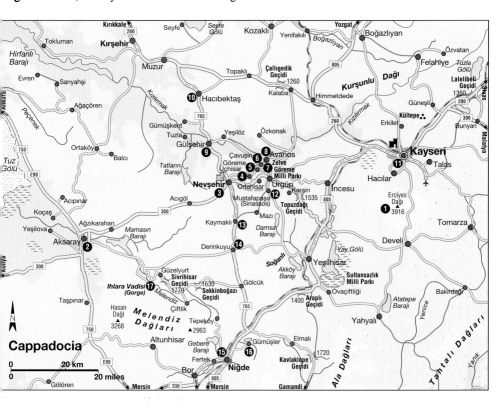

Holy Underground

Altogether there were several thousand churches and monasteries in Cappadocia, along with complex troglodyte towns. Who built them all? The history books don't tell us, but there are clues in the fabric of the cave-houses, the remains of tombs and the extraordinary paintings on the walls.

People have inhabited these underground warrens since the neolithic era, but the soul of the region was forged from the twin powers of religion and repression.

From the 3rd century BC, Cappadocia was a series of small, independent states, ruled by priest-kings. Throughout the Roman era (from AD 18), it became a sanctuary for Christians escaping persecution. The Arab invasions of the 7th–9th centuries again saw the area serve as a refuge, with many thousands flooding into the hills and burrows to escape the terrifyingly relentless sword of Islam.

Cappadocia's isolation also attracted a positive crowd of early hermits and other holy

men, seeking remote corners of the known world, from the Egyptian desert to these tufa towers, in order to serve their god through uninterrupted fasting, prayer and celibacy. Although they became known as monks – literally *monachos* ("solitary ones") – followers inevitably gathered around them and so the first Christian monasteries were born. In AD 360, St Basil of Caesarea laid down a set of rules for these emerging communities. They are still in force in the Greek Orthodox church and helped form the basis of the Rule of St Benedict in the West.

Far from withdrawing from life, many early monks saw themselves as the spearhead of the Christian army. Graffiti crosses scrawled on many classical temples date back to monkish attempts to "disinfect" the great buildings of paganism. At the same time, the monks began to carve an extraordinary series of churches and chapels from the soft Cappadocia rock, basing their architecture on established Byzantine practice, complete with redundant capitals and columns.

Arab rule could have spelled the end of the monasteries. Astonishingly, Islam proved rather more open to religious freedom than the Christians and Cappadocia flourished in relative safety. Over time, however, the influence of the new religion began to be felt as early "puritans" combined Old Testament prohibitions on idols with the Islamic taboo on human representation. From 726–843, the iconoclasts savagely attacked thousands of superb frescoes and mosaics; few of the fragile paintings survived the onslaught.

Cappadocia's last great Christian flowering was from the 9th–11th centuries, as the monasteries were redecorated and the land spawned a warrior aristocracy of Byzantine frontiersmen struggling to fend off the Arabs. Many saints are pictured in battledress.

The Battle of Manzikert (1071) eventually established the Turkish conquest of this part of Anatolia. The Byzantine landowners were able to survive for another couple of centuries, but by the 14th century, the region was firmly under Muslim rule. Only a few small monasteries struggled on in remote corners of the region; the great age was over. ❏

LEFT: extraordinary blood-red figurines decorate St Barbara's Church, Göreme.

The main transport and business hub for the area is the rather scruffy town of **Nevşehir ❸**, which has a ruined **citadel** and small **museum** (open Tues–Sun 8am–noon, 1–5pm; entrance fee), but nothing really to hold the visitor with so much waiting nearby. Even the scenery along the road from Nevşehir to Ürgüp is delightful and mysterious; the turn-off to Üçhisar and Göreme is north of the highway, halfway between the two.

Üçhisar ❹, 7 km (4 miles) east of Nevşehir, is famed for its immense fist-shaped tower of volcanic tuff, honeycombed with chambers. This **citadel** (open daily 8am–sunset; entrance fee), the highest point in Cappadocia, offers a spectacular view of a typical Anatolian village below and the unworldly rock formations in the Göreme Valley. It also has some excellent *pansiyons*, although most people choose to base themselves in **Ürgüp**, a charming town known for its restaurants, wine and carpet weavers; every woman in town is said to have a loom at home to weave carpets as part of her dowry and to earn extra cash for her family. The town is the richest in Nevşehir and the most developed for tourism. It is also handily central to the most fascinating area of Cappadocia.

Göreme village

The village of **Göreme ❺** has the facilities, but also the drawbacks, of a major tourist destination, its charm having been badly dented by a severe outbreak of billboards, despite resistance by local conservationists. Many townspeople still live in cave dwellings, however, and it can be very pleasant to walk among their extraordinary houses, and perhaps meet some modern troglodytes. *Pansiyon* prices are controlled and reasonable, and many include cave rooms with fairy chimneys or are in restored Ottoman or Greek houses.

Map on page 291

TIP

Guided expeditions on horseback are organised by Rainbow Ranch in Göreme while hot-air balloon tours are available from companies in Göreme, Ürgüp and Çavusin. For more information, see Travel Tips.

BELOW: going to town – in this case, Göreme.

Ortahisar, another local village with a towering rock apartment block (open daily 8am–sunset; entrance fee), is a lesser-known, friendly alternative.

Göreme's churches

Two km (just over 1 mile) from Göreme village, on the Ürgüp road, over 30 of the finest churches in Cappadocia are clustered together in the **Göreme Open-Air Museum** (open daily 8am–6pm, to 5pm in winter; entrance fee, with additional fees for Buckle Church and Dark Church – *see below*). Almost all date from the 9th–11th centuries and so escaped the activities of the iconoclasts who gouged the eyes from any human representations. Few visitors can cope with visiting all the churches. Those below are a few of the unmissable highlights.

The **Church of St Barbara** is decorated with red symbols and figurines, including Christ enthroned, and St Barbara, the patron saint of soldiers. Next door is the main dome of the stunningly restored **Elmalı Kilesi** (Church with the Apple). Also nearby is the **Yilanli Kilesi** (Church with the Snake), its walls covered with depictions of St George killing the dragon (or serpent) and paintings of strange creatures. Look also for St Onophrius, a 5th-century Egyptian hermit – a repentant *femme fatale* who was given a beard to make her unattractive to men and went to live in the desert where she wore a loincloth and ate only dates. Empreror Constantine and his mother Helena are pictured holding the True Cross which Helena supposedly discovered in Jerusalem.

The **Karanlık Kilesi** (Dark Church), originally part of a larger monastery, has some of the finest wall paintings in the history of Christian art, including the painting showing the betrayal of Christ by Judas. Another shows the Transfiguration with Christ between Moses and Elias on Mount Tabor. The **Tokalı Kilesi** (Church with the Buckle), also known as the Yeni Kilesi (New Church), has a glorious profusion of well-preserved murals on deep-blue backgrounds, including the *Annunciation*, *Agony in the Garden* and the *Journey to Bethlehem*.

The **Kılıçlar Valley** (the Valley of the Swords), on the high plateau behind Tokalı Kilesi, gets its name from pointed rock formations resembling sabres. The **Kılıçlar Kilesi** (Church of the Swords), about 400 metres (1,312 ft) north of Tokalı, is by far the biggest church complex in the region, but sadly, along with the church of St Eustace and a chapel with a picture of St Daniel in the lion's den, it is closed to visitors.

Çavuşin and Zelve

Çavuşin , 3 km (2 miles) to the north of Göreme town, resembles a gigantic caved-in ant hill. Nearby is a ghost town that was evacuated down the hill after a collapse in the 1960s. The **Church of Çavuşin**, accessible by a metal ladder, has archaic cartoon-style, strip narrative frescoes painted in bright green, pink, orange and dove-blues. Among the vivid portraits are a picture of Melias the Magister, a Byzantine-Armenian general who died as a prisoner of the Arabs in Baghdad in 974, and a Byzantine emperor riding a white horse, identified as John Tzimiskes (968–72).

Ghost towns, cave-houses and churches (few with frescoes) can also be found in and around **Zelve** ,

According to legend, St Barbara's father imprisoned her to prevent his daughter from becoming a Christian. When, despite all his efforts, she converted, he had her tortured and killed – only to be struck down by lightning himself, presumably in divine retribution.

BELOW: Göreme village houses.

Map on page 291

an area made up of three valleys east of Çavuşin. The area is excellent for rock climbing and has a vast underground **monastery** (open daily 8am–7pm, to 5pm in winter; entrance fee), which requires serious physical effort to explore.

Not everything in Cappadocia is Byzantine. **Avanos ❽**, on the northern bank of the Kızılırmak River, north of Zelve, is famed for its pottery, thanks to the rich red clay found along the river banks. The town has scores of shops selling local ware; some of them will let you try your own hand at throwing a pot.

To the west of this, near **Gülşehir ❾**, is the **Karşı Kilesi** (the Church of St John) which postdates Byzantine rule. An inscription records that it was established in 1214. Guillaume de Jerphanion found it still in use when he visited the district before World War I.

About 20 minutes north of Gülşehir, towards Kırşehir, is one of the most impressive antiquities in the region. **Hacıbektaş ❿** (open Tues–Sun 8.30am–12.30pm, 1.30–5.30pm; entrance fee) was the mother convent of the Islamic Bektaşi dervishes who served as chaplains to the janissaries, the storm troops of the Ottoman Empire. Two hundred years ago, it was said that no corner of the empire was more than half a day's journey from a Bektaşi lodge.

They were a free-thinking, tolerant community. Where else in the world will you see a mosque containing a drawing of man – something normally taboo in Islam? There is usually a group of local women praying at the tomb of their founder, **Hacı Bektaş Veli**, and on the annual feast day, August 14, followers from all over Turkey gather in town. This is the last remnant of a great tradition. Rooms in the convent tell their own story: the communal eating hall, with its great cauldrons still hanging by the fireplace, and the meeting room used by the "fathers" of the order, rather like a Western chapterhouse. Each of the senior

BELOW: ancient paintings survive in the churches of Göreme, such as those in Emalı Kilesi.

dervishes had his own place, marked out by an animal fur. The meeting room contains one rather sad reminder of the past – a photograph of the last August 14th meeting of the Turks from Crete in 1924. Soon after it was taken, these people – who a generation earlier had made up over 35 percent of the island's population – were uprooted while the Greeks of Cappadocia were sent to Greece, a land most of them had never seen before.

There are still those here who remember their former homes in Greece with nostalgia and welcome those Greeks who revisit their birthplace in Cappadocia.

East of Ürgüp

Drive east along the Kayseri road from Ürgüp until you see a sign on the right for the Church of St Theodore and keep going for about 10 km (6 miles) along a village road, through the village of **Karain**. People here have been decimated by mesothelioma, a very rare cancer that makes the linings of the lung swell, so both women and men appear pregnant. It is caused by xeolite, a volcanic mineral resembling asbestos found in the stones used to build the village houses.

The outstanding **Church of St Theodore** is located in the village of **Yeşilöz**, previously known as Tagar. Ask the keeper *(bekçi)* to unlock the church for you. The church has a central dome and unique 11th-century frescoes.

Situated on a vast plain facing Mount Erciyes, **Kayseri ⓫** is one of the oldest cities in Anatolia. It served as the capital of the Graeco-Roman province of Cappadocia from 380 BC to AD 17, was conquered by Roman Emperor Tiberius, renamed Caesarea, and remained part of the Roman-Byzantine Empire until 1071, when it came under the control of the Turks. Today, it is a major industrial city, but it does have numerous 13th-century Islamic monuments, such as

BELOW: colourful rag dolls from Derinkuyu.
RIGHT: potter at work in Avanos.

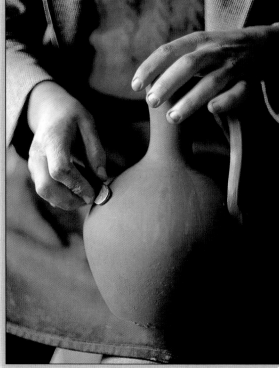

the Çifte Kümbet, tomb of Melike Adile Hatun, wife of the Selçuk Sultan Alâed-din Keykubat, while the Döner Kümbet, built in 1276, contains the tomb of his daughter, Şah Cihan Sultan. The Honat Hatun Camii was built by another of the sultan's wives and contains her tomb, the Honat Hatun Türbesi. It also has a small **Archaeological Museum** (Gültepe Mah. Kilşa Cad.; open Tues–Sun 9am–noon, 1–5.30pm; entrance fee) and a fascinating museum of Ottoman life in the carefully restored 15th-century **Güpüpoğlu Konaği** (Cumhuriyet Mah.; open Tues–Sun 8.30am–noon, 1.30–5pm; entrance fee).

Twenty-two kilometres (14 miles) northeast of the city are the remains of **Kültepe**, a 19th-century BC Assyrian and Hittite trade centre.

Map on page 291

A town of paintings

Largely Greek towns like **Mustafapaşa** ⑫ (Sinassos), southwest of Kayseri, never really recovered from the blow they received with the collapse of the Ottoman Empire. A local *bekçi* will take you to see the 19th-century decorations in the rock-cut **Church of St Basil**, in a meadow above a hauntingly pretty gorge outside the town. In town, ask at the **Hotel Sinassos** to be shown those rooms left as they were decorated by the 19th-century owners of the house. On the wall over the front door is an extraordinary picture which dates from 1893 but seems to have more to do with the Russian-Japanese war.

The painted walls of Mustafapaşa are crumbling from neglect.

Every house has its own stone-sculptured balcony and windows. Inside many of them are late-19th-century frescoes, some with the eyes scoured out by the pious Muslim farmers who inherited these houses in the 1920s. If you can persuade the locals to let you look, you will feast on an extraordinary succession of paintings: young lovers dallying on a swing; the judgement of St Paul at

BELOW: tectonic masterpiece.

Ephesus; 19th-century London as imagined by a Cappadocian artist, with a train running past St Paul's Cathedral; Napoleon fighting Arabs in the desert. Alas, most are doomed. The houses are too large for the farmers, who are therefore fast replacing them with modern houses. The pictures are literally crumbling as you look at them. Leave it another 10 or 20 years, and Mustafapaşa will be just another drab, architecturally anonymous central Anatolian town.

A little further south, the 25-km (16-mile) long **Soğanlı Valley** has numerous 9th–13th century churches, along with a number of Roman rock tombs. The **Kubeli Kilesi**, the most typical of its churches, is built on the top of a pock-marked rock pinnacle; the **Karabaş Kilesi**, on the left-hand side of the valley, has historic frescoes.

Underground cities

An astounding 400 underground cities exist in Cappadocia. Many of these were used at various times by Christians from Kayseri and the countryside escaping from invading Arab and Turkic hordes. Some of the tunnels were probably in use as early as the Bronze Age and Hittite seals show that they took refuge here. As many as 30,000 people could hide in these catacomb-like structures.

The underground city of **Kaymaklı** ⑬, located on the road to Niğde, 20 km (12½ miles) south of Nevşehir, has eight floors. A further 10 km (6 miles) south is the most impressive of the underground cities – **Derinkuyu** ⑭ ("Deep Well" in Turkish). A complex web of settlements including stables, wine presses, kitchens and wells, Derinkuyu has eight undergound floors, reaching a depth of 55 metres (180 ft). Each chamber has been illuminated. Both are open daily 8am–5pm, to 6pm in summer; entrance fee.

BELOW: Derinkuyu, underground city of thousands.

The city of **Niğde** , a historic provincial capital, came to the fore after the 10th-century Arab invasions had destroyed its less defensible neighbours. Sited amid mountains, it has numerous 13th- and 14th-century Islamic shrines and monuments, including a castle, built in the 11th century and once used as a prison. The **Alâeddin Camii**, built in 1203, with a *bedesten* or covered market below it, is worth a visit. The **Akmedrese**, a Seljuk theological school, serves as a museum (open Tues–Sun 8am–noon, 1–4.30pm; entrance fee).

The best of the Christian churches in the area are isolated. One of the very finest, as far as wall painting goes, is the monastery at **Eski Gümüşler** (open daily 9am–6.30pm; entrance fee) in the village of **Gümüşler** , 8 km (5 miles) north of Niğde. If you are a great fan of Byzantine art, it is well worth a visit. The monastery church, which was restored by British archaeologists in the 1960s, has a completely preserved courtyard (the only one to survive in its entirety) and solemn frescoes in its interior which deserve to be better known. A room upstairs springs a surprise: a smoky wall covered with non-religious pictures of animals and birds. Outside a winepress and baths have been discovered.

The Ihlara Valley

To the west of Niğde, over 60 churches have been hewn into the walls of the 10-km (6-mile) long, 80-metres (262-ft) wide **Ihlara Vadisi (Gorge)** . The sheer-sided valley, which runs along the Melendiz River, is excellent for trekking. Most of the churches in this area were built in the 11th century. Only a dozen are open to the public. These include the **Ağaçaltı Kilisesi** (Church Under the Tree), with 10th- and 13th-century frescoes, one of them showing Daniel in the lion's den; and the **Yılanlı Kilesi** (Church of the Serpents), whose frescoes depict the entombment of Mary the Egyptian with St Zosimus and a lion. The **Purenli Seki Kilisesi** (Church with the Terraces) contains a chamber tomb, separated by pillared arcades, and frescoes. The **Eğritas Kilisesi** (Church with the Crooked Stone) is one of the valley's most important Christian shrines, with several frescoes of distinction, most sadly badly damaged.

The **Kırk Damaltı Kilisesi** (the Church of St George) was re-endowed by a Greek nobleman who served the Seljuk Sultan Mesut II at Konya and wore a turban (as the frescoes show) in the last decade of the 13th century. The best approach to Kırk Damaltı Kilisesi is not via the steps at the top of Ihlara Valley, but about 3–4 km (2–3 miles) downstream, on the northeast, near the village of Belisirama. The local children will help to locate it.

South of Niğde, the uplands of Central Anatolia are separated from the southern coast by the magnificent Taurus Mountains. After the town of **Ulukışla**, the road climbs until it reaches the famous **Gülek Boğazı (Cilician Gates)**, a high pass in the mountains which was, for centuries, the only way between the Anatolian plateau and Çukurova (Cilicia). Commercial caravans and invading armies alike had to scale its treacherous heights to reach Tarsus or Adana and the Mediterranean in the south, or to bring goods to the cities of Central and Eastern Anatolia. Most travellers today take a lower, overcrowded expressway, the Adana road. ❏

Map on page 291

About 70 km (44 miles) south of Kayseri, the Sultansazlığı Kuş Cenneti is Turkey's finest bird sanctuary, harbouring around 300 species in a 172 sq km site including freshwater Lake Egri, saltwater Lake Yay and marshlands. Top billing goes to the vast flocks of flamingoes who settle here in Apr–Oct.

BELOW: broom-maker at work.

THE BLACK SEA COAST

*This region is defined by its mountainous isolation,
unpredictable weather and fierce independence*

Ancient Greek accounts of the Black Sea – notably the legendary adventures of the rebel Jason and his Argonauts in around 1000 BC – paint the region as a terrifying place full of killer rocks, sea caves leading to Hades, brutal Amazons, and numerous other bizarre tribes such as the "Mosynoeci", who lived in wooden towers and made love "like swine in the field" wherever and whenever they liked. Medea herself, the betrayed lover of Jason in Euripides' tragic account, may have been a Laz princess of the far eastern Black Sea, where the kingdom of Colchis and Golden Fleece were located, and where her people, many of whom still speak the only pre-Hellenic language in Turkey, maintain a unique culture in the region of Pazar, Ardeşen, Fındıklı, Arhavi and Hopa. Underwater archaeological excavations suggest this could be the site of the great flood of biblical fame, and remains of human settlements more than 7,000 years old are being studied. The Black Sea was once a freshwater lake, until melting glaciers are thought to have raised the level of the Mediterranean, causing saltwater to race through the Bosphorus and widening the lake by as much as 2 km (1¼ miles) a day, causing the population to flee. For this reason, houses are often built on stilts.

Most Black Sea people, though practising Muslims, still consume more alcohol than elsewhere in Turkey. With wild music and dance traditions, the culture and geography of the region make it unlike the rest of the country. Aquiline profiles, fair colouring and a keen sense of humour are frequent amongst the Laz. In the northeast mountain villages near Hopa the people still speak a dialect of Armenian, while those in the valleys near Çaykara and Of speak a form of Greek yet boast the highest proportion of mosques, religious schools and Muslim scholars in Turkey. The Giresun highlands were settled by Türkic tribes in the 13th century, and the inhabitants are Alevi rather than Sunni Muslims, as are those in the Fatsa and Bolaman regions. Georgian is still spoken in some of the valleys of Artvin.

With 1,250 km (780 miles) of coastline, there are still many small and little-visited beaches; one may even find an increasingly rare unspoilt fishing village, west of Samsun. Trade between Turkey and the former Soviet Union is booming and thus there is a four-lane motorway from Samsun to Hopa with enormous trucks thundering continuously, a stone's throw from the beach. The local people may be increasingly well off, but the traveller who has been instilled with visions of tranquillity or the "shimmering towers of Trebizond" may be in for a shock.

Turn inland, however, and a maze of winding roads leads to a feast of unspoiled green, wet wilderness, ancient castles and churches, fairytale forests and villages full of local character. ❑

PRECEDING PAGES: threshing the grain during the autumn harvest in Artvin.
LEFT: fishing boat and its skipper at Ünye.

THE BLACK SEA

The Black Sea Coast is suffering badly from an overdose of development, but for those with time and transport there is still magic to be found

Map on pages 306–7

Technically, the Black Sea holiday resorts begin just outside Istanbul, but there are long stretches worth ignoring. Şile is popular with city dwellers on weekend outings, but horribly crowded; Adapazarı (Sakarya) is the industrial suburb of Istanbul/İzmit; the resort of **Akçakoca ❶** worst hit by the 1999 earthquake. Mostly of interest to Turkish families, Ereğli and Zonguldak are coal-mining and industrial areas.

To avoid this stretch of coast, head inland through **Bolu ❷**. The city is dull, but the surrounding area is stunning. To the south are the spa complex at Abant and the ski resort at Kartalkaya; to the north is the **Yedigöller Milli Parkı ❸** – the Seven Lakes National Forest, worthwhile for the scenic drive alone. **Mengen**, further east, is famous for producing Turkey's finest chefs.

Safranbolu

The first unmissable stop is the city of **Safranbolu ❹**, included in UNESCO's World Heritage List, where some 800 of the finest 19th-century Ottoman houses in Turkey have been beautifully restored, many as *pansiyons*. The houses here are especially grand as the city has been prosperous since the 17th century, the centre of a trade route linking Istanbul and Sinop. The town was and is still famous for its leather, copper and iron craftsmanship, which was quality-controlled under a sophisticated guild system. As its name suggests, Safranbolu is also noted for saffron and other spices. It also produces some of the finest *lokum* (Turkish delight) in the entire country.

There are so many marvellous historic attractions in the old quarter of **Çarşı** that it is impossible to list them all. On arrival, head for the Yemeniciler Arastası, the original leather workers' bazaar. Here, you should be able to pick up a copy of *Museum City Safranbolu*, with complete listings, maps and historical information; as well as buy a marvellous selection of crafts (including traditional Ottoman shoes), fabrics, clothing and herbal remedies. The old Governor's Residence is now host to the **Kaymakamlar Müzesi** (open daily 8.30am–12.30pm, 1.30–5.30pm; entrance fee), near the enormous 350-year-old Cincihanı Caravansaray. The city's largest mansion, Havuzlar Konak, has become a spectacular hotel whose main attraction is a large indoor fountain (the original household's water supply) in the main salon.

There is a craft exhibition in the *Muvakkithane* section of the **Köprülü Mehmet Paşa Camii**, and the 17th-century **Ottoman Cinci Hamam** (bath-house) has been beautifully restored for use with separate male and female sections – a splendid marble setting for the luxury of a Turkish bath.

LEFT: wet and wild, the Black Sea Coast.
BELOW: traditional Ottoman house in Safranbolu.

The coastal route

After Safranbolu, there are two possible routes. The first heads north through Bartın and along the coast road to **Amasra ⑤** (91 km/56 miles), a stunning old town between two fortified promontories with Hellenistic foundations and surviving Byzantine walls. Rarely visited by foreigners, it seems more like a Greek village, with sweeping sea views and steep, cobbled paths from which you can easily view the magnificent 14th-century fortresses, built when Amasra was a Genoese trading colony. At the southern end of the city are Roman ruins which may have been either a provincial parliament house or the gymnasium and bath, and there are several Byzantine churches (later converted to mosques).

A day's catch of fresh brown trout for the intrepid and patient angler.

The winding coast eastwards from Amasra rewards the determined traveller with dramatic scenery and architecture – note especially the timber, shale-roofed dwellings which look as though they would collapse under the weight of the stones. Minibus links are limited and driving conditions are hair-raising, with pot-holed roads twisting along sheer drops to a crashing sea. Some 150 km (90 miles) along the coast towards Sinop, **İnebolu ⑥** and **Ayancık ⑦** are the first beach towns of any note, though they have few antiquities – their remaining Ottoman or Greek houses are either uninhabited or in poor repair, while their *pansiyons* tend to be concrete motel blocks. However, both İnebolu and Ayancık have excellent (cheap) beachside hotels which stay open all year. Ayancık has been trying to promote nature tourism inland and there are hunting and trekking opportunities, good campsites and clear green lakes. Take your own transport.

Sinop ⑧, situated on a peninsula jutting far out to sea, has a superb natural harbour and is the base for underwater excavations. These include beautifully preserved Byzantine shipwrecks as well as human settlements from more than 7,000 years ago (now 19 km/12 miles out to sea), when a great flood inundated the coast. The oldest city on the coast, Sinop was settled by Greeks from Miletus in the 7th century BC, although legend tells us it was founded by the Amazon Queen Sinova, who managed to brush off the ever-amorous Zeus by getting him to grant her one wish: virginity. There are also 39 prehistoric sites in the region, one dating from 4500 BC. The remains of a 2nd-century BC Temple of

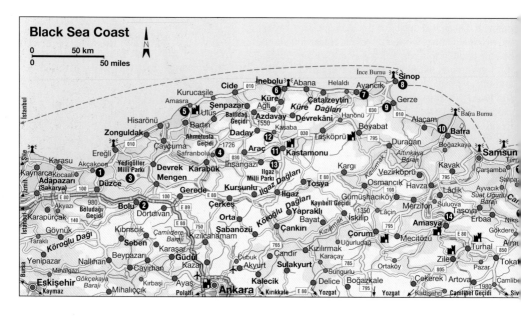

Serapis stand in the town centre, but the mask of the god himself has been removed to the local **museum** (currently closed). On the same street are a 7th-century church, the **Balat Kilise**, and several Seljuk and Ottoman monuments including the 13th-century **Alâeddin Camii** and its accompanying *medrese* (religious school). Most impressive of all are the enormous **city walls**, parts of which stand to a height of 25 metres (80 ft). Even the city prison is studded with Byzantine marble. There are numerous restaurants and *pansiyons*.

Prettiest of all is the tiny fishing village of **Gerze** ❾, some 40 km (24 miles) from Sinop, and mercifully situated well away from the pitiless roar of the motor-way. It has no antiquities or old houses of note, but this calm spot is a genuine haven for true lovers of the sea, though the beach is rather stony. The best places to stay are those situated along the point, where you can sit on a balcony in peace and quiet watching the fishermen harvest *palamut* (type of mackerel).

A little further on, there are camping facilities in the **Çamgölü Forest**, which slopes to the seas, while **Bafra** ❿, at the mouth of the Kızılırmak River, has a thermal spring which once heated a 13th-century *hamam*. There is also a 15th-century mosque-*medrese* worth a stop. **Samsun** does have a reasonable Archae-ology and Ethnographic Museum (Atatürk Bulvari; open Tues–Sun 8.30am–noon, 1–5pm; entrance fee) with a fine collection of 2nd-century BC gold jewellery, but this is a strictly commercial and charmless port city – skip it unless you need to catch a plane in a hurry.

The inland route

If you take the inland route eastwards from Safranbolu, your first stop should be **Kastamonu** ⓫, a 10th-century town which was the feudal stronghold of the Comneni family of aristocratic officers who captured the Byzantine crown in 1081. There are also a number of Seljuk and Ottoman monuments. Fifteen km (9 miles) northwest, in the village of **Kasaba** ⓬, is one of the finest mosques in Turkey – the carved wooden **Mahmut Bey Camii**, a superb Seljuk structure built in 1366 and retaining almost all its original features. Head south from Kastamonu for 63 km (39 miles) and you reach the **Ilgaz Milli Parkı** ⓭

Map on pages 306–7

TIP

Predictably, the most spectacular places in the region are the hardest to reach. Public transport is very limited both on the inland village routes and on the gorgeous, circuitous, coastal road from Sinop to Amasra. Plan seriously, and either hire a four-wheel drive vehicle, go with a tour group, or take stout hiking boots and allow plenty of time.

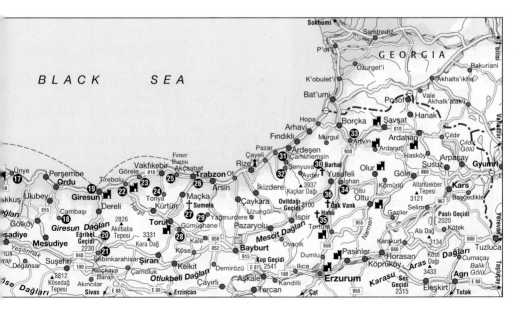

Burial chambers of the Pontic Kings in the cliffs at Amasya.

BELOW: traditional pre-prayer *wudu* ablutions in Amasya.

(National Park), which is growing in popularity as a ski resort. You can continue southeast through the pretty Ottoman villages of **Tosya** and **Osmancık** to Amasya, one of the most attractive towns in all Turkey.

Stunning **Amasya** ⑭, 130 km (80 miles) inland, was the first capital of the self-styled Pontic Kingdom until its rulers moved to Sinop in 120 BC. Overlooking the Yeşılırmak River, old Ottoman houses cluster around the feet of the ancient monuments, while at night floodlights search the cliffs near the citadel for well-preserved Hellenistic cave tombs, above the palace of the first Pontic kings. It was here that the great geographer and historian Strabo was born. Later held as Seljuk territory, it was sacked by Genghis Khan's Mongols in the mid-13th century.

There are two impressive Seljuk mosques – the **Burmalı Minare Camii** (Mosque of the Twisted Minaret) and the **Gök Medrese/Camii**, a 16th-century *bedesten* (inn) in the bazaar, between Ziya Paşı Bulvari and Atatürk Caddesi – as well as a 7th-century Byzantine church converted to a mosque in 1116. Across from the Sultan Beyazıt Camii, on Atatürk Caddesi, the **Amasya Müzesi** (open Tues–Sun 9am–noon, 1.30–5.30pm; entrance fee) contains a wide collection of artefacts from the nine different civilisations that have ruled the city, including wood carvings, astronomical instruments and Mongol mummies. The climb to the **citadel** is a bit steep but at least there is a teahouse at the top. Variously used by Greeks, Romans and Seljuks, there isn't a great deal left of the structure, nor of the Pontic palace, but the view is mind-boggling. The **Hazeranlar Konaği** (Hattuniye Mah.; open Tues–Sun 9am–12.30pm, 1.30–5.30pm; entrance fee) is a restored Ottoman mansion of 1865, carefully furnished in period.

From Amasya, head for the ancient Anatolian temple city of **Niksar** ⑮, some 100 km (60 miles) east, which was also a principal stronghold of Pontic kings. The remains of an impressive fortress still stand on the acropolis.

East of Samsun

Heading east along the coast from Samsun, a ghastly four-lane coastal highway runs along the shore right to the Georgian border. This is now a major trade artery, of interest only to truckers and businessmen; most of its once-charming *pansiyons* or seaside restaurants have become 4-star hotels or discos. But off the beaten track there are still some lovely, wild places. Any combination of side roads from **Terme** ⑯ lead to the wildlife sanctuary marshlands of the Çarşıba Plain and Simelik Lagoon, a hunting and fishing paradise.

Ünye ⑰ has a good beach and tourist facilities, but is rather tacky, as are most of the other local "tourist" towns. Further along the coast, a temple to the leader of the Argonauts once stood at the tip of **Cape Yasun** (**Cape Jason**). Çaka, Perşembe and Ordu have little left to recommend them except as a turn-off to the spectacular beach-encircled crater lake at **Cambaşı** ⑱, about 70 km (45 miles) south. The main attraction of **Giresun** ⑲ is the Aksu Arts and Cultural Festival on Giresun Island (third weekend in May), which has replaced a more ancient event (reputedly Muslim, but probably pagan), the *Hıdrellez*.

For those with a serious interest in history, the time and a suitable vehicle, the spectacularly scenic 93-km (58-mile) trip across the **Eğribel Geçidi (Pass)** ❷⓿ to Şebinkarahisar is highly recommended. A right turn below Dereli brings you to **Hisarköy**, where the badly damaged ruins of a Greek Monastery are perched on the edge of a huge rock, itself on the edge of a forest. **Tamdere Yaylısı** is a friendly place to base yourself if planning a day hike to the glacier lake at **Karagöl**.

Beyond the pass, **Şebinkarahisar** ❷⓵ sits high on a bluff overlooking the beautiful Kelkit Valley. It was identified as Pompey's ancient city of Koloneia, established after the Mithridatic Wars in 63 BC, and there seem to have been settlements here since antiquity. Many prehistoric mounds remain, with Pompey's imposing ruined fortress still crowning the huge basalt rock that towers above the village. The area became part of the Ottoman Empire in 1471, when the now-restored **Fatih Camii** was built.

There are also remains of earlier mosques, several Greek churches and the cave **Monastery of Meryemana**, 7 km (4 miles) across the valley in Kayadibi village, which dates from the 5th century AD but used by the Armenians much more recently. It is a stiff climb up the vertiginous cliff, but the site and view are both breathtaking. Sadly, the area's strategic value, earthquakes and political turmoil (including a showdown between local Armenians and the Ottoman army in 1915) have all damaged the Greek, Armenian and Islamic monuments.

Back on the coast

Tirebolu ❷⓶ (formerly Tripolis) occupies a crescent-shaped bay; on a rocky promontory to the east is the Byzantine fortress of **Kurucakale**, possibly built by the Grand Comneni of Trebizond. This has been a substantial trading port

Map
on pages
306–7

BELOW: night falls over Amasya.

since antiquity, especially for silver mined inland, and became an important Genoese outpost in the Middle Ages. With two other fortresses nearby, it is now considered to be one of the prettiest towns on the central eastern coast.

For the adventurous, **Görele** ㉓ marks the turn-off to the village of **Kuşıöy,** **(Bird Village)**, 28 km (17 miles) away, so named because its inhabitants are famed for long-distance communication by means of an archaic "whistle language". Vakfıkebir, noted for its dairy products, leads 20 km (12 miles) inland to **Tonya** ㉔, a remarkable village inhabited by Greek-speaking Muslims thought to be descended from the fierce, independent tribes who held the region during the time of the Grand Comneni *(see page 307).* Many still carry weapons, and Tonya is notorious for the bloody feuds that have occurred here. In the local graveyard, you can count the bullets carved on the headstones to represent the number of people the deceased had killed before catching a bullet of his own.

Not originally known for getting on with its Laz and Türkmen neighbours, Tonya, most easily reached inland from Akçaabat, is one of several villages to participate in the annual **Kadırga Plateau Festival** (3rd weekend in July), held at the common boundary point with Torul and Maçka and thought to have begun as peace-negotiation after centuries of feuding over grazing lands.

Akçaabat ㉕ still retains a few examples of classic Black Sea architecture, as well as claiming the best *horon* dancers in the region, shown to best effect during the **Hıdırnebi Festival** (also in July), noted for a circle dance of over 500 people.

Tall tales of Trebizond

The medieval empire of Trebizond – **Trabzon** ㉖ – had a bewitching reputation, famed for its wealth, its gold-plated palace domes and cathedrals, and its virtual independence, which lasted for nearly 2,000 years. It pre-dated Byzantium and was the last outpost of Hellenic civilisation seized by the Ottomans. Founded as a Greek colony in the 6th century BC, Trebizond was to reach its cultural zenith when Alexius Comnenus and his Georgian supporters took control in 1204 after the Crusader invasion of Constantinople. The Comneni dynasty lasted 257 years, in part because Mongol raids forced the Silk Road to divert through here, encouraging a flourishing trade with the Genoese and Venetians who were surprised to find this outpost of civilisation in such wild nomadic territory.

George Bessarion (later bishop of Nicaea) carried memories of its magnificence to Rome not long before it fell to the Turks, describing just one part of the Comneni's "golden palace" as "a long building of great beauty, its foundation being all of white stone, and its roof decorated with gold and other colours, painted flowers and stars, emitting beams of light as if it were heaven itself." Rose Macaulay's famed fantasy novel perpetuated this image of Trebizond as a fairytale city of sybaritic splendour, its towers "shimmering on a far horizon in luminous enchantment" – but this is a metaphorical fantasy novel only.

In reality, the glorious days of Trabzon's sea trade all but disappeared in the late 1800s with the completion of the Ankara–Erzerum railway and highways into Iran. Russians occupied the city from 1916 to

Women's markets are a distinct feature of Black Sea culture; the best are in the strip between Vakfıkebir and Çayeli (Wed), Of (Thur), Rize (Mon and Sat), Sürmene (Tues) and Akçaabat (Tues). They are colourful and entertaining and a great way to stock up on locally made cheeses and other produce.

BELOW: no longer romantic, the modern towers of Trabzon.

1918, after which a shortlived attempt at a "Pontic Revival" came to a rude end during the 1923 exchange of populations. Today's **Atatürk House** (open daily 8.30am–4.30pm; entrance fee) was the confiscated mansion of the would-be president of New Pontus.

Trabzon's harbour area and city centre are now far from attractive. No shimmering towers define the horizon, and the few Byzantine remains are little more than a pile of stones, while crumbling, uninhabited Greek mansions line the quay. Yet even though Trabzon has lost virtually all of its former glamour, thriving trade with the CIS is again making the city an international marketplace.

The city has pretty much given up on tourism; there is little left to see of the grandiose city walls or citadel and remains of the Imperial Palace. It is worth stopping at the classic 13th-century **Church of Aya Sofia** (İnönü Cad.; open Tues–Sun 8.30–noon, 1–5.30pm, to 5pm in winter; entrance fee) which was built by Emperor Manual VII Palaeologus. It is beautifully situated on a seaside bluff and has a number of fine mosaics and frescoes. The Chrysocephalos, the cathedral of Trebizond during Comneni rule, is now a mosque, the **Fatih Camii**. Like the Church of St Eugenius (the Yeni Cuma Camii since 1461), it may have contained important mosaics and imperial portraits of the Comneni, but they have been plastered over out of respect for Allah. The oldest church in the city, the 9th-century Church of St Ann, is permanently locked. The **Trabzon Museum** (Zeytinlik Cad.; open Tues–Sun 9am–noon, 1–5.30pm; entrance fee) has a small collection of local archaeological finds housed in a magnificent 19th-century mansion, originally a convent but later the home of a wealthy Greek banker. However, the only really compelling reason to stop in Samsun is for a day trip to the famous monastery at Sumela.

Map on pages 306–7

TIP

Enormous amounts of money change hands daily in Trabzon, lending it a lively "gold rush" atmosphere – complete with a great many prostitutes from the CIS countries. Things have calmed down since the mid-1990s, but female tourists may well find themselves mistaken for streetwalkers.

BELOW: Sumela Monastery.

A monastery to remember

The **Monastery of the Black Virgin** at **Sumela** ㉗, in the depths of an uninhabited forest valley, is an enormous seven-storey structure that perches dramatically on a ledge between heaven and earth, halfway up a sheer rockface above roaring waters. According to legend, it was built by two monks from Athens under instructions from a vision of the Virgin, but some historians claim it was more likely to have been commissioned by 4th-century Byzantine emperors in a move to convert the pagan natives to Christianity. Sumela's glory days, like those of Trebizond, came under the patronage of the Grand Comneni, who granted an edict exempting it from all taxes and restrictions. In Ottoman times, Selim the Grim upheld these rights, but all came to an end when the monks were deported along with the rest of the Greek community in 1923.

The present buildings probably date from the 12th century and contain many layers of frescoes; most of those still visible date from the 1700s. These have been vandalised over the years, but Sumela has been under restoration for some time and remains one of the Black Sea Coast's biggest attractions, with several bus tours each day. Getting there still involves a panting climb up a forest path. The monastery opens daily Nov–Apr 9am–3pm, May–Oct 8am–6pm; entrance fee).

BELOW: the rural idyll still survives, away from the motorway.

Beyond Trabzon

There are many more monastic ruins in the Maçka district, such as **Peristera**, near Şimşili, and **Vazelon**, 14 km (8½ miles) above Maçka, but they are not worth the effort of bad, steep roads. Continuing past Maçka, you travel through the Harşit Valley and over the Zigana Pass, along the old caravan route towards Erzurum and Asia, to **Torul** (with a castle once controlled by a 15th-century mountain lord) and **Gümüşhane ㉘**, once an important trade town whose remains are set among fruit groves and wild rose fields. Likewise **Bayburt**, the provincial capital, boasts the remains of a Byzantine castle, significant mosques, tombs and *hamams*.

Connoisseurs of the altogether out of the way and unexplored will enjoy the lush mountain valley of **Yağmurdere ㉙**, some 40 km (24 miles) east. Those with vehicles (it is a long and tortuous route) can also reach **Barhal ㉚**, with its well-preserved 10th-century church, from this direction, along the Çoruh River valley.

Outdoor enthusiasts may want to head for Barhal/Yusufeli on foot or horseback over the Kaçkar Mountains via **Çamlıhemşin ㉛** and **Ayder** *(see box opposite)*. This means getting away from the dreaded coastal highway and its tea factories. There is not much to see at Of (pronounced "oaf") or Çaykara, both bastions of Islamic piety, while the tea capitals of **Rize** and **Çayeli** are concrete trade strips. Though **Pazar** marks the beginning of the traditional Laz land, you would do as well to meet the people inland. Watch out for men carrying hawks on their wrists; hawking is a traditional Laz sport and there are even teahouses where fanatics bring their "pets" to squawk in competition with the conversation.

The Hemşınlis are not Laz but a very old Turkish tribe whose language is a dialect of Armenian. From early-15th-century accounts, they were nominally Christian but are also referred to as "robbers and brigands" who demanded a toll

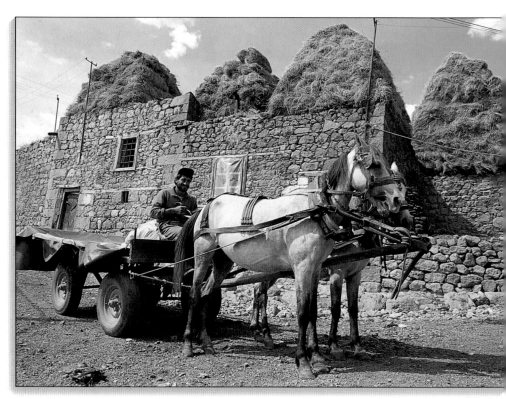

for the right of passage through the mountains. Their conversion to Islam came perhaps 150 years ago – and though some of the older families are deeply religious, the majority have good jobs in sophisticated urban areas and only visit their relatives in summer to maintain traditions or run *pansiyons*. Hemşınlis are gifted people, known for their skill as confectioners and pastry chefs.

Map on pages 306–7

Çamlıhemşın itself is a fairly attractive town built on the roaring Fırtına River (meaning storm) over which, rather further up towards Şenyuva **㉜**, there are several magnificent stone bridges, some dating from the 17th century. The tourist information office in the single main street can recommend trekking guides and accommodation (language may be a problem).

On the rugged road leading onwards from Şenyuva, the impressive **Zilkale** (castle) has fairytale spires and a mysterious history. Some claim it dates from the 6th century, but it has never been established whether it was built by Justinian, the Comneni or a local warlord – or why such an imposing fortress was built in such an obscure location. A steep climb to **Çat** rewards the trekker with a good hotel, after which a right fork leads into serious mountaineer's territory to the Tatos glacier lakes. The high pastures of **Pokut Yayla**, which has a few basic hostels, is good hunting territory, teeming with wild boar and deer as well as mountain goats.

Picking tea on a plantation near Rize.

Artvin: a region with links to Georgia

The Artvin region is still quintessentially Caucasian and offers some of the most impressive 9th–11th century church architecture in the world. **Yusufeli** stands at the centre of a region where a 200-year renaissance of Georgian medieval culture flourished between Tortum, Artvin and Ardahan.

BELOW: boat builders in Hopa.

TREKKING FROM AYDER

With at least half a dozen mountain ranges in the Black Sea region, eco-tourism and trekking are attracting outdoor sports enthusiasts in unprecedented numbers, particularly to the Hemsin area, where guides are readily available, and the lush Kaçkar Mountains, which are particularly good for climbing and hiking.

The ideal base camp is Ayder (17 km/10½ miles above Çamlıhemşın; reached by bus from Trabzon), which has several *pansiyons* specialising in group treks. Most local accommodation is basic, so carry camping gear, but there are some decent shops and restaurants and a recently renovated, seriously hot (57°C/135°F) thermal bath.

There are routes and guides available for all levels of ability and a minibus of sorts runs regularly up the 13 km (8 miles) to the Kavron plateau (which even has a teahouse) where you can easily make a low-stress day outing or picnic. A stiff day hike might take in the loop of the three primary Kavron *yaylas* (summer pastures), and a popular three-day trek takes you to Barhal, which has a good pansiyon, and a minibus to Yusufeli, the only city with decent bus connections anywhere.

Winter trekking is not advised, because the weather conditions are unpredictable and avalanches common.

Georgians have inhabited southern Caucasia, the Kura and Çoruh valleys since antiquity. During the centuries of Greek and Roman expansion, a Georgian kingdom held the region inland as far as today's Baku, while the ancestors of the Laz, close relatives of the Georgians, ruled the kingdom of Colchis by the Black Sea. The king of Georgia adopted Christianity shortly after his Armenian counterpart, but unlike the Armenians the Georgians never broke with the Eastern Orthodox church, and managed to maintain their independence in the face of Roman, Byzantine, Persian, Arab and Turkish incursions.

In the 9th century, a branch of the feudal Armenian Bagratid dynasty gained footholds as far south as Ani, and ultimately acquired Abkhazia and most of Georgia over the next two centuries, proclaiming a kingdom of Georgia in 1008. At its peak, this extended as far as modern İspir. Their heirs reigned from T'bilisi as the world's longest-lasting sovereign dynasty until the Russian occupation in 1811. During the first 200 years, the valleys around Artvin saw a Georgian cultural renaissance which bred some of the finest icon painters, poets and jewellers of the era and resulted in a vast number of fortresses, churches and monasteries, many of which still survive in the forests and valleys – if you can find them. It all came to an abrupt end with the arrival of the Mongols in 1220.

A little visited region

Like Trabzon, the town of **Artvin** ❸ has nothing to recommend it except one decent hotel and some sweeping views, but the surrounding land is beautiful, covered with forests, and walnut, apple, cherry and mulberry orchards. The Kafkasör Festival with its traditional (generally bloodless) bullfights still attracts quite a crowd, but sadly, an unfortunate association with Turkey's eastern

problems has seen tourism in the region dwindle. Getting to the numerous colourful villages and marvellous monasteries has become almost impossible. There are no tour agents, car-rental services, guides or even local *dolmuş* to take you to the furthest reaches of Yusufeli and Tortum, or the six churches and monasteries of note, including Opiza, outside Şıvşı, Hantza, Ahiza and Tbeti. Thus, you either come with your own jeep or rent a taxi at an outrageous daily rate from Artvin. If you're stuck, speak to the knowledgable Yavuz Karahan at the hotel of the same name.

If you are driving, a southern circuit through Yusufeli and Oltu will take in a series of churches and lead eventually to the breathtaking **Tortum Gorge** and lake, famous for its waterfall. **Işhan** ❹ is a good place to begin: a 6-km (4-mile) climb from the parched canyon base reveals a veritable oasis, with the mind-blowing mass of the red-domed church, built in 828, sitting in the backyard of the quaint village schoolhouse with delicate stone carvings on the outer walls.

The 10th-century complex of **Hahuli (Haho)** ❺, 9 km (5½ miles) west of the southern end of Lake Tortum, was once the most celebrated of the Georgian monasteries, and is now one of the best preserved and most impressive, though it has served as the local mosque since the 17th century.

Gigantic **Öşk Vank** ❻, another 10th-century work a little further north, also owes its preservation, save a partly collapsed dome, to being used as a mosque. Now partially filled with debris from the construction of a new mosque, the interior is still spacious enough for the occasional volleyball tournament. The Far Eastern Black Sea is becoming more accessible, and nature lovers may wish to travel on to Av at on Lake Karagöl, a hunting and wildlife paradise with an excellent *pansyion* and camping facilities. ❑

Map on pages 306–7

BELOW: every area has a festival to celebrate the start of summer.

PROPHETS AND PREACHERS

From Noah's perch on Mount Ararat to Abraham's birthplace, Anatolia is steeped in the legends and history of the Bible and early Christianity

Many sites mentioned in the Old Testament are located in eastern or central Anatolia. Indeed, many scholars believe that the Garden of Eden was between the Tigris and Euphrates (ancient Mesopotamia) in southeast Turkey, though all efforts to find it have failed.

The permanently snow-capped Mount Ararat (Büyük Ağrı Dağı), the biblical resting ground of Noah's Ark, is on Turkey's border with Armenia. Muslim tradition believes that the ark came to rest on the slopes of the vast Mount Cudi, in Siirt province, about 350 km (220 miles) further southwest, near the Iraqi border.

According to Genesis, Abraham and his family lived in Harran, about 50 km (30 miles) south of Şanlıurfa. This is also where Abraham took Sarah, where Jacob hid when Esau threatened to kill him, where Rebecca drew water for Abraham's servant, and where Jacob rolled off the stone lid to water Laban's sheep.

Turkey's many New Testament sites tend to be along the coast of Roman Anatolia. Among them are Antioch (Antakya), Seleucia ad Pieria (Çevlik), Iconium (Konya), Tarsus – the birthplace of St Paul – and Myra (Demre), where St Nicholas (Santa Claus) served as a bishop in the 4th century. The so-called Seven Churches of Revelation were actually sites of early Christian communities. They are Smyrna (İzmir), Pergamon (Bergama); Thyatira (Akhisar); Sardis; Philadelphia (Alasehir); Laodicea, near the city of Denizli; and, of course, the great city of Ephesus.

△ **ANTIOCH**
St Peter lived in Antioch (Antakya) for many years. It was here that followers of Jesus first gathered secretly in a cave church and named themselves Christians.

▽ **SECRET SYMBOLS**
The Greek word for fish, *ichtys*, shared letters with the Greek name for Christ; the fish became a secret symbol amongst many of the persecuted early Christians.

THE ROAD TO DAMASCUS

St Paul was probably the greatest of the early Christian missionaries and theologians. Born in Tarsus in about AD 10, a Jew with Roman citizenship, he was a tentmaker by profession and a zealot by nature. He spent his early years as a rabbi and Pharisee, promoting the persecution of Christians.

After a revelation (some say a blinding vision of Jesus) while on the road to Damascus, all his zeal went into proselytising and converting both Jews and Gentiles to Christianity. He never actually met Jesus.

He then criss-crossed Anatolia and the Eastern Mediterranean. His many writings (letters to the Romans, Corinthians, Galatians, Philippians, Thessalonians, Philemon, and possibly also to the Ephesians and Colossians) are the earliest extant Christian texts.

Christ came up with the concept, but it was Paul who laid down the rules of the Church. In AD 58, he was arrested, and sent to Rome, imprisoned and eventually martyred.

△ COUNCIL OF NICAEA
In AD 325, church leaders meeting in Nicaea (Iznik) hammered out the Nicene Creed – the basic tenets of Christian belief.

▽ PRAYER MEETING
As fiery as modern Bible Belt evangelists, St Paul drew huge crowds when he preached in the great theatre at Ephesus.

◁ FLOOD RELIEF
A dove carrying an olive twig showed Noah that the flood waters were finally receding, stranding the ark high up Mount Ararat.

▽ HOME OF THE VIRGIN
The Meryamana, near Ephesus, was supposedly the last home of the ageing Virgin Mary. The Pope has been one of many pilgrims.

▷ FATHER OF THE JEWS
Abraham, father of the Jewish nation, lived as a child in Sanlıurfa. Pilgrims still visit his tomb in Birket Ibrahim Mosque (*detail pictured*).

THE EAST

*Few tourists visit the beautiful but troubled plains of
the "Fertile Crescent" and the mountains of the Far East*

The vast expanse that is eastern Turkey is made up of two very distinct regions. The Near East is dominated by the Euphrates and Tigris rivers, along which the authorities are building a series of giant hydroelectric dams and irrigation canals to turn the neglected barren flatlands into an agricultural power house, discovering – then drowning – a number of remarkable Roman cities and mosaics in the process. Its crowning historic glory is Nemrut Dağı, said by some to be a greater feat of engineering than the pyramids. Even today, the peak is an extraordinary landmark, visible from many miles away. How did King Antiochus of the Commagene and his men build this monumental tomb and drag the statues up the 2,150-metre (7,050-ft) mountain some 2,000 years ago?

The region has several important cities: once backward Kahramanmaraş, now transforming itself into a booming industrial centre; Gaziantep, a regional hub known for producing pistachio nuts, cotton yarn and pasta; and ancient Şanlıurfa, the city of prophets, which Islamic tradition claims as the birthplace of Abraham.

The Far East begins with the southern lowlands, rising through the rugged southeastern corner, broken up by plateau pastures where sheep and cattle are grazed by nomadic tribesmen, to frightening mountain passes and the upper Anatolian plateau, criss-crossed by permanently snow-covered mountain chains, where the average elevation for towns, cities and other settlements is above 2,000 metres (6,560 ft). Mount Ararat, on the Armenian border, dominates the northeast corner of the country.

The urban centres of the East are fascinatingly diverse. Erzurum, the biggest city in the northeast, was once ancient Theodosiopolis, named after the Byzantine Emperor Theodosius, although it has more Muslim shrines than Byzantine relics. In the far south, near the Syrian border, are the overwhelmingly Kurdish cities of Diyarbakır and Mardin. In the east, Van hugs the southeast corner of emerald-green Lake Van, Turkey's largest body of inland water, at an altitude of 1,650 metres (5,500 ft). Ahlat, on the north shore, is famed for its Turkish tombs; Bitlis, to the west, is dominated by a castle; Hakkari, to the southeast, is the capital of one of the poorest provinces in Turkey, bordering Iran and Iraq.

Eastern Turkey is a hard but immensely rewarding place to travel. The terrain can be difficult and the roads remote; any journey must be undertaken with careful planning and forethought. And just as the Turkish war against the Kurdish PKK abated, and tourism to the East was reviving, the upheavals of the 2003 Iraq War have threatened to destabilise the Kurdish regions again. Take advice before travelling here, particularly in the Hakkari area. ❏

PRECEDING PAGES: a desert palace: the Işak Paşa Sarayı, near Mount Ararat, on Turkey's eastern border. **LEFT:** Hercules and Mithridates, Nemrut Dağı.

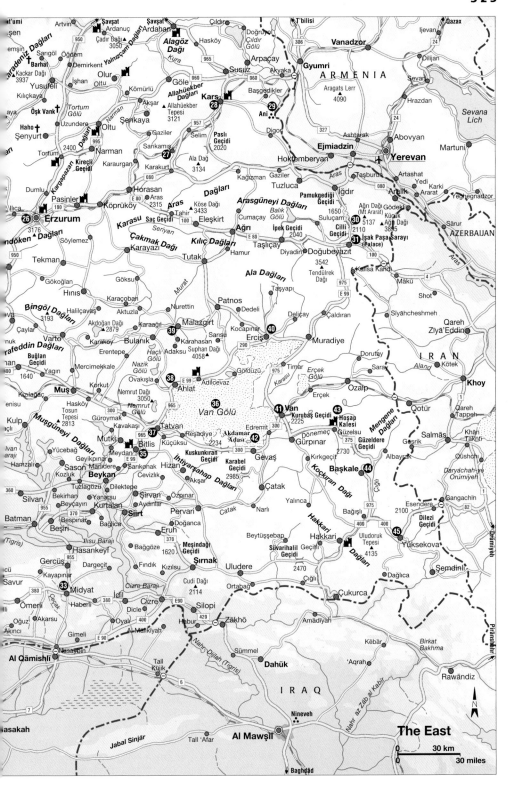

The East

0   30 km
0   30 miles

Map
on pages
322–3

THE NEAR EAST

*This vast unknown tract of central Turkey offers fabulous
scenery, from sprawling plains to towering mountains,
not to mention some of the world's largest dams*

The central plateau extends for many bleak and lonely miles east of Ankara. Patchy wheatfields alternate with bald hills that centuries of soil erosion has fashioned into eerie sculptures. Brown and ochre predominate, except when the brief glory of May covers the land with grass and wildflowers. The land can offer little but solitude and the magnificence of its daybreaks.

Erzincan ❶ is the largest centre in the region, a modern-looking city which was entirely rebuilt after the devastating earthquakes of 1939 and 1992. Beyond it, to the north, the road leads over remote mountain passes to the Black Sea Coast. To the south, the wild canyon of the Upper Euphrates gradually emerges into the high plateau of the northeast – the Roman province of Armenia Major.

The local towns are mostly nondescript, with two exceptions. **Sivas ❷** (known as Sebastia to Rome and Byzantium) deserves a stop for its thriving crafts bazaar and its magnificent clutch of Seljuk architecture: the 12th-century **Ulucamii** and the four theological and medical colleges of **Gök, Çifte Minareli, Şifahiye** and **Bürüciye Medrese**. These all have elaborately decorative 13th-century foundations, built by the Seljuk and Mongol governors. Look for the decorative animals, including pigs, an artistic adaptation from Armenian design that would have been anathema to most iconoclastic Muslims. Some 15 km (10 miles) east of Kangal, the **Balıklı Kaplıca** (hot springs) has become renowned for its varieties of skin-eating fish, said to relieve psoriasis. The sleepy iron-mining town of **Divriği ❸** to the east houses perhaps the most significant work of pre-Ottoman Turkish architecture in Turkey, and certainly calls for a detour. The mosque and hospital complex of the **Ulucamii** was founded in 1228 by the Mengücük dynasty, which ruled the area as vassals to the Seljuks.

Keban

From Divriği a rough country road heads 76 km (45 miles) southeast to the town of **Arapkir ❹**, perched above a gorge with several side streets running precipitously downhill. From here, a cliffside road leads along the lake to **Kemaliye**, a quaint little town on the west bank of the Euphrates at the spot where the river starts to fill the valley behind the Keban Dam.

This central area, formerly dependent on snowfall and rain for dryland farming, has become a major source of grain for Turkey since the construction of the spectacular **Keban Barajı ❺**, a dam at the confluence of the Euphrates and Murat rivers as they churn deep and white out of the mountains of the Central Anatolian plateau. This was Turkey's answer to the Aswan and High dams on the Nile in Egypt until the initiation of the even larger and vastly more ambitious Atatürk Dam project downstream near Şanlıurfa.

BELOW: Çifte Minareli Medrese in Sivas – poetry set in stone.

Those who delight in spectacular cliffs and canyons to rival all but the Grand Canyon itself should head further north: the road winds through increasingly beautiful country – at times appearing dangerously close to the precipice above the Euphrates, at times crossing remote country gouged by lesser rivers and streams, which finally pour into the Shatt-al-Arab and the Persian Gulf thousands of river-miles to the south through Syria and Iraq.

Formerly known by its Armenian name of Egin, **Kemaliye ❻** is an abrupt architectural change from the surrounding traditional Muslim settlements. Fair or unfair as it may seem, it is clear that the Anatolian Christians of the 19th century not only enjoyed a much higher standard of living than most of their contemporaries, but that an eye for outward appearance and private ease was a primary concern. Although their fine houses are now in urgent need of restoration, it is nonetheless clear from the gardens, sluices and delicately carved shutters and balconies that the residents of Egin cared for their environment.

Irrigation is turning the southeast into the bread basket of Turkey.

İliç – the end of the line

Only the criminally irresponsible or insane have any business proceeding further up the Euphrates from Kemaliye by car. Distrust all maps of the area, for they have seduced more than one hapless traveller into the dead-end town of İliç, at a bend in the Euphrates some 32 km (20 miles) as the crow flies but well over an hour's journey over mountain passes from Kemaliye.

İliç ❼ is the closest thing Turkey has to a classic one-horse town, founded solely to service the freight and passenger trains that run through it, with a combined teahouse and flop-house. Locals maintain (despite evidence to the contrary) that a farm road leads west along the railway tracks from İliç to the old

BELOW: Keban Dam: the power of the future.

Ottoman towns of Divriği and Sivas, but the traveller is advised either to park and take the train (there are several each day for the one-hour ride to Divriği) or to double back to Elazığ and continue east from there. İliç has begun to attract canoe and raft enthusiasts, who shoot the rapids of the Upper Euphrates here before gliding downstream towards the Keban Dam.

Tunceli province: a troubled past

Due east, Tunceli province, along the north shore of **Keban Barajı** (**Lake Keban**), is arguably the least developed and most problematic area of Turkey (though this has improved). It may also be one of the most beautiful. The towering Munzur Mountain range, with an average height of over 2,500 metres (8,000 ft), is the source of many small, whitewater streams that eventually merge with either the Euphrates or its major tributary, the Murat. Sadly, the poverty and underdevelopment of the place, coupled with its remoteness, make the province a security problem for the Turkish state, its jagged mountains honeycombed with caves that have hidden brigands, terrorists and separatist guerrillas alike.

Formerly known as Dersim, Tunceli was the site of a dramatic uprising in 1938, when local inhabitants, under the leadership of one Seyyid Riza, revolted against the central government, in protest at the region's economic poverty and high government taxes. They blew up bridges, blocked passes into the alpine valleys, and slaughtered soldiers stationed there. Reinforcements were shuttled down the newly constructed railway to the east, and the Turkish air force dive-bombed those rebel strongholds beyond the reach of the ground forces.

The general carnage and violence on both sides, as well as the mass forced migration of the survivors to different areas of the country, were such that the

BELOW: rocky track in remote Tunceli.

Map on pages 322–3

entire period has, until recently, been effectively erased from official history, only to live on in local memory. It was, in effect, Turkey's Wounded Knee, and only the span of some 60 years has allowed the younger generations to start exploring the roots and consequences of the entire tragic affair.

Tunceli today

Tunceli remains a hard-scrabble province, but for those with time, and ideally, a four-wheel drive vehicle, it is worth exploring. **Elazığ**, on the south shore of Lake Keban, is a natural jumping-off point. A ferry station some 16 km (10 miles) north of Elazığ provides transport across the lake, past **Pertek Kalesi ❽**, which once dominated the valley floor of the Murat River from a high knoll, but which now barely keeps its head above water on an island halfway across the reservoir. For those curious to see what yet another castle might have to offer, small craft service the route for a nominal fee.

Once on the north bank, the road disintegrates into a gravel path leading up to the mountain town of **Hozat**. Stunning views greet you around every turn of the road, but the driver would do best to keep his eyes on the track, and leave any sightseeing to the passengers – who are good to have along, just in case the car gets stuck in a mass of mud, ice and roots from a landslide.

Ovacık

Once over the lesser Munzur mountain range, you are greeted by the fabulous sight of **Ovacık ❾** ("the little valley"), which is arguably as close to Arcadia as anywhere on earth. Slivers of water cascade down the cliffs, rushing together into musically babbling brooks, their banks lined by brilliant alpine flowers and backed by dwarf pines. The valley floor, flanked by high mountains on all sides, is lush with emerald grass, frisky, prancing horses and idly grazing cows. The dairy products of the area, not usually exported more than 50 km (31 miles) are, nonetheless, famous. And through the middle of this exquisite valley runs the Munzur Çayı, a trout fisherman's paradise. The water literally gushes out of the surrounding mountains and is so cold that it is impossible to wade in it for more than a few seconds. Even the heartiest trout choose to live some distance downstream.

Strangely and inexplicably, there is also a rainbow trout-breeding station just downstream of Ovacık itself, which – like every other similar trout-breeding station in the country – has never released a single baby fish into the river rushing past on the grounds that someone is bound to catch it before it grows up.

Tunceli town

The clear, white waters of the Munzur Çayı slowly darken as the silt of scores of mountain streams flush into it, creating a frothing brown river as one proceeds down the mountain towards **Tunceli ❿**. This, sadly, has precious little to recommend it. There are several cheap hotels and an array of rooftop restaurants, enlivened by the relaxed attitude of the local Alevi population towards alcohol. The visitor is advised to stop only for tea before moving on, either by way of

BELOW: Ovacık: an outdoor paradise.

the Pülümür Pass to Erzincan and Erzurum to the northeast, or through Bingöl and Muş eastwards to the waters of Lake Van.

The Euphrates region

Back on the southern shore of Lake Keban, **Elazığ**  is a surprising exception to the general trend of dreary, boring construction sites called towns in the region. A relatively new town, nestled in the hills, now overlooking the lake, Elazığ was established in the mid-19th century by, and named after, Sultan Abdulaziz. The distortion in the original name occurred by design in the early years of the Republic when many of Turkey's place names were changed to fit better with Atatürk's new nationalism.

Like many of the towns and cities of Central and Eastern Anatolia, Elazığ is primarily a military barracks. But unlike Malatya to the south, Erzurum to the north and Van to the east, Elazığ has a most remarkable quality in an eastern Turkish town – it is clean. It has broad avenues, punctuated by traffic lights that actually work, with drivers and pedestrians who obey the signals. This is an excellent centre from which to explore the entire east-central region. The local university hosts a Folk Music Festival each year (early June), when busloads of students from across Turkey descend on the town to strut their cultural stuff. On the university grounds, the local **Archaeological Museum** (open Tues–Sat 9am–5pm; entrance fee) has a rather rag-tag collection of pots and pans, but some good coins, jewellery and carpets, and a number of Urartian items rescued from digs ahead of the flooding of the lake.

BELOW: the leaning minaret of Harput.

The history of **Harput** ⑫, a few kilometres up the road on the lakeshore, neatly sums up the whole complex, contradictory and often violent history of east-central Anatolia. The **citadel**, founded by the Urartus some hours after the dawn of time, was conquered successively by every army that passed from east to west or north to south, including the Hurrites, Mitanis, Hittites, Egyptians, Achaemanids, Macedonians, Parthians, Armenians, Romans, Sassanians, Byzantines, Arabs, Seljuk, Artuk and Akkoyunlu and various other sundry Turks.

Even Baudouin, Crusader king of Jerusalem, spent the month of April, 1193, in Harput, albeit as a captive. He became so fond of the town, that a few months after his release, he reappeared at the head of an army. The Muslim lords returned his affection by taking him and Harput again in September of the same year. The town and fortress were, inevitably, sacked by the Mongols in 1244 in their general rape of civilisation, but re-established as a pivotal control point in the East in 1514 when Sultan Yavuz Selim (the Grim) dragged his newly forged cannons east to crush the Safavid Shah Ismael of Iran at Çaldıran.

Today, the most significant buildings in the town are the **Ulucamii** (Grand Mosque), with its wildly off-balance brick minaret clinging on for grim death, the austere **Tomb of Arab Baba**, a local holy man, and the paltry remains of the churches abandoned by the Armenians during World War I.

Immediately below the citadel, a thriving **mineral spa** has hot baths that allegedly provide an antidote for all manner of maladies, including hepatitis. The road east, above Harput, leads through a series of local cemeteries to a peculiar rock formation known as the **Buzluk**, or "refrigerator" – it possesses the bizarre ability to accumulate ice in summer that melts off in winter. For a happy medium between boiling mineral springs and frozen caves, head for the local crater lake and resort area known as **Hazar Gölü ⓑ**, a long and lovely saline lake 1,200 metres (3,900 ft) above sea level, 30 km (18 miles) south of Elazığ on the Diyarbakır road.

Map
on pages
322–3

South of Elazığ, the upper Euphrates region is dominated, physically and emotionally, by Nemrut Dağı *(see page 330)* – on a clear day, the strange, man-made nipple of Antiochus's tumulus can be seen from nearly 150 km (100 miles) in every direction. It is by no means the only point of interest in this oft-neglected area, but one must often search for charm in the towns and cities.

Malatya

Malatya ⓙ, and to a lesser extent, **Adıyaman** (historic Hisni Mansur) may have an illustrious history, but today, aside from the odd, old mosque and the remains of a citadel, there is little to delay the traveller. Malatya's greatest claim to fame – aside from a medieval battle in which local Muslims and Christians joined together to (unsuccessfully) defend their town from the Mongol hordes – is as the hometown of Atatürk's chief lieutenant, İsmet İnönü. The figure of Turkey's second president surveys the town square from a bronze horse, one of the few places where this honour has been bestowed on someone other than Atatürk. The local **museum** (Fuzuli Cad.; closed indefinitely) has a small but significant Hittite collection. The area's most important cultural event is the annual Apricot Festival (July), a fruit found readily in the Apricot Bazaar.

BELOW: inside the old mosque at Malatya.

Decapitated but still awesome, giant stone gods haunt the terraces of Nemrut Dağı.

About 4 km (2½ miles) north of town, however, archaeologists have been gutting the site of Hittite **Aslantepe** (open daily 8am–5pm). A rich source of treasures to early archaeologists, more thorough excavations in recent years have uncovered a vast mudbrick palace complex dating back to 4000 BC, with wall-paintings from 3200 BC. In late Roman times, the settlement moved 8 km (5 miles) north to **Eski Malatya**, which still has a smattering of Byzantine and Seljuk remains including 6th-century city walls, a 13th-century **Ulucamii** and a 17th-century caravansaray, the **Silahtar Mustafa Paşa Hanı**.

Nemrut Dağı

The country, Commagene, was a blip in history, a tiny buffer state on the Upper Euphrates, pinched between the fleet cavalry of ancient Parthia and the inexorable legions of Rome. It flourished for the briefest instant during the Roman civil wars which pitted the tyrannicides, Brutus and Cassius, against the fragile coalition of Mark Antony and Octavian, only to be crushed and absorbed into the Roman Empire, disappearing from history as Christianity took hold.

Unlike most of the other forgotten states of late antiquity, Commagene carved its place in history from the living rock. Thousands of visitors make the trek to see the fabulous remains atop **Nemrut Dağı** ⑮ (Mount Nemrut). The tumulus was built by the little kingdom's uniquely self-obsessed ruler, Antiochus I, as his own final resting place. Excavations have begun on the tomb, which is hoped to reveal finds equivalent to that of Tutankhamun in Egypt.

The genealogy of the house of Commagene is obscure. Apparently they began as a lesser line of the Seleucids of Antioch, who established themselves in the foothills of the upper Euphrates following the rout of the Seleucids at the Battle

BELOW: the tumulus of Antiochus.

of Magnesia in 190 BC. They styled themselves as the twin of the Achamenians of old Iran on the male side, and the descendants of Alexander the Great on the other – the perfect cultural synthesis of East and West, as sought by Alexander himself.

With the decline of the Seleucids and the rise of Rome during the late Republican era, Commagene seems to have been involved with periodic anti-Roman uprisings along the Eastern marches, usually associated with the nascent power of Parthia in Iran. Following the Roman defeat of the Pontic King Mithridates the Great in 63 BC, Antiochus I of Commagene was confirmed in power by Pompey, either as a token of trust for Commagenean support against Mithridates, or, more probably, as a gesture of realpolitik to help secure the distant marches on the Parthian frontier. Whatever the motive, the arrangement did not have the desired effect, and a mere eight years later, in 53 BC, the Romans suffered their most humiliating defeat when Crassus and his legions were destroyed at Carrhae, literally on the doorstep of Commagene. When Mark Antony arrived to resecure the frontier, Antiochus was obliged to pay a stiff indemnity for neglecting to aid his Roman ally (none dared call it treason).

After a long struggle to maintain its precarious independence between the Rock of Rome and the Hard Place of Parthia, Commagene was finally absorbed into the newly established Roman province of Syria during the reign of Nero. Little remained to mark the position of the country's capital, Samosata (Samsat; about 50 km/30 miles south of Kâhta), and what there was has now been drowned by the Atatürk Dam. Commagene might have disappeared altogether from history, but for the massive tumulus on Nemrut Daği. Built by Antiochus for his own glory and honour, it is a fabulous pile of stones and statuary to rival the greatest efforts of the self-deifying, pyramid-building Egyptian pharaohs.

The summit

The centrepiece of any tour of Commagene (and possibly even of Turkey) is a climb to the summit of the 2,150-metre (7,053-ft) Nemrut Daği, where the statues of the gods of antiquity lie scattered. The route passes a variety of other ruins, including a beautifully preserved Roman bridge and the citadel of Eski Kâhta (Old Kâhta). Allow at least a day for the excursion. Visitors are encouraged to arrive at the tumulus of Antiochus before sunrise to catch the ravishing beauty of the spectacle as the first red rays of dawn flood the summit.

There is now a road up to the summit, but many still prefer to approach on foot (or donkey) after a 20-minute uphill climb that is surprisingly hard on the lungs and is made all the more difficult by the shattered shale and loose rocks. The first glimpse of the terraces is truly astounding. Atop the highest peak in the region, with panoramic views in all directions, Antiochus I had his peons drag huge blocks of cut stone to build twin terraces facing east and west, lined with massive statues of his favourite gods: Apollo, Tyche (the goddess of fortune), Zeus and Hercules, including himself in their illustrious company. The king of Commagene traced his descent to the gods through Alexander the Great.

In addition to the gods and the man-god Antiochus, there are also two fallen statues of an eagle and a lion.

Map on pages 322–3

TIP

Most organised trips to Nemrut Daği start at Kâhta, 100 km (60 miles) away. A full day's guided tour, with driver, costs around $75 for the entire minibus. Public transport is as little as $5 per person, depending on how many can be squeezed into the old vans.

BELOW: a vision of grandeur fit to make history.

The Leo Horoscope, hiding the fortune of a dynasty?

All of the heads of the statues – long toppled from their bases – stand taller than an average man. Of particular note in the line-up of the gods is Apollo, who in the eastern realms of late antiquity was known as Mithras, the god of light and darkness, good and evil, in the cult of Mithraism, to which Christianity is indebted for many of its sacred rites. Baptism, for example, is probably a refined version of the Mithraic initiation ceremony involving a bath of bull's blood. Mithraism took root among the Roman legionaries during Pompey's campaigns in the east against Mithridates the Great, and was briefly declared the official religion of the Roman Empire by Diocletian in a last ditch effort to counter the growing appeal of Christianity.

The Leo Horoscope

In addition to the statues of the gods, there are also numerous reliefs depicting Antiochus shaking hands with various deities. The most special of these is the beautifully carved relief of the constellation of Leo on the west terrace, which allegedly contains the horoscope of Antiochus at the time of the coronation of his father, Mithridates, on 14 July, 109 BC. It is the subject of much speculation among those of the Erik von Daniken-reincarnation school. One Dutch woman, Laura Crijns, maintains she was there on the night of the coronation, and knows the secret entrance to the tumulus and how to get at whatever treasures are thought to lie beneath the tons of fist-sized stone Antiochus had his slave labourers pulverise for the nipple-shaped top of the mountain.

BELOW: guardian eagle hovers over a grave mound.

Planning to succeed with intuition where the American archaeologist, Theresa Goell, had failed with dynamite (the tumulus is 50 metres/160 ft lower than before, thanks to her efforts), Miss Crijns managed to convince the authorities to give her a chance. Sadly, her excavation papers were revoked at the last minute, possibly due to the religious implications for all good Muslims if a zany lady from Holland, who claimed to have attended a coronation ceremony atop the mountain 2,000 years ago, should stumble on Antiochus's tomb, thus "proving" reincarnation to be true.

Eski Kâhta

Down the mountain on the way back to Kâhta and the plains, the first stop on the Nemrut circuit is usually **Eski Kâhta** (Old Kâhta), known in antiquity as Arsameia, the summer capital of Commagene.

In addition to the relief of Apollo/Mithridates pointing the way to the sanctuary, there are several inscriptions and statues of Mithridates pressing the flesh with Hercules. Two tunnels lead to an underground cave clearly used in Mithraic rites, when novices would enter the underworld to worship the goddess Cybele, fasting and praying for several days before re-emerging, enlightened, to the rising sun. Unfortunately, there is little information for the casual tourist, who is left with the impression that the grotto is just another cave where rustics once made their abode.

Also close at hand is the **Yeni Kale** (New Citadel), whose crenellated parapets were built by Mamelukes during the time of the Crusades. The surrounding village has several basic *pansiyons*. Further along the road to Kâhta is a 90-metre (300-ft) long single-span **Cendere Bridge** over the Kâhta Çayı – once known as the Nymphaium River and one of the major tributaries of the Euphrates – a Roman structure built during the period of Septimus Severus (AD 193–211), with three of its four original columns still standing. Nearer still to Kâhta is the **Karakuş** tumulus, surrounded by carved pillars with animal motifs and said to be the burial site of the Commagene royal women.

The GAP: an ambitious plan

The **Southeastern Anatolia Project** (or GAP) is Turkey's most ambitious economic undertaking to date, consisting of a network of 22 dams, 19 hydroelectric plants and hundreds of kilometres of irrigation tunnels and canals in the Euphrates-Tigris basin. It began in 1974 with the aim of transforming this neglected southeastern region into a breadbasket for the Middle East. GAP, which resembles the US Tennessee Valley Authority or Australia's Snowy Mountains scheme, has been described as one of the "Seven Wonders of the Modern World". Its centrepiece is the 84 million cubic-metre (3,000 million cubic-ft) rock and earth-fill **Atatürk Barajı** , the fourth-largest dam in the world, at 80 metres (250 ft) high, 800 metres (2,500 ft) wide at the base and 20 metres (65 ft) wide at the top. It came onstream in 1992.

The twin 26-km (16-mile) long, 1.8 km (1 mile) wide **Şanlıurfa Tunnels** and long distribution canals which feed off the giant reservoir will eventually irrigate over 1.7 million hectares (4.2 million acres) of plains stretching south to the Syrian border, now devoted to wheat but expected in the future to yield tobacco, sugar beet and cotton. Such massive state investment is seen as the last and best hope for the rocky Turkish economy, aimed at providing 1.8 million jobs and

Map on pages 322–3

In the late 1980s, Turkey suggested the creation of two "peace pipelines" to pump water (at a cost) from the Çeyhan, Seyhan, Tigris and Euphrates to Syria, Jordan, Iraq, Saudi Arabia and the Gulf states, all of whom were deeply unimpressed by the concept. As yet, nothing has been done about it.

BELOW: the Mameluke castle of Yeni Kale.

irrigating 3 million hectares (8 million acres). Turkey's downstream neighbours, Syria and Iraq, are furious. Syria, in particular, is a largely desert country which had already lost much of its access to the Jordan River when it lost the Golan Heights to Israel and now feels compelled to accede to Turkey's wishes under the very real threat of having the tap turned off. The impressive scale of the engineering is well worth a look and has become a popular tourist sight among Turks.

Sanlıurfa

About 75 km (50 miles) south of the giant lake lies the venerably old town of **Şanlıurfa ⓱**. According to local tradition, allegedly based on the Qur'an, it is the birthplace of Abraham, the father of Judaism, before his migration to Canaan (now Palestine). Local Muslim legend differs from that of the other great monotheistic faiths through the intervention of the viciously cruel giant King Nimrod, who had Abraham launched from a catapult in the city's citadel, to fall into a pile of burning wood. Happily, God intervened and turned the fire to water and the faggots to fish. Today, visitors can pray at the mosque complex surrounding the **İbrahim Halilullah Dergâhı** (Abraham's Cave; open daily 8am–5.30pm; entrance fee) and visit the lifesaving pools of holy carp. Nimrod's massive slingshot is represented by two Corinthian columns still standing atop the **citadel** walls.

The city's real history is far more complex than mere legend. Known to the ancient Greeks as Orrhoe or Osrhoe, Seleucus Nicator, of Antioch fame, first established the capital of his eastern Hellenistic realm here, populating it with Macedonian veterans who preferred to call it Edessa, after their native province. Şanlıurfa remained an important garrison town into Roman times, and was one

Mythical King Gilgamesh, one-third man, two-thirds god, was supposedly based on a Sumerian king who ruled in 2850 BC. He and his faithful companion, Enkidu, lived with the wild animals before setting out on an epic adventure, vanquishing everything from famine to giants. When Enkidu died, Gilgamesh chose to join him in Irkalla, the place of no return.

BELOW: Şanlıurfa, city of the prophets.

of the first centres of the early church (although it was given over to the mono-physite heresy). It was also in Edessa that the great scientific works of late antiquity were translated, with commentaries, into Syriac/Aramaic, whence they made their way into Arabic after the Muslim conquest, only to find their way back to the west following the reconquest of the city by the Byzantines and then the Crusaders. Under Baldwin I, the city was the first of several Crusader states in the Middle East.

Map on pages 322–3

Edessa was sacked by the Zengi dynasty during the Muslim "*Reconquista*" of the Holy Land in 114; all its men were put to the sword and all the women were sold into slavery. In the 13th century, following the standard Mongol rape of the Middle East, ancient Edessa disappeared from history, re-emerging only after World War I. Thanks for its survival as part of Turkey should go to the local population who brilliantly resisted French attempts to include it in greater Syria. In recognition of this feat, the honorific Şanlı was added to the old name, Urfa.

Today, Şanlıurfa is a surprising mix of the old and new, with Arab and Turk-ish peasants in for a day's shopping from the countryside haggling in the tradi-tional bazaar, while young technocrats and engineers bustle between offices and shops lining the modern downtown area. A city of some 200,000, Şanlıurfa is earmarked to become one of Turkey's largest metropolitan areas since the building of the Atatürk Dam. Already the city has the single highest growth rate in the country, with many indigent farmers and absentee landlords from the nearby Harran plain returning with the promise of making the city the centre of Turkey's new Fertile Crescent.

For tourists, the streets of old Şanlıurfa, with their overhanging medieval houses and warren-like bazaars, are the greatest attraction, but there are, inevitably, several interesting old mosques and a good local **Archaeological Museum** (on S. Nusret Cad.; open Tues–Sun 8.30am–noon, 1.30–5.30pm; entrance fee).

BELOW: ponds of the sacred carp, Birket İbrahim Mosque, Şanlıurfa.

Harran

South of Şanlıurfa, the landscape once more flattens into the Mesopotamian plain, broken only by ancient mounds and obscure, mud-brick villages, many of which are now being connected to the electrical grid. With the prospect of greater wealth, thanks to irriga-tion, locals are gleefully investing in such "luxury" objects as refrigerators and televisions. The pace of change is rapid and sometimes startling.

Some 15 km (9 miles) off the main tarmac road leading to Syria, turn left and ask for **Sultantepe** ⑱, a *höyük* (tell or mound) covering a 7th–8th century BC Assyrian town, where tablets inscribed with the legends of Gilgamesh (*see page 334*) have been unearthed.

Further down the dirt road lies ruined **Sümürtar**, a large mound with a labyrinth of passages and under-ground chambers used by the Sabians, worshippers of the sun, moon and planets, whose culture and reli-gion managed to survive the onslaught of Christianity and Islam until the 11th century. Today, some poorer villagers have been using the chambers as donkey sta-bles. Note the statue of Sin, with a crescent moon on his head, if you can get the donkeys to step aside. The grottos were clearly used for ceremonial purposes;

TIP

To visit Karkamiş, get permission from the military post some 10 km (6 miles) outside Barak. It is easily recognisable by the flags and barbed wire. Don't try to reach the site without stopping, or you may get a dozen automatic rifles jammed in your back.

BELOW: beehive houses on the Harran plain.

some seem to have been later converted into subterranean mosques replete with *mihrab* facing in the direction of Mecca.

Back towards the main road is the village of **Harran** ⑲ itself, with its strange beehive-style mud-built dwellings. Standing above the ruins of the ancient citadel, you overlook the scattered bits of rock that somehow evoke the dawn of time: the very shards crunching underfoot have an immediacy here, the broken vessels having surely been used by some long forgotten ancestor from the land of Ur, an acquaintance of Abraham, a Roman legionary from Gaul.

Harran has an incredibly ancient and illustrious past. Here was the site of the Temple of Sin (erroneously called the first university), famous throughout the ancient world for its star readers and savants. It was in Harran that Rebecca drew water for Jacob, from whence Abraham decided to make his move into the land of Canaan. This was also where the Roman Emperor Crassus was defeated by the Parthians, with the Legion standards captured and brought back in triumph to Ctesiphon to the undying shame of the Romans; Crassus himself reportedly died by having liquid gold poured into his mouth. Later, Emperor Julian the Apostate worshipped the moon here on the way to his fateful encounter with Shapur I further east. And Harran was the last stronghold of the Sabians, their tradition finally killed by the arrival of the fanatic Crusaders.

The South

Returning to Şanlıurfa, the road heads west to **Birecik** ⑳ (ancient Apamaea) which, along with Zeugma on the west bank, was traditionally an important jumping-off point for Roman adventures in the East, including Mark Antony's disastrous campaign against the Parthians in 36 BC. Part of the GAP project,

the Birecik hydroelectric dam made international news in summer 2000, when a rich store of sculptures (including one of the war god Mars), elegant mosaics, frescoes and the remains of several rich Roman mansion houses were discovered just as the dam was to be flooded. Historians and archaeologists hurried to carry what they could to the Gaziantep Archaeology Museum but they were only able to hold back the waters for 10 days, as the cost to the dam consortium and local farmers in need of water was immense. Birecik is also one of the only two places left on earth where the bald ibis nests.

To the west, the area's rolling hills, covered with ripening wheat in early summer, are cut by the tributaries of the Euphrates, flowing southward to the desert flats of Syria and Iraq. It has a subtle but spectacular beauty. In many ways the river marks the point at which Asia really starts – ancient Mesopotamia, the Land Between the Two Rivers, where civilisation as we know it began.

Karkamış

Drive west along the E5 to the town of **Nizip** (ancient Nisibis), then turn left down an asphalt road lined with pistachio orchards towards Barak/Carapolous (Jarabulus). Someone has done a fine job of confusing the issue here, as Carapolous, marked with a big yellow sign designating an historical site, is in fact in Syria, and the tiny Turkish village of Barak holds nothing of interest to the visitor. Fear not. **Karkamış (Carchemish)** ㉑ remains on the Turkish side of the border (defined by the tracks of the Berlin-to-Baghdad railway), albeit in a minefield overlooking the Euphrates.

One of the most important sites in the area, Karkamış was a Hittite capital until it was conquered by the Assyrian King Sargon II (722–705 BC). A century later it became the venue for one of the great battles of the ancient world, which pitted the Egyptian Pharaoh Neco against the Chaldean king of Babylon, Nebuchadnezzar. After crushing the Egyptians, Nebuchadnezzar rolled into Palestine to defeat the Jewish kingdom and carry off the survivors to their Babylonian exile.

Two thousand years later, another major engagement was fought in the same area, when the Ottoman Sultan Mahmud sent his forces against his nominal vassal, the Egyptian Khedive Ibrahim. Fortunes reversed this time, with the Egyptian delivering the Asiatic Turks a crushing defeat. The Ottoman state itself was only saved by European intervention.

A visit to the ruins is well worthwhile, especially for those with the imagination to repopulate the tattered remains of the once great city. Associated throughout history with the cities of the Euphrates Valley, such as Duru Europus, Hierapolis-Bambyce and Samsota, Karkamış bestrides a bluff over the wide expanse of the Euphrates. Stepping gingerly through the minefields with your soldier-guide, you can still see the remains of the main city gate near the river and, just downstream, a bridge defining the border with Syria.

This must have been the St Louis of its day, and one wonders how many Mesopotamian Huckleberry Finns took this route from the Anatolian highlands to the Persian Gulf. It would have been a fabulous trip;

Map on pages 322–3

The number of bald ibis, a protected species for which Birecik is famous, is starting to grow.

BELOW: woman carrying firewood, Harran.

tragically, two borders – those of Iran and Iraq – are now a greater obstacle than any rapids downstream.

Travel notes by travellers such as Gertrude Bell and T.E. Lawrence (of Arabia fame) and photos taken in the early 20th century show Karkamiş as a city of columns, altars and temples. The archaeological rape of the site was apparently conducted with all the methodological might the Germans could muster: the German box cars used in building the railway did not depart empty.

Gaziantep

Heading rapidly back into the "civilisation" of heavy industry, the roads west become ever larger and busier. The next stop, **Gaziantep** ⍟ is one of several cities in the Middle East with a claim to be the oldest continuously inhabited town in the world; little, however, is left of the city's hoary past, and today it is primarily known for its pistachio nuts, as a copper and brass working centre, a bustling industrial city and Turkey's leading producer of pasta, surrounded by fields of golden durum wheat. The Sanko factory on the outskirts of the city is one of the world's biggest manufacturers of cotton yarn.

Like its sister city Kahramanmaraş, Antep (as most continue to call it) enjoys the honorific "Gazi" ("Fighter for the Faith") bestowed upon it by Atatürk in recognition of the Alamo-like stand the inhabitants put up against French and Senagalese forces at the end of World War I.

Although it cannot be called either beautiful or truly exotic, it is strange that Gaziantep remains so neglected; most folks just speed by it at 100 km (60 miles) an hour. This is a mistake, because Gaziantep does have its own charm, and the area around it enjoys its share of antique sights and vistas.

The Euphrates boasts river catfish of such size that the stories seem too outrageous to be true. But local fishermen regularly pull out whiskered monsters, weighing up to 200 kg (440 lb), usually using the net and shotgun method.

BELOW: badlands on Turkey's southern border.

Squarely in the middle of town are the citadel and several fine 15th-century mosques and caravansarays. The **Archaeological Museum** (İstasyon Cad.; open Tues–Sun 8am–noon, 1–5pm; entrance fee) has some worthwhile exhibits including Hittite reliefs and a culture park devoted to recent finds at the Roman garrison town of Zeugma *(see page 336)*. Of much greater interest, however, is the labyrinth of the **old town** just north and downhill of the citadel, consisting of a chaotic tangle of narrow streets, paths and cul-de-sacs. Although illegal destruction and construction have taken their toll, there is still enough of the old town left to get a flavour of what life was once like in a traditional Oriental city. Beat-up wooden doors facing neglected streets open onto beautiful courtyard gardens, replete with orange, plum and pomegranate trees, and tinkling fountains. One of the finest 19th-century mansions now houses the excellent **Hasan Süzer Ethnography Museum** (Hanifioglu Sok.; open Tues–Sun 8.30am–12.30pm, 1.30–4.30pm; entrance fee).

Kahramanmaraş

From here, the E90 slices west to Adana and the Mediterranean coast. The smaller Highway 835 leads northwest through Arcadian scenery of small neat farms and babbling brooks to **Kahramanmaraş ㉓**.

Hawking is still a popular local sport.

Formerly known as Maraş, the city acquired the honorific "Kahraman" ("heroic") due to the large number of casualties it suffered during the Turkish War of Independence. Historically an important outpost guarding the second major pass over the Taurus Mountains, it has been sacked by passing invaders, which may account for the singular dearth of antique buildings in and around the town. The exceptions are the 15th-century **Ulucamii** (Great Mosque), the **Taş Medrese** and the inevitable **citadel**, within which is the municipal **museum** (open Tues–Sun 9am–5pm; entrance fee) with its collection of Hittite reliefs.

BELOW: the old ways may be slower, but they still work.

The most important personality to emerge from Maraş was the Byzantine Emperor Leo the Isaurian, who managed to repel the last great Arab siege of Constantinople in AD 717. It was during his reign that we first hear of the iron chain which closed off the Golden Horn to enemy warships. Today, aside from the pretty mountain scenery in the region, Kahramanmaraş is known primarily for the best ice cream in Turkey – a combination of cold sugar and cream with a peculiar elasticity and longevity; vendors throughout the country are obliged to wear traditional Maraş costumes in accordance with some unwritten law.

The city also owns the dubious distinction of being one of the most conservative cities in the country and having been the scene of Turkey's worst massacre in living memory, when the Sunni Muslim population of the town went on a rampage, slaughtering scores of "heretical" leftist Alevis from the nearby villages, a tragedy regarded as a key stage in the imposition of martial law in 1978 and the military coup in 1980. Since 1990, Kahramanmaraş has emerged as a thriving textile manufacturing city with over 50 mills.

Highway 55, to the northwest of town, leads towards Kayseri and Cappadocia through countryside that demands you stop to hike, climb and fish. ❑

THE FAR EAST

There is no trace of Europe left in this vast, distant swathe of land, bordered by Syria, Iraq, Iran, Armenia and Georgia. The Far East is foreign even to many Turks

Eastern Turkey is best accessed by road either via Trabzon and Gümüshane in the Black Sea region, or via Şanlıurfa in the Near East. This chapter is split into two, to reflect both routes; they meet at Lake Van.

The northeast

Somewhere between the old Silk Road cities of **Gümüşhane** and **Bayburt** the traveller crosses the geographical boundary between the Black Sea and the plateau, as well as the ancient historical boundary between the Pontic-Greek and Armenian cultural zones. An outward sign may be noted in the clothes of the women, through Erzurum and eastward until near Kars and Ağrı, who wear a distinctive brown sacklike *chador*, covering them from head to toe. It is a visible manifestation of the extremely conservative and somewhat xenophobic culture of the region.

Bayburt ㉔ is dominated by a stupendous fortress, first built by Justinian, rebuilt by the Bagratids, fortified by a Turkish lord in the 13th century, and destroyed by the Russian army in 1828. After Bayburt, the road climbs to the bleak grandeur of the **Kop Geçidi (Pass)** ㉕, which commands a stunning panorama of several of the high mountain ranges of the East. The plateau lying below leads to Aşkale, and on to Erzurum *(see page 342),* the largest and the most important city in eastern Turkey.

The high plateau

Higher than the central Anatolian basin by about 1,000 metres (3,000 ft) the northeastern plateau is broken by the gigantic masses of the Kop, Palandöken, Soğanlı and Allahuekber mountain ranges, which give it a vast and terrifying aspect, culminating finally in the single, overwhelming peak of Mount Ararat.

Snow buries all for a good half of the year, cutting off many villages from the rest of the world. Then, in a long spring that lasts well into July, the pastures break into an orgy of grass and wildflowers. Huge herds of brown sheep and cattle cover the endless landscape and underpin the regional economy.

Historically, the plateau provided a natural route between Asia Minor and the Orient. It was here that the ancient east-west trade route crossed into the Roman-Byzantine world; caravans carrying silk and the other riches of Asia from China, made their way through the Taklamakan desert and the bazaars of Bukhara and Samarkand, Nishapur and Tabriz, skirted Erzurum, then continued westward to Sebastea and Caesarea, or crossed the Zigana Pass to Trebizond.

This accessibility proved to be a mixed blessing, as wave after wave of invaders also broke into Anatolia through the northeast, leaving ruin and desolation in

LEFT: church on Akdamar Island, Lake Van.
BELOW: detail on the Yakutiye Medrese, Erzurum.

their wake. Between 1828 and 1918 alone, the region was the scene of at least four wars between the Ottoman Empire and Russia, in each of which the Tzarist armies succeeded in breaching Turkish defenses as far as Erzurum. In the war of 1878, Russia occupied – and held until 1919 – the provinces of Artvin and Kars as far as Sarıkamış. Then, in the winter of 1914, the last of Turkey's imperial dreams came to grief as several hundred thousand soldiers under Enver Paşa froze to death in the Allahuekber Mountains near Sarıkamış, a melancholy tale commemorated by a monument outside that town.

Erzurum

Ancient Theodosiopolis, named after Emperor Theodosius the Great who fortified it in the 4th century, **Erzurum** ㉖ is not distinguished for its prettiness. It is a sombre, sad city, whose outward aura is somehow reflected in the faces of its inhabitants. It has been perhaps best described as a city that has never recovered from winter, and it is indeed one of the coldest places in Turkey. Still, it merits a stop for several reasons: its awesome setting in the shadow of the giant **Palandöken Dağları** is one. Another is the superb ski-run overlooking the city, the best in Turkey, which awaits the hardy soul who dares venture out here in winter.

The city also offers an array of historical monuments, which have surprisingly survived a history of constant warfare and destruction, not to mention serious earthquakes in 1939 and 1983. All existing works are of Islamic origin, as any Christian monuments that survived the depredations of World War I – including the cathedral – were sadly subsequently razed.

There are three *kümbets* (domed tombs), of which one is the oldest historical building in town, ascribed to Emir Saltuk, the feudal lord whose dynasty

The mountainous region of east Turkey – an area three times the size of the Alps – is covered in snow for up to seven months of the year. The authorities are attempting to develop it for winter sports.

BELOW: visiting a historical monument in Erzurum.
RIGHT: native to eastern Turkish hot springs, skin-eating fish are used to treat psoriasis.

Map on pages 322–3

dominated the area for a century after the Turkish conquest. The **Ulucamii** was built in 1179 by his grandson. The town's architectural masterpiece, the **Çifte Minareli Medrese** was built, like its counterpart in Sivas, under Selçuk Sultan Alâeddin Keykubat II. The Mongols, in their turn, built the **Yakutiye Medrese** in 1310, naming it after the local governor of Ogeday, a grandson of Gengis Khan who held court in Tabriz. The Ottomans then rebuilt and resettled the city and, among others, contributed the graceful **Lala Paşa Camii** in 1563.

In more recent times, Erzurum served as the setting for the Congress of July 1919, which marked the beginning of the resistance movement that eventually led to the forming of the Republic.

Beyond Horasan, a short way east of Erzurum, the road forks, the left branch heading northeast to Sarıkamış and Kars, eventually linking up with Artvin, in the Black Sea region. The other heads due east to Doğubeyazıt and Ararat before turning south at the border to Van.

The road to Kars

About 150 km (90 miles) northeast of Erzurum, **Sarıkamış ㉗**, huddled into the surrounding cold, dark taiga of giant pines, teeming with wolves and foxes and the endless rows of old Russian barracks, reminds the visitor that he has entered what used to be an outpost of the Tzarist Empire until the end of World War I. The town is now a leading ski resort, with the longest ski runs in Turkey.

Kars ㉘ confirms the same impression, with a peculiar aura of being utterly out of place and out of time. The grid layout, unique in Turkey, and the dusty, once graceful architecture of the city centre both owe their existence to the Russians during their final, 41-year-long occupation after 1877 – so do the

BELOW: troglodyte houses near Kars.

occasional blond descendants of Russians, Germans, and even Estonians.

The old city, which served as capital to the Bagratids during the early part of the 10th century, is now a slum clinging to the hillside across the Kars stream. It is dominated by a magnificent **fortress** of the usual Urartu-Byzantine-Armenian-Turkish-Mongolian-Russian pedigree, which deserves a visit mainly for its panoramic views of the town and the plateau beyond. The town's other major historical work is the **Cathedral of the Holy Apostles**, built in AD 937, and used alternately as church and mosque for most of the next 1,000 years. It continues to be useful, but only as a timberyard.

The faded elegance of Ani

The skeleton of the medieval metropolis of **Ani** 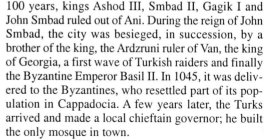, sprawled across the endless meadows of the high plateau, is one of the most impressive sights of the Near East. Once again accessible after being off limits to visitors during the war against the PKK, it is announced by the mighty row of double walls and round towers that loom in the distance, extending more than a mile on the land side. Inside, at the height of its fortunes, it was a city of 100,000 inhabitants and legendary 1,000 churches. Now the dilapidated remains of some 10 churches, which include frescoes of biblical scenes, one mosque and a royal citadel stand in sad and silent testimony to the Ani's vanished glory. Not one house remains, but a single paved avenue suggests what might have been the city centre.

A town evidently existed here in the pre-Christian era, then the Gamsaragan dynasty of Armenian lords held it for several hundred years, before it was acquired in the 9th century by the Bagratids. It began to bloom in AD 961, when it became capital of medieval Armenia at the apogee of its power. For the next

BELOW: to the top of Mount Ararat, the hard way.

100 years, kings Ashod III, Smbad II, Gagik I and John Smbad ruled out of Ani. During the reign of John Smbad, the city was besieged, in succession, by a brother of the king, the Ardzruni ruler of Van, the king of Georgia, a first wave of Turkish raiders and finally the Byzantine Emperor Basil II. In 1045, it was delivered to the Byzantines, who resettled part of its population in Cappadocia. A few years later, the Turks arrived and made a local chieftain governor; he built the only mosque in town.

East to Ararat

The Iran transit road east from Erzurum still follows the line of the ancient caravan route and still carries perpetual convoys of intercontinental trucks heading through Eleşkirt and Ağrı to Iran and Afghanistan.

Just before **Doğubeyazıt**, unwary travellers are jolted by the stupendous apparition of **Ağrı Dağı – Mount Ararat** 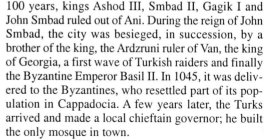 – soaring above the horizon. The grandeur of the view is hard to capture in prose and harder in photographs; there is no substitute for the actual experience.

The towering volcanic peak stands at 5,137 metres (16,853 ft). Its relative elevation over the surrounding plain – over 4,000 metres (13,000 ft) in the north – makes it one of the sheerest profiles in the world. This is further enhanced by the incomparable impact of its single, symmetrical, conical mass. On a typical hazy day, the base of the mountain blends into the blue sky, leaving the enormous white cap of snow hovering eerily in space.

The search for the remains of Noah's Ark has been a growth business since the French nobleman Pitton de Tournefort first scaled the mountain in 1707. In recent years, activity has increased with several dozen groups joining the search each year. To date, however, not one of the many pieces of rotten timber and indefinite shapes sighted under the ice cap has been able to provide conclusive evidence of any boat on the mountain.

For those simply interested in climbing the peak, formalities are long, and best dealt with through local adventure travel agencies like Trek Travel, well in advance. For those who want to see the "ark" without climbing the mountain, another school of bible-pushers say they have found the world's first ocean liner in the hills around Terçeker. Others say it is a big clump of mud. Meanwhile, according to Islamic tradition, the ark came to rest on the slopes of Mount Cudi in the southeastern province of Siirt.

Nearby, the **Işak Paşa Sarayı** ㉛, nestled in a high valley above Doğubeyazıt, was built in the 18th century. Little is known about the families who lived in the palace, except that they held the title of Ottoman governors at a time when Istanbul would have beeen quite content to receive an occasional tribute from such distant provinces. The impregnable position of the palace-stronghold, overlooking the caravan route, suggests the source of their wealth.

The southeast

Heading due east across the plain from Şanlıurfa, below Mardin and Midyat, runs the long and dangerous E-90 highway, and one should take care when driving in this part of the country. From the town of Kızıltepe onwards, the road

Map on pages 322–3

Detailed carving covers the Işak Paşa Sarayı.

BELOW: Mount Ararat, in all its glory.

runs parallel to the heavily patrolled Turco-Syrian frontier. Fortunately, the sights of interest to tourists are situated a little further north.

Standing on a bluff above the Mesopotamian flats, **Mardin** ㉜ is arguably the most Arab town in Turkey, but it has also been the home of Suriyani (Jacobite) Christians since the 5th century. The **Deyrul Zarafan Monastery** (open daily 8am–noon, 1–5pm), 6 km (4 miles) east of the town, was founded in AD 495 on the remains of a temple to the sun. Once the seat of the Syrian Orthodox patriarchate, the monastery includes a 1,500-year-old mosaic floor, a wooden throne and litters once used to carry church dignitaries. Services are held in Aramaic, a proto-Arabic language related to that spoken by Christ. The vista afforded from the town's citadel is nearly magical, stretching across the vastness of the Syrian plain, pancake-flat but for the occasional *höyük* (mound) designating the site of some ancient and forgotten city of the Fertile Crescent. Most of Mardin's monuments share the same style and dates as those in nearby Diyarbakır, but where Diyarbakır's massive walls were often breached by invaders, the Mardin citadel held militarily and only submitted politically once the raping and plunder of the hinterland had stopped and the new rulers of the land had absorbed a modicum of civilisation. About 60 km (37 miles) to the east, **Midyat** ㉝ is the centre of the remaining 40,000-odd Suriyani community.

Diyarbakır

Locals like to call **Diyarbakır** ㉞, about 90 km (56 miles) north of Mardin, "the Paris of the East", and claim its massive black basalt walls are second only to the Great Wall of China in size. Both erroneous claims should be discounted, but no visit to Turkey is complete without a visit to this ancient, walled city on the Tigris.

Known in classical times as Amidiya, the city was annexed by Rome in AD 297, and became a vital part of the line of defence between the Roman and Parthian/Sassanian empires of Persia. Ceded to the Persians after Julian the Apostate's ill-fated campaign down the Euphrates in AD 362, Diyarbakır was conquered once again by the Byzantines and held until the walls were breached by the Muslim armies of Khalid Ibn Walid (The Sword of Islam) in AD 639. The city takes its current name from the Arab clan of Baqr, dubbing itself the "abode of the Baqr", or Diyarbakır.

Conquest by the Arab Muslims was not the end of the city's martial history, however, and it was taken again by the Ummayad and Abbasid Arabs, the Marwani Kurds, Seljuks, White Sheep Turcomans and even the Safavid Persians again, before finally falling to the Ottomans with the rest of eastern Anatolia in 1515. Most of the mosques, *medreses* and houses of interest date from the Ottoman period.

Diyarbakır remains Turkey's pre-eminently Kurdish city. Save for the military, civil servants, a few Arabs, fewer Armenians and Afghanis (refugees from Pakistan in 1982), the population of the city is overwhelmingly Kurdish.

Checkerboard mosques

The most distinctive of the town's 22 older mosques is the **Ulucamii** (Grand Mosque), about halfway down

İzzet Paşa Caddesi, Diyarbakır's main drag, between the Harput and Mardin gates. The oldest place of Muslim worship in Anatolia, this was originally built as the primary Syriac Cathedral of Mar Touma (St Thomas). Similar in design to the much grander Umayyad Mosque in Damascus (a city which Diyarbakır closely resembles), the Ulucamii is built on the courtyard plan of Arabian mosques, unlike the covered and domed buildings familiar throughout the rest of Turkey.

Map on pages 322–3

Up and down İzzet Paşa, one encounters dozens of buildings – mosques, *medreses* or caravansarays – that alternate black and white stone blocks to give the town a decidedly checkerboard look. The first of these structures is the **Peygamber Camii (Mosque of the Prophet Muhammed)**, built by Kasap Hajj Hüseyin ("The Butcher") in 1530, and named thanks to the vocal calisthenics of a 16th-century *muezzin*, whose plaintive invocation of the Prophet's name kept the neighbours awake.

At the end of the street is the entrance to the **İç Kale** (citadel). Nearby is another checkerboard mosque, known variously as the **Nasiriye Camii**, Citadel Mosque or the Mosque of St Süleyman. It was built in 1155 by Abu al-Qassim Ali in honour of the 24 early Muslim martyrs who first breached the walls during Khalid Ibn Walid's conquest of the city in AD 639, one of whom, Süleyman, was Walid's son. Their tombs are now a place of pilgrimage. The interior of the citadel itself provides a good view of the Tigris River (Dicle Çayı in Turkish) down below. Note, too, the peculiar **Lion's Fountain** at the entrance, presumed to date from the late Roman/Byzantine period.

Ancient Christian tradition lives on in this Suriyani wall painting.

The **Sheikh Mutahhar Camii**, better known as the Four-Legged Minaret Mosque, though just one of many 16th-century structures in town, has a peculiar minaret, standing in the middle of a crowded thoroughfare, and local legend has it that wishes come true to those who pass under it seven times. Down a winding and child-clogged street from here is a rickety Armenian church, the **Ermeni Kilisesi**. Built to accommodate over 500 people, it now serves a dozen local families, and the odd Syriac in from Mardin for Sunday prayers.

BELOW: wedding in southeastern Turkey.

The city walls

Stretching for some 5 km (3 miles) around the old city, and once possessing 82 defensive towers, the great basalt walls of Diyarbakır were first built during the reign of Constantinus but have been restored repeatedly since. They are still in remarkably good shape, with inscriptions, geometrical and animal designs, in spite of repeated battering by sundry armies throughout history. The main north entrance to the old town is the **Harput Gate**, once known as the **Bab-al-Arman** (Gate of the Armenians), thanks to the road leading to traditional Armenia.

Upon entering a road leads west along the walls to the **Urfa Gate**, and beyond that, the **Ulu Beden**, from where there is access to the top of the walls through passages which, unhappily, double as public toilets. With courage and a few goat-like leaps, you can continue almost as far as the southern **Mardin Gate**, overlooking the vast, festering slum of **Ben-u-Sen** outside the city. There are also fine views of the Tigris River meandering along a valley east of the city.

From Diyarbakır, the main road northeast towards Van heads through the delightfully named town of Batman to **Bitlis** ㉟, famous for its tobacco. Built along a river gorge that looks much better by night than day, there are several vaguely acceptable hotels, including one with balconies overlooking the river and the 12th-century **Ulucamii**, whose strange profile is due to its Seljuk patron running out of money before the building was complete. A long, winding **castle**, built by one of Alexander's generals, overlooks the town from the ridge.

Lake Van

Turkey's largest inland body of water and one of the world's highest lakes, **Van Gölü** ㊱ stands some 1,650 metres (5,500 ft) above sea level. Flushed with the run-off from innumerable small streams in the surrounding mountains, it has no visible outlet save for evaporation, accounting for the lake's high salinity. The local fish, a type of smelt, add colour (and not a little odour) to local marketdays.

At the western head of the lake is the town of **Tatvan** ㊲, the western station of the Van ferryboat which carries the occasional broken-down truck or odd passenger. As no railway exists between Tatvan and Van, the ferry service also transports railroad box cars destined for Iran. The tracks pick up again in the town of Van itself on the eastern shore. A good road runs round the south shore.

Tatvan is the easiest place from which to reach some of the smaller towns on the north shore of the lake, such as **Ahlat** ㊳, a place with no current amenities but a clear history behind it, judging by the extensive old cemetery west of the town. Scores of apparently wealthy 15th-century Muslims lie buried beneath ornate, rectangular tombstones, most of which stand taller than an average man. Some half-dozen *kümbets* (domed tombs) also stand near the road, or are tucked among the walnut groves at the back of the cemetery.

A summer-only road west leads towards the lesser **Nemrut Dağı**, a volcanic mountain sporting a spectacular triple crater lake. More accessible, if less visually dramatic, is an excursion to **Malazgirt** ㊴, about 50 km (40 miles) north of Ahlat on the Patnos road. It was here that the Seljuks routed the Byzantine host at the Battle of Manzikert in 1071. It became known as one of the greatest battles of history.

Also north of Lake Van is 4,058 metres (13,313 ft) **Suphan Dağı**, a mountain popular with climbers, which is often mistaken for Ararat by the uninformed. Beyond that, the village of **Erciş** ㊵ is an extraordinary place, with a smattering of Urartian ruins and a modern Afghani community who settled here as refugees in the 1970s.

Van: an ancient city

The settlement of **Van** ㊶, once called Tushpa, is hoary with old age, reaching back to the days of Gilgamesh and the primordial deluge. Some would even have it that Van was the original Garden of Eden.

The capital of the Urartu Empire during the reign of Sarduni I (764–735 BC), who built the long castle on the lakeshore (and whose merits are engraved on its south wall), Van was invested by the Assyrian Tiglath-Pileser III, although the citadel held out until conquered in about 590 BC by the Medes. Later, Van

---

The Urartians (from the Land of Ur) had a small empire at roughly the same time as the Hittites, to whom they were related. They were distinguished builders (they left some 30 ruined fortress cities) and fine metalworkers, whose goods were exported throughout the Mediterranean and Middle East.

BELOW: the area between Bitlis and Van is famous for its strong tobacco.

became known as one of the principal cities in Armenia before ceding itself to the Byzantines immediately before the Battle of Manzikert.

During World War I, the old town was levelled by Armenian nationalists who dreamt of an independent Armenia with Tzarist Russian support. This was followed by reciprocal destruction upon the return of the Turkish army. Both sides – probably with justice – accused the other of killing civilians while destroying buildings in the general chaos of the period. Today, all that remains of the old town are the minaret of the **Ulucamii**, two conical tombs and a few scattered fragments of the town wall.

The **citadel** itself is strangely impressive, although nearly inaccessible after rain and certainly off limits in winter. Aside from the Royal Burial Chamber on the south side of the summit which has a bit of barbed wire and fence around it, there are no guard rails to prevent the visitor from pitching off the side.

New Van itself serves mainly as the administrative headquarters for the military and state-security apparatus in the southeastern region. The central market is colourful with cheap leather goods; Van *kilims* are ubiquitous but rather expensive, once again proving the Turkish adage "the stone is heavy in its place". Van and the neighbouring province of Hakkari also specialise in *otlu peynir* (white cheese with bits of parsley and garlic pressed into it).

Akdamar Island

The primary reason for any visit to Van is a trip to the 10th-century Armenian church on **Akdamar Adası (Island)** ❷, reached by a 5-km (3-mile) boat ride from a point along the lakeshore just past the town of **Gevaş**, some 40 km (24 miles) southwest of Van.

Map on pages 322–3

The Urartian castle at Lake Van, one of the world's oldest surviving fortresses.

BELOW: sunset across Old Van.

With the entire edifice of the Byzantine state about to collapse before the Turkish onslaught, and with only his kingdom standing between the warrior hordes and the soft underbelly of Central Anatolia, the Armenian king, Gagil I Artunsi had the church and its palace complex built as a retreat. It probably remains in such good condition today because the famed Turkish horsemen were poor boatbuilders, and the island would have appeared impregnable.

The chief attraction of the church, built in the standard Armenian style with a conical dome atop four axes, is the ornate reliefwork on the façade, depicting the Old Testament: a veritable zoo of animals and birds ring the roof, door and walls in an orgy of iconography. One senses the religious tension that must have existed between the Armenian church and the orthodox Muslim clerics, who saw in such sacral sculpture the influence of the devil himself.

Strangely, however, the Seljuk Turks, as newly converted Muslims, adopted the Armenian style of decoration for their monumental works at Divriği and Sivas *(see Near East, pages 324–39)*. The church's interior has not weathered the winds of time so well, and precious little remains of the glorious murals and frescoes that once adorned its walls. Locals say there are even more impressive churches and monasteries on other islands in Lake Van, but these are largely inaccessible.

So far offshore, take a dip in the sodium waters of the lake and emerge refreshed and with a strange, silky feeling on your skin. The water is six times as salty as the sea and, like the Dead Sea, is said to have healing properties.

Hakkâri province

BELOW: Hosap Castle, near Van.

Just south of Van, a turn-off leads south to Hakkâri, Turkey's remote province, and home to the most astounding mountain range between Switzerland and the

Hindu Kush. It is also Turkey's most problematic province, squeezed between Iraqi and Iranian Kurdistan, with considerable separatist sentiments of its own. Travel in the area is safe on major highways, but dangerous on country roads and in the mountains, where one can still be in real danger of getting shot or kidnapped. Security forces have set up frequent road blocks.

The first site of interest, 48 km (30 miles) south of Van is the dramatic **Hoşap Kalesi** ㊸ (open daily 8.30am–7pm; entrance fee), built by a Kurdish despot, Sarı Süleyman ("the Blonde") in 1643. The extent of the castle area compares a little too favourably with the contemporary village of Güzelsu below.

About 50 km (30 miles) further down the road, now running along the Greater Zap River, a major tributary of the Tigris, is the town of **Başkale** ㊹, which at 2,500 metres (7,500 ft) is the highest urban area in Turkey. The town used to be inhabited by Nestorians, followers of a breakaway Christian sect, whose last remaining members were massacred or scattered by the Kurds in the 1930s.

The road south leads to **Hakkâri**, a town best avoided, and **Yüksekova** ㊺ ("High Meadow" in Turkish), a town with a greater concentration of Mercedes cars than anywhere else in Turkey thanks to the booming border commerce between Turkey and Iran, and the illicit drug trade from northern Iraq. Most cars in Hakkâri province have Istanbul license plates (number 34), designed to prevent the drivers from being harassed by security officials.

As it heads towards the Iranian border, the road suddenly becomes a 12-lane highway for about 2 km (1 mile). This is an airstrip built for use in a rescue operation by the US military during the 1979–81 Iranian Embassy hostage crisis. Now it doubles as a road and an airport for a number of visiting cabinet ministers. ❏

Map on pages 322–3

A new image for an ancient trade route.

BELOW: workers heading home from the fields.

PKK AND KURDISH SEPARATISM

An end may now be in sight to the dirty, relentless war waged since 1984 between Turkish security forces and the separatist Kurdistan Workers' Party (PKK), a Marxist group aiming to form an independent Kurdish state in southeast Turkey. More than 30,000 civilians, soldiers and PKK guerrillas have been killed. Nearly 3,000 villages have been depopulated. Four million people – Turks and Kurds – are refugees. Extraordinary security conditions have existed in 10 southeast provinces since 1991.

In December 1999, the Turkish government was greeted with widespread condemnation for arresting the PKK leader Abdullah Ocalan and then sentencing him to death. His life may have been saved by the government's desire to join the EU: in an effort to present a more acceptable face to the West, the country has now abolished the death penalty.

In 2000, the PKK declared peace with the Turkish state. Ocalan, from his prison cell, has committed himself to finding a solution to the Kurdish question through democratic means. However, the 2003 Iraq War threatens to destabilise the fragile peace as the Iraqi Kurds bargain for autonomy, and the Turks, terrified of incursions, have only been held back from invading northern Iraq by the USA.

INSIGHT GUIDES
Travel Tips

✻ INSIGHT GUIDES Phonecard

One global card to keep travellers in touch. Easy. Convenient. Saves you time and money.

It's a global phonecard

Save up to 70%* on international calls from over 55 countries

Free 24 hour global customer service

Recharge your card at any time via customer service or online

It's a message service

Family and friends can send you voice messages for free.

Listen to these messages using the phone* or online

Free email service - you can even listen to your email over the phone*

It's a travel assistance service

24 hour emergency travel assistance – if and when you need it.

Store important travel documents online in your own secure vault

For more information, call rates, and all Access Numbers in over 55 countries, (check your destination is covered) go to **www.insightguides.ekit.com** or call Customer Service.

JOIN now and receive US$ 5 bonus when you join for US$ 20 or more.

Join today at

www.insightguides.ekit.com

When requested use ref code: **INSAD010**

OR SIMPLY FREE CALL
24 HOUR CUSTOMER SERVICE

UK	0800 376 1705
USA	1800 706 1333
Canada	1800 808 5773
Australia	1800 11 44 78
South Africa	0800 997 285

THEN PRESS **0**

For all other countries please go to "Access Numbers" at **www.insightguides.ekit.com**

* Retrieval rates apply for listening to messages. Savings based on using a hotel or payphone and calling to a landline. Correct at time of printing 01.03

(INS001)

powered by ✻*ekit*

"The easiest way to make calls and receive messages around the world"

CONTENTS

Getting Acquainted

Area 780,000 sq. km (300,000 sq. miles).
Highest point Mt Ararat, 5,165 metres (17,000 ft).
Capital Ankara.
Population 67.8 million (2002 figures); Istanbul 10 million; Ankara 4 million; 32 percent of the population is concentrated in the northwestern Marmara region. About one third of Turks are under 15 years old, less than 5 percent are over 65. In recent years over 300 people per week have been moving from rural and eastern Anatolia to greater Istanbul.
Language Turkish.
Religion Officially 99 percent of Turks are Sunni Muslim, and 1 percent are Orthodox, Catholic or Protestant Christians and Jews.
Time Turkish Standard Time is 2 hours ahead of Greenwich Mean Time. It advances by one hour in summer (Apr–Oct) to GMT+3.
Currency Turkish lira (TL). This has been devalued to such an extent over recent years that it takes

millions of lira to buy even the most simple meal.
Weights and measures Metric.
Electricity 220 volts AC. Two-pronged round plug.
International dialling code 90.

Geography

Turkey is a vast country that is sandwiched – both politically and geographically – between East and West. Bordered by Greece and Bulgaria in the northwest, Georgia and Armenia to the northeast, Iran to the east and Iraq and Syria to the southeast, 3 percent of its land is in Europe and 97 percent in Asia.

The two continents of Turkey are divided by the Bosphorus, the Sea of Marmara, and the Dardanelles in the northwest of the country. To the north lies the Black Sea, to the south the Mediterranean, and to the west the Aegean.

Altogether there is a total of approximately 8,000 km (5,000 miles) of coastline, varying from the misty, mountainous Black Sea coast to the thriving Mediterranean resorts, with yachts, sub-tropical gardens and discos.

Eighty percent of Turkey is 500 metres (1,640 ft) or more above sea level.

Climate

There are three main climatic zones in Turkey:
● The Marmara (which includes Istanbul), Aegean and

Mediterranean regions. These have a typically Mediterranean climate with hot summers and mild winters, with temperatures rising the further south you go.
● The Black Sea region, which has warm summers, mild winters and relatively high rainfall throughout the year.
● The central and eastern Anatolian regions (including Ankara), which have more extreme hot, dry summers and cold winters.

Economy

In the 1990s, a move towards a competitive free market (led by increasing privatisation) generated economic growth of about 7 percent per annum between 1995 and 1998. The end of the decade, however, saw a dramatic drop as earthquakes, higher taxation, world recession and global politics all hit home. After the near collapse of the currency, a massive cash injection by the IMF has helped stabilise the lira, but wages remain low and inflation high. Rising consumer expectations, entry into the customs union with the EU, and a significant drop in tourism have led to higher imports and a massively increased foreign trade deficit.

Government

Turkey has a 400-member Grand National Assembly and a multi-party political system that is largely democratic, though changes can seem volatile from the outside.

Currently, the prime minister is Recep Tayyip Erdogan of the AKP (Justice and Development Party) which came to power in the 2002 elections. It is a religious party and descendent of the banned party Refah, but has agreed to abide by Turkey's secular constitution. The president of the Republic is Ahmet Necdet Sezer, formerly chief justice of the constitutional court, and only the fourth civilian to hold the post.

Turkey is a member of the United Nations, the EU Customs Union, the OECD, the Council of Europe and NATO and a candidate for membership of the European Union.

Average Temperatures (°C/°F)

Region	Jan	Apr	July	Oct
Marmara				
Istanbul	7°	16°	28°	19°
	45°	61°	82°	66°
Aegean				
İzmir	9°	20°	30°	21°
	48°	68°	86°	70°
Mediterranean				
Antalya	11°	22°	32°	23°
	52°	72°	90°	73°
Black Sea				
Trabzon	8°	16°	16°	13°
	47°	61°	61°	56°
Central Anatolia				
Ankara	4°	15°	30°	18°
	39°	59°	86°	65°
Eastern Anatolia				
Erzurum	9°	6°	20°	12°
	48°	43°	68°	54°

Planning the Trip

Visas and Passports

Visa requirements and costs for entering Turkey vary substantially according to your nationality. All travellers need a passport valid for at least six months.

Citizens of the following countries require visas, which can be obtained at the point of entry into Turkey (not in advance from consulates): UK (£10), Canada (US$40), Australia (US$20) and Ireland (€10). You must pay in hard currency at the booth before immigration. Photographs are not required. You will be issued with a multiple-entry tourist visa valid for three months.

US citizens may buy a three-month visa (US$100) either at the point of entry or from a Turkish consulate in advance of travel.

Provided that they have a valid passport, nationals of many countries (including Belgium, France, Germany, the Netherlands and New Zealand) do not need a visa for visits of up to three months. The tourist visa will be stamped into the passport free of charge; it is important to leave the country before the expiry date.

Consulates Abroad

UK: Rutland Lodge, Rutland Gardens, Knightsbridge, London SW7 1BW.
Tel: 020-7589 0949.
USA: 5th Flr, 821 United Nations Plaza, New York, NY 10017.
Tel: 212-949 0159/62/63.
2525 Massachusetts Avenue NW, Washington DC 20008.
Tel: 202-612 6700.

Nationals of South Africa will be issued with a visa for one month on the same basis.

Extending your stay

Anyone wishing to stay in Turkey beyond three months can apply for a residence permit, as long as they can show proof of employment in Turkey, or financial means to support their stay.

Alternatively, foreigners can leave the country before the end of the three-month period, stay outside Turkey (in Greece or Bulgaria, for example) for 24 hours, then re-enter. This has become common practice.

Customs

You are allowed to bring into the country up to 200 cigarettes (400 if bought in a Turkish duty-free shop), 50 cigars, 200g pipe tobacco (500g if bought in Turkey), 75 cl alcohol, 5 litres wine or spirits, 1 kg chocolate and 1.5 kg coffee.

Cars, valuable electronic equipment (such as a laptop computer or mobile phone) or antiques may be entered in the owner's passport on arrival, and then checked on exit to prevent their being sold on in Turkey.

Possession of narcotics is treated as an extremely serious offence; penalties are harsh.

Exporting antiques

It is strictly forbidden to take antiques, including rugs and carpets, out of the country. Should you buy anything old or old-looking, be sure to have it validated by the seller, who should get a clearance certificate from the Department of Antiquities. Respectable carpet dealers should be familiar with the procedure.

Health Matters

Turkey is a pretty safe country, as long as you are sensible. If you do fall ill the standard of healthcare is not high, so it is essential to have medical insurance (see page 356). Most drugs are available without

Health Advice

In the UK, detailed health advice, tailored to individual needs, is available from MASTA (Medical Advice for Travellers Abroad). Tel: (0906) 822 4100. www.masta.org

Alternatively, you could try a British Airways Travel Centre. To find your nearest branch call (0845) 779 9977.

prescription from pharmacies (eczane). For details of these and medical treatment within the country, see page 363.

Health hazards

Traveller's diarrhoea is the main hazard, best avoided by paying attention to food and water hygiene. Drink only bottled water, wash and/or peel all fruit and vegetables, and ensure cooked food is piping hot. It's safest to eat freshly prepared local produce. Refrigeration can be poor, even in tourist resorts. Grilled meat or fish is usually safe if properly cooked through.

Some form of diarrhoea treatment and pre-packaged sachets are a useful addition to your first-aid kit. But should you succumb, it's advisable to resort to drugs only if you absolutely have to. The best treatment is to maintain fluid levels with plenty of non-alcoholic drinks or rehydration salts, eat very plain food and avoid dairy products. Recent advice is that even if fluids are repeatedly vomited, rehydration therapy will eventually work. If the diarrhoea lasts more than 48 hours, seek medical advice.

Sun and heat The other major hazards in summer are heatstroke and sunburn. The answer is pure common sense. Wear a hat and sunglasses, put on a wrap on the beach, use high-factor sunblock and aftersun cream, drink plenty of water and soft drinks, and cut down on alcohol intake. If you or your companions get an overwhelming headache, are dizzy or disoriented and cannot bring your body

Tourist Offices

UK
170–173 Piccadilly (1st Floor),
London W1V 9DD.
Tel: (020) 7355 4207.
Fax: (020) 7491 0773.
USA
821 United Nations Plaza,
New York, NY 10017.
Tel: (212) 687 2194.
Fax: (212) 599 7568.
Suite 306,
2525 Massachusetts Avenue,
NW, Washington DC 20008.
Tel: (202) 612 6800.
Fax: (202) 319 7446.

Web pages *see page 357.*

temperature down, put the patient in a cool bath and get someone to ring for a doctor. True heatstroke is a serious medical condition.

Stings and bites If you stand on a sea urchin or any other sea creature, or are bitten by any animal, it is vitally important to seek medical attention as soon as possible. Stings can produce a severe allergic reaction, while a bite may require vaccination against rabies. While waiting for the doctor, the best first aid is to wash the wound thoroughly; five minutes' scrubbing with soap under running water is recommended.

Inoculations

As a rule, inoculations are not necessary, but it is always wise to be up to date with polio, tetanus and TB when travelling. Should you plan to visit central or eastern Anatolia, consider immunisation against typhoid.

Antimalarial tablets are recommended in summer in the southeastern Anatolian region (Adana, Alanya, Mersin and along the border with Syria and Iraq).

You may wish to consider immunisation against hepatitis A (spread through contaminated food and water). As everywhere else, Aids and hepatitis B are prevalant and precautions should be taken.

Medical insurance

An insurance policy, including cover for medical evacuation, is essential, as medical costs in Turkey are high and EU reciprocal agreements do not apply.

If you already have a general year-round travel policy, check that it will cover you on the Asian side of the country (some companies use Asia as a threshold).

Money Matters

CURRENCY

The currency is the Turkish lira (TL), which has one of the lowest unit values of any currency in the world. Discussions are ongoing as to whether, or when, to knock a few noughts off the end of the huge numbers involved to make them easier for everyone to handle – the situation is so out of control that most calculators cannot cope because they simply don't have enough room for all the digits. The foreign currency exchange rates are published every day.

Unlimited foreign currency can be brought into Turkey. Although you can bring in up to US$5,000 worth of Turkish lira, it is better to arrive with a small amount of Turkish currency (and use your credit or cash card), as you will get a much better rate of exchange within the country, even at the airports. With inflation and commission, you will also get a very poor rate if you try to change your TL back into a harder currency, so use them up during your stay if possible.

OBTAINING CASH

Banks are plentiful in Turkey, but they are slow and with the increasing number of cash dispensers you can easily get through your whole stay without entering one.

Travellers' cheques

These can be cashed at the foreign exchange desks of banks and at post offices, but it is useful to bring

a supply of foreign currency, whether US dollars, sterling or euros, which can be used directly for larger purchases. Most traders are happy to haggle in all three.

To cash travellers' cheques you will need your passport. Note that exchange offices, hotels and shops usually don't accept them.

Credit and debit cards

Most major cards, including Visa and MasterCard, are accepted by more and more shops, restaurants, hotels and petrol stations. Fewer outlets accept Amex, which has significantly higher commission.

ATMs

There are 24-hour cash dispensers, accepting credit cards and bank cards with PIN numbers, on every street corner; Işbank alone has over 1,000 all over Turkey.

The machines usually offer you a choice of five or six languages in which to conduct your transaction, but they issue only Turkish lira. There may be several days' delay

Business Hours

Offices Generally Mon–Fri 9am–6pm.
Government offices 8am–4.30pm in winter; 8.30am–5pm in summer.
Shops Most closed on Sunday, but major stores open all week. The large shopping centres and smart clothes shops open later, at 10am, closing between 8pm and 10pm. Small neighbourhood stores are generally open 8am–8.30/9pm; some only shut up for the night at around 10pm.
Banks Mon–Fri 8.30am–noon, 1.30–5pm; a few main branches also open Saturday morning. Most private banks remain open over lunch. Several banks at Istanbul airport open 24 hours a day.
Post Offices Mon–Sat 9am–5pm. Sirkeci Post Office in Istanbul is open 24 hours.
Garages Larger ones remain open 24 hours a day.

in the transaction reaching your home account.

Foreign exchange offices

Döviz are usually the best places to make a straight exchange of foreign currency, almost always offering a better rate for cash than the banks. US dollars and euros can attract a better rate than less frequently traded currencies. These offices rarely accept travellers' cheques. *For more information, see page 364.*

TAXES

Taxes, chiefly VAT (KDV) at varying rates, are included in the prices of some goods and services. But you may see them itemised separately as a component of the price on a bill or receipt.

Some stores offer VAT-free shopping for tourists living outside the European Union (look out for signs in the window). If you wish to take advantage of this, you need to get an official VAT-free invoice or you will not be able to reclaim the tax at the airport on your way out.

Religious Festivals

Turkish religious holidays are linked to the lunar calendar and move back 11 or 12 days each year. Secular festivals also move to coincide with weekends and precise dates can change annually. Contact your nearest Turkish tourist office to keep up to date.

During these major holidays, shops and businesses are closed,

Public Holidays

- **1 January** New Year's Day
- **23 April** National Sovereignty and Children's Day (folk dancing)
- **19 May** Atatürk's Commemoration and Youth and Sports Day
- **30 August** Victory Day
- **29 October** Republic Day

though local shops will usually reopen on the second or third day.

Ramazan Anyone will tell you that the worst time to travel in Turkey is during the holy month of Ramazan (Ramadan), when a majority of the population (even non-devout Muslims) pride themselves on fasting from dawn to dusk. This includes the intake of water and cigarettes, with the result that taxi drivers may put you out as the sunset approaches so they can stop to eat, and many people are extremely irritable.

Over the next few years, Ramazan will fall in late autumn, which is infinitely preferable to when it is during the long hot days of summer.

Seker Bayram The fast of Ramadan ends with a three-day celebration, Sugar Holiday, when everyone, especially childen, is offered sweets wherever they go.

Kurban Bayram The Feast of the Sacrifice is a four-day holiday celebrating the sacrifice of Isaac. It takes place 20 days after the end of Ramadan and involves the ritual throat-slitting of sheep and cows, often in public.

New Year Most Turks celebrate New Year's Eve and New Year's Day in a way similar to a Western Christmas.

Mirac Kandili, a smaller religious holiday about a month after Kurban Bayram, celebrates the Prophet Mohammed's nocturnal journey to Jerusalem and ascension to heaven on a winged horse. Though not an official holiday, mosques are especially illuminated.

Nevruz (the Festival of Light) is celebrated thoughout eastern Turkey and elsewhere. Originally thought to be a Zoroastrian fire festival, it is now associated with Kurdish tradition in Turkey.

What to Bring

Clothes Your needs will vary greatly according to the part of Turkey you will be visiting and the time of year. In the height of summer, light, cotton clothing for the Marmara, Aegean and Mediterranean areas is

Useful Websites

Republic of Turkey Home Page: www.turkey.org Turkish government site. Useful tourist information, visa requirements and press releases.
Turkish Foreign Ministry: www.mfa.gov.tr
Turkish Ministry of Culture and Tourism: www.kultur.gov.tr
Turkish Press and Information Section www.turkishnews.com
Turkish Daily News Home Page: www.turkishdailynews.com The electronic arm of Turkey's English-language daily.
Turkey hotels: www.onlinehotels-turkey.com
Istanbul hotels: www.istanbulhotels.com Useful accommodation website.
Travel advisories: www.fco.gov.uk www.travel.state.gov/travel_warnings. Regularly updated travel and general health advice from the UK Foreign and Commonwealth Office and US State Department.
Health for travellers: www.dh.gov.uk www.cdc.gov/travel www.masta.org Advice on health from the UK and US governments and the London Hospital for Tropical Diseases.
General tourist information: www.goturkey.com Official Tourist Office site includes extensive information on tourism within the country.
www.turkishodyssey.com Good for facts about Turkey and practical information about everyday life in the country.
www.theguideistanbul.com More or less up-to-date listings magazine, also covers Ankara, Antalya, İzmir and Bodrum. Commercial, but useful.

essential, including a long loose cotton shirt to cover your arms and shoulders against the hottest sun, a shady hat and a high-factor sunscreen, especially if you intend to visit archaeological sites where there can be little or no shade.

For the Black Sea region you may need a light sweater in the evening, a light waterproof mac and water-resistant footwear. Humidity is high. In central and eastern Anatolia, summer evenings can also be cool.

Footwear Comfortable, sturdy shoes are essential for tramping over historical and archaeological sites. Even the pavements on city streets can be uneven or cobbled.

Wet-weather gear Although Turkey is often regarded as hot all year round, winter travellers will soon discover that it has as much rain, snow and ice as most of Europe; parts of the country are very high and should be treated with respect. Especially in the north, tough water-resistant footwear and a raincoat or jacket will prove invaluable.

Insect repellent Mosquitoes (non-malarial) can be a severe annoyance anywhere in summer, so bring a good repellent. Burning coils, or plug-in electric antibug devices that you use with a tablet, are available locally.

Tampons can be difficult to track down, though you will normally find Western brands of sanitary towels. It makes sense to bring your own.

Photography

Taking photographs is perfectly acceptable in almost any context; Turks are generally pleased to be included in photographs, and of course if on holiday themselves will be snapping away. It is polite, however, to ask first and to respect their wishes if they say no. Veiled women sometimes prefer not to be photographed. Some people may ask for a copy; if you take their address, do send the pictures.

The country is immensely photogenic, so take more film than you expect to need; it will get used.

Museums sometimes charge for the use of cameras or videos; flash photography may not be allowed as it can damage paints and textiles.

Mosques usually allow discreet flash-free photography – be tactful.

Developing is readily available and of good quality; fast developing shops have sprung up everywhere. The prices for processing are high, though, and comparable with the equivalent express service at home. In major cities you will find professional-standard processing for black-and-white and slides, as well as colour prints.

Film is expensive, but prices are lower in photographic shops than at tourist sites (which usually have only a limited supply).

Getting There

BY AIR

Flight time to Istanbul from London is about 3.5 hours; from New York about 9 hours.

Most international airlines have regular direct or connecting flights to Istanbul's Atatürk International Airport from major European cities and the US. Turkish Airlines (THY) connects to over 30 European destinations, as well as to cities further afield such as New York. From the UK, the two main scheduled carriers are THY and British Airways (BA).

A smaller number of international carriers also fly direct to the international airports at Ankara, İzmir, Bodrum, Antalya and Dalaman. Numerous summer charter flights fly into İzmir, Bodrum, Dalaman and Antalya, to feed the beach resorts.

To reach the eastern cities such as Adana and Trabzon often involves a connection through Istanbul. For domestic flights, *see page 369.*

Airport Numbers

Istanbul: Atatürk International Airport, Yesilköy.
www.ataturkairport.com
Tel: (0212) 573 2941.
Ankara: Esenboğa International Airport. Tel: (0312) 398 0000.
İzmir: Adnan Menderes Airport. Tel: (0232) 274 2626.
Antalya: Antalya International Airport. Tel: (0242) 330 3030.

Travel to and from the airport

Whichever airport you fly in to, the easiest option to get from the airport into the nearest town is by taxi, of which there is never a shortage. Although cab drivers may not be that good at finding their way around, if you know the name of your hotel, and the area it is in, you will get there.

The fare will be registered on the meter and should come to under US $15/£10. Hotels can arrange transfers, but this can be much more expensive. This may be the only choice on the coast, however, where some hotels are a couple of hours' drive from the airport.

The major cities also have airport buses, often timed to coincide with the arrival or departure of scheduled flights. In Istanbul, there is an efficient bus service from Atatürk Airport to the centre, operating every 30 minutes between 6am and 11pm, and continuing at longer intervals through the night. This makes one stop (at which you should alight for connections to the old-city districts of Sultanahmet and Eminönü) before terminating in the centre of the new city at Taksim Square. Havaş bus service, tel: (0212) 465 4700.

When leaving Turkey, allow plenty of time for checking in, especially in the high season. Long queues can build up both for the security checks and for check-in and passport formalities.

BY SEA

During the summer there are car-ferry crossings between Turkey and Venice, Ancona, Bari and Brindisi on the Italian Aegean coast, taking 30–60 hours to arrive either at İzmir or the nearby seaside resort-cum-port of Çeşme.

Timetables and operating companies are variable from year to year, although Turkish Maritime Lines runs a regular summer service. For details of all the available options, consult travel agencies. Some routes pass through the Corinth Canal, thereby both

Airlines Flying To and From Turkey

Turkish Airlines/THY (overseas)
Australia
600/16 Barrack Street, Sydney,
NSW 2000.
Tel: (02) 9299 8400.
UK
125 Pall Mall, London SW1Y 5EA.
Tel: (020) 7766 9300.
E-mail: info@turkish-airlines.co.uk
USA
Ste 17B, 437 Madison Avenue,
New York 10022.
Tel: 1-800-874 8875.
E-mail: info@tknyc.com

Turkish Airlines/THY (Turkey)
Head Office
Atatürk Airport, Yesilköy, Istanbul.
24-hour Reservations.
Tel: (0212) 444 0849.
THY website (booking):
www.thy.com
Istanbul
Cumhuriyet Cad, Gezidukkanları 7,
Taksim. Tel: (0212) 252 1106.
Cumhuriyet Cad. 199-201,

Harbiye. Tel: (0212) 225 0556.
Recep Peker Cad. 27, Kadıköy.
Tel: (0216) 418 4486.
Adana
Prof. Dr. Nurset Fisek Cad. 22,
Seyhan-Adana.
Tel: (0322) 457 0222.
Ankara
Atatürk Bulvarı 154, Kavaklidere.
Tel: (0312) 428 0200.
Antalya
Cumhuriyet Caddesi,
özel Idare Ishane.
Tel: (0242) 243 4383.
İzmir
Gaziosmanpasa Bulvarı 1/F,
Büyük Efes Oteli.
Tel: (0232) 484 1220.

British Airways
Turkey Tel: (0212) 234 1300
(Istanbul). Tel: (0312) 467 5557
(Ankara).
UK Tel: (0845) 773 3377.
USA Tel: (1-800) AIRWAYS.
www.britishairways.com

---

of the city. For details, see *Getting Around, page 370.*

BY CAR

It is possible to drive to Turkey via Bulgaria or Greece, or via Italy, with a ferry to Turkey *(see above).* The roads leading to or from Russia are often in a bad state.

At the point of entry you will need to show the car's registration documents and your driving licence. Your car details will be stamped into your passport, allowing you to drive it for six months in Turkey duty-free. You must leave the country with it, however; should you write your car off during your stay, you will need special papers to certify that it has not been sold in Turkey. You will be issued with a certificate which you should keep with you at all times.

Documents
In addition to a valid driving licence, you will need the vehicle's log book and proof of ownership (and a power of attorney as proof of permission if you are driving someone else's vehicle), a Green Card (from your insurance company) and insurance (check you are covered for the Asian side of the country and for breakdown). Drivers may use their national licence with a Turkish translation for up to three months, but are advised to take an international licence.

For further details on driving, *see Getting Around, page 373.*

---

cutting hours and adding interest to the journey.

These routes are much used by Turkish migrant workers, returning home for their summer holidays. It's also a good way to get a caravan to Turkey from Western Europe.

Ferries to northern Cyprus run from Taşucu and Mersin, on the Mediterranean coast. **Turkish Maritime Lines**, Istanbul. For information: Tel: (0212) 244 0207 or (0216) 249 9222 for reservations; www.tdi.com.tr

---

BY RAIL

The Istanbul Express comes into Istanbul from Munich, Vienna and Athens, with connecting services in Belgrade and Sofia. There are also weekly departures for Istanbul from Budapest, Bucharest and Moscow. Inter-rail tickets are valid in Turkey; Eurail passes are not.

In the UK, for information on fares, contact Rail Europe: Tel: (08705) 848 848; www.raileurope.co.uk

---

In the US, contact Forsyth Travel Library Inc, 226 Westchester Avenue, White Plains, NY 10604. Tel: 1-800-367 7984; www.forsyth.com

Trains from the West arrive at the Sirkeci Station in Eminönü, in the heart of old Constantinople. Those from the East come in to the Haydarpaşa Station on the Asian side of Istanbul, from where you can take a ferry or a taxi across the Bosphorus to the centre.

For information in Istanbul: Tel: (0212) 527 0050 (European lines); (0216) 336 0475 (Asian lines).

BY BUS/COACH

Bus services operate from major European cities, especially in Germany and Austria, as well as from the Middle East, Russian and Central Asian states. They arrive at the Esenler Coach Station, Bayrampasa, northwest of Istanbul; tel: (0212) 658 0036. There are minibuses from there to the centre

---

PACKAGE TOURS

Unless you are planning to move around a lot, packages are usually much more reasonable than booking independently, particularly if you want to stay in a top hotel. The choice of packages is enormous, whether you are looking for a villa holiday, adventurous mountaineering or white-water rafting, or a simple flight/accommodation deal. It's worth shopping around for the best deals.

Specialist Agents/Operators
United Kingdom
Exodus Travel, Grange Mills, Weir Road, London SW12 0NE.
Tel: (020) 8675 5550.
www.exodus.co.uk
Offers a wide range of tours from gentle blue cruising through heavy-duty sightseeing to active holidays including kayaking, white-water rafting and hiking.
Greentours, Leigh Cottage, Gauledge Lane, Longnor, Buxton, Derbyshire SK17 0PA.
Tel: (01298) 83563.
www.greentours.co.uk
Specialist birdwatching holidays in Turkey's Lake District and Kaçkar Mountains.
Holts Tours, The Old Plough, High St, Eastry, Kent CT13 0HF.
Tel: (01304) 612 248.
www.battletours.co.uk
Gallipoli landings and battlefields tours.
Interest and Activity Holidays Ltd, Hartfield House, 173 Hartfield Road, London SW19 3TH.
Tel: (020) 8251 0208.
www.iah-holidays.co.uk
Interesting range of holidays including mountain walking and olive picking.
Martin Randall Travel, Voysey House, Barley Mow Passage, Chiswick, London W4 4GF.
Tel: (020) 8742 3355.
www.imartinrandall.com
Cultural, art and archaeological tours.
Metak Holidays, 70 Welbeck Street, London W1M 7HA.
Tel: (020) 7935 6961.
Hotel-based packages in a range of coastal resorts.

Savile Tours and Travel, 47 Charlwood St, St John's Wood, London NW8 6JN.
Tel: (020) 7722 2986.
www.saviletours.com
Top-notch villas with pools, luxury hotels, cruises and touring holidays.
Simply Turkey, King's House, Wood Street, Kingston-upon-Thames, KT1 1SG.
Tel: (020) 8541 2204.
Self-catering from rural cottages to villas with pools. Also *gulets*, scuba, kayaking, paragliding, archaeology and painting.
Sunquest, 23 Prince's Street, London W1R 7RG.
Tel: (020) 7499 9991.
www.sunquestholidays.co.uk
Britain's largest specialist operator to Turkey, catering mainly for mass-market, budget/mid-range one- or two-centre holidays, with a huge range of hotels to choose from.
Tapestry Holidays, 286 Chiswick High Road, London W4 1PA.
Tel: (020) 8235 7777.
www.tapestryholidays.com
Good small hotels and *pansiyons*, yachting and watersports.

Other companies include:
Anatolian Sky, 81 Warwick Road, Olton, Solihull B92 7HP.
Tel: (0870) 850 4040.
www.anatolian-sky.co.uk
Includes twin-centre holidays, plus *gulets*.
The Imaginative Traveller
Tel: (020) 8742 8612.
www.imaginative-traveller.com
Sailing, walking, canoeing, cycling and trekking.

Travelbag Adventures, 15 Turk St, Alton, Hampshire GU34 1AG.
Tel: (01420) 541 007.
www.travebag-adventures.co.uk
Walking, sailing and activity tours.

United States
ATC Anadolu Travel & Tours, 420 Madison Avenue, Suite 504, New York, NY 10017.
Tel: (1-800) ANADOLU or (212) 486 4012.
www.atc-anadolu.com
Escorted tours, city breaks, *gulet* cruises and customised itineraries. Specialises in first-time visits.
Blue Voyage Turkish Tours & Travel, 323 Geary Street, Suite 401, San Francisco, CA 94102.
Tel: (1-800) 81-turkey or (415) 392 0146.
www.bluevoyage.com
Tailormade tours including fly-drive, *gulet* charters, and escorted tours.
Club America, 51 East 42nd Street, Suite 1406, New York, NY 10017.
Tel: (1-800) 221 4969 or (212) 972 2865
www.clubamericatravel.com
Escorted and independent tours including historic sights, yacht charters and special interest.
Mountain Travel Sobek, 6420 Fairmount Avenue, El Cerrito, CA 9453.
Tel: (1-888) MTSOBEK (687-6235) or (1-510) 527-8100.
UK office tel: (01494) 448 901.
www.mtsobek.com
Trekking, outdoor and mountaineering adventures in Cappadocia, *gulet* cruises.
Wilderness Travel, 1102 Ninth Street, Berkeley, CA 94710.
Tel: (1-800) 368 2794 or (510) 558 2488
www.wildnernesstravel.com
Adventure tours, including *gulet* cruising, hiking and touring.

Turkey
For Turkish tour operators, see *Getting Around, pages 376–8*.

Maps

Maps are notoriously difficult to come by in Turkey. There are no publicly available large-scale maps as these are seen as a threat to national security. The best at present are the 1:800,000 sheets and road atlas published in Germany by R.V. Verlag, and the 1:500,000 sheets published jointly by the Turkish Ministry of Defence in Ankara and the Kartographischer Verlag Reinhard Ryborsch in Frankfurt. These may be available in the UK from Stanfords and other good travel bookshops, or good foreign-language bookshops in Turkey.
Stanfords, tel: (020) 7836 1321; www.stanfords.co.uk (mail order available).

Practical Tips

Turkey has been enjoying a media explosion. Quantity does not necessarily mean quality, however. The radio waves are so crowded with channels that stations have to take turns; there are dozens of regular TV channels, while apartment buildings bristle with aerials and dishes as people tune in to the world's cable and satellite networks.

Television

From a single state-run TV channel at the beginning of the 1980s, Turkey now has over 12 main channels, the majority of which are privately owned. You will find additional regional channels, depending on where you are. Although entertainment programmes, soap operas, game shows and pop videos dominate the small screen, some channels also show foreign films (sometimes with subtitles) and international sports.

Through satellite and cable, dozens of foreign channels including BBC Prime, MTV and CNN can be viewed (although BBC reception can be erratic). Visitors will find satellite or cable in the major hotels, although you should check before booking if this is important to you.
● **TRT Channel 2** broadcasts the news in English, French and German at 7pm and 10pm.

Radio

Until 1993, only state-run stations broadcast programmes, and these were inclined to be more soporific than stimulating. Today, Istanbul alone has so many private stations playing Western pop and rock, with news broadcasts thrown in, that

Foreign Embassies & Consulates in Turkey

Although the embassies are in Ankara, the Consulates in Istanbul handle visa and passport matters. If you require a visa for somewhere else from Turkey, you must go to Istanbul. In popular tourist areas, you may find an Honorary Consul, a local person appointed to take on Consular responsibilities.

Australia
● Nenehatun Caddesi 83, Gaziosmanpaşa, Ankara.
Tel: (0312) 446 1180.
● Tepecik Yokuşu 58, Etiler, Istanbul.
Tel: (0212) 257 7050.

Canada
● Nenehatun Caddesi 75, Gaziosmanpasa, Ankara.
Tel: (0312) 436 1275.
● Istiklal Caddesi 373, Beyoğlu, Istanbul. Tel: (0212) 251 9838.

Ireland
Honorary Consul: Cumhuriyet Caddesi 26/A, Harbiye, Istanbul.

Tel: (0212) 246 6025.

New Zealand
Iran Cad. 13/4, Kavaklidere, Ankara.
Tel: (0312) 467 9054/6/8.

South Africa
Filistin Sok. 27, Gaziosmanpaşa, Ankara. Tel: (0312) 446 4056.

UK
● Şehit Ersan Caddesi 46/A, Çankaya, Ankara.
Tel: (0312) 455 3344.
● Room 158, Hilton Hotel, Cumhuriyet Caddesi, Harbiye Istanbul (temporary address).
Tel: (0212) 334 6400.

USA
● Atatürk Boulevard 110, Kavaklıdere, Ankara.
Tel: (0312) 468 6110.
● Mesrutiyet Caddesi 104, Tepebaşı, Istanbul.
Tel: (0212) 251 3602.

they jostle for air time, and it can be difficult to get a clear signal on the station you want.
● **Voice FM** (90.6) broadcasts news in English (from *Voice of America*) at 3pm.
● **TRT3** (FM 88.2) The old state channel appeals to more sophisticated listeners, playing jazz, Latin and classical music. TRT3 also broadcasts news in English, French and German following the Turkish bulletin at 9am, noon, 2pm, 5pm, 7pm and 10pm.
● **BBC World Service** can be received if you have a shortwave radio with a good aerial, but reception is not very clear.

Newspapers and magazines

In Turkish There are now 29 major Turkish newspapers, chasing a relatively small reading public and competing with radio, TV and the Internet. Women are especially targeted with ever-more enticing free offers: you can collect a whole

dinner service or set of saucepans from your daily paper.

Sabah and *Hürriyet* are Turkey's best-selling national newspapers and leading public-opinion makers with good news coverage and lots of colour. The left-wing *Cumhuriyet* is considered the most serious newspaper. *Milliyet* is also a dependable, well-established, liberal paper.

The magazine market is also exploding: you will see Turkish editions of many international titles, plus countless popular Turkish weeklies and monthlies. *Atlas* and *Globe* are quality monthly travel magazines with English text summaries.

In English International newspapers (including some British tabloids) and magazines can be found at newsstands and bookshops in tourist areas and hotels. Newspapers are usually a day or two late, and sold at many times the UK cover price.

There is one local English-language daily paper, the *Turkish Daily News* or TDN, which provides coverage of local and international events. As well as listing cinemas showing English-language films, and the main satellite and TV channel programmes, it is useful for its classifieds, should you be looking for an apartment, local travel agent or Turkish lessons.

Cornucopia is a beautifully illustrated English-language magazine featuring Turkish arts, history and culture. It is stocked at Turkish bookshops selling foreign-language publications or you can subscribe on the web at www.cornucopia.net.

Tourist guides

The Guide is a useful English-language city-guide magazine, published bi-monthly in Istanbul, and annually in Ankara, Bodrum and Antalya. It offers visitors practical information, arts news, and restaurant and shopping listings. It also has a website: www.theguideturkey.com, with much of the same information.

The InterMedia publishing company produces several useful reference books in foreign-language editions: guides to eating out in Istanbul, Ankara and İzmir, a step-by-step guide to Istanbul, and the indispensible *Almanac*, packed with vital political and economic statistics. Intended for visiting executives, it includes airlines, car hire, travel agents and consulates, as well as company addresses.

Time Out publishes a weekly listings magazine in Istanbul with a useful English-language supplement.

Books

It can be hard to find foreign-language (most commonly English, French and German) books outside Istanbul and Ankara, although many large hotel shops have a few, often uninspired, titles. You should also bear in mind that they will cost anything up to double their original price.

Dialling Codes

Country code
If dialling Turkey from abroad: 90

Regional codes
You don't dial the area code if calling the area you are in. If calling from abroad, drop the initial 0.

Adana	0322
Aksaray	0382
Ankara	0312
Antalya	0242
Bodrum/Marmaris	0252
Bursa	0224
Çanakkale	0226
Diyarbakır	0412
Edirne	0284
Erzurum	0442
Istanbul Asian side	0216
Istanbul European side	0212

(use these codes if calling from one side of the city to the other.)

İzmir	0232
Kars	0474
Kayseri	0352
Konya	0332
Kütahya	0274
Nevşehir	0384
Samsun	0362
Sinop	0368
Trabzon	0462
Van	0432
Yalova	0226
N. Cyprus	0392

International codes

Australia	61
Canada	1
Ireland	353
New Zealand	64
UK	44
USA	1

Dial 00 and then the country code, followed by the number.

See Further Reading on page 426 for a list of books on Turkey.

Internet
Turks have a passion for new technology, and are very keen on the Internet. Government offices, media, universities and even modest businesses have websites, and late at night the youth of Turkey log on and chat. Every large town is plastered with internet cafés *(see page 397 for listings).*

Postal Services

Post offices *(postane)* are marked by a yellow sign with the black letters PTT, and are usually open Mon–Sat 9am–5pm. Sirkeci Post Office in Istanbul is open daily 24

Useful Numbers

- Directory enquiries (Istanbul) **118**
- International operator **115**
- International directory enquiries **115**
- MCI Connect **00 8001 1177**
- Sprint **00 8001 4477**
- AT&T **00 8001 2277**

hours. Services at the larger PTTs include *poste restante*, foreign-exchange bureaux and metered phones.

For stamps only, the desk is open 8am–8pm; the telephone desk from 8am–midnight. There are also small PTT kiosks in tourist areas where you can get stamps, post letters and buy phonecards. Stamps are available only from PTT outlets.

PTT postboxes are yellow, marked PTT and *şehiriçi* (local), *yurtiçi* (domestic) and *yurtdışı* (international).

Always use airmail; surface mail is slow and unreliable, taking anything from five days to three weeks to reach the UK/US. Express post costs more, but is supposed to take no more than three days to arrive. If you are sending a parcel, the contents will be inspected, so don't seal it beforehand.

Telecommunications

TELEPHONES

Public phones
Most public phones use phonecards *(telefon kartı)* and can be found in the streets or grouped

in busy areas such as bus and railway stations and airports. Some post offices (PTTs) also have metered phones for which you pay after your call.

Phonecards can be bought from PTTS, newsstands and vendors near groups of phone booths. They come in different denominations from 30 to 180 units.

There are also credit-card phones at airports and in the lobbies of some five-star hotels in major cities. These are considerably cheaper than making calls from your room.

Useful national and international codes and operator services are posted in phone boxes. Instructions in card phone boxes are in English, French and German as well as Turkish and these days, the phones may well ask you which language you would prefer when you pick up the receiver.

Mobiles

Huge numbers of Turks have mobile phones and they are on them constantly.

If you have a GSM mobile that allows it (check your account), your phone will log on to the local network and you will be able to use it in almost any reasonably frequented part of Turkey. Making local mobile calls is very cheap; international calls, both in and out of Turkey, and incoming local calls (which will still have to be to your UK number) will be expensive. Visitors from the US will be unable to access the Turkish network on their usual cell-phones.

Emergency Numbers

Ambulance (public)   112
(*see below* for Instanbul services)
Police   155
Fire   110
Emergency   115
Turizm (Foreigners') Police
Istanbul, tel: (0212) 527 4503
Ankara, tel: (0312) 384 0606
Antalya, tel: (0242) 247 0336
Izmir, tel: (0232) 446 1454

TELEGRAMS AND FAX

Telegrams can be sent from any post office. The number of words and speed required determine the cost. There are three speeds: normal, *acele* (urgent) and *yıldırım* (flash). This can be done at PTTS or over the phone by dialling 141 (but you will probably encounter language difficulties).

Faxes can also be sent from many post offices, hotels and photocopy shops.

INTERNET

See websites, *page 357*, and Internet cafés, *page 397*.

Medical Treatment

Pharmacies

These should be your first port of call for treating minor ailments. There is a rota system whereby one pharmacist in every district stays open 24 hours for emergencies. This is referred to in Turkish as a *nöbetçi*, and the address will be noted in pharmacists' windows.

Most standard drugs are available in Turkey without a prescription. Although self-treatment is not recommended, it is easy to replace routine medication at any pharmacy *(eczane)* should it be necessary. It is a good idea to show the pharmacist the empty container, to be sure that you are being given the right drug. Remember that generic drugs can be marketed under different names.

Doctors and dentists

Though some doctors and dentists in the cities do speak English or German, and many have been trained abroad to a high standard, unless it is an emergency, it is better to wait until you return home for treatment. Most four- and five-star hotels have a doctor on call with some English and/or German in case of emergency.

Hospitals

There are a number of excellent private hospitals in the major

Emergency Hospitals

Ankara
● Bayındır Hospital, Söğütözü.
Tel: (0312) 287 9000.
● Çankaya Hospital, Kavaklıdere.
Tel: (0312) 426 1450.
● Baskent Hospital, Fevzi Cakmak Cad. 10 Sok. 45 Bahcelievler.
Tel: (0312) 212 6868.

Antalya
● Akdeniz University Faculty of Medicine, Kepez Mahallesi.
Tel: (0242) 227 4343.
● Antalya Private Hospital, Bayındır Mahallesi 325 Sokak 8.
Tel: (0242) 335 0000.

Bodrum
Özel Hastanesi
Mars Mabedi Caddesi, Çesmebasi Mevkii 22-43.
Tel: (0252) 313 6566.

Istanbul
● American Hospital, Güzelbahçe Sokak, Nisantaşı.
Tel: (0212) 311 2000.
● Florence Nightingale Hospital, Abidei Hürriyet Caddesi 290, Çaglayan, Şişli.
Tel: (0212) 224 4950.
● German Hospital, Sıraselviler Caddesi 119, Taksim.
Tel: (0212) 293 2150.
● International Hospital, Yesilyurt.
Tel: (0212) 663 3000.
● Med American, Piyale Paşa Bulvarı, Okmeydanı.
Tel: (0216) 478 2555.

İzmir
● American Hospital, Hilton Oteli 4, Kat.
Tel: (0232) 484 5360.
● Sağlık Hospital, 1399 Sokak 25, Alsancak.
Tel: (0232) 421 8620.

cities, but healthcare generally does not meet Western standards of nursing and aftercare, though some hospitals are better than others, and are fine in an emergency. The further you go

Foreign Exchange

Foreign currency is in great demand in Turkey so you won't have to look very hard for a place to change it.

Foreign Exchange Offices (Döviz) are usually much more efficient than banks, and offer better rates. They are plentiful and open Mon–Sat 8.30/9am to 7pm. No commission is charged for cash. By far the easiest solution however is to use an ATM of which there are hundreds, most accepting foreign cards, as long as you can remember your PIN.

from the major cities, the more limited medical facilities become.

It is also vital to note that hospitals work on a pay-as-you-go basis, requiring payment on the spot in advance of any required treatment, including scans and x-rays. This has been known to happen even in extreme emergencies. It is one very good reason to keep some cash and a credit card on you at all times.

Ambulances

Certain services operate independently; others are attached to particular hospitals. The average Turkish ambulance is little better than a taxi, and in a minor emergency a taxi can be the best and quickest way to get to hospital.

Istanbul, for example, is relatively well provided with ambulances, but so bad is the traffic during the morning and evening rush hours that many drivers stubbornly refuse to give way to the emergency services. The following are worth ringing, however:
● **Medline** is a private company that serves the American Hospital, Florence Nightingale and others, on both sides of the Bosphorus. Their ambulances have emergency equipment, and a doctor and paramedic on board. Call (0212) 280 3388 or the hospital concerned, which can call the ambulance for you.

● **The International Hospital** has well-equipped ambulances, inlcuding a boat that can navigate the Bosphorus (and beat the traffic) and a helicopter during daylight hours only. Tel: (0212) 663 3000.

Local Tourist Information Offices

Government-run tourist information offices, Turizm Danışma Burosu, are marked with a white "i". They are usually open Mon–Sat 9am–5pm, though the one at Istanbul Airport is open 24 hours a day, and in summer those in busy resorts may stay open into the evening.

Don't expect that much from them, however; there are a few outstanding offices, but in many, staff may not speak even rudimentary English. Some have useful lists of accommodation but may have no facilities to make bookings. In some cities local associations have set up their own rival facilities which can be a great improvement. For instance, the Alanya Hotels Association (ALTID) has regulated prices and standards, organised beach lifeguards and extra security, and staffs its office with English speakers.

Main tourist offices:
● Istanbul – Sultanahmet Square. Tel: (0212) 518 1802.
Also at the airport, station and ferry port.
● Alanya – Damlataş Caddesi 1. Tel: (0242) 513 1240.
● Ankara – Gazi Mustafa Kemal Bulvarı 121A. Tel: (0312) 231 5572.
● Antalya – Cumhuriyet Caddesi, Ozel İdare Altı 2. Tel: (0242) 241 1747.

Credit Cards Hotlines

The numbers to ring if your card is lost or stolen during your stay in Turkey are:
American Express Tel: (0212) 283 2201.
Diners, MasterCard, EuroCard and Visa Tel: (0212) 225 0080.

● Bodrum – Baris Meydanı. Tel: (0252) 316 1091.
● İzmir – Adeniz Mah. 1344. Tel: (0232) 421 3514.

Security & Crime

Turkey has an enviably low crime record. This reflects Turkish society: restricted access to guns, low incidence of drug use, respect for law and order, and most important of all, close-knit communities and enduring family ties. Foreigners and tourists are regarded as guests, so are very well treated; in normal circumstances you can expect the police to be polite and helpful.

Tourist areas are regularly patrolled by special Turizm or Foreigners' Police, who should do their best to help you and should speak some French, English, German or Arabic. For telephone numbers, see box on page 363.

Inevitably, there is still some crime, especially in urban areas blighted by poverty and unemployment. In tourist resorts, other foreigners are not above suspicion – never leave money or cameras in your room. Car crimes and break-ins are possible and purse-snatching and pickpocketing are on the increase in crowded places like the Grand or Covered Bazaar and Istiklal Caddesi in Istanbul. There have even been isolated instances of tourists being drugged and robbed.

So take the same precautions as you would at home – don't leave valuables or your bag visible in a car, use a handbag with a long strap slung diagonally over the shoulder and don't walk down dark streets on your own at night.

Make sure that your holiday and medical insurance covers you for both the European and Asian sides of Turkey.

Drugs

The film Midnight Express is always brought up in this context, much to the annoyance of the Turks. But although the script may have been exaggerated, heavy penalties are exacted on anyone found in possession of drugs. A foreigner on a narcotics charge can expect long-term imprisonment.

Military zones

These are normally clearly marked, often by a sign with a picture of an armed soldier. You should keep clear, and also avoid photographing anything with a military content.

Political security

The political violence associated with the PKK has calmed down in recent years and the southeast of Turkey is far safer for tourists than previously. However, the war in Iraq and the Western war on terrorism have stirred up strong feelings among some Turks and destabilised the future of the Kurds, so it is worth taking up-to-date advice before travelling in Kurdish areas.

Tourist crime

Remember that of the many millions of Westerners who flood into Turkey each year, not all are well behaved. The Turks take a very dim view of drunken tourists scaling the statues of Atatürk, or being anything other than respectful to their national icons, religion, women or football teams.

Etiquette

There are few don'ts in Turkey; there is little interference with foreigners who are regarded as a law unto themselves. Your visit is governed by the rules of hospitality that form a substantial part of the infrastructure of Turkish society, and which mean that you are truly regarded as a guest and (mostly) to be accorded the utmost help. This will show itself in the extent to which people will offer endless cups of tea, personal hospitality, invite you to their home, all of which can be gracefully and tactfully refused if you wish, without giving offence.

Feet are regarded as unclean – so don't put them on a table, or where someone might sit. Should you be invited into a Turkish home, remove your shoes.

On the beach

Beachwear is worn only on the beach, and topless sunbathing is frowned on, although all too many tourists strip off at the first patch of sand. At some family resorts you will still see women entering the water fully clothed.

In mosques

Non-Muslims should not enter a mosque during prayer time, and not at all on Friday, the holy day. The call to prayer from the minaret comes five times a day between dawn and nightfall.

Both men and women should be modestly dressed. For women this means a longish skirt or trousers, and covered shoulders. For men, shorts are not acceptable. Before entering remove your shoes. You can leave them outside, or you can carry them, or you may be given plastic shoe covers instead. Women may be asked to cover their heads, so you should always carry a scarf or hat. Off the beaten tourist track there may not be an attendant to supervise you, but do follow these guidelines to avoid giving offence.

Take care not to disturb, touch or walk in front of anyone who may be at prayer. The larger, more famous mosques will be open throughout the day from the first prayer to the last one at night. Smaller ones may only open at prayer times; you may have to find a caretaker (bekci) or wait for prayer time, and enter as the worshippers leave.

In Turkish baths

The traditional Turkish bath (hamam) has its own etiquette. The sexes are segregated, either in different parts of the bath or by different times or days. Some tourist hamams allow mixed bathing, but you will pay more.

Contrary to popular belief, the vast majority of hamams offer a relaxing and invigorating experience which is nothing to be afraid of. Modesty is the order of the day; both men and women should keep their underpants on and cover themselves with a wrap (pestemel).

The easiest way to enjoy a Turkish bath is to go with someone who has been before and knows the ropes; otherwise just watch your neighbours and copy them.

You don't need to have anything with you, but you can of course take along your own wrap, towels, washmitt and toiletries.

See also page 412 for a list of hamams throughout Turkey that may be worth a visit.

Turkey's toilets

You will probably find Turkish toilet facilities disconcerting. Arm yourself with a supply of paper (which goes in the bin, not the hole, as the drains can't cope with it); if possible use the more commonly available squat toilet.

Public lavatories in cities can be revolting; in rural places sometimes sparkling clean; those at motorway and roadside service stations,

Tipping

It is customary to tip a small amount to anyone who does you a small service: the hotel cleaner, porter, doorman who gets you a taxi and so on. Even in cinemas you give something to the person who shows you to your seat.

The only difficulty is arming yourself with plenty of small notes. For some inexplicable reason, change ("bozuk para") is always in short supply. At the time of writing, anything between

500,000–2,000,000TL (approx. 20–70 pence/US30 cents–$1 would be in order.

In restaurants, round the bill up by 10–15 percent; if service has been included, leave 5 percent on the table in cash for the waiter.

Taxis are the exception: you don't tip taxi drivers and they do not expect it, though you can round the fare up to the nearest suitable figure as change can be a problem.

acceptable. Special nappy-changing or baby rooms are very rare.

You will find clean Western-style facilities in the more upmarket hotels and restaurants, and in the swish new American-style shopping malls such as Akmerkez or Carrefour in Istanbul.

You will usually be charged somewhere between 250,000–500,000TL per visit in public facilities, so keep a supply of small notes available.

Women Travellers

Turkish attitudes towards women are liberal in cosmopolitan cities and tourist areas, but more restrictive in provincial towns.

Country women in rural regions cover their heads with scarves more as a means of protecting their hair from dust and dirt than for religious conservatism, although religious fundamentalism has prevailed among certain groups in recent years. In big cities you will see women wearing anything from a full black veil to smart Western-style dress.

Travelling alone
The major cities in Turkey and tourist areas are liberal and westernised, and are very safe compared with many other countries. Leers and suggestions may be common, but physical attacks are rare. Women visitors should not be afraid to travel alone,

or to go out in the evening, though provocative dress may create problems, and at night you might feel more relaxed with a companion.

In certain situations, however, Turkish culture does segregate the sexes. On buses you will not be permitted to sit next to a male stranger. Restaurants often have a designated *aile salonu* (family room), and sometimes prefer a lone woman to sit there.

No woman, whether on her own or with a male partner, is welcome at a traditional coffee or tea room *(kahvehane or çayhane)* – they are strictly male preserves.

Harassment
You should expect Turkish men to chat you up, often in an outrageously flamboyant fashion, but you can reduce harassment to a minimum by dressing respectably and looking as if you know where you are going. Turkish women get some degree of harassment, too, but they cope by sticking together and giving a firm brush-off.

If you are groped by a stranger, speak up loudly; the shame will usually be enough to fend him off and everyone nearby will make it a point of honour to rush to your defence.

What to wear
As far as dress goes, in the big cities you will see young Turkish girls wearing whatever is the current

fashion, whether shorts, miniskirts or Lycra. Cover up your swimming costume or bikini when you leave the beach.

Travelling with Children

Turkey has very few obvious facilities for children, but the Turks adore babies and children, and will be delighted you have brought yours with you. They will undoubtedly make a huge fuss of them.

City streets, most especially in Istanbul, are far from buggy-friendly, however; high kerbstones and steep and uneven surfaces make them almost impossible to push. Buses are often crowded and their entrances are high and awkward. Bring a rucksack-style baby carrier or papoose; you will quickly realise why most Turkish babies are simply carried in their parents' arms.

Discounts
In Turkey child discounts are different from elsewhere: normally you pay for children over seven years old on public transport, but you may not pay at all for up to 12s at museums. It seems often to be at the whim of the attendant. Hotels will offer anything from a third to 50 percent off both room rates and set-meal charges.

Accommodation
Hotels will almost always put up extra beds if there is space in your room. Most places have family rooms, sometimes for as many as six, and even *pansiyons* may have small apartments/suites with a mini-kitchen included at no extra cost. You need to ask in advance if you need a cot.

Food
There are plenty of plain dishes in Turkish cooking that Western children will find acceptable, without having to resort to fast food, although pizzas, burgers and chips can be found easily.

Restaurants rarely offer meals specifically for children, but they will do their best to find something for

Istanbul Parks and Playgrounds

There are several good parks in Istanbul: at Emirgan and Yıldız, for example. Park Orman at Maslak has a swimming pool among other family facilities. Smaller parks around town have play equipment, but it is usually battered and occasionally downright dangerous.

Tatilya, "The Republic of Fun", Beylikdüzü, 18 km (11 miles) west of the airport on the E5 motorway out of the city, is Istanbul's only theme park. It is fairly small, but clean and well run, with safe rides

for various age groups, plus various eateries and shops all under a glass bubble.

Darica Bird Paradise and Botanical Garden, Darica, is 45 km (28 miles) from Istanbul off the E5 going east. It has 70 hectares (170 acres) of gardens and zoo, with a surprising range of species including zebras, kangaroos, penguins and exotic birds. The zoo is acceptably well kept, and there is also an excellent play area with good equipment, and several cafés.

them to eat, even if you can't see anything obvious on the menu. If you would like something plain, ask for *çok sade*, very plain, or *acısız*, not peppery hot. *Çocuklar için* means "for the children".

Dishes children may like include grilled *köfte* (meatballs), and any grilled meat, lamb or chicken *şiş kebabs*, grilled steak or chicken *(tavuk or piliç ızgara)*; all kinds of Turkish bread; *sade pilav* (rice); and *pide* (Turkish pizza) – the one topped with goat may not appeal to everyone. Chips are *patates tava*.

For dessert, Turkish rice pudding *(sütlaç)* is excellent, or you can always ask for a plate of sliced fresh fruit (fruit should always be peeled, to be on the safe side), or ice cream.

Babies
Breastfeeding mothers need not feel shy, but as Turks are modest in public, you should be discreet. Wear something loose, or use a large scarf or beach wrap to screen yourself and your baby – this is what rural Turkish women do, and it will come in useful to protect you from hot sun.

Ready-made babyfood can only be found in Western-style supermarkets, which are thin on the ground, and formula is expensive, so you may prefer to bring your own supplies. Restaurants will be happy to heat milk for you.

What to bring
You will need plenty of good sunblock, hats and long light clothes for children in summer. July and August will be too hot in southern resorts for children unused to such heat and it can be difficult to get them to sleep.

In case of tummy upsets, bring prepacked sachets of rehydration salts such as Dioralyte; babies can take this from a bottle. Disposable nappies and other baby gear such as Johnson's toiletries are readily available, if expensive for imported brands; there are even branches of Mothercare and BHS in Istanbul and Ankara.

Business Travellers

Visitors on business will often be guests of a Turkish company, and the visit will be governed by the rules of hospitality. You can expect to be whisked from place to place by chauffeured car and thoroughly entertained after hours. Although your hosts may speak good English or German, you may prefer to engage an interpreter.

The top hotels, certainly in the main cities, are geared to business travellers and will be able to provide meeting rooms, office and conference facilities, and be relied on to receive and pass on faxes and telephone messages in English.

Translation/Business services
Istanbul
Bayza Diler.
Tel: (0212) 244 0793.
Çitlembik.
Tel: (0212) 292 3032.
Ankara
Boğaziçi Business Services.
Tel: (0312) 468 3648.

SIGHTSEEING

Very little in Turkey is specifically devised with children in mind, but there are one or two attractions intended for them. Holiday villages, with facilities geared for families, may still have only minimal play equipment. The foreign travel companies, such as Mark Warner and Club Mediterranée, will have good facilities as part of their all-inclusive packages, with childcare for younger children and entertainment for older ones.

Depending on their age and interests, children should enjoy some of the sightseeing. Palaces can be difficult, as you may have to join a guided tour (even if your children like that sort of thing, the guide's English is often difficult to understand), but scrambling around ancient ruins is usually good fun. In the cities, if you get desperate, you can always head for one of the shopping malls where you will find a children's play area, clean lavatories and fast food.

Istanbul
Take a ferry: one of the best things to do with children in Istanbul is to travel anywhere in the city by water, since there is so much to see.

Topkapı Palace is usually a hit with children. There is plenty of space for them to run around, and parents could take turns to join the Harem tour which can be claustrophobic, although older children might be fascinated. The carriages, costumes, miniature paintings and fabulous treasury are all of interest to children.

The Archaeological Museum has a children's section (though the captions are in Turkish), and a mock-up of the Trojan Horse to climb on.

The Rahmi Koç Museum, Hasköy, is a museum of transport and industrial technology, brilliantly converted from an anchor-and-chain factory. There are a number of working models of steam locomotives, engines and mechanical toys with buttons to press to make them work.

Naval Museum, Beşiktaş. Although most of the exhibit here, covering Turkey's naval history, is a bit dry, there are some model warships of various ages, a section on diving, and the fabulous collection of Ottoman *caiques* (the imperial water-transport, rowing galleys with dozens of oars).

Yerebatan Cistern, Sultanahmet. Fantastic, enormous, atmospheric underground water tank from the Byzantine era. Again, children can run around on the wooden walkways among the gigantic marble pillars. There are also fish to spot swimming in the water.

Military Museum, Harbiye. Children may like the sultans' campaign tents on display here,

Privacy is Sacrosanct

Family life in Islam is very private, so public displays of affection, even hand-holding between husband and wife, is rarely seen in the streets outside the main cities. To avoid causing offence, it is wise to honour these traditions.

and the ferocious and beautifully decorated curved daggers. The museum is also the venue for performances by the Mehter, the former janissary, Band.

Rumeli Hisarı. The Castle at Rumeli Hisar, a little way up the Bosphorus, is a good place for a scramble around.

Cappadocia

With its incredible lunar landscape, underground cities to explore, and hundreds of caves and rock-cut churches, plus the possibility of pony trekking and seeing pottery made at Avanos, Cappadocia is packed with interest for young children, and they usually enjoy days spent here enormously.

The coast

There are sand, swimming pools, sea and watersports here. Ancient cities are usually good value as there are plenty of things to climb on, space to run around and, if the parents have done some homework, some cracking stories about what went on there.

Bodrum

The castle of St Peter, home to the Museum of Underwater Archaeology in Bodrum, is a terrific place for kids. It is full of the mysteries of pirates, Crusaders, naval battles and wrecks, and even a restored torture chamber.

Gay Travellers

Turkish attitudes to gays, or to overtly gay behaviour, are contradictory. On the one hand, they adulate their own amazingly exhuberant transvestite or transsexual singers; on the other, they can be publicly intolerant of respectable middle-aged gay couples.

Homosexual acts between adults over 18 are legal, and in Istanbul and coastal resorts such as Alanya, you'll find greater tolerance and even some gay bars and discos. Be circumspect in public and you shouldn't have any problems.

Travellers with Disabilities

Turkey has very few facilities of any kind for the disabled. Even manoeuvring a wheelchair in Istanbul, for instance, is a strenuous challenge. There are next to no disabled toilet facilities, and mosques will usually not allow wheelchairs in. However, as with everything in Turkey, people are exceptionally friendly, kind and helpful, and will do their best to assist you in getting into a museum or building.

The powers that be are aware that they have to do something about this situation, so things may improve. There are now a very few low-level telephone booths, and buses with wheelchair access. The Turkish Tourist Office in London issues a guide to facilities for the disabled in Turkey, and there is a Turkish Association for the Disabled in Istanbul; tel: (0212) 521 4912.

For more detailed information, it is worth contacting your country's own disabled assocation before you travel:

UK: RADAR (Royal Association for Disability and Rehabilitation) 12 City Forum, 250 City Road, London EC1V 8AF. tel: (020) 7250 3222; fax: (020) 7250 0212; www.careline.org.uk.

US: SATH (Society for Accessible Travel and Hospitality) 347 Fifth Avenue, Suite 610 New York NY 10016. tel: (212) 447 7284; fax: (212) 725 8253; www.sath.org.

Religious Services

Turkey is officially a secular state, although 99 percent of the population are Muslim. There are significant Jewish, Armenian and Greek Orthodox minorities, but these remain concentrated in Istanbul and İzmir.

However, due to its long history of mixed races and cultures, Turkey has hundreds of non-Muslim places of worship. Most are now places of historical interest but Istanbul, Ankara and İzmir, still have some functioning churches and synagogues.

Attending a service can be a way of meeting people who live and work in the place you are visiting; and of experiencing the building in its intended setting.

ANKARA

Anglican

St Nicholas,
Şehit Ersan Caddesi, Çankaya.
Tel: (0312) 468 6230 ext. 285.
In the grounds of the British Embassy. Services: Sunday 9.45am; Wednesday 7pm; Thursday 7.45am.

Baptist

Ankara Baptist Church International,
Best Hotel, Atatürk Bulvarı 195, Kavaklidere.
Tel: (0312) 468 0880.
Services: Sunday 10am, Wednesday 7pm.

Catholic

Old French Embassy Chapel,
Kardeşler Sokak 15, Ulus.
Tel: (0312) 311 0118.
Sunday and Holy Days only.
Vatican Embassy Church,
2 Sokak 55, Çukurca Mahallesi, Çankaya.
Tel: (0312) 438 5417.
Services: Sunday 10am (English), 11am (French). Holy days 7pm.

Jewish

Jewish Synagogue of Ankara,
Birlik Sokak 8, Samanpazarı.
Tel: (0312) 311 6200.

ISTANBUL

Protestant
Christ Church (Anglican),
Serdarı Ekrem Sokak 82, Tünel,
Beyoğlu (behind the Swedish
Consulate, off Istiklal Caddesi).
Tel: (0212) 251 5616.
Built by subscription in the
1860s to commemorate those who
died in the Crimean War, and
formerly known as the Crimean
Memorial Church, the church was
designed by famous Victorian
architect C.E. Street and should be
visited by fans of High Victorian and
colonial church architecture. This
little corner of Gothic splendour
offers a liberal, international
atmosphere. Matins 9am; evensong
6pm daily; sung Eucharist 10am on
Sunday.
Dutch Union Church of Istanbul,
Postacılar Sokak Beyoğlu.
Tel: (0212) 244 5212.
Friendly New Zealand pastor and his
wife welcome all comers. Sunday
service at 11am.
St Helena's Chapel,
British Consulate, Galatasaray.
Tel: (0212) 244 4228.
The Anglican chaplaincy in Istanbul.
Eucharist 12.30pm, first
Wednesday of the month (except
July and August).

Catholic
St Anthony of Padua,
Istiklal Caddesi Galatasaray-
Beyoğlu.
Tel: (0212) 244 0935.
One of the city's best-known
functioning Catholic churches.
St Louis des Français,
Postacılar Sokak 11, Beyoğlu.
Tel: (0212) 244 1075.

Greek Orthodox
Aya Triada,
Meşelik Sokak 11/1, Taksim.
Tel: (0212) 244 1358.
St Stephen of the Bulgars,
Fener.
Tel: (0212) 525 9193.
The local patriarchate, this
extraordinary church is in fact a
19th-century prefab, that was
constructed in Vienna and delivered
here in flatpacks.

Armenian
Armenian Patriarchate,
Şarapnel Sokak 20, Kumkapı.
Tel: (0212) 517 0970.
Üç Horon,
Balık Pazarı (fish market), Beyoğlu.
Tel: (0212) 244 1382.

Jewish
The majority of the Jewish
population in Turkey are Sephardic,
and can trace their roots back to
the expulsion of Jews from Spain
during the Inquisition and their
welcome by the Ottoman Empire.
However, over the years the
community has dwindled and
services are irregular, as well as
subject to intense security. Thus it
might be a good idea to phone in
advance and let them know you're
coming.
Ashkenazy Synagogue,
Yüksek Kaldırım 37, Karaköy.
Tel: (0212) 244 2975.
Chief Rabbinate,
Yemenici Sokak 23 Tünel/Beyoğlu.
Tel: (0212) 244 8794.
Neve Shalom Synagogue,
Büyük Hendek Caddesi 67, Beyoğlu.
Tel: (0212) 244 1576.

İZMIR

Anglican
St John's,
Talatpaşa Bulvarı, Alsancak.
Tel: (0232) 463 6608.

Catholic
Notre Dame de St Roserie,
1481 Sokak, Alsancak.
Tel: (0232) 421 6666.
Santa Maria,
Halit Ziya Bulvarı 67.
Tel: (0232) 484 8632.
St Polycarpe,
Gaziosmanpaşa Bulvarı 18 (across
from Büyük Efes Hotel).
Tel: (0232) 484 8436.
The oldest church in the city,
dedicated to a mid-1st-century saint
crucified in İzmir.

Protestant
St Mary Magdelena,
Hürriyet Caddesi 18, Bornova.
Tel: (0232) 388 0915.

Orthodox
Aya Fotini,
1374 Sokak 24, Alsancak.
Tel: (0232) 421 6992.

Jewish
Bet Israel,
Mithatpaşa Caddesi 265, Karatas.
Tel: (0232) 425 1628.
Sinyora İveret Synagogue,
927 Sokak 7, Mezarlıkbaşı.
Shaar Ashamayam,
1390 Sokak 4, Alsancak.
Tel: (0232) 425 1083.

Getting Around

By Air

There is a good network of reasonably priced domestic flights serviced by Turkish Airlines (THY; *see page 359* for details). You need to be flexible about timing if booking at short notice on a popular connection at a busy time (for example, to the Aegean and Mediterranean airports over a public holiday). Early-morning and evening flights between Ankara and Istanbul also fill up quickly.

It is easy to book through any local travel agent. The booking can be made on the computer, and the ticket picked up and paid for on the day of flying at the airport.

Istanbul's international airport, Atatürk Airport, at Yeşilköy to the west of the city centre, is the hub of the network, and has undergone major renovation, including a new passenger terminal and metro connection, to help meet the ever-increasing passenger traffic. THY generally enjoys a reasonable reputation for punctuality, as well as for its on-flight services.

You can fly direct to the following cities from Istanbul: Adana, Ankara, Antalya, Bodrum, Bursa, Dalaman, Denizli, Diyarbakır, Erzurum, Gaziantep, İzmir, Kayseri, Konya, Malatya, Samsun, Trabzon, and Van. For many of the Anatolian destinations, it is necessary to fly via Ankara. Security is strict and you will be asked to point out your baggage before it is transferred to the plane.

Hiring small jets and helicopters for personal charter is a new and booming business in Turkey.

By Bus

Turkey has excellent bus services, both inter- and intra-cities. Not surprisingly, this is the preferred method of long-distance travel since it is cheap, reliable and generally comfortable. For instance, you can leave Ankara at 10pm and be at the south coast by 8am the following morning.

Competition between companies is intense; the best are more expensive and have comfortable, modern buses with proper air-conditioning, clean toilets and refreshments, as well as the traditional libations of lemon cologne. They may well also have lace curtains, an overly efficient sound system blaring out Turkish pop, and videos – not always appreciated when you are hurtling around hairpin bends.

Tickets are easy to obtain; in fact when you approach the ticket offices (which are often next door to one another), touts may pressure you to travel with their company, so choose with care. Places are reserved, and unaccompanied women will not be allowed to sit next to a man they do not know. All companies now have no-smoking zones, or non-smoking buses, but a fog of black tobacco smoke can still be a problem.

There is no comprehensive national or local timetable, so you have to work out the best route and departure time for yourself. Several companies will run services on each route.

Most long-distance buses depart from the main bus station *(otogar)* in each town, and there will be ticket offices nearby and in the

Dolmuş

An economical method of travelling around a city or to a neighbouring town is by *dolmuş* (literally "full", sharing the same root as the Turkish word for the country's stuffed vegetables). A kind of shared taxi, usually a minibus, the *dolmuş* travels along a fixed route for a fixed fare, paid to the driver. At the start of the route, it may not set off until it is full, which can entail a wait. After that, passengers can get on and off whenever they want.

Private Charter

The following are private plane charter companies based in Istanbul:
● Bon Air, Yeşilköy. Tel: (0212) 663 1829.
● Çelebi Air Service, Yeşilköy. Tel: (0212) 663 8700.
● General Aviation Co., Yeşilköy. Tel: (0212) 541 2917.
● Türk Hava Kurumu, Yeşilköy. Tel: (0212) 591 7373.

city/town centre. There will usually be a minibus service to take you from out-of-town bus terminals to the centre. The majority of long-haul journeys take place at night.

Istanbul has two main bus stations: at Esenler, Bayrampasa, northwest of the city, tel: (0212) 658 0036, for southwest Turkey, European and international services; and Harem, on the Asian side tel: (0216) 333 3763, for services to eastern Turkey.

By Train

Major cities and many places between are connected by the Turkish State Railways (TCDD), but the network is limited and fans out from Istanbul, so cross-country connections are virtually non-existent. For instance, there is no coastal railway on either the Aegean or Mediterranean shores.

Although cheap (a first-class ticket from Ankara to Istanbul costs about the equivalent of US$15), travel can be very slow and not always comfortable. As well as having a far more extensive network, buses are generally faster, cheaper and more comfortable.

The best connections are between Istanbul, Ankara and İzmir. The *Mavi Tren* (Blue Train) or *Ekspres* (Express) services reach their destinations in times comparable to going with one of the more upmarket bus companies. The *Mavi Tren* between Istanbul and Ankara leaves Istanbul's Haydarpaşa Station at 11.50pm, and reaches Ankara at 8am the following morning; it has a dining car, couchettes and sleepers. This is an entertaining way to travel if you have the time.

Purchase tickets and reserve seats or sleepers in advance, preferably from the station at which your journey will begin. You should be able to book a ticket to and from anywhere in Turkey in Istanbul, Ankara or İzmir, where the system has been computerised, but it can prove difficult. Sleepers get booked up, especially over public holidays. Choose between a *küşetli* (pull-down couchette-style compartment with six sharing, pillows provided but no bedding); *ortülü küşetli* (four bunks, bedding provided); or *yataklı* (first class, with two or three beds, linen included). The following trips may also be of interest:

● **The Sleeper Express** to Pamukkale (famous for stalactites and hot springs), which departs from Istanbul's Haydarpaşa Station daily at 5.30pm, arriving at 8am.
● **The Fatih Express**, which leaves for Ankara from Haydarpaşa at 10.30am and takes about eight hours, allowing a panoramic view of the Bolu Mountains and the Anatolian Plain.

Reservations and Enquiries
Istanbul
Haydarpaşa Station (Asian side):
Tel: (0216) 336 0475/2063 information; (0216) 348 8020 reservations.

Sirkeci Station (European side):
Tel: (0212) 527 0050 information; (0212) 520 6575 reservations (international trains only).
İzmir
Alsancak Station:
Tel: (0232) 464 7795.
Basmane Station:
Tel: (0232) 458 3131; (0232) 484 5353 reservations .
Ankara
Ankara Station:
Tel: (0312) 311 0620 operator; (0312) 311 4994 reservations.

City Transport

Buses
City buses run by the municipality have the letters IETT on the side. They are red and white with a blue stripe on the side and follow fixed routes. Buy tickets in advance either from one of the many bus-ticket booths or from shops, kiosks

Major Inter-city Bus Companies

Kamil Koç (Istanbul, western and southern destinations, and Ankara):
www.kamilkoc.com.tr
National call centre: (0800) 293 1115.
Istanbul
Tel: (0212) 658 2000.
Ankara
Tel: (0312) 224 1700.
Bursa
Tel: (0224) 261 5000.
İzmir
Tel: (0232) 472 0088.
Antalya
Tel: (0242) 331 1170.

Metro Turizm (Istanbul to destinations in southern and western Turkey):
www.metro.com.tr
Istanbul
Tel: (0212) 658 3232.

Pamukkale (Istanbul, western and southern destinations):
Istanbul, Taksim
Tel: (0212) 249 2791.
Istanbul, Sirkeci
Tel: (0212) 527 1280.
Istanbul, Esenler

Tel: (0212) 658 2222.
Ankara (terminal)
Tel: (0312) 224 1273.
Ankara Kızılay
Tel: (0312) 435 6611.
Antalya
Tel: (0242) 331 1020.
İzmir, Basmane
Tel: (0232) 445 5566.
Alanya
Tel: (0242) 513 3606.

Ulusoy (Istanbul, Ankara, Black Sea region, İzmir and the Aegean, Antalya and the Mediterranean, plus international destinations):
www.ulusoy.com.tr
National call centre: (0212) 658 3000.
Istanbul, Ulusoy Turizm head office
Tel: (0212) 658 0270.
Istanbul, Taksim
Tel: (0212) 249 4373.
Istanbul, Kadıköy
Tel: (0216) 336 4538.
Istanbul, Merter
Tel: (0212) 504 8039.
Ankara, Söğütözü
Tel: (0312) 286 5330.
Ankara, Kızılay

Tel: (0312) 419 4080.
İzmir
Tel: (0232) 441 0607.
Antalya
Tel: (0242) 242 1303.
Alanya
Tel: (0242) 512 2868.

Varan (Istanbul, Ankara, western and southern destinations, international):
www.varan.com.tr
National call centre: (0212) 251 7474.
Istanbul, Bahçelievler
Tel: (0212) 551 5000.
Istanbul, Taksim
Tel: (0212) 251 7474.
Istanbul, Kadıköy
Tel: (0216) 336 9610.
Ankara, Kızılay
Tel: (0312) 417 2525.
Ankara, Söğütözü
Tel: (0312) 287 1212.
İzmir
Tel: (0232) 489 1917.
Antalya
Tel: (0242) 343 1392.
Bodrum
Tel: (0252) 316 7849.

and street sellers near bus stops. They currently cost the equivalent of about £0.70/$1 each. *Tam bilet* means full, i.e. a normal adult ticket. Drop your ticket into a small box as you board the bus (at the front). Some longer urban journeys require more than one ticket.

A new system has been introduced, using the *Akbil* or "intelligent ticket", which uses an electronic token on to which fares can be loaded. You buy a certain number of journeys, and put your token into the special machine at the front of the bus, where the fare is deducted. The token can easily be recharged. Look for the *Akbil* sign at ticket booths.

Bus fares are cheap but journeys can be slow, and it is advisable not to travel during rush hours as buses get extremely crowded.

In Istanbul there are also, confusingly, similar but older-looking orange and cream full-sized private buses *(Özel Halk Ötöbüsü)*. These are, in fact, retired municipality buses, and on them you pay the driver's attendant who sits just inside at the front ready to take your money. The fare is the same as on the public buses.

There are also private minibuses, usually white or pale blue, which are faster. On these you pay a fare to the driver or his assistant, the fare being dependent on your destination. The drivers of these buses go fast and furiously, but you can stop them to get on or off anywhere.

All buses have a board in the front window and at the side listing the main destinations on the route. There are maps of the network at bus-stop shelters.

Metro

Ankara, Istanbul and İzmir all now have efficient, if limited, metro systems. Istanbul's runs from Taksim Square, in front of the Marmara Hotel, to the shopping and business districts of Gayrettepe and Levent 4 and down to the Tünel. There is an overground tram beginning at the Eminönü ferry docks, passing through the main tourist centres before branching off to the intercity bus garages and out to the airport.

A "nostalgic" tram runs up Istiklal Caddeşi between Tünel and Taksim every 20 minutes, while the tiny "tünel" underground saves commuters the steep walk up the hill from the Karaköy ferry docks. For metro and tram information, tel: (0212) 568 9970.

Taxis

Taxis *(taksi)* are bright yellow with a light on top. They are reasonably priced and plentiful. In the cities and big towns, it is often unnecessary to look for one; they will find you, signalling by slowing to a crawl alongside you or hooting. You should check the meter is switched on (one red light on the meter for day rate and two for evening) – it almost invariably will be, but it is worth checking.

Sadly, there are inevitably drivers who do their best to multiply the fare by driving round in circles or simply saying that the meter broke; try and check roughly how much it should be before getting in. There are also a very few dishonest drivers, who generally operate from the airport and in the old area of Istanbul. Their trick is to take advantage of visitors' confusion with Turkish currency and numbers; it is difficult to argue in Turkish that you are sure that you handed over a five-million lira note when the taxi driver says it was 500,000. Most will try their hardest to help you, though, even if they speak little or no English.

It helps to have your destination written down in case of difficulties in comprehension, and also because your driver may also be new to the area. State the area location first e.g. Sultanahmet, and go into detail later. When your driver gets close to his destination, he will ask for directions. If crossing the Bosphorus in Istanbul, the bridge toll will be added to your fare.

Most taxis operate independently around a local base, which may be no more than a phone nailed to a telegraph pole. There are few radio-controlled networks. Hotels and restaurants will always be able to find you a taxi.

Tours For long distances or sightseeing tours with waiting time built in, prices can be negotiated.

Blue Cruises by *Gulet*

A Blue Cruise *(Mavi Yolculuk)* is a delightful way to visit the coastal sights of the southwestern shores of Turkey – sailing on a traditional wooden schooner, or *gulet*, at a leisurely place, stopping to swim or sightsee at places of interest on the way. This can be the best way to visit the classical sites, many of which were originally only accessible by sea.

The boats are fully crewed, and usually very comfortable, with every need catered for. You can either book as a group, taking over a whole boat (they vary in size and number of berths); or individually, in which case you will not be able to choose your travelling companions. Some tour companies offer holiday tours with knowledgeable guides on board.

Cruises start from many different ports, large and small, on the Aegean and Lycian coasts; you can more or less choose where you would like to begin, depending on your arrival point.

July and August are the most expensive months and very popular, but it can be too hot, especially for ruin-tramping on shore. Spring is quieter, but the sea can be cold. Aficionados enjoy September or even October, when the crowds have gone but the sea is still warm for swimming.

Blue Cruises are bookable locally, or through your travel agent. *See also pages 359–60.*

Water Transport

Ferries

Car and passenger ferries sail between the Turkish ports of İzmir, Çeşme (near İzmir), Kuşadası,

Bodrum, Ayvalık, Marmaris and the Greek islands of Rhodes, Kos, Samos, Chios and Lesbos. The timetable and companies operating on these routes vary considerably each year. For details and ticket reservations, contact travel agencies.

Turkish Maritime Lines
Turkish Maritime Lines, or TML, operates an all-year-round service between Istanbul and İzmir, departing on Friday at 3pm and arriving the next morning; and returning on Sunday at noon, arriving in Istanbul the following morning.

TML also serves the ports of the Black Sea region from May to October. Departure from Istanbul is on Monday at 2.30pm, with stops at Zonguldak, Sinop and Samsun on Tuesday, and Giresun, Trabzon and Rize on Wednesday. The return is on Thursday with stops at Ordu, Samsun and Sinop, arriving back in Istanbul on Friday at 1.30pm.

For more information, contact TML:
Istanbul
Tel: (0212) 244 0207 information; (0212) 249 9222 reservations.
İzmir
Tel: (0232) 464 8864.
Antalya
Tel: (0242) 241 2630/7770.

Sea of Marmara ferries
Around the Sea of Marmara, car and passenger ferries cross between Darica and Kartal on the northern shore, east of Istanbul, and Yalova on the southeastern shore; these save driving on a journey south, and faster sea buses between Yenikapı to the west of Istanbul, Yalova and Bandırma, on the route to İzmir and the Aegean. There are also ferry links between Eceabat on the Gallipoli peninsula and Çanakkale, and between Bandırma and the Marmara islands. Timetables for these services can be found at any of the seabus or ferry terminals in Istanbul.

For ferries to Italy, see page 358.

Istanbul boat services
Divided by the Bosphorus and the Golden Horn, Istanbul has a busy network of large steamers, small

Private Cruise Boats
The following companies offer luxury cruises for small groups:
Halas M/S
Tel: (0212) 287 1014
Fax: (0212) 225 1957
www.iliadatourism.com
The *Halas* is a luxurious yacht sleeping 28. Often used by the British Royal Family, it operates in the bay of Fethiye from the end of June until the end of October, and can be chartered for the rest of the year.
Hatsail Tourism & Yachting Inc.
Maçka.
Tel: (0212) 241 6250.
www.hatsail.com
Bosphorus cruises for groups or executive meetings with lunch/dinner and cocktails, plus yacht cruises on the Aegean and Mediterranean seas.
Bitez Tour
Bodrum.
Tel: (0252) 394 3732.
Fax: (0252) 394 3550.
E-mail: aegean98@turk.net
www.holidaybank.co.uk/bitezyachting
Yachting and sailing holidays around the Bodrum Peninsula.

water buses that operate like *dolmuş*, catamarans, hydrofoils, seabuses and water taxis. Crossing the water is an essential part of a visit to the city.

From the main jetties at Beşiktaş or Eminönü, on the European side, you can catch a ferry to Kadıköy or Üsküdar on the Asian side. You buy a *jeton* at the *gişe* and drop it in the slot at the entrance to the jetty *(iskele)*. Each jetty serves one destination which is prominently displayed.

The privately operated *dolmuş* water buses, called "*motors*", cross at certain points, notably between Vskidar and Beşkitaş, mopping up commuter traffic at rush hour, and running until 1am when the state ferries have long closed. You pay on board. Water taxis can be hired privately near the Galata Bridge to go up the Golden Horn.

The hydrofoils serving the outer suburbs are more expensive; the timetable is arranged to suit commuters, so most trips are in the morning and evening, but they can whisk you to the Prince's Islands in 30 minutes.

Bosphorus cruises, tel: (0212) 522 0045, can be a lovely way to view the elegant waterside mansions or *yalı* lining the banks of this channel separating Europe from Asia. Public ferries leave three times daily in summer and twice daily in winter (except Sunday) from the Eminönü jetty and go all the way to Anadolu Kavağı, where a lunch break is given before the return journey (*see also page 135*).

Also from Eminönü, ferries leave at frequent intervals for the Prince's Islands or Adalar, off the Asian shore in the Sea of Marmara. The journey takes an hour and stops at all the islands before terminating at Büyükada, the largest island.

Printed timetable booklets covering the Istanbul water-transport system are available at the ticket windows of the jetties, but they do sell out quickly. The seabuses *(Deniz Otobüsleri)* have their own separate jetties and timetable.

Fast catamaran seabuses offer services from Kabataş and Bostancı to Bakırköy, Yenikapı, Kadıköy, Yalova and the Prince's Islands. For information, call (0216) 410 6633/251 6144.

Driving
Driving in Turkey can be alarming for newcomers. However, if you keep calm and drive cautiously you will be perfectly safe. The condition of the roads is usually reasonable although if you can avoid driving at night, you would do well to do so. The roads are not well lit, nor well-enough signposted, and hazards include unlit trucks and tractors, horses and carts, and even flocks of sheep.

Road conditions
The road network is extensive, with new toll-motorways completed and

Car Hire Companies

In the UK
Avis, tel: (0870) 606 0100.
Budget, tel: (0870) 156 56 56.
Europcar, tel: (0870) 607 5000.
Hertz, tel: (0870) 599 6699.

In the US
Avis, tel: (1-800) 230 4898.
Budget, tel: (1-800) 527 0700.
Europcar (Dollar), tel: (1-877) 940 6900.
Hertz, tel: (1-800) 654 3131.

In Turkey
Avis
www.avis.com
Downtown Istanbul
Taksim (at the Hilton Hotel).
Tel: (0212) 246 5256.
Istanbul Airport
Tel: (0212) 662 0852.
Downtown Ankara
Iel: (0312) 467 2313.
Ankara Airport
Tel: (0312) 398 0315.
İzmir Airport
Tel: (0232) 274 2174.
Antalya Airport
Tel: (0242) 330 3073.

Other Avis offices in Bursaand Samsun.

Budget
www.budget.com
Downtown Istanbul
Tel: (0212) 253 9200.
Istanbul Airport
Tel: (0212) 663 0858.
Downtown Ankara
Tel: (0312) 417 5952.
Ankara Airport
Tel: (0312) 398 0372.
İzmir Airport
Tel: (0232) 274 2203.
Downtown Antalya
Tel: (0242) 322 7686.
Antalya Airport
Tel: (0242) 330 3079.
Bodrum
Tel: (0252) 316 7382.

Europcar
www.europcar.com
Downtown Istanbul
Tel: (0212) 233 7101.

Istanbul Airport
Tel: (0212) 663 0807.
Ankara Airport
Tel: (0312) 398 0503.
İzmir Airport
Tel/fax: (0232) 274 2163.
Antalya Airport
Tel/fax: (0242) 330 3088.
Bursa
Tel: (0224) 236 5133.

Hertz
www.hertz.com
Downtown Istanbul
Tel: (0212) 233 7101.
Istanbul Airport
Tel: (0212) 663 0807.
Ankara Airport
Tel: (0312) 468 1029.
İzmir Airport
Tel: (0232) 274 2193.
Antalya Airport
Tel: (0242) 330 3030.

Other Hertz offices at Adana, Alanya, Bodrum, Dalaman, Kuşadası, Marmaris and Side.

Thrifty-Decar
www.decar.com.tr
Downtown Istanbul
Tel: (0212) 274 7323.
Istanbul Airport
Tel: (0212) 465 4525.
Ankara
Tel: (0312) 426 9737.
İzmir Airport
Tel: (0232) 274 1779.

Other Thrifty-Decar offices in Kapadokya, Kuşadası, Marmaris, Adana, Bodrum, Kemer, Belek, Trabzon and Erzurum.

Sixt Rent a Car
www.sixt.com.tr
Istanbul (Üsküdar)
Tel: (0216) 318 9040.
Istanbul Airport
Tel: (0212) 663 2587.

Other Sixt offices in Ankara, İzmir, Gaziantep, Antalya, Side, Alanya, Belek, Fethiye, Bodrum, Dalaman, Marmaris, Mersin, Kayseri and Konya.

under construction. Otherwise, there are few dual carriageways, and many three-lane roads where the central lane is used for overtaking. (Take care not to overtake over a solid white line, though you may see others do so.)

Surfaces are reasonable, but the overall engineering of the road can be poor, with poor drainage, making roads excessively dangerous in rain and leading to unexpected potholes. Few of the mountain roads have any crash barriers or other protection and most have narrow hard shoulders. For added thrills, many overconfident locals seem happy to overtake at high speed on blind corners.

By far the largest number of vehicles on the road are buses and trucks, and very many of the trucks are elderly, overloaded and underpowered (and often on the wrong side of the road).

Access roads to many of the lesser archaeological sites are single-track pitted gravel. They are usually driveable with extreme care in good weather, but rain can cause mud and rock slides, instant waterfalls and fast-flowing rivers, all in the middle of the road. Some sites are simply not accessible in winter, except on foot.

Rules of the road
Drive on the right and, unless it is signed otherwise, give way to traffic joining from your right, even on a roundabout or multiple junction where you might think you had right of way.

Road marking and signposting is only moderately good: it can be good on the new motorways, and on some rural routes, with historical sites clearly marked with yellow signs.

At motorway junctions, be prepared for traffic coming from unexpected directions, and do not expect to be able to get back on to the motorway easily if you make a mistake. Some dual carriageways have very broad hard shoulders, alarmingly used by locals in the wrong direction, to avoid long distances to the nearest junction.

Traffic lights change straight from red to green. A flashing arrow means you may turn right with care even if the main light is red.

Safety Everyone is supposed to wear a seat belt, and to carry a warning triangle and a first-aid kit. Almost no one does. You will usually see a small cairn of rocks, or similar, in the road to warn of a breakdown, but only at the last minute as they are usually placed very close to the vehicle in question.

Drink driving There is a total ban on alcohol when driving; even one beer will put you over the limit.

Traffic police operate control points on the access roads to many cities. You should always carry your driving licence, passport, the car's log book, insurance certificate and vehicle registration, as you may be asked for any or all of them. They may also run seat-belt checks, breath tests and speed traps and check for faulty vehicles. Almost all traffic offences are punishable by on-the-spot fines; ask for a proper receipt.

Etiquette

Although Turkey has much the same highway code as other countries, the population does not obey it. As a result, the country suffers from 14 times more road traffic accidents per number of vehicles than the UK. There has been a powerful campaign lately to try to cut the horrific toll, not only of accidents involving vehicles, but vehicles and pedestrians as well. "Don't be a traffic monster" urge the posters, recognising the Turkish driver's unacceptable levels of aggression.

Expect the unexpected: sudden stops, reversing, pulling out. Some driver signals mean the exact opposite of their UK equivalent. Flashing your headlights, by day or night, means "I am coming through", not "please go first".

There is a lot of hooting, mostly to warn that you are being passed, or (from behind) to hurry you up. A loud hoot means keep out of the way; two short pips on the hooter sometimes means "thanks".

Do not expect traffic to stop to let you out of a side turning; you have to push in. If you beckon to pedestrians to cross in front of you, they will be confused. By all means pause, but they expect to dodge the traffic. Do not expect people to use their indicators, or their handbrakes on a hill. Cars in front of you on a steep hill will almost always roll back, so leave room.

Expect overtaking on all sides, and cutting in. Everyone drives very closely to one another, so if you leave a reasonable stopping distance ahead of you, someone will fill it.

Breakdowns

The most common breakdowns are punctures and smashed windscreens (due to grit thrown up or dropped by another vehicle). But whatever your problem, you will find people inordinately helpful.

For tyres, you need a *lastikci* (tyre-repair man), a small shop where even fairly severe damage will be repaired. For windscreens and other car parts you will have to find the nearest *oto sanayi*. Even in a small town there will be an area dedicated to motor spares and repairs. Especially if you are driving a local hire car, parts and repairs should be easily available and reasonably priced.

If you break down in your own car, your insurance documents should tell you what to do. British motoring associations have reciprocal agreements with the Turkish Touring and Automobile Association, TTOK; the American AAA does not; other nationalities should check the

Slow Going

Although road networks are improving in Turkey, there is still some way to go, and the country's hilly terrain does not make driving particularly easy. For this reason road journeys can take longer than the distance would seem on the map – allow for an average of no more than 60 kmph (35–40 mph).

Speed Limits

- **Urban areas**
50 kmph (30 mph)
- **Open roads**
90 kmph (55 mph) for saloon cars
80 kmph (50 mph) for vans
70 kmph (40 mph) if towing a trailer or caravan
- **Motorways**
120 kmph
(70 mph) for cars

position before travelling. Hired cars always come with instructions.

TTOK's national 24-hour emergency breakdown number is: (0212) 280 4449

Petrol

The western half of Turkey is well supplied with petrol stations, mostly open 24 hours, some of which are good places to stop for a meal and a rest as they are well equipped and have clean toilet facilities.

Most have fully served forecourts, so you don't have to fill your car yourself. The attendant will check oil, clean the windscreen and so on (and will appreciate a tip).

Petrol (*benzin*) is available in 3-star *normal* and 4-star *süper* grades. Lead-free petrol (*kurşunsuz*) is sold at most petrol stations on the western side of the country. Diesel (*mazot*) is available everywhere. The further east you go, the more infrequent the stations become, and you would be wise not to let your tank run low, especially if your car runs on lead-free; it is hard to come by in the more remote rural areas. Beware of bargain-priced diesel as there has been an influx of cheap fuel from Iraq which is exceptionally dirty.

It is usually possible to use credit cards at petrol stations, but in practice it is much easier to pay by cash, especially in remote areas.

Parking

Take heed of no-parking signs. Although the fines for parking illegally are relatively small, retrieving a car that has been towed away is extremely time-consuming.

Caravan Hire

Let's
Istanbul
Tel: (0212) 254 6973 (Taksim)
İzmir
Tel: (0232) 251 4009 (Airport)
Antalya
Tel: (0242) 242 5309

Anadolu Caravan
Istanbul
Tel: (0212) 260 1480

Hewa Caravan
Istanbul
Tel: (0212) 661 4143
Antalya
Tel: (0242) 346 5203

On-street parking areas (look for an *otopark* sign) are manned by watchmen who will approach as you park, and either give you a receipt or place a ticket on your windscreen. Charges vary, but are not expensive – around US$1.50/£1 for two hours in central Istanbul. There are also some multi-storey car parks, a few on-street meters and ticket machines, and valet parking at the smartest hotels and restaurants.

Car hire

To rent a car you must be over 21, and need to have held a licence for a year. You will also need a credit card or substantial cash sum for the deposit. Services are available in most cities and tourist areas (*see page 364* for companies), or in advance through the multinationals or your travel agent.

Car hire in Turkey is quite expensive (minimum £200/US$320 per week inclusive), and there is a huge variance in price, even between the major companies. It is often cheaper to book in advance as part of a fly-drive package, but whatever method you choose, get several quotations before deciding. Basic insurance will be included in the price but you should check that collision-damage waiver (CDW) is added; it is worth the extra cost.

If you book in Turkey, small local Turkish hire companies may offer a better deal, especially if it is out of season. It is worth trying to bargain a little, especially if you suspect business is slack.

Hiring through an international company will allow you to return the car to a different point for no extra charge. Small local companies will usually allow this only if they have an office at your destination.

Child seats should be available for a small extra charge, but you need to check this when booking.

Hiring other vehicles

Campervans and caravans can be hired locally (*see Caravan Hire box opposite*), but this too is expensive. Motorcycles, scooters and bicycles can all be hired in tourist areas.

Sightseeing Tours

Local travel agents, hotels and pensions can offer, or help you find, a wide choice of worthwhile tours. English-speaking guides can always be provided. Tours vary from half a day for part of a city, to a couple of weeks to cover extensive areas of interest. You can tailor your tour to your needs, and engage a private guide, car or minibus and driver by the day. Be warned that some guides will take you to particular shops or restaurants where they may get commission, so you should arrange in advance if you wish to stop at a particular place for lunch or to do your shopping.

Istanbul

Tours include Byzantine Art Tours with visits to Byzantine churches such as Aya Sofya, walls and aqueducts; and Ottoman Art Tours which include visits to the Blue Mosque, the sultans' palaces and so on. There are plenty of full- and half-day trips, as well as sailing tours of the Bosphorus or to the nearby Prince's Islands.

Elsewhere

Tours of the Aegean include visits to Ephesus, Sardis, Pergamon, Aphrodisias and İzmir, plus the beautiful resorts of Bodrum, Fethiye and Marmaris.

On the Mediterranean, you can visit the ancient ruins of Perge, Aspendos, Alanya, Antalya, Side, Termessos, and the beaches of Kaş, Silifke and so on.

You may be interested in taking a long tour such as along the Aegean and Mediterranean coasts, or into the plains of Anatolia, to include Ankara and Cappadocia, and eastern Turkey.

Faith tourism, which may highlight the seven churches of the bible or historic Jewish sites, is becoming increasingly popular.

Tour Operators and Travel Agents

AEGEAN COAST

Bodrum
Akustik Travel & Yachting
Neyzen Tevfik St. Nr. 200 (right across the marina).
E-mail: info@travelbodrum.com
Tel/fax: (0252) 313 8964.
Sightseeing tours and boat trips.
Arya Yachting
Caferpaşa Caddesi, Mildos Evleri 25/1. Tel: (0252) 316 1580.
www.arya.com.tr
Yachting excursions and holidays.
Botur
Cevat Sakir Caddesi 2
Tel: (0252) 316 88 15/316 90 52.
Fax: (0252) 316 82 08.
Local tours and motorbike rental.

İzmir
Rainbow Tours
Fevzi Pasa Bulvari, Çankaya.
Tel: (0232) 446 1638.
Fax: (0232) 441 4183.
Pilgrimage tours of the holy places of Turkey.

Kuşadası
Yücel Tour
A. Menderes Bulvarı, Kuşadası.
Tel: (0256) 614 6827.
Excursions to Didyma, Milet (Miletus) and Priene, plus yacht charters, vehicle hire and safaris.
Sun Wind
Celai Atik Sokak No 10, Kuşadası.
Tel: (0256) 614 9268.
Local excursions and safaris by jeep or on horseback.

Panda
Sağlık Caddesi, Kuşadası.
Tel: (0256) 614 8631.
As well as the usual local
excursions, ferry tickets to Samos,
car and motorbike hire, and a hotel
reservation service is available.
Sardunya Travel
Candan Tarhan
Blv. Mavi Yaka Sitesi 9.
Tel: (0256) 613 0230.
Fax: (0256) 613 0233.
www.tourturkey.com.
Independent and group travel with
the focus on hiking, bird-watching
and photography.

Marmaris
Turmaris
Atatürk Square, No 48/2,
Marmaris.
Tel: (0252) 413 2610.
Located in the centre of town, this is
a useful place to book a ticket on an
air-conditioned catamaran to Rhodes.

BLACK SEA COAST

Enis Ayar
Ordu
Tel: (0452) 223 1337.
Trekking and mountaineering guide.
Works all year, but specialises in
winter trips to the peak of Karagöl,
one of the highest of the Black Sea
region. Experienced climbers only
for winter climbs.
Agencies in Istanbul that
specialise in Black Sea Tours
include **Abelya Tourism**, **Fest** and
Fotograf Evi *(see Istanbul later)*.

CENTRAL ANATOLIA

Ankara
2M
Karim IsMerkezi, Kavaklidere.
Tel: (0312) 427 0035.
Culture and nature tours.
Aloha
Cinnah Caddesi, 39/B, Çankaya.
Tel: (0312) 440 9855.
Travel agent for flights and tours
worldwide; local car hire.
T&T
Abdullah Cevdet Sokak 22/7,
Çankaya.

Tel: (0312) 440 9234.
Tours throughout Anatolia.
Tanzer
Abdullah Cevdet Sok. 24/2,
Cankaya.
Tel: (0312) 441 4181.

Cappadocia
Kapadokya Baloons Göreme
Nevsehir Yolu 14/A, Nevsehir.
Tel: (0384) 271 2442.
Idyllic hot-air-balloon rides over
Cappadocia's lunar landscape.
Red Valley
Cumhuriyet Meydanı, Ürgüp.
Tel: (0384) 341 5061.
Walking and sightseeing tours and
cave exploration among the fairy
chimneys and lunar landscape.

THE EAST

Gaziantep
Arota Turizm
Değirmicem Mahallesi, Gazi
Mustafa Kemal Paşa Bulvarı 31/C.
Tel: (0342) 230 3010.
Fax: (0342) 230 8400.
Tours of the holy city of Şanlıurfa
and Nemrut Dağı, as well as
southeast Turkey.
Kantara Turizm
Atatürk Bulvarı, Şaban Sokak 2/3.
Tel: (0342) 220 6300.
Fax: (0342) 220 6302.
Special tours of the dam and
irrigation projects of the massive
southeastern Anatolia Project.
Şahinbey Turizm
Gaziler Caddesi, Kirişci Sokak 17/1.
Tel: (0342) 230 3152.
Fax: (0342) 231 2898.
Local tours of Gaziantep, Sanlıurfa
and Nemrut Dağı.
Zöhre Turizm
Ataturk Bulvarı, Ari Sinemasi Karşisi.
Tel: (0342) 220 5857.
Fax: (0342) 231 4238.
Regional tours to archaeological
sites such as Nemrut Dağı.

Van
Erek Turizm
Donat Işhanı Kat 2, Beşyol.
Tel/fax: (0432) 214 3800.
Sightseeing tours of the Van area
including the lake, town, Akdamar
Island and Hoşap Castle.

Çarpanak Turizm
Kazım Karabekir Caddesi, Soydan
Işhanı.
Tel: (0432) 214 4464.
Fax: (0432) 351 5942.
Summer-only tours of the
mountains of eastern Turkey.

ISTANBUL

Arnika
Istiklal Caddesi, Miis Sokak 6/5
Beyoğlu.
Tel: (0212) 245 1593.
Daily and weekend tours to the
countryside around Istanbul.
Art Tours
Valikonağı Caddesi 77/3, Nişantası.
Tel: (0212) 231 0487.
Fax: (0212) 240 4945.
Flight reservations, city tours, car
rental, incentive and congress
organisation.
Fest
Barbaros Bulvarı, Barbaros Apt 44
D.20, Balmumcu.
Tel: (0212) 216 1036/7.
Expert guides arrange tours to
lesser-known corners of the city and
off-the-beaten-track regions of the
country, including the Black Sea.
Fotograf Evi
Istiklal Caddesi Tütüncü Çıkmazı 4,
Galatasaray.
Tel: (0212) 249 0202.
Photography and travel club, geared
towards young people, which
organises weekend nature walks
and slide shows.
Gençtur
Prof. K. İsmail Gürkan Caddesi,
Hamam Sok, Kardeşler Han 14/4.
Sultanahmet.
Tel: (0212) 520 5274.
Fax: (0212) 519 0864.
Student travel agency offering
discount cards, as well as nature
tours near Istanbul.
Grup Günbatmadan
Istkilal Caddesi, Zambak Sokak 15,
4th floor, Beyoğlu.
Tel: (0212) 293 0438.
Fax: (0212) 245 6035.
Organises trekking at all levels
around the country.
Meptur
Büyükdere Caddesi 26/17,
Mecidiyeköy.

Tel: (0212) 275 0250.
Fax: (0212) 275 4009.
Tailormade group tours,
reservations, city packages,
corporate travel.
Plan Tours
Cumhuriyet Caddesi 131/1,
Elmadağ.
Tel: (0212) 230 2272/230 8118.
Fax: (0212) 231 8965.
www.plantours.com
City sightseeing tours, seminars
and congresses, ticketing, hotel
reservations, car and yacht rentals,
hunting trips, Jewish heritage tours.
Setur
Cumhuriyet Caddesi 107, Elmadağ.
Tel: (0212) 230 0336.
Fax: (0212) 230 3219.
www.setur.com.tr
Car rental, aeroplane tickets, tours
and conference organisation.
Sultan Tourism
Cumhuriyet Caddesi 87, Elmadağ.
Tel: (0212) 241 3178.
Fax: (0212) 230 0419.
Incentive and conferences, private
and group tours, aeroplane tickets.
Car, bus, helicopter, aircraft hire.
Sunday Holiday
Abdülhamit Caddesi 82/2, Taksim.
Tel: (0212) 256 4156.
Fax: (0212) 256 8808.
Tailormade group tours, hotel
reservations, city packages,
conventions, corporate meetings.
Trans Orient
Cumhuriyet Caddesi 211/2, Harbiye.
Tel: (0212) 233 6822.
Fax: (0212) 230 6359.
Incoming reservations, incentive
tours, group and individual tours,
seminar and congress organisation.
Türk Ekspress
Cumhuriyet Caddesi 47/1, Taksim.
Tel: (0212) 235 9500.
Fax: (0212) 241 0431.
Long-running full-service travel
agency with offices also in the
Conrad and Hilton hotels, offering
air tickets, car rental and a wide
range of city tours. Local Amex
representative.
Yeşil Bisiklet
Lalezar Caddesi 8/1, Kardelen
Apartment, Selamiçeşme, Kadıköy.
Tel: (0216) 363 5836.
Cycling club/shop with cycling gear
and maintenance. Organises trips.

Viking Turizm
Cumhuriyet Caddesi 271, Harbiye.
Tel: (0212) 334 2600.
A Rosenbluth Network company and
general sales agent of Seaburn
Cruise Lines, offering airline
ticketing, corporate and leisure
travel, conferences and incentives.

MEDITERRANEAN COAST

Adana
Adalı Turizm
Stadyum Caddesi 37/C.
Tel: (0322) 453 7440.
Full-service travel agency handling
flights, packages, accommodation,
car hire and local excursions.

Alanya
Tantur
B Güller Pınarı Mahallesi, 12 Eylül
Caddesi, Akdeniz Apartman.
Tel: (024) 512 0982/513 3362.
Fax: (0242) 513 3368.
One of Turkey's largest tour
operators offering yacht charters,
destination tourism and special-
interest holidays.

Antalya
Akay Travel Service
B Cumhuriyet Caddesi 54, Solmaz
İşhanı, Kat. 1.
Tel: (0242) 243 1700.
Fax: (0242) 241 9847.
Tours to off-the-beaten track
archaeological sights.
Pamfilya
30 Ağustos Caddesi 57/B
Tel: (0242) 243 1500.
Fax: (0242) 242 1400.
Sightseeing tours, yacht charters,
rafting and trekking.
Skorpion Turizm
Fevzi Çakmak Caddesi 12/5.
Tel: (0242) 243 0890.
Sightseeing tours and a host of
outdoor activities, including
mountaineering, jeep safaris,
trekking and village tours.

Fethiye
**Be There Yachting and Travel
Agency**
B Fevzi Çakmak Caddesi 11/1,
Marina, Fethiye.
Tel: (0252) 614 7711.

Fax: (0252) 614 9119.
Daily excursions, travel
reservations, yachting and *gulet*
cruises.
SkySports
Deniz Camp Olüdeniz-Fethiye.
Tel: (0252) 617 0511.
Fax: (0252) 617 0324.
www.paragliding.net/skysports
Experienced tandem pilots,
instructors and international
competition pilots run this outfit.
Simena Travel
Atatürk Caddesi, PTT Santral Sokak,
Urantaş Sitesi, Kat 4.
Tel: (0252) 614 4957.
Island and moonlit cruises, historic
sightseeing and jeep safaris.

Kaş
Bougainville Travel
Ibrahim Serin Caddesi 10.
Tel: (0242) 836 3737.
www.bougainville-turkey.com
Guided cultural sightseeing, boat
tours, diving, trekking and village
safaris.

THRACE & MARMARA

Bursa
Karagöz Tourism & Travel Agency
Kapalı Çarşı, Eski Aynalı Çarşı 12.
Tel: (0224) 221 8727.
Fax: (0224) 220 5350.
Guided tours of Bursa and environs.

Edirne
Sedan Turizm
Talatpaşa Asfaltı Adil 2, Sitesi 60.
Tel: (0284) 213 2146.
Fax: (0284) 213 6742.
Guided tours of Bursa and environs.

Çanakkale
**Hassle Free Tourism & Travel
Agency**
Anzac House, Cumhuriyet Meydanı.
61.
Tel: (0286) 213 5969.
Fax: (0286) 217 2906.
www.anzachouse.com.
Guided tours to Troy, the Troad,
Ephesus and around the World War
I battlefields in Gallipoli.

Where to Stay

Turkey offers all conceivable varieties of accommodation: from campsites to the most luxurious of hotels. Not long ago, most visitors to Turkey were independent travellers, and outside the capital and Istanbul, accommodation was simple, even spartan.

It is still true that there is most choice in the most developed resorts and cities, but the more unusual destinations can offer unique places to stay. On the coast, there are rapidly increasing numbers of huge resorts (in the main indistinguishable from each other), interspersed with equally anonymous small concrete blocks for those on a tighter budget. There are the first glimmerings of a movement towards charming small hotels in some places outside Istanbul, but the options are still extremely limited.

Types of Lodgings

HOTELS

Choosing a hotel
You are the best judge of your needs. Your choice will be affected by the kind of holiday you wish to have, how much money you wish to spend and the amenities you are looking for. Do you want peace or a party?

In busy resorts and cities noise may be a factor: if you are choosing your hotel on the spot, ask to see the room first – this is quite normal and expected. If choosing a hotel during the day, think about the proximity of night-time activity; somewhere that is peaceful at 10 in the morning may be throbbing with disco music through the night.

Hotel categories
The Ministry of Tourism classifies all hotels from one to five stars, with the majority between one and three.

At one-star level you will get an en-suite room that is basic but modern and reasonably comfortable. A three-star hotel will usually have a restaurant and a bar, minibars and TVs in the rooms, and possibly a swimming pool.

The five-star hotels at the top end of the market include the luxury flagships of the major international hotel chains, such as Inter-Continental, Hilton, Hyatt and Swissotel. Although their rooms are expensive, the competition is intense, so that at quiet times these hotels may offer extremely attractive packages.

The Season

Outside Istanbul, tourism in Turkey is highly seasonal and many hotels close between October and April. Of the few that remain open in winter, even fewer will be able to offer either hot water or central heating; check carefully before booking.

Apart-hotels
These offer some of the independence of being in your own flat, but with the services associated with a comfortable hotel. In Istanbul they have been developed as a way of renovating and adapting attractive older apartment buildings without substantially changing their character. One or two of the five-star hotels also offer apartments within the hotel.

PENSIONS

A Turkish pansiyon is somewhere between a simple hotel and a bed and breakfast. They can be lovely places to stay, especially if they are run by a family. At the seaside resorts you will find that they are often used by Turkish families on their summer holidays and only

offer full-board or half-board terms in high season. The more expensive will have en-suite facilities in every room. In some, hot water is heated by solar panels on the roof – and may run out.

YOUTH HOSTELS

Accommodation is so reasonable in Turkey that there are very few youth hostels as such. It is possible, out of term-time, to stay in empty student dormitories or halls of residence or in the teachers' accommodation (ogretmen evi), but the rooms will be spartan and often no cheaper than the cheapest ordinary pansiyon or hotel.

SELF-CATERING

There is now a wide choice of comfortable villas and apartments with pools, including the most luxurious accommodation, with more springing up all the time. Rapid development does mean, though, that you should be a little careful to ensure that your holiday spot is not in the middle of a building site. Some agents specialise in providing quiet, rural, more genuinely Turkish locations, but these may not have pools.

CAMPING

The best camping areas (kampink) are close to the seaside resorts, and have all the necessary facilities, including showers, shops, restaurants and activities. They generally cost around as much as staying in a cheap hotel.

You can actually camp almost anywhere in Turkey except designated historic or natural sites, provided you don't damage farmland or light fires in forests. There are so few campsites that it's worth stressing this; for most trekking activities camping out is necessary.

Hotel Listings

Accommodation is listed region by region, with the pick of hotels, historic hotels and *pansiyons* included for each region. Within each category, hotels are in order of luxury (with the most deluxe and expensive first).

Because of the enormous fluctuations of the lira, price brackets are based on a US$ average and are an indication only; prices may change considerably. Expect to pay at least 30 percent more in Istanbul. Bargaining is usually possible, especially out of high season. Many cheap hotels will not accept credit cards, so check on booking.

ISTANBUL

Istanbul's five-star accommodation is in line with that in New York or any major European city in both quality and price. *Pansiyon* accommodation, however, can be very reasonable.

Hotels

Ceylan inter-Continental ★★★★★
Taksim.
Tel: (0212) 231 2121.
Fax: (0212) 231 2180.
www.istanbul.interconti.com
In the city centre, this luxurious hotel commands superb views of the Bosphorous and city skylines. It has 390 rooms and suites, including 4 suites for the disabled. Restaurants include Turkish, French and Californian, and there are bars and deluxe banqueting and convention rooms, sports facilities and so on. **$$$$**

Conrad International Istanbul ★★★★★
Barbaros Bulvarı, Beşiktaş.
Tel: (0212) 227 3000.
Fax: (0212) 259 6667.
www.conradhotels.com
A huge hotel with 625 rooms and 32 suites. Excellent Italian and Turkish restaurants, French patisserie, and live jazz in the bar every night. Health club with indoor and outdoor swimming pools, 24-hour business centre. Convenient

location with wonderful views of the Bosphorus and Yıldız Imperial Gardens. **$$$$**

Çırağan Palace Hotel Kempinski ★★★★★
Çırağan Caddesi, Beşktaş.
Tel: (0212) 258 3377.
Fax: (0212) 259 6686.
www.ciraganpalace.com
One of Istanbul's most prestigious (and expensive) hotels, reconstructed from Ottoman palace ruins. Superb Bosphorus setting and proximity to the city centre also a plus. Two gourmet restaurants, one Ottoman (Tuğra), one Italian (Bellini). There are 295 rooms and 27 suites, 12 in a restored Ottoman palace. Outdoor swimming pool and outdoor jazz club. **$$$$**

Divan ★★★★
Cumhuriyet Caddesi, Elmadağ.
Tel: (0212) 231 4100.
Fax: (0212) 248 8527.
www.divanhotel.com.tr
A relatively small, first-rate hotel with 169 rooms and 11 suites. The Divan has one of the most distinguished restaurants in Istanbul, serving Ottoman and international dishes, as well as a popular café for quick meals. A few rooms have private terraces. **$$$$**

Four Seasons ★★★★★
Tevkifhane Sokak 1, Sultanahmet.
Tel: (0212) 638 8200.
Fax: (0212) 638 8210.
www.fourseasons.com
There are views of Aya Sofya and the Blue Mosque from this

Historic Hotels

Special licences are granted by the municipality to hotels housed in historic buildings such as old Turkish houses or *caravansaries*. Many are in the oldest and most interesting parts of towns.

They offer the amenities of three-, four- or five-star hotels (and at the same prices), but with some limitations (such as no lift, due to the age of the buildings). Many are very atmospheric, and are decorated in old Turkish style.

Price Guide

Prices are per night for a double room during the high season.
$$$$ = above $150
$$$ = $70 to $150
$$ = $50 to $70
$ = below $50

neoclassical building, with 54 rooms and 11 suites, as well as top-notch service, splendid décor (complete with Ottoman antiques), and all modern conveniences. The restaurant offers top-quality Turkish and Continental cuisine. **$$$$**

Hyatt Regency ★★★★★
Taskışla Caddesi 80090, Taksim.
Tel: (0212) 368 1234.
Fax: (0212) 368 1000.
www.istanbul.hyatt.com
A cross between Turk-Nouveau and Art Deco architecture, this deceptively large (332 rooms and 11 suites) classic is right in the centre of Istanbul's "Conference Valley". Features include Italian, Ottoman and Japanese restaurants, a bar, lounge, business centre, conference facilities, Turkish bath, floodlit outdoor pool and tennis courts. **$$$$$**

Keban ★★★★
Sıraselviler Caddesi 51-A, Taksim.
Tel: (0212) 252 2504.
Fax: (212) 243 3310.
www.kebanhotel.com
In the heart of Istanbul's entertainment district. 84 rooms with satellite TV and air

The concept was introduced by the pioneering director of the Turkish Touring and Automobile Club, Çelik Gülersoy, a tireless conservationist and campaigner for the protection of Turkey's historical and cultural heritage. He intended the hotels to be inspirational examples for others to follow, and under his guidance the first were created about 20 years ago. A stay in one is a unique experience.

Istanbul: New City or Old City?

Most of the best-kept and most famous Byzantine and Ottoman sites are in what is known as the "old city", the area encompassed by the Marmara Sea and Golden Horn. As a consequence, it is where most visitors stay, and the area is home to literally hundreds of small *pansiyons* and hotels, as well as carpet shops, hawkers, overpriced and uninspired eateries, and virtually no sign of real Turkish life outside the tourism industry. As an old religious neighbourhood, there is little nightlife – a boon to some and a disappointment to others. In

recent years, however, Istanbul's hectic economic expansion has attracted a lot of business and incentive visitors who wish to combine conference attending with sightseeing, and consequently there has been a boom in excellent mid-size, mid-range hotels in the Taksim area. It is only a 15-minute taxi ride to the Sultanhmet/Bazaar Quarter, one is spoilt for choice in terms of restaurants, cafés and clubs, and there is a better chance to mix with the city's cultured middle class instead of dodging carpet dealers and con-artists.

conditioning. Efficient, English-speaking staff. **$$$$**
Merit Antique ★★★★★
Ordu Caddesi 226, Laleli.
Tel: (0212) 513 9300.
Fax: (0212) 512 6390/513 9340.
www.meritantiquehotel.com.tr
This lovingly restored early 20th-century apartment complex in the heart of the old city is now a charming hotel with 275 rooms. Superb Chinese, Turkish and Kosher restaurants, patisserie, wine bar and health club. **$$$$**
Mövenpick Hotel Istanbul ★★★★★
Büyükdere Caddesi 4, Levent.
Tel: (0212) 319 2929.
Fax: (0212) 319 2900.
www.movenpickhotels.com
Chic business hotel with 249 rooms with desks and internet connections, state-of-the-art meeting facilities, health club, pool, an excellent restaurant, and Mövenpick ice cream. **$$$$**
Polat Renaissance ★★★★
Sahil Caddesi, Yeşilyurt.
Tel: (0212) 663 1700.
Fax: (0212) 663 1755.
www.polatrenaissance.com
This thoroughly modern business hotel, one of Istanbul's best near the airport and the World Trade Centre, has the added advantage of a location in a quiet residential neighbourhood overlooking the Sea of Marmara. It has the largest in-house conference facility in the city,

354 rooms, 20 suites, two non-smoking floors, numerous bars and restaurants, pool, Turkish bath, fitness and beauty centres. **$$$$$**
Swissôtel The Bosphorus ★★★★★
Bayıldım Caddesi 2, Maçka.
Tel: (0212) 326 1100.
Fax: (0212) 326 1122.
www.swissotel.com
480 rooms and 23 suites. Excellent sports and health facilities (including outdoor and indoor pools, Jacuzzi, sauna, tennis and so on), six restaurants and banqueting facilities. Superb views from a hilltop location. **$$$$**

Historic hotels and pansiyons in Istanbul
Anemon Galata
Büyükhendek Caddesi 11, Kuledibi Beyoğlu.
Tel: (0212) 293 2343.
Fax: (0212) 292 2340.
www.anemonhotels.com
Delightfully restored old house hotel with 23 rooms and 7 suites, in a perfect position right beside the Galata Tower. The rooftop bar and restaurant have one of the finest views in the city, over the Bosphorus and Golden Horn. **$$$**
Arena Hotel
Mehmet Paşa Yokuşu İçler, Hamam Sokak 13–15, Sultanhmet.
Tel: (0212) 458 0364/65.
Fax: (0212) 458 0366.
www.arenahotel.com

Most of the 27 rooms have a sea view. All are decorated with İznik motif ceramics and have air conditioning, direct-dial phones and satellite TV. Public facilities include a *hamam*, restaurants, laundry service and airport shuttle. **$$$**
Armada ★★★★
Ahırkapı Sokak Ahırkapı.
Tel: (0212) 638 1370.
Fax: (0212) 518 5060.
www.armadahotel.com.tr
Surrounded by Byzantine city walls, this 110-room hotel is new, but built in the style of 16th-century row housing. Quiet location near the Marmara coast but within walking distance to all main sites. An ecologically aware hotel that uses only olive oil soaps – no detergents. Authentic Turkish food in acclaimed Ahırkapı restaurants; also offers Greek music nights as well as Turkish classical music *(fasıl)*. **$$$**
Ayasofya Pansiyonlar
Soğukçeşme Sokak, Sultanhmet.
Tel: (0212) 513 3660.
Fax: (0212) 513 3669.
www.ayasofyapansiyonlari.com
A charming cobbled lane full of restored wooden houses furnished with period furniture, located directly behind Aya Sofya. 57 rooms, 4 suites, 3 restaurants (one in a Byzantine cistern), café, bars, Turkish bath and even a research library on old Istanbul. **$$$**
Pera Palas ★★★★
Meşrutiyet Caddesi 198/100, Tepebaşı.
Tel: (0212) 251 4560.
Fax: (0212) 251 4089.
www.perapalas.com
The historic "Orient Express" hotel retains its 100-year-old aura of spy intrigue as well as its original décor and has hosted the likes of Agatha Christie and Mata Hari. **$$$$**
Hotel Splendid Palace
Nisan Caddesi 71, Büyükada (Prince's Islands, hovercraft from Kabataş).
Tel: (0216) 382 6950.
Fax: (0216) 382 6775.
No cars on this spectacular island location, though you can hire a horse and trap. Spectacular sea view outside Istanbul's urban crush,

all amenities, including a garden restaurant and pool, in this historic building. **$$$**

Hotel Kariye
Edirnekapı (beside the Church of Chora or Kariye Museum).
Tel: (0212) 534 8414.
Fax: (0212) 521 6631.
www.kariyeotel.com
Unique, peaceful location for lovers of Byzantium. This elegant hotel in a restored Ottoman mansion is right next to one of Istanbul's most exceptionally preserved churches. Superb restaurant specialising in historic Ottoman dishes and traditional court music, 22 rooms, 5 suites, garden pavillion. **$$$**

Price Guide

Prices are per night for a double room during the high season.
$$$$ = above $150
$$$ =$70 to $150
$$ = $50 to $70
$ = below $50

Sarniç Hotel
Küçük Ayasofya Sok, 26, Sultanahmet.
Tel: (0212) 518 2323.
Fax: (0212) 518 2414.
E-mail: info@sarnichotel.com
www.sarnichotel.com
Simple décor in restored old house, 24-hour medical service, parking, airport pick-up. Small hotel with lovely rooftop terrace in the heart of Byzantine Istanbul. **$$$**

Yeşil Ev
Kabasakal Caddesi 5, Sultanahmet.
Tel: (0212) 517 6785.
Fax: (0212) 517 6780.
www.turing.org.tr
A restored wooden mansion, previously the home of an Ottoman pasha, located between Aya Sofya and the Blue Mosque. 18 rooms and 1 suite with period décor, intimate walled rear garden with conservatory and good restaurant. Book well in advance. **$$$**

Empress Zoë,
Akbıyık Cad, Adliya Sokak 10, Sultanahmet.
Tel: (0212) 518 2504.
Fax: (0212) 518 5699.

www.emzoe.com
American owner Ann Nevins has turned this small hotel (16 rooms, 3 suites) near Topkapı Palace into something unique, complete with Byzantine wall paintings and a garden which incorporates the ruins of a 15th-century Turkish bath. **$$**

Hotel Celal Sultan
Salkımsöğüt Sokak 16, Sultanahmet.
Tel: (0212) 520 9323.
Fax: (0212) 527 2704.
E-mail: csultan@ibm.net
Classically restored, cosy townhouse (16 rooms, 1 suite) with double-glazed windows and filtered water. International cable TV and great view of Aya Sofya from the roof terrace. **$$**

Hotel Fehmi Bey
Üçler Sokak 15, Sultanahmet.
Tel: (0212) 638 9083/85.
Fax: (0212) 518 1264.
www.fehmibay.com
This 18-room restored townhouse has friendly hosts, slick décor, a sauna and a spectacular sea view from its rooftop terrace. **$$**

Hotel Kybele
Yerebatan Caddesi 35, Sultanahmet.
Tel: (0212) 511 7766/67.
Fax: (0212) 513 4393.
www.kybelehotel.com
A treasurehouse of Ottoman antiques with a lobby lit by over 1,000 historic lamps. 16 rooms, restaurant, phone etc. and delightful courtyard. English, Japanese and other languages spoken. **$$**

Hotel Nomade
Divanyolu, Ticarethane Sokak 15, Sultanahmet.
Tel: (0212) 511 1296.
Fax: (0212) 513 2404.
Run by two French-educated twin sisters, this homely 15-room hotel will appeal to well travelled internationalists, intellectuals and solo females. It has a rooftop terrace, and its own bistro (Rumeli Cafe) across the street. **$**

Vardar Palace Hotel
Sıraselviler Caddesi 54-56, Taksim.
Tel: (0212) 252 2888.
Fax: (0212) 252 1527.
Great central location for those in

town for conferences or festival-hopping. Built 100 years ago in the Levantine-Selçuk style, it has been thoroughly restored with 40 en-suite rooms, TV, minibars and so on. **$**

Apart-hotels in Istanbul

Galata Residence Hotel
Bankalar Caddesi, Hacı Ali Sokak, Galata/Karaköy.
Tel: (0212) 252 6062.
Fax: (0212) 292 4841.
www.galataresidence.com
This huge 19th-century Jewish mansion is uniquely located near Galata Tower – the old "international" neighbourhood – and has been elegantly restored with NGO and business conference delegates in mind. 14 five-person suites and 3 doubles with fully equipped kitchens and bathrooms, air conditioning and TV. Rooftop restaurant has spectacular Bosphorus view; atmospheric bar in the basement. **$**

Mega Residence
Eytam Caddesi 33, Maçka.
Tel: (0212) 231 3161.
Fax: (0212) 233 4461.
E-mail: residence@turk.net
The Residence is superbly placed between "Conference Valley" and its concert halls, and the heart of the city's best shops, restaurants and art/antique galleries. 30 rooms, 15 with kitchenette in a classic, bay-windowed apartment building. Boardroom, private parking, all business facilities. **$$**

THRACE & MARMARA

Bursa

Çelik Palas Oteli/Swissôtel
★★★★★
Çekirge Caddesi 79.
Tel: (0224) 233 3800.
Fax: (0224) 236 1910.
www.swissotel.com
Bursa's finest historic hotel has been bought recently by Swissôtel who are building a new 5-star hotel next door then closing down the Çelik Palas for renovation. The whole process will take 2–3 years. The hotel's magnificent marble-clad Turkish bath will remain open and

can be used by guests of both hotels. **$$$$**

Hotel Çeşmeli
Heykel Gümüşçeken Caddesi 6.
Tel/fax: (0224) 224 1511/2.
Small (18-room) comfortable city centre hotel. **$$$**

Diamond Otel ★★
Inönü Caddesi, Toyota Plaza Yan 104.
Tel: (0224) 271 4401.
Fax: (0224) 271 4400.
Clean, quiet, if somewhat spartan. There is rather a steep uphill walk from the hotel to the city centre. Friendly atmosphere. **$**

Safran Hotel
Ortapazar Caddesi, Arka Sokak 4, Tophane.
Tel: (0224) 224 7216.
Fax: (0224) 224 7219.
Lovingly restored wooden house in the old town. Rooms have modern amenities, including TVs and minibars. **$$**

Those preferring to stay out of town could try one of the many ski lodges at nearby **Uludağ**. Options include:

Grand Hotel Yazıcı ★★★★
Tel: (0224) 285 2050.
Fax: (0224) 285 2048. **$$$$**

Kar Hotel
Tel/fax: (0224) 283 2121. **$$**

Çanakkale
Akol Hotel ★★★★
Kordonboyu Caddesi.
Tel: (0286) 217 9456.
Fax: (0286) 217 2897.
www.hotelakol.com.tr

Assos

Assos Harbour (Behramkale) has become a favoured spot of Istanbul's young and rich. Book early and stay in one of the small secluded establishments, usually lovingly constructed from traditional Greek stone houses, which are further out on the coast or in the traditional hilltop village. Assos Harbour tends to be quiet in winter, and the few hotels that remains open attract artists and intellectuals.

Bursa *Hamam* Hotels

Bursa is justifiably famous for its hot springs and Turkish bathhouses, and the best are often part of major hotel complexes. Available to the public as well, prices for the *hamam* are usually considerably cheaper than in Istanbul. They are as modern as any European health facility and usually offer expert massage as well as hot pool and private rooms. If you have just one Turkish bath, take it as part of a leisurely weekend in Bursa.

This seafront hotel has its own swimming pool, good restaurants, disco and satellite TV in the bedrooms. It is open throughout the year. The service is good and the atmosphere friendly. **$$$**

Anzac House
Cumhuriyet Meydanı 61.
Tel: (0286) 217 0156.
Fax: (0286) 217 2096.
www.anzachouse.com
Central, cheap and cheerful Australian-run backpackers' hangout, providing basic facilities. Hostel-style dormitory rooms with shared bathrooms. Book here for local tours and there are films about Gallipolli every evening. Open all year. **$**

Tusan Hotel
Güzelyalı, Intepe.
Tel: (0286) 232 8746.
Fax: (0286) 232 8226.
Popular, simple country hotel on the beach, surrounded by pine forests, 14 km (8.5 miles) south of Çannakale on the road to Troy. Indoor and outdoor restaurants and watersports. Book well ahead. **$**

Edirne
Karam Hotel
Mithatpaşa Mah., Maarif Caddesi, Garanti Bankası Sokağı 6.
Tel: (0284) 225 1555.
Fax: (0284) 225 1556.
Comfortable little new hotel in a restored town-centre mansion. 8 rooms with 24-hour room service, hot water, satellite TV, air-con, phone and minibar. **$$$**

Hotel Rüstem Pasa Caravansaray
Iki Kapılı Han Caddesi 57, Sabuni Mahallesi.
Tel: (0284) 212 6119.
Fax: (0284) 212 0462.
This beautifully restored 16th-century inn, designed by Sinan, is now back in service as a pleasant, if sometimes basic hotel, with airy rooms (bitterly cold in winter), plain furniture and a flowery central courtyard. **$$**

Sultan Oteli ★★★
Londra Asfalti 42.
Tel: (0284) 225 1372.
Fax: (0284) 225 5763.
Located in the city centre, this is one of the best of Edirne's bunch of rather indifferent hotels. The rooms have shower and TV, but those on the front may be noisy. Open all year. The service can be rather surly. **$$**

Truva (Troy)
Hisarlık
Tevfikiye Köyü.
Tel: (0286) 283 0026.
Fax: (0286) 283 0087.
A small hotel (with 11 double rooms, each of which is named after a Trojan hero), serving independent travellers only. Good Turkish meals. **$$**

AEGEAN COAST

Assos/Behremkale
Old Bridge House
P.K. 2, Ayvacik 17860.
Tel: (0286) 721 7426.
Fax (0286) 721 7427.
www.oldbridgehouse.com
Romantic, tiny 4-room hotel in a renovated stone house just outside Behramkale with a huge open fire in the central lobby, and a view over the acropolis of the ancient city. Turkish and Indian cuisine in the restaurant. Rooms and gardens imaginatively decorated with salvaged local materials. **$$$**

Assos Hotel
Iskele Mevkii. Behramkale.
Tel: (0286) 721 7017.
Fax: (0286) 721 7240.
www.assoshotel.com
One of the oldest hotels on the harbourfront, with great views across

to the Greek island of Lesbos. Open all year round, no package tours allowed! Great restaurant right on the seafront where you can watch fishermen bring in the daily catch that will serve your table. **$$$**

Assos Kervansaray
Behremkale.
Tel: (0286) 721 7093.
Fax: (0286) 721 7200.
www.assoskervansaray.com
Attractive, stone-built harbourfront hotel with great views and 50 rooms, all with bathroom, phone and central heating. Nice restaurant and café/bar, swimming pool and sauna. Hunting and fishing opportunities. **$$**

Behram Hotel
Behramkale Iskele.
Tel: (0286) 721 7016.
Fax: (0286) 721 7044.
www.behram-hotel.com
One of the oldest decent hotels in the resort, the Behram has 17 comfortable rooms with bathroom and phone, and a charming seaside fish restaurant. Open all year. **$$**

Ayvalik

Kaptan
Balıkhane Sokak.
Tel: (0266) 312 8834.
A converted soap mill, this is one of the best options in town – clean and basic yet comfortable, with 13 rooms and 2 suites, all with balconies overlooking the sea. **$$**

Taksiyarhis
Mareşal Fevzi Çakmak Caddesi 71.
Tel: (0266) 312 1494.
Fax: (0266) 312 2661.
Run by an Austrian-Turkish couple, this is a large, restored old house with terraces offering wonderful views. Five rooms, shared bathroom and kitchen, plus a Turkish bath. **$**

Yalı
Behind the PTT building, No. 25.
Tel: (0266) 312 2423.
Fax: (0266) 312 3819.
A beautiful 150-year-old Greek building restored with period décor. Shaded waterfront garden with a small pier. Five bedrooms, shared bathrooms and kitchen. **$**

Cunda Hotel
Alibey Island, 5 km (3 miles) from Ayvalık.

Tel: (0266) 327 1598.
Fax: (0266) 327 1943.
Pleasant seafront hotel with a private sandy beach and its own jetty, connected to the mainland by a narrow sand spit and small bridge. **$$**

Grand Hotel Termizel ★★★★★
Sarmısaklı.
Tel: (0266) 324 2000.
Fax: (0266) 324 1274.
One of the largest (with 164 rooms) and certainly the plushest of the local hotels, kitted out in marble and brass, with a casino, spa and private beach. **$$$**

Hotel Kalif
Hürriyet Caddesi 19, Sarmısaklı.
Tel: (0266) 324 4914.
Fax: (0266) 324 5106.
www.kalifhotel.s5.com
Pleasant little resort hotel a couple of blocks back from the beach. Good, plentiful food, and friendly service. **$$$**

Bodrum

Antique Theatre Hotel
Kibris Sehitleri Caddesi 243.
Tel: (0252) 316 6053.
Fax: (0252) 316 0825.
E-mail: theatrehot@superonline.com
www.pathcom.com/~antique
Small luxury hotel and gourmet restaurant affiliated to the prestigious Chaîne des Rôtisseurs Association. **$$$$**

Lavanta Village
P.O. Box 35, TR 48430 Yalikavak.
Tel: (0252) 385 2167.
Fax: (0252) 385 2290.
E-mail: lavanta@lavanta.com
www.lavanta.com
Small boutique hotel with some self-catering suites, 20 km (12 miles) from Bodrum, 1.5 km (1 mile) from the beach. Panoramic sea/mountain views and very quiet. Large swimming pool. Food prepared with vegetables grown on the premises. Home-made bread and wine from the cellar also on offer. Internet access. **$$$**

Karia Princess ★★★★★
Canli Dere Sokak 15.
Tel: (0252) 316 8971.
Fax: (0252) 316 8979.
Probably the best accommodation

in Bodrum. Although it is within walking distance of the town centre, it is away from the noisy discos and bars. A classy place, its Turkish bath is one of the best you'll see along the Aegean coast. Bodrum's largest supermarket is across the road. Open all year. **$$$$**

Merit Altınel ★★★★★
Duvarlı Taria Mevkii.
Tel: (0252) 367 1848.
Fax: (0252) 367 1847.
Nearly 200 rooms, complete with air conditioning and minibars, and a pool and disco. 11 km (6.5 miles) from Bodrum. Attracts package groups mostly and popular with families. Closed over winter. **$$$$**

Manastir Hotel
Barıs Mevkii, Kumbahçe.
Tel: (0252) 316 2854.
Fax: (0252) 316 2772.
E-mail: manastir@unimedya.net.tr
Pleasant, whitewashed Mediterranean-style hotel on the site of a former monastery. All rooms have balconies and the hotel has a pool, fitness centre, sauna and 2 restaurants. **$$$**

Çeşme

Altın Yunus Tatilköyü
Kalemburnu Boyalık Meydanı, Ilıca.
Tel: (0232) 723 1250.
Fax: (0232) 723 2252.
Attractive, low-rise resort built around a sandy bay, with luxurious fittings and all possible mod cons and entertainments. **$$$$**

Çeşme Kervansaray
Çeşme Kalesi Yani.
Tel: (0232) 712 7177.
Fax: (0232) 712 2906.
Romantically restored 16th-century *caravansaray* round a fountain courtyard, 2 suites and 32 rooms, some with a sea view. **$$$**

Sheraton Çeşme ★★★★★
Ilıca.
Tel: (0232) 723 1240.
Fax: (0232) 723 1388.
www.sheraton.com
Luxurious 373-room resort, offering a full range of spa and therapy treatments. Private beach, children's entertainments and wonderful food. **$$$$**

Dalyan

Kilim Hotel
Yali Sokak.
Tel: (0252) 284 2253
Attractive small pension with good-sized rooms, a pool and plenty of the *kilims* that give the place its name. **$$**

Konak Melsa
Köyceğiz Caddesi, Çavuşlar Mah.
Tel: (0252) 284 5104.
Fax: (0252) 284 3913.
Quiet, attractive 24-room hotel decorated in local stone and wood. Internet café and restaurant. **$$**

Foça

Karaçam
Sahil Caddesi 70.
Tel: (0232) 812 3216.
Fax: (0232) 812 2042.
A charming old Greek house with 24 rooms. It is popular with tour groups, so it's advisable to book well ahead. **$$$**

Hanedan ★★
Sahil Caddesi.
Tel: (0232) 812 1515.
Fax: (0232) 812 1609.
A basic, but comfortable 4-storey box on the harbour. **$$**

Evim Pansiyon
216 Sokak 40.
Tel: (0232) 812 1360.
Renovated old house with 7 rooms and a beautiful garden. **$$**

Gökçeada

Barba Yorgo
17763 Tepeköy.
Tel: (0286) 887 3592/4247.
Fax: (0286) 887 3592.
Once a Greek island, the mixed culture is still very much alive on Gökçeada. Barba Yorgo comprises 4 restored original houses, 15 km (9 miles) from the ferry landing. The taverna is full of locals every night – great Greek food, dance and music. The surrounding area offers superb hiking and the beach is not far away. **$$**

Heracleia

Agora ★
Kapıkırı, 10 km (6 miles) north of Çamiçi, a village on the Söke-Milas highway.
Tel: (0252) 543 5445.

Fax: (0252) 543 5567.
A modest and friendly little place amid the inspiring remains of ancient Heracleia. Open all year round. **$**

İzmir

Antik Han Hotel
Anafartalar Caddesi 600.
Tel: (0232) 489 2750.
Fax: (0232) 483 5925.
Charming small city-centre hotel in a restored Ottoman mansion. Can be noisy. **$$**

Büyük Efes ★★★★★
Gaziosmanpasa Bulvarı.
Tel: (0232) 484 4300.
Fax: (0232) 441 5695.
A very attractive interior, full of plants and ethnic designs, gives this quality hotel an individual character. With 3 pools, 5 restaurants and a fitness centre. Open all year. **$$$$**

Hilton ★★★★★
Gaziosmanpaşa Bulvarı.
Tel: (0232) 441 6060.
Fax: (0232) 441 2207.
E-mail: izmhitw@hilton.com
The 34-storey Hilton, a landmark building in the city, has a sports centre and a bar that looks out over İzmir from its 31st floor. Open all year. **$$$$**

Karaca Otel
1379 Sokak 55, at Necatibey and Gaziosmanpaşa Bulvarı.
Tel: (0232) 489 1940.
Fax: (0232) 483 1498.
Centrally located mid-rise hotel with a garden on a quiet side street, with a small pool on the roof terrace. **$$$**

Kuşadası

Kuşadası has over 300 hotels in all categories; the local tourist office can provide a comprehensive list.

Korumar ★★★★★
Just outside the town centre on the road to Selçuk.
Tel: (0256) 614 8243.
Fax: (0256) 614 5596.
www.skymedia.com.tr/korumar
Attractive hotel with excellent pools, restaurants, Turkish bath and an open-air disco. Open all year. **$$$$**

Grand Blue Sky ★★★★★
Kadinlar Denizli.
Tel: (0256) 612 7750.
Fax: (0256) 612 4225.
www.grandbluesky.com
A sea-facing luxury hotel, offering the full range of watersports, including diving, and its own stretch of private beach. Open all year. **$$$**

Imbat ★★★★★
Kadınlar Denizi Mevkii.
Tel: (0256) 614 2000.
Fax: (0256) 614 4960.
One of Kuşadası's big resort hotels with all the amenities one would expect from a 5-star hotel: disco, pool, watersports, restaurant and bar. Situated at the Ladies' Beach end of town and easily reached by *dolmuş* from the town centre. Open all year. **$$$$**

Ökuz Mehmet Paşa Kervansaray
Atatürk Bulvarı 1.
Tel: (0256) 614 4115.
Fax: (0256) 614 2423.
The Hollywood fantasy version of Turkey, in a restored 300-year-old *caravansaray* replete with palm trees, *kilims* and belly dancers. **$$$**

Liman Hotel
Buyral Sokak 4, Kıbrıs Caddesi.
Tel/fax: (0256) 612 3149.
Simple, friendly hotel, with cast-iron balconies overlooking the sea, near the harbour. **$**

Villa Konak
Yıldırım Caddesi 55.
Tel: (0256) 614 6318.
Fax: (0256) 613 1524.
Attractively restored old-town mansion with rooms set around several small courtyards. Bar, restaurant, garden and pool. **$$**

Marmaris and İçmeler

Green Nature ★★★★★
Siteler Mahallesi Armutalan, Marmaris.
Tel: (0252) 413 6054.
Fax: (0252) 413 6052.

Most guests here are on package deals offering half-board. Adult and children's pools, sauna, fitness centre, tennis court, billiards room and a Turkish bath. Closed in winter. **$$$$**

Merit Grand Azur ★★★★★
Kenan Evren Bulvarı, Marmaris.
Tel: (0252) 412 8201.
Fax: (0252) 412 3530.
A popular resort hotel that manages to keep a sense of class about itself. A tempting split-level pool and a pretty garden that leads to the hotel's own stretch of beach. Easy access to Marmaris by *dolmuş*. **$$$$**

Munamar Vista ★★★★★
Kayabal Caddesi, Içmeler.
Tel: (0252) 455 3360.
Fax: (0252) 455 3359.
Spacious rooms and lots of facilities, including a pool, disco and a beach on the doorstep with plenty of watersports. The water *dolmuş* from Marmaris makes a stop here. Open all year and suitable for anyone seeking a location that is relatively peaceful yet close to Marmaris. **$$$$**

Aqua ★★★
Içmeler.
Tel: (0252) 455 3633.
Fax: (0252) 455 3650.
A landscaped garden leads down to the beach, while indoors there is a fitness centre and a tennis court. Open all year. **$$$**

Hotel Begonya
Hacı Mustafa Sokak 101.
Tel: (0252) 412 4095.
Fax: (0252) 412 1518.
Attractive converted barn with a courtyard garden. Expect some noise from the nearby disco. **$$**

Interyouth Hostel ★
Tepe Mahallesi 42, Sokak 45, Marmaris.
Tel: (0252) 412 3687.
Fax: (0252) 412 7823.
Budget accommodation in the main covered market of Marmaris, with some single and double rooms as well as the basic dorms. There is another hostel with the same name on Kemeraltı Mahallesi, tel: (0252) 412 6432, which is outside the centre so it should offer a more peaceful night's sleep. Open throughout the year. **$**

Pamukkale

Kervansaray ★
Inönü Caddesi, Pamukkale Köyü.
Tel: (0258) 272 2209.
Fax: (0258) 272 2143.
The hotels in neighbouring Bergama have little to recommend them but this little place between the town and Pamukkale offers comfortable accommodation for an overnight stay and all the rooms have their own showers. Open all year. **$$**

Price Guide

Prices are per night for a double room during the high season.
$$$$ = above $150
$$$ =$70 to $150
$$ = $50 to $70
$ = below $50

Selçuk

Kalehan ★★★
On the main street that runs through the town.
Tel: (0232) 892 6154.
Fax: (0232) 892 2169.
E-mail: ergirh@uperonline.com
Easily the classiest hotel in Selçuk, combining modern comforts like air conditioning and swimming pool alongside traditional Ottoman décor and design. Open all year. **$$**

Nazhan ★
Saint Jean Caddesi, 1044 Sokak.
Tel: (0232) 892 8731.
There are many attractive features in this elegant 6-room *pansiyon*, including a bar on the rooftop and a tiny courtyard for breakfast in the shade. Open all year. **$$**

MEDITERRANEAN COAST

Many of the giant resort hotels along this coast, between Kemer and Alanya, cater to an almost exlusively German clientele and offer all-inclusive packages designed for people who never move from the premises except when escorted. Prices are very high for casual arrivals and you need to check on the position of

hotels if you want the freedom to move around; some are 20 km (12.5 miles) from the nearest town.

Adana

Hotel Seyhan ★★★★★
Turhan Cemal Beriker Bulvarı 18.
Tel: (0322) 457 5810.
Fax: (0322) 454 2834.
Shiny, mirror-plated tower block in the town centre, with several restaurants and bars, a swimming pool, health club and nightclub. **$$$**

Inci Hotel ★★★★
Kurtulus Caddesi 40, 01060 Kuruköprü.
Tel: (0322) 435 8234.
Fax: (0322) 435 8368.
Large city-centre business-style hotel with friendly staff and a nightclub in the basement. **$$**

Alanya

The main hotel strip for Alanya is about 20 km (12.5 miles) west of the city, along Incekum Beach, where there are at least 20 large hotels, with more still under construction.

Grand Kaptan ★★★★
Oba Gölü Mevkii.
Tel: (0242) 514 0101.
Fax: (0242) 514 0092.
Huge all-encompassing resort hotel with pools, fitness centre, disco, land- and watersports and private beach, right near the marina. **$$$$**

Pasha Bey ★★★★
Konaklı Mevkii.
Tel: (0242) 565 1520.
Fax: (0242) 565 1513.
Very upmarket, flamboyant Disney castle-styled beach hotel with all the trimmings. **$$$**

Bedesten
Içkale.
Tel: (0242) 512 1234.
Fax: (0242) 513 7934.
Restored 13th-century Seljuk *caravansaray* on the castle rock, with heaps of atmosphere, wonderful views and a pool. **$$**

Kaptan
Iskele Caddesi 70.
Tel: (0242) 513 4900.
Fax: (0242) 513 2000.
www.kaptanhotel.com
A small, friendly city-centre hotel

ideally placed near the harbour for sightseeing and nightlife. **$$**

Pansiyon Best
Alaladdinoğlu Sokak 23.
Tel: (0242) 511 0171.
Fax: (0242) 513 0446.
This modest *pansiyon* near the museum offers clean rooms and breakfast at reasonable rates. **$**

Anamur

Hotel Hermes ★★★
Iskele Mevkii 33006.
Tel: (0324) 814 3950.
Fax: (0324) 814 3995.
Friendly, simple seaside hotel. All rooms have central heating, air conditioning and balconies. The hotel also has a pool, sauna and brick-shaking disco. **$$**

Yalı Motel
Yalı Mahallesi, Iskele.
Tel: (0324) 814 1435.
Fax: (0324) 814 3474.
Attractive beachfront motel with shady gardens. 16 bungalows, camping, restaurant and café-bar. Booking advised. Closed in winter. **$**

Antalya

There are numerous small hotels and *pansiyons* in the old town and a few larger properties facing Konyaalti Beach, but most of Antalya's larger hotels and package-tour properties are in Lara, a modern suburb along the seafront about 12 km (7.5 miles) east of the city. A local speciality is the growing number of Special-License (Historic) Hotels (*see page 380*). The local tourist office can provide a complete list.

Sheraton Voyager ★★★★★
100 Yil Bulvarı, Konyaalti.
Tel: (0242) 243 2432.
Fax: (0242) 243 2462.
www.sheraton.com
Happily soaking up Turks and foreigners, business people and tourists, this is one the best hotels on the Turkish coast, on the beachfront near the museum. It has several excellent restaurants and bars, attractive gardens, a jogging track, pool and fitness centre. **$$$$**

Falez ★★★★★
Konyaalti Falez Mekvii, 07050 Antalya.

Tel: (0242) 248 5000.
Fax: (0242) 248 5025.
www.falez.com.tr
Sleek, luxurious, expensive and on Konyaalti Beach, all the 324 rooms and 22 suites have balconies with sea views, and the hotel offers a wide range of land- and watersports for adults and children. **$$$$**

Alp Paşa Hotel
Barbaros Mahallesi, Hesapcı Sokak 30.
Tel: (0242) 247 5676/243 0045.
Fax: (0242) 248 5074.
www.alppasa.com
Atmospheric Ottoman-style old-town hotel, with 60 rooms, Turkish bath, garden bar and excellent restaurant. **$$$$**

Dedekonak Pansiyon
Kılıçarslan Mahallesi, Hısırlık Sokak 13.
Tel/fax: (0242) 247 5170.
Carefully restored Ottoman mansion built around a courtyard with a marble fountain, offering good, cheap old-town accommodation. **$$**

Villa Perla
Kaleiçi.
Tel: (0242) 248 9793.
Fax: (0242) 241 2917.
www.villaperla.com
Atmospheric family-run hotel in a converted Ottoman house, with 16 rooms, private courtyard garden for outdoor eating and small pool. **$**

Otel Tuvana
Karanlik Sokak 18.
Tel: (0242) 241 1981.
Secluded and quiet hotel, beautifully restored, with a relaxed atmosphere and garden with pool. **$$$**

Bagana Park
Yukara Karaman Koyu.
Tel: (0242) 425 2270.
A horse ranch with several excellent chalet rooms around a swimming pool, and an excellent bar and restaurant. Very handy for the ruins of Termessos and walks in the national park, as well as riding. **$$–$$$**

Antakya

Büyük Antakya Oteli ★★★★
Atatürk Caddesi 8.
Tel: (0326) 213 5858.
Fax: (0326) 213 5869.

Ideally located in the city centre, Antakya's finest hotel is comfortable, friendly and efficient, with furnishings stuck in the 1960s. **$$$**

Aspendos

Attaleia ★★★★★
Belek.
Tel: (0242) 725 4301.
Fax: (0242) 725 4324.
Glamorous beachfront holiday village with landscaped gardens, pine forests and a private golf course. Restaurants, bars, fitness centre, pools and many other sporting facilities also on offer. **$$$$**

Fethiye

Letoonia Hotel and Club
4 km (2.5 miles) from the town.
Tel: (0252) 614 4966.
Fax: (0252) 614 4422.
Huge out-of-town resort with hotel block, villas and "club" units; 9 bars, 5 restaurants, 2 pools, 3 beaches, and all the land- and watersports you could dream of. Kids' club and shuttle boat to Fethiye. Parts close down in winter. **$$**

Villa Daffodil
Karagözler Orta Yol 21; 1 km (0.5 mile) from the town centre.
Tel: (0242) 614 2816.
Fax: (0242) 612 2223.
Peaceful, attractive Ottoman-style *pansiyon* with pool and restaurant. Early booking is essential. **$**

Kemal Hotel
Geziyolu.
Tel: (0252) 614 5009.
Fax: (0252) 614 5009.
Simple modern hotel at the quieter end of the waterfront. **$**

Duygu Pansiyon
Ordu Caddesi 54.
Tel: (0252) 614 3563.
A delightful *pansiyon* with spectacular bay views from the roof terrace. **$**

Finike

Presa Di Finica
P.O. Box 31, Sahil Yolu, (4 km/2.5 miles from town centre).
Tel: (0242) 855 5500.
Fax: (0242) 855 5300.

Beachfront hotel with 375 beautiful rooms and 52 private suites, sports facilities and excellent convention facilities. Surrounded by citrus groves. Open all year. **$$$**

Gocek
Creative Cultural Holidays
The Marina, Gocek.
Tel: (0252) 612 3998.
www.worldpeacetravel.co.uk
Five beautiful waterfront cottages sleeping from 2 to 5; ideal for relaxation before or after a *gulet* tour. **$$–$$$**

Iskenderun
Hotel Cabir
Ulucami Caddesi 16.
Tel: (0326) 612 3391.
Fax: (0326) 612 3393.
Iskenderun's best hotel – all 35 rooms are clean and comfortable and there is a bar and disco. **$$$**

Kalkan
Club Patara/Patara Prince ★★★★★
2 km (1 mile) from village centre.
Tel: (0242) 844 3920.
Fax: (0242) 844 3930.
The most luxurious resort in the area, with a 5-star hotel and estate of timeshare houses, tennis courts, diving centre, Italian restaurant and all the other luxuries. Open all year. **$$$$**
Pirat Otel ★★★
Kalkan Marina.
Tel: (0242) 844 3178.
Fax: (0242) 844 3183.
Village-centre resort hotel with a pool deck and balconies overlooking the harbour. Open all year. **$$**
Balıkçihan Pansiyon
Village centre.
Tel: (0242) 844 3075.
Fax: (0242) 844 3641.
This tiny *pansiyon* near the waterfront is one of the prettiest, friendliest and most comfortable hotels in town. Booking essential. Summer only. **$**
Diva Pansiyon
Cumhuriyet Caddesi.
Tel: (0242) 844 3175.
Fax: (0242) 844 3139.
Even though it has only 15 rooms, this charming little hotel has 3 bars

and a pool with a children's section, along with lovely views over the village and harbour. Open in summer only. **$$**

Kaş
Hera Hotel ★★★★
Küçükçakil Mevcii.
Tel: (0242) 836 3062.
Fax: (0242) 836 3063.
Overblown film-set grandeur, with fake columns, 40 rooms with balconies and sea views, on the seafront within walking distance of the town centre. Turkish bath, sauna, Jacuzzi, fitness centre, disco, games room, shopping mall, pool and pocket-sized private beach. **$$$**

Price Guide

Prices are per night for a double room during the high season.
$$$$ = above $150
$$$ =$70 to $150
$$ = $50 to $70
$ = below $50

Hotel Club Phellos ★★★
Lycia Caddesi.
Tel: (0242) 836 1953.
Fax: (0242) 836 1890.
Central, modern concrete box. However, all 80 rooms have balconies with sea views and there is a good pool and sauna. **$$**
Ekici Hotel ★★★
Arisan Sokak 1, 168/B.
Tel: (0242) 836 1417.
Fax: (0242) 836 1823.
Medium-sized comfortable hotel, directly opposite and comparable to the Hotel Club Phellos. A bit smarter, but the view and pool are not as good. Summer only. **$$**
Arpia Pansiyon
Çukurbağ Yarımadası.
Tel: (0242) 836 2642.
Fax: (0242) 836 3163.
Pretty, quiet *pansiyon* with a pool and restaurant, away from the bustle, on the peninsula. Open in summer only. **$$**
Golden Pansiyon
Ilkokul Caddesi (near Lycian tomb).
Tel: (0242) 836 1736.
Popular German-Turkish managed backpackers' stop, with spartan

rooms and shared bathroom in an old Ottoman house in the town centre. Cheap, cheerful and very noisy, with a roof-terrace bar. **$**
Yalı Pansiyon
Hastane Caddesi 11.
Tel: (0242) 836 3226.
Superb sea views from the wide shady terraces; comfortable rooms and cooking facilities. **$**

Kemer
While there are a number of places to stay here, from large hotels to simple *pansiyons* in Kemer itself, the real hotel districts are a few kilometres out of town, to the north and south, at the satellite resorts of Göynük, Beldibi, Tekirova and Çamyuva.

Antalya Renaissance ★★★★★
Beldibi.
Tel: (0242) 824 8431.
Fax: (0242) 824 8130.
338 rooms, 57 suites, 87 garden rooms and 13 villas, multiple restaurants, pools, bars, shops, conference facilities, casino and health club, all surrounded by mountains, pine forests and the sea. Huge, attractive and expensive. **$$$$$**
Royal Resort Hotel ★★★★★
Göynük.
Tel: (0242) 815 2370.
Fax: (0242) 815 1627.
A luxurious resort with 187 balconied rooms, 9 villas and 4 restaurants, pool, sauna, bars and shops. **$$$$**
Sultan Saray ★★★★
Göynük.
Tel: (0242) 815 1480.
Fax: (0242) 815 1499.
Square 500-room complex with 6 bars, tennis and squash courts, several pools, watersports, films, cabaret, a private beach and health club. Clean, comfortable and efficient. **$$$**
Hotel Sport
Beldibi.
Tel: (0242) 824 8549.
Fax: (0242) 824 1176.
A small hotel by local standards, with 70 rooms. Set in beautiful shady gardens, with swimming pool and tennis court. **$$**

Hotel Kaliptus
Kemer.
Tel: (0242) 814 2467.
Small, friendly and attractive with a pool and two restaurants, within easy walking distance of the town centre and beach. Closed in winter. **$$**

Aşkın Motel
Bahçecik Mevkii, Kemer Yolu (main road between Kemer and Beldibi).
Tel: (0242) 824 8171.
Charming, small family-run hotel surrounded by orange groves. A short way from the sea, but it has a pool and restaurant, serving Black Sea specialities. **$**

Kis Kalesi
Club Hotel Barbarossa
Kis Kalesi seafront, 23 km (14 miles) east of Silifke.
Tel: (0324) 523 2364.
Fax: (0324) 523 2090.
Comfortable, pleasantly designed hotel with 103 rooms on a private beach, with views across to Kis Kalesi. Good pool, watersports, disco and indoor and outdoor restaurants. **$$$**

Mersin
Hilton ★★★★
Adnan Menderes Bulvarı 3310.
Tel: (0324) 326 5000.
Fax: (0324) 326 5050.
City-centre tower block with all the usual efficiency and conveniences of the Hilton chain. **$$$**

Ölü Deniz
Club Belcekiz Beach
Tel: (0252) 616 6009.
Fax: (0252) 616 6448.
Colourful, low-rise holiday village with a pool and Jacuzzi, shopping mall, *hamam* and 2 restaurants, on the beach within easy walking distance of the lagoon. Closed in winter. **$$**

Hotel Montana Pine Resort
Ovacık Mahallesi, Ölüdeniz Beldesi.
Tel: (0252) 616 7108.
Fax: (0252) 616 6451.
This delightful low-rise hotel is situated in the pine forests overlooking the lagoon. There are 3 pools, tennis courts, gym and games room, plus a shuttle bus to the beach, 3 km (2 miles) away. Closed in winter. **$$$**

Patara
Beyhan Patara Resort Hotel
Gelemiş Köyü.
Tel: (0242) 843 5096.
Fax: (0242) 843 5097.
Large resort hotel on the hill overlooking Patara; the most upmarket option in town. **$$$**

Patara View Point Hotel
Gelimiş Köyü.
Tel: (0242) 843 5184.
Fax: (0242) 843 5022.
Delightful little *pansiyon* just east of town, with fine views and a shuttle service to the beach. The management also runs the Golden, which has the best restaurant in the village. Closed in winter. **$**

Side
The town has over 25,000 hotel beds – there really is something for everyone, although much of it is sold within package tours. The local tourist office has full details.

Side Palace Hotel ★★★★
Sorgun Mevkii.
Tel: (0242) 756 9321.
Fax: (0242) 756 9320.
Large resort overlooking the beach, with 6 bars, 2 restaurants, several pools, a health club, land- and watersports and all the trimmings. **$$$$**

Robinson Club Pamfilya
Sorgun.
Tel: (0242) 756 9350.
Fax: (0242) 756 9358.
One of the oldest and prettiest of the larger Side resorts, set in a beachfront pine forest. It has 331 rooms, restaurant, bar, disco, *hamam* and a variety of sports. **$$$**

Hanimeli Pansiyon
Turgut Reis Sokak.
Tel: (0242) 753 1789.
Charming small town-centre *pansiyon* with a marble staircase and garden courtyard. **$**

Yıldırım Pansiyon
Tiyatro Arkası (behind the theatre).
Tel: (0242) 753 2398.
Delightful little *pansiyon*, tucked away from view. **$**

Tarsus
Mersin Oteli ★★★★
Şelale.
Tel: (0324) 614 0600.
Fax: (0324) 614 0033.
Large, spacious modern hotel on the edge of the city, near the waterfall. **$$$**

CENTRAL ANATOLIA

Ankara
As capital, Ankara's hotels are particularly geared to business travellers, bristling with air conditioning, phones, satellite TV, minibars and secretarial facilities. Prices often match the convenience, however.

Ankara Hilton S.A ★★★★★
Tarhan Caddesi 12, Kavaklıdere.
Tel: (0312) 468 2888.
Fax: (0312) 468 0909.
One of the city's biggest hotels, geared up for foreign business executives, the Ankara Hilton has 324 rooms and 24 suites, no-smoking rooms and special rooms for the disabled. There are 2 restaurants, a cafeteria, patisserie, bar, conference and banquet facilities with simultaneous translation services, a Turkish bath, sauna, Jacuzzi, solarium, pool, fitness centre, shopping arcade, garage, post office and hairdresser. **$$$$**

Merit Altınel Hotel ★★★★★
Gazi Mustafa Kemal Bulvarı No. 151, Tandoğan.
Tel: (0312) 231 7760.
Fax: (0312) 230 2330.
A flagship hotel of the Net Group, Turkey's leading tourism company, the Merit Altınel has 170 rooms, 25 suites, and 9 rooms for disabled travellers, 2 restaurants, a snack bar, a cafeteria, pastry shop, 4 conference halls, bar, banquet facilities, a beauty parlour, barber, hairdresser, gym, Turkish bath, swimming pool and sauna, and book store. **$$$$**

Grand Hotel Ankara ★★★★
Atatürk Bulvarı 183, Kavaklıdere.
Tel: (0312) 425 6655.
Fax: (0312) 425 5070.

Located across from the National Assembly, the Grand Hotel Ankara is the city's oldest deluxe hotel, with 192 rooms and 14 suites. The hotel also has 2 restaurants, 2 bars, casino, meeting room, a conference hall and banquet facilities, a nightclub, pool and health centre. **$$$$**

Sheraton Ankara Hotel and Towers ★★★★★
Noktalı Sokak, 06700 Kavaklıdere.
Tel: (0312) 468 5454.
Fax: (0312) 467 1136.
One of the best hotels in the city, the Sheraton is connected to the Karun Shopping Centre, which has dozens of gift shops, jewellers, and carpet and copperware sellers. The hotel has 304 rooms, 16 suites, a bar, 3 restaurants, casino, meeting room, beauty centre, pool, sauna and Jacuzzi. **$$$$**

Houston Hotel
Guniz Sokak 26, Kavaklıdere.
Tel: (0312) 466 1680.
Fax: (0312) 466 1674.
Comfortable, efficient and friendly modern hotel in an excellent city-centre location. 50 rooms with private bathroom, telephone, satellite TV, air conditioning. The Houston also has a restaurant, bar, cafeteria, garden and garage. **$$$**

İçkale Hotel ★★★★
Gazi Mustafa Kemal Bulvarı 89, 06570 Maltepe.
Tel: (0312) 231 7710.
Fax: (0312) 230 6133.
This hotel is centrally located, with 122 rooms and 3 suites. It has 3 restaurants, bar, conference room, sauna, Turkish bath, gymnasium and a swimming pool. **$$$**

Angora House Hotel
Kalekapisi Sokak 16–18, Ulus & Citadel,
Tel: (0312) 309 8380.
Fax: (0312) 309 8381.
Charming small hotel with 6 individually decorated rooms in a restored Ottoman house in the citadel. Booking essential. **$$**

Bolu

Hotel Doruk Kaya
Kartalkaya Mevkii.
Tel: (0374) 234 5026.
Fax: (0374) 234 5025.

Located in Kartalkaya, a popular ski resort in the Bolu Mountains, the Hotel Doruk Kaya has 164 rooms and also operates a 35-room ski lodge, connected to the hotel by an underground passage. It has a swimming pool, fitness centre, sauna, restaurant, several bars and 7 ski lifts. Open from December to April. **$$$**

Çankırı

Ilgaz Doruk Hotel
Ilgaz Doruk Mevkii, Kayak Merkezi, Ilgaz.
Tel: (0376) 416 1210.
Fax: (0376) 416 1210.
Located in the Ilgaz Mountains ski resort, the hotel has 52 rooms, 4 suites and 2 special rooms, a restaurant, bar, discotheque, sauna and nightclub. **$$–$$$**

Kayseri

Dedeman Erciyes Hotel ★★★
Erciyes Dağı, Kayseri; 32 km (20 miles) from Kayseri Airport.
Tel: (0352) 342 2116.
Fax: (0352) 342 2117.
Part of a ski resort on the slopes of Mount Erciyes, a 3,917-metre (12,926-ft) extinct volcano. The hotel has 60 rooms, each with satellite TV, air conditioning and minibar. It operates ski lifts in winter and also has a swimming pool, sauna, restaurant, bar and disco. Open all year round. **$$$**

Konya

Hotel Selçuk ★★
Alaadin Caddesi 4.
Tel: (0332) 353 2525.
Located near the main tourist attractions of the city, Hotel Selçuk has 70 rooms and a restaurant. **$$**

Nevsehir

Club Mediterranée Kaya Hotel ★★★
Üçhisar.
Tel: (0384) 219 2007.
Fax: (0384) 219 2363.
Built on the side of a hill, this hotel has a grand view of Üçhisar and the volcanic tuff formations. Part of the hotel is built right into the rocks. With 62 rooms, a swimming pool, meeting room, restaurant and bar. Open 25 April–15 October. **$$**

Dedeman Kapadokya ★★★★★
2 km (1 mile) from Nevsehir on the road to Ürgüp.
Tel: (0384) 213 9900.
Fax: (0384) 213 2158.
Cappadocia's most luxurious hotel with 349 rooms, 34 suites, and a royal suite, plus all the trimmings. It has 3 restaurants, 3 bars, a disco, 2 conference halls with simultaneous translation facilities, and 5 meeting rooms. It also has a sauna, fitness centre, basketball and tennis courts, pool, Turkish bath and so on. **$$$**

Ataman Hotel
Orta Mahallesi, Göreme.
Tel: (0384) 271 2310.
Fax: (0384) 271 2313.
E-mail: ataman@wec-net.com.tr
www.wec-net.com.tr/atamanhotel
This charming small cave hotel has 16 rooms, decorated with kilims and antiques. **$$$$**

Altınöz Hotel ★★★★
Ragıp Üner Caddesi 23.
Tel: (0384) 213 5305.
Fax: (0384) 213 2817.
This hotel has 120 rooms and 12 suites, 3 indoor restaurants, a meeting room and banquet facilities, TV room, roof and disco bars, a sauna, pastry shop and gymnasium. **$$$**

Peri Tower Hotel ★★★★
Nar.
Tel: (0384) 212 8816.
Fax: (0384) 213 9028.
The deluxe Peri Tower, elaborately designed to resemble the fairy chimneys of Cappadocia, has 126 rooms and 20 suites, a restaurant, conference room, meeting rooms, banquet facilities, a café with an open fire, disco, health club and massage parlour, and volleyball and basketball courts. **$$**

Sofa Hotel
Orta Mahalesi, Avanos.
Tel: (0384) 511 5186.
Fax: (0384) 511 4489.
The Sofa Hotel is an old restored Turkish house with 34 rooms. It has an outdoor restaurant, snack bar, cafeteria and outdoor bar. **$**

Ottoman House
Orta Mahalesi, Göreme.
Tel: (0384) 271 2616.
Fax: (0384) 271 2351.

Simple, but clean and cosy accommodation in a friendly hotel, decorated with carpets from the manager's shop. Good restaurant and bar. **$**

BLACK SEA COAST

Ağva
Riverside Club
Yakuplu Mahallesi 2, 81740 Ağva (Black Sea coast above Şile).
Tel: (0216) 721 8293.
Fax: (0216) 414 2103.
Sandy, untrammelled beaches, good fishing and the sense of a true nature reserve from this country lodge-style hotel. Environmentalists are especially welcome and guests can use the hotel's canoes, rowing boats and an outboard to cruise down to the beach or explore the forest upstream. Quiet music and superb seafood in the restaurant. With 10 rooms, open all year. **$$**

Amasra
Amasrist
Büyük Liman Caddesi.
Tel: (0378) 315 2465.
Fax: (0378) 315 2629.
Rather quaint, 1930s spa-style accommodation overlooking the sea; basic en-suite rooms with balconies. Closed in winter. **$$**
Otel Belvü Palas
Küçük Liman Caddesi 20.
Tel: (0378) 315 1237.
Fax: (0378) 315 1310.
Although the accommodation is very basic, the tiny rooms all have balconies and stunning views. Closed in winter. **$**
Yağmur Pansiyon
Zindan Mahallesi, Kemere Sokak 6.
Tel: (0378) 315 1603.
Cheery, newly built, family-run house containing several 3-bedroom apartments with a view, fully fitted kitchens, and bedding and central heating. Open all year round. **$–$$**

Amasya
Emin Efendi Pansiyon
Hatuniye Mahallesi Hazeranlar S 73.
Tel: (0358) 212 0852.
Fax: (0358) 212 1895.

Price Guide

Prices are per night for a double room during the high season.
$$$$ = above $150
$$$ =$70 to $150
$$ = $50 to $70
$ = below $50

Fine 200-year-old Ottoman house jutting out over the Yeşilırmak River, in the town's historical section, below royal tombs. Five rooms, some en suite, with a courtyard and common room containing a piano and an open fire, plus a café. **$$**
Ilk Pansiyon
Gümüşlü Mahallesi Hitit S 1 (opposite the tourist office).
Tel: (0358) 218 1689.
Fax: (0358) 218 6277.
This old Armenian mansion is one of the most beautifully restored houses in Amasya, refurbished by the owner, an architect committed to urban renewal. The 6 rooms are all of different sizes and are individually furnished with various amenities (including bathtubs hidden in the cabinets); all of them are situated around a lovely courtyard. **$**

Çamlihemsin/Ayder

There are now many more places to stay in this trekkers' paradise. A local tourist office may give you some advice, if you can find someone who speaks English.

Türkü Tourism
Inönü Caddesi 47, Çamlıhemsin.
Tel/fax: (0464) 651 7230.
The Turkish tourist own *pansiyon* in Ayder is a neat, modern wooden house, from where they also organise trekking tours.

Those willing to brave more basic accommodation but with more competent English-speaking guides might try out:
Çağlayan Otel
Tel: (0464) 657 2073.
This quaint and clean old wooden

Artvin
Hotel Karahan
Inönü Caddesi 16.
Tel: (0466) 212 1800.
Fax: (0466) 212 2420.
The only comfortable hotel in town. The Karahan brothers have made this place a haven after a long journey from the coast, and if there is sufficient demand they can arrange a taxi to the famous forest monasteries. Although unprepossessing from the outside, this 48-room hotel offers superb mountain views from many of its well-ordered balconied rooms and its good restaurant. The owners speak English. **$$**
Karahan Pension
Barhal Koyu, Yusufeli.
Tel: (0466) 826 2071.
Fax (0466) 212 2420.
Owned by the same family as the Hotel Karahan (see above), this attractive pension is located in a remote and atmospheric spot, famous for its 10th-century Georgian church. It is difficult to get to except by trekking, in a 4-wheel drive or on horseback. There are 2 chalets as well as a covered roof terrace that can sleep up to 15 people. Summer only. **$–$$**

lodge at the top of the village is family run. Contact Mehmet (Niko) Sarı or another member of the family. Closed during winter.
Pirikoğlu Otel
Tel: (0464) 657 2021.
Cheap accommodation available all year. Contact Adnan Pirikoglu. **$**
Kuşpuney Otel
Modern with en suite rooms and central heating, recommended by both Mehmet (Niko) Sarı and Adrian Pirikoğlu. **$$**
If you plan to do the long trek across to Barhal/Yusufeli, contact Mehmet (Niko) Sarı and Adrian Pirikoğlu for details of mountain huts and *pansiyons* in small villages.

Ayancık
Belediye Apart Otel
Gazhane Caddesi 55, Inebolu.
Tel: (0368) 613 1137/3536.
Fax: (0368) 613 1333.
Again, the best-run accommodation in town is the government-run apart-hotel and bungalows, which are new but built to traditional Black Sea design. Hotel section open all year. 8 duplex suites, 5 wooden rooms, 3 bungalows, 1 suite done up in traditional village style. 54-bed capacity, but gets full with local government officials and their families, so best to book. Cooking facilities, bar, restaurant and every convenience. **$$**

Price Guide

Prices are per night for a double room during the high season.
$$$$ = above $150
$$$ =$70 to $150
$$ = $50 to $70
$ = below $50

Gerze
Körfez Turistik Tesişleri
End of point, Gerze village.
Tel: (0368) 718 2476.
A gem for lovers of simplicity and solitude, all the rooms in this small, basic motel complex rooms have balconies overlooking the sea; from those on the right you can watch the fishermen trawling by night. Good restaurant. Closed in winter. **$**

Inebolu
Inebolu Belediyesi Motel and Yakamoz Holiday Village
Boyran Mahallesi, Ismet Paşa Caddesi.
Tel: Motel (0366) 811 4305.
Tel: Yakamoz (0366) 811 3100.
Fax: Motel (0366) 811 3232.
Open all year, this comfortable local government-run seaside motel is open all year and probably the best bet in town. **$$**

Safranbolu
This small museum town is renowned for its beautiful old wooden mansions, many of which have been converted into hotels

and *pansiyons*, each with a distinct quality. A full listing is available from the tourist information office.

Havuzlu Konak
Çarşı Mahallesi.
Tel: (0372) 725 2883.
Fax: (0372) 712 3824.
One of the most elegant mansion hotels in the town, the Havuzlu Konak is famous for its enormous indoor pool and fountain, which provided water for the original 18th-century owners and is now surrounded by café tables. With 14 rooms, 4 suites. **$$$$**

Hotel Uz ★★
İnönü Mahallesi Araphacı Caddesi 3, Kıranköy.
Tel: (0372) 712 1086.
Fax: (0372) 771 2215.
Just outside the town, this is one of the few local modern business hotels, with 30 rooms, 6 suites and all modern conveniences, including TV and car park. **$$$**

Tahsin Bey & Paşa Konağı
Çarşı Mahallesi.
Tel: (0372) 712 6062.
Fax: (0372) 712 5596.
Two connected historic mansions, one 19th century and one 18th century, operated under one personable management. 11 rooms, plus a garden café. **$$$**

Çarşı Han Pansiyon
Baba Sultan Mahallesi, Cinci Hanı Sokak. Tel: (0372) 725 1079.
Modern, bright, cheap and clean; a favourite with trekkers going east. **$**

Sinop
Villa Rose
Ada Mahallesi Kartal C 9.
Tel: (0368) 261 1923.
Fax: (0368) 260 1016.
Comfortable home as much as a hotel, full of the travel memoirs and personality of the owner. Good home-cooking, master suite with sauna, close to beach. 6 rooms. **$$**

Karakum Motel
Gelincik Mevkii, just outside Sinop.
Tel: (0368) 261 8777.
Fax: (0368) 261 1954.
60 basic waterfront bungalows with private beach and restaurant; promises 24-hour hot water. **$**

Trabzon
Zorlu Grand Hotel ★★★★★
Maraş Caddesi 9.
Tel: (0462) 326 8400.
Fax: (0462) 326 8458.
The city's first 5-star hotel, catering to the booming business traffic. Its 160 rooms include 2 minisuites, 8 large suites and a royal suite. Every business convenience. **$$$$**

Hotel Usta ★★★
Telegrafhane Sokak 1, Iskele Caddesi.
Tel: (0462) 326 5704.
Fax: (0462) 322 3793.
The best of Trabzon's middle-range hotels offers 76 well-kept rooms, good service and a convenient location, as well as tours. **$$**

Hotel Anil
Güzelhisar Caddesi (off Iskele Caddesi). Tel: (0462) 321 9566.
Down near the waterfront, this basic hotel is close to some rather seedy action but is comfortable and even offers some harbour-view rooms at rock-bottom prices. **$**

Ünye/Ordu/Karagöl
Kumsal Hotel
Gölevi Köyü, Ünye.
Tel: (0452) 323 4490.
Fax: (0452) 323 4490.
27 clean and simple en-suite rooms; garden, restaurant, bar, private beach. 5 km (3 miles) outside the village. **$$**

Belde Otel ★★★
Kirazlimanı Mahallesi, Ordu.
Tel: (0452) 214 4273.
Fax: (0452) 214 9338.
Located on a small point of land off the highway, this is Ordu's biggest holiday complex, with a pool. **$$**

Uzungöl
Inan Kardeşler Trout Farm and Motel
60 km (37 miles) inland from the town of Of.
Tel: (0462) 656 6021.
Fax: (0462) 656 6066.
A favoured fishing retreat also offering opportunities for day hikes into the higher plateaus, with a regular minibus service in summer. A collection of 33 peaked wooden bungalows with all modern facilities, restaurant and tea garden. **$$**

Karagol/Şavşat
Karagöl Pension
Karagöl Lake, 08780, 23 km
(14 miles) from Şavşat village.
Tel: (0466) 537 2137/2300.
Fax: (0466) 517 1260.
Great facilities in this remote, green
region of the eastern Black Sea
with unspoiled forests and hunting
and fishing opportunities. 4 rooms
and some camping facilities. Brown
bears roam the woods. **$$–$$$**

THE EAST

Dıyarbakır
Dedeman Dıyarbakır Hotel ★★★★
Elazığ Caddesi, Yeni Belediye
Sarayı Yanı.
Tel: (0412) 224 7353.
Fax: (0412) 224 7353.
E-mail: hotels@dedeman.com.tr
The city's best accommodation,
with 98 rooms and 2 suites, a
restaurant-bar, seminar room,
fitness centre and pool. **$$**
Otel Büyük Kervansaray ★★★★
Gazi Caddesi.
Tel: (0412) 228 9606.
Fax: (0412) 223 7731.
A 16th-century sandstone
caravansaray recently refurbished
into atmospheric glory. Courtyard
garden, restaurant and pool. **$$**
Balkar Hotel
Kibris Caddesi 38
Tel: (0412) 228 1233.
Modern central hotel aimed at
business customers, but surprisingly
quiet and tastefully furnished. **$$$**

Doğubeyazıt
Sim-Er Hotel ★★★
Iran Transit Yolu 3 Km, PK 13
Doğubeyazıt, Ağrı.
Tel: (0472) 312 4842.
Fax: (0472) 312 4843.
Hotel with 125 rooms and a
restaurant as well as an excellent
view of Mount Ararat. **$**

Erzurum
Dedeman Palandöken Ski Centre
★★★★
Palandöken Dağı PK 115.
Tel: (0442) 316 2414.
Fax: (0442) 316 3607.
E-mail: hotels@Dedeman.com.tr

Set in a mountainous ski resort
with Turkey's longest ski run, the
hotel has 196 rooms, a restaurant,
bar, cocktail room, sauna, fitness
centre, pool and disco. Open all
year. The ski season is usually from
mid-November to May, but may be
extended if weather permits. **$$$**
Otel Polat ★★
Kazım Karabekir Caddesi 6.
Tel: (0442) 218 1624.
Fax: (0442) 234 4598.
Modern block, centrally located. **$$**

Gaziantep
Tuğcan Hotel ★★★★★
Atatürk Bulvarı 34.
Tel: (0342) 220 4323.
Fax: (0342) 220 3242.
One of the best hotels in eastern
Turkey. Swimming pool, sauna,
beauty parlour, disco, fitness
centre, bar and restaurant, cocktail
room and conference hall. **$$$**
Hotel Tilmen ★★★★
Inönü Caddesi, 168.
Tel: (0342) 220 2081.
Fax: (0342) 220 2091.
Central, with restaurant and bar. **$$**

Kahramanmaras
Otel Kazancı
Kurtuluş Mahalesi, Garajlar
Caddesi.
Tel/Fax: (0344) 233 4462.
Utilitarian and centrally located. **$**

Kâhta
New Merhaba Hotel ★★★
Çarşı Caddesi 49, Kâhta, Adıyaman.
Tel/Fax: (0416) 725 7111.
Boring but convenient for the 3am
hike up to Nemrut Dağı. **$**
Otel Kervansaray Nemrut
Karakut Köyü, Nemrut Dağı; 8 km
(5 miles) from the summit.
Tel: (0416) 737 2190.
Fax: (0416) 737 2085.
Low-slung old stone *caravansaray*
near a waterfall on the slopes of
Nemrut Dağı. with 14 simple but
comfortable rooms, restaurant,
pool and camping. **$$**

Şanlıurfa
Harran Otel ★★★★
Sarayönü Caddesi, Ataturk Bulvarı.
Tel: (0414) 313 2860.
Fax: (0414) 313 4918.

Located in the city centre, the
Harran Otel has a bar, meeting and
conference rooms, Turkish bath,
sauna, Jacuzzi, fitness centre, pool
and table-tennis facilities. **$$$**
Edessa Hotel
Balikligöl Mevkii, Hasanpaşa
Mevkii Karşısı.
Tel: (0414) 215 9911.
Fax: (0414) 215 5589.
A charming hotel built in the style of
the traditional architecture of the
old city. It has a swimming pool,
fitness centre and restaurant. **$$**
Şanliurfa Valılığı Konak Evi
Vali Fuat Bey Caddesi.
Tel: (0414) 215 4678.
Exquisite sandstone mansion,
converted by the local government
into a small hotel and superb
(alcohol-free) restaurant for visiting
dignitaries. Rooms are beautifully
furnished and decorated. Air
conditioning in summer, heating in
winter and within walking distance
of Urfa's famous sites. **$$**

Sarıkamıs
Dedeman Sarıkamış Oberj
Sarıkamış, Kars.
Tel: (0474) 413 6312.
Fax: (0474) 413 6312.
A plush ski lodge in one of Turkey's
best ski resorts. Open October to
May, or longer, weather permitting.
$$$

Van
Büyük Urartu ★★★
Cumhuriyet Caddesi.
Tel: (0432) 212 0660.
Fax: (0432) 212 1610.
Has 75 rooms, 2 restaurants,
2 bars and a disco. **$$**

Where to Eat

Choosing a Restaurant

It is difficult to go hungry in Turkey. From the sesame-sprinkled bread rings (simit) sold in every street to the most elaborate Ottoman palace cuisine, there is something here for all appetites.

There are also plenty of foreign restaurants. Urban Turks have, unfortunately, taken to the international fast-food chains such as Pizza Hut and McDonald's, which have an upmarket image, since for Turks they are relatively expensive. Many affluent Turks have travelled, with the result that they love more sophisticated eating out too, so you can find numerous fashionable restaurants offering anything from sushi to spaghetti.

The best hotels often have excellent restaurants of different nationalities, plus lavish buffets available in their coffee shops, especially for Sunday brunch. However, don't assume that fancy décor and well-dressed waiters necessarily mean a good meal; often, you will find the simpler restaurants give you better service and more delicious food.

RESTAURANT TYPES

The word restoran is applied to almost anywhere where food is served, and Turkish restaurants fall into several clearly defined specialist categories:

● **Balık lokantası:** fish restaurants serving hot and cold meze (a mixed selection of starters, which can make up a whole meal, see Order As You Go page 398), freshly caught fish and shellfish. You will be welcome to look at the fish available in order to

choose. Fish is more expensive than other meals in Turkey, and is normally priced by weight.

● **Çayhane/Kahvehane:** local tea or coffee houses. Some Turkish men seem to spend their lives in them, smoking and playing backgammon, but these are not usually places where foreigners (especially women) would be welcome.

● **Et lokantası:** restaurants specialising in meat dishes.

● **Kebapçı:** a kebab house.

● **Köfteci:** a meatball specialist.

● **Lokanta:** the basic neighbourhood restaurant, feeding local businessmen at lunchtime, as well as visitors. These are reliable places to eat, and it is easy to choose as the food is displayed in hot cabinets. A waiter will bring your choice to your table.

● **Mantı/Gözleme Evi:** serves Turkish ravioli and filled pancakes.

● **Meyhane:** translated somewhat inadequately as "tavern". Some of these places are smoky drinking dives, dedicated to wine (and sometimes song) over food, but the

best are in fact also famous for their delicious cooking. Meze are often especially good here.

● **Muhallebici:** Turkish pudding shop – for milk puddings and baklava, plus chicken dishes.

● **Ocakbaşı:** grill restaurants, where you can sit at a table set around a charcoal fire and cook your own choice of meat (though, of course, if you prefer, the restaurant will do it for you). Breads, rice and salads will also be on offer.

● **Pastane:** at a Turkish pastane – the word "pasta" means pastry or gâteau in Turkish – you can buy flaky su böreği (baked layers of pastry with cheese and parsley), gâteaux and desserts, and often sit and eat there, but sometimes they will not serve coffee and tea.

● **Pideci/Lahmacun:** specialises in the Turkish equivalent of pizza.

Restaurant Listings

Places to eat are listed alphabetically region by region, in descending order of price.

Cafés and Bars

Many smart cafés turn into bars at night. In the cosmopolitan cities and resorts these are as subject to fashion as they would be in London or New York. Some will have live music.

Expensive hotels have glamorous expensive bars: sometimes offering a spectacular view, for which you pay in the inflated price of the drinks. Some offer a "British pub" or other theme to bring in custom. In most you can find snacks; in some a full meal will be available.

Cafés There are plenty of elegant European-style cafés springing up, offering Turks an experience that is not quite Turkish, with French-style baguette sandwiches, Italian cappuccinos and American cheesecake on offer. You'll find the "ladies who lunch" here since they are smart places to be seen.

ISTANBUL

Fish restaurants
Balıkçı Sabahattin
Hasankuyu Sok. 1, Sultanahmet.
Tel: (0212) 458 2302.
Popular old-town seafood restaurant serving an excellent variety of regional specialities since 1927. **$$**
Kıyı
Kefeliköy Caddesi 126 Tarabya.
Tel: (0212) 262 0002.
Swish fish restaurant featuring original Turkish art and photography by contemporary masters. Open noon–midnight. Cards: Amex, Diners Club, Visa, MasterCard. **$$$**
Körfez
Körfez Caddesi 78, Kanlıca.
Tel: (0216) 413 4314/4098.
A chic fish restaurant on the Asian side, with a romantic seaside setting. Sea bass is recommended. A private boat runs across the Bosphorus from Rumeli Fortress by appointment. Open noon–3pm, 7pm–midnight. Closed Monday. All major cards except Prestige. **$$$**

Price Guide

The following price categories are an indication only, based on a two-course meal for one (such as *meze*, kebab, salad and bread, with non-alcoholic drinks).

Outside the major cities and the top hotels, there is very little variation in price among restaurants, with charges merely changing according to whether you eat meat or fish.

Few cheaper restaurants accept credit cards outside the resorts.

$$$ = $15–30
$$ = $10–15
$ = $5–10

Traditional Turkish

Çatı
Istiklal Caddesi, Orhan Apaydın Sokak 20/7.
Tel: (0212) 251 0000.
The top floor has city views in this popular theatre- and cinema-goers' restaurant, often with live Turkish folk music. Open noon–1am. Cards: MasterCard, Visa. **$$$**

Güney Kardeşler
Kuledibi Şah Kapısı Sokak 6.
Tel: (0212) 249 0393.
Cheap and friendly, this lunchtime restaurant is a real Istanbul workers' "caff" and offers better, cheaper food (mostly stews or *sulu yemek)* than anywhere nearer Istiklal. Open 11am–7pm; closed Sunday. **$**

Hacı Baba
Istiklal Caddesi, 49/Meşelik Sokak, Taksim.
Tel: (0212) 244 1886.
This classic Turkish restaurant offers a superb selection of *şiş kebab* and a generally varied menu. In summer the balcony overlooking the garden of a Greek church makes it especially appealing. Booking advised. Open noon–midnight. Cards: Amex, Visa. **$$**

Havuzku
Gani Çelebi Sokak PTT Yani 3, Kapalı Çarşı.
Tel: (0212) 527 3346.
Best of the restaurants in the Covered Bazaar, specialising in kebabs and delicious *meze*. **$**

Kallavi Taverna
Istiklal Caddesi, Kallavi Sokak 20, Beyoğlu.
Tel: (0212) 251 1010.
Aytor Caddesi 1, Levent.
Tel: (0212) 282 7070
Sefik Bey Sokak 9, Kadiköy.
Tel: (0216) 414 4468.
Three small, upmarket but lively Turkish *meyhane* each offering a reasonable all-in price for the night, including excellent food, drinks and live music. Extremely popular with local yuppies and office parties; reservations essential. Closed Sunday.
No cards. **$$**

Refik's
Sofyalı Sokak 10–12, Tünel.
Tel: (0212) 243 2834.
A popular spot with Turkish and foreign intellectuals, embassy sorts and the occasional celebrity. Part of the charm is the secluded off-street location and a complete lack of concern for décor. Specialises in Black Sea dishes, especially fish. Closed Sunday. No cards. **$$**

Hacı Abdullah
Sakız Ağa Caddesi 17, Beyoğlu.
Tel: (0212) 293 8561.
A famous long-established Turkish restaurant serving authentic home-style Ottoman Turkish cuisine. Menu changes daily. Try the *hünkar beğendi kebab* (beef stew served on a bed of aubergine purée) or the *kuzu tandır* (roast lamb). No alcohol. Open 11.30am–10pm. Cards: Amex, MasterCard, Visa. **$**

Şemsiye
Şeybender Sokak 18, Asmalımescit, Tünel.
Tel: (0212) 292 2046.
A health/vegetarian interpretation of traditional Turkish home-cooking and an upmarket décor. Open 8.30am–10.30pm. **$**

Yakup 2
Asmalımescit Sokak 35/37.
Tel: (0212) 249 2925.
When Refik's (around the corner) gets crowded and service is slow – which happens often – try here. Owned by a relative of the avuncular Refik, and similar but open later. Cards: Amex, MasterCard, Visa. Closed Sunday. **$$**

Evim
Büyük Parmakkapı Sokak 32/2, Beyoğlu.
Tel: (0212) 293 4025.
Superb Black Sea home-cooking (including corn bread) as well as some imaginative international food. Cheap, cosy and popular with students. No cards. **$**

Oriental

Ming Garden
Hotel Lamartin, Lamartin Caddesi 25, Taksim.
Tel: (0212) 254 6270.
Friendly atmosphere, authentic cuisine and very reasonable prices compared to Istanbul's more chic Chinese restaurants. The plum brandy is a literal knock-out. Open noon–3pm, 6–11pm; closed Sunday. Cards: Visa, Amex, MasterCard. **$$–$$$**

Street Cuisine in Istanbul

● Easily recognisable by the swanky, high-domed opera-set interior built at the turn of the century, the Çiçek Pasajı (Flower Seller's Alley) is now a raucous, touristy covered lane full of basic *meyhanes* and the sound of gypsy music. It runs parallel to the Fish Market and both open out on to the main pedestrian thoroughfare of Istiklal.

● The Fish Market also has a number of good restaurants, some slightly more upmarket (such as Degustasyon), and some more traditional (such as the studenty Cumhuriyet).

● But if you're looking for real street theatre, head for the bustling Nevizade Sokak (a right turn near the bottom of the Fish Market), jammed with tables in summer.

● Try Boncuk for Armenian specialities, Asır for Greek, and remember that the less decorated eateries tend to have the better food.

Chinese Unlimited
Ahmet Fetgari Sokak, 164/1
Tesvikiye.
Tel: (0212) 240 3166.
Excellent selection of dishes using authentic ingredients at affordable prices. Contemporary Asian décor. Cards: Visa, MasterCard. **$$**

Sai Thai
Aytar Caddesi, Levent Işhanı 3/6, 1, Levent.
Tel: (0212) 283 5346.
Best Thai cuisine in town, served in a traditional setting, complete with kneeling tables. Open every day noon–3pm, 6.30–11pm; lunch on weekdays only. All major cards accepted. **$$$**

French/Mediterranean

Café du Levant
Rahmi M. Koç Museum, Hasköy Caddesi 27, Sütlüce, Golden Horn.
Tel: (0212) 235 6328.
French-style bistro set in the grounds of this unique urban industrial museum, with excellent food prepared by French chefs. Lunch noon–2.30pm, afternoon tea 2–7.30pm, dinner 9.30–10.30pm. Closed Monday. All cards. **$$$**

Le Select
Manolya Sokak 21, Levent.
Tel: (0212) 268 2120/281 7100.
One of Istanbul's most exclusive, European-style gourmet restaurants set in a prosperous area of the city. Reservations essential. Open noon– 3pm, 8pm–1am. All cards. **$$$**

Yirmidokuz (29)
Adnan Saygun Caddesi, Ulus Park.
Tel: (0212) 265 6181/6198.
Stunning Bosphorus view and gourmet French cuisine prepared by a French chef, as well as (pricy!) imported wines and champagne. Open noon–4pm, 8pm–1am. Brunch on Sunday, no lunch on Saturday. All major cards. **$$$**

International

Hünal's Brasserie
Araketler Sıraevleri, Spor Caddesi 1, Beşiktaş.
Tel: (0212) 259 3030.
Set in a restored mansion, this trendy restaurant offers international cuisine and an outdoor

Istanbul's Fishermen's Quarter: Kumkapi

At times the atmosphere in Kumkapı is like a carnival. The former fishermen's quarter, located off the coast road behind Sultanahmet (and rather wild as a result) boasts 50 restaurants all bunched together along a few narrow streets. You will undoubtedly cross paths with strolling musicians, alcohol soaked revellers and even a few ladies of the night.

Among the restaurants worth trying here are: Kör Agop, Olimpiyat, Cemal'in Yeri, Çamur Sevket and Evren (**$$** price range).

summer terrace. The North Shield English Pub is below the restaurant. **$$**

Laledan
Çiragan Palace Hotel Kempinski, Bosphorus.
Tel: (0212) 258 3377.
Highest-quality international cuisine, in a fabulous setting – a palace hotel on the shore of the Bosphorus. Terrace open in summer, live music, seafood specials on Monday and Tuesday. Open daily 7am–11pm. The hotel also has an excellent Turkish restaurant: Tuğra. **$$$**

Sunset Grill & Bar
Ahmet Adnan Saygun Caddesi, Yol Sokak 2, Ulus Parkı.
Tel: (0212) 287 0357.
A Californian-style restaurant set on a hill with an exquisite view of the Bosphorus. Very trendy, it serves mainly grill dishes. Enjoy the bar after sunset 7pm–midnight. All major credit cards. **$$$**

Süreyya
Istinye Caddesi 26, Istinye.
Tel: (0212) 277 5886.
One of the city's oldest-established international gourmet restaurants, founded by a Russian émigré. Closed Sunday; booking essential. Open noon–3pm, 8pm–midnight. Cards: Amex, Diners, Visa. **$$$**

Price Guide

The following price categories are an indication only, based on a two-course meal for one (such as *meze*, kebab, salad and bread, with non-alcoholic drinks).

$$$ = $15–30
$$ = $10–15
$ = $5–10

Four Seasons
Istkilal Caddesi 509, Tünel.
Tel: (0212) 293 3941.
Classy English/Turkish-owned restaurant serving outstanding international cuisine for more than 20 years. Superb service on Ottoman-style copper trays and a scrumptious dessert trolley. A bit pricy at night, but lunch set menus are excellent value. Open noon–3pm, 6pm–midnight. All major credit cards, booking advised. **$$**

Pars
Mesrutiyet Caddesi 187, Tepebaşı.
Tel: (0212) 292 1846.
The only Persian restaurant in town, across from the Pera Palace Hotel. Breakfast at 7am, lunch noon–3pm, and dinner 7pm–1am. **$$**

Rejans
Emir Nevruz Sokak 17, Galatasaray.
Tel: (0212) 244 1610.
Untouched faded grandeur in this nostalgic favourite, founded in the 1920s by White Russian refugee aristocrats. Major write-ups in French guidebooks, however, should tell you something about the quality of the food – try the *piroshki*, *borscht*, beef stroganoff and stewed duck. Reservations are recommended for dinner. Open noon–3pm, 7–11pm. Closed Sunday. Cards: Visa, MasterCard. **$$**

Cafés and patisseries

Andon
Sıraselviler Caddesi 89, Taksim.
Tel: (0212) 251 0222.
Different floors offer different specialities, from drinks to snacks to disco. A favourite with film buffs, the bar upstairs serves deli pastries and coffees.

Cadde-i-Kebir
Istkilal Caddesi, Imam Adnan Sokak 7, Beyoğlu.
Tel: (0212) 251 7113.
A café/bar owned by one of Turkey's more controversial film directors, Reis Çelik. Imported German beer and light meals.
Cafeist
Takkeciler Sokak 41–45, Grand Bazaar.
Tel: (0212) 527 9853.
With its arty décor, this is the only café in the Grand Bazaar that doesn't look like a men's teahouse. Serving typical bistro fare and beverages, it's worth the search.
Dulcinea
Istiklal Caddesi, Meşelik Sokak 20, Beyoğlu.
Tel: (0212) 245 1071.
www.dulcinea.org
Creative modern décor and very trendy. Offers a wide selection of imported drinks and light meals, live jazz at weekends. A bit pricy.
Kaktüs
Imam Adnan Sokak (off Istiklal).
This tiny Parisian-style bistro and bar attracts an arty clientele.
Paul
Valikonağ Caddesi 36, Nişantaşı.
Tel: (0212) 223 9978.
Just in case you didn't know that Istanbul had its fair share of sleek, Parisian-style pastry houses, Paul will leave you in no doubt. Expensive and very French. Branches also in Etiler and Yeniköy.

Pia
Bekar Sokak 4, (off Istkilal).
Tel: (0212) 252 7100.
Similar to Kaktüs, but with a younger crowd and second-floor seating.
Urban
Istkilal Caddesi, Kartal Sokak 6A, Beyoğlu.
Tel: (0212) 252 1325.
Hidden down a back alley, this relaxed café/bar is in a beautifully restored historic building. It originally opened in the 1920s as a Jewish patisserie, constructed on earlier Ottoman foundations, so it has interesting interior décor. Quieter than most Beyoğlu bars, with a good selection of imported drinks, coffees and light meals.

THRACE & MARMARA

On the whole, restaurants in this area are average provincial establishments, with no frills, quite unlike the luxury restaurants found in Istanbul, Ankara and the coastal resorts. Telephone reservation is unusual and rarely necessary.

Bursa
In addition to several restaurants in the Kültürpark, which serve traditional Turkish food, there are several fish restaurants tucked away behind the fishmonger's in Alt Parmak in the city centre. These restaurants serve alcohol and have something of the lively atmosphere of Istanbul's *meyhanes*.

Cumurcul
Çekirge Caddesi.
Tel: (0224) 235 3707.
Attractively converted old house in Çekirge, with the usual range of *meze*, kebabs and grills. Reservations at weekends. **$$**
Inegol Köfteci
Atatürk Caddesi 48.
For a change from kebabs, try the *Inegol köfte* (grilled meatballs served with raw onion rings). Open all year. **$**
Kebabçi Iskender
Unlü Caddesi 7, Heykel.
Tel: (0224) 221 4615.
Popular with the people of Bursa. The owners claim to be descended from the inventor of the famed *Iskender kebab*. Open all year. No credit cards. **$**

Çanakkale
Akol Hotel Restaurant
Kordonboyu Caddesi.
A varied menu of Turkish and International dishes, and fine views of shipping passing through the straits. Open all year. Major credit cards accepted. **$$**
Yalova
Liman Caddesi
Tel: (0286) 217 1045.
The best seafood restaurant in town, on the quay, near the ferry. **$$**

Istanbul's Internet Cafés

Backpacker's Internet Café
22 Yeni Yeni Akbiyik Caddesi, Sultanahmet (across from Orient Youth Hostel).
Tel: (0212) 638 6343.
E-mail: backpackers@turk.net
Fast Pentium computers combined with warm Turkish décor.
Caffinet
Kurabiye Sokak, Beyoğlu (behind Fitaş Cinema).
Upmarket place that plays jazz and doubles as a pasta and seafood restaurant at night.
Sanal Internet Café
14/1 Imam Adnan Sokak, Beyoğlu.

Tel: (0212) 245 6345.
E-mail: sanalc@aidata.com.tr
Reasonable rates and kindly helpers. Coffees, teas and simple meals.
Sinera Internet Café
Mis Sokak, Taksim.
Cheap rates 9am–1pm and comfortable atmosphere for lounging around while you download. Also sells computer components if something you've got is on the blink.
Yağmur
Şeybender Sokak 18, Asmalımescit, Tünel, Beyoğlu.

Tel: (0212) 292 3020.
E-mail: cafe@citlembik.com.tr
One of the most popular cyber-cafés in town, thanks to the American owner and multilingual staff. Offers speedy internet access, e-mail addresses and assorted computing facilities in a calm environment. English reading selection also available. A popular meeting place for foreigners living or travelling through the city. Good restaurant and English-language book exchange on ground floor. Open 11am–11pm.

Order As You Go

In many Turkish restaurants there is no printed menu, or if there is one, it may not relate to what is available.

In fish restaurants and *meyhanes* large trays with assorted plates of *meze* will be brought round, and you just point to the ones that take your fancy. Later, you will be asked for your choice of hot *meze (sıcak mezeler)*, and later still for what you'd like as a main course. You can order as you go, and it is quite all right to stop after the *meze* if you have had enough.

Bread and bottled drinking water will be brought automatically but usually attract a modest cover charge.

Other good hotel restaurants include the **Otel Anafartalar ($)**, which is conveniently close to the ferry and has a wide range of *meze*, kebabs and fish, and the **Anzac Hotel ($)**, a popular meeting and eating place for backpackers, a few minutes' walk from the ferry, which serves good snacks and light meals.

Edirne
Çatı Lokantası
Hürriyet Meydanı.
Tel: (0284) 225 1307.
Shabby but good, with a standard range of Turkish dishes, well cooked at reasonable prices. Serves alcohol. Open all year. **$**
Lalezar Restaurant
South of the city on the road to Karaağaç.
Excellent *meze* and kebabs; fine views of the Meriç River and an Ottoman bridge. Open all year. A nearby alternative is the Villa Restaurant. **$**

Gelibolu (Gallipoli)
Gelibolu Restaurant
Near the harbour.
Well known for its fish dishes, particularly Gelibolu's speciality, *sardalya* (sardines). Open all year. **$–$$**

Ipek Urfa Kebab Salonu
Towards the town centre.
Tasty, spicy kebabs at low prices. **$**

AEGEAN COAST

Look also at the hotel list for many of the best local restaurants *(see page 383–6)*. Alternatively, head for the harbours. Most are lined with small fish restaurants with outdoor terraces.

Ayvalık
Öz Canlı Balık
Gazinolar Caddesi.
Excellent *meze* and fish, near the seafront. No credit cards. **$$**

Bergama
Sağlam
Cumhuriyet Meydanı 29.
Tel: (0232) 632 8897.
A short distance from the tourist office on the other side of the street, with regional specialities, a courtyard and a second dining area upstairs. Open till 8pm all year. **$$**

Bodrum
Kocadon
Neyzen Tevfik Caddesi 160.
Tel: (0252) 614 3705.
Turkish dinners, no lunch, served in a romantic setting that evokes a Turkey of bygone years. Open all year. Credit cards accepted. **$$$**
Picante
Türkkuyusu Mahallesi Külcu Sokak 8.
Tel: (0252) 316 0270.
It is worth seeking out this place for its intimate setting and appealing Mexican cuisine. Credit cards accepted. Open all year. **$$$**
Buğday
Türkuyusu Caddesi.
Tel: (0252) 316 2969.
The best vegetarian restaurant along the Turkish Aegean coast, using local recipes and ingredients and serving meals in a rustic-inspired setting. Open all year. **$$**
Nur
Cumhuriyet Caddesi, Eski Adilye Sokak 5.
Tel: (0252) 313 1065.
Meat and fish dishes are served for lunch and dinner in this smart

restaurant with a pleasing Mediterranean atmosphere. Open all year. **$$**
Sandal
Atatürk Caddesi 74.
Tel: (0252) 316 9117.
Renowned for its Thai and Chinese food, the Sandal offers both set meals and à la carte dining. Open all year. **$$**

Çesme
Körfez
On the waterfront.
Tel: (0232) 712 6718.
This popular restaurant has a good range of *meze* and fish dishes. Western dishes are also available but they may prove disappointing. Open all year. **$**

Heracleia
Agora
Tel: (0252) 543 5445.
The few restaurants in Heracleia are fairly equally priced, but the Agora has a pleasant patio dining area in the shade, serving a small selection of local and Western meals. Open all year. **$**

İzmir
Deniz
Atatürk Caddesi 188-B.
Tel: (0232) 422 0601.
Very highly regarded by the citizens of İzmir, who return here regularly for the specialist fish dishes. Reservations often necessary. Cards accepted. Open all year. **$$$**
Chinese Restaurant
1379 Sokak.
Tel: (0232) 483 0079.
The largest Chinese restaurant in town, offering the usual wide range of meat, rice and noodle dishes. Easy to find, along the street that runs behind the Hilton Hotel. Credit cards accepted. Open all year. **$$**
Seçkin
M. Kemalettin Caddesi 16/A, Konak.
Tel: (0232) 489 2404.
Upstairs is the first internet café to open in İzmir, while at street level there is an efficient restaurant offering a host of traditional Turkish dishes and desserts. Open all year. **$**

Kuşadası
Club Cappello
Akyar Mevkii.
Tel: (0256) 614 4043.
Within walking distance from the centre, just before the Korumar Hotel. Intimate atmosphere. Local fish and meat dishes. Open all year. Reservations advisable. **$$**

Golden Pizzeria
Ismet Inönü Bulvarı 19.
Tel: (0256) 614 5417.
In the centre of town, this pleasant and clean restaurant serves a wide range of pizzas; also open for breakfast. Open all year. **$**

Sultan Han
Bahçe Sokak 8.
Tel: (0256) 614 6380/3849.
Touristy, but so what? A variety of local dishes and an appetising selection of meze in a restaurant that aims to evoke a traditional Turkish-style atmosphere. Credit cards accepted. Open all year. **$$$**

Marmaris
Alba
Kaleiçi 30, Sokak 10.
Tel: (0252) 412 4299.
Delicious European cuisine, well complemented by a wonderful panoramic hilltop view. **$$$**

Dede
Barbaros Caddesi.
Tel: (0252) 413 1289.
Fairly typical of the sea-facing restaurants lining the promenade near the tourist office, with a large menu featuring familiar Western dishes as well as local fish and meze. Open all year. **$$**

Mr Zek
Barbaros Caddesi 49.
Tel: (0252) 413 4123.
Popular, laid-back Italian restaurant on the harbourfront. Open for lunch and dinner all year. **$$**

Taraça
30 Sokak No. 11.
Tel: (0252) 411 3999.
Imaginative backstreet bistro in a restored house in the old Greek quarter of Marmaris. **$$**

Pamukkale
Motel Koru
Tel: (0258) 272 2429.
The choice of restaurants in Pamukkale is limited. Although the Motel Koru can be overrun by coach parties, the view from the window tables is terrific. Open all year. **$–$$**

Priene
Şelâle
Güllübahçe.
Tel: (0256) 547 1009.
A pleasant place for lunch in between visiting the sites, close to Kuşadası; choose from the kebabs, meatballs and fish dishes displayed at the counter. Open all year. **$**

Selçuk
Selçuk Köftecisi
Vergi Dairesi altı 37/J.
Tel: (0232) 892 6696.
This café specialises in meatballs, though the kebabs are good as well, and is often overlooked by visitors (partly due to its unassuming décor). Worth a visit. **$$**

Kalehan
Kalehan Hotel.
Tel: (0232) 892 6154.
Turkish dishes served as set meals or à la carte in this comfortable restaurant with the benefit of air conditioning, reasonable prices and character. Open all year. **$–$$**

MEDITERRANEAN COAST

Antakya
Antakya Evi Restoran
Silahlı Kuvvetler Caddesi No. 3.
Tel: (0326) 214 1350.
A traditional Antakya mansion with a choice of rooms for dining on hot and spicy eastern Turkish food, in the tradition of the east, but this is like a family home and attracts a congenial mixture of locals and visitors. Open for lunch and dinner all year round. **$$**

Fethiye
Anfora
Paspatur Hamam Sokak 5.
Tel: (0252) 612 1282.
Trendy décor, good Turkish and continental food, popular with groups. There are many other good restaurants also huddled into this buzzing old-town street; take time to stroll and read the menus. **$$**

Meğri Lokantası
Ordukan Aş, Eski Cami Geçidi, Likya Sokak 8–9.
Tel: (0252) 614 4046.
Excellent seafood, meze and grills served alfresco. Shut in winter. **$$**

Ratef Restaurant
Kordon Boyu.
Tel: (0252) 614 1106.
Long-established favourite fish restaurant on the promenade, near the fishing harbour. Open all year. **$$**

Spinecker Café and Restaurant
Kordon Boyu.
Tel: (0252) 612 0432.
Excellent seafood restaurant near the marina. Open all year. **$$**

Finike
Deniz 2
Kordon Caddesi.
Tel: (0242) 855 2282.
A cheerful local restaurant frequented by Turkish lorry drivers and locals alike. Good plain Turkish cooking. Open all year. **$$**

Price Guide

The following price categories are an indication only, based on a two-course meal for one (such as meze, kebab, salad and bread, with non-alcoholic drinks).
$$$ = $15–30
$$ = $10–15
$ = $5–10

Kalkan
There are several good restaurants down beside the harbour, all of which have outdoor terraces and good seafood.

Aubergine (Patlican)
Harbourfront.
Tel: (0242) 844 3332.
Attractive seafront restaurant serving Turkish, Ottoman and international dishes. Open summer only, for lunch and dinner. **$$**

Belgin's Kitchen
Yaliboyu Mahallesi.
Tel: (0242) 844 3614.
Opulent surroundings, with diners heaped in among the carpets and cushions to sup on fine Turkish cuisine. Closed in winter. **$$**

Kaş

Chez Evy
Terzi Sokak 2.
Tel: (0242) 836 1253.
A unique blend of French country cooking and Turkish staples make this small backstreet restaurant one of the most popular on the Lycian coast; book ahead. Closed in winter for meals. **$$**

Eriş
Gürsoy Sokak No. 13.
Tel: (0242) 836 2134.
Excellent food, some very unusual Turkish dishes and helpful service.

Oba Ev Yemekleri
Çukurbağli Caddesi.
Tel: (0242) 836 1687.
Charming, laid-back family-run restaurant with a shady garden terrace and ever-changing variety of nourishing stews. Open all year. **$**

Kemer

Derya Turk Muttaği
Liman Caddesi.
Tel: (0242) 814 4775.
Basic local café with excellent food, Formica tables and friendly staff; some might like to avoid a few specialities such as lamb's brains and tripe soup. Open all year. **$$**

Kemer Marina
Yat Limanı (on the edge of the marina).
Tel: (0242) 814 1192.
Upmarket, slick restaurant catering mainly to the international yachting crowd, with good Turkish food and a small bar. Summer only. **$$**

Ölü Deniz

Beyaz Yunus
Belcekiz, near Padirali.
Tel: (0252) 617 0068.
Fabulous views and elegant, colonial-style furnishing complement an imaginative menu that fuses the best of Turkish and international cuisine. **$$**

Olympos

Park Restaurant
Ulupınar Köyü, Ulupınar (near the turning off the main road, 30 km /19 miles west of Kemer).
Tel: (0242) 825 7213.
Delightful trout and seafood restaurant in a converted mill, with a shady terrace. Lunch and dinner, all year round. **$$**

Patara

Golden Restaurant
Gelemis Köyü.
Tel: (0242) 843 5162.
The best of a number of basic Turkish restaurants in the village, serving fish and grills. Closed in winter. **$**

Saklıkent

Yaka Park
Yaka Köyü.
Tel: (0252) 638 2011.
Trout so fresh they swim up to the table at this trout farm/restaurant housed in a restored windmill set in cool, green parkland. Closed in winter. **$$**

Hüseyin Güseli'in Yeri
On the approach road to Saklıkent Gorge.
Tel: (0252) 636 8113.
Turkish pancakes and grills cooked over an open fire are the highlights of this basic, but friendly family-run restaurant. Closed in winter. **$**

PAMPHYLIA

Adana

Anatolian Restaurant and Bar
Atatürk Caddesi 182, Incirlik.
Tel: (0322) 332 8022.
Hollywood-style Turkish restaurant hung about with carpets and cushions and with a buffet designed to cater for the appetites of the American airforce personnel next door. **$$**

Mesut
Vali Yolu, Ekin Sk, Vizon Apt Alti.
Tel: (0322) 453 3468.
Quiet suburban indoor restaurant, famous for its classic Turkish food menu featuring a wide range of meze and wonderful kebabs. Open all year. **$$**

Büyük Onbasilar Restaurant
Gazipasa Bulvarı.
Airy first-floor restaurant offering good food and efficient service, overlooking one of the city's main squares. **$$**

Alanya

Arzum Mantı Evi
Atatürk Caddesi.
Tel: (0242) 513 9393.
Simple but delicious home-cooking, with mantı and vegetarian dishes. **$**

Garden Restaurant
Keykubat Caddesi 5.
Tel: (0242) 513 8561.
Peaceful haven with live guitar music or jazz, good food and a garden. Open all year. **$$**

Iskele Bar and Restaurant
Iskele Caddesi.
Tel: (0242) 513 1822.
Noisy, brash but immensely popular harbourfront hangout with a wide range of Turkish and international food, seafood and live music. **$$**

Other good options along the harbour include the equally vibrant Bistro Bellman and the marginally calmer Yakamoz. **$$**

Antakya

Anadolu
Hurriyet Caddesi 50/C.
Tel: (0326) 215 1541.
Drab town favourite where delicious food more than makes up for the poor décor. Broad range of meze, grills and kebabs. Open all year. **$$**

Sultan Sofresı
Istiklal Caddesi 18.
Tel: (0326) 213 8759.
This local restaurant serves an incredible range of Syrian/Turkish specialities. Often packed as the locals appreciate the reasonable prices and snappy service. **$$**

Didem Turistik Tesisleri
Reyhanli Yolu Uzeri.
Tel: (0326) 212 1928.
A good range of Turkish dishes. **$**

Price Guide

The following price categories are an indication only, based on a two-course meal for one (such as meze, kebab, salad and bread, with non-alcoholic drinks).
$$$ = $15–30
$$ = $10–15
$ = $5–10

Samlioğlu Künefe Salonu
Next to Ulu Camii.
Serving only *kunefe*, the local delicacy made of spun wheat, cream cheese and honey, and served piping hot. **$$**

Anamur

Astor Restaurant
Iskele Mahallesi, Inönü Caddesi.
Tel: (0324) 814 2280.
Shady beachfront terrace, serving simple *meze*, grills and fish. Closed in winter. **$**

Çelikler/Kale
Mamure Kalesi Karşısı, Iskele.
Tel: (0757) 71358.
One of several small terraced restaurants near the castle, which are ideal for lunch before the chef turns tour guide. Shady parking is a major benefit in summer. Open all year; small *pansiyon* in summer. **$**

Antalya

As one would expect, the harbour restaurants specialise in seafood. In addition to such standards as sea bass, red mullet and swordfish, you can sample the Turkish version of bouillabaisse, *tarança şiş* (not skewered fish, as the name would suggest, but a stew using grouper, grida or sea bass as its base).

Back above the walls, near the corner of Atatürk and Cumhuriyet Caddesi, is an alley of outdoor restaurants serving a variety of Turkish dishes, including *tandır*, or oven-baked lamb served with flat *pide* bread. A 150g portion of *pide* should satisfy a sightseer's hunger.

The colourful jars lining the windows of the pickle seller *(turşucu)* are proof of the ingenuity of Turkish cuisine. Not confined to the usual peck of pickled peppers, there is a wide range of Turkish pickles, sold by the piece so sampling is simple. Jams and jellies find favour in Antalya too, with the enormous variety of local fruit lending themselves happily to the confection. A speciality is rose jam.

Kırk Merdiven Restaurant
Selçuk Mahallesi, Musalla Sokak 2.
Tel: (0242) 242 9686.
Unpretentious old-town restaurant

serving fish, international and Turkish dishes. The food is carefully prepared, the service friendly and the prices fair. Terrace in summer. Open all year, for lunch and dinner. **$–$$**

Kral Sofrası (King's Table)
Old Harbour, Kaleiçi.
Tel: (0242) 241 2198.
Well-loved, long-lived place with excellent Turkish and international food and a terrace overlooking the old harbour. Open all year. **$$**

Met Fish Restaurant
Lara Yolu.
Tel: (0242) 321 1828.
One of Lara's best, offering delicious fish, sea views and a friendly family atmosphere. **$$**

The Orange Tree
Atatürk Caddesi 1251 Sokak 8.
Tel: (0242) 244 3765.
Tiny bistro with tasty lunches and snacks. **$–$$**

Stella's Bistro
Fevzi Çakmak Caddesi 3/C (opposite the Belediye).
Tel: (0242) 243 3931.
Trendy Turkish-English owned Italian restaurant. Heaps of delicious pasta, stodgy puddings, friendly and efficient service. **$$$**

Yedi Mehmet
Hasan Subasi Park.
Tel: (0242) 241 1641.
Slick new marble and pine décor, but the same excellent-quality Turkish food. This is where Antalya's politicians and businesspeople cut their deals. **$$**

Aspendos

Belkıs Restaurant
Belkıs Köyü, on the road to the ruins.
Tel: (0242) 735 7263.
Simple riverfront restaurant, near the ruins, specialising in traditional Turkish stews. Closed in winter. **$$**

Iskenderun

Hasan Baba
Ulucami Caddesi 43/E.
A good, simple kebab house. **$**

Köprülü Kanyon

Ada Insel
Köprülü Kanyon Yolu Üzeri, Beskonak.

Tel: (0242) 765 3389.
Shady riverside terrace, where you can enjoy some peace before you reach the hubbub of Beşkonak. The food is simple (trout, kebabs and salad) but well cooked, with friendly, helpful owners. Open all year. **$**

Mersin

Ali Baba Restaurant
Uluçarsi Otopark Girisi Karşısı.
Tel: (0324) 223 3088.
Good standard Turkish menu. Right by the main car park. **$$**

Pizzeria Ocin
Bahri Ok Işhani 39, off Atatürk Caddesi.
Rustles up reasonable spaghetti, pizzas and the like for a young crowd. **$$**

Side

Nergiz
Liman Caddesi, Selimiye Köyü.
Tel: (0242) 753 1467.
This large, two-storey restaurant, on the main square beside the harbour, is where most tourists gravitate. The décor is attractive, it has a large terrace and good seafood. Prices are marginally higher than others along the strip, but not exorbitant. Open all year. **$$**

Liman
71 Liman Caddesi (towards the temple).
Tel: (0242) 753 1168.
Much simpler than the Nergiz, this is one of the best of the many fish restaurants lining the waterfront. Go en masse and ask for the fish platter – I won't spoil the surprise, but it's worth it. Open all year. **$$**

Tarsus

Şellale
Tel: (0324) 624 8010.
The poshest of several restaurants and cafés clustered around the waterfall where Alexander the Great supposedly swam and caught a chill that put his campaign back two months. It is by far the nicest place to eat in the hot, dusty city – here or at the simple café next door, which confusingly shares its name. Open all year. **$$**

CENTRAL ANATOLIA

Afyon
Ikbal Restoran
Özdilek Tesisleri Yanı, Kütahya Yolu.
Tel: (0272) 252 5500.
Döner kebab specialist. Also, try its *kaymaklı ekmek*, a sweet and thick Anatolian cream made by boiling the milk of water buffaloes. **$**

Ankara
Cafemiz
Arjantin Caddesi 19 Kavaklidere.
Tel: (0312) 467 7921.
Charmingly converted old house with a conservatory café, serving French-style crêpes, salads and desserts. Closed Mon. **$$**
Gusto
Mega Hotel.
Tel: (0312) 468 5400.
Intimate Italian restaurant, a happy-hour bar and delicious food. Live music at weekends. **$$**
Kale Washington
Doyran Sokak 5/7, Kaleiçi.
Tel: (0312) 311 4344.
Delightful restaurant with excellent Turkish food and fine views in a restored Ottoman mansion within the castle. Terrace in summer. Open noon–midnight. **$$$**
Kebap 49 Bulten
Sok. 5 Kavaklidere.
Tel: (0312) 428 4949.
Traditional 3-storey kebab house also offering great desserts. Garden in summer. **$**
Merkez Lokantası
Çiftlik Caddesi, 72/A, Atatürk Orman Çiftliği.
Tel: (0312) 213 1750/4696.
Set in a farm 15 km (10 miles) from central Ankara, this is a favourite of the government's top bureaucrats in a relaxed outdoor atmosphere. It has excellent grilled meat and vegetable dishes. **$$**
Zenger Paşa Konağı
Demirkıran Mahalesi, Doyuran Sokak 13, Kale Ulus.
Tel: (0312) 311 7070.
Perched up on Ankara's citadel in a restored 19th-century Turkish mansion, Zenger Paşa serves delicious grilled meats with *pilav* (specially cooked Turkish rice),

with a bird's-eye view of the city. **$$**
Boyacızâde Konağı Kale Restaurant
Berrak Sokak 9, (next to the Museum of Anatolian Civilizations), Ankara Kalesi.
Tel: (0312) 310 2525/311 1945.
Turkish cuisine, including *manti*, a ravioli-like dish served with a spicy tomato sauce. Outdoors there is a fountain and splendid city views. **$**
Piri Reis
Ahmet Mithat Efendi Sok. 4 Cankaya.
Tel: (0312) 441 4119.
Excellent seafood, friendly service and a charmingly elegant setting. **$$$**.

Wiener Kaffehaus
Budak Sok. 5, 1st floor Gaziosmanpaşa.
Tel: (0312) 428 6927
Elegant Viennese coffee house, with a tantalising choice of cakes.

Eskişehir
Ekrem Restoran
2 Eylül Caddesi, Esnaf Sarayı Kat 4.
Tel: (0222) 231 4538.
Serving a range of chicken, fish and meat dishes. **$$**

Kayseri
Tuana Restoran
Mehmet Alemdar Iş Hanı, Sivas Caddesi, Cumhuriyet Meydanı.
The Tuana Special, a *filet mignon* steak with mashed potatoes, is the choice of most locals. **$$**

Konya
Horozlu Han Kervansaray
Konya-Ankara Yolu Üzeri, TNP Yanı.
Tel: (0332) 248 3115.

Restored medieval *caravansaray*, with floor shows on many evenings. **$$**
Sammaz Usta
Marangozlar Sanayi, Baskisla Caddesi 35.
Tel: (0322) 236 2918.
Specialises in Mevlana kebab and *etli ekmek*, a kind of local pizza. **$**

Kutahya
Dedem Ocakbaşı Restoran
Cezaevi'nin bitişiği, Eskişehir Yolu.
Tel: (0274) 216 7675.
Meat and chicken dishes cooked on skewers over flaming charcoals. **$**

CAPPADOCIA

Amasra
Canlıbalık
Küçük Liman Caddesi 8.
Tel: (0378) 315 2606.
Coastal restaurant serving fresh, unusual fish dishes. Lively atmosphere and sea views. **$**

Üçhisar
Yemeni Restoran
Tandir Evi Karşisi.
Tel: (0384) 219 2374.
The speciality here is tender lamb over *pilav*. **$**
Harmandalı Restoran
Kavak Yolu Üzeri.
Tel: (0384) 219 2364.
Specialist in *kuzu fırın* (lamb roasted in an oven on a skewer). **$**

Ürgup
Şömine Restoran
Cumhuriyet Meydanı, Merkez Pasajı Üstü.
Tel: (0384) 341 8442.
Tradional Turkish fare, with *testi kebab* (spicy lamb with tomatoes, onions, peppers) a house special. **$**
Karakuş Restoran
Mustafa Paşa Yolu Üzeri, Pancarlık Mevkii.
Tel: (0384) 341 5353.
The most famous of several all-inclusive "Turkish evenings" in the area, with plenty of *meze*, folk and belly-dancing, and the occasional whirling dervish. Expect many tour groups. **$**

BLACK SEA COAST

Most decent restaurants here are in the hotels *(see page 391–3)*.

Safranbolu
Kadıoğlu Şehzade Sofrası
Çeşme Mah, Arasta Sokak 8.
Tel: (0372) 712 5091.
Fax: (0372) 712 2624.
Specialities include *kuyu kebab* (lamb roasted in a clay pit). **$$**

THE EAST

Dıyarbakır
Beyzade
Lise Caddesi 10.
Tel: (0412) 221 1221.
Specialises in the spicy kebabs of southeast Turkey. **$**
Selim Amca
Yenişehir.
Tel: (0412) 221 7378.
Offers spicy kebabs and *meze* appetisers. **$**

Erzurum
Güzelyurt Restoran
Cumhuriyet Caddesi 54.
Tel: (0344) 218 5697.
Famed for its kebabs. **$–$$**
Tufan Restoran
Cumhuriyet Caddesi.
Tel: (0344) 218 3107.
A good choice of grilled meat, chicken and *meze*. **$$**

Gaziantep
Imam Cağdaş Restoran
Eski Gümrük Caddesi 14.
Tel: (0342) 231 2678.
Wide range of meat and vegetable dishes. **$**
Turkuaz Restoran
Il özel Idare Caddesi, Müdürlüğü, özel Hizmet, Binasi Altı.
Tel: (0342) 220 3801.
Try its spicy *ali nazik* kebab and *lahmacun* (a kind of Turkish pizza), with *baklava* for dessert. **$**
Turumin Kebap Salonu
Büyük Şehir Belediyesinin Karşısı.
Tel: (0342) 231 8155.
Tasty Turkish dishes. Try the special *ali nazik* kebab and *ufakli kofte* (a meatball dish). **$**

Iğıdır
Beyoğlu Café
Faikbey Caddesi, Atatürk Işhanı, Sosyal Tesis.
Good choice of mixed grilled meats. **$–$$**

Kahramanmaraş
Avşaroğlu Restoran
Gözde 2 Sitesi 14, Şehir Merkezi.
Tel: (0344) 223 3888.
Centrally located, it specialises in local dishes, such as *icli kofte* (a bulgur and meat dish), and *dolmaş* (stuffed vegetables). Try *kahramanmaraş* ice cream or dessert. **$**
Samdan Restoran
Trabzon Caddesi 11.
Tel: (0344) 225 4996.
Try the various kebabs and *kahramanmaraş* ice cream. **$**
Osman Usta Restoran
Trabzon Caddesi, 8/A.
Tel: (0344) 214 0879.
More tasty traditional snacks. **$**
Mazicioğlu Restoran
Milli Egemenlik Bulvar.
Tel: (0344) 321 8055.
Good for a spicy *gaziantep kebab* and *baklava* for dessert. **$**

Şanlıurfa
Tandır Restoran
Sarayonu Caddesi.
Tel: (0414) 215 5378.
12 varieties of *urfa* kebabs, *lahmacun* and *ciğ kofte*. **$–$$**
Urfa Sofrasi
Şehirmerkezi.
Tel: (0414) 315 6130.
Urfa kebabs. **$–$$**
Haran Otel Restoran
Sarayonu Caddesi, Atatürk Bulvar.
Tel: (0414) 313 2860.
Famed for its *urfa* kebabs and vegetable dishes. **$**

Culture

Developing the Turkish people's interest in Western arts and culture was an important part of Atatürk's raft of reforms in the early years of the Republic. The most fundamental was the change from Arabic to Roman script, together with modernisation of the language; others included the introduction of Western art forms such as classical music, ballet and opera.

Cinema is very popular, and contemporary Turkish filmmaking is interesting, though of course you won't find English subtitles on Turkish films. Antalya and İzmir also host film festivals.

Traditional Turkish folk music is a living art, and immensely popular – you will hear some form of it everywhere. It has blended inextricably with Western pop and rock, to give Turkish pop a decidedly ethnic flavour.

Music & Dance

CLASSICAL

Western art forms such as ballet, classical music and opera are now well established among the educated, secular classes. The opportunities for seeing performances vary from city to city; Istanbul, Ankara and İzmir have large cultural centres and their own symphony orchestras, ballet and opera companies, which tour elsewhere. The standard is variable, especially for opera and ballet.

It is not easy to find out about programmes much in advance, and tickets can be difficult to get hold of. Sometimes seats are sold out, or given to sponsors before the public can buy them.

The annual cultural highlight in Turkey is the Istanbul Festival (April–July), which incorporates four linked festivals of music, theatre, cinema and jazz. It is organised by the Istanbul Foundation for Culture and Arts, which also runs the International Istanbul Biennial art exhibition. Banks and institutions sponsor other jazz, blues and classical festivals which attract top performers. At international festivals you will get the opportunity to hear world-renowned soloists, orchestras and conductors, plus the cream of home-grown talent.

TRADITIONAL TURKISH

Music has an exceptionally rich tradition in Turkey. Academics and folklore groups sponsor interest in *halk müziği* (folk music), which is still played spontaneously and genuinely at village weddings and festivals, but which visitors are most likely to encounter at a concert or dance display organised for tourists. A "village" music and dance performance will often include a belly dancer – popular even with the most sophisticated.

Although some of the shows put on for tourists at resorts, complete with dinner, can be shoddily done, some of the most expensive hotel restaurants in Istanbul have folk music and dancing performed to the highest standards, to accompany your Turkish dinner.

Types of music

Sanat and *Fasıl* music (both traditional Turkish styles) are best heard live, and are played in numerous bars and *meyhanes*.

Arabesk, melancholic and sentimental oriental pop ballads will probably be the first thing you hear in Turkey, and will haunt you from every taxi and minibus.

Classical Ottoman and religious music is played by distinguished groups such as that of the Istanbul Municipal Conservatory, and can be heard in concert halls, and on radio and television, often broadcast live.

At some dervish *tekkes* or lodges, visitors are permitted to watch the remarkable meditational whirling dance.

JAZZ, ROCK AND POP

Istanbul is beginning to creep on to the international rock-band circuit. Home-grown bands thrive and you can hear live jazz in bars and nightclubs, and more formally in a concert hall.

ISTANBUL

Performing arts venues
Atatürk Cultural Centre (AKM)
Taksim Square.
Tel: (0212) 251 5600/243 3261.
State-owned opera house shared by the State Opera and Ballet, Symphony Orchestra and State Theatre Company.
Cemal Reşit Rey Concert Hall
Harbiye.
Tel: (0212) 232 9830.
www.crrks.org.
Large hall with varied programmes.
Lütfi Kırdar Convention & Exhibition Centre
Next to the Hilton Hotel and CRR Concert Hall, Harbiye.
Tel: (0212) 256 3055/212 7880.
One large hall (capacity 2,000); four smaller halls (capacity 500 each), plus meeting rooms, a large restaurant and terrace.
Turkish Cultural Dance Theatre
Firat Culture Centre, Divanyolu Caddesi Çemberlitaş.
Tel: (0212) 517 8692.
Excellent programme of Turkish dance from 10 different regions of the country, performed every Mon, Wed and Sat night, including whirling dervishes and belly-dancing.

Cultural centres
Many foreign cultural centres maintain libraries, offer language classes and sponsor concerts, cultural activities and films.
Aksanat Cultural Centre
Istiklal Caddesi, Akbank Building, Beyoğlu.
Tel: (0212) 252 3500.

Listings Information

Programmes are not published very far in advance, even for the state opera and ballet. The *Turkish Daily News* carries the cinema listings for Istanbul, İzmir and Ankara. *Time Out* has weekly listings for Istanbul and a useful English-language supplement. Ordinary Turkish newspapers carry arts listings, obviously in Turkish, but it is fairly easy to work out what is being listed.

Festival-ticket booking is always centralised, which makes things easier. However, the festival organisers try out new systems and locations every year in an attempt to improve both service and sales, so things can change from season to season.
Istanbul
Atatürk Cultural Centre (AKM)
Taksim
Tel: (0212) 251 5600.
Istanbul Foundation for Culture and Arts (for information on and tickets to the Istanbul Festivals and Biennial).
Istiklal Cad. 146, Luvr Apt. 10, Beyoğlu.
Tel: (0212) 334 0700.
www.istfest.org
Biletix
Tel: (0216) 454 1555.
www.biletix.com.tr
Phone and internet booking for all major arts and sporting events. Open Mon–Fri 8.30am–9pm, Sat–Sun 10am–9pm. Also sales outlets across the city.
Ankara
Opera and ballet tickets can be purchased from **Atatürk Bulvarı Opera Meydanı**, Ulus.
Tel: (0312) 324 2210.
For musical events, contact the **SCA Music Foundation**, Tunalı Hilmi Caddesi 114/26, Kavaklıdere.
Tel: (0312) 427 0855.
İzmir
İzmir Culture Foundation,
Şair Eşref Bulvarı, Park Apt 58/4, Alsancak.
Tel: (0232) 463 0300.

Interesting programmes of recorded jazz and classical music via a large laser-disc screen. Also painting and sculpture exhibitions and drama.

American Library and Computer Centre
Meşrutiyet Caddesi 108, Tepebaşı. Tel: (0212) 251 2675. CD Rom, internet, books. Open Mon–Fri 10am–3.30pm. USIS (US Information Service), tel: (0212) 251 3602.

British Council
Barbaros Bulvari, Akdoğan Sokak 43/2-7, Beşiktaş. Tel/Fax: (0212) 327 2700. E-mail: bc-istanbul@ britishcouncil.org.tr www.britishcouncil.org.tr

Economics And History Foundation
Vali Konağı Caddesi, Samsun Apt. 57, Nişantaşı. E-mail: tarihvakfi@tarihvakfi.org.tr www.tarihvakfi.org.tr This leftish intellectual think-tank puts on eye-opening exhibitions in the city (most in the Imperial Mint, next to Aya Irini in the Topkapı complex), as well as publishing books and magazines, with an emphasis on social history.

French Cultural Centre
French Consulate, Istiklal Caddesi, Beyoğlu. Tel: (0212) 249 0776. Short film festivals and other cultural events – in French.

Goethe Institute (German Cultural Centre)
Yeni Çarşı Caddesi 52, Beyoğlu. Tel: (0212) 249 2009. www.goethe.de/istanbul Good reference library and regular events.

Topkapı Palace Library
Sultanahmet (inside the palace). Tel: (0212) 511 1315. A valuable collection of handwritten Ottoman books. Open Mon–Fri 9.15am–4.30pm.

Süleymaniye Library
Ayşekadın Hamam Sokak 35, Beyazıt. Tel: (0212) 520 6460. Thorough reference collection on Ottoman culture and history.

The Women's Library
Across Fener Jetty on Golden Horn. Tel: (0212) 534 9550.

Diverse works for and about women, with regular cultural events. Open Mon–Sat 9am–5.30pm.

Cinema

Screens are dominated by international films, mostly recent releases from the US, and they are usually shown in the original language with Turkish subtitles (*alt yazılı*) – though the title will be translated into Turkish. If the film has been dubbed, *Turkçe* (Turkish) or *ilk gösterim* (dubbed) will appear on the programme listing or poster outside the cinema – this will usually be the case with cartoons and films suitable for children. At any one time there will be a choice of a dozen or so foreign films in Istanbul, Ankara, İzmir and Antalya. Across the rest of Anatolia, most places of any size have a screen.

If you want to see the latest Turkish movies with English subtitles, you'll have to visit during one of the major international film festivals, such as the Golden Orange in Antalya (autumn) or the Istanbul Film Festival (spring).

The free weekly sheet, *Sinema*, which you can pick up at any cinema, lists the current week's programme.

Ankara
Akün
Atatürk Bulvarı 227, Kavaklıdere. Tel: (0312) 427 7656.

Major Entertainment Producers

As it can be very difficult to find out about forthcoming cultural events in Turkey, this brief list might help you find out what's on before you arrive.

hip Productions
www.hipproductions.com.tr Head of the league for rave, techno and contemporary music events.

Istanbul Foundation for Culture and the Arts
Istiklal Caddesi 146, Luvr Apt., Beyoğlu. Tel: (0212) 334 0700. www.istfest.org

Travellers' Club

A Travellers' Club has been organised in the Sultanahmet area by people who want to write about their journey and share their observations. The group provides information to travellers, and organises discussions and slide and video shows. It also runs tours. Tel: (0212) 518 5409/02.

Çinepol
Ümitköy Galleria Iş Merkezi. Tel: (0312) 235 4580.

Kavaklıdere
Tunalı Hilmi Caddesi 105/B, Kavaklıdere. Tel: (0312) 426 7379.

Metropol
Selanik Caddesi 76, Kızılay. Tel: (0312) 425 7479.

Antalya
Altın Portakal
Kaleiçi. Tel: (0242) 248 6302. Book here for the film festival.

Kent
Şarampol Caddesi. Tel: (0242) 243 2342.

Kültür Sineması
Atatürk Caddesi. Tel: (0242) 241 6239.

Megapol Sineması
Özlem Sokak. Tel: (0242) 237 0131.

Organises world-class events such as the International Film, Theatre, Classical Music and Jazz Festivals, as well as the Istanbul Biennial (in odd-numbered years).

Pozitif Promotions
Havyar Sokak 54, 80060, Cihangir. Fax: (0212) 249 4176. E-mail: pozitif@superonline.com.tr www.pozitif-ist.com The brains (and taste) behind much of Istanbul's avant-garde jazz and world-music scene also runs Istanbul's live world music and jazz club, Babylon.

Prestige
Metin Kasapoğlu Caddesi, Metropol
Çarşısı.
Tel: (0242) 312 0543.

Bodrum
Karya
In the basement of the Karya Hotel.
Tel: (0252) 316 6272.
Sinema Bodrum
Tel: (0252) 313 3000.
Outdoors; shows start at 10pm.

Istanbul
There are over 30 cinemas in
Istanbul, many of which are
multiplexes attached to the major
shopping areas. Istiklal Caddesi in
Beyoğlu has the largest cluster, and
certainly the most "alternative"
films. Check the *Turkish Daily News*
or *Sinema* for programme details.
AFM Akmerkez
Akmerkez Shopping Centre
Etiler.
Tel: (0212) 282 0505.
Four screens.
AFM Fitaş
Fitafl Pasajı, Beyoğlu.
Tel: (0212) 249 0166.
Alkazar Cinema Centre
Istiklal Caddesi 179, Beyoğlu.
Tel: (0212) 293 2466.
An old cinema with three screens
and a café/bar.
Beyoğlu
Istiklal Caddesi Halep Pasajı 140,
Beyoğlu.
Tel: (0212) 251 3240.
Two screens. The cinema runs a
mini-festival from July to September
showing the most popular art-house
releases of the year.
Capitol Shopping Centre
Altunizade.
Tel: (0216) 391 1935.
Eight screens.
Movieplex Etiler
Nispetiye Caddesi 1, Levent.
Tel: (0212) 284 3004.

İzmir
AFM EGS Park
Tel: (0232) 373 7320.
AFM Deniz
Tel: (0232) 381 6461.
Cinecity Kipa
Mavişehir.
Tel: (0232) 386 5888.

Şan
Şan Pasajı, Konak.
Tel: (0232) 483 7511.

Art

The huge Biennial Exhibition brings
together a heady mix of
international contemporary artists;
with the emphasis also on
showcasing Turkish artists.
Turkish painting and sculpture
have a short history, but Turkish
artists are now experimenting with
conceptual art and video. In
architecture and design, some
contemporary or recent buildings
and interiors are of interest.

COMMERCIAL ART GALLERIES

Every financial institution seems to
have decided to sponsor modern
art, including decorative arts and
art jewellery, so you will find many
small art galleries tucked into the
ground or reception floor of office
headquarters in the big cities. Here,
the art exhibited may or may not be
for sale. There are many other
small commercial galleries, some of
which double up as bars or cafés
and are good places to meet
people. Current exhibits will be
featured in city-guide magazines
such as *City Plus Istanbul* and *The
Guide* series.

Istanbul
Istanbul is richly endowed with
galleries large and small.
Borusan Kültür ve Sanat Merkez
Istiklal Caddesi 421, Beyoğlu.
Tel: (0212) 292 0655.
E-mail: info@borusanat.com
www.borusanat.com
Exciting contemporary art, as well
as concerts and recitals.
Contemporary Art Marketing (cam)
Abdi Ipekçi Caddesi 48/5,
Nişantaşı.
Tel: (0212) 234 3902.
Fax: (0212) 248 3692.
Trendy gallery with corporate flair.
Dulcinea
Meşelik Sokak 20, Beyoğlu.
Tel: (0212) 245 1071.

E-mail: art@dulcinea.org
www.dulcinea.org
One of Istanbul's newest and most
stylish galleries, below the popular
restaurant of the same name.
Galatea
Sofyalı Sokak 16, Asmalımescit,
Tünel (bottom of Istiklal Caddesi).
Tel: (0212) 292 5430.
E-mail: konak@turk.net.com.tr
Gallery showcasing contemporary
Turkish artists. Also a good
restaurant and bar.
Galeri Baraz
Kurtuluş Caddesi 191, Kurtuluş.
Tel: (0212) 240 4783.
Fax: (0212) 231 6258.
Off the beaten track, but worth
seeking out for those with an
interest in Turkish Abstract. Huge
collection dating from the 1950s.
Galeri Nev
Maçka Caddesi 33, Maçka.
Tel: (0212) 231 6782.
www.galerinev.com
Perhaps the best gallery for Turkish
contemporary art. Young English-
speaking owners.
Milli Reasürans Gallery
Teşvikiye Caddesi 43/57, Teşvikiye.
Tel: (0212) 230 1976.
Fax: (0212) 231 4730.
One of Istanbul's posher galleries
featuring popular Turkish masters;
run by a multilingual Dutch woman.
Pamukbank Gallery of Photography
Teşvikiye Caddesi 105/3, Teşvikiye.
Tel: (0212) 236 6790.
Fax: (0212) 236 6791.
E-mail: ays.bil@pamukbank.com.tr
Historic and contemporary shows
by Turkish/foreign photographers,
plus a photo-album library.
Tem
Orhan Ersek Sokak 44/2, Nimet
Apt., Niıantaşı.
Tel: (0212) 247 0899.
Fax: (0212) 247 9756.
One of Istanbul's best galleries,
with an excellent collection of
Turkish contemporary art. Also
holds international exhibitions. The
owner Besi Cecan speaks good
English.

Ankara
Akpınar Sanat Galerisi
Güneş Sokak 31, Kavaklıdere.
Tel: (0312) 468 7960.

Galeri Nev
Gezegen Sokak 5, Gaziosmanpaşa.
Tel: (0312) 437 9390.
Same owners as Galeri Nev in
Istanbul.
Hobby Café Sanat Galerisi
7 Caddesi 3, Bahçelievler.
Tel: (0312) 215 1014.
Vakıfbank Sanat Galerisi
Uğur Mumcu Caddesi 78,
Gaziosmanpaşa.
Tel: (0312) 446 8554.
Vakko
Atatürk Bulvarı 113, Kızılay.
Tel: (0312) 417 4445.

Antalya
Antalya Güzel Sanatlar Galerisi
Cumhuriyet Caddesi.
Art House
Pamir Caddesi 26/A.
Tel: (0242) 242 4141.
Falez Hotel Gallery
Konyaaltı Falez Mevkii.
Tel: (0242) 248 5000.
Turkuaz Sanat Galerisi
Tel: (0242) 242 0176.

Cultural Festivals

January
Ağrı – Troubadour Celebration.
Selçuk (İzmir) – Camel Wrestling
Festival; camel wrestling also takes
place in Denizli and Aydin.

February
İzmir – Camel Wrestling.

March
Çanakkale – 1915 Sea Victory
Celebration.
İzmir – European Jazz Days.

April
Ankara – International Music and
Arts Festival.
Çanakkale – Anzak Days.
Istanbul – International Film
Festival; Tulip Festival.
Manisa – traditional *Mesir*
(traditional sweet) Festival.

May
Alanya – International Rafting and
Triathlon Organization.
Ankara – International Film Festival
and International Caricature
Festival.

Aydın – Erik Culture and Arts
Festival.
Bartın – Strawberry Festival.
Bergama – Festival of Pergamon
(with drama in the amphitheatre).
Birecik (Sanlıurfa) – Kelaynak
Festival (dedicated to a pelican-like
bird unique to Turkey).
Bursa – International Tulip Festival.
Çiğli (İzmir) – Bird Sanctuary
Celebration.
Edirne – Kakava Festival.
Ephesus (Selçuk) – Festival of Art
and Culture.
Eskişehir – Yunus Emre Arts and
Culture Week (a 13th-century
humanitarian poet and mystic).
Giresun – Aksu Arts Festival.
Istanbul – International Theatre
Festival.
Karacasu (Aydın) – Afrodisias
Culture and Arts Festival.
Konya – Javelin and Jousting
Competition.
Kırklareli – Arts, Culture and
Humour Festival.
Marmaris – International Yacht Week.
Silifke – Music and Folklore
Festival.

June
Adıyaman – Commagene Tourism
and Cultural Festival.
Antakya – Saint Pierre Mass.
Artvin – Kafkasör Bullfights, Culture
and Arts Festival.
Aspendos – Opera and Ballet
Festival.
Bandırma – "Bird Paradise" Culture
and Tourism Festival.
Bursa – International Music and
Dance Festival.
Edirne – traditional Kırkpınar Oil
Wrestling Competitions (late June or
early July).
Foça (İzmir) – Music, Folklore and
Watersports Festival.
Istanbul – International Classical
Music Festival.
Kemer (Antalya) – International
Golden Pomegranate Festival.
Köyeceğiz – Tourism Festival.
Marmaris – International Music and
Arts Festival.
Rize – International Tea and Tourism
Festival.
Safranbolu – Architectural
Treasures and Folklore Week.

July
Abana (Kastamonu) – Sea Festival.
Akşehir (Konya) – Nasreddin Hodja
Festival.
Antakya (Hatay) – Tourism and
Culture Festival.
Bursa – International Folk Dance
Competition.
Çeşme – Sea Festival and
International Song Contest.
Çorum – Hittite Festival.
Datça-Knidos – Arts and Culture
Festival.
Foça – Watersports Festival.
Gerze (Sinop) – Sea Festival.
Ihlara (Aksaray) – Tourism and
Culture Festival.
İskenderun – Culture and Tourism
Festival.
Istanbul – International Jazz Festival.
Kabaoguz (Amasya) – Yayla Festival.
Kadırga (Giresun) – Yayla Festival.
Kargı-Tosya-Taşköprü – Yayla Festival.
Kuşadası (İzmir) – Music Festival.
Malatya – Apricot Festival.
Mesudiye (Ordu) – Yayla Festival.
Samsun – International Folk Festival.

August
Alanya – International Beach
Volleyball.
Ankara – International Anatolian
Music Festival.
Antalya – 30 August, Zafer Bayrami
(Victory Day).
Avanos (Nevşehir) – Tourism and
Handicraft Festival; Hacı Bektaş Veli
Commemoration (Bektaşi and Alevi
ritual singing and dancing).
Bozcaada (Troy) – Arts and Culture
Festival.
Canakkale – Troy Festival.
Keçiborlu (Isparta) – Türkmen
Nomad Feast Days.
Kütahya – Traditional Tile-making
and Ceramics Festival.
Mengen (Bolu) – Traditional Turkish
Cooking and Chef's Festival.

September
Aksaray – Yunus Emre Culture and
Art Week.
Diyarbakır – Watermelon
Competitions.
Eskişehir – Meerschaum (White
Gold) Festival.
Istanbul – Tüyap Arts Fair.
İzmir – International Fair.
Safranbolu – Festival.

October

Alanya – Arts and Culture Festival; Triathlon Competition.
Antalya – Golden Orange International Film Festival.
Bodrum – International Sailboat Race.
Bozburun (İzmir) – International *Gulet* Sailing Festival.
Istanbul – International Arts Biennial (odd-numbered years).
Istanbul, Ankara, Adana – Akbank Jazz Festival.
Konya – Troubador Celebration.
Ürgüp – Wine Competition.
29th – Cumhuriyet Bayrami (Republic Day). Everywhere.

November

Bursa – International Karagöz and Shadow Theatre Festival.
Marmaris – International Yacht Races.
Nationwide – Anniversary of Atatürk's death (10th).
Nationwide – Teacher's Day (24th).

December

Demre (Kaş) – St Nicholas' Festival.
Konya – Mevlâna Festival (10th–17th; whirling dervish shows).

Nightlife

Nightlife traditionally revolves around *meyhane* (taverns), bars, restaurants and *gazinos* (places where *meze* are served with accompanying Turkish cabaret or dancing). In the major cities and resorts, though, discos and nightclubs exert a powerful pull on the young and more affluent; they are as vulnerable to fashion as clubs in New York or London.

You'll find a range of bars from the simple to exotic and elegant; some have live music, others a theme (Mexican, British pub...)

The best dance clubs and discos are as good, with as up-to-date sounds, as you'd find anywhere. Along the coast, many of the larger hotels have their own discos and cabarets, most of which are open to non-residents.

Venues

ISTANBUL

Babylon
Seyhbender Sok. 3, Asmalımescit, Tünel.
Tel: (0212) 292 7368.
Istanbul's best and most famous live-music club serving up an inspirational mix of world music, jazz and electronica.

Hayal Kahvesi
Büyükparmakkapı Sokak 19, Beyoğlu.
Tel: (0212) 243 6823.
By day a cosy café, by night a live-music venue featuring jazz and rock, with a young clientele. Open every day 11–2am. No credit cards.

Hayal Kahvesi Çabuklu
Burunbahçe, Beykoz.
Tel: (0216) 413 6880.
Upmarket cousin to the Beyoğlu rock café of the same name, this is an elegant, isolated summer spot for the well-heeled, right on the water's edge, but still in the city. In summer a private boat runs every half-hour from Istinye on the European side of the Bosphorus. Restaurant and café open noon–midnight, bar until 2am; live music after 11pm and a large dance floor. Sunday brunch 10.30am–3.30pm. All major cards.

Historical Pano Wine House (*Tarihi Pano Şaraphanesi*)
Balık Pazar, junction of Meşrutiyet Caddesi, Hamalbaşı and Kalyoncu Kulluşu Caddesi.
Tel: (0212) 292 6664.
An old Greek wine house dating from 1898 that has been renovated with sensitivity to its original layout, complete with the old wooden vats and rough but drinkable wine on tap at low prices. Old Istanbul atmosphere.

James Joyce – The Irish Pub
Tarlabaşı Boulevard, Dernek Sokak, Taksim.
Tel: (0212) 238 8892.
The oldest and best-established Irish pub in Istanbul offers ceilidh dancing, live Irish music as well as blues and African rhythms most nights. Rooftop barbecue on Sunday in summer run by Eamonn, the Irish owner. Imported Guinness and classic Irish pub grub. Very popular with foreigners.

Millennium
Nizamiye Caddesi 14, Taksim.
Tel: (0212) 256 4437.
One of Istanbul's most-frequented, celebrity-packed clubs, and also one of the priciest – minimum US$25/£15 entrance free and expensive drinks. Two spacious rooms offer house, garage, techno and the scent of the city's richest youth. Open Wed, Fri and Sat midnight–6am. All major credit cards.

Neo
Lamartin Caddesi 40/2, Taksim.
Tel: (0212) 254 4526.
Fax: (0212) 245 6821.
Istanbul's newest gay and lesbian venue.

New Yorker Balo Bar
Istiklal Caddesi Balo Sokak 6, Beyoğlu.

Smart new venue with a New York restaurant, cocktail bar, the Balo Bar which features live cabaret and the Balo Club with international guest DJs.

North Shield
Fitaş Sineması, Istiklal Caddesi 24–26, Beyoğlu.
Tel: (0212) 292 9698.
Part of a growing chain of English pubs with a good range of English beer and whisky. Open noon–1am.

Pupa's
Caddesi 17 Arnavutköy.
Tel: (0212) 265 6533.
Nowadays, Pupa's is only nominally African in theme, but it is still one of the few places in town for reggae. African food on Tuesday night, reggae disco on Friday and Saturday. Credit cards not accepted.

Q Bar
Çırağan Palace Hotel, Beşiktaş.
Tel: (0212) 236 2121.
One of Istanbul's top classical jazz venues is imaginatively run, featuring debut shows by young up-and-coming Turkish painters on Blue Monday nights in winter. Music outdoors along the Bosphorus in summer. Expensive, but far more interesting than hotel lounges and attractive to Istanbul's older élite.

Roxy
Arslan Sokak, Sıraselviler, Taksim.
Tel: (0212) 249 4839/234 3236.
Trendy, expensive youth venue with great live international bands. Open 6pm–3.30am. No credit cards.

Switch
Muammer Karaca Sokak 3, Beyoğlu.
Tel: (0212) 292 7458.
E-mail: info@switchclub.net/
www.switchclub.net

Cover Charges

Istanbul's nightclubs often have extremely high cover charges (on the grounds that Turkish girls don't drink much) which may not be well displayed and yet appear infuriatingly on your bill at the end of the evening, especially if there is live music. The charge usually includes a few drinks, however. Check before you enter.

Gay/straight industrial techno club with international DJs, open Thur–Sat 10pm–4am.

19–20
Tepebaşı, Taksim.
Tel: (0212) 235 6197.
Mixed gay and straight late-night haunt of the young and wild. One room for rock, another for techno.

THRACE & MARMARA

Apart from a few local discos, there is little or no nightlife – as Westerners understand the term – in Thrace or Marmara. Notices of occasional concerts and plays appear on posters and in shop windows. In Bursa the desperate might try:

The Club S
Kültür Park (Ipekiş entrance).
Weekends only.

Bongo Bar
Clup Altınceylan, Kültür Park.

Karagöz Theatre
Çekirge.
Details of performances and tickets from lenal Çelikkol at the Karagöz Antique Shop, Eski Aynalı Çarsı 1–17.
Tel: (0224) 222 6151.

AEGEAN COAST

Bodrum
Halikarnas
Cumhuriyet Caddesi.
Tel: (0252) 316 8000.
The most famous disco on the Turkish Aegean coast. It starts moving after the midnight laser-and-light show.

M&M Dancing
Dr Alim Bey Caddesi.
Tel: (0252) 316 2725.
The closest rival to the Halikarnas in terms of popularity. The music keeps playing until around 4am.

Ora
Dr Alim Bey Caddesi 19/21.
Tel: (0252) 316 3903.
Attracts a lively crowd of young people intent on enjoying themselves until the early hours of the morning.

Çesme
Lowry's Irish Pub
İzmir Caddesi, Ilica.
Tel: (0232) 723 0425.
Authentic Irish-managed pub with live music and food.

İzmir
Windows on the Bay
Hilton Hotel, Gaziosmanpaşa Bulvarı.
Tel: (0232) 441 6060.
Looking out over the city from the 31st storey and open till the early hours of the morning with live music.
The more downmarket nightlife is centred on Barlar Sokak, where the Irish should feel right at home.

Kuşadası
Emperor
Barlar Sokaği (Beer Street) 21.
Tel: (0256) 612 2575.
Elbow space is at a premium in this very popular disco in the heart of Kuşadası's entertainment area, surrounded by pubs.

Marmaris
Crazy Daisy Bar
Bar Street.
Tel: (0252) 412 4856.
Ear-shattering music, lasers and piles of heaving bodies make this one of the best venues on Bar Street, the centre of all Marmaris nightlife.

Cabaret

Though expensive, cabaret is often worth it. This form of entertainment, which can include expertly performed traditional music and belly-dancing, should not be dismissed since it is not always designed to liberate the hapless tourist's wallet. Cabaret is a genuine, popular Turkish celebration, often laid on as part of lavish family events, and at its best it can be very very good.

Dinner and show together will come to US$50–90 (£30–55) a head, more if you find yourself lavishly tipping the belly dancer.

MEDITERRANEAN COAST

Alanya
Auditorium Open Air Disco
Dimçayi Mevkii.
Noisy, lively open-air disco. Summer only.
Janus Restaurant and Café-Bar
Rıhtım Girişi.
Tel: (0242) 513 2694.
Large, lurid pink harbourfront café/restaurant/bar through the day, with late-night dancing. Open round the clock.

Antalya
Birdland Jazz Club
Hıdırlık Kulesi Arkası, Hesapçı Sokak 78, Kaleiçi.
Tel: (0242) 242 01507.
For those who prefer something a little more sophisticated, this trendy jazz club in a restored konak (mansion) positively oozes cool.
Çizgi Café and Bar
Uzun Çarşı 28, Kaleiçi.
Tel: (0242) 248 1549.
With a yachting-Ottoman theme that sounds – and is – peculiar, this is nevertheless a great place to hang out, with low tables, cushions and cocktails.
PM Bar and Underground
Cumhuriyet Caddesi 59, Sokak 8.
Tel: (0242) 247 3256.
Young, loud and energetic club serving a popular mix of rock and Turkish pop.
Şaziye Bar
Cumhuriyet Caddesi, 59 Sokak.
Classy bar designed for those with the wealth and years to support it.

Fethiye
Disco Marina
Yat Limanı Karşısı, opposite the Yacht Harbour.
Tel: (0252) 614 9860.
Popular with the young Turks and tourists; an odd but entertaining mix of modern music, mirror balls and professional dancers (including belly-dancing).
Yes!
Cumhuriyet Caddesi 9.
Tel: (0252) 614 9289.
Trendy and highly successful English-Turkish venture mixing traditions, ages, disco and live

shows. Entrance free; happy hour 9pm–midnight; open until 4am.
Ottoman Café
Karagözler Caddesi 3/B.
Tel: (0252) 612 1148.
Ottoman-style, with carpets, kilims, cushions and copper pots aplenty. Live Turkish folk music and tour groups. Visit in the afternoon or early evening.

Kalkan
Aquarium Bar
Town centre.
Tel: (0242) 844 3453.
Three floors of entertainment, a lively bar, excellent music, games (billiards) room, and live shows with transvestite belly dancers.

Kaş
Fullmoon Disco
Fullmoon Hotel, 1 km (0.5 mile) out of town, on the Kalkan road.
Tel: (0242) 836 3241.
Popular, seafront open-air disco whose brain-numbing beat is carefully sited a little from town.
Sun Café Bar and Restaurant
Hükümet Caddesi.
Tel: (0242) 836 1053.
With a terrace overlooking the harbour and a wood stove in winter, this is a favourite year-round drinking spot for locals and tourists alike.

Side
Blues Bar
Cami Sokak.
Tel: (0242) 753 1197.
Friendly bar that prides itself on being safe for single women. Sit on the breezy outdoor terrace and work your way through the 100 cocktails.
Zeppelin Barr
Barbaros Caddesi, 68.
Tel: (0242) 753 4323.
Loud, hot and sweaty, with sea views.

CENTRAL ANATOLIA

Ankara
Agora Restaurant-Bar
Kale Kapisi 14 Sokak Kale, Ulus.
Tel: (0312) 310 7675.
Live Turkish music (fasil) in a restored mansion.

Cabare
Atakule Cankaya.
Tel: (0312) 440 2374.
Elegant club with glorious views, on the second floor of Atakule tower. Live pop music at weekends. Closed Sun.
Club So
Turan Gunes Bulvari 274, Or-An.
Tel: (0312) 491 1250.
Crowded dance club featuring Turkish and foreign music and video screen. Live music at weekends. Open 11pm–4am. Closed Sun and Mon.
Cult
Ugur Mumcu Caddesi Kupe Sok. 8/A Gaziosmanpaşa.
Tel: (0312) 447 6390.
Hard rock and heavy metal for Turkish yuppies. Popular with locals, Mind-boggling people-watching.
North Shield
Guvenlik Caddesi 111, Asagiayranci.
Tel: (0312) 466 1266.
English pub Turkish-style, with English beer, whisky, pub grub and international food. Pleasant and popular. Open daily noon–1am.
Section
Nenehatun Caddesi 53, Gaziosmanpaşa.
Tel: (0312) 446 2030.
Popular, young, upmarket bar with live Turkish pop music and a garden in summer. Closed Sun.
Seğmen Bar
Merit Altınel Hotel, Gazi Mustafa Kemal Bulvari 151, Tandoğan.
Tel: (0312) 231 7760.
Live entertainment. Western music. Good place to socialise with Turks.

Sport

Spectator Sports

Soccer is the national obsession; the fortunes of favourite teams are closely followed, with much celebration after a victory. Galatasaray, Beşiktaş and Fenerbahçe are all Istanbul-based teams with a national following. Small boys wear the strip, and you'll see coloured scarves and flags flying and hear car horns blaring on the night of a match. A Turkish soccer match is a thrilling event, and the atmosphere inside the ground dramatic and emotional. Trouble is always anticipated, so you can expect to see armoured vehicles and water cannon in readiness outside the ground.

Basketball is also a popular spectator sport, and is played by youths all over the country.

Ice hockey The national team is surprisingly successful considering the country has only one proper rink, in Ankara.

LOCAL SPORTS

Oil wrestling

This ritualised form of wrestling, *Yağlı güreş*, in which contestants wear nothing but leather shorts and are coated with olive oil, is described on page 149. The year's highlight is the (late June or early July) Kırkpınar Festival near Edirne, when up to 1,000 people compete. For tickets, try the Edirne tourist office, tel: (0284) 225 1518; www.kirkpinarwrestling.com

Camel wrestling

An annual camel-wrestling festival takes place at Selçuk in January. Two adult male camels are pitted against each other. Other bouts take place in the Aydın region in December and January.

Cirit (jirit)

A wild, ruthless game vaguely akin to polo, played on horseback. *Cirit* ponies are trained to gallop from a standing start and turn on the spot. It is exciting but cruel, as ponies are sometimes treated roughly.

Birdwatching

Although not strictly a sport, bird-watching is an increasingly popular outdoor activity. Several places in Turkey are designated as a "bird paradise" *(kuş cenneti)*, a flamboyant name for a sanctuary, which come in varying standards.

One of the best places for serious birders is the complex of freshwater marsh, salt lakes and mudflats in the area known as Sultan Sazlığı, southeast of Cappadocia. At the crossroads of two important migrating routes, 250 species have been recorded as visiting, and 69 have settled to breed. Autumn is the best time to visit. Most exciting for the lay person are the vast flocks of flamingoes and other interesting birds such as pelicans and storks. You can spend the night on the edge of the marshy area and be taken out onto the water at dawn.

Golf

In a bid to draw more wealthy foreign tourists to Turkey, the country has rapidly developed golf. It has eight courses, four in Belek, in the Mediterranean coastal province of Antalya, three in Istanbul and one in Ankara. By the year 2005, Turkey is expected to have 25 golf courses.

The Klassis Golf and Country Club, the Kemer Golf and Country Club in Istanbul and the National Golf Club in Belek have all been settings for senior European Professional Golf Association (PGA) tournaments. Most accept day visitors and many top hotels have arrangements for their guests. In spite of this activity, only about 1,000 people, of whom 300 are expatriate foreigners, actually play the game in Turkey.

Alternative Travel & Holidays
146 Kingsland High Street, London E8 2NS.
Tel: (020) 7923 3230
Fax: (020) 7923 3118
www.turkishgolf.com
UK tour operator specialising in golfing holidays in Turkey.

Ankara
Ankara Golf Club
Erkeksu Çiftliği, Yenikent, Sincan.
Tel: (0312) 490 3255.
Ankara's only golf club; the 9-hole course is open Apr–Nov.

Belek
A purpose-built golf resort, built to the highest level, with 4 excellent golf courses (so far) and around 23 four- or five-star hotels, all with players' privileges. This is golfing heaven. The Turkish tourist office publishes a brochure on golf-based holidays in Belek.

National Golf Course
Tel: (0242) 725 4620.
Tat Golf Belek International Golf Course
Tel: (0242) 725 4128.
Gloria Hotel Golf Resort
Tel: (0242) 715 1368.

Istanbul
Istanbul Golf Club
4 Levent.
Tel: (0212) 264 0742.
Turkey's oldest course, established in the late 19th century by British businessmen living in the city. Members and guests only.
Kemer Golf and Country Club
Tel: (0212) 239 7913.
Golf and tennis.
Klassis Golf and Country Club
Silivri.
Tel: (0212) 748 4600.
Magnificent 18-hole course designed by Tony Jacklin, 100 km (97 km/60 miles) outside Istanbul. Tennis, swimming, riding and a health farm.

Horse Riding

Facilities vary enormously, but horse riding can be a wonderful way to explore the landscape. Short treks, from 2 hours to a full day, can be

Turkish Baths (Hamams)

As a spectator sport, nothing surpasses a *hamam* – be sure to visit one during your stay. Many people are put off the idea because they simply don't know what to expect (or what to do). Don't worry. The locals will happily steer you straight. The rules are simple, based on the old Roman baths or the Scandinavian sauna. The sexes are usually segregated either in different baths or by set hours for each. Nudity is not the norm, so wear underpants or ask for a sarong *(peştamal)*. You will also be given a towel and wooden clogs *(takunya)*.

Change in the reception area *(camekân)*. From here, you move through to a private sideroom to wash down before entering the central hot steam room *(hararet)*. In the old baths, this is often a spectacular room with domes, arches, marble and tiles, at the centre of which is a large marble slab. You lie down on this and are given an energetic face, foot and/or full-body massage, or a scrubdown with a camel-hair glove.

Most five-star hotels offer luxurious, modern *hamams*, but some of the more traditional bathhouses are well worth a visit for the atmosphere.

Istanbul (old city)
Cağaloğlu Hamam, Prof. Kazım Gürkan Caddesi 34, Cağaloğlu.
Tel: (0212) 522 2424.
Priced for tourists (up to US$50/£30 for the works), but superb care is offered in this 400-year-old bathhouse. Fabulous bar around the old courtyard, full of antiquities and almost Moorish in feel. Men: 7am–10pm; women: 8am–8pm. Group bookings taken.
Çemberlitaş Hamam, Vezirhan Caddesi 8, Çemberlitaş.
Tel: (0212) 522 7974/520 1850.
E-mail: contact@cemberlitashamami.com.tr
www.cemberlitashamami.com.tr
Another bath of great antiquity, built by the great Ottoman architect Sinan. Traditional bathing with separate sections for the different sexes. Open 6am–midnight.

Aegean Coast
Bodrum
Haman, Cevat Sakir Caddesi Fabrika Sok.
Tel: (0252) 213 4129.
www.hamam.com
Surprisingly traditional for touristy Bodrum, with some afternoons set aside for women. Open daily 6am–10pm. Shuttle service from many hotels.

Marmaris
Armutalan
off Datça Caddesi, 2 km (1.3) miles from the centre.
Tel: (0252) 412 0710.
A clean, modern tourist-oriented bath. Shuttle bus from the Tansas Shopping Centre. Open daily 9am–10pm Apr–Nov.

Mediterranean Coast
Alanya
Mimoza Turkish Bath, Sugözü Caddesi 19.
Tel: (0242) 513 9193.
All-in-one experience for the body, mind and social life; with a café.
Antalya
Antalya Yeni Hamami, Sinan Mahallesi 1255, Sokak 3/A.
Tel: (0242) 242 5225.
Modern, shiny and professional. You may not experience the atmospheric delights of Ottoman marble, but you will be clean.
Fethiye
Old Turkish Bath, Hamam Sokak 2, Paspatur Bazaar.
Tel: (0252) 614 9318.
Unusually there is some mixed bathing at Fethiye's 16th-century bathhouse, in the middle of the bazaar, and now geared almost entirely towards tourists. Open daily 7am–midnight.

arranged at centres in Cappadocia and from the southern coastal resorts. There are also riding stables in the vicinity of Istanbul, but on the whole these are open to club members only.

In all cases, you should be upfront about your experience or lack of it, and you will have to use your judgment on the safety of the horses and the establishment. There are almost no ponies in Turkey, and the high level of Arab blood in the horses makes them pretty but skittish.

Ankara
Ankara Atlı Spor Kulübü
Çiftlik Caddesi, 260; Gazi Mahalesi.
Tel: (0312) 213 2192.

Antalya
Bagana Ranch
On the road to Termessos.
Tel: (0242) 425 2270.
Fax: (0242) 425 2244.
Ride up into the mountains on a day trail with picnic lunch.

Cappadocia
A number of hotels and individuals offer horse-riding tours – often the best way to see individual churches.
Kapadokya Lodge Country Club
Üchisar, Nevşehir.
Tel: (0384) 213 9945.
Fax: (0384) 213 5092.
Rainbow Ranch
Göreme, Nevşehir.
Tel: (0384) 271 2413.

Istanbul
Ferhat Bey Binicilik Club
Sile Yolu-Alemdağ Mevkii.
Tel: (0216) 429 5031.
istanbul Altı Spor Club
Maslak.
Tel: (0212) 276 2056.
Istanbul Riding Club
Binicilik Sitesi Ucyol, Maslak.
Tel: (0212) 276 1404.
Samandıra Atlıspor Club
Samandıra.
Tel: (0216) 311 4333.

Ice Skating

Ankara
Bel-Pa Eğlence Tesisleri
Bahçelievler Sondurak, Adnan Ötüken Park.

Tel: (0312) 222 2291.
Year-round ice skating at Turkey's only Olympic-sized ice rink. Open usually 9am–11pm. Amateur hockey matches at weekends.

Atatürk Buz Pateni Lokantasi
Kurtulus Parki İci.
Tel: (0312) 431 9202.
Ice skating is also possible at this outdoor rink, set in a pleasant park in the city centre. Open Oct–Apr. The restaurant is open year round.

Istanbul
Galleria Shopping Mall
Ataköy.
Tel: (0212) 560 8550.
Cheerful shopping-centre ice rink for fun rather than serious sport. Open daily 9am–10pm.

Skiing

Around 60 percent of Turkey lies at an elevation of 1,000 metres (3,300 ft) or more, and the rugged mountainous areas to the east are three times the size of the Alps. Snow blankets the country's sparsely populated eastern provinces for around seven months of the year.

Skiing was first introduced in Turkey at the end of World War I. The Russian army, retreating from the mountains of occupied eastern Turkey, left behind hundreds of skis that Turkish troops began to use. The first ski clubs were established in the 1930s in the northwestern city of Bursa.

Today, thousands of people ski in Turkey, and the country attracts winter tourists from the European Union and the former Soviet Union. Skiing is steadily becoming more popular and is considered chic, but is generally overpriced by Turkish standards – and under-equipped. Little of the skiing is particularly challenging for the experienced.

Ski Resorts
There are 24 ski resorts, but only a couple of real significance – Uludağ, in northwest Anatolia, and Sarıkamış, in Kars province in eastern Turkey. Many of the resorts lack either hotels or mechanical ski lifts. But both problems are being

solved. Mount Erciyes, near Cappadocia, has the longest ski season (mid-Nov to mid-Apr). Other resorts include Kartalkaya, in the northwestern Bolu province; Palandöken Dağı in Erzurum, to the northeast; and Ilgaz Dagı, in the northwest.

Due to its proximity to Istanbul, Uludağ is Turkey's most developed ski resort, with 14 hotels. In the Saklıkent area, 50 km (31 miles) northwest of Antalya, there is snow from December to March, and it is possible for hardy visitors to ski in the morning and swim in the Mediterranean in the afternoon. Skis can be rented, and prices are moderate by European standards.

Specialist Tour Operators

These cover a range of activities, including trekking, canoeing, rafting, paragliding, diving, jeep safaris, mountain biking, horse-riding and motorbikes. The Turkish Tourist Office in the UK publishes an excellent list of specialist tours and activities.

Alanya
Alraft Rafting and Riding Club
Biçakçı Köyü Mevkii.
Tel: (0242) 513 9155.
Martin Türkay
Atatürk Caddesi 95/C.
Tel: (0242) 513 5666.

Antalya
Medraft
Gençlik Mahallesi, Tevfik İ±ık Caddesi, Mehmet Kesikçi Apart.
Tel: (0242) 248 0083.
Stop Tours
Dr Burhanettin Onat Caddesi, Yılmaz Sitesi, A Blok, No. 14.
Tel: (0242) 322 6557.
Trek Tourism
Kızılsaray Mahallesi, 61 Sokak Alanya Is Merkezi 10-16.
Tel: (0242) 248 1629.

Bodrum
Askin Dive Centre
Tel: (0252) 316 4247.
www.askindiving.com

Cappadocia
Middle Earth Travel
Gaferli Mah. Cevizler Sokak No. 20, 50180 Goreme, Nevşehir.
Tel: (0384) 271 2559/28
Fax: (0384) 271 2562.
www.middleearthtravel.com

Fethiye
Cadianda Tours
Babataşı Mahallesi, M. Kemal Bulvarı.
Tel: (0252) 614 4150.
Fax: (0252) 612 8655.
Explora
Hisarönü, Fethiye.
Tel: (0252) 616 6890.
Han Camp, Ölüdeniz.
Tel: (0252) 616 6316.

Kaş
Bougainville
Ibrahim Serin Caddesi.
Tel: (0242) 836 3737.
www.bougainville-turkey.com

Marmaris
Alternatif Turizm
Çamlik Sok.
Tel: (0252) 413 5994.
www.alternatifraft.com

Side
Get Wet
Tel: (0242) 753 4071.

Tennis

Tennis is popular among the members of swanky private clubs. Visitors can sometimes book courts by the hour. Holiday villages and complexes and five-star hotels will usually feature tennis courts.

Ankara
Kavaklidere Tennis and Sports Club
Iran Caddesi 4, Kavaklıdere.
Tel: (0312) 427 5092.

Antalya
Antalya Tennis Ihtisas ve Spor Kulübü
100 Yıl Bulvarı, Konyaaltı (next to the Sheraton Hotel).
Tel: (0242) 243 3537.

Istanbul
ENKA Sports Centre
Istinye Yolu.
Tel: (0212) 276 5084.
Indoor and outdoor tennis, as well as swimming, basketball and volleyball.
Levent Tennis Club
Akasyalı Sokak 34, Levent.
Tel: (0212) 279 2710.
TED Tennis Club
Tarabya Caddesi, Tarabya.
Tel: (0212) 262 9080.

Walking & Mountaineering

Turks are just beginning to become interested in recreational walking, but the emphasis tends to be on organised group walks (there are some popular local rambling clubs).

Independent walkers are severely hampered by the lack of good large-scale maps, and the country's first proper signed long-distance hiking route snakes across inland Lycia. Tour companies can take you to good areas for hill and mountain walks, but you can also get a great deal of pleasure in striking out for a short distance on your own.

Mount Ararat has opened up to mountaineering again but you must go with a guide. There are specialist agencies that can take you to climb the extinct volcanoes of the Central Anatolian Plain and there is a growing interest in the Kaçkar Mountains along the Black Sea coast (see page 313). The Taurus Mountains along the south coast are generally less formidable and several national parks, such as Olympos and Termessos, offer good day treks for the reasonably fit. Cappadocia has a huge variety of walking, from easy day trips to more vigorous climbs on Mount Erciyes.

Watersports

Turkish resorts can now offer sailing, surfing, windsurfing, scuba diving and snorkelling, paragliding and waterskiing to a much higher and safer standard than was previously the case. Diving in particular is popular.

SWIMMING

Swimming in the sea should always be undertaken with caution. There are some areas, such as parts of the Black Sea coast, where seemingly inviting beaches harbour dangerous currents. Plenty of places offer perfect conditions, but it's safest to check.

Some areas are also home to sea urchins, so a pair of flip-flops or espadrilles for wading may be a good investment. Turkish beach hygiene can leave a lot to be desired, too, and busy beaches will be marred by litter.

The big resort hotels all have pools. In winter, indoor hotel pools can be fun, though expensive.

DIVING

The larger resorts have clubs and schools offering properly supervised instruction leading to internationally recognised certificates. There are also numerous independent schools.

Fish are few and far between, but in some places underwater attractions include archaeological remains or ancient sunken vessels, though since these are often unexcavated diving is strictly controlled by the government. Foreigners may dive only with those certified by the Ministry of Tourism.

You should bring any international certificates with you. For simple snorkelling, you can normally hire a boat for the day to take you to secluded spots.

Alanya
Active Divers Club
Iskele Caddesi 80.
Tel: (0242) 512 8811.
Diving tours, underwater photography and PADI courses, from the Pasha Bay Hotel.
Active Diving Centre
Tel: (0242) 511 3662.

Dolphin Dive
Tel: (0242) 512 3030.

Antalya
Ilter Diving Centre
Tel: (0242) 311 8677.

Fethiye
European Diving Centre
Atatürk Caddesi.
Tel: (0252) 614 9771.
Run by Englishmen with US and UK trained intructors; PADI courses.

Kemer
Eurasia Diving Centre
Tel: (0242) 814 3250.
British intructors.

Marmaris
European Diving Centre
Içmeler.
Tel: (0252) 455 4733.
A British-owned diving school offering a one-day introductory course, plus complete PADI courses.

White-Water Rafting

Turkey's rivers are rapidly growing in popularity, with rafting on offer in the Kaçkar Mountains, which run parallel with the Black Sea, and the Taurus or Beydağları Mountains, a short distance inland from Antalya, Alanya and Fethiye, as well as several points in the Central Anatolian plateau and even along stretches of the Euphrates.

None of the rapids is especially dangerous, so you can even consider rafting for an exciting family day out! All the same, you should always wear the helmets provided and distrust any company that does not insist on their use.

You can organise white-water rafting with local companies yourself, or book through a travel agent, either at home or locally.

Shopping

Shopping in Turkey can be a delight, it is always fascinating and is sometimes even educational.

High-fashion clothes can be bought very cheaply, as Turkey has a booming cotton industry and has become a cheap source of manufacture for the West. Turkish leather is well known, but the clothing and bags are usually better value than shoes.

Look carefully at the quality of what you are buying; it varies enormously and when you pay more, you often get something that is much better made.

It is hard to find a good bargain in the tourist areas; try to shop in the more out-of-the-way villages and towns, where you will probably find better quality products.

Where to Shop

Turkey offers many different shopping experiences, from the glitzy to the gritty. There are vast user-friendly shopping centres, like American shopping malls, complete with parking, supermarket, cinemas, food courts and international designer labels.

There is the older version of the same idea, the amazing Grand (or Covered) Bazaar in Istanbul, a veritable labyrinth of shops and workshops, selling every imaginable product. Excellent local weekly street markets, best for Turkey's wonderful fresh produce if you are self-catering, plus flea markets (bit pazarı) can be found.

If you prefer more sophisticated, individual and independent shops, you will find them, too, offering high-quality fashion, interior design and gifts.

What to Buy

Textiles, clothing, carpets, pottery, metalwork, semi-precious and precious stones and jewellery, leather and glass all fall into various categories of quality and price. You could easily go home with a bag full of shoddily made but amusing souvenirs with a Turkish flavour. Or you could spend some serious money and kit out a small museum with the finest craft work.

ANTIQUES

Rummaging in junk shops and flea markets is very entertaining, and although you are not supposed to take antiques out of Turkey, there is no clear definition of what constitutes an antique.

Old Turkish things used to be dirt cheap because newly wealthy Turks wanted everything modern, Western and glitzy. Stylish Turks have recently become keen on old Ottoman pieces for their interior décor, so prices are rising.

For items of European origin, it is possible to get export permission, and good shopkeepers will know the procedure and be able to tell you if you may legally export any

Opening Times

Shops are generally open from Mon–Sat 9am–6/8pm (later in summer, especially in resorts). A selection of local shops in any busy neighbour-hood, and more so in the cities, will be open late into the evening. Large shops open later, and the US-style shopping malls are open seven days a week from 10am–10pm.

Shops do not close for lunch, but small shops may shut briefly for prayers, especially for the midday prayers on Fridays.

Street markets begin around 8am, and may start packing up in the mid-afternoon.

The Grand Bazaar and Spice Bazaar in Istanbul are open 8.30am–7pm (closed Sun).

particular item. Antiquities and antique Turkish things are another matter, and there are severe penalties for anyone caught trying to take these out of the country without a special export licence.

BOOKS

The best large coffee-table-sized Turkish-published books on Turkey, with good photographs and English or bilingual text, are usually very expensive – often over US$100 (£60). Çelik Gülersöy, the doyen of Turkish conservation, has written many titles on the various palaces and historic areas of Istanbul, plus other areas in Turkey, and his books are reasonably priced and available in museum bookshops, though not terribly well produced.

You will find cheap and not particularly good illustrated guidebooks in several languages at tourist sites. New imported English books can now be bought at their sterling price at good urban bookshops. In Istanbul check out the English-language one-for-one book exchange under the Yağmur Cybercafé (see cybercafé listings, page 397) which is open 5–7pm on weekdays. Small pansiyons in tourist areas may also offer book exchanges in summer.

There's a thriving second-hand and antiquarian book trade, and some very good dealers who run shops in Istanbul and elsewhere and stalls at flea markets. However, the appetite for foreign-language books is great and prices are not so low. You'll also find maps and prints, but anything with a Turkish subject has become fashionable and will be very expensive.

CARPETS & KILIMS

A carpet is a hand-made rug with a raised pile, a kilim is flat woven. They can be made from cotton, wool, silk or a mixture. Designs and techniques are regional.

You do not have to be an expert to buy a good carpet, but it helps. It is worth remembering that London and New York are world-class carpet markets in their own right, and that department stores and chains all over the world buy new and antique Turkish carpets and flat-woven *kilims* and offer them at competititive prices, so there is no special reason why your find should be a bargain.

On the other hand, if you let yourself be guided by what you like, and most important, do some research before making a commitment, you can go home with something you really love.

Within Turkey, certain places are carpet-trading centres. The Grand or Covered Bazaar and surrounding area in Istanbul is one, but Cappadocia in Central Anatolia is another, as dealers travel there to buy and makers to sell.

Buying a carpet can rarely be done in a hurry, and can take half a day of tea-drinking and discussion, enjoyed by both customer and dealer. If you are serious, it would be worth doing a little background reading beforehand. *See also pages 100–103.*

METALWORK

You will find many wonderful things made of hand-beaten copper or brass: samovars, lunch boxes, pots and pans, cauldrons and so on. Craftsmanship is excellent, and since antiques are popular but illegal to export, many items are convincingly and attractively "antiqued".

Everyday household and functional metalware items can also be extremely attractive and sometimes very cheap: stainless steel and aluminium saucepans are much less expensive than in Europe and well made, and in street markets you will find pretty enamel tin trays, metal pots for making tea and coffee Turkish-style, and many other appealing things.

CHINA & GLASS

Turkey has a thriving industry churning out household glass and china at extremely good prices: if your luggage allowance can take it. At a more rarefied level, some factories are making beautiful replicas of traditional and museum pieces.

The Yıldız factory by the Yıldız Palace and Park in Istanbul makes delicate pretty porcelain in royal, Ottoman style. Pasabahçe, with shops all over Turkey and its product in every store, makes not only the household stuff but also the pretty blue-and-white swirled *çeşmibülbül* glass vases and ornaments.

Elsewhere, you will also see vast numbers of decorated plates and tiles in supposed "Kütahya" or "Iznik" style, which will be cheaper if you can get to Kütahya itself.

Some are mass produced, some are hand done, and the price will reflect this.

At Avanos, in Cappadocia, you can watch potters working the local red clay into shapes that haven't changed since classical times. Prices are very reasonable. Artist potters are beginning to use traditional decorative motifs in a freer, inspirational way, and their work is on sale at the better-quality shops.

JEWELLERY, GOLD & SILVER

Some of the most skilled craftsmen anywhere in the world are based in the jewellery workshops of the Grand or Covered Bazaar in Istanbul. You can find silversmiths, too, working to the highest standards. It is also possible to order something to be made specially. The choice can be overwhelming.

Gold and silver are sold by weight, with something added on for the work involved. You can still haggle. Precious and semi-precious stones are also said to be well priced, but you do need to know what you are doing.

Amber and turquoise are common, but real gems are also there if you want them.

LEATHER

There will undoubtedly be leather-goods shops wherever you decide to go. Jackets, coats, bags, briefcases and small leather goods such as wallets and card cases can all be good buys, but look hard at the styling and finish and not just the price tag. Shoes tend to be poor quality, and anything likely to catch your eye may well be imported.

Wealthy Turks are charmed by international labels, so you will see these in expensive shops at astronomical prices. However, markets may well have convincing copies of this season's Prada or Gucci style.

Haggling

Don't be afraid to haggle – the shop owners expect it in Turkey and often you can get items down to a very reasonable price over a glass or two of tea.

There is a subtle etiquette to haggling, which many Westerners find awkward and embarrassing at first, but then, if they get good at it, learn to love.

Tradesmen in tourist areas start their prices high, especially for tourist goods, so you usually can begin bargaining at at least half the initial stated price. It may well turn out that after a bout of intensive haggling, and several glasses of tea, the shopkeeper will respect you all the more when you finally reach an agreed price.

You can haggle a little even if you have no intention of buying, but once you have agreed a price it is very bad form to walk away.

Look out, too, for signs spelling out that prices are fixed. They usually mean what they say.

MUSIC & MUSICAL INSTRUMENTS

CDs and cassettes, either made under licence, remaindered from mainstream producers or bootleg, can be very cheap. Remember that if you are caught importing bootleg copies, they will be confiscated and you may face a fine.

Up-to-date releases, though plentiful, are just as expensive, if not more so, than at home. Traditional Turkish instruments, wind, percussion and strings, can be a good buy, and are available in specialist shops. Avoid buying them in tourist places since they will be overpriced.

FASHION

Turkey has its own established and sought-after fashion labels. Limon Company, Yargıcı and Mudo are among the top young(ish) and trendy designer names; Vakko and Beymen are equivalent to Harvey Nichols or Saks; while "diffusion" ranges, such as Vakkorama and Beymen Club, offer more youthful, cheaper styles.

Local fashion houses, however, do tend to be overwhelmed with one idea each season, which can make for a cloned effect both inside the shop and out in the fashionable streets.

Prices are more reasonable than in London, although it is harder to find pure natural fabrics. But in Kaş, several local designers will custom-make clothes from handwoven fabrics over the course of your holiday, for prices that needn't necessarily break the bank.

Turkey is also a manufacturing base for many foreign companies, so you can find very cheap jeans, T-shirts, sweatshirts and other casual gear. Down several alleys in Istiklal, in Istanbul, you will find massive outlets of overstock or 'seconds' (defolv), some in designer brands. There is a particularly big collection near Odakule (Galatasaray) in the alley adjoining the Paşbahçe glass shop.

TEXTILES

Bursa is famous both for producing silk and for its excellent cotton towels and bathrobes, but you can also find reasonably priced pure cotton sheets and pillowcases. Women's scarves are available everywhere, from lavishly decorated silk to simple rustic cotton. Soft-cotton 1970s-style cheesecloth is made at Şile on the Black Sea and other places; you'll find tablecloths, lace-edged scarves and embroidered cotton blouses.

Everyday items that might be useful include cotton "peştemel"

(sarong-style wraps worn in the hamam), which are good for the beach, and attractive cottons that can be bought by the metre.

Specialist dealers in the Grand or Covered Bazaar in Istanbul and elsewhere may be able to offer you ravishing old textiles: costumes from some forgotten harem, brocade coats and waistcoats, delicately edged handkerchiefs, but these things are getting rarer (and dearer) every day.

Shop Listings

ISTANBUL

Antiques and Curios

Antikarnas
Faik Paşa Yokuşu 15.
Tel: (0212) 251 5928/4135.
Ottoman and European antiques, as well as religious and decorative objects.

Antik Palas
Spor Caddesi Talimyeri Sokak, Maçka.
Tel: (0212) 230 5017.
www.antikpalas.com
Superb collection of Ottoman and European paintings and antiques; monthly auctions. Also Nişantaşı sales room.

Atlas Pasajı
Istiklal Caddesi 209, Beyoğlu.
Enter through a historic cinema complex into this unique arcade filled with everything from

Gifts and Souvenirs

The range of presents you can go home with from Turkey is huge:
● Bowls, vases and ornaments carved in green or gold onyx, mined in Cappadocia.
● Embroidered or brocade leather-soled slippers, fezes, embroidered and beaded hats, and for the fancy-dress cupboard any number of gaudy costumes including belly-dancing outfits for all ages and sizes. Check out the bazaars for all of these.
● A functioning nargile, or hubble bubble pipe (still routinely smoked by many contented Turks).

● Meerschaum, a soft white stone, traditionally intricately carved to make pipes. Although quarried in the Eskişehir region, the pipes are sold everywhere. Look carefully at the quality of the stone and the carving, and shop around to make sure you pay the right price.
● Backgammon sets (tavla). These are plentiful and not too heavy.
● The mavi boncuk, or blue glass beads used to warn off the evil eye (nazar), come attached to key rings and dog collars, as large ornaments, bracelets and tiny earring pendants.

● Karagöz shadow puppets. Made of painted leather, they originally came from Bursa but can be found elsewhere.
● Consumables, such as a bag of pistachios; spices, such as vanilla pods or saffron; boxes of Turkish delight (lokum); dried fruit; Black Sea tea; or a jar of delicious Turkish honeycomb.
● The Doşem shops attached to the country's museums have on offer some wonderful reproductions of ancient pottery, glass and figurines at very affordable prices.

antiques to costumes to Central Asian jewellery and alternative music.

Atrium

Tünel Pasajı 5 & 7.
Tel: (0212) 251 4302.
Fax: (0212) 249 8983.
Old Turkish ceramics, miniatures, calligraphy, prints and maps, paintings, frames, textiles, jewellery and gifts. Branch at the Swissôtel. Open Mon–Sat 9am–7pm.

Beyazıt Sahaflar Çarşısı

Antiquarian books and much more in this old market on the Beyazıt side of the Grand/Covered Bazaar.

Cendereci

Eytam Caddesi 27/1, Maçka.
Tel: (0212) 231 0942/231 7286.
Beautifully handcrafted silver.

Çukurcuma

A T-shaped intersection of streets in central Beyoğlu containing at least 50 shops from basic second-hand furniture and junk dealers to top-price antiques. Follow Turnacıbaşı Sokak (sign marked Galatasaray Hamam) around to the left, where you have a choice to continue straight for the cheaper, bohemian alleys, or take a left and down the hill at Faik Pasa Yokuşu for the more upscale shops.

Döşem

Topkapı Palace Complex.
The state-owned gift-shop chain truly has some of the best bargains and unquestionably the best collection of Ottoman and ancient reproduction jewellery, textiles, ceramics, silks and glassware.

Eren

Sofyalı Sokak 34, Tünel.
Tel: (0212) 251 2858.
Old and new art and history books, maps and miniatures.

Horhor Bit Pazarı (flea market)

Kırık Tulumba Sokak 13/22, Aksaray.
A five-storey, upscale antique market with marvellous selection.

Istanbul Handicrafts Centre

Sultanahmet, beside Yeşil Ev Hotel.
Tel: (0212) 517 6782.
A series of crafts workshops in a restored religious school (medrese). Visitors can watch the artisans at work as well as purchase wares.

Kapalı Çarşı (The Grand/Covered Bazaar)

Once next to the slave market, Istanbul's legendary bazaar is a labyrinth of over 4,000 tiny shops offering everything from tourist trash to gold to icons, textiles and antiques. Competition keeps prices keen but beware of touts. Open Mon–Sat 9am–7pm.

Librairie de Pera

Galip Dede Sokak 22, Tünel.
Tel: (0212) 252 3078.
One of the oldest and best antiquarian bookshops in Istanbul. Turkish, Greek, Armenian, Arabic, and European books, maps of the Ottoman Empire, Old Istanbul etchings and prints, photographs and original watercolours.

Rölyef Art Enterprises

Emir Nevruz Sokak 16, Galatasaray, Beyoğlu.
Tel: (0212) 244 0494/293 9397.
Ottoman ornaments, engravings, Islamic miniatures, calligraphy, gilding and marbling.

Paşabahce

Büyükdere Caddesi, Maslak.
Tel: (0212) 276 1079.
Turkey's main manufacturer of

Sales Tax/VAT

VAT (KDV), at rates between 8 and 15 percent, is included in the price of most goods (you will see a sign saying kdv dahildir).

You will be able to obtain a tax refund only on goods bought from shops authorised for tax-free sales, which will have to be sales in Turkish lira (rather than in hard currency) to holders of foreign passports. There are not many of these shops around, but it is worth asking.

There is a laborious procedure to go through, whereby you obtain a special invoice from the shop and submit it to customs on departure. Eventually, the shop is supposed to send you your refund in your own currency (a very few will offer on-the-spot cash or cheque refunds).

It is probably only worth doing this for larger purchases.

glass, with many of their jugs, glasses and vases in a distinctive blue-and-white striped design.

Urart

Abdi Ipekçi Caddesi 18/1, Nişantaşı.
Tel: (0212) 246 7194.
Distinctive silver and gold jewellery as well as metalwork, painting and sculpture often based on designs of great antiquity but with modern flair. Branch at the Swissôtel.

Books

Dünya Bookstores

Istiklal Caddesi 469, Beyoğlu.
Tel: (0212) 249 1006.
Books, magazines and newspapers in major European languages. Branches at the Swissôtel, Hilton and Holiday Inn.

Homer

Yeni Çarşı Caddesi 28/A, Galatasaray.
Tel: (0212) 249 5902.
Great stock of books (many academic titles) in English.

Pandora

Büyükparmakkapı Sokak 3, Beyoğlu.
Tel: (0212) 245 1667.
E-mail: pandorainfo-ist.comlink
www.pandora.com.tr
Large selection of foreign books including many academic and regional titles.

Robinson Crusoe

Istiklal Caddesi 389, Tünel-Beyoğlu.
Tel: (0212) 293 6968/77.
Great selection of English-language books, many of local interest. Also French- and German-language publications available.

There are also small news-stands around Taksim Square and the Sultanahmet district in Istanbul which sell a selection of foreign newspapers and magazines.

Music

Galip Dede Sokak

The neighbourhood around the tram stop at Tünel, at the bottom of Istiklal Caddesi, is Istanbul's music district, with the best selection of Turkish CDs, traditional instruments and rock-and-roll gear. Zühal is an international distributor with four branches here and one in Antalya.

Carpets

Gördes Halı
Nurosmaniye Caddesi 85–7,
Cağaloğlu.
Tel: (0212) 522 6152/527 3942.

Güneş Öztarakçı
Mim Kemal Öke Caddesi 5,
Nisantasi.
Tel: (0212) 225 1954.

Fashion and Leather

Punto
Sahilyolu Beşkardesler 4, Sok. 4,
Zeytinburnu.
Tel: (0212) 546 8750.
www.puntoleather.com
Factory-outlet shop for one of
Turkey's biggest and best leather
designers. This is only one of a
number of excellent leather shops
in this small shopping district
halfway between the Old City and
the airport.

THRACE & MARMARA

Bursa

Karagöz Antique Shop
Bazaar Eski Aynalı Çarşı 1–17.
Tel: (0224) 222 6151.
Fax: (0224) 220 5350.
Karagöz (Bursa shadow puppets)
and other traditional articles.

Koza Han
The centre of the Bursa silk trade
for several hundred years, with
masses of tiny shops selling
material, shirts, ties, scarves and
fashion at knock-down prices.

AEGEAN COAST

Bergama

Sadirwan Hali
Küçükkaya Köyü, PK 35.
Tel: ((0232) 633 2719.
Fax: (0232) 632 1820.
www.sdadirvancarpet.com
Carpet warehouse and weaving
centre where you can see how they
are made before choosing your own.

Bodrum

Ifos
Çarşi Mahallesı, Çarı Içı 6,
Sokak 16.
Tel: (0252) 316 4961.

Hookahs, kilims, copper pots and
other antiques fill the two floors of
this shop.

İzmir

Sevgi Youlu Market,
Sevgi Youlu.
A pedestrianised street behind the
Hilton Hotel, filled at weekends with
small stalls selling rings and other
jewellery. Inexpensive.

Kuşadası

Asia Shop
Kibris Caddesi 4.
Tel: (0256) 614 1393.
The perfect place when it comes to
shopping for souvenirs and small
presents for the folks back home.
Fixed prices clearly marked.

Çerge
Kemal Ankan Caddesi 16.
Tel: (0256) 612 5821.
One of the better gift shops in town,
selling imported crafts from Italy
and Turkish items for the home.

Faberce
Söförler Sokak 3, Grand Bazaar.
Tel: (0256) 614 8885.
One of the more agreeable carpet
stores in town. Two floors. Staff
keep the chat within acceptable
limits. Open till midnight.

Galeri Sultan
Grand Bazaar 5.
Tel: (0256) 612 4569.
A well-established leather store that
sells jackets for men and women.

Music Box
Yıldırım Caddesi 13.
Tel: (0256) 614 7522.
Traditional Turkish musical
instruments for sale in this small
shop at the end of Bar Street.

Marmaris

İlkay Leather Fashion Centre
Gözpınar Sokak 36.
Tel; (0252)-412 9466.
Fax: (0252) 413 1290.

Nur-Bal
Fevzi Paşa Caddesi 9/C.
Marmaris is famous for its honey
and this small shop behind the post
office, has a good selection.

Oriental
Yat Limanı 3.
Tel: (0252) 412 4818.
Located on the waterfront, close to

the tourist office, this store has a
large selection of *kilims* and
carpets. Bargaining for the best
price is in order.

Ottoman
Çeşme Meydanı, Grand Pazar 1.
Tel: (0252) 412 5911.
One of the better antique shops in
Marmaris, this shop is crammed with
copper pots, old watches and clocks,
antique jewellery and assorted other
relics from bygone days.

**Vogue Jewellery and Diamond
Centre**
Kemal Elgin Bulvarı.
Tel: (0252) 413 4875.
Fax: (0252) 413 7205.
Upmarket emporium with stunningly
displayed jewellery and precious
stones. A few kilometres from the
town centre with a free shuttle
service.

Priene

Onyx Factory
Tel: (0256) 547 1123.
In the square where buses and
taxis congregate, this busy little
workshop allows visitors to observe
the process of cutting, shaping and
polishing the onyx. Open all year.
No obligation to buy.

MEDITERRANEAN COAST

Antalya

Almost the entire Old Town has
become a tourist bazaar, with every
second shop selling carpets,
jewellery, ceramics and fashion,
while the streets are the province of
increasingly persistent and
annoyingly aggressive touts, sellers
of postcards, pistachios and fake
watches. The big daily produce
market, Halk Pazar, is next to the
municipal bus terminus.

Ardıc Kitabevi
Selekler Çarşısı 67.
Tel: (0242) 247 0356.
Foreign-language books, magazines
and newspapers.

Antik Bazaar
Selçuk Mahallesı, İzmirli Ali Efendi
Sokak 12.
Tel: (0242) 242 0306.
Established reliable stockist of
carpets and *kilims.*

Bazaar 54
Yat Limani, Kaleiçi 4.
Tel: (0242) 241 0290.
The local branch of Turkey's (i.e. the world's) largest retailer of Turkish carpets. Quality is reliable and you can pay a deposit, with the balance due only when your carpet arrives safely at your home.
Dösem
Yat Limanı, 24.
Tel: (0242) 241 4667.
Superb Ministry of Culture souvenir shop; other branches at Antalya museum and Aspendos.
Kırcılar Leatherland
İsmet Paşa Caddesi, Dölen İşhanı 4.
Tel: (0242) 241 1892/242 7110.
Leather jackets for men and women, skirts and coats, reasonably priced and good quality.

Aspendos
Aspendos Jewellery Centre
Küçükbelkis Köyü, Serik.
Tel: (0242) 735 7250.
A glittering jewellery empire offering workshop tours of the largest jewellery manufacturers in Turkey, custom-crafted and off-the-peg jewellery. Open daily 9am–6pm.
Bazaar 54
Küçükbelkis Köyü, Serik.
Tel: (0242) 735 7281.
Sprawling upmarket shopping centre, including carpets, jewellery and leather shops. Carpets are woven on site and tours are on offer. Open daily 9am–6pm.

Fethiye
There is a colourful daily market, between Çarşı Caddesi and Tütün Sokak, selling food, souvenirs and high-quality fakes. It grows hugely and becomes irresistible when villagers swarm in by the busload on Tuesday morning.
Imagine
Cumhuriyet Caddesi 9.
Tel: (0252) 614 1983.
Large supply of English-language novels, local guides, Turkish and Western music.
Old Orient Kilim Bazaar
Karagözler Caddesi 5.
Tel: (0252) 612 1059.
Kilims gorgeously displayed in an old Ottoman mansion.

Telmessos Gold Galerie
Atatürk Caddesi 2.
Tel: (0252) 612 2809/10.
Fine selection of gold and precious stones. European and Turkish designs.
Tunç Leather
Paspatur Mevkii, Hamam Sokak C.
Tel: (0252) 612 3744.
Good selection of leather jackets and bags.

Kaş
This pretty little town is crammed with fabulous designer boutiques guaranteed to make even the reluctant shopper salivate. It is one of the finest and certainly most convenient shopping centres in Turkey, specialising in carpets, jewellery and designer fashion. Every Friday, there is a big market behind the bus station on the Elmalı road.

Carpets
The two main carpet shops both have two outlets. All have excellent stock, are reliable and honest and can be relied on to ship your carpet for you. Bargaining is still the order of the day, however.
Kaş and Carry
Bahçe Sokak.
Tel: (0242) 836 1662.
Magic Orient
Hükümet Caddesi 15.
Tel: (0242) 836 3150.

Fashion
All three boutiques have resident designers who make up clothes using local hand-loomed fabrics. Summer only.
Butik Sera
Bahçe Sokak.
Tel: (0242) 836 1501.
Papilio Butik
Uzunçarşı Sokak 16/B.
Tel: (0242) 836 2895.
Tufan Designer
İbrahim Serin Sokak.
Tel: (0242) 836 2917.

Jewellery
Argentum
Uzunçarşı Caddesi.
Tel: (0242) 836 1673.
Silver specialists, with antiques, modern and traditional designs.

Silver Art
İbrahim Serin Caddesi 3/A.
Tel: (0242) 836 1186.
Silver specialists, as the name suggests.
Topika
Uzunçarşı Sokak 11.
Tel: (0242) 836 2172.
Fabulous modern and custom designs with silver and precious stones.
Xtra Kuyumcular
Elmalı Caddesi.
Tel: (0242) 836 2372.
Traditional Lycian design with a contemporary twist.

Leather
Premier Leather Collection
İbrahim Serin Sokak 13/B.
Tel: (0242) 836 2186.
A wide range of leather goods.

CENTRAL ANATOLIA

Ankara
abc Kitabevi
Selanik Caddesi 1/A, Kızılay.
Tel: (0216) 434 3842.
Dost Book Shop
Konur Sokak 4, Kızılay.
Tel: (0312) 428 8327.
The Book
Karum İş Merkezi 287, Kavaklıdere.
Tel: (0312) 427 3477.
All the above bookshops stock some English-language titles.
Seç Leder
Menekse Sokak, Menekse Pasaji 6/38, Kizilay.
Tel: (0312) 425 5440.
Leather.
Zeki-Ismet Candan
Ataturk Boulevard 67/18, Kizilay.
Tel: (0312) 433 7726.
Jewellery.
The Flying Carpet Shop
Filistin Sokak, 3/A, Gaziosmanpaşa.
Carpets.
Güzel İş Bakır
Salman Sokak 31, Samanpazari.
Tel: (0312) 324 1436.
Gifts.

Language

Atatürk's great language reform took place in 1928, when Arabic script was replaced by the Roman alphabet, and Persian and Arabic vocabulary was ousted by words of Türkic origin, with the intention of simplifying the language to boost literacy.

One legacy of the flowery elaborations of late-Ottoman speech is in the way Turkish people exchange formal greetings: these pleasantries and politenesses follow a set routine in which both sides of the exchange follow formulaic patterns of questions with set answers.

Turkish is undoubtedly a difficult language for Europeans to learn. Although the grammar is consistent and logical, with few irregularities, and pronunciation follows phonetic spelling, both the vocabulary and structure are very different from any language that English-speakers may have tackled before. The vocabulary in particular is very difficult to remember and use, especially over a short visit. There are a very few words, mainly of French or English origin, that you will recognise once you have deciphered the Turkish spelling.

It is probably most useful to try to master basic pronunciation, so you can say addresses and place-names correctly, and read and use some set phrases. Off the tourist track English is hardly spoken, so if you are travelling further afield you will need to know a little more.

Pronunciation

As spelling is phonetic, pronunciation is the easiest part of learning the language, once you have mastered the few different Turkish vowel and consonant sounds.

Letters are always pronounced in the same way. One of the difficult ones is the "c", which is always pronounced "j" as in "jump", so the Turkish word "camii" (mosque) is pronounced "jah-mi", and "caddesi" (road, street) is pronounced "jah-des-i". The soft "g" is never voiced, but lengthens the preceding vowel. Also, look out for the dotless i, "I (ı)", which makes an "er" sound; it is quite different from the dotted "İ(i)". Compare "ızgara" (grill, pronounced uh-zgara) with "incir" (fig, pronounced in-jeer). Double consonants are both pronounced. Each syllable in a word carries equal stress, as do words in a phrase.

The basic rules of pronunciation are as follows:

c "dj" as in jump
ç "ch" as in chill
s s as in sleep
ş "sh" as in sharp
g g as in good
ğ is silent, lengthens the previous vowel, never begins a word
a "ah" as in father
e e as in let
i with a dot as in sit
ı without a dot is an "er" or "uh" sound, like the second "e" in ever
o is pronounced "o" as in hot
ö with diaeresis is similar to "ur" as in spurt, or German "oe" as in Goethe
u is pronounced like "oo" as in room
ü is like the "ew" in pew, or u-sound in French "tu" (impossible without pursing your lips).

Useful Words & Phrases

DAYS OF THE WEEK

Monday *Pazartesi*
Tuesday *Salı*
Wednesday *Çarşamba*
Thursday *Perşembe*
Friday *Cuma*
Saturday *Cumartesi*
Sunday *Pazar*

MONTHS

January *Ocak*
February *Şubat*
March *Mart*
April *Nisan*
May *Mayıs*
June *Haziran*
July *Temmuz*
August *Ağustos*
September *Eylül*
October *Ekim*
November *Kasım*
December *Aralık*

NUMBERS

1	*bir*
2	*iki*
3	*üç*
4	*dört*
5	*beş*
6	*altı*
7	*yedi*
8	*sekiz*
9	*dokuz*
10	*on*
11	*on bir*
12	*on iki*
20	*yirmi*
21	*yirmi bir*
22	*yirmi iki*
30	*otuz*
40	*kırk*
50	*elli*
60	*altmış*
70	*yetmiş*
80	*seksen*
90	*doksan*
100	*yüz*
200	*iki yüz*
1,000	*bin*
2,000	*iki bin*
1,000,000	*bir milyon*

To make a complex number, add the components one by one e.g. 5,650,000 = *beş milyon altı yüz elli bin* (in Turkish these would normally be run together). Managing huge numbers has become routine for Turks in dealing with their currency.

Greetings

Hello *Merhaba*
Good morning (early) *Günaydın*
Good day *İyi günler*
Good night *İyi geceler*

Good evening *Iyi aksamlar*
Welcome! *Hoş geldiniz!*
Reply: **Happy to be here!** *Hoş bulduk!*
Please, with pleasure, allow me, please go first (multi-purpose, polite expression) *Buyrun*
Don't mention it *Rica ederim*
Pleased to meet you *Çok memnun oldum*
How are you? *Nasılsınız?*
Thank you, I/we am/are fine *Tesekkürler, iyiyim/iyiyiz*
My name is... *Adım...*
I am English/Scottish/American/ Australian *Ben İngilizim/İskoçyalım/ Amerikalım/Avustralyalım*
We are sightseeing *Geziyoruz*
We'll see each other again ("see you") *Görüşürüz*
God willing *İnşallah*
Goodbye *Hoşça kalın* or *Allaha ısmarlardık*
Reply: **"Go happily"** *Güle güle* (only said by the person staying behind)
Leave me alone *Beni rahat bırakin*
Get lost *Çekil git*
I don't want any *Istemi yorum*

Essentials

Yes *Evet*
No *Hayır/yok*
OK *Tamam*
Please *Lütfen*
Thank you *Teşekkür ederim/sağolun/mersi*
You're welcome *Bir sey değil*
Excuse me/I beg your pardon (in a crowd) *Affedersiniz*
Excuse me *Pardon*
I don't speak Turkish *Türkçe bilmiyorum*
Do you speak English? *İngilizce biliyor musunuz?*
I don't understand/I haven't understood *Anlamıyorum/ Anlamadım*
I don't know *Bilmiyorum*
Please write it down *Onu benim için heceleyebilir misiniz?*
Wait a moment! *Bir dakika!*
Slowly *Yavaş*
Enough *Yeter*
Where is it? *Nerede?*
Where is the...? *... Nerede?*
Where is the toilet? *Tuvalet nerede?*
What time is it? *Saatiniz var mı?*

At what time? *Saat kaçta?*
Today *Bugün*
Tomorrow *Yarın*
Yesterday *Dün*
The day after tomorrow *Obür gün*
Now *Şimdi*
Later *Sonra*
When? *Ne zaman*
Morning/in the morning *Sabah*
Afternoon/in the afternoon *Oğleden sonra*
Evening/in the evening *Akşam*
This evening *Bu akşam*
Here *Burada*
There *Şurada*
Over there *Orada*
Is there a newspaper? *Gazete var mı?*
Is there a taxi? *Taksi var mı?*
Is there a telephone? *Telefon var mı?*
Yes, there is *Evet, var*
No, there isn't *Hayır, yok*
There is no ticket *Bilet yok*
There is no time *Zaman yok*

Sightseeing

Directions
How do I get to Bodrum? *Bodrum'a nasıl giderim?*
How far is it to...? *...'a/'e ne kadar uzakta?*
Near *Yakın*
Far *Uzak*
Left *Sol*
On the left/to the left *Solda/sola*
Right *Sağ*
On the right/to the right *Sağda/ sağa*

Road Signs

Dikkat *Beware/Caution*
Tehlike *Danger*
Yavaş *Slow*
Yol ver *Give way*
Dur *Stop*
Araç giremez *No entry*
Tek yön *One way*
Çıkmaz sokak *No through road*
Bozuk yol *Poor road surface*
Tamirat *Roadworks*
Yol kapalı *Road closed*
Yaya geçidi *Pedestrian crossing*
Şehir merkezi/Centrum *City centre*
Otopark/Park edilir *Parking*
Park edilmez *No parking*

Emergencies

Help! *İmdat!*
Fire *Yangın!*
Please call the police *Polis çağırın*
Please call an ambulance *Ambulans çağırın*
Please call the fire brigade *Itfaiye çağırın*
This is an emergency *Bu acıldır*
There has been an accident *Kaza vardı*
I'd like an interpreter *Tercüman istiyorum*
I want to speak to someone from the British Consulate *İngiltere konsoloslugundan biri ile görüşmek istiyorum*

Straight on *Doğru*
North *Kuzey*
South *Güney*
East *Doğu*
West *Batı*

Sights/places
City *Şehir*
Village *Köy*
Forest *Orman*
Sea *Deniz*
Lake *Göl*
Farm *Çiftlik*
Church *Kilise*
Mosque *Camii*
Post Office *Postane*
What time does it open/close? *Kaçta açılıcak/kapanacak?*

Travelling

Car *Araba*
Petrol/gas station *Benzin istasyonu*
Petrol/gas *Benzin (super/ normal)*
Fill it up, please *Doldurun, lütfen*
Flat tyre/puncture *Patlak lastik*
My car has broken down *Arabam arzalandı*
Bus station *Otogar*
Bus stop *Emanet*
Bus *Otobüs*
Train station *Gar/İstasyon*
Train *Tren*
Taxi *Taksi*
Airport *Havalimanı/Havaalanı*
Aeroplane *Uçak*

Port/harbour *Liman*
Boat *Gemi*
Ferry *Feribot/Vapur*
Quay *İskele*
Ticket *Bilet*
Ticket office *Gişe*
Return ticket *Gidişdönüs*
Can I reserve a seat? *Reservasyon yapabilir miyim?*
What time does it leave? *Kaçta kalkıyor?*
Where does it leave from? *Nereden kalkıyor?*
How long does it take? *Ne kadar sürüyor?*
Which bus? *Hangi otobüs?*

Health

Remember that in an emergency it can be quicker to get to hospital by taxi.
Clinic *Klinik*
Dentist *Dişçi*
Doctor *Doktor*
Emergency service/room *Acil servis*
First aid *İlk yardım*
Hospital *Hastane*
Pharmacist *Eczacı*
Pharmacy *Eczane*
I am ill *Hastayım*
I have a fever *Atesim var*
I have diarrhoea *İshallım*
I am diabetic *Şeker hastasıyım*
I'm allergic to... *Karşı alerjim var...*
I have asthma *Astim hastasıyım*
I have a heart condition *Kalp hastasıyım*
I am pregnant *Gebeyim*
It hurts here *Burası acıyor*
I have lost a filling *Dolgu düştü*
I need a prescription for... *İçin bir reçete istiyorum...*

Accommodation

Hotel *Otel*
Pension/guesthouse *Pansiyon*
Single/double/triple *Tek/çift/üç kişilik*
Full board *Tam pansiyon*
Half board *Yarım pansiyon*
With a shower *Duşu*
With a bathroom *Banyolu*
With a balcony *Balkonlu*
With a sea view *Deniz manzaralı*
Lift *Asansör*
Room service *Oda servisi*

Air conditioning *Havalandırma*
Central heating *Kalorifer*
Key *Anahtar*
Bed *Yatak*
Blanket *Battaniye*
Pillow *Yastık*
Shower *Duş*
Soap *Sabun*
Plug *Tıkaç*
Towel *Havlu*
Basin *Lavabo*
Toilet *Tuvalet*
Toilet paper *Tuvalet kağıdı*
Hot water *Sıcak su*
Cold water *Soğuk su*
Dining room *Yemek salonu*
I need/...is necessary *lazım/...gerek*
I have a reservation *Reservasyonım var*
Do you have a room? *Odnız var mı?*
I'd like a room for one/three nights *Bir/üç gece için bir oda istiyorum*
I'm sorry, we are full *Maalesef doluyuz*

Shopping

Price *Fiyat*
Cheap *Ucuz*
Expensive *Pahalı*
No bargaining (sign) *Pazarlık edilmez*
Old *Eski*
New *Yeni*
Big *Büyük*
Bigger *Daha büyük*
Small *Küçük*
Smaller *Daha küçük*
Very nice/beautiful *Çok güzel*
This *Bu*
These *Bunlar*
That *Şu*
I would like... *İsterim...*
I don't want *İstemem*
There isn't any *Yok*
How much is it? *Ne kadar?*
Do you take credit cards? *Kredi karti alır mısınız?*
How many? *Kaç tane?*

Eating Out

Basics
Table *Masa*
Cup *Fincan*
Glass *Bardak*

Money

Bank *Banka*
Credit card *Kredi kartı*
Exchange office *Kamiyo büroso*
Exchange rate *Dövis kuru*
Post office *Postane*
Travellers' cheque *Seyahat çeki*

Wine glass *Kadeh*
Bottle *Şişe*
Plate *Tabak*
Fork *Çatal*
Knife *Bıçak*
Spoon *Kaşık*
Napkin *Peçete*
Salt *Tuz*
Black pepper *Kara biber*
Starters *Meze*
Soup *Çorba*
Fish *Balık*
Meat dishes *Etli yemekler*
Grills *Izgara*
Eggs *Yumurta*
Vegetarian dishes *Etsiz yemekler*
Salads *Salatalar*
Fruit *Meyva*
Bread *Ekmek*
Peppery hot *Acı (a-je)*
Non-spicy *Acısız (a-je-suz)*
Water *Su*
Mineral water *Maden suyu*
Fizzy water *Soda*
Beer *Bira*
Red/white wine *Kırmızı/beyaz sarap*
Fresh orange juice *Portakal suyu*
Coffee *Kahve*
Tea *Çay*
A table for two/four, please *İki/dört kisilik bir masa, lütfen*
Can we eat outside? *Dışarıda da yiyebilir miyiz?*
Waiter! *Garson!*
Excuse me *(to get service or attention) Bakar mısınız?*
Menu *Menü*
I didn't order this *Ben bunu ısmarlamadım*
Some more water/bread/wine, please *Biraz daha su/ekmek/sarap, rica ediyoruz*
I can eat... *Yiyorum...*
I cannot eat... *Yiyemiyorum...*
The bill, please *Hesap, lütfen*
Service included/excluded *Servis dahil/hariç*

Menu Decoder

Kahvaltı/Breakfast
Beyaz peynir *White cheese*
Kaşar peyniri *Yellow cheese*
Domates *Tomatoes*
Zeytin *Olives*
Salatalık *Cucumber*
Reçel *Jam*
Bal *Honey*
Tereyağ *Butter*

Extra dishes which you may order
for a more substantial breakfast:
Haşlanmış yumurta *Hard-boiled
eggs*
Rafadan yumurta *Soft-boiled eggs*
Menemen *Scrambled-egg omelette
with tomatoes, peppers, onion and
cheese*
Sahanda yumurta *Fried eggs*
Pastırmalı yumurta *Eggs fried with
pastırma, Turkish cured beef, like
pastrami*
Sade/peynirli/mantarlı omlet
Plain/cheese/mushroom omelette

Çorbalar/Soups
Haşlama *Mutton broth*
Tavuk çorbası/tavuk suyu *Chicken
soup*
Düğün çorbası *Wedding soup
(thickened with eggs and lemon)*
Ezogelin çorbası *Lentil soup with
rice*
Mercimek çorbası *Red lentil
soup*
Domates çorbası *Tomato soup*
İşkembe çorbası *Tripe soup*
Paça çorbası *Lamb's feet soup*
Şehriye çorbası *Fine noodle soup*
Yayla çorbası *Yoghurt soup*
Tarhana çorbası *Soup made from a
dried yoghurt base*

Soguk meze/Cold starters
These are usually offered from a
large tray of assorted dishes, or
you can choose from a cold cabinet;
there are dozens of variations.
Beyaz peynir *White cheese*
Kavun *Honeydew melon*
Zeytin *Olives*
Patlıcan ezmesi *Aubergine purée*
Piyaz/pilaki *White bean salad with
olive oil and lemon*
Acı *Spicy hot red paste or salad of
chopped peppers and tomato*
Taramasalata *Purée of fish roe*

Çerkez tavugu *Shredded chicken
in walnut sauce*
Haydari *Dip of chopped dill and
garlic in thick yoghurt*
Fava *Purée of beans*
Dolma *Vegetables or other things
stuffed with rice mixed with dill,
pinenuts and currants*
Yalancı yaprak dolması *Stuffed
vine leaves*
Midye dolması *Stuffed mussels*
Biber dolması *Stuffed peppers*
Lakerda *Sliced smoked tuna*
Hamsi *Fresh anchovies preserved
in oil*
Zeytinyağlı *Vegetables cooked with
olive oil, served cold*
Zeytinyağlı kereviz *Celeriac in
olive oil*
İmam bayıldı *Aubergine stuffed
with tomato and onion, cooked with
olive oil*

Sıcak mezeler/Hot starters
Sigara böreği *Crisp fried rolls of
pastry with cheese or meat filling
(can also be triangular:* **muska**)
Arnavut ciğeri *Albanian-style fried
diced lamb's liver*
Kalamar tava *Deep-fried squid
rings*
Midye tava *Deep-fried mussels*
Tarator *Nut and garlic sauce
served with above, or with fried
vegetables*
Patates köfte *Potato croquettes*

Common Signs

Giriş/Çıkış *Entrance/Exit*
Tehlike çıkışı *Emergency exit*
Giriş ücretsiz/ücretli *Free/paid
admission*
Açık *Open*
Kapalı *Closed*
Varış *Arrivals*
Kalkış *Departures*
Askeri bölge *Military zone*
Sigara icilmez *No smoking*
Girmek yasaktır *No entry*
Giriş *No photographs*
Lütfen ayakkabılarınızı çıkartınız
Please take off your shoes
Bay *Men*
Bayan *Women*
Tuvalet/WC/Umumi *WC*
Bozuk *Out of order*
İçme su *Drinking water*

For Vegetarians

I eat only fruit and vegetables
Yalnız meyve ve sebze yiyorum
I cannot eat any meat at all
Hiç et yiyemiyorum
I can eat fish **Balık yiyorum**

Salata/Salads
Karışık *Mixed*
Çoban salatası *"Shepherd's salad"
(chopped mixed tomato, cucumber,
pepper, onion and parsley)*
Yeşil salata *Green salad*
Mevsim salatası *Seasonal salad*
Roka *Rocket/arugula*
Salatalık *Cucumber*
Domates *Tomatoes*
Marul *Cos/romaine lettuce*
Semizotu *Lamb's lettuce/purslane*
Söğus *Sliced salad vegetables with
no dressing*

Et yemekleri/Meat dishes
Kebap *Kebab*
Döner *Sliced, layered lamb grilled
on revolving spit*
Tavuk döner *As above, made with
chicken*
Şiş kebap *Cubed meat grilled on
skewer e.g.* **kuzu şiş** *(lamb),* **tavuk
şiş** *(chicken)*
Adana kebap *Minced lamb grilled
on skewer, spicy*
Urfa kebap *As above, not spicy*
Bursa/İskender/yoğurtlu kebap
*Dish of döner slices laid on pieces
of bread with tomato sauce, melted
butter and yoghurt with garlic*
Pirzola *Cutlets*
Izgara *Grill/grilled – usually over
charcoal*
Köfte *Meatballs*
Köfte ızgara *Grilled meatballs*
Bıldırcın ızgara *Grilled quail*
Kuzu tandır/fırın *Lamb baked on
the bone*
Hünkâr beğendili köfte *Meatballs
with aubergine purée*
Kadınbudu köfte *"Ladies' thighs",
meat and rice croquettes in gravy*
Karnıyarık *Aubergines split in half
and filled with minced lamb mixed
with pine nuts and currants*
Kavurma *Meat stir-fried or braised,
cooked in its own fat and juices*
Çoban kavurma *Lamb fried with
peppers, tomatoes and onions*

Saç kavurma *Wok-fried meat, vegetables and spices*
Etli dolması *Dolma stuffed with meat and rice* (eaten hot)
Etli kabak dolması *Courgettes stuffed with meat*
Etli nohut *Chickpea and lamb stew*
Etli kuru fasuliye *Haricot beans and lamb stew*
Kağıt kebabı *Lamb and vegetables cooked in paper*
Kıymalı *with minced meat*
Güveç *Casserole*

Balık yemekleri/Fish dishes

Most fish is eaten plainly grilled or fried, and priced by weight. It will be less expensive if it is local and in season. Always ask the price, "ne kadar?" before ordering.
Balık ızgara *Grilled fish*
Balık kızartması *Fried fish*
Balık şiş *Cubed fish grilled on skewer*
Alabalık *Trout*
Levrek *Sea bass*
Lüfer *Bluefish*
Hamsi *Anchovies*
Sardalye *Sardines*
Karagöz *Black bream*
Uskumru *Mackerel*
Palamut *Tuna*
Kalkan *Turbot*
Gümüş *Silverfish* (like whitebait)
Barbunya *Red mullet*
Kefal *Grey mullet*
Kılıç balığı *Swordfish*
Dil balığı *Sole*
Karides *Shrimp, prawns*
Karides güveç *Prawn casserole with peppers, tomato and melted cheese*
Hamsi pilav *Rice baked with anchovies*
Levrek pilakisi *Sea bass stew with onion, potato, tomato and garlic*
Kiremitte balık *Fish baked on a tile*
Kağıtta barbunya *Mullet (or other fish) baked in a paper case*

Other things that may be on menus:
Makarna *Macaroni, noodles*
Patates puresi *Mashed/puréed potatoes*
Patates kızartması/tava *Chips/ french fries, sometimes eaten with meze*
Pilav *Cooked rice, can be a rice dish with meat, chicken, pulses or noodles*

Tost *Toasted cheese sandwich*
Turşu *Pickles – Turkish pickles are sour and salty, sometimes spicy but never sweet, and are eaten with meze*

Tatlı/Desserts

Baklava *Layers of wafer-thin pastry with nuts and syrup*
Ekmek kadayıf *Bread pudding soaked in syrup*
Güllaç *Dessert made with layers of rice wafer, sugar and milk*
Tavuk göğsü *Milk pudding made with pounded chicken breast*
Kazandibi *Glazed, with browned, caramelised top*
Dondurma *Ice cream*
Muhallebi *Rice flour, milk and rosewater blancmange*
Sütlaç *Rice pudding*
Aşure *"Noah's pudding" made with dried fruits, nuts, seeds, pulses*
Kabak tatlısı *Candied pumpkin*
Ayva tatlısı *Candied quince*
Kaymaklı *with clotted cream*
Komposto *Poached fruit*
Krem caramel *Caramel custard, French crème caramel*
Pasta *Gâteau-style cake, patisserie*

Soft or cold drinks

Su *Water*
Memba suyu *Mineral water*
Maden suyu gazoz/soda *Sparkling water*
Ayran *Yoghurt whisked with cold water and salt*
Meyva suyu *Fruit juice*
Visne suyu *Sourcherry juice*
Kayısı suyu *Apricot juice*
Taze portakal suyu *Freshly squeezed orange juice*
Şerbet *Sweetened, iced fruit juice drink*
Limonata *Lemon drink*
Buz *Ice*

Hot drinks

Çay *Tea*
Açık *Weak*
Demli *Brewed*
Bir bardak çay *Glass of tea*
Bir fincan kahve *Cup of coffee*
Ada çayı *"Island tea" made with dried wild sage*
Elma çayı *Apple tea*
Kahve *Coffee*
Neskafe *any instant coffee*

Alcohol

Turkish wine labels: Doluca, Villa Doluca, Doluca Antik, Kavaklıdere Yakut (red), Kavaklıdere Çankaya (white), Kavaklıdere Lal (rosé), Turasan (Cappadocian)
Turkish beers: Efes Pilsen, Efes Light (low alcohol); Venus, Marmara, Tuborg
Spirits are made in Turkey by Tekel, the state tobacco and liquor concern, and a variety of other private companies.

Sutlu *with milk*
Şeker *Sugar*
Türk kahvesi *Turkish coffee*
Az şekerli *with little sugar*
Orta *Medium sweet*
Şekerli *Sweet*
Sade *without sugar*
Süzme kahve *Filter coffee*
Sahlep *Hot, thick sweet winter drink made of **sahlep** root, milk and cinnamon*

Alcoholic drinks

Bira *Beer*
Siyah *Dark* (beer)
Beyaz *Light* (beer)
Cintonik *Gin and tonic*
Votka *Vodka*
Yerli *Local, Turkish*
Şarap *Wine*
Şarap listesi *Wine list*
Kırmızı şarap *Red wine*
Beyaz şarap *White wine*
Roze şarap *Rosé*
Sek *Dry*
Antik *Aged*
Özel *Special*
Tatlı *Sweet*
Şişe *Bottle*
Yarım şişe *Half bottle*
Rakı *Turkish national alcoholic drink, strongly aniseed-flavoured*
Yeni Rakı *Chief brand of rakı*

Further Reading

There are plenty of books in English about all aspects of Turkey: such a complex country with so many layers of history and culture couldn't fail to generate a wealth of histories, memoirs, poetry, fiction, biographies and travel writing. Not much Turkish writing has been translated into English, however. Some good books in English have been written and issued by Turkish publishers, but are difficult to obtain outside Turkey.

History

Alexander of Macedon, by Peter Green (Penguin, 1970).
Atatürk: The Rebirth of a Nation, by Lord Kinross (Weidenfeld and Nicolson, 1964).
Black Sea, The Birthplace of Civilisation and Barbarism, by Neal Ascherson (Vintage, 1996). Compelling, brilliantly written book about the cultures surrounding this great inland sea; from Herodotus to the fall of Communism.
Byzantium, three volumes: *The Early Centuries*, *The Apogee* and *The Decline and Fall*, by John Julius Norwich (Penguin, 1993–6). Thorough, accessible, readable and entertaining account of the history of the empire up to the Ottoman conquest of 1453.
Constantinople, City of the World's Desire, 1453–1924, by Philip Mansel (Penguin, 1997). Outstandingly researched portrait of the imperial city. Scholarly and gripping, with a mass of information, anecdote and analysis.
History of the Byzantine State, by Georg Ostrogorsky (Blackwell, 1968).
History of the Ottoman Empire and Modern Turkey, by Stanford J. Shaw and Ezel Kural Shaw. (Cambridge University Press, 1976).
Istanbul, The Imperial City, by John Freely (Viking, 1996). Illustrated introductory "biography" of the city and its social life through 27 centuries. The most recent publication by this long-time resident and knowledgeable lover of Turkey.
Julian, by Gore Vidal (Signet, 1962).
Orientalism, Western Conceptions of the Orient, by Edward W. Said (Penguin, 1995). Highly acclaimed overview of Western attitudes towards the East, analysing literature, arts and culture.
On Secret Service East of Constantinople, by Peter Hopkirk (Oxford Paperbacks, 1995). Brilliant account of Turkish and German conspiracies against Britain and Russia after 1914, by the author of *The Great Game*.
The Armenians, by Sirapie der Nersessian (Thames and Hudson, 1979).
The Emergence of Modern Turkey, by Bernard Lewis (Oxford University Press, 1968).
The Fall of Constantinople, 1453, by Steven Runciman (Cambridge University Press, 1965). Great British medieval historian, also author of the classic three-volume history of The Crusades.
The Greeks in Ionia and the East, by John Cook (Thames and Hudson, 1962).
The Harvest of Hellenism, by F.E. Peters (Simon and Schuster, 1970).
The Hittites by O.R. Gurney (Penguin). Classic history of the earliest Anatolian civilisation for non-specialists. Gurney practically invented Hittite studies single-handedly.
The Ottomans, Dissolving Images, by Andrew Wheatcroft (Penguin, 1995). Colourful, readable account of the development of Ottoman power and empire, with good detail about social life.
The Ottoman Centuries, by Lord Kinross (Morrow Quill, 1977).
The Ottoman Empire: The Classical Age, 1300–1600, by Halil Inalcik (Weidenfeld and Nicolson, 1973).
Troy and the Trojans, by Carl Blegen (London: Thames and Hudson, 1963).
Turkey Unveiled, Atatürk and After, by Nicole and Hugh Pope (John Murray, 1997). Excellent, readable account of the intricacies of Turkish political affairs in the recent past, written by journalists who have been living in and covering the country for the past 10 years.

Lives & Letters

A Village in Anatolia, by Mahmut Makal (Valentine, Mitchell, 1954).
An English Consul in Turkey, Paul Rycaut at Smyrna 1667–78, by Sonia Anderson (Clarendon Press, 1989). Rycaut spent 17 years in Turkey, 11 as consul in Smyrna, whose contemporary English community is vividly described in this biographical study.
Everyday Life in Ottoman Turkey, by Raphaela Lewis (B.T. Batsford, 1971).
Portrait of a Turkish Family, by Irfan Orga (Eland Books, 1993). Vividly and movingly describes the author's family life and his growing up first as a child in Ottoman Turkey before World War I, then through the war and the years of Atatürk's reforms.
The Imperial Harem of the Sultans, The Memoirs of Leyla Hanımefendi (Peva Publications, 1995, available in Istanbul). The only contemporary account of daily life at the Çirağan Palace during the 19th century, originally published in French in 1925, which gives a vivid portrait of this hidden world.
The Turkish Embassy Letters, by Lady Mary Wortley Montagu (Virago, 1995). Collection of lively and intelligent letters, written in 1716 when the writer's husband had just been appointed ambassador. One of the most fascinating of early travel writers.

Art & Architecture

A History of Ottoman Architecture by Godfrey Goodwin (Thames and Hudson). Comprehensive and definitive, covering every kind of building all over Turkey. Goodwin's other great book is a monograph on Sinan, the greatest of the Ottoman architects (Saqi Books).

Ancient Civilizations and Ruins of Turkey

Ancient Civilizations and Ruins of Turkey, by Ekrem Akurgal (Haset Kitabevi, 1973, available in Istanbul).
Catal Höyük, by James Mellaart (Thames and Hudson, 1967).
Early Christian and Byzantine Architecture, by Richard Krautheimer (Penguin, 1965).
Hattusa, The Capital of the Hittites, by Kurt Bittel (Oxford University Press, 1970).
The Art of the Hittites, by Ekrem Akurgal (Thames and Hudson, 1962).
The Palace of Topkapı, by Fanny Davis (Scribners, 1970).
Turkish Art and Architecture, by Oktay Aslanapa (Faber and Faber, 1971).

Carpets

Halı Magazine (Halı Publications). Six issues a year dedicated to rug commerce and scholarship, with frequent articles on Turkish textiles and carpets. They also publish *Istanbul, The Halı Rug Guide* and *Orient Stars*, by E. Heinrich Kirchheim, lavishly illustrated with 250 colour plates of classical Turkish carpets.

Travel Writing

A Fez of the Heart, by Jeremy Seal (Picador, 1996). The author travels around Turkey in search of a real fez, the red felt hat banned in 1925; and offers a perceptive alternative view of modern Turkey.
From the Holy Mountain, A Journey in the Shadow of Byzantium, by William Dalrymple (Flamingo, 1998). Starting from Mount Athos in Greece, the author follows the trail of Eastern Christianity, travelling into eastern Turkey and beyond. Dalrymple has been hailed as a successor to Patrick Leigh Fermor; he is certainly adventurous and his writing is lively and erudite.
The Crossing Place, A Journey among the Armenians, by Philip Marsden (Flamingo, 1994). Travels in search of this remarkable people, one of Turkey's most important minorities, the remaining traces of their culture and their diaspora.

Anthologies

Istanbul, A Traveller's Companion, selected and introduced by Laurence Kelly (Constable). A wonderful collection of extracts from 14 centuries of writing, arranged around landmark buildings to act as a background guide, which brings to life sites that visitors can still see.
Istanbul, Tales of the City, selected by John Miller (Chronicle Books, 1995). Pocket-sized eclectic collection of prose and poetry, including pieces by Simone de Beauvoir, Disraeli and Gore Vidal.
Turkish Verse, by Nermin Menemencioğlu (Penguin, 1978).

Fiction

Greenmantle, by John Buchan (Penguin). First published in 1916, the immortal Richard Hannay adventures across the Balkans into Anatolia. Based on a true story.
Mehmet My Hawk, by Yasar Kemal (Harvill). The best-known Turkish novelist in translation. This is just one, the most famous, of many novels, some set in and around Istanbul, some epics set in rural Anatolia.
The Rage of the Vulture, by Barry Unsworth (Granada). Historical novel by the best-selling author, set in the twilight years of the Ottoman Empire and focusing on the sultan Abdülhamid.
The White Castle, The Black Book, The New Life. Novels by Orhan Pamuk, translated by Güneli Gün (Faber). Introspective, perceptive, sometimes over-complex but much lauded contemporary Turkish writer. *The New Life* was the fastest selling book in Turkish history.

Food & Cooking

Classic Turkish Cookery, by Ghillie and Jonathan Basan, introduced by Josceline Dimbleby (Tauris Parke Books, 1997). A beautiful illustrated book which places Turkish cooking in its geographical and cultural context; the recipes are a practical and authentic introduction to the best of Turkish dishes, gleaned from sources all over the country.
Timeless Tastes, Turkish Culinary Culture, project director Semahat Arsel (Vehbi Koç Vakfı and Divan Istanbul, 1996). Published to celebrate the 40th anniversary of the Divan Hotel, long renowned for its kitchen and its patisserie. The book has several authors: experts on culinary art and history, and professional chefs who give their recipes. This history of Turkish cooking at the most elevated level is illustrated with Ottoman miniatures and engravings.
The Art of Turkish Cooking, by Neşet Eren (Hippocrene Books, 1996). Written in 1969, the excellence of this book lies in its simple instructions, and the use of simple ingredients that are readily available (a characteristic of Turkish cooking anyway). The style is a little dated, but the recipes are authentic. A less lavish choice than the above two books.

Guides

Aegean Turkey, Lycian Turkey, Turkey's Southern Shore, Turkey Beyond the Maeanders, by George E. Bean (John Murray). Scholarly specialist guides to the archaeological sites of Turkey, compiled from Professor Bean's research.
Blue Guide Turkey, by Bernard McDonagh (A&C Black, 1999). Latest edition of the classic fount of all wisdom on history and archaeology.
Eastern Turkey: A Guide and History, by Gwynn Williams (Faber and Faber, 1972).
Istanbul, An Archaeological Guide, by Christa Beck and Christiane Forsting (Ellipsis, 1997). Neatly designed, tiny pocket-sized book with black-and-white photographs. The only guide to include some of Istanbul's most interesting recently built, renovated or redesigned buildings and structures.
Strolling through Istanbul, A Guide to the City, by Hilary Sumner-Boyd and John Freely (Redhouse Press,

Istanbul, 1996). First written and published in the early 1970s and one of the first proper guides to the city, this book is still valuable, though it has outlived one of its authors. The other, John Freely, still lives and works in Istanbul, and few are more knowledgeable than he.
The Companion Guide to Turkey, by John Freely (HarperCollins, 1996). This was first published in 1979 but has since been revised. Freely's knowledge of and affection for the country is palpable in its pages.

Other Insight Guides

There are a number of other Insight Guides which highlight destinations in this region.

In the original Insight Guides series are *Insight Guide: Turkish Coast* and *Insight Guide: Istanbul*. Both books include background essays, comprehensive Places chapters and fact-packed practical information sections. Lavish photography supports the text. There are also *Pocket Guides* and *Compact Guides* to Istanbul and the Turkish Coast.

Feedback

We do our best to ensure the information in our books is as accurate and up-to-date as possible. The books are updated on a regular basis, using local contacts, who painstakingly add, amend and correct as required. However, some mistakes and omissions are inevitable and we are ultimately reliant on our readers to put us in the picture.

We would welcome your feedback on any details related to your experiences using the book "on the road". Maybe we recommended a hotel that you liked (or another that you didn't), as well as interesting new attractions, or facts and figures you have found out about the country itself. The more details you can give us (particularly with regard to addresses, e-mails and telephone numbers), the better.

We will acknowledge all contributions, and we'll offer an Insight Guide to the best letters received.

Please write to us at:
   Insight Guides
   APA Publications
   PO Box 7910
   London SE1 1WE
Or send e-mail to:
insight@apaguide.co.uk

ART & PHOTO CREDITS

Picture Spreads

INSIGHT GUIDE TURKEY

Cartographic Editor **Zoë Goodwin**
Production **Linton Donaldson**
Design Consultants
Carlotta Junger, Graham Mitchener
Picture Research **Hilary Genin, Monica Allende**

Map Production Lovell Johns
© 2005 Apa Publications GmbH & Co.
Verlag KG (Singapore branch)

Index

Numbers in italics refer to photographs

A
B
C
D
E
G
H
I
J
b
c
d
e
f
g
h
i
j
k
l

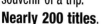

INSIGHT GUIDES

The world's largest collection of visual travel guides & maps

A range of guides and maps to meet every travel need

Insight Guides

This classic series gives you the complete picture of a destination through expert, well written and informative text and stunning photography. Each book is an ideal background information and travel planner, serves as an on-the-spot companion – and is a superb visual souvenir of a trip. **Nearly 200 titles**.

Insight Pocket Guides

focus on the best choices for places to see and things to do, picked by our local correspondents. They are ideal for visitors new to a destination. To help readers follow the routes easily, the books contain full-size pull-out maps. **125 titles.**

Insight Maps

are designed to complement the guides. They provide full mapping of major cities, regions and countries, and their laminated finish makes them easy to fold and gives them durability. **133 titles.**

Insight Compact Guides

are convenient, comprehensive reference books, modestly priced. The text, photographs and maps are all carefully cross-referenced, making the books ideal for on-the-spot use when in a destination. **133 titles.**

Different travellers have different needs. Since 1970, Insight Guides has been meeting these needs with a range of practical and stimulating guidebooks and maps